Multidisciplinary Approach to Modern Digital Steganography

Sabyasachi Pramanik
Haldia Institute of Technology, India

Mangesh Manikrao Ghonge
Sandip Foundation's Institute of Technology and Research Centre, India

Renjith V. Ravi
MEA Engineering College, India

Korhan Cengiz
Trakya University, Turkey

A volume in the Advances in Information Security, Privacy, and Ethics (AISPE) Book Series

Published in the United States of America by
   IGI Global
   Information Science Reference (an imprint of IGI Global)
   701 E. Chocolate Avenue
   Hershey PA, USA 17033
   Tel: 717-533-8845
   Fax: 717-533-8661
   E-mail: cust@igi-global.com
   Web site: http://www.igi-global.com

Library of Congress Cataloging-in-Publication Data

Names: Pramanik, Sabyasachi, 1978- editor. | Ghonge, Mangesh, 1984- editor.
  | Ravi, Renjith, 1985- editor. | Cengiz, Korhan, editor.
Title: Multidisciplinary approach to modern digital steganography /
  Sabyasachi Pramanik, Mangesh Ghonge, Renjith Ravi, and Korhan Cengiz,
  editors.
Description: Hershey, PA : Information Science Reference, [2021] | Includes
  bibliographical references and index. | Summary: "This book gives an
  insight to the different latest techniques and state-of-the-art methods,
  algorithms, architectures, models, methodologies, and case studies of
  steganography in the domain of Cloud, IoT and Android Platform"--
  Provided by publisher.
Identifiers: LCCN 2020052339 (print) | LCCN 2020052340 (ebook) | ISBN
  9781799871606 (hardcover) | ISBN 9781799871613 (paperback) | ISBN
  9781799871620 (ebook)
Subjects: LCSH: Data encryption (Computer science) | Computer security.
Classification: LCC QA76.9.D335 M85 2021 (print) | LCC QA76.9.D335
  (ebook) | DDC 005.8/24--dc23
LC record available at https://lccn.loc.gov/2020052339
LC ebook record available at https://lccn.loc.gov/2020052340

This book is published in the IGI Global book series Advances in Information Security, Privacy, and Ethics (AISPE) (ISSN: 1948-9730; eISSN: 1948-9749)

British Cataloguing in Publication Data
A Cataloguing in Publication record for this book is available from the British Library.

All work contributed to this book is new, previously-unpublished material. The views expressed in this book are those of the authors, but not necessarily of the publisher.

For electronic access to this publication, please contact: eresources@igi-global.com.

Advances in Information Security, Privacy, and Ethics (AISPE) Book Series

Manish Gupta
State University of New York, USA

ISSN:1948-9730
EISSN:1948-9749

MISSION

As digital technologies become more pervasive in everyday life and the Internet is utilized in ever increasing ways by both private and public entities, concern over digital threats becomes more prevalent.

The **Advances in Information Security, Privacy, & Ethics (AISPE) Book Series** provides cutting-edge research on the protection and misuse of information and technology across various industries and settings. Comprised of scholarly research on topics such as identity management, cryptography, system security, authentication, and data protection, this book series is ideal for reference by IT professionals, academicians, and upper-level students.

COVERAGE

- Telecommunications Regulations
- IT Risk
- Tracking Cookies
- Data Storage of Minors
- Technoethics
- Computer ethics
- Device Fingerprinting
- CIA Triad of Information Security
- Network Security Services
- Global Privacy Concerns

IGI Global is currently accepting manuscripts for publication within this series. To submit a proposal for a volume in this series, please contact our Acquisition Editors at Acquisitions@igi-global.com or visit: http://www.igi-global.com/publish/.

Titles in this Series

Security and Privacy Solutions for the Internet of Energy
Mohamed Amine Ferrag (Guelma University, Algeria)
Information Science Reference • © 2021 • 325pp • H/C (ISBN: 9781799846161) • US $195.00

Privacy and Security Challenges in Location Aware Computing
P. Shanthi Saravanan (J.J. College of Engineering and Technology, Tiruchirappalli, India) and S. R. Balasundaram (National Institute of Technology, Tiruchirappalli, India)
Information Science Reference • © 2021 • 298pp • H/C (ISBN: 9781799877561) • US $195.00

Revolutionary Applications of Blockchain-Enabled Privacy and Access Control
Surjit Singh (Thapar Institute of Engineering and Technology, India) and Anca Delia Jurcut (University College Dublin, Ireland)
Information Science Reference • © 2021 • 297pp • H/C (ISBN: 9781799875895) • US $225.00

Multidisciplinary Approaches to Ethics in the Digital Era
Meliha Nurdan Taskiran (Istanbul Medipol University, Turkey) and Fatih Pinarbaşi (Istanbul Medipol University, Turkey)
Information Science Reference • © 2021 • 369pp • H/C (ISBN: 9781799841173) • US $195.00

Handbook of Research on Digital Transformation and Challenges to Data Security and Privacy
Pedro Fernandes Anunciação (Polytechnic Institute of Setúbal, Portugal) Cláudio Roberto Magalhães Pessoa (Escola de Engenharia de Minas Gerais, Brazil) and George Leal Jamil (Informações em Rede Consultoria e Treinamento, Brazil)
Information Science Reference • © 2021 • 529pp • H/C (ISBN: 9781799842019) • US $285.00

Limitations and Future Applications of Quantum Cryptography
Neeraj Kumar (Babasaheb Bhimrao Ambedkar University, Lucknow, India) Alka Agrawal (Babasaheb Bhimrao Ambedkar University, Lucknow, India) Brijesh K. Chaurasia (Indian Institute of Information Technology, India) and Raees Ahmad Khan (Indian Institute of Information Technology, India)
Information Science Reference • © 2021 • 305pp • H/C (ISBN: 9781799866770) • US $225.00

Advancements in Security and Privacy Initiatives for Multimedia Images
Ashwani Kumar (Vardhaman College of Engineering, India) and Seelam Sai Satyanarayana Reddy (Vardhaman College of Engineering, India)
Information Science Reference • © 2021 • 278pp • H/C (ISBN: 9781799827955) • US $215.00

701 East Chocolate Avenue, Hershey, PA 17033, USA
Tel: 717-533-8845 x100 • Fax: 717-533-8661
E-Mail: cust@igi-global.com • www.igi-global.com

Editorial Advisory Board

Table of Contents

Detailed Table of Contents

Chapter 1
    Samir Kumar Bandyopadhyay, GLA University, India
    Vishal Goyal, GLA University, India
    Shawni Dutta, The Bhawanipur Education Society College, Kolkata, India
    Sabyasachi Pramanik, Haldia Institute of Technology, India
    Hafiz Husnain Raza Sherazi, University College Cork, Ireland

In this digital era, most of the daily works of users are captured in digital forms like image, audio, video, or even text. These may contain sensitive, confidential, or private information as well. To keep these, there are different techniques exercised over the years like chest, coffer, repository, treasury, etc. Sometimes such ways of hiding information attract unintended users. Therefore, steganography has been applied to digital objects in a new form called digital steganography. This chapter enforces identifying methods in digital steganography. The basic model of any type of digital steganography is composed of three types of objects: cover object, text to be hidden, and stego object. Depending on the type of cover object, different types of digital steganography methods have been defined. Only data hiding in text is discussed.

Chapter 2
    Sana Parveen K, MEA Engineering College, India
    Renjith V. Ravi, MEA Engineering College, India
    Basma Abd El-Rahiem, Menoufia University, Egypt
    Mangesh M. Ghonge, Sandip Foundation's Institute of Technology and Research Centre,
        India

Steganography is the process used hide the existence of information during transmission. Cover mediums like text, image, audio, and video protocols are used to hide the secret information. This process helps to provide secret communication between two parties. As data is unknown, it is challenging to attract the attention of any third parties. Therefore, steganography becomes the best and most secure method for data transmission. Digital images are the most common cover media or carriers in steganographic processes, where the secret payload is embedded into images. Several techniques are coming under image steganography, and there includes a different method to ensure the secrecy of messages. This chapter gives an overview of the different commonly used techniques in this area and the latest existing image steganography methods and the comparison of techniques.

Chapter 3

Gurunath R., CHRIST University (Deemed), India
Debabrata Samanta, CHRIST University (Deemed), India

There is an immense advancement in science and technology, and computing systems with the highest degree of security are the present hot topic; however, the domination of hackers and espionage in terms of disclosing the sensitive information are steadily increasing. This chapter presents a theoretical view and critical examination of the few text steganography methods in the contemporary world. It tells the direction in which research has developed over the past few years. Cryptography, the encipherment to a certain extent, protects the data by making it unreadable but not safe. Improvisation of the same can be done using another layer of protection that is steganography in which the secret embedded inside the cover text will not be revealed.

Chapter 4

Ankur Gupta, Vaish College of Engineering, Rohtak, India
Sabyasachi Pramanik, Haldia Institute of Technology, India
Hung Thanh Bui, School of Engineering and Tecnology, Thu Dau Mot University, Vietnam
Nicholas M. Ibenu, ESCAE University of Technology, Benin

Steganography is the way to conceal data inside a normal (non-mystery) record to keep it from discovery. While encryption expects to conceal the substance of data, steganography means to shroud the presence of data. Information security is significant when touchy information is communicated over the internet. Steganography and steganalysis methods can take care of the issue of copyright, possession, and discovery of malevolent information. Steganography is to conceal mystery information without contortion, and steganalysis is to distinguish the presence of shrouded information. In this chapter, steganography and steganalysis methods are depicted along with AI structures to show that AI systems can be utilized to recognize the mystery information covered up in the picture utilizing steganography calculations.

Chapter 5

Ajay B. Gadicha, P. R. Pote College of Engineering and Management, Amravati, India
Vrinda Beena Brajesh Gupta, Goverment College of Engineering, Amravati, India
Vijay B. Gadicha, G. H. Raisoni University, Amravati, India
Krishan Kumar, National Institute of Technology, Srinagar, India
Mangesh M. Ghonge, Sandip Foundation's Institute of Technology and Research Centre, India

The information technology era or the third industrial revolution began around the 1960s; has changed the ways we live, work, and play; and brought substantial challenges that include loss of privacy, fake news, digital divides, and significant information security risks. With billions of connections and systems, security vulnerabilities are abundant including the opportunity for criminals to exploit any gaps that present themselves. Eventually, we'll need a groundbreaking technology to gain the upper hand against these threats. Protecting data, systems, and networks assumed a more specific term: cybersecurity. The goal of cybersecurity today is to protect information while it's at rest and in motion. One of the most interesting ways to deliver hidden information is through steganographic technique.

> Swaroop Shankar Prasad, University of Stuttgart, Germany
> Ofer Hadar, Ben-Gurion University of the Negev, Israel
> Ilia Polian, University of Stuttgart, Germany

Steganographic channels can be abused for malicious purposes, thus raising the need to detect malicious embedded steganographic information (steganalysis). This chapter will cover the little-studied problem of steganography and steganalysis over a noisy channel, providing a detailed modeling for the special case of spatial-domain image steganography. It will approach these issues from both a theoretical and a practical point of view. After a description of spatial-domain image steganography, the impact of Gaussian noise and packet loss on the steganographic channel will be discussed. Characterization of the substitution-insertion-deletion (SID) channel parameters will be performed through experiments on a large number of images from the ALASKA database. Finally, a steganalysis technique for error-affected spatial-domain image steganography using a convolutional neural network (CNN) will be introduced, studying the relationship between different types and levels of distortions and the accuracy of malicious image detection.

Chapter 7

> Binay Kumar Pandey, College of Technology, Govind Ballabh Pant University of Agriculture
>   and Technology, India
> Deepak Mane, Tata Consultancy Services, Australia
> Vinay Kumar Kumar Nassa, Department of Computer Science Engg, South Point Group of
>   Institutions, Sonepat, India
> Digvijay Pandey, Department of Technical Education, Dr A.P.J. Abdul Kalam Technical
>   University, Lucknow, India
> Shawni Dutta, The Bhawanipur Education Society College, Kolkata, India
> Randy Joy Magno Ventayen, Pangasinan State University, Philippines
> Gaurav Agarwal, Invertis University, Bareilly, India
> Rahul Rastogi, Invertis University, Bareilly, India

This work's primary goal is to secure the transmission of text hidden within the cover image using steganography over a public network of computers. Steganography is a powerful tool for concealing information within a cover image so that the concealed message remains undetectable. As a result, steganography refers to concealed writing. The secure transmission of information over a public network communication channel using steganography occurs in two stages, the first on the sender side and the second on the receiver side. In the first phase, steganography is normally applied to conceal the encrypted information within the image as a cover. The encrypted data is implanted inside the cover image using an improved least significant bit steganography method. The secret key obtained by the embedding algorithm is shared with the message retrieval algorithm on the receiver side to retrieve the message. Finally, the embedded text message is identified using a hybrid convolution regression adaptive integrated neural network (CRAINN) approach.

Chapter 8

Vladimir N. Kustov, Saint Petersburg State University of Railway Transport of Emperor
Alexander I, Russia
Alexey G. Krasnov, Nexign, Russia
Ekaterina S. Silanteva, NST LLC, Russia

This chapter's primary goal is to provide a comprehensive approach to the development of new highly undetectable stegosystems that greatly complicate their steganalysis. The authors propose several implementations of highly undetectable stegosystems, the so-called HUGO systems, using an integrated approach to their synthesis. This approach most fully considers the features of transmitting hidden messages over highly noisy communication channels. At the stage of embedding hidden messages, the authors suggest actively using their discrete transformations. The authors also propose increasing the secrecy of secret messages by converting them to a form that resembles natural noise. The authors use a discrete chaotic decomposition of the Arnold cat map (ACM) to do this. The authors also suggest using highly efficient noise-tolerant encoding and multi-threshold decoding to combat interference in the communication channel and an embedding algorithm. The authors also describe two original stegosystems $\pm$HUGO and $\oplus$HUGO and test results confirming their effectiveness.

Chapter 9

Atrayee Majumder Ray, Netaji Subhash Engineering College, India
Anindita Sarkar, Netaji Subhash Engineering College, India
Ahmed J. Obaid, University of Kufa, Iraq
Saravanan Pandiaraj, King Saud University, Saudi Arabia

Internet of things (IoT) is one of those emerging technologies, which are going to rule the world in the next few decades. Due to the advancement of low-cost computing systems and mobile technologies, these physical things are now capable of sharing and collecting data with minimal human interference. However, these devices are exposed to various security threats regarding privacy and data confidentiality as they are openly accessible to all in the network. Moreover, many IoT devices have low processing power and weak security level which could be the main targets for hackers. Lightweight cryptographic schemes are used to meet the security needs in IoT environment. Steganography is used as another security tool for IoT devices. This chapter is an attempt to analyze the various steganography techniques used to strengthen the security needs of IoT devices as per their applications. IoT security schemes using different steganography models and algorithms are outlined here with their relative advantages and disadvantages.

Protected stored data as well as transfer in this virtual environment have been a significant thing since this world wide web has been used for information exchange. The need for data security rises as the level of personal data exchanged on the web is becoming more susceptible. To protect information from malicious use as well as alteration, services like confidential information but also data integrity have been needed. So many traditional cryptographic methods have been proposed by numerous studies throughout recent times to maintain multimedia data communicated over public networks. The chapter proposes a novel keyless picture encryption algorithm focused on a chaotic map. Almost every picture element is encoded by shuffling pixel values, which would be measured by an adapted cat map. In this suggested technique, steganography is used to transfer keyless encrypted information using a cover picture with encrypted information inserted in picture, audio, and video files.

This research consists of three phase. The first model includes a crystal payload encryption method watermarking scheme and an attack-free encryption scheme called international data encryption algorithm (IDEA). The second model is a binary grey scale image in chicken swarm optimization (CSO) applied to copyright production parameter optimized swarm intelligence domain-based approach, which is compared to conventional approaches. The work performance has been evaluated for conventional machine learning approach using MATLAB. The simulation results show that proposed hybridized crystal payload algorithm with chicken swarm optimization (HCPECSO) scheme achieves a high copyright production with the lowest mean square error values and highest peak signal noise ration when compared with the existing approaches schemes like machine learning SVM, logistic regression, and neural network. The proposed HCPECSO attained less processing time of 32.33s and processing cost compared to existing schemes.

Chapter 12
Kannadhasan S., Cheran College of Engineering, India
R. Nagarajan, Gnanamani College of Technology, India

The exponential development of the internet and the internet of things (IoT) applies to the next step of the information transition, which entails billions of integrated smart devices and sensors to enable the speedy sharing of information and data under soft real-time restrictions. Significant improvements in data sharing also sparked the digital information movement. This transmission of data can include private, reliable, and often private communication. The exponential development of the internet and the internet of things (IoT) applies to the next step of the information transition, which entails billions of integrated smart devices and sensors to enable the speedy sharing of information and data under soft real-time restrictions. Significant improvements in data sharing also sparked the digital information movement. This transmission of data can include private, reliable, and often private communication.

Chapter 13
Kylyn Fernandes, Dwarkadas J. Sanghvi College of Engineering, India
Ankit Rishi Gupta, Dwarkadas J. Sanghvi College of Engineering, India
Pratik Panchal, Dwarkadas J. Sanghvi College of Engineering, India
Ramchandra Mangrulkar, Dwarkadas J. Sanghvi College of Engineering, India

Steganography is the art of hiding messages or files in a way that prevents the detection of the existence of these hidden messages. It encompasses several techniques, including physical methods like invisible ink on paper and digital techniques like hiding text on multimedia files like images and music files. In the modern digital era, steganography has become a useful tool to evade detection and perusal of secret messages. With the advent of social media, it is very easy to encode a message or file onto an image and upload it online for the intended recipients to access, decode, and read or use. In this case of digital steganography of messages or files onto images, an important factor to consider is the effect of image compression on the hidden message. Since most social media and other online image posting websites run some sort of compression, cropping, and other image transformations on the uploaded images, understanding these techniques and their effect on the hidden text can help one choose the most suitable steganography technique to use for a particular use case.

Chapter 14
Mahip M. Bartere, G. H. Raisoni University, Amravati, India
Sneha Bohra, G. H. Raisoni University, Amravati, India
Prashant Adakane, G. H. Raisoni University, Amravati, India
B. Santhosh Kumar, GMR Institute of Technology, India

Data security is one of the most important aspects in today's scenario. Whenever we send our data from source to destination, data protection is one of the prime components. With the help of data hiding and data extraction techniques, we are able to provide the solution of different types of problems whenever we transfer our data. Steganography is a process where we can hide our data and maintain the quality of the image. At the same time, we think about data alteration. With the help of stegtanalysis method, we reverse engineer and extract the original data. In this chapter, data hiding and data extraction techniques are explained in the combination of machine learning architecture. The combination of steganography and steganalysis along with machine learning is used to identify protected data using different techniques.

Chapter 15
Abhishek Rajeshkumar Mehta, Parul Institute of Computer Application, Parul University,
India & DCIS, Sabarmati University, India
Trupti Pravinsinh Rathod, Vidyabharti Trust College of Master in Computer Application,
India

Internet of things (IoT) is a typical thing (object) in this day and age, which fills in as a component of our standard life exercises. In spite of the fact that it benefits the private region in a few different ways, different difficulties, for example information classification and protection, are made. Web of things (IoT) is all over the place and utilized in a lot more advantgeous functionality. It is utilized in our homes, clinics, fire counteraction, and announcing and controlling of ecological changes. Information security is an urgent prerequisite for IoT since the number of late advances in various spaces is expanding step by step. Different endeavors have been set to sate the client's expectations for greater security and protection.

Preface

OVERVIEW OF THE SUBJECT MATTER

Steganography is the art of secret writing. The purpose of steganography is to hide the presence of a message from the intruder. This book gives an insight to the different techniques and state of the art methods, algorithms, architectures, models, methodologies and case studies of steganography in the domain of Cloud, IoT and Android Platform. Security aspects of cloud computing and IoT are related to the external data storage, dependency on the "public internet," inability to control and incorporation with internal security mechanisms. The book proposes a new approach to secure data storage on cloud infrastructure and IoT by hiding secret data in multimedia. Besides, it also includes discussions on machine learning/ deep learning based steganography approaches, steganography in cyber attacks, security control in android platform, optimization models in steganography. Various traditional security aspects such as authentication, identity, and authorization are elaborated based on neural network, optimization models and cryptography.

A DESCRIPTION WHERE MY TOPIC FITS IN THE WORLD TODAY

Though Security controls in Cloud Computing, IoT and Android Platform are not much different than security controls in an IT environment, still they might present different type of risks to an organization than the classic IT solutions. Therefore, a detailed discussion is needed in case there is a breach in security. This book will for the first time will review the security aspects of Could, IoT and android platform related to steganography in a convincing way. In a nutshell, this book is a handy reference for the security engineers and security analysts to solve practical problems.

This book, as a whole, is a guide to the researches and professionals in the area of data privacy and security. The interdisciplinary approaches of steganography enhance the strengths of security in the area of Cloud, IoT and android. It addresses some newer security concerns, proposes new algorithms and discusses some case studies.

DESCRIPTION OF THE TARGET AUDIENCE

Primary Audience

1. Professionals working as a Forensic Engineer, Forensic Analyst, Cyber security Analyst, Cyber Forensic Examiner, Security Engineer, Cyber security Network Analyst, Cyber Network Defense Analyst and Digital Forensic Examiner.
2. Researchers: University Professors, scholars, instructors focusing on digital enterprise, and teaching & researching in courses such as management, marketing, accounting & finance, banking, information technology, education, healthcare and many others.

Secondary Audience

1. Postgraduate and undergraduate computer science and management students focusing on cyber security as a specialization. It can also be included in the curriculum of students who take elective paper choice as "Computer Security /Network Security/Cryptography."
2. Scientists
3. Ethical Hackers
4. Fraud Detection Experts
5. Consultants
6. General Public

BENEFITS TO AUDIENCE

The professionals including the security analysts, forensic engineers, digital forensic examiners will gain an in-depth knowledge of the security algorithms, principles, architecture and approaches in a convincing manner. It will also provide them with a solution in their domain of expertise.

The researchers will grasp new ideas of steganography. They can also enhance the algorithms and look for a better solution in future.

- Gives an insight of machine learning/deep learning approach of steganography
- It has an in-depth analysis of steganography in the domain of cloud and IoT

A new concept of Quantum steganography has been proposed

The first chapter, "Unseen to Seen by Digital Steganography: Modern Day Data Hiding Techniques," highlights the importance of identifying newer approaches in Digital Steganography in the modern era. In this modern age, the majority of users' everyday tasks are captured in digital formats such as images, audio, video, and even text. They may also contain important, confidential, or private information. Various methods, such as chest, coffer, repository, and treasury, have been used to hold these over the years. Such methods of concealing information can also attract unintended users. Steganography is the modern name for the ancient method of secret sharing. It has been rediscovered and applied to restructured digital objects in a new form known as Digital Steganography. The authors Samir Bandyopadhyay, Vishal Goyal, Shawni Dutta, Sabyasachi Pramanik and Hafiz Husnain Raza Sherazi in this chapter describe the various multidisciplinary approaches ranging from the domain of IoT, Machine Learning and Deep Learning. Every kind of digital steganography starts with three types of objects: the cover object, the text to be covered, and the Stego object. Various types of innovative and secured Digital Steganography methods have been identified based on the types of cover items.

The authors of the research work "Image Steganography: Recent Trends and Techniques" are Sana Parveen K, Renjith V Ravi, Basma Abd El-Rahiem and Mangesh M Ghonge. Steganography is a technique for concealing the presence of data during transmission. Text, image, audio, and video protocols are used to conceal the sensitive information. This procedure aids in the transmission of confidential information between two parties. Since the data is unknown, attracting the interest of some third parties is difficult. As a result, steganography emerges as the most effective and reliable form of data transmission. An innovative image steganography technique is discussed here in the Android platform to portray the confidential transmission. In the steganographic processes, where the hidden payload is embedded in photographs, digital images are the most common cover medium or carrier. Image steganography encompasses a number of methods, each of which uses a different approach to ensure message confidentiality. This chapter provides an overview of the various widely used techniques in this field in the Android domain, as well as the most recent image steganography methods and a technique,

In the research "Advances in Text Steganography Theory and Research: A Critical Review and Gaps," Gurunath R. and Debabrata Samanta provide a theoretical and practical discussion and critical assessment of the various text steganography methods which may be applied in the modern day in the domain of Fuzzy Logic. While there has been tremendous progress in science and technology, the current issue is computer systems with the highest level of security; nevertheless, the dominance of hackers and espionage in terms of revealing confidential information is increasingly growing. This exemplifies the direction in which career research has progressed in recent years. Encryption protects data to some degree by rendering it unreadable, but it is not secure. Another layer of security, Steganography, may be used to improvise the same, in which the secret knowledge found within the cover text is not revealed. This paper considers text data hiding methods for the analysis, and the authors choose four key methods: linguistic synonym-based digital steganography, low-tech steganography, a unique number system, and text steganography with a picture. In addition, some new diagrams are proposed and tested using the C and Python languages to aid the review process. The review's findings point to important research deficiencies in the respective text steganography techniques and suggest areas for further investigation. Also included is a study of different text steganographic approaches, as well as their advantages and disadvantages.

The authors of Chapter 4, "Machine Learning and Deep Learning in Steganography and Steganalysis," are Ankur Gupta, Sabyasachi Pramanik, Hung Bui and Nicholas Ibenu. Although encryption aims to hide the content of data, steganography aims to hide the fact that data exists. When sensitive information is transmitted over the Internet, information security is critical. Copyright, retention, and discovery of malicious information can all be addressed using steganography and steganalysis techniques. In this chapter, steganography and steganalysis methods are shown alongside deep learning and artificial intelligence structures to demonstrate how steganography calculations can be used to identify the mystery information hiding in the image. The use of Scikit Learn – A Software for machine learning library for Python programming language has been implemented. It describes some innovative clustering and regression algorithms. Keras, the Python Deep Learning API has been discussed and its functionality is shown in the concept of steganography. Also some state-of-the-art comparison techniques have been discussed which portrays the superiority of the suggested technique.

The authors of the work "Multimode Approach of Data Encryption in Images Through Quantum Steganography" are Ajay Gadicha, Vrinda Gupta, Vijay Gadicha, Krishan Kumar and Mangesh Ghonge. Since the 1960s, the information technology age, also known as the third industrial revolution, has changed the way we live, work, and play, posing major challenges such as lack of privacy, false news, digital divisions, and significant information security threats. With billions of links and networks, security vulnerabilities abound, giving criminals plenty of opportunities to exploit any holes that arise. To gain the upper hand against these challenges, we'll eventually need ground-breaking technology. The term "cybersecurity" was coined to describe the process of safeguarding data, systems, and networks. The aim of today's cybersecurity is to secure data while it is in transit and at rest. In the field of quantum communication, quantum steganography is one of the most important branches of quantum information hiding. Quantum noises are unavoidable in a realistic quantum communication environment, and they will have a significant impact on the protection and efficiency of the quantum steganographic system. Quantum mechanics can deliver a compelling collection of solutions in the cyber security domain, just as it promises to change our paradigm for classical computing and usher in a new generation of capability and efficiency. Unlike classical methods, which rely on mathematical algorithms that are difficult but not impossible to decipher, these quantum solutions are based on physical laws. Quantum steganography has many advantages over traditional approaches. In this chapter, the authors go through the fundamentals of quantum computing before discussing its role in knowledge concealment. The laws of quantum computation are also discussed and how they can be used for hidden communication is also suggested. The BB84 protocol, Error correcting code, Least Significant Qubit, and Prior entanglement are then discussed as the various quantum steganographic methods. The authors also go into how these protocols keep the secret channel imperceptible and data private.

In "Detection of Malicious Spatial-Domain Steganography Over Noisy Channel," Swaroop Shankar Prasad, Ofer Hadar and Ilia Polian present us that steganographic channels can be exploited for malicious purposes, necessitating the detection of maliciously embedded steganographic data (steganalysis). This chapter will look at the understudied problem of steganography and steganalysis over a noisy channel, with a comprehensive modeling for the special case of spatial-domain image steganography. It will take a theoretical and realistic approach to address these problems. The effect of Gaussian noise and packet loss on the steganographic channel will be addressed after a review of spatial-domain image steganography via experiments on a large number of images from the ALASKA database, the substitution-insertion-deletion (SID) channel parameters will be characterized. Finally, using a convolutional neural network (CNN), a steganalysis technique for error-affected spatial-domain image steganography will be implemented, examining the relationship between various forms and levels of distortions and the accuracy of malicious image detection.

The authors of Chapter 7, "Secure Text Extraction From Complex Degraded Image by Applying Steganography and Deep Learning," are Binay Pandey, Deepak Mane, Vinay Kumar Nassa, Digvijay Pandey, Shawni Dutta, Randy Joy Ventayen, Gaurav Agarwal and Rahul Rastogi. The primary aim of this project is to use steganography to protect the transmission of text concealed inside the cover image over a public network of computers. Steganography is a sophisticated technique for hiding information inside a cover picture such that the hidden message remains undetectable. The protected transmission of information over a public network communication channel is accomplished in two steps, the first on the sender side and the second on the receiver side, using steganography. In the first step, steganography is usually used to hide the encrypted data inside an image that serves as a mask. Using an improved Least Significant Bit steganography process, the encrypted data is implanted inside the cover picture. To retrieve the message, the secret key obtained by the embedding algorithm is shared with the message retrieval algorithm on the receiver side. Finally, a hybrid Convolution Regression Adaptive Integrated Neural Network (CRAINN) approach is used to identify the embedded text message. Furthermore, an optimization technique improves the performance of the HCNN (hybrid convolution neural network).

The authors of Chapter 8, "Modern Approaches to Creating Highly Undetectable Stegosystems (HUGO Systems)," are Vladimir Kustov, Alexey Krasnov and Ekaterina Silanteva. The primary aim of this chapter is to use steganography to protect the transmission of text concealed inside the cover image over a public network of computers. Steganography is a sophisticated technique for hiding information inside a cover picture such that the hidden message remains undetectable. As a consequence, steganography refers to writing that is hidden. The protected transmission of information over a public network communication channel is accomplished in two steps, the first on the sender side and the second on the receiver side, using steganography. In the first step, steganography is usually used to hide the encrypted data inside an image that serves as a mask. Using an improved Least Significant Bit steganography process, the encrypted data is implanted inside the cover picture. To retrieve the message, the secret key obtained by the embedding algorithm is shared with the message retrieval algorithm on the receiver side. Finally, a hybrid Convolution Regression Adaptive Integrated Neural Network (CRAINN) approach is used to identify the embedded text message. Furthermore, an optimization technique improves the performance of the HCNN (hybrid convolution neural network).

In Chapter 9, "IoT Security Using Steganography," a new model in IoT is presented by Atrayee Majumder Ray, Anindita Sarkar, Ahmed Obaid and Saravanan Pandiaraj. Internet of Things (IoT) is one of the next-generation technologies that will dominate the world in the coming decades. These physical objects can now share and collect data with minimal human interaction thanks to the advent of low-cost computing systems and mobile technologies. However, since they are publicly available to all on the network, these devices are vulnerable to a variety of security risks relating to privacy and data confidentiality. Furthermore, many IoT devices have low processing power and poor security, making them prime targets for hackers. To meet the security needs of the IoT environment, lightweight cryptographic schemes are used. Another protection option for IoT devices is steganography. This chapter aims to examine the different Steganography techniques that have been used to improve the protection of IoT devices based on their applications. Here are some IoT protection schemes that use various steganography models and algorithms, along with their relative benefits and drawbacks. A new methodology in IoT is devised using steganography.

In the research work "An Integration of Keyless Encryption, Steganography, and Artificial Intelligence for the Secure Transmission of Stego Images," the authors, Digvijay Pandey, Vinay Nassa, Ayushi Jhamb, Dashrath Mahto, Binay Pandey, A.S. Hovan George, A. Shaji George and Samir Bandyopadhyay, confer that as the World Wide Web has become more widely used for information sharing, secure data storage and transfer in this virtual environment has become increasingly important. As the amount of personal data exchanged on the Internet becomes more vulnerable, the need for data protection grows. Services such as classified information, as well as data integrity, have been required to protect information from improper use and modification. Numerous studies have introduced numerous conventional cryptographic methods to preserve multimedia data communicated over public networks in recent years. The entire article proposes a new Keyless Picture Encryption algorithm that works even with a chaotic-map. Shuffling pixel values, which would be calculated by an adapted cat-map, is used to encode almost every picture feature. Steganography is used to transmit key-less encrypted information using a cover image, with encrypted information embedded in picture, audio, and video files in this suggested technique. On the other hand, retrieving text encoded on the receiver side has long been thought to be a difficult job. Furthermore, the sender would exchange a justification with the receiver instead of a key, despite the fact that accessing the embedded text hidden inside the cover image to boost performance would be difficult. Steganography was made simple by integrating data bits of the hidden textual information into the cover-least image's important bit of pixels. The picture quality, on the other hand, suffers as a result of the inclusion of an encoded message. From time to time, images can cause some distortion. As a consequence, the image's non-smooth areas are considered smooth. Inadequacies like these often minimize overall achievement by using various algorithms. As a result, a well-formulated high-performance technique for concealing the hidden textual data embedded within the cover-image without interfering with noise must be used. As a consequence, it has been discovered that the enhanced approach is capable of statistical analysis. It must also achieve a sufficient correlation value and perform adequately against attacks. The technique is being simulated with MATLAB.

The research titled "Multimedia Data Protection Using Hybridized Crystal Payload Algorithm With Chicken Swarm Optimization" has been developed by the following authors: Sivanantham Kalimuthu, Farid Naït-Abdesselam and Jaishankar B. The rapid advancement of technologies and technological systems ensures that different applications are protected indefinitely. Data is an advantage that should be ensured. Cipher text is the process of encrypting data or images by converting plaintext into an unreadable format. The message can only be decoded into plain text by those who have a secret key. In the ever-improving world of multimedia, security plays a critical role in communication and image power. It transforms the material into an incomprehensible and impenetrable mass. The security of digital content is required by the modification of digital media and the distribution of information over the internet. Other authentication mechanisms, such as digital watermarks, offer additional security to digital information in addition to encryption. The primary goal of this proposed research project is to improve copyright digital content security. The Chicken Swarm Optimization was used to encrypt images using crystal payload encryption. The proposed method is a development of the well-known wavelet theory. MATLAB 2013a was used to test the job output with a traditional machine learning approach. When compared to current approaches schemes such as only machine learning SVM, Logistic Regression, and Neural Network, simulation results show that the proposed Hybridized Crystal Payload Algorithm with Chicken Swarm Optimization scheme achieves a high copyright production with the lowest Mean Square Error Values and highest Peak Signal Noise Ration. When compared to current systems, the proposed HCPECSO achieved a processing time of 32.33 seconds and a lower processing cost.

The chapter "Secure Framework Data Security Using Cryptography and Steganography in Internet of Things" is a research carried out by Kannadhasan S and R Nagarajan to portray the Internet's exponential growth and the Internet of Things (IoT) referring to the next phase in the knowledge transformation, which involves billions of connected smart devices and sensors that allow for rapid sharing of data and information under soft real-time constraints. The digital knowledge revolution was also triggered by significant developments in data sharing. This data transmission may include safe, dependable, and often private communication. Cryptography and steganography are two of the most popular methods for encrypting information in communication. Cryptography defends against threats by stopping eavesdroppers from obtaining anything useful from the device and providing an insecure communication channel. Cryptography, on the other hand, has a number of drawbacks, and cryptographic expertise can raise suspicion. The first and third strategies use three (R, G, B) channels for information transport, while the second method uses G and B channels for transmission. Both approaches choose a higher-order position in the channel for embedding data. Steganography, on the other hand, protects data by concealing it inside a carrier and preventing attackers from detecting it. Since it conceals the very presence of secrets rather than just protecting the content, it offers more identity protection and safety than encryption.

"Application of Steganography for Secure Data Transmission using Lossless Compression" is a chapter authored by Kylyn Fernandes, Ankit Gupta, Pratik Panchal and Ramchandra Mangrulkar that presents research on Steganography being the practice of concealing messages or files in a way that prevents their presence from being discovered. With the advent of social media, encoding a message or file onto an image and uploading it digitally for intended recipients to view, interpret, read, or use has never been easier. The effect of image compression on the hidden message is an important factor to consider in this case of digital steganography of messages or files onto images. Since most social media and other online image-sharing websites apply compression, cropping, and other image transformations to the uploaded images, knowing how these techniques affect the hidden text will aid in selecting the most appropriate steganography technique for a given use case.

"Applications of Machine Learning in Steganography for Data Protection and Privacy" is a chapter authored by Mahip Bartere, Sneha Bohra, Prashant Adakane and B Santhosh Kumar which shows that data protection is one of the most critical aspects in today's world. When we send data from one location to another, one of the most important factors to consider is data security. We can solve a variety of problems by using data hiding and data extraction techniques whenever we move data. Steganography is a method of concealing data while maintaining image quality. At the same time, we consider data manipulation. We can reverse engineer and remove the original data with the aid of the steganalysis process. Data Hiding and Data Extraction techniques in the context of an innovative Machine Learning Architecture are discussed in this chapter. To classify protected data using various techniques, a combination of steganography and steganalysis, as well as a machine learning approach, is used.

The authors of the work titled "Design and Development of Hybrid Algorithms to Improve Cyber Security and Provide Securing Data using Image Steganography with Internet of Things" are Abhishek Mehta and Trupti Rathod. The Internet-of-Things (IoT) is a common thing (object) in today's world, and it is a part of our everyday activities. Despite the fact that it helps the private sector in a variety of ways, it poses a number of challenges, such as information classification and security. IoT is used in our homes, hospitals, firefighting, and announcing and monitoring environmental improvements, among other places. Since the number of recent developments in different fields is steadily increasing, information security is an essential requirement for IoT. Various initiatives have been launched in order to raise the client's demands for increased security and privacy. However, any one of those advantages could come with a significant risk of security and safety issues. Since they are disseminated, replicated, and exposed through widespread use of communication innovations, computerized archive protection and copyright assurance are also significant issues in IoT to schedule a half breed calculation for using steganography to improve digital security. The problem of clinical information transmission protection and trustworthiness in clinical applications is addressed in this application. This chapter proposes a steganography technique to ensure the confidentiality of clinical data using 2-D discrete wavelet transform. For safe and efficient knowledge transmission and collection of clinical pictures in medical services systems, the proposed model combines cryptography, steganography, and Orthogonal Frequency Division Multiplexing.

Acknowledgment

We wish to acknowledge the help of all the people involved in this project and, more specifically, the authors and reviewers who took part in the review process. Without their support, this book would not have become a reality. We thank God for the opportunity to pursue this highly relevant subject at this time, and each of the authors for their collective contributions. Our sincere gratitude goes to all the chapter authors around the world who contributed their time and expertise to this book. We wish to acknowledge the valuable contributions of all the peer reviewers regarding their suggestions for improvement of quality, coherence, and content for the chapters. Some authors served as referees; we highly appreciate their time and commitment. We'd like to express our gratitude to the production team at IGI-Global, who have delivered the highest level of service and have been extremely helpful and encouraging during this research process; without their perseverance, this publication would not have been possible. A successful book publication is the integrated result of more people than those persons granted credit as editor or author. We would also like to dedicate this book to our parents and spouse for their constant inspiration and support.

Sabyasachi Pramanik
Haldia Institute of Technology, India

Mangesh Manikrao Ghonge
Sandip Foundation's Institute of Technology and Research Centre, India

Korhan Cengiz
Trakya University, Turkey

Renjith V. Ravi
MEA Engineering College, India

Chapter 1
Unseen to Seen by Digital Steganography:
Modern-Day Data-Hiding Techniques

Samir Kumar Bandyopadhyay
GLA University, India

Vishal Goyal
GLA University, India

Shawni Dutta
https://orcid.org/0000-0001-8557-0376
The Bhawanipur Education Society College, Kolkata, India

Sabyasachi Pramanik
https://orcid.org/0000-0002-9431-8751
Haldia Institute of Technology, India

Hafiz Husnain Raza Sherazi
University College Cork, Ireland

ABSTRACT

In this digital era, most of the daily works of users are captured in digital forms like image, audio, video, or even text. These may contain sensitive, confidential, or private information as well. To keep these, there are different techniques exercised over the years like chest, coffer, repository, treasury, etc. Sometimes such ways of hiding information attract unintended users. Therefore, steganography has been applied to digital objects in a new form called digital steganography. This chapter enforces identifying methods in digital steganography. The basic model of any type of digital steganography is composed of three types of objects: cover object, text to be hidden, and stego object. Depending on the type of cover object, different types of digital steganography methods have been defined. Only data hiding in text is discussed.

DOI: 10.4018/978-1-7998-7160-6.ch001

1. INTRODUCTION

Today the Internet has become a trusted process of information transmission for everyone. The healthcare industry also upgrades itself by sharing electronic health records of patients digitally and can transmit to other places, if necessary. E-Governance (Aithal, P. S., 2016). system is the basic moto of all sectors in the globe. This information is the burning target of intruders in today's e-world. Therefore secure communication becomes a challenge today. This challenge brings information security to a level that now-a-days is treated as a subject to academics and a challenging research area to the researcher of every corner in the world. The chapter is also dedicated to secure communication using steganography (Pramanik, S. et al, 2019) (Pramanik, S. and Raja, S. S., 2017) methods. The main focus of the chapter is to explain thoroughly image steganography based on histogram. Three steganography methods are explained briefly and results are also given after each method. However, method for data hiding within the text is only defined since it may itself a chapter.

1.1. Brief Overview

The concept of steganography is to hide messages during transmission so that it is not noticeable in the naked eye. Secret message is hidden inside the entire message in such a way that it is only visible to the particular person. It works based on the invisible communication. The process of steganography system is shown in box 1.

Box 1. The Steganography System

Process:
Step 1: Cover image and target secret image are the input to the process of embedding.
Step 2: The output is stego image.
Step 3: It is input to process of extraction.
Step 4: The output is target secret image.

Steganography system is a function of M, method, and is defined by S = M (C, I) where C is cover media and I is secret information. The reverse process is called extraction (Mahato, S., Khan, D. A. and Yadav, D. K, 2020) of the secret message.

An effective steganographic scheme should meet following challenges. These are given below.

Imperceptibility (Mukherjee S. and Sanyal G., 2020) indicates the stego file (Hambouz, A., et al. 2019) is not distinguishable from the original cover file.

Capacity (Duan, X. et al, 2020) contains the maximum amount of secret information in a cover file.

Robustness (Eyssa, A.A., Abdelsamie, F.E. and Abdelnaiem, 2020) ensures that it is not possible to extract secret information from stego file.

Robustness is the ultimate goal of steganography for hiding the secret text properly.

1.2. Image Steganography

In image steganography the secret data is hidden within an image and images are popular cover media in this approach. Here a large amount of secret data can be confined within an image. Image steganography works in both spatial as well as in frequency domain. Pixel intensity is used to hide data in the time domain. The transformed coefficient is to store secret data in the frequency domain.

1.3. Audio Steganography

In this approach the secret data is embedded within an audio file called cover media. In this process it is difficult to identify small distortion in target data embedded in the audio. In the audio signal there is a gradual change in the amplitude as well as the frequency so that the proper suppression of target data can be confined in the signal very safely. Environmental factors may cause distortions (Chaharlang, J., Mosleh, M. and Rasouli-Heikalabad, S, 2020).

1.4. Steganography Using Text

Text media is used as cover to hide the secret data using different schemes. Text has a less redundant portion than image or audio so it is the most difficult kind of steganography. Linguistics method is the most popular method. Syntax and Semantics are both required in the Linguistics method. The synonyms of certain words are used to hide the secret text.

1.5. Video Steganography

In this method a data file is embedded within a video i.e. carrier file. A novel technique involving Discrete Cosine Transformation (DCT) and Discrete Wavelet Transform (DWT) has been implemented in recent works. This method is also robust against any types of attacks and supports blind key-based extraction of secret message. As the embedding has been performed in a specific video frame, it would add an extra layer of security as it will be difficult for any intruder to identify - out of several hundred video frames, which one is Stego.

2. BASICS AND USES OF STEGANOGRAPHY

Now-a-days Steganography applies legitimately for securing many daily life applications. Political persons and journalists use it for sending valuable messages by keeping their contacts in dark. Photographers protect their pictures from copyright stealing. People prevent piracy of e-books, MP3 files, DVD movies by applying this security technique. It can protect confidential documents from industries as well as governmental departments. Researchers in their works introduce a secure e-government system by hiding confidential governmental documents within an image. Researchers can hide their confidential contribution in journals through steganography before final publications [9].

Steganography also covers a very responsible part in the field of healthcare security today. Steganography also shows interest in various fields but the challenges are the capacity of carrier file as well as strength of security techniques.

3. LITERATURE REVIEW

Least Significant Bit (LSB) (Pramanik, S., 2013) (Pramanik, S. et al. 2020) substitution method exploits the fact that the human eye can't perceive small changes of text in the hiding media. LSB of every byte of an image contains the secret message bit. Stego key in secret message is shared between the sender and the receiver for encoding and decoding process [11]. 2nd bit, 3rd bit, 4th bit and 5th bit of LSB can be used to hide data.

Robert, Sobel and Prewitt operators are the most popular methods for image steganography for finding edge for embedding secret data. A successful signal transformation technique is DCT. It decomposes an image into a series of cosine functions. In the method the image is divided into matrix in terms of blocks. Researchers developed Bit-Plane Complexity Segmentation (BPCS) Steganography for hiding secret data using hamming distance. Two numerical values such as 7 and 8 have large hamming distance and it indicates small change in pixel values and output is distinguishable. In case of Gray code (Rashid, A. and Rahim M. K., 2016), two successive numbers are changed by a single bit and it is better to use it instead of hamming distance (Taha, M. S., Rahim, M. S. M., Lafta, S. A., Hashim, M. A. and Alzuabidi, H. M., 2019).

Researchers described different spatial and frequency domain techniques of audio steganography. Some researchers broke the audio signal into a number of samples in a parity encoding (Pramanik, S. et al., 2020) approach. In phase encoding phase, the components are used to hide data and it is difficult to understand whether there is any secret data (Handoko, W. T. et al, 2020). Researchers also used difference between the phase values of the selected component frequencies and their adjacent frequencies of the cover signal as a medium to hide secret data bits and are called Spread Spectrum (Kumar, S., Singh, A. and Kumar, M., 2019).

Four frequency components are decomposed in DWT. Low-Low (LL), Low-High (LH), High-Low (HL), and High-High (HH) is the sub bands. The LL sub-band describes the approximation details. The horizontal details are found in HL band. Vertical details are represented by LH sub-band. Researchers used to hide the low frequency part of DWT of the cover audio (Antonio, H., Prasad, P. W. C. and Alsadoon, A., 2019) media.

DCT is used to convert a signal of cosine series from spatial domain to frequency domain. The two-dimensional DCT can be performed by executing one dimensional DCT twice, initially in the x direction and next in y direction. SMS (Short Messaging Service) text contained secret data in text steganography method. The meaning of COLOR and COLOUR is same in UK and USA. It is possible to hide text in the cover media and retrieve using this fact. Researchers have used different words for describing the same object. Researchers proposed a method of hiding text through short form of words. The secret message was stored in a Sudoku puzzle and sent by SMS through mobile phones. Consider the following texts that are sent as the secret message:

"Again boating? At forest mind intelligent advice! Circumvent lakeside"

It reads as - "gotoindia" if second letter of each word is taken out to form secret message.

In video steganography, LSB is decomposed into a number of frames and then a particular frame is converted to an image. The secret bit is embedded in LSB of each byte of the image. Recently Artificial Neural Networks (ANN) is used to hide data within the layer of the network. Deep learning based methods are also implemented for hiding data.

4. DATA SET

Data set plays a vital role for testing and verification of the methods for any type of research based on data. Data collection is the major part of the research. Again the validation of data is done through testing and performance analysis. Both of these processes require data for successful execution of the methods. The performance analysis is required to be done for comparison with the existing works. This comparison is done based on some parameters that work with data.

It is composed of a set of data of similar category with the fulfilment of all the required information for testing. The concept of database (i.e. the set of similar data) arises from this necessity. The comparison will be fair if comparison of all the methods is made from the same data set. So it is required to collect standard data set for analysis and comparison.

A test image can be chosen based on many parameters like size, colour, textured/smooth areas, synthesis with straight edges, sharp, blurring (Sah H. R. and Gunasekaran, G., 2015), brightness/contrast, etc. The main requirements should be common among different data sets. These points are addressed in the chapter for testing and validation using same data sets for steganography research.

Petitcola's Photo Database is the free database/dataset which is purely created for watermarking (Embaby, A. A., Mohamed A., Shalaby, W. and Elsayed, K. M., 2020) and steganography research purpose. The database contains various type of .TIFF (Douglas, M., Bailey, K., Leeney, M. et al., 2018) images like Computer generated images (3 images), Bright colours photos (3 images), Reduced colour set & dark colours photos (4 images), Photos with textures & fine details (5 images), Photos with lines & edges (6 images), Photos with smooth areas (1 images), Other photos (1 images) and Classics Photos (5 images) of different size. The freely available images in internet are shown in figure 1.

The photo database of DECSAI was first introduced by the department of Computer and Artificial Intelligence of the University of Granada. The database contains many standard images, both gray level and colour. The gray image database contains several categories of images like illusion, contours, biomedical, astronomical and Miscellaneous includes images of different size. Similarly the colour database, USC-SIPI, contains Biomedical, marble and miscellaneous standard images in TIFF format generally used for testing. It is shown in figure 2.

The database consists of different volumes based on the characteristics of the images. It consists of 16 colour and 28 mono images and the sizes are 256×256, 512×512 (26 images) and 1024×1024 (4 images). Two images (San Diego (512×512), Oakland (512×512)) from Vol. 2: Aerials are also used. The sample images from this database are shown in figure 3.

The database, Kodak, contains 24 colour images of PNG (Zenati, An., Ouarda, W. and Alimi, A. M., 2019) format where each image size is either 768×512 or 512×768. The sample images from this database with information like photographer, date, location, are shown in figure 4.

UCID Database has been created for content based image retrieval (Gupta, M.K., Chandra, P., 2020, Ritala, P. et al., 2020). It basically designed to investigate the effect of image compression on content retrieval. Although the initial intention of this database is to provide test images for content retrieval algorithms, the database (Setyono, A. and Setiadi, D. R. I. M, 2019), is also suitable for any kind of steganography research where the hidden data should be retrieved at the receiver (Gowda, S. N., 2016) side. The sample images from UCID database are shown in Figure 5.

Photography Image Dataset is created for research on image retrieval. The database contains 2360 images of size 384x256 or 256x384. The images are of JPEG format and each one is manually annotated. Some sample images from this database is shown in figure 6.

Figure 1. Shows some sample images from Petitcola's Photo Database

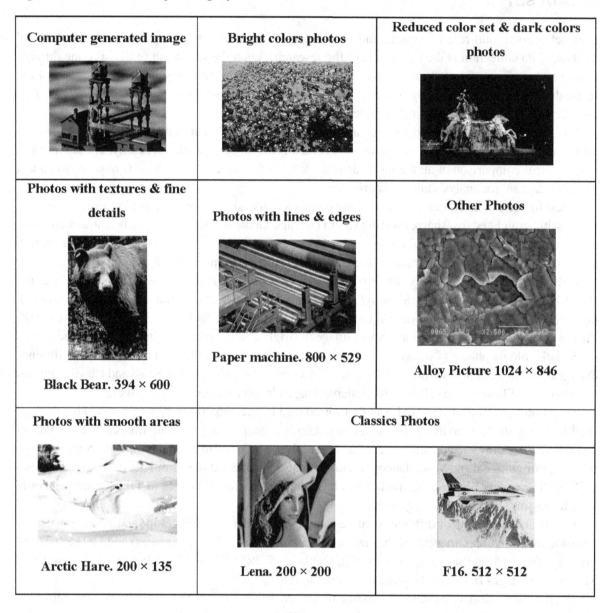

Table 1. Information regarding database

Gray level Images		Color Images	
No. of Images	Size of Images	No. of Images	Size of Images
68	256 × 256	15	128 × 128
96	512 × 512	11	256 × 256
4	1024 × 1024	64	512 × 512
6	Variable size		

Figure 2. Sample Images from the photo database of DECSAI

Free sound is an audio database containing a huge collaborative database of audio snippets, samples, recordings, bleeps, etc. The database contains both mp3 and .wav file of different sizes and durations. But only the .wav files are considered here. Some sample audio plots collected from free sound database are shown in figure 7.

A brief overview of databases and the parameters used in this chapter is given in this section. It is not possible to know the use of databases without a basic introduction of them. At the same time it is not possible to perform fare comparison without knowing the characteristics, format of the test date set. Similarly a basic understanding mainly the threshold (Lanza, C. I., 2018) value for analysis is needed to know clearly before performing test based on certain parameters.

5. COMMONLY USED QUALITY METRICS

In this section commonly used Quality metrics (Panwar, S. et al, 2018) for Image, Audio and Video are discussed. There are few exclusive metrics are also exercised in this paper. These metrics are Peak to Signal Noise Ratio (PSNR), Mean-Square Error (MSE), Structural Similarity Index Method (SSIM), Bit Error Rate (BER) and Correlation Coefficient (CC).

The first one is given by the equation (1). In which Max_{sf} is maximum signal value and is the maximum pixel value of cover image.

$$\text{PSNR} = 10 \log_{10} \left(\frac{\text{Max}_{sf}^{2}}{MSE} \right) \tag{1}$$

The second one is specified in equation (2).

Figure 3. Sample Images from USC-SIPI Image Database

$$MSE = \frac{1}{mn}\sum_{i=0}^{m-1}\sum_{j=0}^{n-1}\left[S_{Ref} - S_{Test}\right]^2 \tag{2}$$

S_{Ref}=original signal; S_{Test}= degraded signal;

Figure 4. Sample Images from Kodak Lossless True Colour Image Suite

Kodak Image 23 (768x512)
Description: two macaws
Photographer: Steve Kelly
Location: Maui, Hawaii, USA
Film: KODACOLOR Gold 100 Plus (35mm)

Kodak Image 8 (768x512)
Description: market place
Photographer: Alfons Rudolph
Location: Essligen, Germany
Film: KODAK VR 100 (35mm)

Kodak Image 3 (768x512)
Description: hats
Photographer: Don Cochran
Location: Bahamas
Film: KODAK EKTAR 25 (35mm)

Kodak Image 9 (512x768)
Description: sailboats under spinnakers
Photographer: John Menihan
Location: Anapolis, MD, USA
Film: KODAK EKTAR 25 (35mm)

Kodak Image 4 (512x768)
Description: portrait of girl in red
Photographer: Bob Clemens
Location: studio
Film: KODAK EKTAR 25 (35mm)

Kodak Image 19 (512x768)
Description: lighthouse in Maine
Photographer: Alan Fink
Location: Maine, USA
Film: KODAK EKTACHROME 64 Pro (35mm)

m, n, I, and j represent number of rows, number of columns of the signal matrix, index of row and index of column.

SSIM is represented in equation (3).

$$SSIM(S,E) = \frac{\left(2\tilde{1}_S\tilde{1}_E + c_1\right)\left(2\tilde{A}_{SE} + c_2\right)}{\left(\tilde{1}_S^2 + \tilde{1}_E^2 + c_1\right)\left(\tilde{A}_S^2 + \tilde{A}_E^2 + c_2\right)} \tag{3}$$

Figure 5. Sample Images from UCID database

μ_S and μ_E are the mean of reference signal S and distorted signal E.

Figure 6. Sample Images from Compressed image database

Figure 7. Sample Audios from Free sound Audio Databases

σ_S =standard deviation of S

σ_E = standard deviation of E

σ_{SE} = correlation of S and E.

BER is presented by the equation (4):

$$BER = \frac{N_{ErrorBit}}{N_{BitsTransmitted}} \times 100 \qquad (4)$$

Consider the transmitted bit sequence is -

0 1 1 0 0 0 1 0 1 1

and the following are the received sequence of bits -

0 0 1 0 0 0 0 0 1 0

Here bit error obtained is 3. So, BER in this case is 3/10, i.e. 0.3

CC is given by paired measurements $(X_1, Y_1), (X_2, Y_2) \ldots (X_n, Y_n)$ in equation (5):

$$Corr_p = \frac{\sum_{i=1}^{n} \left(X_i - \bar{X} \right)\left(Y_i - \bar{Y} \right)}{\sqrt{\sum_{i=1}^{n} \left(X_i - \bar{X} \right)^2 \sum_{i=1}^{n} \left(Y_i - \bar{Y} \right)^2}} \qquad (5)$$

6. METHODS OF STEGANOGRAPHY

In this subsection the method for Histogram based Image Steganography is discussed in detail. Other methods such as Audio Steganography, Text Steganography and Video Steganography are described briefly.

6.1. Image Steganography

Steganography is primeval form of invisible communication. With the advent of technologies, different digital objects like image, audio, text and video are used in Steganography. The basic representation of digital image is a collection of binary bit called picture elements, in short pixels. LSB Substitution, Blocking (Damrudi, M. and Aval, K. J. 2019), and Palette Modification are the basic methods for this steganography. The images are binary, greyscale and colour image. An image is composition of pixels. A greyscale image of 8 bit representation has 2^8=256 shades of grey. Red, Green and Blue are in colour image. The databases contain greyscale as well as colour RGB (Bandekar, P. P. and Suguna, G. C., 2018) images. Example of the three types of images is shown in Figure 8.

Figure 8. Three types of images are shown in (a), (b) and (c)

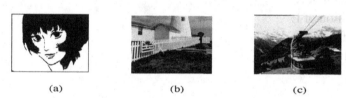

6.2. Histogram Based Image Steganography

The information can hide in any digital media like image, audio, video or text in histogram based on steganography. It allows only intended user to decode hidden information. Histogram contains secret text message and LSB of DCT (Damrudi, M. and Aval, K. J. 2019) is cover image. In the histogram (Padmavathi, B. and Kumari, R. 2013) the binary stream of data has been embedded. It is treated as Stego image.

Here, a 4x4 transformation equation is used which is given by -

$$t_{ij} = f(x) = \begin{cases} \dfrac{1}{\sqrt{N}} \, if \, i = 0 \\ \dfrac{\sqrt{2}}{\sqrt{N}} \cos\left[\left(2j+1\right)i\Pi\right)/2N\right] if \, i > 0 \end{cases} \tag{6}$$

The various steps involved in generation of Stego image is shown in Figure 9.

From cover image, each of pixel values is taken. Next 128 have been subtracted from each of the pixel values. An image block of 4X4 has been taken where equation (6) had been applied. Then DCT of

Figure 9. Steps involved in Stego image generation

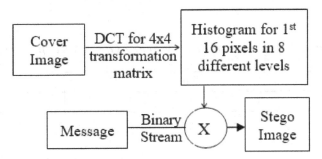

Table 2. Histogram of Eight different grey levels values (From 2ⁿᵈ Column to 9ᵗʰ column)

0-15	2	5	1	0	2	4	0	2
16-31	5	0	3	2	0	0	6	0
.	.	.	.	.	.	.	.	.
496-511	3	0	0	8	4	1	0	0

cover image has been obtained. Table 2 shows a matrix of histogram containing 8 different levels with first column contains number of pixels.

If the message is 'ABC......' then get the first character and convert it into binary stream. It is shown in Table 3. Figure 10 shows the binary stream character is added to Grey Levels.

Table 3. Binary stream for character 'A'

Character	Binary stream of character							
A	0	1	0	0	0	0	0	1

Figure 10. Histogram of DCT of cover image after addition of binary stream of message

No of pixel	Grey level 0	Grey level 1	Grey level 2	Grey level 3	Grey level 4	Grey level 5	Grey level 6	Grey level 7
0-15	2	5	1	0	2	4	0	2
.	.	.	.	.	.	.	.	.

Character	Binary stream of character							
A	0	1	0	0	0	0	0	1

Histogram which has been obtained after embedding binary stream of message is shown in Table 4.

Table 4. Histogram obtained of Number of Pixels vs 0 to 7 Grey levels after embedding text

0-15	2	6	1	0	2	4	0	3
.	.	.	.	.	.	.	.	.

Table 5. Cover image Pixel value

162	150	160	155	130	145	160	180	.
185	100	155	140	130	148	162	155	.
138	120	160	168	150	125	132	162	.
.	.	.	.	.	.	.	.	.

Table 6. Binary Format of Pixel value of cover image

10100101	10010110	10100000	10100000	10011011	10010001	10100000	10110100	.
10111001	01100100	10011011	10001100	10000010	10010100	10100010	10011011	.
.	.	.	.	.	.	.	.	.

Table 7. Binary stream of Histogram

0-15	0010	0110	0001	0000	0010	0100	0000	0011
.	.	.	.	.	.	.	.	.

Table 8. Binary streams obtained after embedding message

10100**010**	10010**110**	10100**001**	10100000	10010**010**	10010**100**	10100**000**	10110**011**	.
10111001	01100100	1001101	10001100	10001100	10010100	10100010	10011011	.
.	.	.	.	.	.	.	.	.

Table 9. After embedding Pixel value of Stego image

162	**150**	**161**	**160**	**146**	**148**	**160**	**179**	.
185	100	155	140	130	148	162	155	.
.	.	.	.	.	.	.	.	.

Now this cover image pixel values have been transferred into binary stream as shown in Table 5. Each of the pixels is now transferred in binary stream as shown in Table 6.

Now binary stream of histogram is shown in Table 7. Table 8 generates Stego image.

The data of Table 8 are transferred to decimal form for obtaining pixel value of Stego image. It is shown in Table 9.

The extraction technique is just the reverse of the embedding technique. The detailed steps of extraction technique are shown in Figure 11.

Figure 11. Steps involved in Extraction

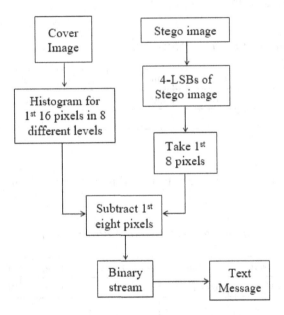

Here using the below equation (7), a 4x4 transformation matrix has been created.

$$t_{ij} = f(x) = \begin{cases} \dfrac{1}{\sqrt{2}} \; if \; i = 0 \\ \dfrac{2}{N} \cos(2j+1) \end{cases} \tag{7}$$

Now considering the cover image, 128 from each of the pixel value has been subtracted and then a block of 4x4 from modified pixel value has been taken to transform the matrix for obtaining the DCT of the image.

Then the histogram of 1st 16 pixels has been created in 8 different gray levels in such a manner that the range of histogram should lie between the lowest and highest value of grey level (Bhargava, S. and Mukhija, M. 2019). Now a matrix of histogram containing 8 different levels as shown in Table 10 has

Table10. Histogram of cover image

0-15	2	5	1	0	2	4	0	2
16-31	5	0	3	2	0	0	6	0
.	.	.	.	.	.	.	.	.
496-511	3	0	0	8	4	1	0	0

been created. If there are values which are greater than 14 in the histogram, then set it to 14 as similar to the process of embedding.

Pixel values of Stego images are shown in Table 11.

Table 11. During extraction Pixel values of Stego image

162	150	161	160	146	148	160	179	.
185	100	155	140	130	148	162	155	.
.	.	.	.	.	.	.	.	.

Each of pixels is transferred now in binary form and it is shown in Table 12.

Table 12. Pixel values of Stego image are converted into Binary stream

10100**010**	10010**110**	10100**001**	10100**000**	10010**010**	10010**100**	10100**000**	10110**011**	.
10111001	01100100	1001101	10001100	10001100	10010100	10100010	10011011	.
.	.	.	.	.	.	.	.	.

4 LSB bits of Table 12 contain binary stream of message and it is shown in Table 13.

Table 13. Stego image contains 4-LSB bits of message

0-15	0010	0110	0001	0000	0010	0100	0000	0011
16-31	.	.	.	.	.	.	.	.
.	.	.	.	.	.	.	.	.

After obtaining this, it has been converted to decimal followed by it which has been subtracted from histogram of Cover image to obtain binary message stream, as shown below in Figure 12.

Binary stream of messages which has been obtained after subtraction are shown in Table 14.

Figure 12. Histogram (in decimal) of Secret is subtracted from Histogram of Cover image

No of pixel	Grey level 0	Grey level 1	Grey level 2	Grey level 3	Grey level 4	Grey level 5	Grey level 6	Grey level 7
0-15	2	6	1	0	2	4	0	3
.	.	.	.	.	.	.	.	.

No of pixel	Grey level 0	Grey level 1	Grey level 2	Grey level 3	Grey level 4	Grey level 5	Grey level 6	Grey level 7
0-15	2	5	1	0	2	4	0	2
.	.	.	.	.	.	.	.	.

Now this binary stream has been converted to character stream to get the text which was embedded. The above value is 65 and it is "A" in ASCII (Ozighor, E. R. and Izegbu, I., 2020). The embedding method and extraction method are shown below and the results are shown in Table 15.

Embedding Method

STEP 1:   Obtain the binary stream of the given text.

STEP 2:   Construct a 4x4 matrix of cover image for DCT.

STEP 3:   DCT is Performed on the given cover image.

STEP 4:   Histogram is now constructed by DCT of the cover image. Take 16 pixels from 8 different levels. If the value of histogram in a given level is more than 14 then set it to 14. 4-LSBs of cover image are used to embed text.

STEP 5:   Take first 8 bit of the binary stream of message and add it to the given eight level of histogram.

STEP 6:   1st 4 Least Significant Bits of cover image are embedded in histogram containing message.

STEP 7:   Make 4 Least Significant Bits of 8 successive pixels to 0 and this will be used as terminating condition.

Extraction Algorithm

STEP 1:   Cover image of 4*4 matrixes are constructed for DCT.

STEP 2:   DCT of the cover image is made.

STEP 3:   Histogram of the cover image is constructed.

STEP 4:   Stego image obtains 4 LSBs of each pixel and now it is converted to decimal.

STEP 5:   Each decimal value of stego image is subtracted from corresponding histogram value of the cover image to get the binary stream.

Table 14. Binary stream of retrieved Secret message

Binary stream of character							
0	1	0	0	0	0	0	1

Table 15. Result Analysis for Cover vs. Stego and Original with Secret Extracted Image

Cover Image	Original Secret	Stego Image	Extracted Secret	PSNR	SSIM
				49.5026	0.9432
				45.3315	0.9977
				43.4010	0.9141

Table 16. PSNR and BER of secret message

No. of characters in secret message	PSNR	BER
30	61.288	.000412
40	59.678	.000587
50	58.346	.000700
60	57.342	.008890

Table 17. Comparison Results

No. of hidden characters in the proposed method	BER of the proposed method	Depth of Hiding of the existing method	BER of the existing method
30	0.000412	1	2.780208
40	0.000587	2	8.330555
50	0.000700	3	8.315001
60	0.008890	4	8.326388
100	0.282738	5	8.347917
500	0.500095	6	8.265972
1500	0.500961	7	8.359446

STEP 6:   Convert binary stream into text stream.

STEP 7:   This process is repeated until it generates four 0's in Least Significant Bit of 8 consecutive pixels.

6.3. Result Analysis

Table 16 shows the values of PSNR and BER

BER value of proposed method has been used for comparison with the steganography methods published by. It is shown in Table 17.

7. AUDIO STEGANOGRAPHY

The blind audio steganography on a key based method is used on DWT and DCT. The message is hidden while a group of people are talking to each other and it is impossible to extract message from the chaos. It can happen in any party such as in Cocktail Party. The process is more robust and wrapping (Debnath, B., Das, J. C. and De, D., 2018) Stego-audio is done easily. The entire process is shown in figure 13.

8. RESULTS

There is a possibility of injection of noise in secret communicate for reducing detecting the message. The quality analysis of Secret image, Scrambled (Ramalingam, M., Isa, N. A. M. and Puviarasi, R. 2020) Secret Image, Extracted Scrambled Image and Extracted Image are shown in Table 18.

9. TEXT STEGANOGRAPHY

In this approach the transmission of secret data is used by the cover text. In image, audio and video steganography there are plenty of redundant (Achkoun, K., Hanin, C. and Omary, F. 2019) spaces that are available to hide data. This is not possible in text steganography since small modification can be notified easily. Normally any language is chosen to hide data provided that both sender and receiver can understand the language. In most cases English language is chosen. The basic method relies on lexical substitution techniques. The word in 2nd, 3rd, 4th … places of each sentence of cover text is replaced by the secret text. Suppose the cover text is:

"Then speaker *starts to speak before audience about happiness in life. It is* happening *in many times in lives. Everyone is frantically* for *happiness all around his/her life. Our happiness lies in* the *happiness of other people. Give them sky happiness and* you *will get your own happiness."*

"It is time to touch sky" is the secret text.

The resultant passage after embedding process is given below:

Figure 13. The Scenario of Embedding and Extraction Process

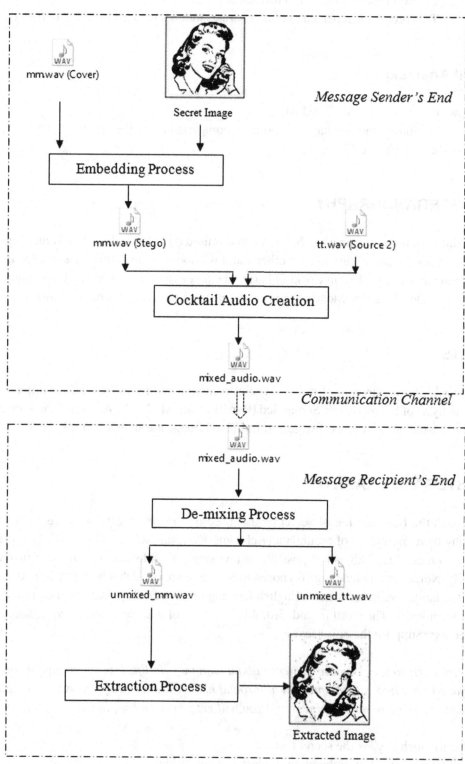

Table 18. Quality Analysis of Types of Images

Secret Image (I_S)	Scrambled Secret Image	Extracted Scrambled Image	Extracted Image (I_E)	PSNR (I_S, I_E)	SSIM (I_S, I_E)	BER (I_S, I_E)	CC (I_S, I_E)
				72.8714	0.9999	1.0925	0.9717
				70.9007	0.9999	1.0620	0.9729
Keep the Gun under the shed			Keep the Gun under the shed	68.3717	0.9998	0.9460	0.9597
				72.3511	0.9999	0.3174	0.9852

"Then It starts to speak before audience about happiness in life. It is is in many time in lives. Everyone is frantically time happiness all around his/her life. Our happiness lies in the to happiness of other people. Give them sky happiness and touch will get your own happiness. It is the purpose of human sky".

Since it does not have any meaning so it is easy to detect that there is something hidden in it. It is required to write cover text in such a way that after hiding the secret message shall have a proper meaning. Researchers used part-of-speech (POS) to ensure meaningful message. The method along with results is not discussed here since the chapter concentrates on histogram based image steganography.

10. VIDEO STEGANOGRAPHY

In this method a collection of still images called, frame, is used to hide any secret in the video. MPEG format is most popular. The process is shown in Figure 14.

Figure 14. Stego video creation technique

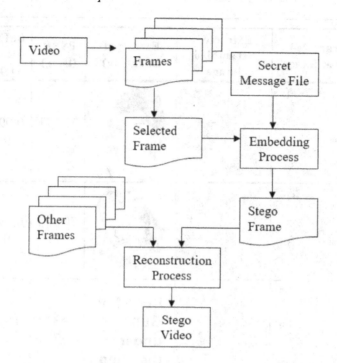

Video is a collection of frames which is nothing but a still image. An image is composition of picture elements or pixels. The quality of any image is measured by resolution and aspect ratio. Researchers consider pixel resolution of 640 × 480 pixels. Full High Definition (HD) can have resolution of 1920x1080. Ultra HD (Pramanik, S. et al. 2014) can be of 2k, 4k and 8k.

A video can be treated as a sequence of frames. Each frame is nothing but a still image. Rapid succession of collection of frames creates an impression of movement. At first, one of the frame cover video is selected for data hiding. It is known as Stego frame once embedding is completed. Now the question arises how that Stego frame is chosen to hide data. There is a concept called Shot transition detection (simply, shot detection) or cut detection or scene change detection or scene boundary detection in video processing. A shot or scene or cut is series of frames shot at a stretch with one camera. There are several existing methods for scene change detection. Still all these algorithms generally follow two steps:

Scoring: A score which is basically a number of excellence is calculated between a pair of frames (frame$_i$ and frame$_{i+1}$). These scores can be evaluated through Histogram Differences, Sum of Absolute Differences and Edge Change Ratio generally.

Decision: The frame which scored highest in scene change detection has been chosen for further processing.

Figure 15 and figure 16 demonstrate the approach of the proposed technique of video steganography.

Here the secret image is processed through Arnold Transform (Kui, X. S. and Wu, J. 2018) which creates a scrambled image. The advantage of using Arnold Transform in steganography is that it rearranges the pixel in such a way that random cropping Steganalysis attack on Stego object doesn't destroy the secret image.

The four sets of test results have been shown Table 19 and Table 20. Table 21 shows the resultant image.

Figure 15. Block Diagram of embedding algorithm

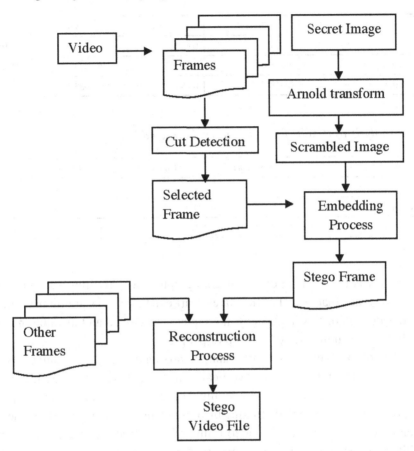

11. CONCLUSION

Figure 16. Block Diagram of decoding algorithm

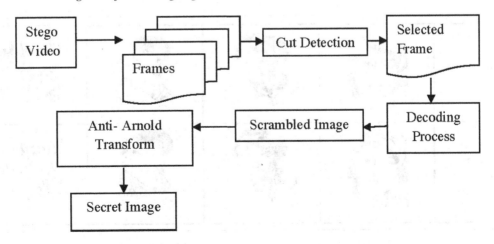

Table 19. Analysis of Results for Videos

Full HD Cover Video →	Video #1	Video #2	Video #3	Video #4
Mean Square Error	0.5342	0.6604	0.4468	0.2129
Peak Signal to Noise Ratio	50.8535	58.1707	53.2739	50.5931
Structural Similarity Index	0.9184	0.8989	0.5083	0.6512

Table 20. Quality Analysis of Results for Original vs. Extracted Secret

Secret Binary Image →	Image #1	Image #2	Image #3	Image #4
Mean Square Error	0	0	0	1.2346e-04
Peak Signal to Noise Ratio	99	99	99	87.2157
Structural Similarity Index	1	1	1	1.0000

The aim of this chapter is to enlighten digital steganography specially Image Steganography. The literature survey demonstrates that not all of the state-of-art existing works are robust, imperceptible and have high capacities in one go. Next audio steganography is discussed and its implementation will find secret data to be hidden through party of a group of people.

The common flaw of existing text steganography approaches are visual changes like space, use of colour or different fonts in text, horizontal or vertical arrangement etc. These are highlighted.

Video is used for secret communication by hiding data. Here a novel blind technique of hiding image has been proposed and implemented utilizing the redundant bits of cover video object. An effective function has been used to opt for specific video frame where some scene change occurs. This makes identification of Stego frame very difficult for any intruder out of several thousand frames. It also provides additional layer of security for data hiding. In the next level secret image is scrambled which ensures another layer of security. At last the secret hiding is done in transform domain. Other than quality data extraction, this method has also been tested against Steganalysis attacks like random cropping (Azza,

Table 21. Images for Original Secret vs. Extracted Secret

A. A. and Lian, S. 2020), rotation, resizing, noise addition and histogram equalization, the results of which are very affirmative. All the methods of steganography are discussed but the main stress is on image steganography.

REFERENCES

Achkoun, K., Hanin, C., & Omary, F. (2019) SPF-CA: A new cellular automata based block cipher using key-dependent S-boxes. *Journal of Discrete Mathematical Sciences and Cryptography.* Doi:10.10 80/09720529.2019.1649031

AithalP. S. (2016). A Review on Various E-Business and M-Business Models & Research Opportunities. *International Journal of Management, IT and Engineering, 6*(1), 275-298. Available at SSRN: https://ssrn.com/abstract=2779175

Antonio, H., Prasad, P. W. C., & Alsadoon, A. (2019). Implementation of Cryptography in Steganography for Enhanced Security. *Multimedia Tools and Applications*, 78, 32721–32734. doi:10.100711042-019-7559-7

Azza, A. A., & Lian, S. (2020). *Multi-secret image sharing based on elementary cellular automata with steganography. Multimed Tools Appl.* doi:10.100711042-020-08823-8

Bandekar, P. P., & Suguna, G. C. (2018). LSB Based Text and Image Steganography Using AES Algorithm. *3rd International Conference on Communication and Electronics Systems (ICCES)*, 782-788. doi: 10.1109/CESYS.2018.8724069

Banik, B. G., & Banik, A. (2020). Robust, Imperceptible and Blind Video Steganography using RGB Secret, Maximum Likelihood Estimation and Fibonacci Encryption. *International Journal of Electronic Security and Digital Forensics, 12*(2), 174–199.

Bhargava, S., & Mukkhija, M. (2019). Hide Image and Text using LSB, DWT and RSA based on Image Steganography. *ICTACT Journal on Image and Video Processing, 9*(3), 1940–1946.

Chaharlang, J., Mosleh, M., & Rasouli-Heikalabad, S. (2020). A novel quantum steganography-Steganalysis system for audio signals. *Multimedia Tools and Applications, 79*, 17551–17577. doi:10.100711042-020-08694-z

Damrudi, M., & Aval, K. J. (2019). Image Steganography using LSB and Encrypted Message with AES, RSA, DES, 3DES and Blowfish. *International Journal of Engineering and Advanced Technology, 8*(63), 204–208.

Debnath, B., Das, J. C., & De, D. (2018). Design of Image Steganographic Architecture using Quantum-Dot Cellular Automata for Secure Nanocommunication Networks. *Nano Communication Networks, 15*, 41–58.

Douglas, M., Bailey, K., & Leeney, M. (2018). An overview of steganography techniques applied to the protection of biometric data. *Multimedia Tools and Applications, 77*, 17333–17373. doi:10.100711042-017-5308-3

Duan, X. (2020). A New High Capacity Image SteganographyMethod Combined with Image Elliptic Curve Cryptography and Deep Neural Network. *IEEE Access: Practical Innovations, Open Solutions*, *8*, 25777–25788.

Embaby, A. A., Mohamed, A., Shalaby, W., & Elsayed, K. M. (2020). Digital Watermarking Properties, Classification and Techniques. *International Journal of Engineering and Advanced Technology*, *9*(3), 2742–2750.

Eyssa, A. A., Abdelsamie, F. E., & Abdelnaiem, A. E. (2020). An Efficient Image Steganography Approach over Wireless Communication System. *Wireless Personal Communications*, *110*, 321–337. doi:10.100711277-019-06730-2

Gowda, S. N. (2016). An advanced Diffie-Hellman approach to image steganography. *2016 IEEE International Conference on Advanced Networks and Telecommunications Systems (ANTS)*, 1-4. doi: 10.1109/ANTS.2016.7947849

Gupta, M.K., & Chandra, P. (2020). A comprehensive survey of data mining. *Int. J. Inf. Tecnol.* doi:10.100741870-020-00427-7

Hambouz, A., Shaheen, Y., Manna, A., Al-Fayoumi, M., & Tedmori, S. S. (2019). Achieving Data Integrity and Confidentiality Using Image Steganography and Hashing Techniques. *2nd International Conference on new Trends in Computing Sciences (ICTCS)*, 1-6. doi: 109/ICTCS.2019.892306010.1

Handoko, W. T. (2020). IOP Conf. Ser. *Mater. Sci. Eng., 879.*

Kalubandi, V. K. P., Vaddi, H., Ramineni, V., & Agilandeeswari Loganathan, A. (2016). A Novel Image Encryption Algorithm using AES and Visual Cryptography. *Proceedings of NGCT 2016*. DOI: 10.1109/NGCT.2016.7877521

Kui, X. S., & Wu, J. (2018). A Modification Free Steganography Method Based on Image Information Entropy. *Security and Communication Networks*, 1–8. doi:10.1155/2018/6256872

Kumar, S., Singh, A., & Kumar, M. (2019). *Information Hiding with Adaptive Steganography based on Novel Fuzzy Edge Identification*. Defence Technology.

Lanza-Cruz, I., Berlanga, R., & Aramburu, M. J. (2018). Modelling Analytical Streams for Social Business Intelligence. *Informatica (Vilnius)*, *5*, 33.

Mahato, S., Khan, D. A., & Yadav, D. K. (2020). A Modified Approach to Data Hiding in Microsoft Word Documents by Change-Tracking Technique. *Journal of King Saud University-Computer and Information Sciences*, *32*(2), 216–224.

Mukherjee, S., Roy, S., & Sanyal, G. (2018). Image Steganography using Mid Position Value Technique. *Procedia Computer Science*, *132*, 461–468. doi:10.1016/j.procs.2018.05.160

Ozighor, E. R., & Izegbu, I. (2020). Information Protection against Security Threats in an Insecure Environment using Cryptography and Steganography. *Computing in Science & Engineering*, *8*(5), 1671–1692.

Padmavathi, B., & Kumari, R. (2013). A Survey on Performance Analysis of DES, AES and RSA Algorithm alongwith LSB Substitution Technique. *International Journal of Scientific Research*, *2*(4), 170–174.

Panwar, S., Damani, S., & Kumar, M. (2018). Digital Image Steganography using Modified LSB and AES Cryptography. *International Journal of Recent Engineering Research and Development, 3*(6), 18–27.

Pradhan, A., Sekhar, K. R., & Swain, G. (2018). Digital Image Steganography Using LSB Substitution, PVD and EMD. *Mathematical Problems in Engineering.* Advance online publication. doi:10.1155/2018/1804953

Pramanik, S., Bandyopadhyay, S. K., & Ghosh, R. (2020). Signature Image Hiding in Color Image using Steganography and Cryptography based on Digital Signature Concepts. *2020 2nd International Conference on Innovative Mechanisms for Industry Applications (ICIMIA),* 665-669.

Pramanik, S., & Bandyopadhyay, S. (2013). Application of Steganography in Symmetric Key Cryptography with Genetic Algorithm. *International Journal of Computers and Technology, 10*(7).

Pramanik, S., & Bandyopadhyay, S. K. (2014). Hiding Secret Message in an Image, International Journal of Innovative Science. *Engineering & Technology, 1*(3), 553–559.

Pramanik, S., & Singh, R. P. (2017). *Role of Steganography in Security Issues. International Journal on Advance Studies in Engineering and Science.*

Pramanik, S., Singh, R.P., & Ghosh, R. (2019). A New Encrypted Method in Image Steganography. *Indonesian Journal of Electrical Engineering and Computer Science, 14*(3), 1412–1419. .v13.i3.pp1412-1419 doi:10.11591/ijeecs

Pramanik, S., Singh, R. P., & Ghosh, R. (2020). *Application of bi-orthogonal wavelet transform and genetic algorithm in image steganography. Multimed Tools Appl.* doi:10.100711042-020-08676-1

Ramalingam, M., Isa, N. A. M., & Puviarasi, R. (2020). A Secured Data Hiding using Affline Transformation in Video Steganography. *Procedia Computer Science, 171,* 1147–1156. doi:10.1016/j.procs.2020.04.123

Rashid, A., & Rahim, M. K. (2016). Critical Analysis of Steganography "An Art of Hidden Writing". *International Journal of Security and Applications, 10*(1), 259–282. doi:10.14257//ijsia.2016.10.3.24

Ritala, P., Schneider, S., & Michailova, S. (2020). Innovation management research methods: embracing rigor and diversity. *R&D Management.* doi:10.1111/radm.12414

Sah, H. R., & Gunasekaran, G. (2015). Privacy preserving data mining using visual steganography and encryption. *10th International Conference on Computer Science & Education (ICCSE),* 154-158. doi:10.1109/ICCSE.2015.7250234

Setyono, A., & Setiadi, D. R. I. M. (2019). Article. *Journal of Physics: Conference Series, 1196,* 012039.

Swain, G. (2018). *High Capacity Image Steganography Using Modified LSB Substitution and PVD against Pixel Difference Histogram Analysis.* Security and Computer Networks. doi:10.1155/2018/1505896

Taha, M. S., Rahim, M. S. M., Lafta, S. A., Hashim, M. A., & Alzuabidi, H. M. (2019). Combination of Steganography and Cryptography: A Short Survey. *ICSET, 2019.* Advance online publication. doi:10.1088/1757-899X/518/5/052003

Von Leipzig, T. (2017). Initialising customer-orientated digital transformation in enterprises. *Procedia Manufacturing, 8,* 517–524.

Wang, M., Gu, W., & Ma, C. (2020). A Multimode Network Steganography for Covert Wireless Communication based on BitTorrent. *Security and Communication Networks*. Advance online publication. doi:10.1155/2020/8848315

Zenati, A., Ouarda, W., & Alimi, A. M. (2019). SSDIS-BEM: A New Signature Steganography Document Image System based on Beta Elliptic Modeling. *Engineering Science and Technology, an International Journal, 23*(3), 470-482.

Chapter 2
Image Steganography:
Recent Trends and Techniques

Sana Parveen K
MEA Engineering College, India

Renjith V. Ravi
https://orcid.org/0000-0001-9047-3220
MEA Engineering College, India

Basma Abd El-Rahiem
Menoufia University, Egypt

Mangesh M. Ghonge
https://orcid.org/0000-0003-0140-4827
Sandip Foundation's Institute of Technology and Research Centre, India

ABSTRACT

Steganography is the process used hide the existence of information during transmission. Cover mediums like text, image, audio, and video protocols are used to hide the secret information. This process helps to provide secret communication between two parties. As data is unknown, it is challenging to attract the attention of any third parties. Therefore, steganography becomes the best and most secure method for data transmission. Digital images are the most common cover media or carriers in steganographic processes, where the secret payload is embedded into images. Several techniques are coming under image steganography, and there includes a different method to ensure the secrecy of messages. This chapter gives an overview of the different commonly used techniques in this area and the latest existing image steganography methods and the comparison of techniques.

DOI: 10.4018/978-1-7998-7160-6.ch002

INTRODUCTION

Technology and internet usage have entirely changed in every social field. Social evolution is growing each and every day and affects our daily life also. Without the internet and technologies, a day will not pass (Hossen et al., 2020). As the internet revolution is increasing higher, the main challenge is to provide information security. People give more importance to privacy in life. Hidden communication is a difficult thing in this internet era. It is important to keep information secure from hackers or cyber-thieves so that a proactive security system is necessary (Kalaichelvi V et al., 2020). In such situations, security methods like cryptography, watermarking etc., gain attention. In this chapter, such a security strategy named Steganography and its latest existing methods are briefly discussed.

Steganography is an art of communication that provides a healthy means of security to information transmission and reception. It hides the existence of the information, which is the main factor which differ steganography from other hiding methods (Al-Sanjary O I et al., 2020). Steganography is a way of inserting a secret message in text/ image/ audio/ video or protocol. The main concept of steganography is illustrated in Figure 1.

Figure 1. Concept of Steganography

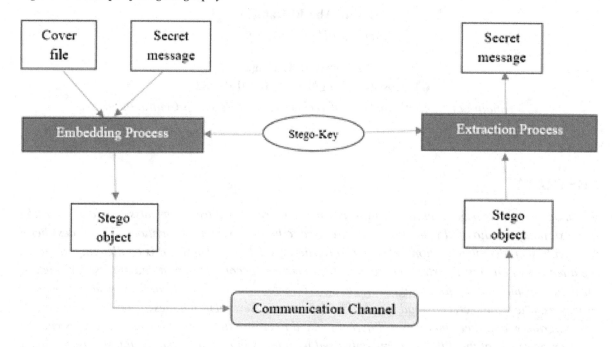

Figure 1. shows the basic concept of steganography, the term cover file indicates the carrier like image, text, video or audio etc. The secret message is embedding in the cover file with the help of stego-key. Stego key is an optional key that uses in both the embedding and extraction process. After embedding, the output is obtained as a stego object or stego file containing the secret information in the cover file. At the extraction process, the secret message is extracting from stego object with the provided stego key. That stego key must be the same which used for embedding (Pramanik S et al., 2020).

Image steganography, text steganography, audio Steganography, video steganography or protocol steganography etc. are disparate kinds of steganographic means (Anusha M et al., 2020). Just as the cover file changes the method of Steganography will be different.

In the image steganography, a cover file that hides the secret message is an image. And stego-object becomes stego-image, which is the output image that contains a secret message (Kaur et al., 2020). The hiding process will not affect the physical properties of the carrier image. Therefore, it doesn't attract any attention of outside parties other than the sender and recipient. The basic concept of image steganography is shown in Figure 2.

Figure 2. Concept of Image Steganography

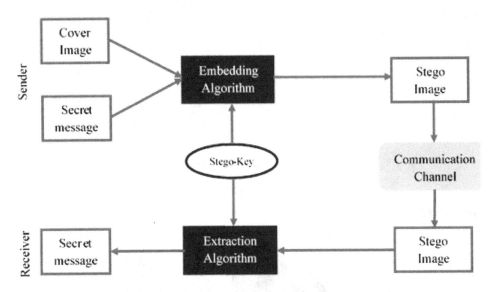

The hierarchical tree diagram of image steganography is given in Figure 3. to obtain a brief idea about basic technologies (Dhawan S & Gupta R., 2021).

The Figure 4. shows the percentage of general image steganographic techniques in total percentage of surveyed papers. Out of 52 research papers, the half percentage is spatial domain techniques i.e., 50%. And 24% is transform domain techniques, 26% shows of other techniques.

Out of total 50% of spatial techniques, 76% is Least significant bit insertion method because of the easiness. And the second most commonly used method is Pixel value differentiation scheme which is as 24% of total. The pie-diagram is shown in Figure 5.

In the case of Transform domain techniques i.e., in Figure 6, Discrete wavelet transformation is with 33%, Dual tree complex wavelet transformation and Discrete cosine transformation carries equal percentage of 25. And other transform domain techniques are 17%.

As the existence of communication is unknown, steganographic methods provide a high guarantee of confidentiality for information (Debnath et al., 2020). Media, transportation of information among companies, digital watermarking are very commonly using steganographic schemes. Smart identity cards are available which hides the details of a person in their photographs. Image steganography has applications in medical fields like patient's information such as patient name, patient's ID, and doctors remarks

Figure 3. General hierarchical tree diagram of image steganography

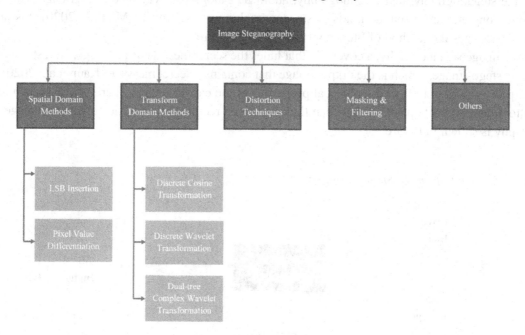

Figure 4. General Pie-chart of all methods

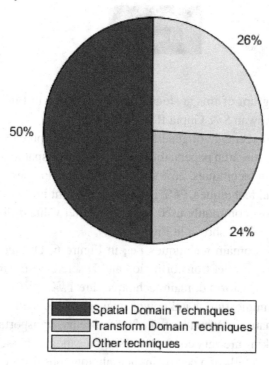

Figure 5. Pie-chart of Spatial domain techniques

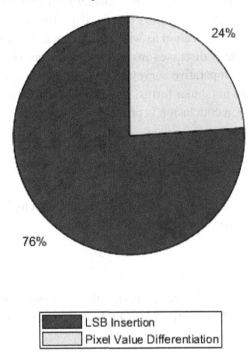

Figure 6. Pie-chart of Transform domain techniques

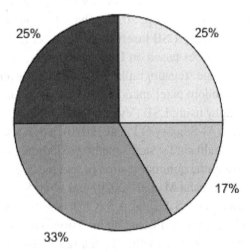

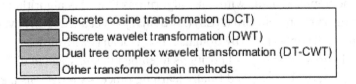

i.e., patients medical record is embedding in medical images (Stoyanov et al., 2020). It is also used by investigation agencies, police department, Military defense department (Duan et al., 2020), International Governments for confidential communication as well as in many more fields.

The next section, Section 2, briefly discusses an overview of Image steganography with basic security algorithms as sub-sections and comparative survey of the performance of distinct currently innovated image steganographic techniques in tabular forms. It will be showing the recent researches on the area of Image Steganography. Finally, a conclusion is provided in Section 3.

AN OVERVIEW OF IMAGE STEGANOGRAPHY

Image steganography includes different types of techniques and data hiding methods nowadays. Some of the vital data confidential schemes are explained in this section.

Spatial Domain Methods

In spatial domain methods, the secret information is straightly inserted in the carrier image pixel values without affecting the same physical properties (Anusha M et al., 2020). It includes different classifications as follows:

LSB Insertion

Hiding data using LSB insertion is one of the most repeatedly used image steganographic techniques. The method is done by replacing LSB of a randomly selected cover image with the secret message to be transmitted (Kalaichelvi T & P Apuroop, 2020). The selection of random pixels can be done by stego key. An illustration of the primary LSB insertion method is given in Figure 7.

Many steganographic analyses based on LSB insertion are available in the last few years. Some of them include changeable image steganography by using dual-layer LSB matching (Sahu A K & Swain G, 2020), using LSB and random pixel encoding process with encryption (Soni T et al., 2020), object-oriented image steganography using LSB (Vyas A O & Dudul S V., 2020), an optimum steganographic algorithm for secure image (Al-Sanjary O I et al., 2020), a dynamic 3-bit image steganographic scheme for medical systems and e-healthcare systems method (Siddiqui et al., 2020). Anusha M et al. conducted a study on providing confidential communication of text messages and audio messages using the image steganographic algorithm (Anusha M et al., 2020) and blind feature image steganography based on local binary pattern by Chakraborty S & Jalal A S (Chakraborty S & Jalal A S, 2020). Another scheme is differential evolution and the least significant bit insertion-based method (Kaur et al., 2020) as a study to get a structured image steganographic method by using a multi-objective differential evolution process.

Researchers also approached a novel image steganographic scheme by using the least significant substitution (LSB) steganographic scheme with other algorithms like RSA algorithm (Kalaichelvi V et al., 2020) and Advanced Encryption Standard (AES) (Al-Sanjary O I et al., 2020). A variable neighborhood search (VNS) based method is introduced by Boughaci D & Douah H with the least significant bits method (LSB). In this, VNS chooses suitable pixel positions to embed the message in different neighborhoods. LSB insertion process inserts the data, and finally learning process strengthens the performance of the process (Boughaci D & Douah H, 2020). A secure algorithm to identify the receiver is not a machine

Figure 7. Basic LSB insertion method

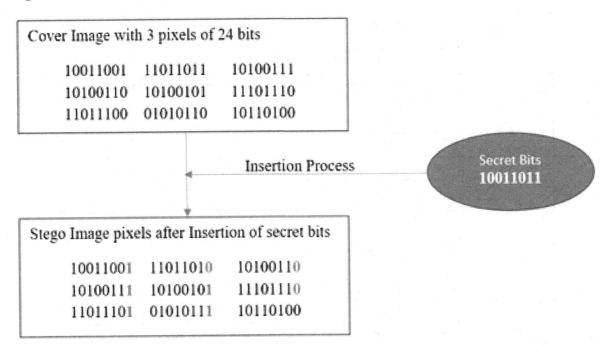

using CAPTCHA codes (Kalaichelvi T & P Apuroop, 2020). In this method, the encrypted CAPTCHA message within the cover image is transmitting. Once the authenticated receiver side is identified, the secret message will be sent using the LSB method. Neogi P P G et al. 's work explained steganographic scheme named as complex region determination based on intelligent water drop (IWD-CRD) (Neogi P P G et al., 2020). They applied the Intelligent water drops algorithm (IWD) for finding the complex region on the input image. And the implantation of secret information is done by Least significant bit algorithm. Recently (Nolkha A et al., 2020) presented a comparative analysis of LSB image steganography on different colour models like RGB, YCbCr, YUV, and CMY. Comparing the PSNR values of each color model concluded that RGB and CMY show good image quality than other color models. Image Region Decomposition (IRD) algorithm and LSB scheme are used for Medical and e-Healthcare Systems to secure the patients' information inside a cover image. Siddiqui G F et al. explained by portioning the cover image into three main regions: lower, middle, and higher based on intensity levels and utilizes the secret image pixel point bits till three least significant bit (Siddiqui G F et al., 2020). Pandey J et al. (Pandey J et al., 2020) introduced interpolation and cyclic LSB substitution-based image steganographic scheme in digital Images. The RGB channels of the carrier image are utilized to conceal the secret detailed bits. Color image component channels acting as the red channel, green channel, and blue channel hide the first bit, second bit, and third bit of the message, respectively. It continued as a cyclic process. Hence it is named as cyclic LSB substitution technique. As mentioned by every researcher, the LSB insertion method provides high payload capacity and simple information recovery.

Table 1.LSB Insertion based image steganographic algorithms

Sl.No	Author &Year	Title of Work	Methods/Techniques used	Findings
1	(Sahu et al., 2020)	"Reversible Image Steganography Using Dual Layer LSB Matching".	Least significant bit (LSB) matching.	High embedding efficiency. Reduces the distortion caused to the images.
2	(Chakraborty et al., 2020)	"A novel local binary pattern based blind feature image steganography."	Least significant bit (LSB) insertion method.	Very high PSNR value with better embedding capacity.
3	(Kaur et al., 2020)	"An efficient image steganography method using multi-objective differential evolution."	Differential evolution and LSB substitution method.	Better robustness PSNR, SSIM, and BER, quality of stego image and message carrying capacity.
3	(Anusha M et al., 2020)	"Secured Communication of Text and Audio using Image Steganography."	Least significant bit (LSB) Embedding.	High PSNR value.
5	(Kalaichelvi V et al., 2020)	"A stable image steganography: a novel approach based on modified RSA algorithm and 2–4 least significant bit (LSB) technique."	Modified RSA algorithm and LSB insertion algorithm.	High imperceptibility data efficiency and security.
6	(Kalaichelvi T & P Apuroop, 2020)	"Image Steganography Method to Achieve Confidentiality Using CAPTCHA for Authentication."	Least significant bit (LSB) substitution Algorithm.	More secure and reliable.
7	(Soni T et al., 2020)	"Using Least-Significant Bit and Random Pixel Encoding with Encryption for Image Steganography."	Least significant bit (LSB) insertion method and random pixel encoding process.	High robustness and security. Hide any kind of data.
8	(Neogi P P G et al., 2020)	"Intelligent Water Drops Based Image Steganography."	Least significant bit (LSB) insertion method.	Better security of data.
9	(Vyas A O & Dudul S V 2020)	"A Novel Approach of Object-Oriented Image Steganography Using LSB."	Least significant bit (LSB) steganography method.	More secure.
10	(Elharrouss O et al., 2020)	"An image steganography approach based on k least significant bits (k-LSB)."	k LSB based method using LSB coding.	High robustness and very less data loss during transmission or reception.
11	(Boughaci D & Douah H, 2020)	"A Variable Neighbourhood Search-Based Method with Learning for Image Steganography."	Variable neighbourhood search (VNS) and least significant bits insertion (LSB) technique.	Better performance with good image quality.
12	(Chandra N S R et al., 2020)	"A Novel Image Steganography Model Using LSB with Extended ASCII Codes."	LSB with Extended ASCII Codes.	High payload capacity and robustness with strong data security.
13	(Brar R K & Sharma A, 2020)	"Improved Steganography Using Odd Even Substitution."	Least significant bit (LSB) insertion method using odd-even pixel substitution.	More Secure.
14	(Patani K & Rathod D, 2020)	"Advanced 3-Bit LSB Based on Data Hiding Using Steganography."	Least significant bit (LSB) insertion method.	High PSNR value with better performance and accuracy.
15	(Al-Sanjary O I et al., 2020)	"A New Approach to Optimum Steganographic Algorithm for Secure Image."	Advanced Encryption Standard (AES) with Least Significant Bit (LSB) insertion process.	Improved data security with accuracy in reception process.
16	(Pramanik S et al., 2020)	"Signature Image Hiding in Colour Image using Steganography and Cryptography based on Digital Signature Concepts."	Cryptography & LSB method in Steganography.	High secrecy and safety of data transmission.
17	(Nolkha A et al., 2020)	"Image Steganography Using LSB Substitution: A Comparative Analysis on Different Colour Models".	LSB Substitution method.	RGB and CMY colour model provides good image quality also shows better results and performance.
18	(Siddiqui et al., 2020)	"A Dynamic Three-Bit Image Steganography Algorithm for Medical and e-Healthcare Systems."	Image Region Decomposition (IRD) algorithm and LSB insertion process.	Highly imperceptible and non-attractive.
19	(Pandey J et al., 2021)	"Steganographic Method Based on Interpolation and Cyclic LSB Substitution of Digital Images."	Cyclic Least Significant Bit Substitution	Assured security and better embedding capacity.

Pixel Value Differentiation

In this method, the secret information is hiding by comparing two consecutive pixels' pixel value differences. The difference decides the amount of information that could be hidden. It is widely used in data-concealing fields (Vishnu B et al., 2020). Firstly, the cover image is partitioning into non-overlapping and consecutive groups of two neighboring pixels. From each group, the difference is calculating. Then all the sets of values are grouping into different ranges and creating a range table. The secret bit is adding

Figure 8. Basic Pixel Value Differentiation method

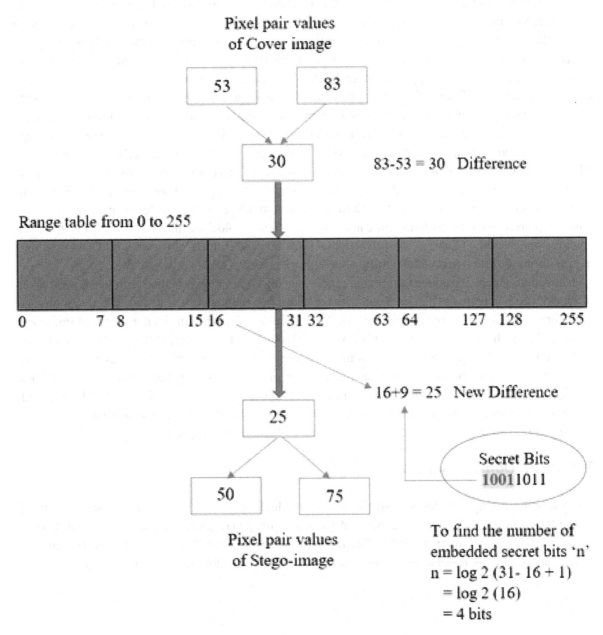

different values to get a new difference. This new difference decides the amount of information that can hide to get stego image. The primary pixel value differentiation method is shown in Figure 8.

The Figure 8 explains the necessary procedure in the pixel value differentiation process. Here the secret bit adds 10011011 but, only 4 bits can be embedded from the range table. The pixel pair values of the cover image are assumed as 53 and 83. The difference value is 30, which is in the range of 16 to 31, which defines that it can embed four bits of secret information. The integral value of secret bits 1001 is 9, is added to the lower range 16 to get the new difference value 25. This new difference is making use to get pixel pair values of stego image.

Researchers (Nisha C D & Monoth T, 2020) conducted pixel value differencing based study on spatial domain image steganographic techniques with detailed analysis. The analyzed the recently introduced PVD techniques with performance matrices like imperceptibility, payload embedding capacity, robustness…etc. Kukharska N et al. 's work focused on securing approaches by using Arnold algorithm with pixel value differencing scheme. Arnold algorithm is made use to reposition the pixels of the porter image. After applying the Arnold algorithm to BMP color image matrices, it separates to blocks. The Arnold algorithm was again applied to shuffle the block with confidential data to ensure better confidentiality. Pixel value differencing is the scheme used here for data insertion (Kukharska N et al., 2020). A method was proposed that secures information by combining pixel value differentiation with an edge detection method named Canny edge detection (Vishnu B et al., 2020). In this work, the secret message is first converted to binary format and embedded to the edge pixels of the carrier image using Canny edge detection. Since the human eye can't detect the changes in sharp edges, it ensures more security and better image quality. Das D & Basak R K explained robust data securing strategy by rearranging all the bitstreams before implanting every data bit to each block in the pixel value differencing process. At the initial step, the carrier image divides into non-overlapping pixel blocks with certain ranks. Furthermore, a unique pin is setting to carry each private data. Each bit is selecting from several pins based on rank matrix during insertion procedure, which assures more security (Das D & Basak R K, 2020).

Chowdhuri P et al. introduced a repeated pixel value difference based method with overlapped pixels of block. The porter image here is a color image and its components such as red, green and blue are used here to insert data by overlapping pixels. After splitting the porter image, the secret information is implanted to each block to expand by pixel value differencing (Chowdhuri P et al., 2020). Pixel value differencing based steganographic algorithm introduced by Mukherjee N et al. (Mukherjee N et al., 2020) for data embedding in the non-sequential position of pixel pairs. Here the researchers selected low contrast pixel pairs also with high contrast pairs. PVD is considered an embedding method by randomly selecting the pixel pairs to increase security. PVD ensures the security of information from various attacks caused to an image and also higher robustness and embedding capacity.

Transform Domain Methods

This method is highly complex than spatial domain methods in which the secret information is embedded in the transform or frequency domain of the porter image (Duan et al., 2020). Different types of transformation algorithms are available. Discrete cosine transform (DCT) and discrete wavelet transform (DWT) are usually used techniques. These methods also provide more robust security to information.

Table 2. Pixel Value Differentiation based image steganographic algorithms

Sl.No	Author &Year	Title of Work	Methods/Techniques used	Findings
1	(Nisha C D & Monoth T, 2020)	"Analysis of Spatial Domain Image Steganography Based on Pixel-Value Differencing Method."	Pixel Value Differentiating (PVD) scheme.	High robustness, imperceptibility and payload embedding capacity.
2	(Kukharska N et al., 2020)	"The Steganographic Approach to Data Protection Using Arnold Algorithm and the Pixel-Value Differencing Method."	Pixel Value Differentiating (PVD) scheme.	Ensures image quality with better performance.
3	(Vishnu B et al., 2020)	"Enhanced Image Steganography with PVD and Edge Detection."	Canny edge detection algorithm and Pixel Value Differentiating (PVD) scheme.	High robustness, more secure and high image quality.
4	(Das D & Basak R K, 2020)	"Rank Based Pixel-Value-Differencing: A Secure Steganographic Approach."	Pixel Value Differentiating (PVD) scheme.	Highly efficient with strong security.
5	(Chowdhuri P et al., 2020)	A New Repeated Pixel Value Difference-Based Steganographic Scheme with Overlapped Pixel."	Pixel Value Differentiating (PVD) scheme.	Better data embedding capacity and good quality.
6	(Mukherjee N et al., 2020)	"A PVD based high capacity steganography algorithm with embedding in non-sequential position."	Pixel Value Differentiating (PVD) scheme.	High PSNR value with high payload capacity.

Discrete Cosine Transformation (DCT)

DCT covers an input image from the spatial domain to the frequency domain by separating the image into sub-bands like low, middle, and high. For better data hiding, it chooses the middle band because compression, cropping, and processes are less effective than middle-frequency components of selected images. Duan et al. (Duan et al., 2020) invented deep learning-based an unknown high-capacity image steganographic system. The discrete cosine transformation method helps transform the input image and then encrypted by ECC, i.e., Elliptic Curve Cryptography technique, to advance the anti-detection

Table 3. Discrete cosine transformation-based image steganographic algorithms

Sl.No	Author &Year	Title of Work	Methods/Techniques used	Findings
1	(Duan et al., 2020)	"A New High Capacity Image Steganography Method Combined with Image Elliptic Curve Cryptography and Deep Neural Network".	Discrete Cosine Transform (DCT) and Elliptic curve cryptography (ECC) techniques.	Anti-detection features improved. High steganographic capacity.
2	(Ayub N & Arvind Selwal, 2020)	"An improved image steganography technique using edge-based data hiding in DCT domain."	Edge situated data bit insertion in discrete cosine transform domain	Better performance with PSNR and SNR values.
3	(Singh P K et al., 2021)	"Robust Watermarking Scheme for Compressed Image Through DCT Exploiting Superpixel and Arnold Transform."	DCT and Arnold Transform	High robustness, imperceptibility, and embedding efficiency.

feature of the output image. SegNet deep neural network with a set of insertion and extraction networks is used to improve steganographic capacity. On the next paper researchers are focused on providing a clear idea about edge-based data hiding in DCT domain (Ayub N & Arvind Selwal, 2020). Singh P K et al. presented a robust watermarking scheme through DCT using superpixel and Arnold transform for compressed image (Singh P K et al., 2021). Arnold transform is to perform the test for heterogeneity to select the image's non-uniform regions for the confidential data implanting process. DCT ensures more robustness than the LSB method.

Discrete wavelet transformation (DWT)

DWT also changes an image or signal from the spatial domain to the transform domain, where the wavelets are discretely sampled (Evsutin O & Kultaev P, 2021). It contains only higher and lower sub-bands. The lower frequency parts will again divide to higher and lower components. The higher transform components are used to carry edge components of an image that is less attentive to human eyes. Patil A S et al. proposed discrete wavelet transform (DWT) based mosaic image steganography. The secret image first converts to the mosaic image (Patil A S et al., 2020). The mosaic image is with splatted fragments and with colour transformation is embedding into the cover image. It is difficult to identify or read the message of the sender. The embedding is based on DWT method. Yadahalli et al. detailed explained the execution and study of image steganographic system using LSB and DWT schemes (Yadahalli et al., 2020), Debnath et al. proposed a novel key-based multiple images hiding blind scheme image steganography for RGB color images, which is based on combined DCT and DWT methods (Debnath et al., 2020). Researchers Evsutin O & Kultaev P introduced a technique based on discrete wavelet transform and learning automata for implanting messages in digital porter images. For embedding operation, a block version of QIM, i.e., quantization index modulation, is proposed. The distortion optimization problem of DWT coefficients blocks is solved by this method with a better quality of embedding (Evsutin O & Kultaev P, 2021).

DWT provides better quality for images after compression processes than the DCT technique, also more accurate.

Table 4. Discrete wavelet transformation-based image steganographic algorithms

Sl.No	Author &Year	Title of Work	Methods/Techniques used	Findings
1	(Patil A S et al., 2020)	"DWT Based Mosaic Image Steganography."	Discrete Wavelet Transform (DWT)	High quality compression.
2	(Yadahalli et al., 2020)	"Implementation and analysis of image steganography using Least Significant Bit and Discrete Wavelet Transform techniques."	Least-Significant Bit (LSB) insertion & Discrete Wavelet Transform (DWT).	High degree of security for communication.
3	(Debnath et al., 2020)	"Multi-Image Hiding Blind Robust RGB Steganography in Transform Domain."	Discrete Cosine Transformation (DCT) and Discrete Wavelet Transformation (DWT) methods.	Very less data loss during data extraction and better image quality.
4	(Evsutin O & Kultaev P, 2021)	"An algorithm for embedding information in digital images based on discrete wavelet transform and learning automata."	Discrete Wavelet Transformation (DWT).	High quality of embedding.

Dual Tree Complex Wavelet Transformation (DT-CWT)

Kadhim et al. proposed a compatible embedding scheme on DT-CWT sub-bands using optimization techniques based on machine learning to adapt edge-based image steganography (Kadhim et al., 2020). DT-CWT uses two dissociate filter trees of DWT decompositions to calculate the complex transform of a signal. Another paper is DT-CWT based image steganography method with more sub-bands to embed more secret data bits hence providing high payload embedding capacity (Atta et al., 2021). According to the human visual system, the method gives more importance to implant bits in image edge-areas because edges are less sensitive to human eyes.

Table 5. Dual tree complex wavelet transformation-based image steganographic algorithms

Sl.No	Author &Year	Title of Work	Methods/Techniques used	Findings
1	(Kadhim et al., 2020)	"High-capacity adaptive image steganography with cover region selection using dual-tree complex wavelet transform."	Dual tree complex wavelet transformation (DT-CWT).	High imperceptibility, payload capacity.
2	(Atta et al., 2021)	"A high payload data hiding scheme based on dual tree complex wavelet transform."	Dual tree complex wavelet transformation. (DT-CWT).	High embedding capacity and more secure.

Other Transform Domain Methods

Hidden Markov Tree (HMT) Contourlet transform is used for image steganography by considering bio-medical images as cover files introduced (Jeevitha et al., 2020). Canny edge detection method and PSO, i.e., Particle Swarm Optimization algorithm, also proposed to find the suitable non-attractive areas of the porter image to conceal information. Reshma et al. (Reshma et al., 2020) explained optimized support vector neural network and contourlet transform for medical images. The support vector neural network identifies the appropriate pixels using pixel features and contourlet transforms to embed the secret data to

Table 6. Other transform methods with image steganographic algorithms.

Sl.No	Author &Year	Title of Work	Methods/Techniques used	Findings
1	(Jeevitha et al., 2020)	"Effective payload and improved security using HMT Contourlet transform in medical image steganography."	Hidden Markov Tree Contourlet Transform.	Higher imperceptibility and robustness. Provides more security to the medical images.
2	(Reshma et al., 2020)	"Optimized support vector neural network and contourlet transform for image steganography."	Pixel prediction-based image steganography.	Excellent performance with good PSNR and SSIM value.
3	(Lu et al., 2020)	"Secure Robust JPEG Steganography based on Auto Encoder with Adaptive BCH Encoding."	An autoencoder based JPEG steganographic scheme with a commutable BCH encoding.	High robustness, statistical security with better performance.

carrier image. Another scheme is an autoencoder based JPEG steganographic scheme with a commutable Bose-Chaudhuri-Hocquenghem encoding which provide high robustness and security (Lu et al., 2020).

Distortion Techniques

Distortion techniques are done by applying a sequence of modifications to the carrier image to insert the concealed message (Anusha M et al., 2020). The cover image properties should be available during decoding to measure the difference of the distorted carrier image to the original cover image for reconstructing the sequence of modifications. It distorts the input signal for embedding. This method is more robust than the LSB insertion process (Laishram D & Tuithung T., 2020).

Masking and Filtering

For licenses or copyright materials like documents, a user is provided with watermarks to avoid data copying. Like that in image steganography, it is a way of masking a cover image using digital watermarks. So, the watermarked images will not be copied by unauthorized users or can easily be identified (Singh P K et al., 2021). Here the digital watermarks cover the presence of secret information. Watermarks change the images and ensure the security of hidden data better than the LSB insertion algorithm (Dhawan S & Gupta R., 2021).

Other techniques of Image steganography.

Qin J et al. (Qin J et al., 2020) 's paper focused on Generative Adversarial Network (GAN) based coverless image steganography, which includes neural networks such as generator and discriminator. The discriminator discriminates the fake image from real images and provides feedback to the generator to generate fakes images with the properties of real images. By continuing this process, the discriminator cannot identify the image is real or not. This is the process that happens in GAN. Here this method is used to clear the common problems of coverless steganography. A novel image steganographic method called BOOST using a nuclear spin generator (Stoyanov et al., 2020) to implement in medical fields to implant patient's information such as patient name, patient's ID, and doctors remarks, i.e., patients medical record in medical images. Addition and subtraction-based quotient value differencing (ASQVD) and side match (SM) techniques are the basic techniques used in the study conducted by Pradhan et al. (Pradhan et al., 2020). It is a two-stage process in which the initial stage is addition and subtraction based quotient value differencing of adjacent pixels. The reminders are substitutes on a pixel and also in the four surrounding pixels. After getting new values of these five pixels on the second stage, the side match implementation of secret data on four neighbouring corner pixels occurs. A Thakur et al. (A Thakur et al., 2020) presented bit-based image steganography by inserting the secret message data bits to the bits of carrier image pixels. By analysing the performance of the method, the results show high PSNR and high payload capacity. Shah et al.'s work focused on detailed analysis of an image steganographic algorithm for encrypted text and non-encrypted text implantation into an image. For encrypted data transfer, the advanced encryption standard (AES) method is used (Shah et al., 2020). AES is a symmetric key encryption scheme that uses one secret for input and output processes. Jan et al. introduced a new approach with Laplacian of Gaussian (LoG) and chaotic encryption-based image steganographic method (Jan et al., 2020).

Laplacian of Gaussian (LoG) is an edge-situated operator to spot appropriate edge areas for hiding. The researchers use a logistic map, one of the chaotic encryption methods for the encryption process at the initial stage. Sharma et al. (Sharma et al., 2020) 's work explained Generative Adversarial Network (GAN) based image encryption technique. The cover image is first converting to image matrices and later to string is carved to different images using Steganography, and the process repeats for new images then transmits. The reverse of this occurs in decryption steps to get the output image. Randomly GAN hides the secret bit combined with image steganography. Hossen et al. proposed a different approach to hide confidential data based on AES and RC5 algorithm cryptosystem for digital images using steganographic strategies. To avoid the attention of outsiders, they ensure high visual quality for transmitting stego images. AES uses the same key for encryption and decryption, and RC5 cipher also secure because of including more blocks. They include watermarks to establish a sealed projection of the message (Hossen et al., 2020). Improved particle swarm optimization (PSO) algorithm-based image steganographic embedding method is introduced by Ali & Y M B (Ali & Y M B, 2021). Improved Particle swarm optimization (PSO) algorithm finds the best and suitable pixels of cover image to insert secret message as text or image without compromising the quality of the carrier. Jan A et al. (Jan A et al., 2021) 's work explained logistic map-based image steganographic scheme. It gives more importance to edge portions of the cover file for not to identify quickly. Logistic maps are used for the encryption process of data, and the method provides higher imperceptibility. Ahmad et al. presented a modular arithmetic operation-based confidential data communication framework for data embedded in color images. The first step is to divide the carrier image into different planes of its parts. Then inserting the data bits into each of the planes using modular arithmetic operation. These steps experimented in different color images to get better results (Ahmad et al., 2021)

Next method explained a different scheme to avoid steganography problems without embedding based on generative adversarial network (GAN) (Yu et al., 2021). To avoid the loss of accuracy during recovery process of data, method named attention GAN is proposed. The generator creates images with fewer image distortion errors and the advanced correlation between pixels. Mathivanan P uses three security assurance levels in the proposed paper with stego-crypto strategies using dynamic bit replacement and logistic map based on QR code for color images. The method involves a QR code generator in addition to the base 64 encoding technique. On the first level, the QR codes are generating corresponds to the message. Secondly, using a dynamic bit substitution scheme, each respective QR codes' insertion into color image fundamentals acting as red, green, and blue develops. On the third level, random pixel mix-ups and the logistic chaos map encryption occur with a high-security guarantee (Mathivanan P, 2021).

This whole section gives a clear and comparative analysis of the performance output of abundant recently designed steganographic techniques in tabular forms under each sub-sector description. To analyze the recent developments, around 52 research papers were surveyed. All the provided tables give a brief comparison of the technique used or algorithm, findings with author name, year, and title of the research paper.

Most of the survey papers detailly explained the method used for image steganography. From the given tables, it is clear that the LSB insertion technique is the most repeatedly used method. The second most commonly used methods are Transform domain methods such as Discrete Cosine Transform (DCT) and Discrete Wavelet Transform (DWT) and spatial domain method Pixel value differentiation.

Most of the researchers are analyzed and finalized the results based on parameter matrices like robustness, imperceptibility, PSNR value, SSIM, payload(message) capacity...etc.

The performance parameter matrices can define as follows

Table 7. Other techniques of image steganography with algorithm

Sl.No	Author &Year	Title of Work	Methods/Techniques used	Findings
1	(Qin et al., 2020)	"Coverless Image Steganography Based on Generative Adversarial Network."	Generative adversarial network (GAN).	High payload capacity and high image quality.
2	(Stoyanov et al., 2020)	"BOOST: Medical Image Steganography Using Nuclear Spin Generator."	Pseudo Random byte output scheme based on the nuclear spin generator.	Excellent PSNR value and desirable security properties.
3	(Pradhan et al., 2020)	"Image steganography using add-sub based QVD and side match."	Add-sub based quotient value differencing (ASQVD) and side match (SM) technique.	Hides a greater number of messages through transmission.
4	(Thakur et al., 2020)	"Analysis of Image Steganography Performance Check Using Bit Selection."	Bit based Steganography.	More secure. Better PSNR and SSIM values.
5	(Shah et al., 2020)	"Design, Development, and Implementation of an Image Steganography Algorithm for Encrypted (Using AES) and Non-encrypted Text into an Image."	Advanced Encryption Standard (AES) Method.	High image quality.
6	(Jan et al., 2020)	"A Novel Laplacian of Gaussian (LoG) and Chaotic Encryption Based Image Steganography Technique."	Logistic map and Laplacian of Gaussian operator.	Strong security and high payload capacity.
7	(Sharma et al., 2020)	"Generative Network Based Image Encryption."	Generative Adversarial Network (GAN).	More secure because of Stegano Gan function, without its message can't decode.
8	(Hossen et al., 2020)	"A New Approach to Hiding Data in the Images Using Steganography Techniques Based on AES and RC5 Algorithm Cryptosystem."	Advanced Encryption Standard (AES) method and RC5 algorithm cryptosystem techniques.	High flexible embedding capacity of data. Algorithm has no complication.
9	(Ali and Y M B, 2021)	"A Steganographic Embedding Scheme Using Improved PSO Approach."	Improved particle swarm optimization (PSO) algorithm.	Higher imperceptibility, robustness and strong security.
10	(Jan et al, 2021)	"Logistic Map Based Image Steganography Using Edge Detection."	Logistic map and Edge detection.	Better security for data transmission and higher imperceptibility.
11	(Ahmad et al., 2021)	"Data Embedding in Color Images: A Secure Data Communication Framework Based on Modular Arithmetic."	Modular Arithmetic Operation.	Higher imperceptibility and high data hiding capacity.
12	(Yu et al., 2021)	"An improved steganography without embedding based on attention GAN."	Generative Adversarial Network (GAN).	Assures quality of image and more accurate on recovery process.
13	(Mathivanan P, 2021)	"QR code based color image stego-crypto technique using dynamic bit replacement and logistic map."	Dynamic bit substitution and logistic map.	Better security, robustness and message embedding capacity.

1. Robustness is the total amount of information that can be hidden without any distortion (Jeevitha et al., 2020).
2. Imperceptibility is the ability of information to show good quality after undergoes several procedures.
3. PSNR, i.e., Peak Signal to Noise Ratio, calculates the quality between the porter image and output stego image (Kaur et al., 2020). A high PSNR value indicates a higher quality of stego image.
4. Structural Similarity Index Measurement (SSIM) shows the measure of similarity of two images (Kaur et al., 2020).
5. Payload/ message capacity is the capacity of the cover image to hide secret information.
6. Bit Error Ratio (BER) is the ratio of error bits to the total amount of bits in the cover file.
7. MSE, i.e., Mean Square Error, calculates the average squares of total error characteristics between a cover image values and a stego image values. Low MSE indicates a low error rate and higher quality of the image (Kalaichelvi V et al., 2020).

CONCLUSION

In this chapter familiarized various types of techniques of Steganography. In the last years, the LSB insertion method is the most extensively and commonly used confidential scheme. Researchers have also adapted the techniques like Pixel Value Differentiation (PVD), Discrete Cosine Transformation (DCT), Discrete Wavelet Transformation (DWT), Generative adversarial network (GAN) etc, in their work and provided an effective, secure data transmission. The researchers analyzed the performance analysis of several image steganography schemes based on parameters like robustness, embedding efficiency, payload capacity, imperceptibility, PSNR value etc.

Based on the brief review of papers, this chapter concludes that, newly introduced methods cover and protects the information efficiently by limiting the demerits of present systems. In the upcoming years, the field of Image steganography will develop with more and more new technologies to carry away all the drawbacks of existing embedding strategies. And those technologies will act as the best shield for the secret communication.

REFERENCES

Ahmad, B., Kamili, A., Gull, S., & Parah, S. A. (2021). Data Embedding in Color Images: A Secure Data Communication Framework Based on Modular Arithmetic. In *Multimedia Security* (pp. 157–176). Springer. doi:10.1007/978-981-15-8711-5_8

Al-Sanjary, O. I., Ibrahim, O. A., & Sathasivem, K. (2020, June). A New Approach to Optimum Steganographic Algorithm for Secure Image. In *2020 IEEE International Conference on Automatic Control and Intelligent Systems (I2CACIS)* (pp. 97-102). IEEE. 10.1109/I2CACIS49202.2020.9140186

Ali, Y. M. B. (2021). A Steganographic Embedding Scheme Using Improved-PSO Approach. In *Heuristics for Optimization and Learning* (pp. 199–210). Springer. doi:10.1007/978-3-030-58930-1_13

Anusha, M., Bhanu, K. N., & Divyashree, D. (2020, July). Secured Communication of Text and Audio using Image Steganography. In *2020 International Conference on Electronics and Sustainable Communication Systems (ICESC)* (pp. 284-288). IEEE. 10.1109/ICESC48915.2020.9155715

Atta, R., & Ghanbari, M. (2021). A high payload data hiding scheme based on dual tree complex wavelet transform. *Optik (Stuttgart), 226*, 165786. doi:10.1016/j.ijleo.2020.165786

Ayub, N., & Selwal, A. (2020). An improved image steganography technique using edge-based data hiding in DCT domain. *Journal of Interdisciplinary Mathematics, 23*(2), 357–366. doi:10.1080/09720 502.2020.1731949

Boughaci, D., & Douah, H. (2020). A Variable Neighborhood Search Based Method with Learning for Image Steganography. In *Sustainable Development and Social Responsibility—Volume 2* (pp. 7–18). Springer. doi:10.1007/978-3-030-32902-0_2

Brar, R. K., & Sharma, A. (2020). Improved Steganography Using Odd Even Substitution. In *Cognitive Computing in Human Cognition* (pp. 1–8). Springer. doi:10.1007/978-3-030-48118-6_1

Chakraborty, S., & Jalal, A. S. (2020). A novel local binary pattern based blind feature image steganography. *Multimedia Tools and Applications, 79*(27-28), 1–14. doi:10.100711042-020-08828-3

Chandra, N. S. R., Sneha, V., & Paul, P. V. (2020). A Novel Image Steganography Model Using LSB with Extended ASCII Codes. In *Smart Intelligent Computing and Applications* (pp. 107–116). Springer. doi:10.1007/978-981-13-9282-5_11

Chowdhuri, P., Pal, P., Jana, B., & Giri, D. (2020). A New Repeated Pixel Value Difference-Based Steganographic Scheme with Overlapped Pixel. In *Intelligent Computing: Image Processing Based Applications* (pp. 103–118). Springer. doi:10.1007/978-981-15-4288-6_7

Das, D., & Basak, R. K. (2020). Rank Based Pixel-Value-Differencing: A Secure Steganographic Approach. In *Proceedings of the Global AI Congress 2019* (pp. 501-514). Springer. 10.1007/978-981-15-2188-1_39

Debnath, D., Ghosh, E., & Banik, B. G. (2020). Multi-Image Hiding Blind Robust RGB Steganography in Transform Domain. *International Journal of Web-Based Learning and Teaching Technologies, 15*(1), 24–52. doi:10.4018/IJWLTT.2020010102

Dhawan, S., & Gupta, R. (2021). Analysis of various data security techniques of steganography: A survey. *Information Security Journal: A Global Perspective, 30*(2), 63-87.

Duan, X., Guo, D., Liu, N., Li, B., Gou, M., & Qin, C. (2020). A New High Capacity Image Steganography Method Combined with Image Elliptic Curve Cryptography and Deep Neural Network. *IEEE Access: Practical Innovations, Open Solutions, 8*, 25777–25788. doi:10.1109/ACCESS.2020.2971528

Elharrouss, O., Almaadeed, N., & Al-Maadeed, S. (2020, February). An image steganography approach based on k-least significant bits (k-LSB). In *2020 IEEE International Conference on Informatics, IoT, and Enabling Technologies (ICIoT)* (pp. 131-135). IEEE. 10.1109/ICIoT48696.2020.9089566

Evsutin, O., & Kultaev, P. (n.d.). An algorithm for embedding information in digital images based on discrete wavelet transform and learning automata. *Multimedia Tools and Applications*, 1-23.

Hossen, M. S., Islam, M. A., Khatun, T., Hossain, S., & Rahman, M. M. (2020, September). A New Approach to Hiding Data in the Images Using Steganography Techniques Based on AES and RC5 Algorithm Cryptosystem. In *2020 International Conference on Smart Electronics and Communication (ICOSEC)* (pp. 676-681). IEEE. 10.1109/ICOSEC49089.2020.9215442

Jan, A., Parah, S. A., & Malik, B. A. (2020, June). A Novel Laplacian of Gaussian (LoG) and Chaotic Encryption Based Image Steganography Technique. In *2020 International Conference for Emerging Technology (INCET)* (pp. 1-4). IEEE.

Jan, A., Parah, S. A., & Malik, B. A. (2021). Logistic Map-Based Image Steganography Using Edge Detection. In *Innovations in Computational Intelligence and Computer Vision* (pp. 447–454). Springer. doi:10.1007/978-981-15-6067-5_50

Jeevitha, S., & Prabha, N. A. (2020). Effective payload and improved security using HMT Contourlet transform in medical image steganography. *Health and Technology*, *10*(1), 217–229. doi:10.100712553-018-00285-1

Kadhim, I. J., Premaratne, P., & Vial, P. J. (2020). High-capacity adaptive image steganography with cover region selection using dual-tree complex wavelet transform. *Cognitive Systems Research*, *60*, 20–32. doi:10.1016/j.cogsys.2019.11.002

Kalaichelvi, T., & Apuroop, P. (2020). Image Steganography Method to Achieve Confidentiality Using CAPTCHA for Authentication. In *2020 5th International Conference on Communication and Electronics Systems (ICCES)* (pp. 495-499). IEEE. 10.1109/ICCES48766.2020.9138073

Kalaichelvi, V., Meenakshi, P., Devi, P. V., Manikandan, H., Venkateswari, P., & Swaminathan, S. (2020). A stable image steganography: A novel approach based on modified RSA algorithm and 2–4 least significant bit (LSB) technique. *Journal of Ambient Intelligence and Humanized Computing*, ●●●, 1–9.

Kaur, M., Kumar, V., & Singh, D. (2020). An efficient image steganography method using multi-objective differential evolution. In *Digital Media Steganography* (pp. 65–79). Academic Press. doi:10.1016/B978-0-12-819438-6.00012-8

Kukharska, N., Lagun, A., & Polotai, O. (2020, August). The Steganographic Approach to Data Protection Using Arnold Algorithm and the Pixel-Value Differencing Method. In *2020 IEEE Third International Conference on Data Stream Mining & Processing (DSMP)* (pp. 174-177). IEEE. 10.1109/DSMP47368.2020.9204108

Laishram, D., & Tuithung, T. (2020). A novel minimal distortion-based edge adaptive image steganography scheme using local complexity. *Multimedia Tools and Applications*, 1–24. doi:10.100711042-020-09519-9

Lu, W., Zhang, J., Zhao, X., Zhang, W., & Huang, J. (2020). Secure Robust JPEG Steganography based on AutoEncoder with Adaptive BCH Encoding. *IEEE Transactions on Circuits and Systems for Video Technology*, 1. doi:10.1109/TCSVT.2020.3027843

Mathivanan, P. (2021). QR code based color image stego-crypto technique using dynamic bit replacement and logistic map. *Optik (Stuttgart)*, *225*, 165838. doi:10.1016/j.ijleo.2020.165838

Mukherjee, N., Paul, G., Saha, S. K., & Burman, D. (2020). A PVD based high capacity steganography algorithm with embedding in non-sequential position. *Multimedia Tools and Applications*, 79(19), 13449–13479.

Neogi, P. P. G., Goswami, S., & Mustafi, J. (2020). Intelligent Water Drops Based Image Steganography. In *Proceedings of the Global AI Congress 2019* (pp. 363-375). Springer. 10.1007/978-981-15-2188-1_29

Nisha, C. D., & Monoth, T. (2020). Analysis of Spatial Domain Image Steganography Based on Pixel-Value Differencing Method. In *Soft Computing for Problem Solving* (pp. 385–397). Springer. doi:10.1007/978-981-15-0184-5_34

Nolkha, A., Kumar, S., & Dhaka, V. S. (2020). Image Steganography Using LSB Substitution: A Comparative Analysis on Different Color Models. In *Smart Systems and IoT: Innovations in Computing* (pp. 711–718). Springer. doi:10.1007/978-981-13-8406-6_67

Pandey, J., Joshi, K., Sain, M., Singh, G., & Jangra, M. (2021). Steganographic Method Based on Interpolation and Cyclic LSB Substitution of Digital Images. In *Advances in Communication and Computational Technology* (pp. 731–744). Springer. doi:10.1007/978-981-15-5341-7_55

Patani, K., & Rathod, D. (2020). Advanced 3-Bit LSB Based on Data Hiding Using Steganography. In *Data Science and Intelligent Applications* (pp. 383–390). Springer.

Patil, A. S., Patil, R. M., & Shinde, M. M. (2020). DWT Based Mosaic Image Steganography. In *Techno-Societal 2018* (pp. 95–107). Springer. doi:10.1007/978-3-030-16848-3_10

Pradhan, A., Sekhar, K. R., & Swain, G. (2020). Image steganography using add-sub based QVD and side match. In *Digital Media Steganography* (pp. 81–97). Academic Press. doi:10.1016/B978-0-12-819438-6.00013-X

Pramanik, S., Bandyopadhyay, S. K., & Ghosh, R. (2020, March). Signature Image Hiding in Color Image using Steganography and Cryptography based on Digital Signature Concepts. In *2020 2nd International Conference on Innovative Mechanisms for Industry Applications (ICIMIA)* (pp. 665-669). IEEE.

Qin, J., Wang, J., Tan, Y., Huang, H., Xiang, X., & He, Z. (2020). Coverless Image Steganography Based on Generative Adversarial Network. *Mathematics*, 8(9), 1394. doi:10.3390/math8091394

Reshma, V. K., Kumar, R. V., Shahi, D., & Shyjith, M. B. (2020). Optimized support vector neural network and contourlet transform for image steganography. *Evolutionary Intelligence*, 1–17. doi:10.100712065-020-00387-8

Sahu, A. K., & Swain, G. (2020). Reversible image steganography using dual layer LSB matching. *Sensing and Imaging*, 21(1), 1. doi:10.100711220-019-0262-y

Shah, V., & Kumbharana, C. K. Design, Development, and Implementation of an Image Steganography Algorithm for Encrypted (Using AES) and Non encrypted Text into an Image. In *Rising Threats in Expert Applications and Solutions* (pp. 313–320). Springer. doi:10.1007/978-981-15-6014-9_36

Sharma, V., Shukla, M., Srivastava, S., & Mandal, R. (2020, May). Generative Network Based Image Encryption. In *2020 4th International Conference on Intelligent Computing and Control Systems (ICICCS)* (pp. 1-5). IEEE. 10.1109/ICICCS48265.2020.9121060

Siddiqui, G. F., Iqbal, M. Z., Saleem, K., Saeed, Z., Ahmed, A., Hameed, I. A., & Khan, M. F. (2020). A Dynamic Three Bit Image Steganography Algorithm for Medical and e-Healthcare Systems. *IEEE Access: Practical Innovations, Open Solutions, 8,* 181893–181903. doi:10.1109/ACCESS.2020.3028315

Singh, P. K., Jana, B., & Datta, K. (2021). Robust Watermarking Scheme for Compressed Image Through DCT Exploiting Super pixel and Arnold Transform. In *Proceedings of the Sixth International Conference on Mathematics and Computing* (pp. 43-54). Springer. 10.1007/978-981-15-8061-1_4

Soni, T., Baird, R., Lobo, A., & Heydari, V. (2020, June). Using Least Significant Bit and Random Pixel Encoding with Encryption for Image Steganography. In *National Cyber Summit* (pp. 139–153). Springer.

Stoyanov, B., & Stoyanov, B. (2020). BOOST: Medical Image Steganography Using Nuclear Spin Generator. *Entropy (Basel, Switzerland), 22*(5), 501. doi:10.3390/e22050501 PMID:33286274

Thakur, A., Gill, G. S., & Saxena, S. (2020, February). Analysis of Image Steganography Performance Check Using Bit Selection. In *2020 7th International Conference on Signal Processing and Integrated Networks (SPIN)* (pp. 1-5). IEEE. 10.1109/SPIN48934.2020.9071251

Vishnu, B., Namboothiri, L. V., & Sajeesh, S. R. (2020, March). Enhanced Image Steganography with PVD and Edge Detection. In *2020 Fourth International Conference on Computing Methodologies and Communication (ICCMC)* (pp. 827-832). IEEE. 10.1109/ICCMC48092.2020.ICCMC-000153

Vyas, A. O., & Dudul, S. V. (2020). A Novel Approach of Object Oriented Image Steganography Using LSB. In *ICDSMLA 2019* (pp. 144–151). Springer. doi:10.1007/978-981-15-1420-3_16

Yadahalli, S. S., Rege, S., & Sonkusare, R. (2020, June). Implementation and analysis of image steganography using Least Significant Bit and Discrete Wavelet Transform techniques. In *2020 5th International Conference on Communication and Electronics Systems (ICCES)* (pp. 1325-1330). IEEE.

Yu, C., Hu, D., Zheng, S., Jiang, W., Li, M., & Zhao, Z. Q. (n.d.). An improved steganography without embedding based on attention GAN. *Peer-to-Peer Networking and Applications,* 1-12.

Chapter 3
Advances in Text Steganography Theory and Research:
A Critical Review and Gaps

Gurunath R.
CHRIST University (Deemed), India

Debabrata Samanta
https://orcid.org/0000-0003-4118-2480
CHRIST University (Deemed), India

ABSTRACT

There is an immense advancement in science and technology, and computing systems with the highest degree of security are the present hot topic; however, the domination of hackers and espionage in terms of disclosing the sensitive information are steadily increasing. This chapter presents a theoretical view and critical examination of the few text steganography methods in the contemporary world. It tells the direction in which research has developed over the past few years. Cryptography, the encipherment to a certain extent, protects the data by making it unreadable but not safe. Improvisation of the same can be done using another layer of protection that is steganography in which the secret embedded inside the cover text will not be revealed.

INTRODUCTION

Steganography is a way in which a secret (private or sensitive) data is concealed into other non-secret text or data at the source, for the purpose of avoiding the tendency of attack from a third party; that the text can only be spotted by its intended recipients and to protect the legitimate data. Later, embedded data is sent to the destination through insecure channels of the Internet; and it is then extracted at the destination.

DOI: 10.4018/978-1-7998-7160-6.ch003

The data hiding or steganography is a skillful technique of covert communication. (Dhawan, 2020), an unremarkable cover medium is used to disguise the text so as not to doubt it. The use of this technique was witnessed in ancient times. People were using a type of ink to create images on the body and embed the text in it. It could only be understood by the people who believed to be the trusted parties on the other side. With the evolution of computer power, the combination of the Internet and e-processing turned manual Steganography into digital (Anand, 2020).

Steganography is the process of hiding in a trusted carrier of critical data without sharing it with third parties with the knowledge that information exists. Steganography has two forms: one in which the message is securely retrieved and the medium is shielded (reversible). Secondly, the message may be properly retrieved, but the cover medium could be skewed (irreversible) (Douglas, 2018). Cryptography provides the data with confidentiality, although steganography does not reveal that even the message exists. By combining it with cryptography, the power of steganography can be increased (Alajmi, 2020).

The section of Background and Literature survey, discusses the origin of Steganography, contemporary steganographic methods, characteristics of strong Steganography, text steganographic forms, Cryptography and Steganography, and Steganalysis types.

In this paper, Text Steganography is chosen for our analysis because it is the most difficult form of steganography; this is due to the absence of repetitive bit sequences in comparison to the image and sound (Kamaruddin, 2018).

Linguistic steganography is one of the modes of text steganography that this paper focuses more on. It is a collection of techniques that enables any digital information to be concealed within texts based on certain linguistic features (Lingyun Xiang, 2020).

To conceal the secret, the corresponding covert text should not be invisible but grammatically accurate and semantically cohesive. The methods of linguistic steganography use fonts, alphabets, lexicon, word structure, phrase structure, and word order to camouflage the message.

In Format based Steganography methods, the data hiding is done by character space assignment, line shifting, and word shifting, changing font are some sole characteristics (Xiang, 2017).

This paper explores few Steganographic approaches, paper by (Mahato, 2020), proposes a steganography technique by using Microsoft word document to adjust tracking function.

Low-tech steganography operations, which do not use digital transfer (Nag, 2019) use only manual, are the second method talked about. To create and interpret it needs some form of human intelligence. Low-tech methods, therefore, are often difficult to detect using only automated techniques and, indeed, maybe improvisational. These low-tech methods include Semagrams and concealment Ciphers.

Another type of steganography mentioned here in this paper is to use mathematical formulas or a particular number system to convert text into some kind of numbers (Mandal K. K., 2020).

The last method discussed in this paper is based on text steganography within image data (Joshi, 2018). This method is simple and has more capacity for hiding data. Finally, a comparison of text steganography methods concerning to their merits and demerits is given as table format.

BACKGROUND AND LITERATURE SURVEY

The word Steganography is borrowed from the Greek word "Steganos" meaning hidden writing (Al-Huwais, 2020). Terms that can be used interchangeably; "cover data" is non-secret data and "secret data" is data to hide. Hundreds of years ago, these styles of ancient forms of steganographic methods were used.

The proposed Steganographic technique is centered on the Fibonacci series. The secret text is encrypted and its cipher text is encoded as a hidden message inside an image; two layers of security are provided here (Mukherjee, 2014).

The idea of hidden transmission is as early as communication technologies. In the early days, messages were sent to the intended people by messengers who used to go by walk or horse to convey the message, often it had to be delivered in a hidden manner, so either the messenger had to memorize it or conceal it on the messenger. The history of steganography started way back in 440 BC by a Greek ruler Histaeus. The story goes like this; he bald the head of the messenger and made design of the communication on his scalp and delayed for the hair to grow and later directed him to the receiver; the head was shaved again by the receiver to disclose the message.

In 480 BC, there is another story about the hiding message; in his book "Investigator guide to Steganography" a writer Gregory Kipper recorded a story written in his book "The Histories" by the Greek historian Herodotus. Xerxes, a Persian Ruler wanted to extend his empire, and wanted to conquer Greece. Demaratus, the exiled Spartan king of Greece, was the person who set up the military framework in Greece. He lived in Susa, a Persian city. Even after he was an expatriate, he was very faithful to Greece. He decided to move on to the king of Greece a secret plan concerning the Persian invasion of Greece. He did so by secretly sending a message. By scraping the wax off a pair of wooden folding tablets, writing on the wooden hull about the details of the Persian king's plan and again waxing over it, and sending the messenger to Greece, he intended to send the message via the messenger. The mission was successful, and the Greeks were able to grasp Persia's dirty plan. This is proof of the method of steganography used in ancient times (Nechta, 2017).

It is assumed that the ancient Arabic manuscripts on secret scripting, written in the eighth century and these scripts were found in Turkey and Germany (Madhavi, 2018).

Chinese ancient method of hiding data was used 500 years ago, this was found by an Italian mathematician Jerome Cardan (Dhawan, 2020). The process is, sender supplied with a paper mask with some cuts. The sender is allowed to write secret words through these cuts and the mask put on a clean paper, and then the mask is taken off and the gaps were filled with other information. The entire text so obtained appears to be an innocuous text.

The first steganography usage occurred in the year 1499, and this is mentioned in a book called 'Steganographia' (Easttom, 2021), book is basically on Cryptography, Steganography, and magic. The book gives a description of hidden secrets under picture, text, or shopping lists. The secret might have written in these using an invisible ink; this is documented in that book. These invisible inks are made out of milk, vinegar, and fruit juices have been used by spies (Dalal, 2020). To decode the message hidden on a page using the ink and is heated to few degrees, to reveal the secret, at the destination.

Sir Francis Bacon during 1605 (Bonavoglia, 2020), introduced an encoding method called Bacon's Cipher or Baconian Cipher, a steganography method, hiding a secret message. The pictorial representation is shown in Figure 1.

It's a substitution encryption function in which every letter is replaced by a series of five letters. For example, the letter 'D' was substituted by 'aaabb' and the letter 'O' by 'abbab', likewise, all the alphabets and numbers were assigned strings of 5 letter words. The following diagram shows the process of Bacon's Steganography. "DATA" is the secret word and is encoded as "aaabb aaaaa baabb aaaaaa". The recipient decodes as a secret word to extract the "DATA".

Gaspar Schott (1608-1688), German scientist in his book "Schola Steganographica", documented a message hiding technique by generating pseudo-logical texts, for original text messages. This could be

Figure 1. Baconian Cipher, a steganography method for hiding a secret message

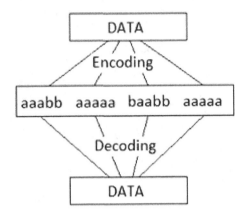

done by inserting a word or phrase that somehow correlates to a specific letter in the original message (Liu, 2018). In a drawing in 1945, Morse code was hidden and is encoded on a few of the objects on the drawing along with the shape of the object (Kadhim, 2019).

Characteristics of Strong Steganography

The steganography algorithm can be measured in terms of several parameters. These include a volume of data to be concealed, invisibility or unable to find out intentional biases made in the cover text. Further, un-detectability or highly difficult for computer/ computing methods to comprehend secret data inside cover text. Robustness or information capability to endure even after compression or other normal modification. Tamper- resistance or text-ability to withstand despite unauthorized alteration, and signal to noise ratio.

The idea of Steganographic characteristics understood better through Figure 2. Even though the parameters, capacity, un-detectability, and robustness are essential for steganography to be strong, any elevation or decrease in one of these causes the algorithm to be weak. The conclusion here is none of the data hiding algorithms are perfect (Abdulla, 2015).

Text Steganographic Forms

There are few ways of steganography; image, audio, video, and text are used. In this article, the study discusses only the text Steganography. The authors focus more on text steganography since the data hiding in the text is an uphill task compared to other forms of Steganography. Text steganography divided into three types: Format-based, Random and Statistical generation, Linguistic methods as shown in the following Figure 3.

Format Based Methods

These methods tap the structure of the text to cover the information, however, it has its shortcomings; easy detection is possible when the original message is available, and compared with Stego text file, fabrications can be viewed. The categories under Format based methods belong to Line shifting, Word

Figure 2. (a) Opposed Properties for a Good Steganography (b) All properties

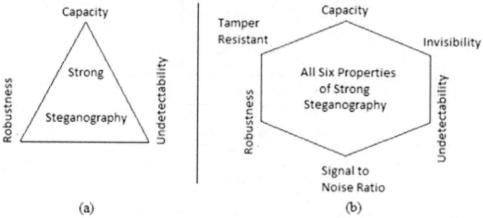

Shifting, Feature Coding, and White/Null space methods. The cover text information itself is used as the property, namely, punctuation, White spaces, spelling, and non-printing characters are used to mask the message (Lockwood, 2017). For example1, four characters are assigned in the following manner: a full stop might interpret bits 00, comma 01, exclamation mark 10, and question mark as 11. Example 2, based on the English words used in the UK and US, i.e., British-English word "color" and the US-English word 'color' represent 0 and 1 respectively. Some of the other examples, using HTML as a cover text medium, coloring of whitespaces, in document files line space character is used to encode bits, fonts to hide information, and features of the text; 0 for affected and 1 for not affected as the encoding mechanism.

Random and Statistical Generation

Here the cover text is produced using the statistical features i.e. character sequences and word sequences. Embedding the data in the sequence of characters will appear to be a random sequence of characters.

Figure 3. Text Steganographic Forms

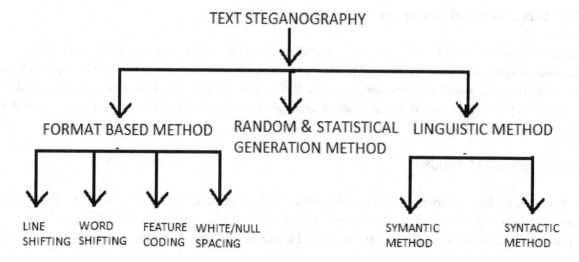

Another approach uses word sequences to produce characters that add word-length and letter frequency statistical properties to construct words (Aman, 2017). The obtained sequence looks random for any third party. The word generation uses a codebook of mappings among words and bit sequences, or words themselves can encode the concealed material.

Linguistic Steganography

The features of a certain language or verbal or lexical or vocabulary or wordy text or even the space in which the hidden text is concealed are ultimately looked at. The sub-types under the Linguistic approach semantic and syntactic methods (Mansor, 2018). One example, consider the sentence in italics below (Krishnan, 2017):

Apparently neutral's protest is thoroughly discounted and ignored. Is man hard hit. Blockade issue affects pretext for embargo on by-products, ejecting suets and vegetable oil.

The hidden message is tagged with the cover text shown above, which is extracted by selecting the second letter from each word that looks like the one given below.

Pershing sails from NY June 1

Cryptography and Steganography

The combination of Steganography and cryptography are made for each other; one is secret communication and the other is secret information respectively.

Cryptography and Steganography provide privacy and secrecy to the data, respectively. Encryption is a process of Cryptography used to convert sensitive information into some non-readable format, cipher-text, with a secret key, so that the data can be kept ordinarily somewhere or transmitted over the Internet without any cover. Here, the intruder learned very well that the hidden data was being passed on. However, it is not possible to read and comprehend the data in a normal way.

On the other hand, the Steganography, a mechanism of covert communication, uses an appropriate carrier to hide the secret data. The hidden data inside the carrier is then made to travel towards the destination, the hidden message inside the carrier will not be known to anyone else but the communicating parties. The main objective of this mechanism is not only to foreclose the message being read, however, to conceal its existence. In other words, it is not only sufficient to encipher the data/traffic, as the crooks uncover, and react to, the presence of encrypted communication. The Stego-key (Pramanik, S and Singh, R. P., 2017) is rarely used in the hiding process to control and restrict detection and/or recovery of embedded data. The Stego object is the product of the embedding process; it is eventually sent to the destination on the unreliable communication channels and thus retrieved by the recipient. The two technologies listed to above are aimed at preserving privacy and information confidentiality (Hadipour, 2020).

Cryptography

Cryptography provides a kind of defense to legitimate users from the attackers, who normally alter, delete, impersonate, and destroy the valuable data remotely. Cryptography provides security to the data which is stored as well as transmitted over insecure networks. To have protection to the legitimate data one should have the security in place. The source of vulnerabilities, (Rashid, 2014) are due to cyber-attacks. The model comprising of: types of security attacks, Security services, and Security mechanisms.

Security attacks are categorized into Active attacks and Passive attacks. A Passive attack is intended not to harm the data rather obtain and analyze data and traffic respectively. The main attack namely: Release of message contents and Traffic Analysis.

In active attack, the opponent is very much intended to cause problems/destruction to the lawful system of communication. There are certain activities belong to this are passive capture and subsequent retransmission (Replay) of the data, pretending to be a different entity (Masquerade), Altering/Modification /Fabrication of data, and disrupting of entire network / disabling the network.

Services: A procedure or communicative service, adds security to the informatics of an organization. These services are designed to negate the security attacks, to delineate security policies, and implement security mechanisms. The Security services include Authentication, Access Control, Confidentiality, Integrity, Non-repudiation, and Availability.

Authentication

It is a service and as well a mechanism, to identify and allow the legitimate process, system, person, and event to utilize the resources of any communication network. The process needs certain credentials from every entity in the form of passwords, login details, smart cards, biometric, etc. These details are verified and access to the resources given on the basis of the outcome, whether to allow or disallow. Some of the Authentication services are SSL Certificates, Kerberos, and Digital signature.

Access Control

Process control is controlling access to computer resources that are formally permitted or limited. The operation saves against the unlawful exercise and exploitation of resources; it offers confidentiality, integrity, and authorized use of a system.

Confidentiality

Encryption has two sections of Algorithms namely: Symmetric key encryption and asymmetric key encryption. Data Encryption Standard, Advanced Encryption Standard, International Data Encryption Algorithm, Blowfish, etc. are Symmetric or secret key algorithms. Here a single shared key is used for both encryption and decryption processes. Public key algorithms include private and public keys, one for encryption and the other for decryption. The popular algorithms are RSA, Diffie-Hellman, Rabin cryptosystems, El-Gamal cryptosystems, etc.

Integrity

It is the property that information is altered only in a stated and lawful manner. It is the freedom of data from damage or deliberate manipulation Integrity is a property of any information which can be seen as data, program, system, and network. The integrity of information can be of data, program, system, and network. The data which is accurate, consistent, and complete in all aspects is called data Integrity. The degree of quality design of the software is related to program integrity. The ability of any system which does a purposive job with reasoned, and authorized control. In terms of network integrity, it follows the way of system integrity perspective to network. The integrity of any data at rest or at transit can be checked using a method called hashing, which is an irreversible process unlike encryption, yields a fixed quantity of code, used to check whether an unauthorized modification has occurred or not.

Non-Repudiation

Repudiation meaning, declare not to be true. It is very tough to deny the act made by someone and there is always a record of such an act. This service is called non-repudiation. Using the digital signature can prove the unlawful act of someone by the system. Non-repudiation is possible 100% with public-key cryptography.

Availability

Availability service requires that the resources be available to authorized people when needed. The cryptographic attacks can lead to a compromise in availability; one such is the Denial of Service attack (DoS). These attacks reduce the availability of resources to the legitimate user and are challenged byways of countermeasures, such as authentication and encryption mechanisms.

Security Mechanisms: Some techniques for realizing security are listed here: Figure 4

Figure 4. Mechanisms for realizing Information Security

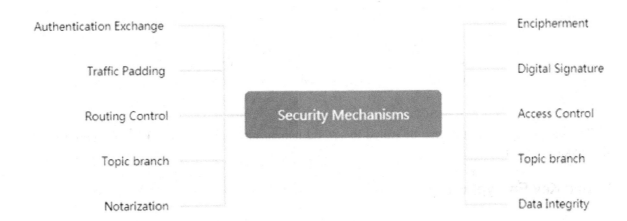

Block Ciphers and Stream Ciphers

Conventional Cryptography is classified into Block Cipher algorithms and Stream cipher algorithms. The algorithms are classified based on their volume of input to the encryption algorithm.

The Block ciphers take the input in terms of a block of bits at a time. Different algorithms follow different volume bits called blocks. For example DES, a block cipher takes plain-text of 64 bits, AES having variations, takes 128 bits, 192 bits, and 256 bits as input, etc. While the stream ciphers convert plain-text digits on the fly.

A Stream cipher is a secret key cipher; the individual data bits are combined with keystream bits to form a cipher bit-stream. The XOR operation is used to generate the cipher stream. A function called pseudorandom number Generation (PRNG) is intended to generate a keystream from a random-looking data called an initial vector (IV). For Example RC4, A5, CryptMT, etc. are Stream ciphers.

Secret Key Encryption

The secret key is a small quantity of data supplied to an encryption algorithm to generate cipher-text. The secret key is shared between the source and the destination. The converted text is unreadable and transmitted over insecure channels to the recipient. Even if the cipher-text accessed by a third party (attacker) will not be in a position to know the substance of the transmitted data. The receiver uses a decryption algorithm to decipher the data into plain-text using the shared secret key as given in the Figure 5.

Figure 5. Shared / Secret key Encryption Process

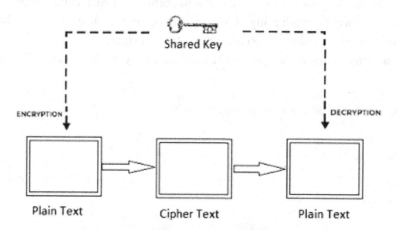

The secret key encryption can be called in several names such as symmetric key, conventional, or shared key encryption.

Public Key Encryption

Public key Encryption is a very recent technology and not historical like symmetric key Encryption. It is more secure than symmetric key encryption. The development of public-key encryption technology is due to the challenges faced in the areas of key management in symmetric Key. The Asymmetric key encryption has properties: different keys used for encryption and decryption provides a very good authentication system, complex enough so that adversary finds it difficult to attack, both the keys are mathematically related, and not easy to calculate the private key from the public key.

Figure 6. Public-Key / Asymmetric Key Cryptography

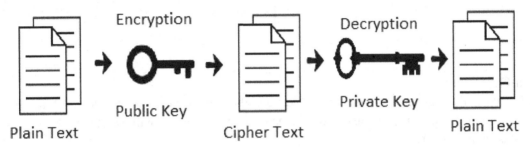

In the recent past, almost all the Internet applications such as chat applications email, voice, and video calls, and file sharing are protected with encryption from source to the destination. The messages originated from these applications are made unreadable to the hacker on the channel as well as to the service vendors. These end-to-end applications depend mainly on public-key cryptography or public-key encryption.

In public key encryption outlined in Figure 6, anyone receiving the encrypted message from any authorized user must be decrypted using the receiver's private key. Any user in the public key domain must have generated two keys of their own, public, and private keys using certain well-known algorithms. The public key is distributed to all the intended users to encrypt messages. The private key is kept secret by the user only; it should not be shared with anyone. The private key is used for decryption of the message and signing the document in the process of a digital signature. A public key is used for encrypting the message and verifying the authenticity of the digital signature.

Steganalysis

It is the study; all about the detection of hidden content using Steganalysis depicted in Figure 7. It corresponds to Cryptanalysis in Cryptography. In other ways, it is a set of techniques and methods used to reveal the existence of secrets in an embedded digital object and to retrieve it. Steganalysis has two processes first, detecting the message, and second, is to extract the message. The difficult part is the extraction of messages. There are known types of Steganalysis: The basic idea of Steganalysis is to suspect the cover media then determine the existence of the secret, finally, recover the message. In most cases, the suspicion originates because of deformed Stego media, or unusual factors of the media. This is not always correct. One example might be in the case of IP based steganography, the process is defeated when Intrusion Detection is used on the Stego media. Offending Stego media involves identifying, retrieving, and destroying the secret object of it. There are certain types of attacks depending on the information present for the analysis (Samanta S. &., 2020).

Figure 7. Process of Steganalysis and Steganography

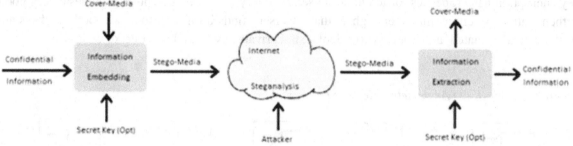

Known-Carrier Attack:

In this method of attack; the original cover-object and the Stego object are considered for the analysis. A difference component obtained after comparing the above two will lead to the detection of the message in Stego text.

Steganography-only attack:

In this case, the hidden information is detected only when Stego media is available for analysis in the absence of the original file. This is possible when an attacker analyzes Internet traffic.

Chosen-steganography attack:

The attacker analyzes Stego media and the respective steganographic algorithm. The weakness of the algorithm is exploited here to detect the hidden information.

Chosen-message attack:

Here the attacker tries to build Stego-media when the message and the steganographic algorithm are known. This is kept and used for future attacks or comparisons.

Known-message attack:

In this, the message to be embedded before the steganography process is known to the attacker. This is done to analyze the known patterns of the future.

Known-steganography attack:

In this case, every detail of the steganography process is known to the attacker. This is a very rare case, and it damages more.

Literature Review - *Some of the significant literature surveys related to digital text steganography methods taken from 5 years back to date are given in the following section of the article.*

(Sedeeq, 2017) Proposed a format based text steganography and open space method. It's mainly based on manipulation of whitespace characters. This method exploits inter-sentence, end-of-line, and inter-word spacing in justified text. However, the method is vulnerable, when some word processors format commands are used; the encoded hidden text will be destroyed. In fact the methods above hide data but not to the extent of bulk volume, i.e. several bits per kilobytes of the text.

(Sharma S. G., 2016)The paper exploits the features of the English language for hiding the secret text inside another text. The author presents certain schemes to embed data.

Firstly, the letters of English are made into two groups, letters with curvature, and letters without curvature. For example - The first letter of the sentence starts with a letter, namely, B, C, D, G, etc.; are having a curvature, embed bit value 0. The letters without any curvature, for instance, A, E, F, H, etc. embed bit values as 1.

Let say '110' is the data to hide and the cover sentence is "All birds can fly. Ostrich is a bird. Ostrich can also fly". There are 3 sentences and the starting letters of these do not match with the bits '110'. Little modification required i.e."All birds can fly. This is a bird. Ostrich can also fly".

Secondly, in this Approach (Vertical Straight line) no. of vertical lines not equal to each other are: e.g. A, C, G, H, M, etc. encoded as bit 0. Bit 1 takes characters with vertical lines is equal to each other. For example, the letter B, D, E, F, etc. belong to this category.

Thirdly, Quadruple categorization has four divisions of English letters that can embed two bits at a time i.e. 00, 01, 10, 11. The bit 00 falls under curved letters say, C, D, G, O, etc. Bits 01, middle horizontal straight line, the characters: A, B, E, F, H, etc. The bits 10, one vertical straight line characters: I, J, K, L, etc. The Bits 11, letters with the diagonal line: M, N, V, W, etc. The approaches mentioned above have pros and cons. The advantage is time and memory overheads have been removed. The disadvantage lies in the frequent applicability that leads to the identification of the used method and becomes easy prey for the attackers.(Ahvanooey, 2018)This paper presents a kind of text steganography using SMS or Social media between mobile users, called "AITSteg''. The secret message (SM) and cover message (CM) are assumed. SM's characters are converted to ASCII value. From the ASCII value a pair of values generated using Godel function. Then a binary stream is constructed and symmetric key and hash value are concatenated. The resultant binary stream is grouped into two bits each. Then the corresponding pair of bits are encoded into hexadecimal and made hidden; concatenated with the cover data as SMS Message. This approach provides a reasonable security to the secret text, robustness and more hiding capacity, and invisibility.

(Khosravi, 2019) The paper proposes an algorithm to hide data and implemented it in a PDF file. The Structure of the PDF file 3 parts namely: Header, Body part - I contain objects, and Body part - II containing reference tables. The header is the very first line that indicates the version of PDF; the user can modify this and apply font and the texts. Body part II contains objects that refer to the actual content of PDF. Objects are image, fonts, text, annotations and etc. of PDF. Here user can able to insert the hidden objects along with other data and this can be made secure from alterations by unknown people. The cross-reference table has links to the objects mentioned in part I. This is used to circumvent the entire PDF by the user. If any time the PDF is modified then automatically Part II links are also modified. Apart from these there is a space in PDF called "trash space" contains some special characters and there is a way to embed our secret data. In this technique, before embedding the message encryption is done and the outcome is embedded and appended after the Body part II. This appended data has no relation with the actual PDF data and it is not visible also. Using this method one can hide a large volume of secret data. After the embedding process, it's sent to the receiver. Again at the other end, the extraction of hidden data is done.

(Al-Nofaie, 2020) Text pseudo-spaces operation and extended characters in Arabic language steganography techniques have been introduced in this paper. The positive factor of this method is that it provides high data hiding volume and also security of the message taken care of as well. Approximately, 53% of the secret message is been able to embed into the cover text. This is a little improvement compared to earlier methods. The authors have to explore more on their language so that even better methods can be devised.

(Wang, 2019) This steganography method does not use the cover text, and applicable to Chinese language text. There are different techniques followed in this method such as preprocessing the message, exploitation of parity, and statistical features of the character, space mapping with the help of binary search tree, segmentation, and matching. The final output is in the form of some texts and URLs. The output so obtained processed again to extract the original secret message by the receiver. The main motive of this method to have a higher concealed rate, no altering cover text, and the same technique can be ported to other languages as well.

(Gupta Banik, 2020) The proposed technique is a new technique for the text steganography based on part-of-speech Tagger of NLP. For this, a Penn POS tagger concept is applied, and a table of different tags having 36 entries devised. This table is been used to hide the secret. Also, RSA security is applied to protect the message from intruders. This method is good for short messages and bulk data cannot be handled by the method. Roughly around 3-10% of secret messages can be concealed.

(Zhou, 2019)This scheme of text steganography is based on typographical errors, introduced in the Chinese language. The process of data hiding involves inserting typos intentionally to pave way for concealing the secret message with the application of BERT (Devlin, 2018). The cover text here chosen to hide messages is Internet data such as chat messages of Chinese Internet Applications, and social network information. The embedding rate is very low and requires large computing power.

(Majumder, 2020) A Sudoku puzzle-based, text steganographic method; uses cover text information to generate a Sudoku puzzle. In these puzzles, the secret message is hidden at different positions of other words. From the positions of the hidden characters, a random Sudoku puzzle is generated and sent to the destination. Using these positional values secret message is extracted. This method is considered to be the reliable one and secured.

A Modified Approach to Data Hiding in Microsoft Word Documents by Change-Tracking Technique

This method (Mahato, 2020) uses modified Huffman coding for improved embedding capacity and follows linguistic synonym based digital steganography type. To hide the secret it tracks the changes made into the word document and reduces the suspicion about the message. Since the earlier method used the rare words which were too lengthy and taking much space as compared to words used here are most common. The core change here is the utilization of the most common words people use every day.

The basic method of Huffman code steganography (Raghavendra, 2019) also uses a change tracking technique. Huffman coding is a lossless compression technique (Yang, 2018) based on the frequency occurrence of data.

The basic objective is to assign variable length codes to input characters; it is based on the frequency of those characters. The highest frequency characters get the smallest code and fewer frequency characters get bigger code. This paper uses the non-occurrence frequency technique and minimizes the lengthy codes into shorter ones thereby increases the embedding capacity further. As per the author test results are giving approximately a 9% increase in the embedding capacity compares to the previous technique.

Here the process has two folds embedding process and extraction (Pramanik, S. and Bandyopadhyay, S. K., 2014) process. Embedding process Figure 8 (proposed diagram) starts with selecting a message for encoding and converts it to binary equivalent.

The embedding process uses a cover text, an MS-Word document. Identify and select the words having proper synonym words. Generate the Huffman codes due to the non-occurrence probability for

Figure 8. Message Embedding Process using Synonym Substitution

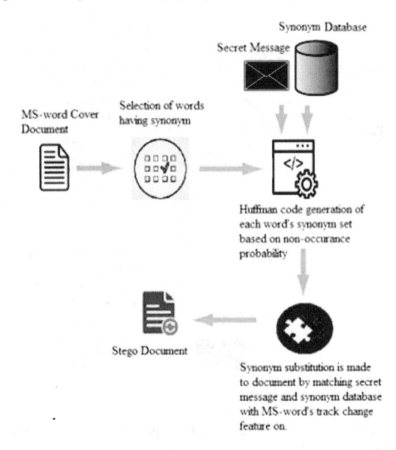

the words selected. Generate a synonym table for the words selected earlier. Each word should have a proper synonym equivalent and apply Huffman's non-occurrence probability to generate the binary codes.

Then the synonym replacement instead of the word, to hide the message is done. This process takes the binary bits from the message stream and matches the synonym code in the synonym table. The synonym word is then embedded into the cover text. If there is no proper match found then it moves to the next word.

Finally, after all the words have been substituted the Stego-text will be ready to send shown in Figure 9 (Proposed diagram). At the receiver end, the Stego-text is accepted and the receiver generates synonym words. This subjected to Huffman's non-occurrence probability to generate and modifications are traced and message bits are extracted from the Stego-text to make messages again.

Shortfalls

1. The suspicions cannot be ruled out and further studies might improve the results.
2. The algorithm is customized to the English language and studies are required may be to generalize it.
3. Embedding ratio is very low.
4. Synonym paraphrasing tools can reveal the presence of the secret in the cover text.

Figure 9. Message Extraction Process using Synonym Substitution

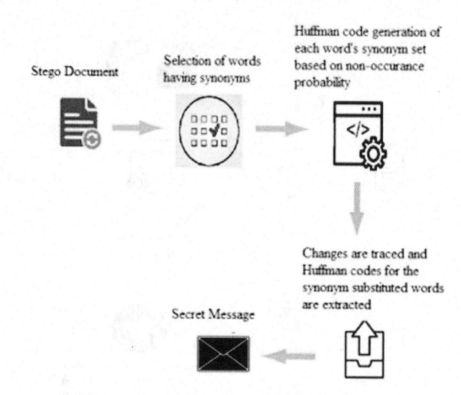

5.   In synonym Steganography, certain times do not preserve the meaning of the cover text after embedding.

"Low-Tech Steganography for Covert Operations"

Low-tech Steganography (Nag, 2019) provides a much-secured way of a manual covert operation. Over the years digital Steganography has taken the upper hand. There are certain reasons why Digital steganography cannot be used for sending secrets to destinations. The Internet is always prone to attacks on information due to easy access and modification. The Stego-text which is generated through some automated tools can be modified or destroyed in the transit by any arbitrator and even the suspicion arises that some secrets have been transferring. In addition, there are certain software tools such as checkers and scanners that disclose the existence of secret data inside the cover text. In some situations, the formatting options of software can change the structure of the Stego text itself. During war times to save the interest of the nation there may be interruption of the Internet and other message transfer facilities. During this period digital steganography cannot be used when the Internet is down. Steganography cannot be used when the Internet is down.

In these conditions, manual Steganography or low-tech covert operation can be used very effectively. This paper elucidates every aspect of low-tech covert operations. The following diagram gives the visual representation of the method.

STEGASSIST is the implementation of the method mentioned above of covert operation. The user inputs two quantities, Message, and initial cover text to the system and checks the cover text for the suitability to conceal the message into it. In case the cover text entered is not meeting the conditions to embed data then the execution terminates with some suggestions and modification. After the required modifications, the process is repeated and this will continue till the cover text is made suitable. Further, the user has two options to choose from, shown in Figure 10 (proposed diagram); either whole word or partial word embedding or both. Whole word embedding uses the complete word for the process, whereas the partial word option conceals partially.

Figure 10. Embedding Process in Low-tech for Covert Operation

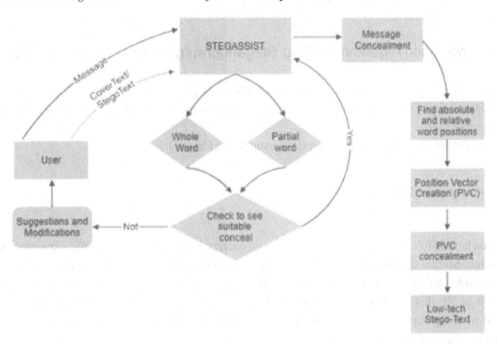

The process of embedding starts with the first word of the message and it's scanned in the cover text. The position number of the word in the cover text is recorded, and then the second word follows the same way. Likewise, all the words of the secret message are scanned and the position number is recorded. The relative position of the words is calculated thereafter. This is done by counting the number of words from the previous word. From the above data, a vector is generated containing the word positions which are converted to binary signed magnitude form and apply base-23 number systems to get PVC (Position Vector Code). PVC is prefixed with a header containing 4-bit data as follows: First bit from MSB 1 for the start of the header always, Second bit 1 for partial word and 0 for the whole word, Third bit 1 for Encryption and 0 for no encryption, Fourth bit 1 for Hashing and 0 for no hashing.

The above header data along with PVC both will encode into cover text. For this process, an interactive method is employed. The system asks the user, a series of words to make a meaningful sentence and it is then appended to the cover text which becomes Stego text on a paper. At the receiver end, the extraction process follows based on the header and PVC values embedded.

Shortfalls

1. The present algorithm uses the static position embedding and a bit inefficient; further research can be taken by improving partial word embedding using dynamically selecting the position inside the word.
2. If the presence of the number and time in the message part; will be more suspicious.
3. Through some OCR devices the lines of the cover text can be scanned and put to Steganalysis to detect the existence of a secret.
4. This kind of manual Steganography is very rarely used due to the fact that the message cannot be sent immediately or for longer distances.
5. The chances of Stego object exposing to the atmospheric conditions resulting in a damaged Stego object.

Applying Encryption Algorithm on Text Steganography Based on Number System

According to the paper (Mandal K. K., 2020), the method employed stands out from conventional types of text steganography. This method uses a unique number system, Figure 11(Proposed diagram) to conceal the message.

To generate the sequence of numbers, the formula used here is:

$$y * \frac{y+1}{2} + z \text{ for an ordered pair (y, z).} \tag{1}$$

The idea here is to send a number sequence pairs; each pair of a number indicates a specific character of a message. So that the complete message is converted to sequence pairs and it becomes Stego-text.

For example, let's pick a character from the message; say, 'p' and convert it to its hexadecimal. In this case, it is 50; this number is expressed in the form of the formula mentioned above. Find out 50 belongs to which group? According to the number system, it belongs to group 10, and then y is 10-1=9. Apply the equation (1) as under:

$$\frac{9*10}{45} = 2 \tag{2}$$

So, the sequence for character 'p' can be represented as ordered pair:

$$(y, z) \text{ è } (9, 5) \tag{3}$$

This way any character can be represented and put in the ordered form(y, z). If the hexadecimal number is above 9, then it has to be converted to an octal number system.

The number system proposed in this paper and the groups of numbers are shown as under.

The Message "COMMUNICATED" as a specimen is transformed to the ordered pair, Stego text as following:

Figure 11. A New Number System for the Steganography Algorithm

```
Proposed Number System (K.K.Mandal, 2020)

Group 1 ==>   1
Group 2 ==>   2,3
Group 3 ==>   4,5,6
Group 4 ==>   7,8,9,10
Group 5 ==>   11,12,13,14,15
Group 6 ==>   16,17,18,19,20,21
Group 7 ==>   22,23,24,25,26,27,28
Group 8 ==>   29,30,31,32,33,34,35,36
Group 9 ==>   37,38,39,40,41,42,43,44,45
Group 10==>   46,47,48,49,50,51,52,53,54,55
Group 11==>   56,57,58,59,60,61,62,63,64,65,66
Group 12==>   67,68,69,70,71,72,73,74,75,76,77,78
Group 13==>   79,80,81,82,83,84,85,86,87,88,89,90,91
Group 14==>   92,93,94,95,96,97,98,99,100,101,102,103,104,105
```

$(8, 7)\ (14, 2)\ (14, 10)\ (14, 10)\ (9, 10)\ (14, 11)\ (9, 4)\ (8, 7)\ (8, 5)\ (9, 9)\ (8, 9)\ (8, 8)$

The decoding algorithm scans all the coordinates received from left to right. The y and z coordinate substituted in the formula mentioned above and the result in the hexadecimal or if possible octal value. Value then converted back to character. Similarly, other coordinates are converted to the respective characters. These characters are organized to get the final message.

Shortfalls

1. The main problem is the algorithm itself; if it is exposed to Steganalysis then the purpose is defeated.
2. Though the AES security is provided however not sufficient.
3. The numbers or encrypted text always leads to suspicion and more tendencies of Steganalysis.
4. Very less embedding capability.
5. Less secured.

A New Approach of Text Steganography using ASCII Values

This method of text steganography uses the image as the cover text to embed text messages. This method makes use of the alteration of the RGB value to conceal the message. To do this the message's ASCII values are extracted and eventually minor changes are made to the original RGB values of an image (Joshi, 2018).

Any pixel is a combination of RGB values. Each of these pixel values is ranging from 0 to 255. The pixel color in the image is formed based on the variation in the RGB values. The proposed method exploits the characteristic of an image that small changes in the pixel values will not distract the quality of the image. The method yields more embed data compare to any other text based steganography methods.

The process stores individual ASCII characters inside the RGB values by slight modification. As a part of the literature survey, message embedding is implemented in python language. An image of matrix 1024X768 is taken as cover media. The program output having original RGB values, values corresponds to each character, and the modified RGB values are given. A series of such values running up to the length of the message.

As an illustration in Figure 12, the first original pixel value of RGB is 101, 90, and 58 respectively. Then the first character of the message (It's our little secret) is 'I' and its ASCII value is 073. The individual digits of this number are replaced as the last digits of the RGB value mentioned before. The modified RGB will become 100, 97, and 53.

Figure 12. Embedding Process

```
Message :  It's our little secret
           101 90 58
           0 7 3
           (100, 97, 53)
           102 89 57
           1 1 6
           (101, 81, 56)
           106 95 65
           1 3 9
           (101, 93, 69)
           110 95 66
           1 1 5
           (111, 91, 65)
           107 91 65
           1 3 2
           (101, 93, 62)..........
```

The following images are shown in Figure 13 are original and embedded (Stego image). As one can see there is no change can be detected between them; even though a text message is concealed inside of it. This process is applied to lossless techniques only.

Figure 13. a) The Image Before Embedding and b) The Image After Embedding

(a) Original Image   (b) Embedded Image

The extraction process is done by iterating over the pixels up to the message length of the Stego image accepted at the other end. Then pull the last digits of the RGB values to combine and convert back to the ASCII character. This process is repeated till all the characters are constructed.

Shortfalls

1. This method suitable only for lossless format embedding (Pramanik, S., Singh, R. P., and Ghosh, R. 2020), however lossy format might scramble the message.
2. The method is secure as long as there is no suspicion about the Stego object.
3. As the method is relying on the image pixels and the tendency of hiding huge volume is always there, provided too much of concealment lead to diminish quality of the image.
4. If the Stego image object is subjected to compression then after the decompression, extracting the secret is difficult; because, the compression algorithms are non-deterministic in nature.
5. Even encrypted secret message concealment also suffers due to compression.

COMPARISON OF TEXT STEGANOGRAPHIC METHODS

Steganography has several types; however, text steganography is a difficult one. Other media such as Image or video data have an abundance of repetition values; text does not have the redundant data. On the other hand the organization of image or video has a definite structure and that with text is not. Image can easily be inserted with additional information without altering the image quality. In text it is difficult to achieve. One of the advantages of text steganography is its inexpensive and takes less memory. The following *Table 1* highlights the merits and demerits of text steganographic methods.

CONCLUSION

This research aimed to study the theory behind text Steganography techniques, and their shortcomings. Authors had taken four different text steganography methods namely, the Linguistic method, low-tech method, using a number system, and embedding within an image, and showed some weaknesses of these methods. While making the detailed study, researchers proposed new diagrams, and tiny application development using python and C language. Out of all the methods, text hiding inside image had resulted in a high embedding rate, however suitable only for lossless; otherwise, it scrambles the message. Based on the number system method reasonable embedding capacity can be achieved, yet it cannot hide the suspicion. STEGASSIST method is completely manual and very much secured compare to digital methods, even so, static and embedding number and date leads to suspicion. The linguistic method discussed is not a generalized method suitable to English and suspicion cannot rule out. One major drawback of all these steganography methods is skeptical. Further study is required for the improvisation of these methods. The future scope of this work projects the positivity of the methods discussed and the limitations further motivate the researchers. It is very relevant nowadays that, steganography along with cryptography provides powerful protection to sensitive information over the Internet channels.

Table 1. A general comparison of the methods of text steganography in relation to their merits and demerits

Text Steganography Methods	Type of the Method	Merits	Demerits
Line Shift Encoding steganography (Kumar, 2020)	Bit-level & Alignment Modification, Format Based	This method is applicable to printed text only not for soft copies.	Hidden information in soft copies are altered and/or lost through word processing tools.
Word Shifting (Alwan, 2019)	Bit-level & Alignment Modification, Format Based	Difficult to detect secret due to the minute alteration in the spacing between the words.	If any detecting application is used when there is a suspicion about the Stego-text; that time it is vulnerable.
Syntactic Method (Ganiev, 2020)	Bit-level &, Linguistic Based	Hard to notice embed data since the punctuation marks in the Stego text are coded 0 or 1.	The secret can be detected if a specific scanner tool is used upon suspicion.
Semantic method (Zhang, 2020)	Bit-level &, Linguistic Based	The binary secret stream is encoded based on the actual word as 1 and synonym as 0 respectively. This method is superior to previous methods. Steganalysis is hard to do.	Any sort of scanners having synonym knowledge built-in can disclose the embedded secret.
Abbreviation or acronym method (Naqvi, 2018)	Bit-level &Miscellaneous	By replacing word-phrases with abbreviations indicating a secret bit for each bit of secret binary stream.	A very small amount of text can be embedded
Exploiting case insensitivity (Khairullah, 2019)	Bit-level & Technical or Format based	Applicable for data embedding inside Web pages. Browsers take no notice of cover distortion, further the user is unnoticed the same. Inserting secrets is easy in this method. Ex:HTML	This method is not suitable when the systems use case sensitivity.
Steg-Hash (Szczypiorski, 2016)	Linguistic + miscellaneous	This method is advantageous in embedding large amounts of data through social networks files.	The main disadvantage is sender linked to other users; they might suspect sender due to the behavior.
Feature coding method steganography (Chaudhary, 2016)	Bit-level & Format/ Feature coding	This exploits the features of characters such text size, color, vertical line, horizontal characters. Secret bits added by embedding these features. Improvement of this method is that a large amount of data must be embedded.	The disadvantage lies in reformatting and or retyping of the data then secret data will be deleted. To extract secrets from Stego text needs an original document.
Open space method (Nasereddin, 2016)	Bit-level & Format/ Feature coding	Here whitespace characters are used to encode secret bits. Three subtypes: Inter-sentence space method, End-of-Line space method and Inter-word space method.	Any word processing software changes the entire arrangement of secret encoding and extraction of secret data is impossible
Novel Linguistic Steganography Based on Character-Level Text Generation (Xiang L. Y., 2020)	Character-level & Linguistic based	A character-level linguistic steganographic method (CLLS) generates Stego text by embedding characters. the method yields high concealing volume of message with faster rates, and better imperceptibility	This method customized to English language but not for other languages.

ACKNOWLEDGMENT

This research received no specific grant from any funding agency in the public, commercial, or not-for-profit sectors.

REFERENCES

Abdulla, A. A. (2015). *Exploiting similarities between secret and cover images for improved embedding efficiency and security in digital steganography.* Buckingham E-Archive of Research.

Ahvanooey, M. T. (2018). AITSteg: An innovative text steganography technique for hidden transmission of text message via social media. *IEEE Access: Practical Innovations, Open Solutions, 6*, 65981–65995. doi:10.1109/ACCESS.2018.2866063

Al-Huwais, N. H. (2020). An Improved Least Significant Bit Image Steganography Method. In *International Conference on Multimedia Computing, Networking and Applications* (pp. 90-96). IEEE.

Al-Nofaie, S. M., & Gutub, A. A.-A. (2020). Utilizing pseudo-spaces to improve Arabic text steganography for multimedia data communications. *Multimedia Tools and Applications, 79*(1-2), 19–67. doi:10.100711042-019-08025-x

Alajmi, M. E.-S., Elashry, I., El-Sayed, H. S., & Farag Allah, O. S. (2020). Steganography of Encrypted Messages Inside Valid QR Codes. *IEEE Access: Practical Innovations, Open Solutions, 8*, 8. doi:10.1109/ACCESS.2020.2971984

Alam, S. S. (2014). Entropy Based Visual Cryptographic Encryption Technique for Medical Images Security. ERCICA, 75-78.

Alwan, A. A. (2019). *A Survey On Combined Various Data Hiding Techniques.* Open International Journal of Informatics.

Aman, M. K. (2017). *A hybrid text steganography approach utilizing Unicode space characters and zero-width character.* International Journal on Information Technologies and Security.

Anand, A. (2020). Watermarking techniques for medical data authentication: A survey. *Multimedia Tools and Applications*, 1–33.

Bonavoglia, P. (2020). A Partenio's Stegano-Crypto Cipher. In *International Conference on Historical Cryptology HistoCrypt* (pp. 36-45). Linköping University Electronic Press. 10.3384/ecp2020171006

Chakrabarti, S. D. S. (2015). A Novel Approach to Digital Image Steganography of Key-Based Encrypted Text. Communication and Optimization (EESCO), 24 - 25.

Chaudhary, S. D. (2016). Text steganography based on feature coding method. In *The International Conference on Advances in Information Communication Technology & Computing* (pp. 1-4). ACM.

Dalal, M. (2020). Steganography and Steganalysis (in digital forensics): A Cybersecurity guide. *Multimedia Tools and Applications*, 1–49.

Devlin, J. C. (2018). *Bert: Pre-training of deep bidirectional transformers for language understanding.* arXiv preprint.

Dhawan, S. (2020). Analysis of various data security techniques of steganography. A survey. Information Security Journal: A Global Perspective, 1-25.

Douglas, M. B. (2018). An overview of steganography techniques applied to the protection of biometric data. Multimed Tools App, 77, 17333–17373. doi:10.100711042-017-5308-3

Easttom, W. (2021). Steganography. In *Modern Cryptography*. Springer. doi:10.1007/978-3-030-63115-4_16

Ganiev, A. A. (2020). The analysis of text steganography methods. *International Scientific Journal of Theoretical & Applied Science*, 85-88.

Gupta Banik, B. (2020). Novel text steganography using natural language processing and part-of-speech tagging. *Journal of the Institution of Electronics and Telecommunication Engineers*, 12.

Gupta Banik, B., & Bandyopadhyay, S. K. (2020). Novel text steganography using natural language processing and part-of-speech tagging. *Journal of the Institution of Electronics and Telecommunication Engineers*, 66(3), 384–395. doi:10.1080/03772063.2018.1491807

Hadipour, A. &. (2020). Advantages and disadvantages of using cryptography in steganography. In *International ISC Conference on Information Security and Cryptology* (pp. 88-94). IEEE.

Joshi, K. (2018). A new approach of text steganography using ASCII values. *International Journal of Engineering Research & Technology*, 7(5).

Kadhim, I. J., Premaratne, P., Vial, P. J., & Halloran, B. (2019). Comprehensive survey of image steganography: Techniques, Evaluations, and trends in future research. *Neurocomputing*, 335, 28. doi:10.1016/j.neucom.2018.06.075

Kalsi, S. K., Kaur, H., & Chang, V. (2018). DNA cryptography and deep learning using genetic algorithm with NW algorithm for key generation. *Journal of Medical Systems*, 42(1), 17. doi:10.100710916-017-0851-z PMID:29204890

Kamaruddin, N. S., Kamsin, A., Por, L. Y., & Rahman, H. (2018). A review of text watermarking: Theory, methods, and applications. *IEEE Access: Practical Innovations, Open Solutions*, 6, 6. doi:10.1109/ACCESS.2018.2796585

Khairullah, M. (2019). A novel steganography method using transliteration of Bengali text. *Journal of King Saud University-Computer and Information Sciences*, 348-366.

Khosravi, B. K. (2019). A new method for pdf steganography in justified texts. Journal of Information Security and Applications, 61-70.

Krishnan, R. B. (2017). An overview of text steganography. In *International Conference on Signal Processing, Communication and Networking* (pp. 1-6). IEEE.

Kumar, R. (2020). *Recent Trends in Text Steganography with Experimental Study*. Springer. doi:10.1007/978-3-030-22277-2_34

Lingyun Xiang, S. Y. (2020). Novel linguistic steganography based on character-level text generation. *Mathematics*, 18.

Liu, J. C., Chen, W., & Wen, Y. (2018). A Robust and Flexible Covert Channel in LTE-A System. *Journal of Physics: Conference Series*, 1087, 6. doi:10.1088/1742-6596/1087/6/062027

Lockwood, R. (2017). Text based steganography. *International Journal of Information Privacy. Security and Integrity, 3*(2), 134–153.

Madhavi, K. K. (2018). A Robust and Efficient Steganography Using Skin Tone as Biometric for Real Time Images. *International Research Journal of Engineering and Technology,* 4.

Mahato, S. K., Khan, D. A., & Yadav, D. K. (2020). A modified approach to data hiding in Microsoft Word documents by change-tracking technique. *Journal of King Saud University-Computer and Information Sciences, 32*(2), 216–224. doi:10.1016/j.jksuci.2017.08.004

Majumder, A. C. (2020). A New Text Steganography Method Based on Sudoku Puzzle Generation. In *Proceedings of ICETIT* (pp. 961-972). Cham: Springer. 10.1007/978-3-030-30577-2_85

Mandal, K. K. (2014, March). A new approach of text Steganography based on mathematical model of number system. *International Conference on Circuits, Power and Computing Technologies [ICCPCT-2014],* 1737-1741. 10.1109/ICCPCT.2014.7054849

Mandal, K. K. (2020). Applying Encryption Algorithm on Text Steganography Based on Number System. In Computational Advancement in Communication Circuits and Systems (pp. 255-266). Springer.

Mansor, F. Z. (2018). An Antonym Substitution-based Model on Linguistic Steganography Method. *Indonesian Journal of Electrical Engineering and Computer Science,* 12.

Mukherjee, M. (2014). Fibonacci Based Text Hiding Using Image Cryptography. Lecture Notes on Information Theory, 2(2).

Nag, A. (2019). Low-tech steganography for covert operations. *IJCNIS, 2*(1), 21–27.

Naqvi, N. A. (2018). *Multilayer partially homomorphic encryption text steganography (MLPHE-TS): a zero steganography approach.* Springer.

Nasereddin, H. H. (2016). Enhancing Open Space Method in Data Hiding. *International Journal of Computers and Applications,* 5–17.

Nechta, I. (2017). Steganography in social networks. *Siberian Symposium on Data Science and Engineering,* 33-35. 10.1109/SSDSE.2017.8071959

Pramanik, S., & Bandyopadhyay, S. K. (2014). Hiding Secret Message in an Image. *International Journal of Innovative Science, Engineering & Technology, 1*(3), 553–559.

Pramanik, S., & Singh, R. P. (2017). Role of Steganography in Security Issues. *International Journal of Advance Research in Science and Engineering, 6*(1), 1119–1124.

Pramanik, S., Singh, R. P., & Ghosh, R. (2020). Application of Bi-Orthogonal Wavelet Transform and Genetic Algorithm in Image Steganography. *Multimedia Tools and Applications, 79*(25-26), 17463–17482. doi:10.100711042-020-08676-1

Raghavendra, C. S., Sivasubramanian, S., & Kumaravel, A. (2019). Improved image compression using effective lossless compression technique. *Cluster Computing, 22*(S2), 6. doi:10.100710586-018-2508-1

Rashid, M. R.-H. (2014). Combining SPF and source routing for an efficient probing solution in IPv6 topology discovery. In *Global Information Infrastructure and Networking Symposium*. IEEE.

Samanta, M. M. (2014). Fibonacci Based Text Hiding Using Image Cryptography. *Lecture Notes on Information Theory*, 2(2), 172–176. doi:10.12720/lnit.2.2.172-176

Samanta, S. (2020). A Significant Survey on Text Steganalysis Techniques. *International Journal on Computer Science and Engineering*, 187–193.

Sedeeq, I. C. (2017). A prediction model based approach to open space steganography detection in HTML webpages. *International Workshop on Digital Watermarking*, 235-247. 10.1007/978-3-319-64185-0_18

Sharma, S. G. (2016). Analysis of different text steganography techniques: a survey. In *International Conference on Computational Intelligence & Communication Technology* (pp. 130-133). IEEE. 10.1109/CICT.2016.34

Singh, R. K., T. B. (2017). Text Encryption: Character Jumbling. *Proc. of IEEE International Conference on Inventive Systems and Control*, 19-20.

Syed, K. A., & Khadri, D. (2014). Message Encryption Using Text Inversion plus N Count: In Cryptology. International Journal of Information Science and Intelligent System, 3(2), 71-74.

Szczypiorski, K. (2016). *StegHash: new method for information hiding in open social networks*. arXiv preprint.

Thangadurai, K. &. (2014, January). An analysis of LSB based image steganography techniques. In *International Conference on Computer Communication and Informatics* (pp. 1-4). IEEE. 10.1109/ICCCI.2014.6921751

Wang, K., & Gao, Q. (2019). A coverless plain text steganography based on character features. *IEEE Access: Practical Innovations, Open Solutions*, 7, 95665–95676. doi:10.1109/ACCESS.2019.2929123

Xiang, L. W. (2017). A novel linguistic steganog-raphy based on synonym run-length encoding. *IEICE Transactions on Information and System*, 100(2), 313-322.

Xiang, L. Y., Yang, S., Liu, Y., Li, Q., & Zhu, C. (2020). Novel linguistic steganography based on character-level text generation. *Mathematics*, 8(9), 1558. doi:10.3390/math8091558

Yang, Z. L. (2018). RNN-stega: Linguistic steganography based on recurrent neural networks. *IEEE Transactions on Information Forensics and Security*, 6.

Zhang, S. Y. (2020). *Linguistic Steganography: From Symbolic Space to Semantic Space*. Signal Processing Letters.

Zhou, L. (2019). Study of Chinese Text Steganography using Typos. In *Asia-Pacific Signal and Information Processing Association Annual Summit and Conference* (pp. 1351-1357). IEEE.

Chapter 4
Machine Learning and Deep Learning in Steganography and Steganalysis

Ankur Gupta
https://orcid.org/0000-0002-4651-5830
Vaish College of Engineering, Rohtak, India

Sabyasachi Pramanik
https://orcid.org/0000-0002-9431-8751
Haldia Institute of Technology, India

Hung Thanh Bui
School of Engineering and Tecnology, Thu Dau Mot University, Vietnam

Nicholas M. Ibenu
ESCAE University of Technology, Benin

ABSTRACT

Steganography is the way to conceal data inside a normal (non-mystery) record to keep it from discovery. While encryption expects to conceal the substance of data, steganography means to shroud the presence of data. Information security is significant when touchy information is communicated over the internet. Steganography and steganalysis methods can take care of the issue of copyright, possession, and discovery of malevolent information. Steganography is to conceal mystery information without contortion, and steganalysis is to distinguish the presence of shrouded information. In this chapter, steganography and steganalysis methods are depicted along with AI structures to show that AI systems can be utilized to recognize the mystery information covered up in the picture utilizing steganography calculations.

DOI: 10.4018/978-1-7998-7160-6.ch004

INTRODUCTION

Steganography is to camouflage the clandestine information inside intuitive media substance, for instance, archive, message, picture, or tape. Steganography is stressed over camouflaging the way that the underground information is being sent cryptically similarly as hide the substance of the clandestine information. Steganalysis is the accomplice of steganography that described as the specialty of investigation of perceiving the covered clandestine information in envelops objects. All things considered, steganalysis is to recognize secret information disguised by means of steganography, anywhere steganalysis is to perceive supposed groups, choose if the clandestine information is entrenched or not. ML is a field of man-made mental ability to enable to be trained lacking being adjusted and DL is a compartment of ML. In this document, steganalysis and ML procedures are give details and the cycle and open doors for steganalysis in an assortment of ML structure are depicted. Some datasets on stego-pictures are organized and planning representation is attempted.

With the fast advancement of data innovation and the quick promotion of the Internet, computerized medium has become a huge carrier for martial, business and various affiliations similarly as persons to get and communicate data. And yet, in light of the fact that the advanced correspondence in the Internet is helpless against the danger of snooping, vindictive obstruction and different exercises, individuals give more consideration to the security issues, for example, security assurance and information trustworthiness during the time spent data transmission than any time in recent memory. The conventional plan makes use of encryption advancement to change the information over to cipher text for broadcast. In any case, its inadequacy is so as to the scrambled cipher text is typically scattered. It is simple for an assailant to see the presence of mystery correspondence, which invigorates the aggressor's energy for deciphering. Simultaneously, it might likewise prompt data being meddled or blocked, bringing about the disappointment of data transmission. In the above setting, another idea of correspondence security has been slowly acknowledged and perceived: correspondence security implies not just that the substance of data to be sent is secured, yet in addition that the presence of the demonstration of sending mystery data is obscure. Hence, steganography, which is depicted by ''mask'' in the communication of in order, has pulled in progressively more thought.

The essential standard of steganography is to shroud the mystery data which should be communicated into the excess data by utilizing the coldhearted repetitive data of human observation structure existing in like manner transporters, and to understand the transmission of mystery data by methods for transporter transmission. Since the cycle of data stowing away into the transporter typically doesn't change the ordinary observation qualities of the transporter, it is hard for possible aggressors to identify the presence of mystery data, in this manner guaranteeing the data security secretive transmission. Simultaneously, it can likewise join encryption (Pramanik, S. and Singh, R. P. 2017), scrambling, coding and different advancements, making it hard to remove shrouded data regardless of whether it is identified by outsiders, accordingly further guaranteeing the security of data transmission. To clarify steganography all the more clearly, we depict the ''detainee issue'' for instance. Detainees in various cells in a similar jail they are beneath the consideration of Warden Eve will examine plans for a joint escape. Explicit plans should be haggled through the trading of data. In any case, as indicated by jail guidelines, their correspondences should be checkered by the superintendent, so they can't convey in plaintext. For this situation, Bob and Mice necessitate to take more secretive correspondence actions. One thought is to utilize encryption innovation, so as to is, to shroud the substance of data, other than since the scrambled data is a wreck of system; it is anything but difficult to stimulate Eve's doubt. Along these lines, for this situation, a more secure thought is to conceal data in regular items, furthermore, make the covered items look common, which can diminish Warden Eve's watchfulness and assurance the level broadcast of data.

In any case, steganography is additionally a genuine twofold edged blade, which gives individuals dependable and secure methods for Internet correspondence, simultaneously, it might likewise give accommodation to associations and people with pernicious goals or ill-advised purposes. Truth is told, as of late, there have been reports about the utilization of steganography in reconnaissance, psychological militant assaults, wrongdoings and different exercises. In 2001, some established press in the United States, for example, CNN and US Today, announced the information on mystery correspondences stuck between Al Qaeda individuals utilizing steganography. Detailed that receptacle Laden posse will assault the objective guide, activity guidelines and other data covered up in sexual entertainment, sports talk and different sites. As per Die Zeit, an al-Qaida presume was captured in Berlin and police discovered him conveying a memory card. Afterward, in the wake of being broken by specialists accountable for PC criminal examination in the German Federal Criminal Police Bureau, it be discovered so as to on a superficial level, just a single explicit video named ''KickAss'' showed up on the card, however truth be told, 141 content archives were covered up in the video, including countless Al-Qaida activity reports, future activity designs, etc.

The FBI alleged that by snooping on the discussion connecting the Murphy couple, who were all imagine, they bring into being that Murphy had sent his loved one Cynthia to South America to hand over more than amazing ''imperceptible'' to an important person. According to the FBI assessment, these asserted ''impalpable things'' are probable going to be recorded by automated steganography. In April 2014, customary press in China, for instance, CCTV and Xinhua News Agency, uncovered that the adaptable Trojan Horse ''exceptional Trojan Horse II'' polluted enormous number of PDAs, and finished fishing attacks, regulator of customers' wireless photos, taking customers' online silver and various activities that really in danger of extinction customers' own individual pledge and possessions security. It is represented that, not at all like the normal Trojan horse direct request form, the Trojan horse adroitly veils harmful system rules as a run of the mill depiction from side to side steganography, to keep away from the ''interest'' of wireless security programming

Steganography

Steganography be able to be arranged as what sort of rules is utilized. In Figure 1, steganography procedures are partitioned by sight and sound data types and areas.

Figure 1. Steganography

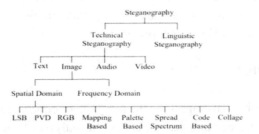

In alternate manner, steganography can be segregated into irreversible and reversible data concealing procedures whether the envelop article can be recuperated, wherever the substance of mystery information can unequivocally wipe out. In irreversible information stowing unendingly, the most minimal basic pieces substitution and pixel-regard differencing strategies are utilized in custom. In reversible data stowing perpetually, capability expansion, histogram moving and desire goof augmentation are recognized in the spatial space. Reversible data concealing system are utilized to deal with the issue of lossless presenting in delicate pictures, for example, military pictures, clinical pictures, and show-stopper defending.

Steganalysis

Steganalysis is to recognize suspected information, choose hid information, in addition, and recuperate the covered information. Steganalysis can be allocated four requests: visual, colleague, genuine, and knowledge steganalysis. Illustration steganalysis is to explore visual old pieces in the stego images, where attempt to get illustration separation by assessing stego images. Right hand steganalysis investigates suspected signs in the medium plan portrayal since the game-plan is reliably misrepresented when the mystery memorandum is installed. RS assessment and two of a kind examination are related with the crucial steganalysis. Genuine steganalysis uses quantifiable replicas to recognize steganography philosophy. Quantifiable steganalysis can be confined into express undeniable and expansive quantifiable steganalysis. Knowledge steganalysis in addition call stun steganalysis is one of all over irrefutable steganalysis because envelop up pictures and stego-pictures are utilized as preparing datasets. Additional strategy of steganalysis can be allocated into six classes as appeared in Figure 2. It is relying on what sort of assaults criminological master occupations.

Figure 2. Steganalysis

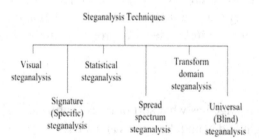

In figure 2, general or visually impaired steganalysis procedures depend on distinguishing the mystery messages regardless of steganography strategies. Contrasting and different steganalysis procedures, all-inclusive steganalysis strategy is hard to track down extraction highlights, where ML strategies are regularly used to construct, train, and assess replica.

Steganalysis Techniques

Steganalysis is the strategy, which distinguishes the presence of concealed information; this interaction can be ordered by various kinds, for example, Statistical steganalysis which contains spatial area. Change space and Feature based steganalysis. The Statistical steganalysis assists with identifying the presence of the shrouded message, factual examination is finished with the pixels and it is additionally delegated spatial space steganalysis and changes area steganalysis. In spatial area, the pair of pixels is thought of and the contrast between them is determined. The pair might be any two adjoining pixels. They might be chosen inside a square in any case across the two squares. At long last the histogram is plotted that shows the presence of the shrouded message. In change area, recurrence checks of co-efficient are determined and afterward histogram examination will be performed at the hour of steganalysis. With the assistance of this, the cover and stego pictures can be separated. Notwithstanding, this strategy isn't giving data about the installing calculations. To beat this issue, we may pick include based steganalysis. The steganalysis strategies are appeared in fig 3.

Figure 3. Steganalysis methods

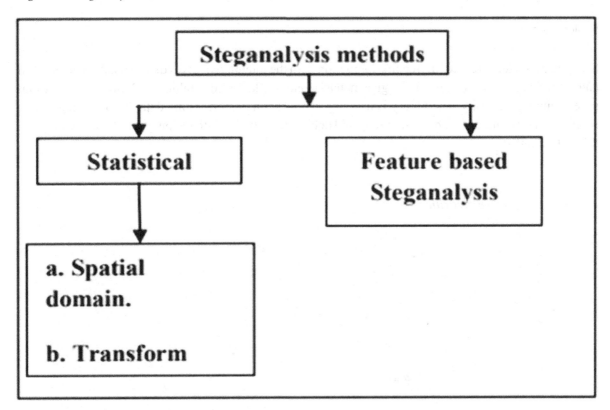

In the feature based steganalysis approach, the highlights of the given picture will be acquired for choosing and holding significant data from the cover picture. These separated highlights are utilized to distinguish shrouded message in a picture. They can likewise be utilized to prepare classifiers.

ML

ML is one of electronic thinking investigates which is a PC based procedure for knowledge as the limit of person personalities. ML can be isolated into three essential classes: directed knowledge, solo knowledge and backing knowledge. Coordinated knowledge is to get familiar with a limit that maps a commitment to a yield by giving information yield sets, which is used regularly in talk affirmation, spam distinguishing proof and thing affirmation. Solo knowledge is the commission of gaining from test information that has not been named, gathered or ordered. Essential usage of solo knowledge is in the field of pack examination, head part investigation, vector quantization and self-affiliation. Backing knowledge is stressed over how to take proceedings to support some thought of total prize. Backing knowledge is used in mechanical innovation, adventure decisions, and stock organization to learn exercises to be carried out. Profound knowledge is a bit of ML which relies upon knowledge information depictions.

To make ML figuring's, various structures are used, for instance, TensorFlow, Theano, Keras, Caffe, Torch, DL 4j, MxNet, CNTK, Lasagne, BigDL, and so forth the going with region put in plain words several of structures in existing. In this document, three structures are giving details cries because scikitlearn, TensorFlow, and Keras are second-hand to test stego-pictures.

Scikit-Learn

Scikit-learn system is a free ML records for python with the intention of gives depiction, descend into sin and gathering figuring's. Scikit-learn give managed and free knowledge tallies by Python boundary that relies winning the SciPy. The library is listening carefully on demonstrating data. For free knowledge, scikit-learn gives unmistakable assembling and debilitating checks with the purpose of are anything but difficult to utilize.

Figure 4. Scikit-learn algorithm

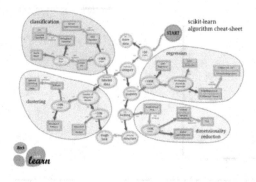

TensorFlow

TensorFlow is an unbolt records to permit strategy of assessment over another stages similar to as CPUs, GPUs, and TPUs. The runtime records are a cross-stage and the C API limits client plane regulations in various dialects beginning the center runtime appeared in Figure. 4. The runtime records surround more than 200 average endeavors together with numerical, show control, control stream, and express the chief's exercises. Tensor Flow is valuable for DL applications.

Figure 5. Architecture of TensorFlow

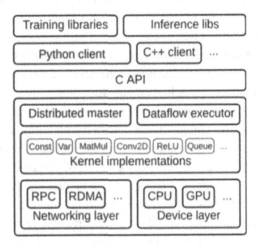

Keras

Keras is a significant height neural association's library on document in Python and fit for organization on pinnacle of TensorFlow, CNTK, or Theano. The center information organization is a replica to sort out coating. Keras enclose neural association construction squares, for example, layers, destinations, initiation capacities, streamlining agents to actualize with image and text data simpler.

DL for Steganalysis

Steganalysis has been broadly amassed in the most recent decade. Its standard setup is to perceive the occurrence of mystery communication in electronic envelop, for example, advanced pictures approaching from a well-known starting place. All around, this undertaking is figured as a twofold depiction issue to see envelop and stego objects. Beneath this container, existing philosophies fundamentally construct steganalysis identifiers in two stages: include extraction (Pramanik, S., Bandyopadhayay, S. K. and Ghosh, R. 2020) and blueprint. In the segment pulling out step, a ton of extraordinary highlights is secluded from every representation to get the effect of embedding's works out. The achievement of steganalysis overall depends upon the component plan. Regardless, the nonappearance of exact replicas of ordinary pictures jumbles this work. Consequently, unique heuristic strategies are planned. The most dependable component plan worldview begins with processing a commotion lingering and afterward replicas the remaining utilizing restrictive or joint likelihood dispersions of nearby components. With the expanded modernity of steganography strategies, more perplexing factual conditions among singular components are thought of. As of late, scientists use more sorts of commotion residuals to get rich image portrayals. To sum up, to acquire a more precise discovery on intricate picture starting place, high-dimensional portrayal is central in present day steganalysis, which makes join game plan dynamically risky. In the social event step, classifiers, for example, SVM or organization classifiers are found out dependent on the eliminated highlights. Since the part extraction and plan steps are restricted, they can't be upgraded at the same time. This suggests the bearing of plan can't be making use of to get significant in sequence in the component taking out step.

The entire subject examined higher than persuade us to be taught join portrayals for steganalysis as opposed to contributing energy trying to arrangement new highlights by hand. Profound knowledge representation is such a course group of machinery that can gain knowledge of highlight portrayals typically. Pushed by the way that human cerebrum gauges data in reformist propensities with a profound arrangement, specialists had expected for a genuine long an ideal occasion to prepare profound multi-layer neural affiliations. In any case, no achievement was spoken to awaiting 2006, when a progress was started. In that employment, Hinton presented Deep confidence system with a ravenous layer wise solo pre-arranging structure that can gain proficiency with a solicitation for highlights each level in this way. Different other profound knowledge replicas were proposed with the comparable way, for example, Deep Boltzmann Machines, significant auto encoders, and (CNNs). Those replicas have profound plans that contain different degrees of non-straight tasks and can be prepared utilizing either oversaw or solo ways to deal with oversee learn reformist portrayals by building gigantic level highlights from low down stage ones. Generally, profound replicas can address certain cutoff points which are not proficiently represented by shallow structures. They have in each down to earth sense, end up being significantly more critical knowledge plans for some mechanized thinking tries, for example, object attestation and typical language managing.

At any rate the steganalysis task is interesting according to these ML ones. For sure, the stego upheaval to oversee in steganalysis is such a weak sign which normally can't be seen by the human perceptual structure, and such a racket is unnoticed in AI farm duties. Consequently, the segment depiction in steganalysis should be exceptionally not equivalent to that in standard AI endeavors. Taking everything into account, we have attempted the current CNN replicas delivered for ML endeavors as steganalysis replica. However, it winds up being a mistake, which infers these CNN replica are unbreakable to get the stego indication that is critical for steganalysis.

1. This dissertation presents profound knowledge for steganalysis, and we think about highlight knowledge for steganalysis as an as of late out of the container new point of view.
2. We suggest a patch up CNN replica describe GNCNN which believe some remarkable follows accomplished by steganography. It and can become skilled at highlight portrayals for steganalysis. Also, the course of solicitation can be used in the section removal venture by bringing together the two stages under a solitary design.
3. We exhibit that, by utilizing highlight portrayals learned consequently from a DL replica, we can get tantamount execution with present status of-the-craftsmanship location techniques utilizing advanced handmade highlights.

DNN

In the accompanying sub-areas, we glances reverse at the significant ideas of a Convolutional Neural Network (CNN). In any case, explicitly, we will review the essential structure squares of an organization dependent on the Yedroudj-Net2 system so as to was distributed in 2018 and which obtain up the thoughts there in Alex-Net, just as the ideas there in organizations produced for steganalysis counting the absolute first organization and organizations of Xu-Net, and Ye-Net.

Figure 6. Yedroudj-Net networks

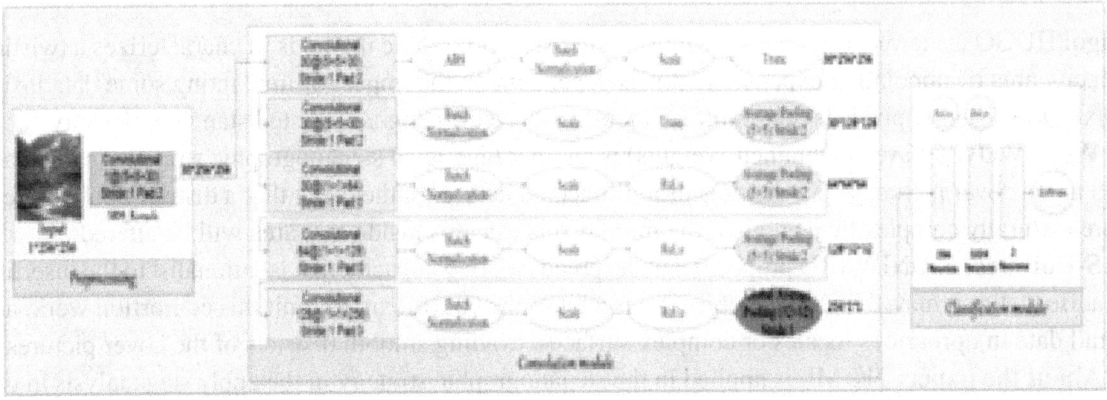

Convolution Neural Network

Prior to portraying the structure of a neural organization just as its rudimentary segments, it is helpful to recall that a neural organization has a place with the AI family. By virtue of managed realizing, which is the circumstance that most concerns us, it is imperative to have a data base of pictures, with, for each image, its imprint, all in all, its group of students. Profound Knowledge complex are huge neural associations that can clearly take unrefined data. In picture setting up, the association is clearly energized by the pixels outward appearance the image. Consequently, a profound knowledge system be taught in a combined method in cooperation the decreased innate individuality of a representation (we examine incorporate guide or of inert space) and all the while, as far as possible allowing the course of action (we moreover talk about separator plans). The knowledge show resembles old style AI strategies. Each image is given as commitment to the association. Each pixel (Pramanik, S. and Bandyopadhyay, S. K. 2014) regard is shipped off in any event one neurons the association contains a given quantity of squares. A square involves neurons that take certifiable information regards, carry out tallies, and a short time later sends the genuine decided characteristics to the accompanying square. A neural association can, as such, be addressed by an arranged diagram where every center addresses a figuring unit. The knowledge is then wrapped up by giving the association replicas made out of a representation and its name, and the association adapts the limits of these figuring component (it learns) because of the instrument of back-spread.

Convolution Module

Inside the difficulty component, we locate a few plainly visible calculation components that we motivation call lump. A square is made the most of out of units that take certifiable data regards, perform assessments, and come again genuine characteristics, which are given to the accompanying square. Specially, a square takes a lot of quality maps (= a lot of pictures) as data and income a lot of characteristic chart as yield (= a lot of pictures). Surrounded by a square, there are different assignments including the going with four: the convolution, the commencement, the pond, ultimately the normalization.

Definitions

Hugo: HUGO is viewed as perhaps the most secure steganographic methods. It characterizes a twisting capacity area by appointing expenses to pixels dependent on the impact of implanting some data inside a pixel; the space of pixels is dense into an element space utilizing a weighted standard capacity.

Wow: WOW (Wavelet Obtained Weights) is another high level steganographic strategy that installs data into a cover picture as per districts of multifaceted nature. In the event that a district of a picture is more texturally complex than another, the more pixels esteems inside that area will be altered.

S-Uniward: S-UNIWARD proposes a widespread twisting capacity that is rationalist to the inserting area. Be that as it may, the ultimate objective is a lot of the equivalent: to limit this contortion work, and install data in uproarious locales or complex surfaces, evading smooth districts of the cover pictures.

About the paper: The ML is applied in the steganographic strategy in the apply steganalysis in two settings: enterprise and personal where the ML tests aren't agreeable; however it tends to be enhanced when numerous replica datasets are readied.

LITERATURE REVIEW

Hussain, Israr & Zeng (2020) steganalysis and steganography have seen gigantic advancement in the course of recent a long time by the development of profound convolution neural affiliations. In this document, we eviscerated repeating design investigate condition from the most recent picture steganography and steganalysis systems dependent on profound knowledge. We will most likely oblige future specialists the occupation being through on profound knowledge-based picture steganography and steganalysis and features the attributes and insufficiency of existing forefront strategies. The possible result of this examination opens new structures for approaching examination and may fill in as wellspring of proposition for additional fundamental appraisal on profound knowledge-based picture steganography and steganalysis. At last, specific difficulties of stream techniques and two or three promising headings on profound education steganography and steganalysis are recommended to plot how these difficulties can be moved into advantageous prospect investigation streets.

Chahar, Vijay & Laddha (2020) steganography has been utilized since quite a while for veil of mail in a wrap medium where communication was truly concealed. The objective in our manuscript is to envelop modernized messages utilizing present day steganography philosophy. An N * N RGB pixel mystery communication (either text or picture) is to be bestowed in an added N * N RGB holder picture with least transform in its substance. The envelop picture in like way name the transporter can be straightforwardly conspicuous. In this manuscript, close by LSB encoding, profound knowledge modules utilizing the Adam calculation are utilized to set up the replica that incorporates a concealing affiliation and an unenvelop set of connections. The encoder neural affiliation figures out where and how to put the message, scattering it all through the pieces of envelop picture. The decoder system on the enduring surface, which is at the same time set up with the encoder, uncovers the mystery picture. The focal bit of this employment is it produces irrelevant contortion to the mystery message. In that capacity, protecting its tolerability Also, other steganography programming adventures can't be utilized to unenvelop the memorandum since the reproduction is prepared utilizing a profound knowledge assessment which bewilders its steganalysis. The affiliation is basically masterminded once, paying little brain to the indisputable holder pictures and mystery messages given as information sources. Hence, this employment has extensive and secure submission in different fields.

Tran, Ngoc & Pham (2019) over the latest couple of years, steganography has pulled in growing thought from a colossal numeral of specialists given that its claim are extending farther than simply the field of data security. The most standard technique depends upon mechanized sign taking care of (DSP, for example, least basic piece encoding. Beginning late, there have been some new systems employing profound figuring out how to address the issue of steganography. In any case, the vast majority of the current structures are normal for picture in-picture steganography. In this document, the utilization of profound knowledge methods to envelop mystery sound into the genuine pictures is planned. We utilize a joint profound neural affiliation planning including two sub-replicas: the essential affiliation conceals the mystery sound into an image, and the following one is liable for unraveling the image to get the fundamental sound. Broad starters are facilitated with a ton of 24K pictures and the VIVOS Corpus sound dataset 1. From side to side test consequences, it will as a rule is seen that our procedure is more sensible than standard systems. The uprightness of both picture and sound is commonly protected, while the most uncommon length of the covered sound is on a very basic level improved.

Chaumont, Marc (2019) for pretty much 10 years, the area of a covered message in an representation has been commonly did by the assessment of Rich Replicas (RM), trailed by social occasion utilizing an Ensemble Classifier (EC). In 2015, the central assessment utilizing a convolutional neural association got the basic possible results of steganalysis by DL pushing toward the introductions of the two-experience approach (EC + RM). In between 2015-2018, unique flows have demonstrated that it is conceivable to get improved introductions, astoundingly in spatial steganalysis, JPEG steganalysis, Selection-Channel-Aware steganalysis, and in quantitative steganalysis. This part directs profound taking in steganalysis from the perspective of current strategies, by introducing specific neural relationship from the period 2015-2018 that have been assessed with a strategy unequivocal to the solicitation for steganalysis. The part isn't needed to go over the essential considerations of AI or profound knowledge. Subsequently, we will introduce the arrangement of a profound neural relationship, in a standard system and in attendance the affiliations projected in obtainable creation for the various conditions of steganalysis, at last, we will examine steganography by profound knowledge.

Tabares Soto, Reinel & Pollán (2019) steganography contains disguising communication contained by a quantity of article known as a transporter to set up a furtive correspondence conduit so the show of correspondence itself goes ignored by onlookers who approach that conduit. Steganalysis is given to the territory of covered messages utilizing steganography; these messages can be seen in various kinds of media, for example, robotized pictures, video reports, sound records or plain substance. All things considered, steganalysis has been allocated two separate stages, the fundamental stage includes manual extraction of bleeding edge highlights and the subsequent stage is planning utilizing Ensemble Classifiers or Support Vector Machines. Beginning late, the progress of DL has caused it conceivable to integrate to and robotize the two normal stages into a start to finish approach with promising outcomes. These dissertations show the progression of steganalysis of late utilizing DL strategies. The possible results of these strategies have defeated those gotten with standard methods both in the spatial and rehash (JPEG) spaces. Since 2014, scientists have utilized difficulty Neural Networks to manage this issue making orchestrated arrangements and approaches to improve the unmistakable evidence movements of stegano-graphic pictures on the last age calculations. Profound Knowledge, living being applied to steganalysis, is starting at now during the time spent unforeseen development and results so far are connecting with for specialists that are enthused about the subject.

Zou, Ying & Zhang (2019) in spite of the truth that steganalysis has urbanized rapidly recently; it really faces various difficulties and challenges. Taking into account the speculation of all around knowledge procedure and picture base universal steganalysis, this document makes a profound investigation of the sizzling and inconvenient issue of steganalysis attribute verbalization, and endeavors to develop another steganalysis perspective from incorporate knowledge. The key responsibilities of this document are according to the accompanying: 1. A Creative steganalysis perspective subject to through and through knowledge is proposed. Considering the specialist profound knowledge procedure CNN, the reproduction is arranged and changed by the uniqueness of steganalysis, which make the planned representation more powerful in catching the measurable attributes, for example, neighborhood connection. 2. A steganalysis highlight knowledge technique dependent on worldwide data imperatives is proposed. In view of the past examination of steganalysis strategy dependent on CNN, this work centers around the significance of worldwide data in steganalysis include articulation. 3. An element knowledge technique for low introducing rate steganalysis is projected. 4. A universal steganalysis technique for multi-class steganography is proposed. A complete objective of all-purpose steganalysis is to fabricate steganalysis locaters without perceiving express kinds of steganalysis calculations.

Jung, Ki-Hyun (2019) information security is huge when delicate information is sent in excess of the Internet. Steganography and steganalysis structures can deal with the issue of exclusive rights, proprietorship, and unmistakable confirmation noxious data. Steganography is to envelop mystery information lacking bowing and steganalysis is to see the company of shrouded data. In this manuscript, steganography and steganalysis methodology are portrayed close by AI systems to show that AI structure can be utilized to recognize the mystery data stowing constantly in picture utilizing steganography counts.

Wu, Pin & Yang (2018) customary image steganography frequently inclines interests towards securely inserting shrouded data into envelop pictures with payload limit nearly dismissed. This document sets late profound convolutional neural association strategies with picture into-picture steganography. It suitably covers a similar size pictures with a deciphering development of 98.2% or bpp (bits per pixel) of 23.57 by changing just 0.76% of the envelop picture in general. Our procedure obviously picks up start to finish mappings sandwiched between the envelop picture and the presented picture and between the covered picture and the decode picture. We extra explain that our inserted picture, while with upper payload limit, is up to this point liberal to quantifiable investigation.

Zhang, Yiwei & Zhang (2018) profound neural association based steganalysis has grown quickly beginning late, which addresses a test to the security of steganography. In any case, present is no steganography system that can adequately repudiate the neural associations for steganalysis beginning at now. In this document, we suggest another structure that makes updated covers against neural associations with the procedure of not all around masterminded replicas. The overhauled covers and their relating all stego will undoubtedly be picked as covers by the associations. Plus, we utilize both profound neural association support steganalysis and high-dimensional part classifiers to assess the introduction of steganography and propose another exhaustive wellbeing exertion. We in like way make an exchange sandwiched between the two examination structures and get better the serious safety. The abundance of the future plot is checked with the proof got from the starters on the BOSS base utilizing the steganography figuring of WOW and acclaimed steganalyzers with wealthy replica and three top tier neural organizations.

Meng, Ruohan & Cui (2018) with the progress of information discipline and advancement, data safety has been besides worried. To manage affirmation issues, for example, singular security being peeped and copyright being encroached, data concealing calculations has been made. Picture data stowing incessantly is to utilize the emphasis of the envelop picture to envelop mystery data in it. Guaranteeing that the stego picture can't be seen from the envelop picture, and distribution mystery data to recipient through the broadcast of the stego picture As of now, the replica dependent on profound knowledge is additionally exhaustively practical to the pasture of data stowing unendingly. This document makes a general end on picture data camouflaging subject to profound knowledge. It is secluded into four pieces of steganography calculations, watermarking presenting assessments, coverless data concealing checks and steganalysis figuring's dependent on profound knowledge. From these four viewpoints, the top tier information hiding progresses subject to DL are spoken to and dismembered.

Ying Zou (2018) in spite of the fact that steganalysis has grown quickly of late; it truly faces different challenges and inconveniences. Considering the hypothesis of beginning to end knowledge technique and picture bottom universal steganalysis, this manuscript makes a profound examination of the hot and hazardous issue of steganalysis include clarification, and attempts to build up another steganalysis viewpoint from consolidate knowledge. The standard obligations of this document are as indicated by the going with 1.) An inventive steganalysis point of view subject to beginning to end knowledge is proposed. Considering the expert profound knowledge system CNN, the reproduction is masterminded and changed by the qualities of steganalysis, which construct the future representation more reasonable in getting the quantifiable attributes, for example, neighborhood relationship. 2.) A steganalysis recollect knowledge strategy subordinate for in general data goals are proposed. Considering the past evaluation of steganalysis procedure subject to CNN, this work rotates around the centrality of in general data in steganalysis fuse verbalization. 3.) A part knowledge structure for low embedding rate steganalysis is projected. 4.) A general steganalysis methodology for multi-class steganography is future. An indisputable objective of universal steganalysis is to build steganalysis identifiers without seeing unequivocal sorts of steganalysis counts.

Ozcan, Selim & Mustacoglu (2018) steganalysis investigates for the procedures used to unenvelop the inserted messages that are covered up in a computerized medium – as a rule in images. The innovative work exercises in Image Steganalysis have increased more footholds as of late. Despite the fact that ML strategies have been utilized for a long time DL is another worldview for the representation Steganalysis region. The accomplishment of the profound knowledge measure relies upon the readiness of the replica for a satisfactory proportion of and with an astounding, different and gigantic extension informational index. Precisely when the arranging cycle needs dataset as for quality, gathering and total, Transfer Knowledge arises as an achievable game-plan from DL techniques. In Transfer Knowledge, a lacking replica positive conditions from some time back masterminded replica and its dataset. Base cutoff is depicted to move the cutoff points from the prepared replica to the lacking replica. Thus, it would develop the accomplishment of profound knowledge replica on Image Steganalysis. In this work, we consider the possible results of two strategies of replicas that are prepared both with and without Transfer Knowledge system. The update system for the replica preparing measure is picked as exploratory Adam W progress technique. Appraisal of preparing, testing, assessing and F1 scoring depend upon the replicas masterminded with various steganography payload respects which begins from simple too difficult to recognize. We researched for the best strategies for broadening the achievement rate and decreasing the blunder rate on seeing stego pictures and envelop pictures self-governing with this assessment. Consequences show with the intention of move knowledge applied replica is more profitable on perceiving stego pictures on each uncommon assessed consignment dataset stood apart from the regular masterminded replica.

Couchot, Jean-François & Couturier (2016) for as far back as couple of a long time, in the contest between picture steganography and steganalysis, profound knowledge has arisen as an extraordinarily encouraging option to steganalyzer approach dependent on rich picture replicas got along with pack classifiers. Indispensable data on picture steganalyzer, which merges material picture features and imaginative game plan strategies, can be found by a profound knowledge approach called Convolutional Neural Networks (CNN). Such profound knowledge networks is so suitable for gathering tasks reliant on the recognizable proof of assortments in 2D shapes that it is the top tier in many picture affirmation issues. In this article, we plan a CNN-based steganalyzer which is not exactly equivalent to the past investigation and its substitution, explicitly proposed configuration embeds fewer convolutions, with a lot bigger channels in the last convolutional layer, and is broader: it can manage bigger images and lower payloads. Our proposition beats all different steganalyzers, specifically the current CNN-based ones, and thrashings many cutting edge image steganography plans.

Adnan M. Alattar (2015) present employment on steganalysis for mechanized pictures is pivoted around the progress of complex inconceivable skin texture. This document proposes another perspective for steganalysis to learn joins along these lines through significant knowledge replicas. We eccentricity propose an adjusted Convolutional Neural Network for steganalysis.

The proposed replica can find the stunning conditions that are critical for steganalysis. Isolated and existing plans, this replica can normally learn incorporate depictions with a couple convolution deposits. The part drawing out and portrayal steps are joined under a single game plan, which suggests the course of combination, can be used during the segment extraction step. We show the reasonableness of the planned representation on three top tier spatial space steganographic checks - HUGO, WOW, and S-UNIWARD. Showed up unmistakably as per the Spatial Rich Replica, our replica accomplishes essentially unclear execution on BOSS base and the reasonable and gigantic Image Net data base.

OBJECTIVES OF STUDY

a.   To study the deep and ML in the steganalysis and steganographic
b.   To determine the Evaluation System for steganalyzers on test sets for steganographic embedders and steganalyzers

PROPOSED METHODOLOGY

Evaluation System for Steganalysis Tests

In this section, we portray the turn of events and use of StegBench, a Python library that empowers the vigorous assessment of steganalysis. StegBench can consistently coordinate into existing steganography and steganalysis assessment arrangements through its incredible and effective design the executive's stage. StegBench is at present under dynamic turn of events and is accessible upon demand for more data on the StegBench structure and API particulars.

Steganographic Dataset Generation

Steganographic embedders and steganalyzers are assessed by how well they either implant or recognize data in a transmission medium. Hence, appropriate data handling and data age is basic for successful assessment since the transmission medium is vital to the steganographic structure. Steganalysis assessment datasets are characterized by three key boundaries: the source dataset, the steganographic embedder, and the implanting proportion. In our structure, we might want to create different steganographic datasets by adjusting every one of these boundaries. Subsequently, we diagram the accompanying three standards that our structure must meet:

1.   **Source Diversity:** The structure must have the option to get to an enormous, various arrangements of source disseminations. Moreover, the structure must give an enormous choice of dataset and image preparing apparatuses for data enlargement.
2.   **Steganographic Embedder Diversity:** The structure must coordinate with a huge and assorted arrangement of steganographic embedders.
3.   **Embedding Ratio Diversity:** The structure must have the option to apply steganographic embedders with a wide choice of implanting proportions.

Standard Steganalysis Evaluation

For a steganalysis assessment structure to be helpful, it must hold fast to standard assessment approaches for double order errands and produce reproducible measurements that can be decently contrasted with different steganalysis research. To accomplish these prerequisites, we distinguish the accompanying replicas:

❖ **Comparable Metrics:** The structure must deliver standard double order measurements that are exact and equivalent to different steganalysis exploration to empower important and reasonable examinations.
❖ **Reproducible Metrics:** The structure must create reproducible measurements so that steganalysis execution can be decently checked on.
❖ **Steganalyzer Diversity:** The structure must coordinate with a huge and different arrangement of steganalyzers to empower far reaching and hearty correlations.

Figure 7. Steganalysis process of ML

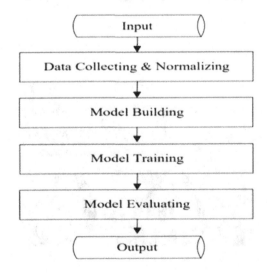

Steganalysis Flowchart

The cycle to be relevant the ML for steganography examination is showed up in Figure 7. It contains four phases: information gathering, mock-up structure, preparing and assessing.

Many preparing data also, test information should be gathered and standardized to manufacture precision. Specifically, vectorization is obliged to be execute from beginning to end portion withdrawal from pictures in view of the fact that pictures are utilized in steganography and steganalysis when everything is said in done. In replica structure, arranging, and looking over advances, different checks can be used relying on ML system.

Preparing Data

For the basic examination, wrap pictures and stego-pictures (Pramanik, S. and Bandyopadhyay, S. K. 2014) were ready so as to introduce the secret information with 3-cycle least basic pieces substitute. The secret information was made by unpredictable limit. Datasets can be set up by consolidating descriptions and the mystery data in different manners.

Figure 8. Guidance above pictures

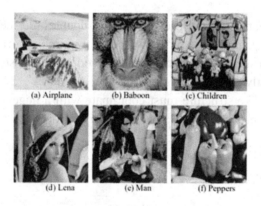

Figure 9. Guidance stego- pictures

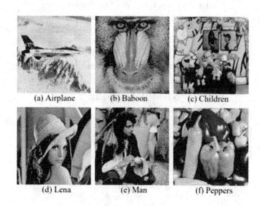

The envelop up pictures in Fig 8 and stego-pictures in Fig 8 are second-hand getting ready datasets and test datasets arbitrarily.

For examination pictures, the assessments embedding's limit and illustration picture excellence PNSR (Pramanik, S., Singh, R. P. and Ghosh, R. 2020), Q index on typical for 3-digit least gigantic pieces replacement are showed up in Table. 1. Test pictures are changed over into python information by means of Numpy bunch plans. Getting ready and examination datasets are set up by embed the secret information by sporadic, and alienated by scikit-learn documentation.

Table 1. Stego- pictures for 512x512 pictures

Images	Embedding capacity (bits)	PSNR (dB)	Q index
Airplane	786,432	35.75	0.7153
Baboon	786,432	35.70	0.9772
Children	786,432	35.67	0.8314
Lena	786,432	35.70	0.8320
Man	786,432	35.66	0.9167
Peppers	786,432	35.69	0.8668

Figure 10. Stego- pictures for 512x512 pictures

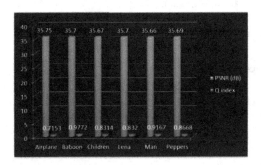

Q index

Q index is the measurement of the 3-bit least significant bits substitution.

Figure 11. Preparation process

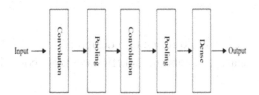

Figure 12. Pseudo algorithm

```
Understand pictures;

Standardize input pictures and incognito keen on datasets;

Separate preparing and test information;

Assemble replica;

replica.Sequential();

replica.add(Convolution2D() ... );

replica.add(Activation() ... );

replica.add(MaxPooling() ... );

replica.add(Dropout() ... ); ...

replica.add(Flatten() ... );

replica.add(Dense() ... );

replica.add(Activation() ... );

replica.add(Dropout() ... );

replica.add(Dense() ... );

replica.add(Activation() ... );

replica.compile();

Train replica;

replica.fit();

Assess yield;

replica.evaluate ();
```

Training Replica

Keras and TensorFlow are utilized to build replica, to design replicas, and to review the yields. As appeared in Figure 9, arranging measure is contained difficulty, pond, convolution, pooling, and thick for contribution information to get yields.

Table 2. ML results

Loss	5.34341287612915
Accuracy	0.6666666865348816

Datasets are standardized prior to displaying, where worth is set from 0 to 255 for every R, G, and B pixels.

RESULTS

Experimental Results

As ML measure as depicted in Fig 12, pseudo code to execute is appeared in Fig 9, somewhere Keras structure was utilized to experiment stego -pictures.

Exactness of ML tests isn't agreeable; however it tends to be enhanced when numerous replica datasets are readied.

In this document, the cycle and open doors for various ML structure are measured, so the exactness was not critical. To assemble the correctness, various datasets must be masterminded and standardized.

We first lead an investigation to benchmark our steganalyzers, ArbNet and FastNet, against a few best in class steganalyzers. We utilize the accompanying system:

1. Train YeNet steganalyzer utilizing the accompanying datasets:
   a. Source Specification: COCO: 9,000x2 preparing, 1,000x2 approval
   b. Steganographic Embedder Specification: WOW at 0.1 bpp
2. There will be one YeNet steganalyzer toward the finish of stage 1. Test it on the accompanying dataset:
   c. Source Specification: COCO: 5,000x2 test. The test dataset is created with the equivalent steganographic embedder: WOW at 0.1 bpp
3. Repeat steps 1-2 for [0.2 ® 0.5] bpp.
4. Repeat steps 1-3 for steganographic embedders: S UNIWARD and HILL.
5. Repeat steps 1-4 for XuNet, SRNet, ArbNet, and FastNet.

Figure 13. Identification blunder for five steganalyzers on test sets implanted with three distinctive steganographic embedders

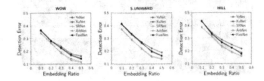

6.   The coming about recognition blunders on the test sets can be found in Table B.1. The discovery mistake pattern lines are appeared in Figure 5-1. The occasions a particular steganalyzer accomplished the best execution for a given installing proportion over the three steganographic embedders is accounted for in Table 1.

Utilizing the outcomes from the investigation, we mention the accompanying objective facts:

d.   Trends concur with the writing - We disenvelop great arrangement between the patterns in Figure 13 and the patterns settled upon in the writing. In particular, we find that YeNet and XuNet perform likewise over all steganographic embedders and implanting proportions. We likewise find that SRNet consistently has a lower location blunder over these setups. These patterns coordinate with those that have regularly been found in different steganalysis review documents.

SRNet and ArbNet consistently play out the best over each test set arrangement contrasted with the different steganalyzers. YeNet, XuNet, and FastNet all perform comparably, aside from at higher implanting proportions where YeNet gets a somewhat higher identification blunder.

Table 3. Number of wins over every one of the three steganographic embedders (WOW, S UNIWARD, HILL) for a given implanting proportion Bold numbers relate to the steganalyzer that had the best number of wins for a given inserting proportion over the three steganographic embedders

Detectors	0.1	0.2	0.3	0.4	0.5
YeNet	0	0	0	0	0
XuNet	0	0	0	0	0
SRNet	0	2	2	2	3
ArbNet	3	1	1	1	0
FastNet	0	0	0	0	0

Figure 14. Number of wins over every one of the three steganographic embedders (WOW, S UNIWARD, HILL) for a given implanting proportion. Bold numbers relate to the steganalyzer that had the best number of wins for a given inserting proportion over the three steganographic embedders

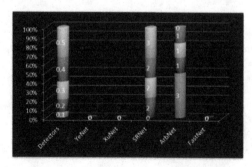

e. SRNet and ArbNet are the best performing steganalyzers - SRNet and ArbNet are the best performing replicas over all steganographic embedders and inserting proportions. Contrasted with different networks, SRNet and ArbNet both use skip associations and can all the more viably process leftover commotion signal.

f. ArbNet is acceptable at low installing proportions - ArbNet shows more grounded execution at lower inserting proportions. In particular, in, we see that ArbNet shows its most grounded execution at 0.1 bpp. This recommends that utilizing methods found in ArbNet could help take care of the low implanting proportion issue. More exploration is expected to distinguish why these procedures are compelling here.

g. FastNet performs similarly to different steganalyzers - FastNet performs equivalently to different steganalyzers. FastNet depends on the Efficient Net engineering, which was planned explicitly for the handy need of preparing and execution productivity. Consequently, this outcome gives a promising indication that FastNet could be an approach to produce a steganalyzer that meets this reasonable need.

Image Size Mismatch Problem

Issue Definition: Most steganalyzers are restricted to just recognizing images of a particular size. Those that do identify discretionary image sizes use procedures, for example, worldwide normal pooling that lead to less exact outcomes.

Proposed Solution: Train a steganalyzer which has a spatial pyramid pooling layer, for example, ArbNet on different image sizes.

Experimental Procedure: To test this arrangement, we utilize the accompanying advances:

1. Train SRNet and YeNet on the following datasets:
   a. Source Specification: COCO(256x256): 9,000x2 training, 1,000x2 validation
   b. Steganographic Embedder Specification: WOW at 0.5 bpp
2. Repeat step 1 for the following image sizes: 512x512 and 1024x1024
3. Train ArbNet on the following dataset:
   c. Source Specification: COCO(256x256,512x512, and 1024x1024): 9,000x2 training, 1,000x2 validation
   d. Steganographic Embedder Specification: WOW at 0.5 bpp
4. There will be three SRNet, three YeNet, and one ArbNet steganalyzer toward the finish of stages 1-3. Test everyone on the accompanying datasets:
   e. Source Specification: COCO (256x256, 512x512, or 1024x1024): 5,000x2 test. The test dataset is produced with the equivalent steganographic embedder: WOW at 0.5 bpp
5. Repeat stages 1-4 for steganographic embedder HILL at 0.5 bpp
6. The coming about recognition mistakes can be found in Table B.2
7. For each steganalyzer, we take away the 256x256 test set recognition blunder from the 1024x1024 test set discovery mistake. This number is accounted for in Figure 15

Figure 15. Execution gain from 256x256 to 1024x1024 across three diverse steganalyzers for two steganographic embedders (WOW, HILL). The exhibition gain is the distinction in recognition mistake between these two test sets. No matter how you look at it, steganalyzers improved in execution when distinguishing images of higher sizes

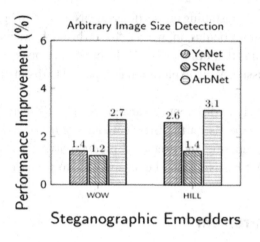

CONCLUSION

In this manuscript, distinctive ML scaffold encompass be dissected to explain the likelihood to steganography assessment. Want consequences and exactness would be varying depending whereupon structure was utilizing and the amount of datasets was utilized. Another representation will be made with attempts to redevelop precision by masterminding particular datasets to be relevant ML systems to steganalysis.

To guard against steganography-empowered assaults, we examine how to appropriately apply steganalysis in two settings: enterprise and personal. In the enterprise setting, we recognize basic controls that security structures can use to moderate steganographic dangers. These controls are recorded. In the personal setting, despite the fact that there are controls that can alleviate security weaknesses, we accept that these controls force severe ease of use limits by hindering registering cycles and restricting other usefulness. In this manner, to moderate steganalysis on a personal setting, we contend that the best protection comprises of network-level steganalysis that checks regular transmission medium administrations for steganographic content.

REFERENCES

Chahar, V. (2020). Steganography Techniques Using Convolutional Neural Networks. *Review of Computer Engineering Studies*. doi:10.18280/rces.070304

Chaumont, M. (2019). *DL in steganography and steganalysis from 2015 to 2018*. Academic Press.

Couchot & Couturier. (2016). *Steganalysis via a Convolutional Neural Network using Large Convolution Filters*. Academic Press.

Han, J., Ji, X., Hu, X., Zhu, D., Li, K., Jiang, X., Cui, G., Guo, L., & Liu, T. (2013). Representing and retrieving video shots in humancentric brain imaging space. *IEEE Transactions on Image Processing*, 22(7), 2723–2736. doi:10.1109/TIP.2013.2256919 PMID:23568507

Hussain & Hussain. (2013). *A survey of image steganography techniques*. Academic Press.

Hussain, I. (2020). A Survey on Deep Convolutional Neural Networks for Image Steganography and Steganalysis. *Transactions on Internet and Information Systems (Seoul)*, 14(3), 1228–1248. doi:10.3837/tiis.2020.03.017

Jung. (2019). *A Study on ML for Steganalysis.* . doi:10.1145/3310986.3311000

Lerch-Hostalot, D., & Meg'ıas, D. (2016, April). Unsupervised Steganalysis Based on Artificial Training Sets. *Engineering Applications of Artificial Intelligence*, 50(C), 45–59. doi:10.1016/j.engappai.2015.12.013

Li, B., Wang, M., Huang, J., & Li, X. 2014. A New Cost Function for Spatial Image Steganography. *Proceedings of IEEE International Conference on Image Processing, ICIP'2014*, 4206–421.

Li, B., Wei, W., Ferreira, A., & Tan, S. (2018, May). ReST-Net: Diverse Activation Modules and Parallel Subnets-Based CNN for Spatial Image Steganalysis. *IEEE Signal Processing Letters*, 25(5), 650–654. doi:10.1109/LSP.2018.2816569

Li, W., Zhang, W., Chen, K., Zhou, W., & Yu, N. (2018). Defining Joint Distortion for JPEG Steganography. *Proceedings of the 6th ACM Workshop on Information Hiding and Multimedia Security, IH&MMSec'2018*, 5–16. 10.1145/3206004.3206008

Li, X., Kong, X., Wang, B., Guo, Y., & You, X. (2013). Generalized Transfer Component Analysis for Mismatched JPEG Steganalysis. *Proceedings of IEEE International Conference on Image Processing, ICIP'2013*, 4432–4436. 10.1109/ICIP.2013.6738913

Li, Wang, Li, Tan, & Huang. (2015). A Strategy of Clustering Modification Directions in Spatial Image Steganography. *IEEE Transaction on Information Forensics and Security,* 10(9), 1905–1917. doi:10.1109/ICIP.2014.7025854

Liu, Zoph, Neumann, Shlens, Hua, Li, Li, Yuille, Huang, & Murphy. (2018). Progressive Neural Architecture Search. In *Proceedings of the European Conference on Computer Vision, ECCV'2018: Vol. 11205. Lecture Notes in Computer Science*. Springer. 10.1007/978-3-030-01246-5_2

Lubenko, I., & Ker, A. D. (2012). Going From Small to Large Data in Steganalysis. *Proceedings of Media Watermarking, Security, and Forensics III, Part of IS&T/SPIE 22th Annual Symposium on Electronic Imaging, SPIE'2012*, 8303. 10.1117/12.910214

Lubenko & Ker. (2012). Steganalysis with Mismatched Covers: Do Simple Classifiers Help? *Proceedings of the 14th ACM Multimedia and Security Workshop, MM&Sec'2008, MM&Sec'2012*, 11–18.

Mallat. (2016). Understanding Deep Convolutional Networks. *Philosophical Transactions of the Royal Society. Series A, Mathematical, Physical, and Engineering Sciences, 374.*

Meng, Ruohan & Cui, et al. (2018). A Survey of Image Information Hiding Algorithms Based on DL. *Computer Replicating in Engineering & Sciences., 117*, 425–454.

Ozcan, S., & Mustacoglu, A. (2018). *Transfer Knowledge Effects on Image Steganalysis with Pre-Trained Deep Residual Neural Network Replica.* doi:10.1109/BigData.2018.8622437

Pramanik, S., Bandyopadhayay, S. K., & Ghosh, R. (2020). Signature Image Hiding in Color Image using Steganography and Cryptography based on Digital Signature Concepts. *IEEE International Conference on Innovative Mechanisms for Industry Applications (ICIMIA)*, 665-669.

Pramanik, S., & Bandyopadhyay, S. K. (2014). An Innovative Approach in Steganography, Scholars. *Journal of Engineering Technology*, 2(2B), 276–280.

Pramanik, S., & Bandyopadhyay, S. K. (2014). Hiding Secret Message in an Image, International Journal of Innovative Science. *Engineering and Technology*, 1(3), 553–559.

Pramanik, S., & Singh, R. P. (2017). Role of Steganography in Security Issues. *International Journal of Advance Research in Science and Engineering*, 6(1), 1119–1124.

Pramanik, S., Singh, R. P., & Ghosh, R. (2020). Application of bi-orthogonal wavelet transform and genetic algorithm in image steganography. *Multimedia Tools and Applications*, 79(25-26), 17463–17482. doi:10.100711042-020-08676-1

Soto, Reinel & Pollán. (2019). DL Applied to Steganalysis of Digital Images: A Systematic Review. IEEE Access. doi:10.1109/ACCESS.2019.2918086

Tran, N. (2019). *Deep Neural Networks Based Invisible Steganography for Audio-into-Image Algorithm.* doi:10.1109/GCCE46687.2019.9015498

Wu, P., Yang, Y., & Li, X. (2018). StegNet: Mega Image Steganography Capacity with Deep Convolutional Network. *Future Internet.*, 10(6), 54. Advance online publication. doi:10.3390/fi10060054

Zakaria, A. (2018). Quantitative and Binary Steganalysis in JPEG: A Comparative Study. *Proceedings of the European Signal Processing Conference*, 1422–1426. 10.23919/EUSIPCO.2018.8553580

Zeng, J., Tan, S., Li, B., & Huang, J. (2018). Large-Scale JPEG Image Steganalysis Using Hybrid Deep-Knowledge Structure. *IEEE Transactions on Information Forensics and Security*, 13(5), 1200–1214. doi:10.1109/TIFS.2017.2779446

Zhang, D., Han, J., Li, C., Wang, J., & Li, X. (2016). Detection of co-salient objects by looking deep and wide. *International Journal of Computer Vision*, 120(2), 215–232. doi:10.100711263-016-0907-4

Zhang, L., Gao, Y., Xia, Y., Dai, Q., & Li, X. (2015). A fine-grained image categorization system by cellet-encoded spatial pyramid replicaing. *IEEE Transactions on Industrial Electronics*, 62(1), 564–571. doi:10.1109/TIE.2014.2327558

Zhang, Yiwei & Zhang. (2018). *Adversarial Examples Against Deep Neural Network based Steganalysis.* . doi:10.1145/3206004.3206012

Zou, Y. (2018). *Research on image steganography analysis based on DL.* doi:10.1016/j.jvcir.2019.02.034

Zou, Y., Zhang, G., & Liu, L. (2019). Research on Image Steganography Analysis Based on DL. *Journal of Visual Communication and Image Representation*, 60, 266–275. Advance online publication. doi:10.1016/j.jvcir.2019.02.034

Chapter 5
Multimode Approach of Data Encryption in Images Through Quantum Steganography

Ajay B. Gadicha
P. R. Pote College of Engineering and Management, Amravati, India

Vrinda Beena Brajesh Gupta
Goverment College of Engineering, Amravati, India

Vijay B. Gadicha
G. H. Raisoni University, Amravati, India

Krishan Kumar
National Institute of Technology, Srinagar, India

Mangesh M. Ghonge
iD https://orcid.org/0000-0003-0140-4827
Sandip Foundation's Institute of Technology and Research Centre, India

ABSTRACT

The information technology era or the third industrial revolution began around the 1960s; has changed the ways we live, work, and play; and brought substantial challenges that include loss of privacy, fake news, digital divides, and significant information security risks. With billions of connections and systems, security vulnerabilities are abundant including the opportunity for criminals to exploit any gaps that present themselves. Eventually, we'll need a groundbreaking technology to gain the upper hand against these threats. Protecting data, systems, and networks assumed a more specific term: cybersecurity. The goal of cybersecurity today is to protect information while it's at rest and in motion. One of the most interesting ways to deliver hidden information is through steganographic technique.

DOI: 10.4018/978-1-7998-7160-6.ch005

Figure 1. Data Hiding classification (Minati Mishra, 2014)

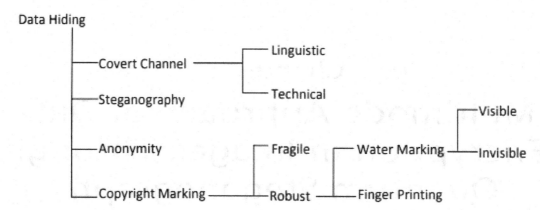

INTRODUCTION

Quantum cryptography is an approach to securing communications by way of applying the phenomena of quantum physics. Unlike conventional classical cryptography, which makes use of mathematical strategies to restrict eavesdroppers, quantum cryptography is targeted at the physics of statistics. Quantum cryptography presents relaxed verbal exchange, whose safety depends simplest on the validity of quantum theory that means it is guaranteed without delay by means of the legal guidelines of physics. This is a great distinction from any classical cryptographic techniques. This article summarizes the cutting-edge kingdom of quantum cryptography and gives potential extensions of its feasibility as a mechanism for securing current structures.

Quantum cryptographic systems need to be analyzed at a diploma of detail this is close pr ical implementation. Computer scientists have evolved various strategies and tools for the evaluation and verification of communication structures and protocols. Those especially applicable to safety evaluation are surveyed with the aid of Ryan et al. This technique has key capabilities. The first is the use of formal languages to precisely specify the conduct of the gadget and the houses which it is supposed to satisfy. The second is the usage of computerized software program equipment to both verify that a tool satisfies a specification or to find out flaws.

There are classical answers to insecure communication to all rely on making a few assumptions, approximately the computational power of a cheater, approximately the wide variety of cheaters, or something of this type. Based on quantum key distribution, one could in all likelihood wish that a quantum computer may permit us to weaken or remove these assumptions. For example, it is feasible to make a quantum digital signature that is comfortable towards all attacks allowed by means of way of quantum mechanics.

Along with advancement of information technology, it brought significant information security risk, leading to growth of cyber security and several crucial information hiding techniques. Information hiding technique is way of communication involving two or more parties who may not trust each other. For instance, while making payments to merchant through credit card to buy goods, third party should not be able to intercept your credit card number. Classification of information hiding techniques is shown in figure1.

Steganography is the science of hiding or encrypting a secret message within an innocent-looking message and transmitting the result so that the steganographic message is readable only by the intended receiver. The remark "Steganography" is originated from Greek word *steganographia, steganos* meaning "concealed" or "covered" and *graphia* meaning "writing" (Jian Wang, 2017). In the past, secret message was used to be concealed on any letter, painting or any other object in reliable and completely inconspicuous way. The Da Vinci Code, we all are familiar with is an example. However, new era of digital information processing has brought new breakthroughs in the field of steganography. Everyday people are using steganography to improve the safety of their messages or more specifically their personal data. Steganography can be further classified into mainly four types namely image, audio, video and text. The classification is made on the basis of cover medium.

Description of words that are going to be used commonly in the chapter

1. Alice: wants to share secret information; the sender
2. Bob: recipient of secret information; the receiver
3. Eve: who wants to gain access to secret information unethically; the eavesdropper
4. Cover Image: Images in which secret information is to be hidden
5. Stego message: Obtained by combining secret information into cover image
6. Secret Key: secret code shared between Alice and Bob
7. Encrpytion(embedding process) and decryption(Extraction process):process to conceal secret message inside cover and recover it respectively.

Figure 2. Block diagram of steganography (Minati Mishra, 2014)

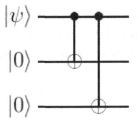

Now, at this point, it's crucial to explain the difference between steganography and cryptography. Both cryptography and steganography have same motive of sharing secret message from sender to receiver while hiding it from eavesdropper, but their techniques are different. In cryptography sender encrypts secret message with "secret key" which is shared to receiver who uses it to decrypt message. The essential difference between them is that, steganography wouldn't even allow eavesdropper to get idea that secret message is being shared.

What is Quantum Mechanics?

Quantum theory, on very broad perspective describes how mechanics of light and matter at the atomic and subatomic scale behaving differently from other objects in real world. It is branch of physics which gives entirely new perspective in field science, technology and even information processing.

The quantum bit, or *qubit* for short is basis of quantum computation and information, just like bit in case of classical. Qubit also has state $|1\rangle$ and $|0\rangle$, just like state 1 and 0 in case of classical bits. Notation '$|\ \rangle$' is known as the Dirac notation. A qubit can also be in a state other than $|0\rangle$ or $|1\rangle$.

Qubit is a vector parameterized by two complex numbers a and b which satisfies equation $|a|^2 + |b|^2 = 1$. Qubit is represented as equation 1

$$|\psi\rangle = a|0\rangle + b|1\rangle \tag{1}$$

On measuring qubit, probability of getting 0 is $|b|^2$, and 1 is $|b|^2$.

Fundamental concepts for quantum computing which we are going to use in this chapter are:

- Qubit – Fundamental information about a computer in quantum aspect. Qubit represents the elements in superposition of all possible states.
- Superposition - The goal of quantum particles to be a mixture of all possible states.
- Quantum measurement – The practice of examining many irregularities and creating a single possible situation.
- Entanglement - The goal of quantum particles to associate their measurement results with other quantum particle.

QUANTUM MODEL HAS TWO SIGNIFICANT PROPERTIES

Property 1

Measurements (read operations) in the quantum computational model are destructive. -Reading quantum register yields classical state i.e. any other state they were in superposition is lost. There is no way to recover the state. Therefore, measurements in quantum are destructive and there is no way to reverse their effect.

Property 2

Quantum information cannot be copied. - That is, it is impossible to "copy" the superposition in one quantum register into another quantum register.

These properties empower us to maintain scrutiny and security while sending the message; if the eavesdropper attempts observing or copying data being sent, the quantum state of information is essentially changed, hence notifying the sender and simultaneously making the data wasteful and inappropriate. So, secure communication would be established.

Quantum steganography basically integrates steganography and quantum cryptography. The figure 3 stated below illustrate the concept of different verticals of quantum steganography. These are import vertical which mainly used in image enhancement and de-noising purpose.

There are 3 important aspects of quantum steganography.

1. Communication-There should be communication between Alice and Bob to share classical or quantum information

2. Secrecy-The information being shared should not be able to detect by Eve.
3. Security- This can or cannot be imposed; Even if Eve detects the presence of secret information, he should not be able to access the information

Figure 3. Three Verticals of Quantum Steganography

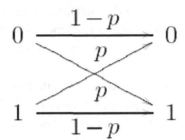

LITERATURE SURVEY

The word "steganography" is largely believed to have been coined by Johannes Trithemius in 1499 in his book Steganographia, a treatises on data hiding techniques. Steganography is not a new concept. Some example might include secret message written with secret inks on paper, message hidden behind the area covered by stamps on letter envelopes. Various indigenous steganographic techniques were used during World War II to share secret information.

The history of Steganography and Cryptography is full of stories about how several encryption techniques have evolved over time to prevent any breach of security. But interestingly, intruders have managed to access the data by their own set of ingenious ideas, and every time this aspect of story has stimulated individuals to think about more solid ways of securing the data. (J. Trithemius, 1606)

In 1983 with advent of PC's being used for applying steganography problems, modern steganography was introduced whose inception was marked by Simmons oeuvre (G.J. Simmons, 1983).

Very first of technique was data hiding in *Least Significant Bit (LSB)i.e 8* th bit of cover image by Younes and Jantan . Although this technique is vulnerable as information can easily be decoded from LSB of image but is remarkable in journey of steganography. (M. A. B. Younes, 2008)

L. Kothari et al. presents idea of "HTML Steganography" i.e. information hiding on internet by combining cryptography and steganography. The results showed that proposed method has better imperceptibility, large embedding capacity and high security as information taken cover behind HTML pages is less suspicious.(L. Kothari, 2017)

D. Stanescu et al. tests and presents comparison using 3 hosts: multi-core processor, microcontroller, PC and it proved that safe data transfer can happen between mobile devices also, offering great performance. The test was made using images as secret information and mainly upon decoding part of steganographic process. (D. Stanescu, 2010)

J. A. R. Kazi et al. used novel method of pixel-based algorithm in which each bit of secret text is embedded into cover image's pixel until last bit of secret text. Then data is hidden under image and sent to client and client reverses process to obtain original text. (J. A. R. Kazi, 2020)

J. Gaba used technique called Compress Encrypt-Stego that modifies the message before hiding behind an image. The modification includes pre-processing text in which text is first compressed using dictionary based compression to reduce its size, altered using a key and then hid behind cover image. (J. Gaba and M. Kumar, 2013)

H. M. Kelash used video sequences to hide data in which color histograms are used for data embedding into Video clips directly. (H. M. Kelash, 2013)

K. Joshi and R. Yadav proposed a new XNOR operation between message and original image based data hiding technique. It eliminates the drawback of LSB method as if the attacker extracts the last three bits he will not be able to retrieve the hidden message because it is in decrypted form. (K. Joshi and R. Yadav, 2016)

Nedal M. S. Kafri and H. Y. Suleiman proposed a technique called "transform domain steganography technique" in which image is changed to frequency domain using DCT. Hidden message bits are written in 4th bit of DCT coefficients. Inconsistency between original and altered coefficient is minimized by modifying 1st, 2nd 3rd or 5th bits of the coefficient called SSB-4 technique. (Nedal M. S. Kafri, 2009)

The message to be transmitted securely can get damaged during preprocessing operations like format conversion, compression etc. avoids this damage and enhance the security, provides robust embedding by using random permutation puzzle based method to insert secret information into the cover image. Receiver has to solve the puzzle to retrieve the message. The intruder is unable to solve the puzzle because of lacking of information about original image order. (Nedal M. S. Kafri, 2009)

T. Denemark and J. Fridrich improve steganographic security by investigating a different form of side information through two JPEG images of the same scene. (T. Denemark and J. Fridrich, 2017)

With evolving network applications, steganographic techniques shifted from image to streaming media. Example of streaming media includes Voice Over Internet Protocol (VoIP).

Huang and Tang proposed a new steganographic algorithm that realise real time cover VoIP steganography. They used codec parameters as cover object.Quantum computation has also improved the speed and performance of performing several image processing related tasks often referred to as quantum image processing (QuIP).

Z. Qu et al proposed a new method for secure quantum communication. They prepare quantum image through quantum log-polar image representation (QUALPI). The carrier image is selected with some expansion angle to encode the secret data. Then data is retrieved through Grover's search algorithm. Simulation is performed on MATLAB and this new protocol is proved to be efficient in all three aspects-security, capacity and imperceptibility. (Z. Qu, 2019)

M. S. Hossain et al.presents way for secure data sharing in mobile-edge and fog computing. In this approach sender embeds secret information in fog cloud using quantum steganography protocol based on hashing and entanglement, and receiver extracts the message using extraction procedure. (M. S. Hossain, 2018)

Z. Qu et al. put forward a novel method for quantum color images secure communication through matrix based coding system. Two encoding methods are proposed namely- single and multiple pixel embedding. Previous method encode 2 qubit secret data in 3 LSQbs of single pixel carrier image and in later they are encoded in 3 LSQbs multiple carrier quantum pixel. Experiments are performed on MATLAB shows good performance in security and imperceptibility. (Z. Qu, 2019)

J. A. Mazumder and K. Hemachandra in their paper present a way for security of quantum data through wavelet transformation and hybridization. They transform and embed secret information into high frequency band without distorting stego-image. This protocol proves to be difficult for eavesdropper to detect and acquire the secret information. (J. A. Mazumder, 2019)

Quantum image encryption and quantum image processing are closely linked fields of research. The storage of image data using quantum states is revealed by quantum image representation. There are plenty ways to model quantum images. Venegas-Andraca et al. proposed an electromagnetic wave mapping based image representation procedure in 2003. The memory cell is referred to as a quantum grid because it maps monochromatic electromagnetic waves into quantum states. Yuan et al. proposed the SQR (Simple Quantum Representation) quantum image representation approach for infrared images, which was based on the quantum grid concept.

Venegas-Andraca et al.proposed a quantum image representation method based on entanglement in 2010, using the maximally entangled state to segment the image. It can solve the entangled state image processing problem more effectively and rapidly. The entanglement-based quantum image representation system, but in the other hand, can only store and handle binary images of basic shapes, limiting the range of applications. (Venegas-Andraca, 2010)

The versatile representation of quantum images (VRQI) was introduced by Le et al. in 2011, and it represents the image's gray-scale and location as a normalized quantum superposition state. Since then, Zhang et al. have proposed the NEQR (novel enhanced quantum representation) method, which makes it easier to extend certain classical image processing algorithms to quantum images in order to achieve its purpose. GQIR (the generalized quantum image representation) was proposed as a new quantum image representation method. GQIR is a step forward from NEQR's representation process. (Le et al, 2011)

Color images can also be interpreted using the GQIR representation. Many quantum image transformations, such as quantum Arnold and Fibonacci image scrambling, geometric transformation, quantum Hilbert image scrambling, quantum image compression, and others, have been proposed at the same time. Many quantum image encryption algorithms have been suggested, based on various quantum image representation methods. There are two types of encryption algorithms. Image transformations such as the Fourier transform, random phase encoding, and quantum wavelet transform are used in one process. (Zhang, 2015)

Wang suggested a quantum wavelet transform and diffusion-based encryption algorithm for quantum pictures. (Wang, 2010)

Yan et al. proposed a quantum video encryption algorithm based on various transforms in 2015. The iterative framework for quantum image encryption was proposed by Wang and et al. This type of encryption technique scrambles the image's position and color information using various transformations. It's a no-secret-key encryption technique. Another form of quantum image encryption method is based on the cipher, which uses the cipher to encrypt the image. (Wang, 2010)

Gong suggested a quantum image encryption algorithm using quantum image XOR operations. A analysis of quantum image encryption was given by (Gong, 2016)

Quantum computational models for a variety of information-theoretic constructs, including image processing and big data analysis have shown promise in improving computational performance. Big data is a term that refers to incredibly large databases that can be analyzed to uncover trends or draw conclusions and comparisons. Since the data is so big, it necessitates a lot of calculations. Big data clustering and classification algorithms for quantum computers and topological data processing have been suggested (Lloyd et al. 2016).

In the latter case, the quantum algorithm for evaluating the data's topological shape outperforms the corresponding classical algorithms by a factor of ten. For example, if a space has n points and k scales, performing the classical persistent homology takes O'(22n). The quantum algorithm, on the other hand, requires O(n5) time to complete. Big data can take several forms, one of which is images. On conventional computers, image processing has been extensively studied, from image acquisition to image analysis, including enhancement, segmentation, transformations, and protection.

The use of quantum computation in visual signal processing will theoretically enable the simultaneous processing of millions of visual signals using the quantum mechanical theory of superposition without compromising computational demand. Quantum image processing models, for example, can significantly improve the results of many image processing tasks in terms of speed and efficiency, regardless of image size, by adjusting existing classical techniques (Dubey et al. 2014). However, the first steps taken toward exploring the possibility of manipulating image pixels as quantum states have made the field of QuIP quite promising. This has primarily involved major improvements in hardware, such as the development and use of quantum computers (Beach et al. 2003)

METHODOLOGY

Quantum Error Correcting Codes (QECC)

Concept of QECC was brought to protect quantum information against effect of noise, bane to information processing system. These codes makes encodes quantum states to make them robust against the effects of noise, and then they can be decoded when the original state is needed. The data that is being sent by sender is subjected to some unwanted altercations due to noise prevailing in the system, so QECC are used to check the aforesaid problem. The idea is to add some redundant information to original message so, even if altercated message is received, original message can be retrieved out of it.

If we wish to send a bit through noisy transmission medium, it is likely that bits get flipped say with probability p, so probability of not being flipped is 1-p. Such channel is called as "binary symmetric channel".

Figure 4. Model of noisy quantum channel

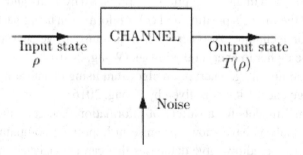

Noise cannot be prevented, so idea to recover correct information is send the bits redundantly also called as "repetition code". For example, we want to send a bit, instead we send three copies of it

Figure 5. Illustrates the functioning of BSC (Jian Wang, 2017)

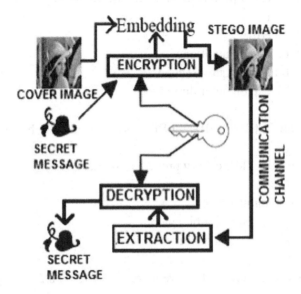

0->000 (ii)

1->111 (iii)

And suppose receiver received 110, considering p is not high, it is possible that channel flipped last bit and bit 1 was sent. This is also called as "majority voting" and it fails if 2 or more bits are flipped by the channel. Using similar principles, QECC are also developed to protect quantum states from effect of noise.

There are two approaches - bit flip and phase flip, discussed below.

Bit Flip Code

For encoding single qubit $|\psi\rangle = p|0\rangle + q|1\rangle$, we use three qubit as $p|000\rangle + q|111\rangle$

To recover correct quantum state two stage error correction procedure is followed

Figure 6. 3 qubit bit flip encoding circuit

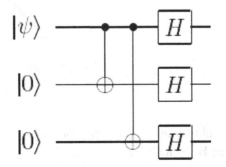

1: **Error Detection**-measurement is performed in quantum states called as error syndromes. There are 4 error syndromes possible:

P_0=|000<000|+|111<111| no error

P_1≡|100<100|+|011<011| bit flip on qubit one

P_2≡|010<010|+|101<101| bit flip on qubit second

P_3≡|001<001|+|110<110| bit flip on qubit three

It means if corrupted state is |010><010|, bit flip has occurred on qubit two.

2: **Recovery**: There are four possible recovery procedure for each case

0: no error – not anything

1: first qubit bit flip – flip first qubit again

2: second qubit bit flip – flip the second qubit again

3:third qubit bit flip – flip the third qubit again.

Though, this procedure doesn't prove effective there are more than 2 bit flips on qubit.

Phase Flip Code

In phase flip error model, the relative phase of qubit is flipped say with probability P, so 1-P is probability that qubit is unflipped. For ex: the state p|0⟩ - q|1⟩ is changed to the state p|0⟩ + q|1⟩ if phase flip operator Z is applied.

Error-correction operations – Encoding, error-detection, and recovery are same as for the bit flip channel except instead of |+⟩, |-⟩ basis, |0⟩, |1⟩ basis is applied with help of Hadamard gate.

Figure 7. Encoding circuit for phase flip Z

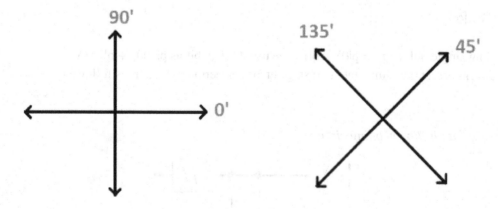

Protocol

Basic idea is to hide secret classical message in quantum data file.

Approach as explained by Gea-Banacloche is

1. Using QECC encode original data file
2. Deliberately, secret message is encoded as "errors" in qubits using for ex: three qubit repetition code
3. Read it as "error syndrome".

Eve can interpret that principal used is 3 qubit repetition code and can hamper with message. So, the solution is to modify code from one qubit to another randomly according to secret key already mutually decided between Alice and Bob but, issue of this approach is that message doesn't look innocent.

Shaw and Brun present a steganographic protocol that hides quantum information can be in noise of depolarization channel (DC) using classical secret key shared between Alice and Bob.

DC is represented as

$$\tilde{n} \rightarrow N_P^{DC}(\tilde{n}) = (1-p)\tilde{n} + \frac{p}{3}X\tilde{n}X + \frac{p}{3}Y\tilde{n}Y + \frac{p}{3}Z\tilde{n}Z$$

Each qubit has identical possibility of going through X, Y or Z error (called canonical Pauli matrices) which flips the bits. The state of a qubit is represented by density matrix $\tilde{n}$

$$X = \begin{pmatrix} 0 & 1 \\ 1 & 0 \end{pmatrix}, Y = \begin{pmatrix} 0 & -i \\ i & 0 \end{pmatrix}, Z = \begin{pmatrix} 1 & 0 \\ 0 & -1 \end{pmatrix}$$

The actual physical channel is considered as noiseless and all the noise that Eve detects are because of the errors, Alice deliberately induces in her codewords.

1. Alice encodes "innocent" quantum message in QECC. Random key is shared between Alice and Bob
2. Depolarizing channel is applied to secret message qubit or covertext, which will convert it into maximally mixed state I/2 called as twirling and inserted at random location in codeword according to shared random key. This makes protocol more transparent. Twirling can be thought as one-time pad
3. Alice transmit codeword to Bob. Using secret key, he decodes or untwirls secret message.

Eve will detect nothing suspicious because even if she gets codeword she will measure it as error syndrome.

Figure 8. Rectilinear basis and conjugate basis

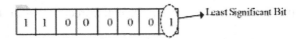

BB84 Protocol

BB84 is first quantum key distribution protocol developed in 1984 by Charles Bennett and Gilles Brassard. In BB84 protocol, polarisation state of a photon is used to encode the secret bits.

BB84 requires measurement in two different orthogonal bases-Rectilinear basis with vertical 0° polarization and horizontal 90° polarization; and Diagonal basis with vertical 45° polarization and horizontal 135° polarization.

Protocol consist of Alice and Bob sharing via communication channel-private quantum channel and public classical channel. Alice sends photons representing bit strings to Bob. Eve tries to intercept the photons sent by Alice. So, when Eve receives a photon, Bob receives nothing and thus Alice and Bob will soon find out that some photos sent by Alice were lost. If this situation happens, they will agree that they have an intruder and the key has not generated. To avoid that when Eve intercepts a photon she must send some photons to Bob, so Alice and Bob would not notice the intrusion. Eve could duplicate the photon, then she might send the exact copy of the photon she received. But it's not possible due to no cloning theorem. So the best thing she can do is to measure the photon and send Bob the same photon as she just measured. But Eve doesn't know which basis to choose. So, the probability of every bit correctly guessed by Eve becomes extremely small.

Protocol

1. Alice chooses random bit string (say length 4n)
2. Through quantum channel, Alice sends photons representing the bit string. Photons are polarized into any of the four possibility.
3. Bob on receiving, decides whether to measure the photon in rectilinear or diagonal polarization and deduces the result of the measurement as a binary zero or binary one, and generate his bit string of say 2n length.
4. For each bit, Bob announces his choice of measurement basis through the open and insecure classical communication channel to determine if encoding and measurement basis are same, but he does not announce the result of his measurement.
5. If their basis agrees, the bit is kept; otherwise, it is discarded.

6. Next step involves testing for eavesdropper by publicly comparing a few bits (say n bits) called as check bits, on which Alice and Bob both have used the same basis.
7. Meanwhile, Eve can try to intercept the photons sent by Alice and determine the measurement basis.
8. If Alice and Bob find no inconsistencies, they assume there is no attempt of eavesdropping in-between the transmission. Secure communication is established over the public channel. The protocol is repeated when this one-time pad is used up, the protocol is repeated again to produce a new one. Else if, they find much inconsistencies the protocol is aborted.
9. Alice and Bob do privacy amplification and information reconciliation for selecting only m-bits from left out n bits.

Figure 9. Steps of BB84 protocol (without eavesdropping)

QUANTUM TRANSMISSION

Alice's random bits	0	1	1	0	1	1	0	0	1	0	1	1	0	0	1
Random sending bases	D	R	D	R	R	R	R	R	D	D	R	D	D	D	R
Photons Alice sends	↗	↕	↘	↔	↕	↕	↔	↔	↘	↗	↕	↘	↗	↗	↕
Random receiving bases	R	D	D	R	R	D	D	R	D	R	D	D	D	D	R
Bits as received by Bob	1		1		1	0	0	0		1	1	1		0	1

PUBLIC DISCUSSION

Bob reports bases of received bits	R		D		R	D	D	R		R	D	D		D	R
Alice says which bases were correct			✓		✓			✓				✓		✓	✓
Presumably shared information			1		1			0				1		0	1
Bob reveals some key bits at random					1									0	
Alice confirms them					✓									✓	

OUTCOME

Remaining shared secret bits			1					0				1			1

But, there is little possibility of attack by Eve because displacement between information bit and check bit is same.

On basis of BB84 protocol, Martin proposed a novel protocol considered as first quantum steganographic protocol. Idea is: before Alice and Bob starts communication, they agree upon initial value of displacement d (say =1), For next time to transfer next bit, the value of displacement will be the key generated in previous QKD. Any such scheme can be used. So, when Bob and Alice equate their bits to check for eavesdropping, point 6 can be changed as follows

*6. Alice randomly selects a information bit which she wants to transmit from the group of 2n bits. Then she arbitrarily selects n − 1 check bits from the remaining 2n − 1. The nth check bit is chosen with displacement d from information bit, the remaining n + 1 bits.

Lets understand by taking example

Alice and Bob takes 2n bits
00101011100101011101011101100
An information bit is selected by Alice
00101011100101011 $\overline{1}$ 0101101100
Now n − 1 check bits are selected arbitrarily
00101011100101011 $\overline{1}$ 0101101100
n + 1 bits are remaining
0*10*01*1*0*0*0**1 $\overline{1}$ *10*1*11**
Alice now selects the bit to the immediate left of the information bit i.e last check bit:
0*10*01*1*0*0*0 $\overline{1}$ **1 $\overline{1}$ *10*1*11**

Eve detecting the existence of this communication depends only upon the secrecy of quantum key distribution i.e if there exists no correlation between information bit and last check bit, then there is no way Eve can know presence of communication channel.

Quantum LSQb

Younes and Jantan used approach in which 8th bit of every byte of cover image is used to hide one bit of secret message. Figure [10] In new approach developed by, authors used novel enhanced quantum representation (NEQR) for hiding quantum image

Figure 10. Least Significant Bit

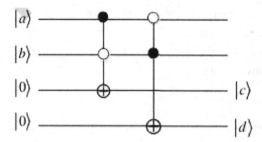

This method involves the color-encoding qubit of cover image being substituted with sensitive information i.e same last qubit of both cover and secret information is used. Also, the length of secret information must be equal to cover image, if not they are made equal.

Algorithm

1. The color-encoding last qubit of cover image is compared with qubit of secret information using quantum comparator. Quantum comparator is the circuit which can compare two quantum states. The figure shows the circuit.

If $|c\rangle|d\rangle=|1\rangle|0\rangle$ or $|c\rangle|d\rangle=|0\rangle|1\rangle$, then quantum state $|a\rangle$ is not equal to $|b\rangle$; and If $|c\rangle|d\rangle=|0\rangle|0\rangle$, then $|a\rangle$ is equal to $|b\rangle$.

2. Do nothing if output of two values from quantum comparator are same, else perform unitary transformation (CNOT operation) on quantum cover image. This operation is applied for all position from i=0,1,...... 2^{2n-1} .This way secret information is embedded inside cover.
3. 3. Now, Bob will have to extract the secret information. LSQb stego image complex vector can be represented as X.

$$ X = C_1 \otimes \begin{pmatrix} 1 \\ 0 \\ 0 \\ 0 \end{pmatrix} + C_2 \otimes \begin{pmatrix} 0 \\ 1 \\ 0 \\ 0 \end{pmatrix} + C_3 \otimes \begin{pmatrix} 0 \\ 0 \\ 1 \\ 0 \end{pmatrix} + C_4 \otimes \begin{pmatrix} 0 \\ 0 \\ 0 \\ 1 \end{pmatrix} $$

Figure 11. Quantum Comparator

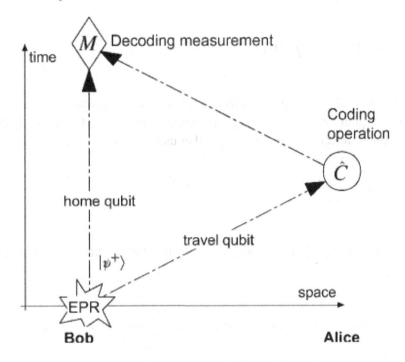

4) Bob convert first part of X into binary i.e. converting C_1, C_2, C_3, C_4 to the appropriate binary data C_{1b}, C_{2b}, C_{3b}, C_{4b} and extracting binary data's last bit, forming a binary code stream. Rearranging these bits gives hidden secret information.

Ping Pong Protocol

Boström and Felbinger devised a deterministic approach of sending secret. In undeterministic approach, Alice does not know what bit value Bob will decode. This approach

Bob creates qubit in bell state. Bells state can be defined as-

$$\left|\psi^+\right\rangle = \frac{1}{\sqrt{2}}\left(\left|0\right\rangle\left|1\right\rangle + \left|1\right\rangle\left|0\right\rangle\right) = \frac{1}{\sqrt{2}}\left(\left|+\right\rangle\left|+\right\rangle - \left|-\right\rangle\left|-\right\rangle\right)$$

$$\left|\psi^-\right\rangle = \frac{1}{\sqrt{2}}\left(\left|0\right\rangle\left|1\right\rangle - \left|1\right\rangle\left|0\right\rangle\right) = \frac{1}{\sqrt{2}}\left(\left|+\right\rangle\left|-\right\rangle - \left|-\right\rangle\left|+\right\rangle\right)$$

$$\left|\phi^+\right\rangle = \frac{1}{\sqrt{2}}\left(\left|0\right\rangle\left|0\right\rangle + \left|1\right\rangle\left|1\right\rangle\right) = \frac{1}{\sqrt{2}}\left(\left|+\right\rangle\left|+\right\rangle + \left|-\right\rangle\left|-\right\rangle\right)$$

$$\left|\phi^-\right\rangle = \frac{1}{\sqrt{2}}\left(\left|0\right\rangle\left|0\right\rangle - \left|1\right\rangle\left|1\right\rangle\right) = \frac{1}{\sqrt{2}}\left(\left|+\right\rangle\left|-\right\rangle + \left|-\right\rangle\left|+\right\rangle\right)$$

Where

$$|+\rangle = \frac{1}{\sqrt{2}}\big(|0\rangle + |1\rangle\big), |-\rangle = \frac{1}{\sqrt{2}}\big(|0\rangle - |1\rangle\big)$$

These states are maximally entangled and therefore the states cannot be distinguished from another by accessing only one qubit i.e. measurement on both qubits are required to perfectly distinguish state from one another. Any state can be converted to another using unitary operations U_{ij}, where U_{ij} are

$$U_{00} = \begin{pmatrix} 1 & 0 \\ 0 & 1 \end{pmatrix}, U_{01} = \begin{pmatrix} 1 & 0 \\ 0 & -1 \end{pmatrix}, U_{10} = \begin{pmatrix} 0 & 1 \\ 1 & 0 \end{pmatrix}, U_{11} = \begin{pmatrix} 0 & 1 \\ -1 & 0 \end{pmatrix}$$

$|\psi^-\rangle$ can be converted into $|\psi^-\rangle, |\psi^+\rangle, |\phi^+\rangle, |\phi^-\rangle$ using 00,01,10 and 11 codes respectively.

Protocol

This protocol works in two modes - *message mode*(MM) and *control mode(CM)*.

0. Set n=0; Let the message to be transmitted is a sequence $x^N=(x_1,\ldots,x_N)$, where $x_n \in \{0,1\}$.
1. Increment n, n=n+1; Bob creates two qubits in bell state. Both Alice and Bob are default in MM. Bob then saves one qubit ("*Home qubit*") and through quantum channel sends another qubit ("*Travel qubit*") to Alice ("Ping").
2. Alice gets travel qubit. If she decides to change mode to CM goto 3b, else go to 3a.
3. a. Message mode(MM):

    1. In MM, Alice performs coding operation to encode her information and sends back to Bob("Pong").
    2. Bob on receiving the travel qubit and does Bell-basis measurement to decode Alice's information.
    3. If n<N goto 1; else when n=N goto 4.

    b. Control mode(CM):

    1. If Alice changes it mode randomly to CM, to check if message is being transferred securely, she measures the travel qubit in $B_z = \{|0\rangle, |1\rangle\}$ or basis and acquires $i \in \{0,1\}$.
    2. She then directs it through public channel to Bob.
    3. Bob on receiving, changes its mode to CM and measures i in same basis and obtains j.
    4. If i==j; intruder, Eve is present; the communication is halted; else, set n=n-1 and goto 1.

4. Message x^N is transferred securely from Alice to Bob.

Dashed lines are qubit transfers and Solid lines are classical transfers.

Figure 12. Message Mode

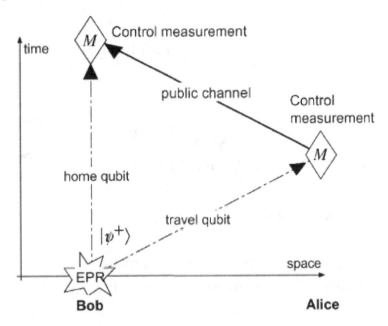

This protocol is modified by Qing-yu Cai* and Bai-wen Li by improving capacity of Boström-Felbinger protocol. They improve capacity to double by introducing two additional unitary operations (Cai, Qing-yu., 2004).

Figure 13. Control Mode

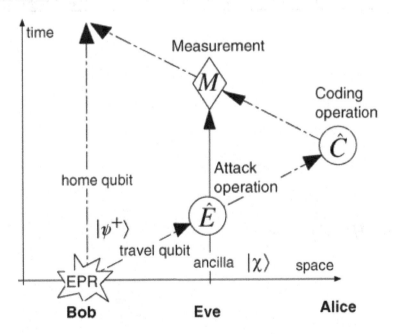

Figure 14. Eavsdropper present

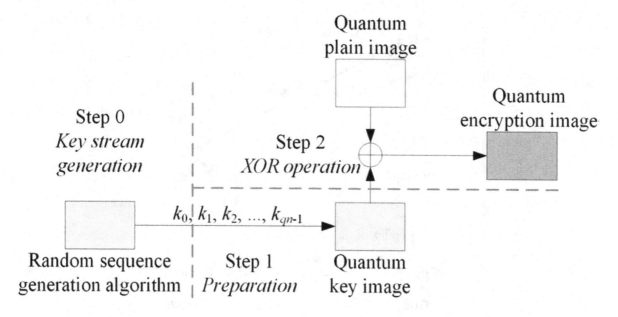

Figure 15. Singular quantum image encryption

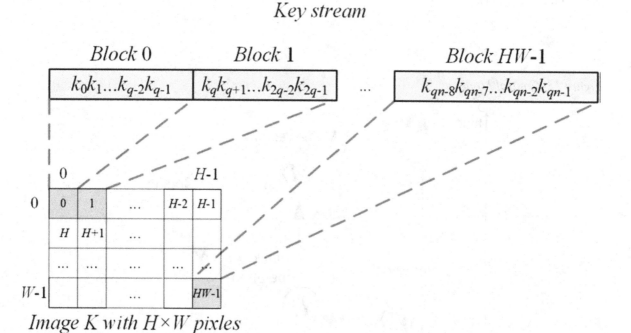

RESULT ANALYSIS

In this segment, we propose singular quantum image encryption set of rules primarily based on quantum key image. The algorithm consist of three steps as proven in Figure 15.

Step 0: Key Stream Generation:

A steganographic algorithm is used to create a key stream .Assume the key stream is: $K = \{k0, k1, k2, \ldots, kqn-1\}$, where $ki \in \{0, 1\}$, $i \in \{0, qn - 1\}$ and $n = HW$, the length of key stream, which is the same as the size of the plain image i.e the image to be encrypted.

Step 1: Preparation of Quantum Key Image

This step organizes the K into a quantum computer as the quantum key image, which is based on GQIR. The K is a 1-D data and the key image is a 2-D data. The conversion is achieved as in Fig 15. Each pixel sequentially uses q bits from K as its gray value. Therefore, K is divided into $H \times W$ blocks, and each block has q bits.

The preparation of GQIR has three steps.

Primarily $h + w + q$ qubits are prepared and set all to $|0\_$. The initial state can be shown as:

$$\left|\psi^{+}\right\rangle = \frac{1}{\sqrt{2}}\left(|0\rangle|1\rangle + |1\rangle|0\rangle\right) = \frac{1}{\sqrt{2}}\left(|+|+-|-\rangle|-\rangle\right)$$

Figure 16. Key Image Preparation

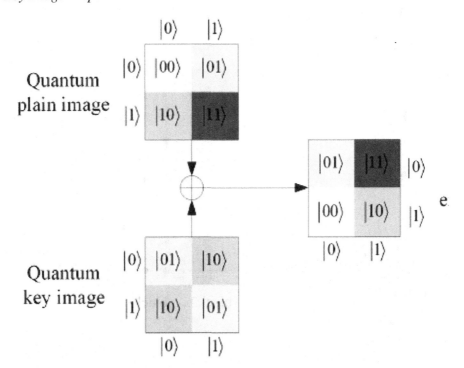

Figure 17. XOR Representation of Quantum Key Image

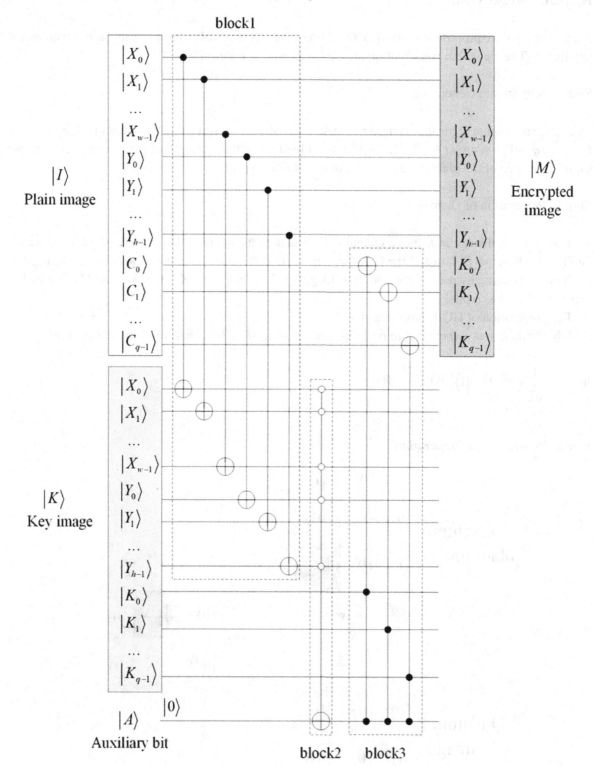

Figure 18. Representation of Image in Quantum Cryptography

$$(1) \qquad\qquad\qquad\qquad (2)$$

$$(3) \qquad\qquad\qquad\qquad (4)$$

Step 2: XOR Operation

We get the encrypted quantum image M by XOR operation between quantum key image K and the plain image I. The operation is shown below:

$$\left| I \right\rangle \oplus \left| K \right\rangle = \frac{1}{\sqrt{2}^{h+w}} \sum_{Y=0}^{H-1}\sum_{X=0}^{W-1} \otimes_{i=0}^{q-1} \left| C_{YX}^{i} \right\rangle \left| Y X \right\rangle \oplus \frac{1}{\sqrt{2}^{h+w}} \sum_{Y=0}^{H-1}\sum_{X=0}^{W-1} \left| K_{YX} \right\rangle \left| Y X \right\rangle$$

$$= \frac{1}{\sqrt{2}^{h+w}} \sum_{Y=0}^{H-1}\sum_{X=0}^{W-1} \otimes_{i=0}^{q-1} \left| C_{YX}^{i} \right\rangle \left| Y X \right\rangle \oplus \frac{1}{\sqrt{2}^{h+w}} \sum_{Y=0}^{H-1}\sum_{X=0}^{W-1} \otimes_{i=0}^{q-1} \left| K_{YX}^{i} \right\rangle \left| Y X \right\rangle$$

Figure 19. Quantum Cryptography on "Boat" and "Vegetables" images

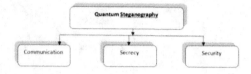

Figure 20. Quantum Experimental Result

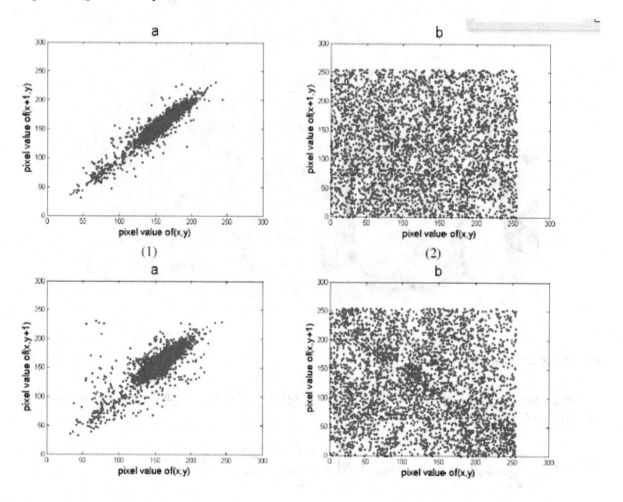

$$= \frac{1}{\sqrt{2}^{h+w}} \sum_{Y=0}^{H-1} \sum_{X=0}^{W-1} \otimes_{\cdot i=0}^{q-1} \left| C_{YX}^i \right\rangle \oplus \left| K_{YX}^i \right\rangle \left| Y\,X \right\rangle = \left| M \right\rangle$$

EXPERIMENT AND ANALYSIS

As this quantum cryptography is a contemporary technological understanding in a cryptosystem generation and plenty of researchers from round the arena are coming across a way of incorporating some gadgets and function already made a jump ahead seems quantum cryptography can be an advanced code- making generation that's theoretically un-crackable. This is because of the legal guidelines of quantum physics that dictate an eavesdropped could not diploma the residences of a single photon without the risk of changing those homes. In distinctive phrases, despite the fact that an

eavesdropper is capable of eavesdrop on a line might be now not capable of study a good buy about the communications traversing it. In this proposed work, it finally give detailed numerical and theoretical analysis of proposed encryption algorithm.

Table 1. Image correlation

Image	Direction of Image (Horizontal)	Direction of Image (Vertical)	Diagonal Direction of Image (Horizontal)	Diagonal Direction of Image (Vertical)
Boat	0.93362	0.92258	0.78223	-0.36922
Vegetables	0.97552	0.93669	0.85229	-0.0.1142

From Table 1 it can be concluded that there is a strong correlation between the adjacent pixels in each direction of the plain image, meanwhile the correlation is often weak for the encrypted image.

REFERENCES

Bennett, C. H. (1984): Quantum cryptography: public key distribution and coin tossing. *IEEE International Conference on Computers, Systems and Signal Processing*, 175(1), 175-179.

Cai. (2004). Improving the capacity of the Boström-Felbinger protocol. *Phys. Rev. A, 69.* . doi:10.1103/PhysRevA.69.054301

Cao, Y., Zhou, Z., Sun, X., & Gao, C. (2018). Coverless information hiding based on the molecular structure images of material. *Computers. Materials & Continua, 54*(2), 197–207.

Denemark, T., & Fridrich, J. (2017). Steganography with two JPEGs of the same scene. *2017 IEEE International Conference on Acoustics, Speech and Signal Processing (ICASSP)*, 2117-2121. 10.1109/ICASSP.2017.7952530

El-Latif, A. A. A., Abd-El-Atty, B., Hossain, M. S., Elmougy, S., & Ghoneim, A. (2018). Secure Quantum Steganography Protocol for Fog Cloud Internet of Things. *IEEE Access: Practical Innovations, Open Solutions, 6*, 10332–10340. doi:10.1109/ACCESS.2018.2799879

Fortes, R., & Rigolin, G. (2015). Fighting noise with noise in realistic quantum teleportation. *Physical Review A, 92*(1), 1. doi:10.1103/PhysRevA.92.012338

Gaba, J., & Kumar, M. (2013). Design and analysis of Compress-Encrypt-Stego technique for steganography. *IEEE International Conference in MOOC, Innovation and Technology in Education (MITE),* 32-36. 10.1109/MITE.2013.6756300

Geabanacloche, J. (2002). Hiding messages in quantum data. *Journal of Mathematical Physics, 43*(9), 4531–4536. doi:10.1063/1.1495073

Guan, X. W., Chen, X. B., Wang, L. C., & Yang, Y. X. (2014). Joint remote preparation of an arbitrary two-qubit state in noisy environments. *International Journal of Theoretical Physics, 53*(7), 2236–2245. doi:10.100710773-014-2024-x

Guo, G. C., & Guo, G. P. (2012). Quantum data hiding with spontaneous parameter down-conversion. *Physical Review A, 68*(4), 4343–4349.

Huang, Y. F., Tang, S., & Yuan, J. (2011, June). Steganography in Inactive Frames of VoIP Streams Encoded by Source Codec. *IEEE Transactions on Information Forensics and Security, 6*(2), 296–306. doi:10.1109/TIFS.2011.2108649

Joshi, K., & Yadav, R. (2016). New approach toward data hiding using XOR for image steganography. *2016 Ninth International Conference on Contemporary Computing (IC3),* 1-6. 10.1109/IC3.2016.7880204

Kazi, J. A. R., Kiratkar, G. N., Ghogale, S. S., & Kazi, A. R. (2020). A novel approach to Steganography using pixel-based algorithm in image hiding. *International Conference on Computer Communication and Informatics (ICCCI),* 1-6. 10.1109/ICCCI48352.2020.9104072

Kelash, H. M., Abdel Wahab, O. F., Elshakankiry, O. A., & El-sayed, H. S. (2013). Hiding data in video sequences using steganography algorithms. *2013 International Conference on ICT Convergence (ICTC),* 353-358. 10.1109/ICTC.2013.6675372

Kothari, L., Thakkar, R., & Khara, S. (2017). Data hiding on web using combination of Steganography and Cryptography. *International Conference on Computer, Communications and Electronics (Comptelix),* 448-452. 10.1109/COMPTELIX.2017.8004011

Ma, S. Y., Gao, C., Zhang, P., & Qu, Z. G. (2017). Deterministic remote preparation via the brown state. *Quantum Information Processing, 16*(4), 93. doi:10.100711128-017-1542-x

Martin, K. (2007). Steganographic communication with quantum information. *International Conference on Information Hiding,* 4567(1), 32-49. 10.1007/978-3-540-77370-2_3

Mazumder, J. A., & Hemachandra, K. (2019). Image Steganography Using the Fusion of Quantum Computation and Wavelet Transformation. *2019 3rd International Conference on Computing Methodologies and Communication (ICCMC),* 226-232. 10.1109/ICCMC.2019.8819681

Meng, R., Rice, S. G., Wang, J., & Sun, X. (2018). A fusion steganographic algorithm based on faster R-CNN. *Computers, Materials & Continua, 55*(1), 1–16.

Mihara, T. (2012). Quantum steganography embedded any secret text without changing the content of cover data. *Journal of Quantum Information Science, 2*(1), 10–14. doi:10.4236/jqis.2012.21003

Mihara, T. (2015). Quantum steganography using prior entanglement. *Physics Letters. [Part A], 379*(12-13), 952–955. doi:10.1016/j.physleta.2015.01.038

Mishra, Mishra, & Adhikary. (2014). *Digital Image Data Hiding Techniques: A Comparative Study.* Academic Press.

Nedal, Kafri, & Suleiman. (2009). Bit-4 of Frequency DomainDCT Steganography Technique. *IEEE Proc. 1st Int. conf. on Networked Digital Technologies*, 286-291.

Nie, Q., Xu, X., Feng, B., & Zhang, L. Y. (2018). Defining embedding distortion for intra prediction mode-based video steganography. *Computers, Materials & Continua, 55*(1), 59–70.

Pradeep, A., Mridula, S., & Mohanan, P. (2016). High security identity tags using spiral resonators. *Computers, Materials & Continua, 52*(3), 185–195.

Qu, Z., Chen, S., & Ji, S. (2017). A novel quantum video steganography protocol with large payload based on MCQI quantum video. *International Journal of Theoretical Physics, 56*(2), 1–19. doi:10.100710773-017-3519-z

Qu, Z., Chen, S., Ji, S., Ma, S., & Wang, X. (2018). Anti-noise bidirectional quantum steganography protocol with large payload. *International Journal of Theoretical Physics, 1*(2), 1–25. doi:10.100710773-018-3716-4

Qu, Z., Cheng, Z., Luo, M., & Liu, W. (2017). A robust quantum watermark algorithm based on quantum log-polar images. *International Journal of Theoretical Physics, 56*(11), 3460–3476. doi:10.100710773-017-3512-6

Qu, Z., Cheng, Z., & Wang, X. (2019). Matrix Coding-Based Quantum Image Steganography Algorithm. *IEEE Access: Practical Innovations, Open Solutions, 7*, 35684–35698. doi:10.1109/ACCESS.2019.2894295

Qu, Z., Li, Z., Xu, G., Wu, S., & Wang, X. (2019). Quantum Image Steganography Protocol Based on Quantum Image Expansion and Grover Search Algorithm. *IEEE Access: Practical Innovations, Open Solutions, 7*, 50849–50857. doi:10.1109/ACCESS.2019.2909906

Shankar, S. S., & Rengarajan, A. (2017). Puzzle based highly secure steganography. *2017 International Conference on Algorithms, Methodology, Models and Applications in Emerging Technologies (ICAMMAET)*, 1-5. 10.1109/ICAMMAET.2017.8186742

Simmons, G. J. (1983). The prisoners problem and the subliminal channel. In D. Chaum (Ed.), Advances in Cryptology – CRYPTO 83 (pp. 51–67). Academic Press.

Stanescu, D., Stangaciu, V., & Stratulat, M. (2010). Steganography on new generation of mobile phones with image and video processing abilities. *International Joint Conference on Computational Cybernetics and Technical Informatics*, 343-347. 10.1109/ICCCYB.2010.5491253

Trithemius, J. (1606). Steganographia. Academic Press.

Wang, J., Geng, Y.-C., Han, L., & Liu, J.-Q. (2017). Quantum Image Encryption Algorithm Based on QuantumKey Image. *International Journal of Theoretical Physics*. Advance online publication. doi:10.100710773-018-3932-y

Wei, Z. H., Chen, X. B., Niu, X. X., & Yang, Y. X. (2013). A novel quantum steganography protocol based on probability measurements. *International Journal of Quantum Information*, *11*(7), 1350068. doi:10.1142/S0219749913500688

Wei, Z. H., Chen, X. B., Niu, X. X., & Yang, Y. X. (2015). Erratum to: The quantum steganography protocol via quantum noisy channels. *International Journal of Theoretical Physics*, *54*(8), 2516–2516. doi:10.100710773-015-2686-z

Younes, M. A. B., & Jantan, A. (2008). A New Steganography Approach for Image Encryption Exchange by using the LSB insertion. *Int. J. of Comput. Sci. and Network Security*, *8*(6), 247–254.

Zhou, Q., Qiu, Y., Li, L., Lu, J., & Yuan, W. (2018). Steganography using reversible texture synthesis based on seeded region growing and LSB. *Computers, Materials & Continua*, *55*(1), 151–163.

Chapter 6
Detection of Malicious Spatial–Domain Steganography Over Noisy Channels

Swaroop Shankar Prasad

University of Stuttgart, Germany

Ofer Hadar

Ben-Gurion University of the Negev, Israel

Ilia Polian

University of Stuttgart, Germany

ABSTRACT

Steganographic channels can be abused for malicious purposes, thus raising the need to detect malicious embedded steganographic information (steganalysis). This chapter will cover the little-studied problem of steganography and steganalysis over a noisy channel, providing a detailed modeling for the special case of spatial-domain image steganography. It will approach these issues from both a theoretical and a practical point of view. After a description of spatial-domain image steganography, the impact of Gaussian noise and packet loss on the steganographic channel will be discussed. Characterization of the substitution-insertion-deletion (SID) channel parameters will be performed through experiments on a large number of images from the ALASKA database. Finally, a steganalysis technique for error-affected spatial-domain image steganography using a convolutional neural network (CNN) will be introduced, studying the relationship between different types and levels of distortions and the accuracy of malicious image detection.

DOI: 10.4018/978-1-7998-7160-6.ch006

INTRODUCTION

Among numerous cybersecurity threats, malicious steganography is a potentially powerful and yet often-overlooked attack vector. Malicious steganography is a threat for systems with a protected part that is isolated from the outside world. The adversaries can define steganographic channels through which they leak sensitive data to unauthorized parties located outside the system while overcoming existing isolation mechanisms. Perhaps even more disturbing, it was recently shown how a malicious steganographic channel can work in the opposite direction, namely to control malware in an isolated system by instructions sent by an attacker located in the outside world (Segal et al., 2017). Figure 1 illustrates both scenarios. In Figure 1a, the protected system sends images through a legitimate communication channel called *cover channel*. For instance, the system may transmit a video stream (sequence of images) meant to be viewed by the general public, but it has no other connections with the outside world. The first adversary, Alice, is assumed to be inside the protected perimeter and has access to the server. She intends to send some sensitive information, e.g., an encryption key, to the second adversary, Bob, who is located outside and

Figure 1. Malicious steganography between Alice (who has access to a protected system but no communication channel to outside world) and Bob (located in the outside world). Passive scenario (information leakage) is shown in (a); active scenario (controlling malware) in (b).

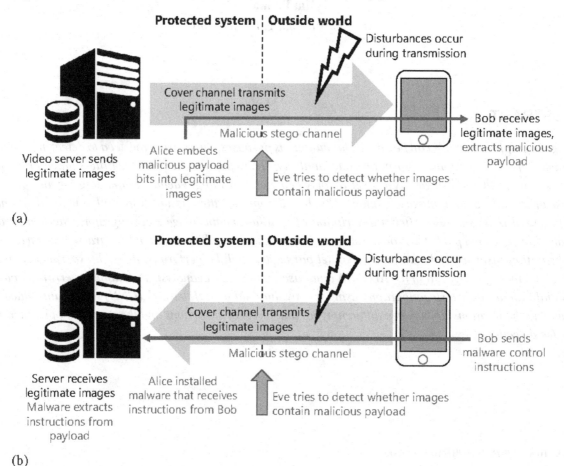

126

does not have access to the system's internal information. To this end, Alice embeds the bits she wants to send (*payload*) into the *cover images* (original images) being sent through the cover channel. Bob, who is allowed to see the transmitted images but has no other means of communicating with Alice, receives the images and extracts the bits of the encryption key sent by Alice, thus overcoming the isolation.

Figure 1b shows the active manipulation scenario based on malicious steganography. Here, Alice and Bob intend to have a piece of malware installed on the protected server such that it can be controlled from outside. The role of Alice (the adversary with access to the server) is to pre-install malware on the server, the role of Bob is to send control instructions. The cover channel in this case transmits images in the other direction than in Figure 1a, namely from outside to inside the protected system. For example, the sender may be a surveillance camera that sends the recorded video stream to the protected server for analysis. Bob has gained access to the camera and embeds control instructions for malware as payload into the images that the camera is transmitting. Alice's malware automatically extracts this payload, recognizes such instructions and acts accordingly.

Different steganographic algorithms for embedding payload into cover images are known. This chapter focuses on *spatial-domain steganography* (Morkel et al., 2005; Hussain et al., 2018), where payload bits are directly written into low-significance bits of the cover image. Its findings are likely extendable to other types of stego approaches, such as the transform-domain steganography, where the image first undergoes DCT (Discrete Cosine Transform) and payload bits are incorporated into the coefficients (Kaur et al., 2011). Several methods for spatial-domain steganography were introduced recently (Boromand et al., 2018; You et al., 2020; Zhang et al., 2018 and 2019), including approaches that leverage quantum computations (Abd El Latif et al., 2019; Li et al., 2019). In this chapter, three classical state-of-the-art stego algorithms, WOW (Holub & Fridrich, 2012), HUGO (Filler & Fridrich, 2010; Pevny et al., 2010) and S-UNIWARD (Holub et al., 2014), are used for experiments. These algorithms embed the payload information into carefully selected pixels of the cover image where small modifications are not directly noticeable, helping the adversaries Alice and Bob to avoid detection.

To defend the system against the malicious steganography threat, it is desirable to detect the presence of unauthorized steganographic (or *stego*) channels by analyzing the transmitted, or received, images. This detection problem, called *steganalysis*, has attracted significant attention of researchers (Qian et al., 2015; Pibre et al., 2016; Baluja, 2017; Ye et al., 2019). The role of the defender is indicated in Figure 1 by the party named Eve, who analyzes the images being transmitted through the cover channel.

In contrast to previous works, this chapter opens up a new dimension of the problem: Steganography and steganalysis over communication links that are noisy, that is, affected by distortions. For example, the surveillance camera used by Bob in the example of Figure 1b can be connected by a wireless link of marginal strength, such that not all bits sent by the camera arrives at the server. The physical distortions, indicated by lightning symbols in Figure 1, introduce problems for both: the adversaries who try to establish a malicious stego channel, and the defender who tries to detect the presence of such a channel. In this chapter, distortions are formalized by Gaussian noise and packet loss, as will be explained further below. It is important, however, that the distortions are affecting the cover channel and their impact on the stego channel is indirect. As it will become apparent, this relationship leads to interesting effects. For example, distortions can lead to desynchronization in the stego channel even if the cover channel is perfectly synchronized. It turns out that, when state-of-the-art stego algorithms are used, the stego channel is a *substitution-insertion-deletion* (SID) channel in an information-theoretical sense.

Figure 2 summarizes the scope of this chapter. Steps ①, , and ƒ relate to investigating the behavior of a steganographic channel under distortions. Steps ,, and … constitute steganalysis of images that had

Figure 2. Overview of steps and experiments in this chapter

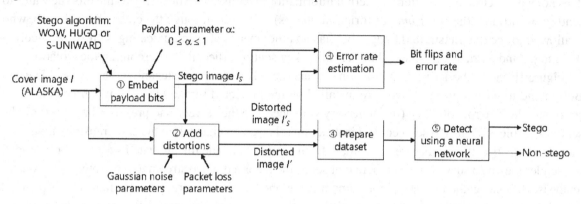

arrived through a distorted channel. These five steps and the structure of the remainder of this chapter are listed next.

- The next section "Spatial-domain Steganography" focuses on embedding payload bits into the cover image (Step ① of Figure 2) by means of a stego algorithm. An overview of different stego approaches is given, but the three above-mentioned algorithms, WOW, HUGO and
- S-UNIWARD, are later used for actual experiments. These algorithms use a *payload parameter* α, which will later turn out to be essential for the performance of steganalysis.
- Section "Spatial-domain Steganography over Distorted Channels" starts with a discussion of the considered distortion mechanisms, Gaussian noise and packet loss, and their effects on the affected cover image (Step , of Figure 2). It discusses in detail the desynchronization problem and the potential role of error-correcting codes. Experimental results reported in this section show empirical findings for error rates and study the influences of the individual distortion mechanisms on the SID channel (Step ƒ of Figure 2).
- Section "Steganalysis of Distorted Images" discusses a convolutional neural network to distinguish manipulated from stego-free images (Step … of Figure 2). An extensive empirical study on a dataset constructed from the distorted images (Step ,, of Figure 2) investigates the possibilities and the limits of NN-based detection.

SPATIAL-DOMAIN STEGANOGRAPHY

An image I can be viewed as an array $I[0] \ldots I[n-1]$ of bits. In most cases, images consist of pixels and consecutive 8 bits of I constitute one pixel. The pixels of an image are arranged in two dimensions, and steganographic algorithms can make use of both coordinates of individual pixels to, e.g., determine their neighbors. Following the raster-scan principle, the information contents of the one-dimensional array used here and the two-dimensional image are identical: Every bit of the array belongs to one specific pixel (or one color component of a pixel) of the image. In spatial-domain steganography, the payload bits P are incorporated by the sender (Alice in Figure 1a, Bob in Figure 1b) into the cover image I; the image is then transmitted to the receiver, who recovers the payload bits. More precisely, the sender and the receiver agree to use a steganographic (or stego) algorithm S that embeds the payload into the cover image:

$$I_S = S(I, P) \tag{1}$$

Spatial-domain stego algorithms place payload information directly into bits $I[0] \dots I[n-1]$. Note that all stego algorithms lead to a deterioration in image quality, though modern algorithms aim at keeping this deterioration small. One can distinguish between different types of spatial-domain stego algorithms, which in the context of malicious steganography have different properties with respect to the attack model, detectability and performance under distortions:

1. **Fixed-key, image-independent** stego algorithms. The payload is inserted by overwriting bits of I at pre-defined positions that are known to both sender and receiver.
2. **Variable-key, image-independent** stego algorithms. The positions where payload bits will be inserted are determined by a key k, a secret shared between Alice and Bob but not known to Eve. For such algorithms, Eq. 1 becomes $I_S = S(I, P, k)$.
3. **Image-dependent** stego algorithms. Modern algorithms (Holub & Fridrich, 2012; Filler & Fridrich, 2010; Pevny et al., 2010; Holub et al., 2014) attempt to determine bit positions where payload insertion will not be noticed by a human viewer or by automatic detection routines. For example, an algorithm might detect edges within an image and pick positions close to edges, to avoid singular payload-carrying pixels within a uniform image region.

Example 1: The first transformation in Figure 3a illustrates a fixed-key, image-independent stego algorithm. Payload bits (1; 0; 1; 1) are inserted into the least-significant bit (LSB) of pixels (1, 2), (2, 2), (3, 2) and (4, 2) of a 4×4 pixel image. This means that the values of pixels (1, 2), (2, 2) and (4, 2) of the stego image are odd and the value of pixel (3, 2) is even. Figure 3b shows an example of a variable-key, image-independent algorithm, where the key specifies four positions (1, 2), (2, 1), (3, 2) and (3, 3). The receiver can again recover the payload from the LSBs of these pixels. Figure 3c shows an image-dependent stego algorithm, where pixels with low values adjacent to high-value pixels are selected.

Fixed-key, image-independent stego algorithms are simple schemes that do not require extra information to establish the stego channel. However, they are rather easy to detect, as a stego pixel in a single-colored region will be salient. For example, a completely black image (value 000 for each pixel) will have pixels 001 on stego bit positions; they might not be perceptible by a human eye but will be easily identified by analysis software. Once the defender (Eve in Figure 1) will discover the stego bit positions, she will be able to read all information communicated between Alice and Bob and also fool them by strategically replacing that information. Variable-key, image-independent stego algorithms make the defender's task harder, as stego bits now can be placed at different positions during each transmission. However, this scheme is difficult to implement, because the only means of communication Alice and Bob have at their disposal is the stego channel. They would need an alternative communication channel inaccessible to Eve to transmit the key, but if they had such a channel, they could use it to transmit the payload in the first place, thus avoiding steganography altogether.

This leaves the image-dependent algorithms as the only choice for adversaries who aim at avoiding being detected. Modern image-dependent algorithms preselect a number of candidate locations and use a pseudo-random matrix RandChange of the same size as the cover image and a *payload parameter* α

Figure 3. Illustration of three types of spatial-domain steganography: fixed-key (a), variable-key (b) and image-dependent (c), of different types of distortions and their effects to the payload. Images are shown as 4 × 4 arrays of bytes.

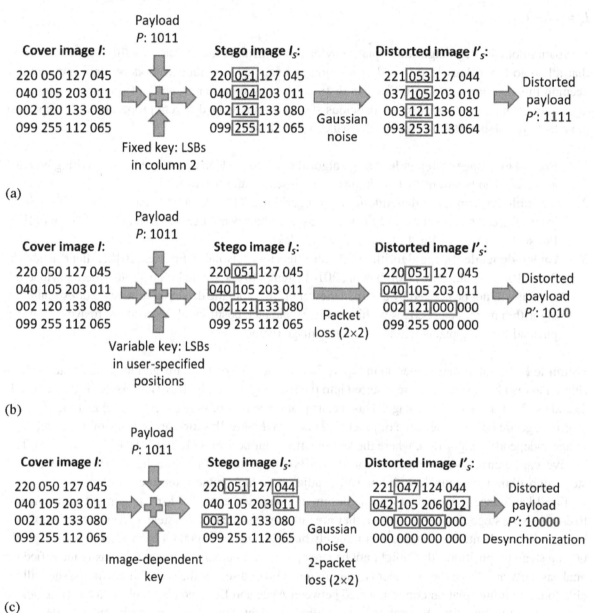

(a)

(b)

(c)

to select actual positions. A cost function is calculated for each cover image position and is compared with the corresponding entry of RandChange, weighted by α. Alice and Bob must agree on RandChange (actually, the seed of the pseudorandom generator used to create it) and α; the higher the latter value, the more payload bits will be embedded, leading to a higher throughput of the stego channel but also a better detectability. For the experiments in this chapter, three state-of-the-art spatial-domain algorithms are used: WOW (Holub & Fridrich, 2012), HUGO (Filler & Fridrich, 2010; Pevny et al., 2010) and S-

Figure 4. (Shankar Prasad et al., 2020). Examples of Gaussian noise (a) and packet loss (b)

(a)   (b)

UNIWARD (Holub et al., 2014). All three follow the image-dependent stego algorithm paradigm. As will be discussed later, only image-dependent algorithms are affected by the desynchronization problem, in contrast to the former two scenarios.

It should be noted that detection is not the only countermeasure against malicious steganography. In *active prevention* (Segal et al., 2017), the defender applies random perturbations to the pixels where the adversary could have embedded payload bits. This approach is challenging, because the defender does not know the type of the stego channel chosen by the attackers: the payload bits can be stored in the spatial domain (as discussed in this chapter), in the transform domain (Kaur et al., 2011) or, in case of a video, in motion vectors (Cao et al., 2011). Therefore, the defender must hit the bits in *all* stego domains that come in question, which can lead to a substantial quality deterioration. Moreover, steganography *per se* has legitimate applications as well, e.g., watermarking for copyright protection or authentication data to identify Deepfake attacks (Dolhansky et al., 2019), so removing *all* stego information from images may be undesired in principle.

SPATIAL-DOMAIN STEGANOGRAPHY OVER DISTORTED CHANNELS

Fundamental Distortion Mechanisms

A number of specific scenarios subsumed by the generic malicious-steganography scheme of Figure 1 can be affected by physical disturbances. One example has been discussed already: a low-power surveillance camera that transmits images over wireless links using signals of marginal strength. Here, the sender may not be able to transmit all packets of data constituting an image (packet loss), or the signal may be so weak that the receiver interprets erroneous symbols (Gaussian noise). Another example emerging application is data being transmitted from or to an autonomous vehicle operating in a smart city. It might be producing a video stream from the front camera that is usable as a cover channel. It is perhaps unrealistic that a adversary called Alice will physically occupy a seat in this car along with its legitimate passengers. But the role of Alice can be taken by a piece of malicious software that runs on the vehicle's board computer, takes, e.g., the owner's credit card number used to pay for parking and embeds it into the transmitted images. This vehicle-to-infrastructure transmission can be distorted when the vehicle drives through locations that are shielded, thus degrading the wireless transmission channel, or which are located close to a source of electromagnetic noise, such as a power distribution line.

A multitude of factors can lead to erroneous generation or transmission of digital objects, including images (Koren & Mani Krishna 2010). Here, the focus is only on natural factors, such as radiation, electromagnetic noise, transient power supply fluctuations, or insufficient transmission signal. These factors are random in nature, and can be described by statistical parameters. To avoid misunderstandings, the word "distortions" is used to describe the considered effects, rather than the terms "errors", "faults", "defects" or "failures", which can have deviating meanings in different scientific communities. This notion of distortion does not include advertent modification of the image, such as compression, cropping or resizing. Alice and Bob are using an existing cover channel and have no possibility to, e.g., change the resolution of the transmitted images. Instead, two specific distortions mechanisms are assumed:

1. Gaussian noise (due to the transmission) and
2. packet loss (due to buffer overflows or severe channel degradation).

Figure 4 illustrates both mechanisms, and their parameters are discussed next in more detail.

Gaussian noise is applied to each pixel individually and independently of other pixels. Its only parameter is its standard deviation σ. In contrast, packet loss has several parameters. The underlying assumption is that pixels are transmitted in packets of size 2×2, 4×4, 8×8 or 16×16, and that one or several such packets are lost during transmission (or do not arrive in time for real-time processing). If this happens, the missing pixels are replaced by values 0, possibly affecting embedded payload bits that happen to be located within the missing packets. Packet loss is characterized by three parameters: the size of the packet; the *average burst length* ABL (the number of consecutive packets that are lost) and the *packet loss ratio* PLR (the probability that a burst of lost packets will start). It is possible to combine Gaussian noise and packet loss.

Example 2: Gaussian noise applied to pixels in Figure 3a can increase or reduce the numerical values of pixels in the transmitted image; rather many pixels are affected but the individual changes are limited. In this specific example, noise has affected and flipped bit 2 of the payload, i.e., pixel (2, 2). Note that noise also affected pixels (1, 2) and (4, 2) but not its LSB, thus leading to no modification of the payload, as well as many other pixels of I_s that do not carry payload. Figure 3b shows a single lost 2×2 packet (burst length of 1). Figure 3c shows a combination of Gaussian noise and a burst of two lost 2×2 packets. Note that the desynchronization observed there is due to the image-dependent algorithm and not due to the combined distortion, as will be discussed in detail in Example 3.

Example 2 clearly illustrates how there are two communication channels: the cover channel, through which image I_s is transmitted, and the stego channel within the cover channel, through which the payload is transmitted. The cover channel is affected by the distortions directly, and the stego channel "inherits" the bit-flips that occur in the cover channel.

Desynchronization Problem

As was discussed further above, modern stego algorithms are image-dependent: they find suitable positions for embedding payload bits in a given cover image. This implies that the number of payload bits that can be embedded can vary for different cover images. Distortions modify the image and can mislead the stego algorithm: The algorithm run on the distorted image may find different locations of payload bits than the same algorithm run on the undistorted version of the same image. That is, the stego algorithm on the receiver side will recover payload bits from different positions than they were embedded. It may even recover more or less bits than were sent!

Example 3: Consider Figure 3c, where the stego image is affected by both: Gaussian noise and a burst of two lost 2×2 packets. Assume that the stego algorithm looks for low-value pixels with a large value difference to their neighbors (edge pixels). The outcome of the algorithm without and with distortions is indicated by the green rectangles. The following effects of distortions to the payload (1; 0; 1; 1) are observed:

- Bit 1 of the payload is encoded as the LSB of pixel (1, 2) with value 51, which is replaced by 47 due to Gaussian noise, but the LSB is kept intact and the correct bit 1 is recovered.
- The position of bit 2, namely pixel (1, 4), is overlooked after the distortions have been applied. This bit is missed, and no payload bit is recovered.
- The stego algorithm erroneously identifies (2, 1) as the next pixel and recovers bit 0, which by coincidence happens to be the correct value stored in the overlooked pixel (1, 4).
- It correctly identifies the next pixel (2, 4) but the bit recovered from its LSB is incorrect, because the pixel's value had been affected by Gaussian noise.
- It misses pixel (3, 1) but erroneously identifies pixels (3, 2) and (3, 3), recovering two wrong values 0.

After this procedure, more bits were received than sent, leading to desynchronization. Without recovery actions, all subsequent received bits will shift by one. The presence of such desynchronization in the stego channel is remarkable, because the cover channel that contains it is fully synchronized: distortions can replace values 1 or 0 by their respective opposite, but not add or remove bits. The size of the transmitted images always remains constant; even if packets do not arrive, they are automatically filled with 0s.

Channels where bits (or, in general, symbols) can not only flip but also appear or disappear, are called *substitution-insertion-deletion* (SID) channels. In the example above, there is one substitution error on bit 3 on pixel (2, 4); three insertion errors on bits 2, 4 and 5 or, respectively, pixels (2, 1), (3, 2) and (3, 3); and two deletion errors on pixels (1, 4) and (3, 1). There are special error-correcting schemes for SID channels (Davey & McKay 2001), which are far more complex and expensive compared with the conventional substitution-only channels where all distortions result in bit flips from 1 to 0 or vice versa. Note that the cover channel has only substitution errors.

Using Redundancy to Counter Distortions

Distortions can, in principle, be countered by redundancy, i.e., retransmitting multiple copies of the same image or using error-correcting codes (Koren & Mani Krishna 2010). It is important to distinguish between redundancy applied to the cover and through the stego channel. The cover channel is controlled by the actual communication parties (e.g., the video server and the receiving device in Figure 1a) and not by the adversaries Alice and Bob. The owners of that channel can agree upon a fault-tolerant protocol where multiple copies of the same cover image I (or I_s if the image has payload bits embedded) are transmitted. They can encode the image using an error-correcting code to obtain its version enc(I) or enc(I_s) which incorporates redundant bits. They can use error-detection instead of error-correction and initiate retransmission upon any detected distortion. All these measures will decrease the error rate, bringing it either down to zero (i.e., all distortions are fully compensated) or to a non-zero value (the effects some distortions are eliminated while others remain).

From Alice and Bob's perspective, this process is fully transparent: They see a channel with certain error characteristics, but it makes no difference to them whether the errors that occur are actual physical failures, or whether further errors had happened but were corrected by a fault-tolerant protocol. Note that if the redundancy solution has perfect efficacy and no distortions "slip through it", the channel is not noisy anymore and the analysis of distortions is no longer needed. At the same time, Alice and Bob cannot directly initiate retransmissions of images through the cover channel or add redundant bits for error-correction to the images being transmitted.

Alice and Bob are, however, free to add redundancy on the stego channel level, i.e., add redundancy to the payload *before* embedding and run the stego algorithm using the larger payload. For example, they embed two copies of the same payload, or calculate redundant bits of an error-correcting code and embed them before or after the actual payload. They cannot, however, use fault-tolerant protocols where the receiver sends an acknowledgment that the payload has been received and successfully recovered, or request a retransmission of payload data parts that did not arrive. This is because the stego channel is, in both cases of Figure 1, unidirectional: The information flows from Alice to Bob (Figure 1a) or from Bob to Alice (Figure 1b), but not in both directions.

The decision whether to use an error-correcting code involves an undesirable (from the attackers' point of view) trade-off. On the one hand, more powerful codes lead to more data that need to be embedded into cover images, thus increasing the chances of being detected. They also require more sophisticated decoding routines that need to be run by the malicious communicating parties (sender and receiver), especially when the effects of desynchronization need to be countered. Executing complex routines, like LDPC (low-density parity code) decoding, can be detectable by Eve on its own through, e.g., an unusually high power consumption or unusually long response times of Alice's and Bob's tasks. On the other hand, using a too simple error-correcting code will leave many errors uncorrected. For instance, a code not designed for insertion and deletion errors will not eliminate desynchronization, which can lead to a large residual error rate.

The two considered types of distortions have a total of four parameters: standard deviation for Gaussian noise; packet size, ABL and PLR for packet loss. To have a reasonable number of comparable experiments, the following two scenarios are defined:

1. **Low-distortion scenario:** the values of the four afore-mentioned parameters are set such as to obtain images with peak signal-to-noise ratio PSNR » 60 dB compared to the undistorted image.
2. **Medium-distortion scenario:** the parameters are set such as to obtain images with PSNR » 30 dB compared to the undistorted image.

In the next section, the effects of distortions will be studied experimentally for these two scenarios.

Experimental Results

17,000 512 × 512-pixel images from the ALASKA dataset (Cogranne et al., 2019) were made subject to distortions: Gaussian noise, packet loss, or both. Several sets of distortion parameters (standard deviation of Gaussian noise; packet size, average burst length ABL and packet loss ratio PLR for packet loss) were used. They were selected such as to obtain PSNR of around 60 dB (low-distortion scenario) or around 30 dB (medium-distortion scenario). The results are summarized in Table 1 for one of the considered stego algorithms, S-UNIWARD, with payload parameter $\alpha = 0.4$ (other algorithms produced similar results). It turned out that even minimal packet loss leads to PSNR far below 60 dB (see, e.g., Figure 4b: even very few lost packets are very well visible and deteriorates the image quality significantly). As a consequence, the low-distortion scenario was obtained by choosing the (comparatively small) value 0.3 for Gaussian noise's standard deviation while disabling packet loss altogether. Keeping packet loss disabled, the average value of PSNR » 30 dB was achieved by standard deviation of 11. These two scenarios (and the absence of any Gaussian noise) were considered in combination with packet loss (for different values of ABL and PLR) as well.

The first four columns of Table 1 specify the used distortion parameters, and the subsequent column contains the average number of lost packets out of their total number (for example, when images were organized in 2 × 2 pixel packets, the total number of packets per image was 65536 and 202 out of them were lost). The observed PSNR (average over all images) is reported in the next column. It is interesting

Table 1. Analysis of distortions on S-UNIWARD ($\alpha = 0.4$). ABL: average burst length; PLR: packet loss ratio; PSNR: peak signal-to-noise ratio (» 60 for low-distortion, » 30 for medium-distortion scenario); substitution errors; I: insertion errors; D: deletion errors; Max I / Max D: Maximum observed burst of insertion / deletion errors.

Gaussian noise	Packet loss				Avg. PSNR [dB]	Avg. bit flips	SID errors				
Std. dev.	Size	ABL	PLR	Packets lost			S [%]	I [%]	D [%]	Max I	Max D
0.3	—				61.49	899	4.69	1.54	1.65	2	2
11					30.52	4804	25.05	20.53	28.20	3	4
—	2 × 2	11	0.0032	202/65536	32.40	30	0.16	2.02	1.69	4	2
0.3					32.40	927	4.83	2.96	2.75	4	2
11					28.38	4822	25.15	20.98	28.45	3	4
—	4 × 4	18	0.0041	65/16384	31.95	37	0.19	0.76	0.64	3	2
0.3					31.95	932	4.86	2.07	2.09	3	2
11					28.27	4822	25.15	20.72	28.34	3	4
—	8 × 8	18	0,005	21/4096	32,00	55	0,29	0,59	0,53	3	3
0,3					32,00	947	4,94	1,97	1,99	3	3
11					28,26	4832	25,20	20,70	28,28	3	4
—	16 × 16	14	0,0051	5/1024	32,84	47	0,25	0,56	0,43	2	2
0,3					32,84	941	4,91	1,90	1,87	2	2
11					28,42	4828	25,18	20,65	28,23	3	4

that only very few packets (between 0.3% and 0.5% of their total number) can be lost without significantly exceeding the PSNR target: almost every packet is extremely well visible (see Figure 4b) and deteriorates the visible image quality by a lot.

The remainder of Table 1 contains the data on the observed effects of the errors in the arriving payload: the number of flipped bits (0 arriving where 1 was sent or vice versa) without investigating their actual cause, and a detailed breakdown of substitution (S), insertion (I) and deletion (D) errors. This is the first such investigation in the context of malicious steganography. It is remarkable that the parameters of packet loss have almost no influence on the observed error rates. As discussed above, there are only very few lost packets (due to their high impact on PSNR), and the chance that payload bits are located in these packets and get affected by their loss is rather small. In contrast, the intensity of the Gaussian noise has a dominant influence on error rates. Recall that the parameters in the first six columns on the table relate to the cover channel (transmission of the image with payload embedded to it) and the error rates in the remaining columns are with respect to the stego channel (the bits of payloads).

Figure 5. Average error rates (G: Gaussian only, PL: Packet loss only, PL + G: Gaussian noise and Packet loss)

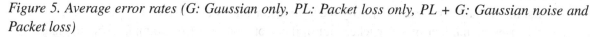

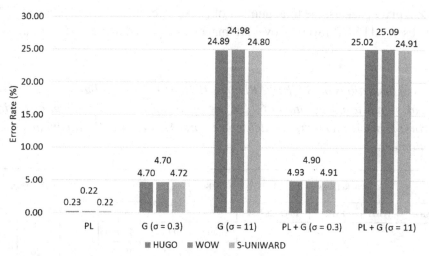

Somewhat surprisingly, insertion and deletion errors are only minimally less prominent than substitution errors. The error rates of up to 28% for the largest standard deviation that still leads to an acceptable PSNR can be considered extremely high. They would necessitate a large amount of redundancy or large error-correcting codes even for the simple case of substitution errors. Insertion and deletion errors are even more difficult to handle. A key parameter in the complexity of SID error-correcting schemes is the expected number of deletions or insertions that can come in a burst (directly one after another). The last two columns of the table report these numbers observed in the experiment. They show that multiple insertion or deletion errors are showing up regularly; therefore, error-correcting codes based on the single-error assumption will not be effective.

Figure 5 shows error rates averaged over different packet loss and Gaussian noise parameters for the three considered stego algorithms. It can be seen that the choice of the algorithm and the presence of packet loss have almost no influence on the results; the main driver for the error rate is the presence of Gaussian noise and its intensity.

In summary, it can be seen that distortions, even when they lead to acceptable PSNR values, greatly impact the quality of the stego channel. Especially in combination with the disadvantage of the attackers who cannot acknowledge problem-free receipt of payload and initiate its retransmission when needed, distorted communication channels seem to limit the attacker's capabilities significantly.

STEGANALYSIS OF DISTORTED IMAGES

Steganalysis Based on Deep Learning

From the defender's (Eve in Figure 1) point of view, the detection procedure must distinguish the malicious effects of steganography from the (unavoidable) consequences of Gaussian noise and packet loss. Deep learning based on convolutional neural networks (CNNs) is the technique of choice for a multitude of image processing and analysis tasks, and steganalysis is no exception. In this section, a CNN from an earlier publication (Salomon et al., 2017) is used for classification. In contrast to this and other previous works on deep-learning based steganalysis (Qian et al., 2015; Pibre et al., 2016; Baluja, 2017; Ye et al., 2019), the network is trained using cover and stego images affected by different types and intensities of distortions. The focus of this chapter is on the investigation of effects of distortions on CNN-backed steganalysis. To this end, this section does not systematically compare the performance of different CNNs for steganalysis as such. Instead, it uses one specific CNN, but puts its behavior under scrutiny for various assumptions about Gaussian noise and packet loss affecting the images under analysis. Consequently, the problem considered in this section is: Given a distorted image Γ, decide whether the image includes steganographic payload bits or not. Recall that the image is distorted because it has been transmitted through a channel affected by Gaussian noise and packet loss, and that the payload bits had been embedded *before* this transmission. That is, distortions can affect the embedded payload bits as well.

Figure 6 shows the CNN used for steganalysis. It includes two convolutional layers, one with a single 3×3 kernel and one with 64 kernels of size 509×509, including the hyperbolic tangent activation function. Interestingly, the network does not include a pooling layer; this is a design decision in (Salomon et al., 2017) that aims at reducing the danger of missing minimal differences between cover and stego

Figure 6. (Salomon et al., 2017). Neural Network used for steganalysis

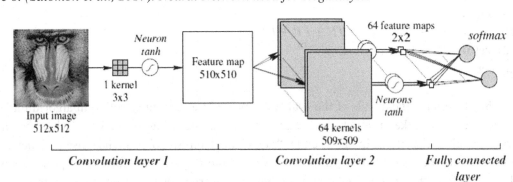

image. The output layer is then a fully connected layer consisting of two softmax neurons. This network was modeled using TensorFlow 2.0.

To train the network, the Stochastic Gradient Descent (SGD) optimization algorithm with a batch size of 100 samples, learning rate of 5×10^{-3}, decay of 5×10^{-7} and zero momentum were employed. Different from (Salomon et al., 2017), the early-stopping strategy was applied, as the experiments showed its benefits in overcoming overfitting; the patience parameter was set to 5.

Experimental Results

To practically evaluate the performance of the network from Figure 6 in detecting steganographic payloads in distorted images, a database of distorted cover and stego images was created. For 512 × 512-pixel greyscale images from the ALASKA dataset (Cogranne et al., 2019) that were used for error rate investigations further above, one distorted cover version and one distorted stego version were created. 11,000 such stego/cover image pairs were employed for training the network, 4,000 different image pairs were used for validation (to decide when to terminate the training of the network), and further 2,000 different image pairs were used for testing, i.e., generating the results reported here. That is, all results are on images that were unseen during training. This procedure was repeated for each of the three stego algorithms considered and for each type of noise. All images were normalized to [0, 1] before use.

Algorithm 1. Generating detection results
Inputs: Image database *IDB*, stego algorithm *Steg-Alg*, payload parameter α,
pre-trained neural network *NN*, noise parameters σ, packet_size, ABL, PLR.
Outputs: Numbers of true positive *TP*, true negative *TN*, false positive *FP*, false negative *FN*,
Average detection accuracy *Acc*.
begin gen_dict
    (1) $TP := TN := FP := FN := 0$;
    (2)   **for each** image $I \hat{I} IDB$;
    (3)   **begin**
    (4)   Generate random payload bits P;
    (5) $I_s := Steg\text{-}Alg(I, P, \alpha)$
    (6) $I' := $ add_distortions$(I, \sigma, $ packet_size, ABL, PLR$)$;
    (7) $I_s' := $ add_distortions$(I_s, \sigma, $ packet_size, ABL, PLR$)$;
    (8)   **if** $(NN(I') == $ "Non-Stego"$)$ **then** $TN := TN + 1$; **else** $FP := FP + 1$;
    (9)   **if** $(NN(I_s') == $ "Stego"$)$ **then** $TP := TP + 1$; **else** $FN := FN + 1$;
    (10) **end for**
    (11) $Acc := (TP + TN) / (TP + TN + FP + FN)$;
    (12) **return** TP, TN, FP, FN, Acc;
end gen_dict

Algorithm 1 presents the details of the evaluation procedure from this section in algorithmic form. The algorithm gen_dict takes as inputs the image database; the stego algorithm with payload parameter; the neural network to classify an image as either "Stego" or "Non-Stego"; and the noise parameters. The algorithm generates the distorted versions of the cover and the stego image (lines 5-7), applies the neural network to classify both versions, and counts the number of true positive, true negative, false positive and false negative classifications (lines 8-9). These numbers are aggregated into the average detection accuracy *Acc* and returned. To generate the results in this chapter, this algorithm is run for the image database ALASKA; three stego algorithms HUGO, WOW or S-UNIWARD with two representative α values 0.1 and 0.4; the NN from Figure 6 trained using 11,000 (different) stego/cover image pairs as described above; and noise parameters set according to the low-distortion and medium-distortion scenarios.

Figure 7 visualizes the average detection accuracy, defined as the ratio of correct, i.e., true positive and true negative classifications among all classifications. It is clear that the determining factor for good detection accuracy is the payload parameter α. For $\alpha = 0.4$ (even bars in Figure 7), the accuracy is around 97-98% in most cases, whereas for $\alpha = 0.1$ it is between 79 and 86%. This is not unexpected, as a higher α means that more payload bits are embedded and more significant modifications are made to the image that are easier to detect. The stego algorithm has almost no influence on the detection accuracy. As for distortion mechanisms, the combined effect of Gaussian noise and packet loss seems to lead to a slight deteriorating impact on the detection accuracy. Table 2 provides, in addition, the complexity of learning (quantified in the number of required epochs). Furthermore, it includes a comparison with the study in (Shankar Prasad et al., 2020) on a different dataset: a combination of BOSSBASE (Bas et al., 2011) and RAISE (Dang-Nguyen et al., 2015) that were in use before the ALASKA challenge.

Figure 7. Detection results for the ALASKA dataset

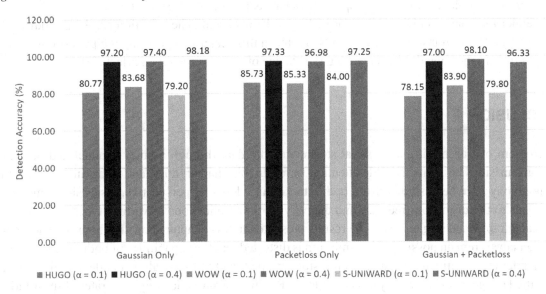

With regard to learning complexity, the training time scaled almost perfectly linearly with the number of epochs reported in Table 2, taking about 4 minutes per epoch using a Tesla K80 GPU (Graphics Processing Unit) with 12 GB memory. The complexity trend is essentially the same as for detection accuracy: the number of required epochs is substantially lower for $\alpha = 0.4$ than for $\alpha = 0.1$; all other factors are secondary. The comparison to earlier results on BOSSBASE and RAISE leads to an interesting observation: The more modern ALASKA dataset is less challenging in the context of distorted images. The achieved detection accuracy is significantly higher for ALASKA, and the number of required epochs is roughly the same in most cases (though it deviates in both directions for some scenarios). Interestingly, the number of embedded bits is systematically (by 11 – 17%) smaller for images in the ALASKA dataset for all algorithms, as shown in Figure 8.

Figure 9 shows how the detection accuracy evolves over the number of epochs for a few representative scenarios. One can see that for $\alpha = 0.1$, the training has to overcome quite some overfitting during early epochs (evidenced by seemingly chaotic up and down accuracy on the testing set). Here, the early stopping strategy seems to be beneficial in overcoming the overfitting problem. Figure 10 elaborates on these scenarios by showing their confusion matrices. Analyzing the cases of misclassification, the distribution between false-positives and false-negatives is rather balanced. In five out of six scenarios, more cover (manipulation-free) images are misclassified as suspicious than stego images that are not identified as such.

If the adversarial parties Alice and Bob are to use the findings from this section to reduce their chance of being detected, they will face a difficult choice related to the number of payload bits to be embedded into an image (controlled by parameter α). Increasing α makes steganalysis decisively simpler; the deep learning approach used in this chapter routinely achieved over 96% accuracy for $\alpha = 0.4$. Decreasing α reduces the chances of the defender to detect malicious payload bits in one image, but at the same time increases the number of images required to transmit a complete payload, thus giving the defender more attempts. However, one could imagine a scenario in which the defender has to monitor not one but a long stream of transmitted images, each of which could be affected by malicious steganography or not. It may not be feasible to apply the complex steganalysis procedure to every transmitted image, so that the defender may have to pick a subset of images to be analyzed. The selection can be periodic (e.g., analyze every 100-th transmitted image) or random. In this scenario, spreading the payload over more images will help the defender by increasing the chance of actually seeing an affected image.

CONCLUSION

The problem of transmitting adversarial steganographic data through a noisy channel and detecting such transmissions has attracted little attention so far. In this chapter, noise and errors in the context of steganography have been studied from both attacker and defender perspective, discussing conceptual differences to the distortion-free case and quantifying the implications of various types of distortions on steganography and steganalysis. The results presented in this chapter show that both steganography and steganalysis remain possible if transmission is distorted, but the capabilities of both the attacker and the defender are negatively affected. Even distortions that lead to minimal visible degradations of the transmitted image (as evidenced by a very moderate PSNR) can have relatively large rates of substitution, insertion and deletion (SID) errors. The precise rates of these errors and their distribution is presented in this chapter for the first time. From the attacker's point of view, distortions necessitate error-correction and fault-tolerance, especially if the payload being transmitted requires perfect accuracy. For instance, when Alice sends Bob a cryptographic secret key, even one bit-flip in this key makes it useless. Steganalysis based on convolutional neural networks has proven quite effective in detecting stego payloads in distorted images, and unexpectedly, its performance when for more recent image databases were used. More research is needed in both: Understanding how the attackers can meaningfully operate through a distorted channel, and how to improve detection through such channels, e.g., by finding better neural networks for classification.

Table 2. Detection accuracy of ALASKA results compared with (Shankar Prasad et al., 2020).

			BOSSBASE & RAISE		ALASKA	
	Stego Algorithm	**Payload param. α**	**Number of epochs**	**Detection Accuracy (%)**	**Number of epochs**	**Detection Accuracy (%)**
Gaussian Noise Only	HUGO	0.1	84	74.05	89	80.77
		0.4	60	97.5	60	97.20
	WOW	0.1	84	75.58	81	83.68
		0.4	58	96.55	50	97.40
	S-UNIWARD	0.1	75	74.98	81	79.20
		0.4	60	95.75	60	98.18
Packet Loss Only	HUGO	0.1	95	77.93	85	85.73
		0.4	60	96.45	60	97.33
	WOW	0.1	85	78.63	85	85.33
		0.4	50	93.48	60	96.98
	S-UNIWARD	0.1	80	76.9	97	84.00
		0.4	58	95.6	58	97.25
Gaussian Noise and Packet Loss	HUGO	0.1	98	73.2	95	78.15
		0.4	47	96.68	47	97.00
	WOW	0.1	94	74.85	94	83.90
		0.4	45	94.1	45	98.10
	S-UNIWARD	0.1	97	73.65	80	79.80
		0.4	48	94.45	48	96.33

Figure 8. Average numbers of embedded payload bits in BOSSBASE and RAISE dataset used in (Shankar Prasad et al., 2020) and in ALASKA dataset in this chapter

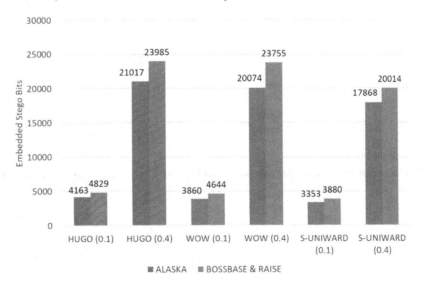

Figure 9. Detection accuracy for different stego algorithms with payload parameter α and different assumed distortions

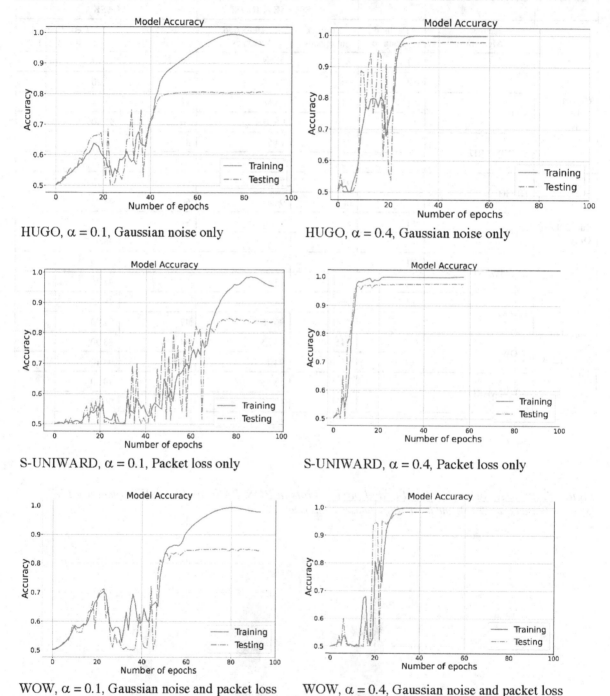

HUGO, α = 0.1, Gaussian noise only

HUGO, α = 0.4, Gaussian noise only

S-UNIWARD, α = 0.1, Packet loss only

S-UNIWARD, α = 0.4, Packet loss only

WOW, α = 0.1, Gaussian noise and packet loss

WOW, α = 0.4, Gaussian noise and packet loss

Table 4

Figure 10 Confusion matrices for scenarios of Fig. 8. The numbers of true positive, true negative, false positive and false negative misclassifications are reported on bottom right, top left, top right, and bottom left, respectively.

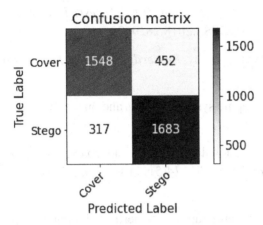

HUGO, α = 0.1, Gaussian noise only

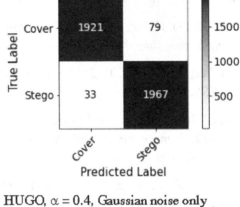

HUGO, α = 0.4, Gaussian noise only

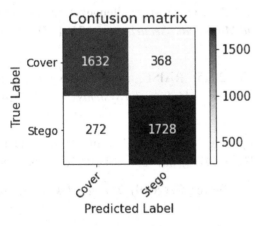

S-UNIWARD, α = 0.1, Packet loss only

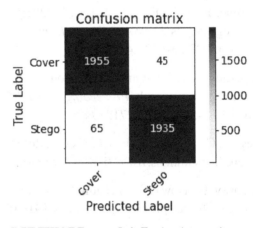

S-UNIWARD, α = 0.4, Packet loss only

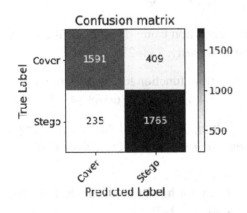

WOW, α = 0.1, Gaussian noise and packet loss

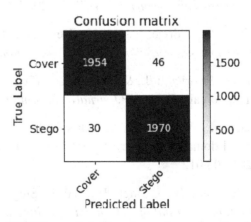

WOW, α = 0.4, Gaussian noise and packet loss

Table 5

REFERENCES

Abd El-Latif, A. A., Abd-El-Atty, B., Hossain, M. S., Rahman, M. A., Alamri, A., & Gupta, B. B. (2018). Efficient quantum information hiding for remote medical image sharing. *IEEE Access: Practical Innovations, Open Solutions, 6*, 21075–21083. doi:10.1109/ACCESS.2018.2820603

Baluja, S. (2017). Hiding images in plain sight: Deep steganography. *Proceedings Neural Information Processing Symposium*, 2069–2079.

Bas, P., Filler, T., & Pevny, T. (2011). Break our steganographic system: The ins and outs of organizing BOSS. *LNCS, 6958*, 59–70.

Boroumand, M., Chen, M., & Fridrich, J. (2018). Deep residual network for steganalysis of digital images. *IEEE Transactions on Information Forensics and Security, 14*(5), 1181–1193. doi:10.1109/TIFS.2018.2871749

Cao, Y., Zhao, X., Feng, D., & Sheng, R. (2011). Video steganography with perturbed motion estimation. *Proceedings Information Hiding, 6958*, 193–207.

Cogranne, R., Giboulot, Q., & Bas, P. (2019). The ALASKA steganalysis challenge: A first step towards steganalysis. In *Proceedings Information Hiding and Multimedia Security* (pp. 125–137). ACM., doi:10.1007/978-3-642-24178-9_14.

Dang-Nguyen, D., Pasquini, C., Conotter, C., & Boato, G. (2015). RAISE: a raw images dataset for digital image forensics. In *Proceedings ACM SIGMM Conference on Multimedia Systems* (pp. 219–224), ACM. 10.1145/2713168.2713194

Davey, M. C., & MacKay, D. J. C. (2001). Reliable Communication over Channels with Insertions, Deletions, and Substitutions. *IEEE Transactions on Information Theory, 47*(5), 687–698. doi:10.1109/18.910582

Dolhansky, B., Howes, R., Pflaum, B., Baram, N., & Canton-Ferrer, C. (2019). *The deepfake detection challenge (DFDC) preview dataset.* abs/1910.08854.

Filler, T., & Fridrich, J. J. (2010). Gibbs construction in steganography. *IEEE Transactions on Information Forensics and Security, 5*(4), 705–720. doi:10.1109/TIFS.2010.2077629

Holub, V., & Fridrich, J. J. (2012). Designing steganographic distortion using directional filters. *Proceedings International Workshop on Information Forensics and Security*, 234–239.

Holub, V., Fridrich, J. J., & Denemark, T. (2014). Universal distortion function for steganography in an arbitrary domain. *EURASIP Journal on Information Security, 2014*(1), 1. doi:10.1186/1687-417X-2014-1

Hussain, M., Wahab, A. W. A., Idris, Y. I. B., Ho, A. T. S., & Jung, K. (2018). Image steganography in spatial domain: A survey. *Signal Processing Image Communication, 65*, 46–66. doi:10.1016/j.image.2018.03.012

Kaur, B., Kaur, B., & Singh, J. J. (2011). Steganographic approach for hiding image in DCT domain. *International Journal of Advances in Engineering and Technology, 1*, 72–78.

Koren, I., & Mani Krishna, C. (2010). *Fault-tolerant systems.* Morgan Kaufmann.

Li, L., Hossain, M. S., Abd El-Latif, A. A., & Alhamid, M. F. (2019). Distortion less secret image sharing scheme for Internet of Things system. *Cluster Computing, 22*(1), 2293–2307. doi:10.100710586-017-1345-y

Morkel, T., Eloff, J. H. P., & Olivier, M. S. (2005). *An overview of image steganography.* Proceedings Information Security for South Africa.

Pevny, T., Filler, T., & Bas, P. (2010). Using high-dimensional image models to perform highly undetectable steganography. *LNCS, 6387,* 161–177.

Pibre, L., Pasquet, J., Ienco, D., & Chaumont, M. (2016). *Deep learning is a good steganalysis tool when embedding key is reused for different images, even if there is a cover source mismatch. In Proceedings Media Watermarking, Security, and Forensics.* Ingenta.

Qian, Y., Dong, J., Wang, W., & Tan, T. (2015). Deep learning for steganalysis via convolutional neural networks. *SPIE Proceedings, 9409.*

Salomon, M., Couturier, R., Guyeux, C., Couchot, J.-F., & Bahi, J. (2017). Steganalysis via a convolutional neural network using large convolution filters for embedding process with same stego key: A deep learning approach for telemedicine. *European Research in Telemedicine, 6*(2), 79–92. doi:10.1016/j.eurtel.2017.06.001

Segal, Y., Hadar, O., Birman, R., & Hadas, E. (2017). Defence from Covert Channel Cyber-attack over video stream payload. *Proceedings RESCUE 2017 – Workshop on Reliability, Security and Quality.* https://www.academia.edu/download/53973023/Cyber_abstract_v-3.7.pdf

Shankar Prasad, S., Hadar, O., & Polian, I. (2020). Detection of malicious spatial-domain steganography over noisy channels using convolutional neural networks. In *Proceedings International Symposium on Electronic Imaging 2020: Media Watermarking, Security, and Forensics.* Society for Imaging Science and Technology.

Ye, D., Jiang, S., Li, S., & Liu, C. (2019). Faster and transferable deep learning steganalysis on GPU. *Journal of Real-Time Image Processing, 16*(3), 623–633. doi:10.100711554-019-00870-1

You, W., Zhang, H., & Zhao, X. (2020). A Siamese CNN for Image Steganalysis. *IEEE Transactions on Information Forensics and Security, 16,* 291–306. doi:10.1109/TIFS.2020.3013204

Zhang, R., Zhu, F., Liu, J., & Liu, G. (2018). *Efficient feature learning and multi-size image steganalysis based on CNN.* arXiv preprint arXiv:1807.11428.

Zhang, R., Zhu, F., Liu, J., & Liu, G. (2019). Depth-wise separable convolutions and multi-level pooling for an efficient spatial CNN-based steganalysis. *IEEE Transactions on Information Forensics and Security, 15,* 1138–1150. doi:10.1109/TIFS.2019.2936913

Chapter 7
Secure Text Extraction From Complex Degraded Images by Applying Steganography and Deep Learning

Binay Kumar Pandey

College of Technology, Govind Ballabh Pant University of Agriculture and Technology, India

Deepak Mane

iD https://orcid.org/0000-0003-4369-6514

Tata Consultancy Services, Australia

Vinay Kumar Kumar Nassa

iD https://orcid.org/0000-0002-9606-7570

Department of Computer Science Engg, South Point Group of Institutions, Sonepat, India

Digvijay Pandey

iD https://orcid.org/0000-0003-0353-174X

Department of Technical Education, Dr A.P.J.

Abdul Kalam Technical University, Lucknow, India

Shawni Dutta

iD https://orcid.org/0000-0001-8557-0376

The Bhawanipur Education Society College, Kolkata, India

Randy Joy Magno Ventayen

Pangasinan State University, Philippines

Gaurav Agarwal

Invertis University, Bareilly, India

Rahul Rastogi

iD https://orcid.org/0000-0001-8278-8257

Invertis University, Bareilly, India

ABSTRACT

This work's primary goal is to secure the transmission of text hidden within the cover image using steganography over a public network of computers. Steganography is a powerful tool for concealing information within a cover image so that the concealed message remains undetectable. As a result, steganography refers to concealed writing. The secure transmission of information over a public network communication channel using steganography occurs in two stages, the first on the sender side and

DOI: 10.4018/978-1-7998-7160-6.ch007

the second on the receiver side. In the first phase, steganography is normally applied to conceal the encrypted information within the image as a cover. The encrypted data is implanted inside the cover image using an improved least significant bit steganography method. The secret key obtained by the embedding algorithm is shared with the message retrieval algorithm on the receiver side to retrieve the message. Finally, the embedded text message is identified using a hybrid convolution regression adaptive integrated neural network (CRAINN) approach.

1. INTRODUCTION

Improving data communication mechanism and the widespread use of multimedia technology has resulted in rapid advances in everyday life (Abdel Wahab, O. F. et. al., 2019). The process of protecting confidential information from unauthorized access has been practiced since ancient times. There were two methods for dealing with such a problem: cryptography and steganography (Zaynalov, N. R. et al., 2019).

Cryptography is defined as a process of comprehensive information security that involves encoding messages at the sender end to make them incomprehensible. In cryptography, data is safely transmitted on a public network of computers by using cryptographic techniques that make it much more difficult for intruders to access classified non-public information (Rahmani, M. K. I. et al., 2014).

The main techniques used in cryptography are encryption and decryption; during the encryption process, plaintext is converted into cipher text. The cipher text is converted to plain text during the decryption process. Plain text is essentially a text that contains original information that has not been encoded, whereas cipher text is the encoded text obtained immediately after the encoding of plain text (Mishra, A., 2013). A key is used to perform both data and message encryption and decryption (Chief, Z. S. et al., 2020)

Steganography involves passing confidential information through original files to keep the message hidden. The term "steganography" comes from a Greek language word that signifies "covered writing" in English. The innocent files used here may also be referred to as cover text, cover image, or cover audio, depending on the requirements (Abikoye, O. C. et al., 2012). Once a secret message implanted in a cover-image, this is referred to as stego-medium.

In this case, a stego key is normally used to control the detection and recovery processes in implanted data. Steganography is a method of concealing information within a digital image, video file, or audio file (Rashmi, N. and Jyothi, K., 2018). The basic proposed steganography-based method holds primarily two types of files. The first file is known as a cover image file, and a private key for encryption will encode the second secret file.

The encrypted secret file is then implanted in the cover image using the embedding technique, and it is compressed to minimize the number of spaces used and the data size even further. The resulting digital image, which contains a secure message hidden within it, is known as a stego image. The acquired stego image is then sent to the receiver via a computer network communication channel. Following that, using the secret key and extracting rules, the receiver will obtain the encrypted information available in the stego-image (Tyagi, M. V., 2012).

Steganography in images can be divided into two categories based on their domains: spatial domain and transform domain. Spatial domain steganography is accomplished by simply altering direct pixel values and attaching secret data to them. Some benefits, such as quick and easy implementation, make spatial domain type steganography one of the most useful steganography types (Hussain, M. et. al., 2018 and Singla, D. and Juneja, M., 2018).

Steganography techniques are the least significant among the existing spatial domain, based, palette-based, pixel value differencing, etc. However, implanting in LSB (Pramanik, S., Bandyopadhyay, S. K., 2014) is a widespread method used in spatial domain steganography (Pramanik, S. et. al., 2020).

Visual attacks (Biswas, R. et al., 2018), altered LSB attacks (Sreekutty, M. S., and Baiju, P. S., 2018), chi-square analysis (Kaur, S. et. al., 2020), and other factual examinations are used to evaluate the success of the rate of hiding in steganography (Jalood, N. S. et. al., 2019). Capacity, robustness, quality, and embedding rate are the most important steganography components (Farrag, S. and Alexan, W., 2019)

- **Robustness:** Steganalysis is used in stego image to determine the rate of strength. As a result, the robustness is completely dependent on the embedding rate. The measure of privacy for hiding the text is reduced if the PSNR value is reduced during the steganalysis.
- **Embedding:** is the main procedure of steganography, and the rate of embedding primarily determines the rate of success and efficacy of steganography. To conceal the secret image, various embedding techniques such as mid-frequency and pixel-based embedding are used.
- **Quality of stego image:** The stego image quality improves as the rate of the least significant bit increases. Furthermore, the cover image and embedded image reflect the same image, but each image's quality varies depending on the embedding procedure. Due to an ineffective embedding algorithm in a few cases, a stego image has a lower quality than the cover image.

The following are some examples of image steganography applications.

- It is used for two-way secure communication.
- It is employed in the creation of a copyright shield for digital records.

Transfer of top-secret and high-level forms among international governments (Pramanik, S. et. al., 2020) Many scientists may give various methods such as artificial bee colony (Fakhredanesh, M. et. al., 2019), u net (Zhao, C. et. al., 2020), discrete wavelet transforms (DWT) (Taburet, T. et al., 2020), image interpolation (Duan, X. et. al., 2020) hash function (Mansour, R. F. and Abdelrahim, E. M., 2019) to end security issues related to steganography. However, the precise solution has not been discovered. Consequently, the proposed research sought to create a new encryption and embedding method to address this security concern.

The secret message is primarily encoded in the proposed method by utilizing some novel encryption method. It is then entrenched into a cover image using the heuristic approach's cover image mid-frequency. Finally, steganalysis is used to extract the secure text hidden within the cover image. Additionally, the proposed model's efficacy is validated by launching several attacks (Rather, M. and Sengupta, A., 2020). Various types of Steganography and Steganalysis techniques are shown below.

1.1 Steganography

As shown in Figure 1, depending upon the nature of cover object or in other wards the actual object in which secret data implanted, steganography can divided in various types

Figure 1. Different type of steganography

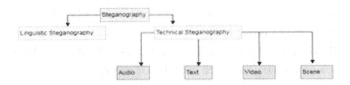

1.2 Steganalysis

Figure 2, shows different classes of steganalysis. The division of class depends upon the types of steganography used to identify the existence of conceal implanted information.

Figure 2. Different type of steganalysis

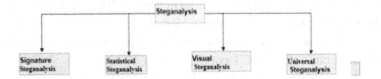

2. LITERATURE REVIEW

The confidential message is hidden within the digital image using image steganography. Its primary goal is to protect the hidden message from attackers. In (Pramanik, S., Bandyopadhyay, S. K., 2013), a new IHED (Image hiding encryption and decryption) for image encryption and decryption was developed. After that, the mid-frequency (MF) values were determined using the mid search African buffalo model (MSABM). The encoding process was completed with such matters. Finally, several attacks such as the chi-square attack, visual attack, white floor square attack (WFSA), and steganalysis were used to validate the IHED method.

Data security was achieved through the use of steganography and cryptography. As a result, security was deemed to play the most critical role in data concealment, which improves data confidentiality. In (Patani, K., Rathod, D. 2021) created a 3-bit least significant bit for encoding the cover image's secret image. Using visual cryptography, the stego image was then securely transmitted over the internet. The use of ECC makes data extraction difficult for a variety of attackers. This method works well for those with large sizes and achieves better color image performance.

As a result of the current massive growth in natural language processing, steganographic methods based on automatic text generation technology have evolved. Such models use neural networks' self-learning and feature extraction abilities to learn large normal feature expressions of text. Following that, it generates heavy steganographic texts that satisfy statistical distribution based on the learned statistical patterns. In this (Yang, Z., et. al., 2019) it is observed that after adding the information to hide, the distribution of the conditional probability of each word in the resulting steganographic texts will be contorted. Using recurrent neural networks retrieves such types of feature distribution differences and classifies them as normal text or cover text.

In (Feng, B. et. al., 2017), detail about the large percentage of cutting-edge binary image information hiding methods focuses on l-shape sequence centers for incorporating alterations. Such an embedding requirement, on the other hand, does have an unstable impact on boundary structures. This article suggests the steganalysis system that uses the embedding effect associated with both the l-shape sequence embedding criterion to identify newly invented content-adaptive binary image data stealing. First, an analysis of how various l-shape patterns affect the distribution of a single 4x3 sized pattern. A 32-dimensional steganalysis feature set is defined based on the findings, using four classes of patterns to model the distribution of two pixels oriented in the pattern changing direction.

According to (Attaby, A. A. et. al., 2019) cryptography is the primary method of data protection, with steganography able to serve as a replacement in some cases. The science and art of steganography is the art and science of confidential communication between two parties that attempt to maintain the message from being discovered. There has been much image steganography that support the idea. Most of them provoke statistically meaningful changes in the cover carrier's properties, particularly whenever the text payload is huge. This study proposes a novel transform domain JPEG image steganography technique that effectively improves embedding performance whilst also needing minor modifications to the cover carrier image. The DCT-M3 method incorporates two bits of the compact form of a hidden code utilizing modulus 3 of the difference of two DCT coefficients.

The author of this paper (Marc, Antonini and Michel, Barlaud., 1992) described a novel method for image compression in both the time and frequency domains. The wavelet transform is used to generate various sub-bands of images and decompose them into different levels. A noise shaping bit allocation procedure is used to encode the wavelet, assuming that details in high-resolution images are less visible to the naked eye.

The author of this paper (Shapiro, J. M., 1993) presented a compression algorithm with the property that the bits in the stream bit generated to obtain embedded code. The binary value sequences available in embedded code distinguish an image of interest from a null image. On test images obtained from a standard source, an image compression scheme known as EZW consistently outperforms all other compression algorithms. Until now, such performance has been achieved with a method that requires no additional training, no additional pre-stored tables, or prior knowledge of the image's source.

In this work (Strom, Jacob & Cosman, Pamela., 1997), presents that image compression methodologies for better picture quality restoration are available for the essential parts of an image. The tiny proportion of even an image could be helpful for medical testing in the case of medical images. However, the price of incorrect assessment is incredibly high. The approach to ensuring accurate and efficient picture coding methodologies for medical diagnosis may be lossless compression throughout interest regions.

The author worked on a discrete wavelet-based, deficient bit-rate video coding scheme, block matching motion estimation, and overlapped block motion compensation in this paper (Detlev, Marpe and H. L. Cycon., 1999). It is discovered in this work that if quantized wavelet coefficients are pre-processed using a procedure that takes advantage of the redundancies available in wavelet sub-band structure, the coding mechanism works more effectively. As a result, a new context of pre-coding techniques based on the concepts of accretion sectionalization and conditional coding is introduced.

The author develops an image filtering scheme based on a wavelet in this paper (Duchowski, A. T., 1998), which maintains high resolution in the ROI-based matching fovea vision and then gradually decreases resolution value in the image's periphery. The proposed method provides multiple ROI representations, extending previous work based on the Mapping to the wavelet domain. Image degradation is achieved by scaling the wavelet coefficient and Voronoi portioning the image.

A method known as Scalable Adaptive Motion Compensated Wavelet (SAMCoW) compression is described in this paper (Fayez, I. and Ferat, A., 2006). The SAMCoW-based method is best suited for communication channels with data rates less than 32 kbps. Various methods for improving the subjective quality of images for SAMCoW are investigated in this work. It also employs B frames, half-pixel accuracy, and unrestricted motion vectors.

The author of this paper presents a novice compression technique based on a scalable video compression algorithm. To reduce temporal type redundancy, this method employs motion compensation. Besides providing a broad range of scalability rates, the encoder used here may outperform existing hybrid traditional video coders such as MPEG1 and H.263. Furthermore, the coding scheme described here allows the data rate to be changed dynamically during decoding, appealing for network-oriented applications.

This paper (Shen, Ke. and Edward, J. D., 1999) and ROI-based coding feature are added to the set partitioning in the hierarchical trees method used for wavelet-based image coding. With a greater emphasis on the coefficients in the transform relating to the ROI, the ROI is encoded with greater fidelity than the rest of the image in the very early stages of progressive coding. This work aims to retrieve the required coefficients from the decoder's wavelet-transform domain to reconstruct the expected region. When compared to previously existing methods, the method proposed here yields better results.

This paper (Keun, H. P. and Hyun, W. P., 2002) discussed an integer wavelet transform, and backward adaptive temporal prediction has been used in the whole adaptive lossless compression technique for colored video streams. In color video streams, there have been two main types of redundancies: spatial and temporal redundancies. An adaptive method that takes full advantage of twin redundancies does provide considerably better compression performance than lossless frame compression, as per this research.

This work (Park., et. al., 2004) describes video compression techniques for greater compression. The region-of-interest (ROI) and frames-of-interest (FOI) based coding techniques may prioritize ROI or FOI by allocating more bits than others. For the reconstruction of the ROI, related coefficients are generally calculated as a function of filter length. However, it is inefficient, so a novel wavelet-based ROI and FOI scheme is proposed.

In this work (Changqing, L., 2004), the author describes a technique for compressing full-image data with such a compression ratio better quality. This research's main objective is to maintain picture quality elevated in the medically important portion while also enabling major loss in the rest of the image. This work's primary focus is on the region of interest-based coding, which allows for the multiple use of the ROI coding research goal to enable the use of multiple and absolute shaped regions of interest within images.

The significance of each region of interest has been defined, utilizing arbitrarily defined weights. Arbitrary weights are often used to highlight each region of interest's application, including the image region. If another image region is also not linked to the region of interest, the image region is not really interested. As a result, other regions may have a higher or lower degree of performance.

This paper (Charalampos, D. and Ilias, M., 2007) describes advanced image compression techniques based on partial EZW algorithms. This process is based on the EZW image compression method's more additional capabilities. The embedded zero tree wavelet methodology has been assumed to be an extended version of an EZW image compression method. The article's proposed a partial EZW Algorithm that significantly lowers these same EZW issues that have a detrimental effect itself on productivity throughout lower bit plane transmission. The Partial EZW presently contains an integer-based wavelet transformation and ROI, making this a much better option for EZW and SPIHT algorithms.

This paper (Babu, D. V. and Alamelu, N. R., 2009) discusses wavelet-based video coding instead of traditional block-based discrete cosine transform (DCT) coders. Wavelet-based video encoding is free of block artifacts and has multi-resolution scalability, both of which are highly desired features in existing multimedia video applications. Similarly, a simple video coding system based on wavelet and new pointers is proposed to evaluate wavelet use in video coding systems. The performance of the wavelet-based compression method is defined by four different indicators, each representing another aspect. Furthermore, the data handled by the various wavelet functions and the quantization function are analyzed in this work. A new concept for sensitivity coefficients is presented, which elucidates video applications' features using the wavelet transform.

The author of this provides an embedded zero tree wavelet algorithm to decrease a picture frame by applying various wavelet filters such as Haar, Bi-orthogonal, Coiflets and Daubechies. Using a context-appropriate threshold level, the picture noise can be reduced during the decryption stage. Image compression methods are significant in tele-health because they decrease the number of bits needed per image pixel to reflect the picture accurately. Consequently, the picture's shorter length, the required storing data space is reduced and increased data transmission performance. As a result, the EZW algorithm is viewed as a picture technique that is both computationally efficient and effective.

The author of this work (Vellaiappan, E. et. al., 2012) discusses regions-of-interest based coding, which is regarded as an important feature required in scalable video coding in future applications. As technology advances, various heterogeneous systems arise that could be very useful for observing a huge streaming video spectrum. An effective customizable ROI video compression scheme has been described in this work, enabling for both the extraction of desired regions-of-interest and the adaptive setting of ROI location, size and resolution.

The discrete Haar wavelet transform (DWT) for image compression is presented in this paper (Angelopoulos, G. and Pitas, I., 1991). The article uses the Haar discrete wavelet transform to compact the signal (HDWT). Image compression methods have been categorized depending on whether the compressed image could reconstruct an identical copy of an original image. The image signal has been condensed using redundant coding information, inter-pixel redundancy, and perceptual redundancy. At various decomposition levels, the simulated studies for dimensionality reduction with Haar wavelet are described.

In (Restrepo, Alfredo & Bovik, Alan., 1988), the use of trimmed mean filters was proposed as a means for image enhancement. Image enhancement is by far the most critical and vital pre-processing phase almost in every Image Processing. Various methods including the Median filter and the trimmed mean filter have been proposed. The median and mean filters were shown to be amended by the trimmed mean filter. The suggested algorithm's de-noising productivity has also been revealed to be outstanding.

This paper (Sauvola, J. and Pietikäinen, M., 2000) gives a novel process that rapidly separates a page's local contents into three main categories: background, pictures, and text. The soft decision method (SDM) is used for backgrounds and photos, and a specialized text binarization method (TBM) is used for text-based and line sketching regions. The SDM is worthy of noise removal and signal monitoring, while the TBM has been used in low-light or noisy environments to detach text elements from the background. The outcomes of such methodologies will then be integrated.

According to (Westin, C. F. et. al., 2000), it isn't easy to instantly achieve fetching indexing details from color paper records. Human editing has been typically needed throughout bibliographic databases to provide details about title, authors, and keywords. Text features should be identified for all the indexing method to be automated. This article suggests the methodology for retrieving document from color book and journal covers instantly. Text extraction methodologies have been introduced in 2 ways. The outcomes from both methodologies have been coupled to establish a clear separation between text and non-text components.

In (Bhoi, N. and Meher, S., 2008) present another good approach for retrieving text from grayscale scanned documents by leveraging edge information. The primary objective is to isolate and distinguish textual and graphical areas in strongly noised newspapers pictures. The process utilizes the local features throughout various entities and afterwards gatherings and edge point of text-based areas. This can effectively retrieve positional text blocks by utilizing lines approximate solution and layout classification techniques. Ultimately, feature-based connected element merging has been used to aggregate together relatively homogenous textual regions within the bounding rectangles. This suggested method was tested on a large number of newspapers pictures with multiple page configurations and promising results confirming that method's effectiveness.

The paper (Chen, D. et. al., 2001) presents a speedy and reliable method to identify textual data in image or video frames with intricate backgrounds and compression effects. Depending upon edge analysis, baseline location, and heuristic constraints, an algorithm initially gathers a candidate text line. The Support Vector Machine can then be used to recognize text throughout the edge-based distance map feature vector from candidates. Experimental studies with such a large number of pictures and video frames of various sources revealed that this algorithm outperformed traditional image/video frame identification performance and computational power.

For colored document images, a novel binarization method has been presented in (Jagtap, K. and Manjare, C., 2015). In documents containing closed or blended foreground and background colors, traditional adaptive threshold procedures do not deliver adequate binarization outcomes. As a start, a luminance distribution is being used to collect statistics image attributes. Next, through selecting various color features, the decision-tree derived binarization method is proposed to binarize color documentation images. Saturation has been used first because the colors throughout the document image are concentrated within a narrow range. Second, luminance is used because the image's foreground colors are essential. Third, if the image background colors are focused within such a small spectrum, luminance is used. Fourth, if the cumulative number of low-luminance pixels is less than 60, saturation is used; else, both luminance and saturation are used. 519 color images were used in research studies, majorities of which have been standardized invoice and name-card document images. Throughout shaped and connected-component measurement, the suggested binarization method outperforms other existing procedures. Moreover, in a commercial OCR system, the binarization approach achieves higher recognition accuracy than similar techniques.

As per (Gllavata, J., et. al., 2003) discussed, a crucial step in retrieving multimedia content, text identification in images or video is conducted. This paper describes a fast method for detecting, classifying, and extracting horizontally aligned text in complex backgrounds of photos (and digital videos). A proposed method uses a color reduction approach, an edge detection method, and text area localization using projection profile analyses and geometrical properties. The algorithm's outputs are text boxes with a simplified background, ready to be fed into an OCR engine for character recognition. Promising experimental results for just a sequence of pictures collected from various video sequences demonstrate the method's efficacy.

In (Kim, K. I. et. al., 2003), a unique texture-based method of detecting text in pictures was presented in this paper. Text-based attributes become assessed using a support vector machine. The intensity levels of a raw pixel, which mainly comprise a textural characteristic, is directly fed to the SVMs, which also functions very well in high-dimensional spaces instead of using external features. Using just a continuously adaptive mean shift method, the texture analysis results will then be used to identify text regions. A combo of CAMSHIFTs and SVMs produces in both adaptable and efficient text recognition, although time-consuming textures studies with less significant pixel are restricted, leaving a small portion of an input image texture-analyzed.

As per (Jung, K., et. al. 2004), identification, localization, surveillance, excavation, enhancement, and recognizing texts from input images are parts of an extraction method. Excavating such information requires identification, localization, surveillance, extracting, improvement, and recognizing text from a given image. Text data in pictures and videos and videos contain helpful information of automatic annotations, indexing, and structuring of images; extracting such information entails identification, localization, tracking, extraction, enhancement, and text recognition (Pandey, D., et. al., 2019) from a given image. Text variables like shape, styling, orientation, alignment, and poor visual contrast and a complex background make automatic text extraction difficult. Although comprehensive evaluations on related problems like face recognition, analysis of documents, and audio/video indexing are available, the text information extraction is not properly covered.

This article (Angelopoulos, G. and Pitas, I., 1991) suggests two local Wiener filtering processes that treat the doubly localized Wiener filtering method. Elliptic directional windows have been used to approximate the signal deviations of noisy wavelet coefficients of different aligned sub-band and the noise image. As per the findings of the research, this proposed algorithm significantly improves de-noising efficiency.

For this work during pre-processing, a low pass filter such as a Wiener filter used to make a reasonable approximation of fore-ground regions for estimation of background surface, interpolation of adjacent background levels of intensity for background surfaces measurement, thresholding by merging the estimated background surfaces in the main image while including picture up sampling, and ultimately a post-processing steps for enhancement of picture quality.

The words written down steganography have risen to prominence as a leading research field in information sharing, with various studies being conducted to advance this field. For "steganography" purpose, this article gives an enhanced least significant bit eLSB procedure for implanting textual data in cover image. As compared to the conventional LSB algorithm used in steganography, the cover picture's fidelity is higher.

In the first step, the metadata formed in the first few bytes of the cover-image. The following phase is responsible for the process optimization of secure textual message and further storing it in the cover image, which is made possible by analyzing the secret text's character sequences. The proposed work takes up less space in the cover image for the given hidden text, resulting in improved quality of stego image compared to pre-existing LSB-based methods. This technique allows for a maximum size of implantation rate and additional confidentiality as a result of the confidential (Attaby, A. A. et. al., 2019) messaging pre-processing. An improved quality of the cover image is obtained because it optimizes secret messages during the implantation phase.

The practice of implanting textual data in multimedia documents like image is known as text steganography. The image used as an input is divided into four sub-bands by applying discrete wavelet transform and saving memory. The image was compressed after the text information was hidden.

The discrete wavelet transforms based method used for size reduction of image and the inverse type discrete wavelet transform method for convalescing the real image and obtaining a secret code. A wide range of experiments has demonstrated the method's suitability and evaluated the fulfillment in the PSNR ratio and NPCR. Stenography attains information hiding by replacing random noise with a secret bit of information and embedding secret information at the lowest plane to avoid noise and security attacks.

3. HYPOTHESIS OF PROPOSED METHOD

Steganography is being used in a variety of information security systems at the moment. Steganography's primary goal is to transfer secret text by embedding it in image, audio, and video files. Steganography is performed using a jpeg image in this proposed method. The retrieval of text embedded at the receiver end, on the other hand, is regarded as the most difficult challenge. Nonetheless, the sender will share the secret key with the receiver, even though extracting the embedded text hidden in the cover image with high efficiency is difficult. Steganography is accomplished simply by converting the text into a less significant bit value in the discrete matrix.

On the other hand, the image quality degrades due to the insertion of the embedded message. The images may contain some noise from time to time. As a result, smooth regions in images are regarded as non-smooth regions. Such inadequacies also reduce the overall success of various algorithms. As a result, a high-performance method for embedding secret textual data implanted within cover-image without interfering with noise presented should be used.

The procedure of fetching the implanted textual data from a steganographic pictorial image is known as steganalysis. This process may be divided into three stages: detecting hidden messages, estimation of messages, and messages extraction. The only one that does not impose itself on the cover-image noise is the fetching of implanted textual data. Resulted, noise must be removed from the image at the beginning of the process. In steganalysis, three major steps are included: noise removal, feature extraction, and message extraction.

4. SUGGESTIVE OBJECTIVES OF PROPOSED METHOD

Following are few objectives of the proposed method for secure text extraction from complex degraded image by applying steganography and deep learning.

- To create an algorithm that extracts text from a cover image with minimal error and high accuracy.
- Using an adaptive optimization algorithm improves the effectiveness of the text extraction technique.
- To create new methods for providing high-quality stego images in data security via image steganography.
- Using new techniques, extracting secret data from stego images with high quality.
- After modeling and simulation, the proposed approaches must be validated.

Finally, the performance of the proposed approaches will be compared to all currently available methods.

5. METHODLOGY USED

The extraction of text hidden within the cover image is regarded as the primary goal of this work. The text extraction process is divided into two stages, the first stage happens on the sender end, and the second stage happens on the receivers end. During the first stage, steganography is normally utilized to implant the secret-text inside the cover-image. The encrypted textual data is implanted within image layers using an improved LSB steganography procedure. Figure 3 depicts a proposed methodology that employs e-LSB (enhanced LSB) to maximize image quality so that the following process can be carried out properly. The proposed embedding process operates in the spatial domain and is divided into two stages. The metadata is created in the first phase. The header data is embedded in the cover image's first few bytes, and the secret message is stored in an optimized way in the cover-image. A secret-key generated by an embedding algorithm is then passed to the receiver side's message retrieval algorithm. The message is retrieved using the secret key, and a hybrid Convolution Regression Adaptive Integrated Neural Network (CRAINN) based approach may deploy to obtained the implanted textual data from the cover image. Convolution Regression Adaptive Integrated neural network (CRAINN), through generating the lowest prediction error, delivers the better prediction performance. Basically, all evaluation metrics such as time and PSNR, and other quality attributes like accuracy, F1 score, and so on, are being used for prospective measures of performance assessment. The whole potential is being used to assess the growth of an enhanced LSB-based stegography for secure text extraction from complex degraded images, and also a tailored method for secure text extraction on a public network. Using an optimization technique, the performance of the used neural network architecture is improved.

Figure 3. Proposed Methodology with CRAINN Steganography technique

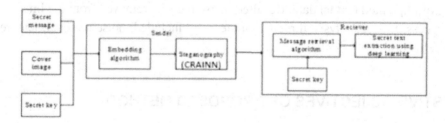

6. DATA SET

For examination of proposed algorithms below set of complex degraded images (Pandey, D., et. al., 2020) are used for analysis of performance parameter such as embedding capacity, computational time, PSNR. Below Dog, Cat, Lion, Lena and Monalisa complex degraded images are used because embedded text in image cannot be easily predicted by hacker.

7. PERFORMANCE ANALYSIS

Figure 4. Dataset used for performance analysis

Figure 5. Comparison analysis in term of computational time

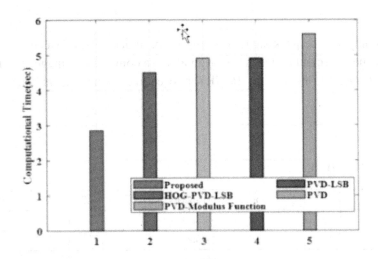

Figure 6. Comparison analysis in term of embedding capacity

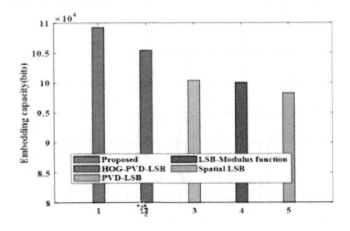

7.1. Computational time and Embedding Capacity

The comparison analysis shown in figure 6 gives excellent performance(Pandey, B. K., et. al., 2011) in regards embedding capacity than the previous pixel value differencing (PVD) with modulus function, pixel value differencing (PVD), Histogram of oriented gradients with pixel value differencing HOG-PVD-LSB methodologies. The comparison analysis in regards of computational time is shown in figure 5.

The comparison analysis depicted in figure 4 gives excellent performance in regards computational time than the previous pixel value differencing (PVD) with modulus function, pixel value differencing HOG-PVD-LSB. This is because of proposed optimization based cryptography has enhanced the effectiveness of proposed steganography process. The effectiveness achieved by proposed algorithm is not yet achieved by any other traditional algorithms as its combination of neural network architecture for image analysis which enhanced the performances of enhanced LSB technique.

7.2. PSNR

The PSNR block computes the peak signal-to-noise ratio, in decibels, between two images. This ratio is used as a quality measurement between the original and a compressed image. The mean-square error (MSE) and the peak signal-to-noise ratio (PSNR) are used to compare various image qualities.

Table 1. Comparison Analysis

Images	Embedding capacity (bits)	PSNR (dB)
Dog	786,432	77.35
Cat	786,432	77.21
Lion Images	786,432	77.11
Lena	786,432	78.70
Monalissa	786,432	68.34

Figure 7. PSNR for various image

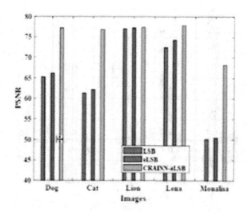

8. CONCLUSION

In this method, enhanced LSB (e-Least Significant Bit) Steganography, a hybrid convolution neural network (CRAINN), adaptive optimization technique is utilized for secure transmission and extraction of images on public network of computers. Steganography and deep learning (Manne, R. et. al., 2020) are used to secure data transmission in a public network-based data transmission channel in two stages—the first on the sender side and the second on the receiver side. In the first phase, the confidential data is implanted inside the cover image using steganography. The encrypted data is implanted inside the cover-image by utilizing an improved LSB steganography procedure, the secret-key obtained by the embedding algorithm is shared with the message retrieval algorithm on the receiver side to retrieve the message, and the embedded text message is finally identified using a hybrid convolution neural network (CRAINN) approach. Furthermore, the hybrid convolution neural network's performance is enhanced through the use of an optimization technique. The MATLAB framework would be used to implement a comprehensive encrypted text extraction process. The measures used to calculate the proposed approach's overall accuracy, mean-square-error, root-mean-square-error, F1 score and precision for future prospective. Performance analysis is used to review and assess the effectiveness of existing approaches and it is found that the proposed algorithms has a better result than the traditional algorithms for performance parameter PSNR, computational time and embedding capacity.

REFERENCES

Abdel Wahab, O.F., Hussein, A.I., Hamed., H.F., Kelash., H.M., Khalaf., A.A., & Ali, H.M. (2019). Hiding data in images using steganography techniques with compression algorithms. *Telkomnika*, *17*(3), 1168-1175. . doi:10.12928/telkomnika.v17i3.12230

Abikoye, O. C., Adewole, K. S., & Oladipupo, A. J. (2012). Efficient data hiding system using cryptography and steganography. *International Journal of Applied Information Systems (IJAIS)*, *4*(11), 6–11.

Angelopoulos, G., & Pitas, I. (1991). Multichannel Wiener filters in color image restoration based on AR color image modelling. *IEEE International Conference on Acoustics, Speech, and Signal Processing, ICASSP-91*. 10.1109/ICASSP.1991.150913

Attaby, A.A., Ahmed, M.F.M., & Alsammak, A.K. (2018). Data hiding inside JPEG images with high resistance to steganalysis using a novel technique: DCT-M3. *Ain Shams Engineering Journal, 9*(4), 1965-1974.

Babu, D. V., & Alamelu, N. R. (2009). Wavelet-Based Medical Image Compression Using ROI EZW. *Int. J. of Recent Trends in Engineering and Technology*, *1*(3), 97–100.

Bhoi, N., & Meher, S. (2008). Circular spatial filtering under high-noise-variance conditions. *Computers & Graphics*, *32*(5), 568–580. doi:10.1016/j.cag.2008.07.006

Biswas, R., Mukherjee, I., & Bandyopadhyay, S. K. (2019). Image feature-based high capacity steganographic algorithm. *Multimedia Tools and Applications*, *78*(14), 20019–20036. doi:10.100711042-019-7369-y

Changqing, L. (2004). ROI and FOI algorithms for Wavelet-Based Video Compression. *Proceedings Of The 5th Pacific Rim Conference On Advances In Multimedia Information Processing, 3*, 241-248.

Charalampos, D., & Ilias, M. (2007). Region of Interest Coding Techniques for Medical Image Compression. *IEEE Engineering in Medicine and Biology Magazine*. PMID:17941320

Chavada, P., Patel, N., & Patel, K. (2014). Region of Interest Based Image Compression. *IJIRCCE, 2*(1), 10-20.

Chen, D., Bourlard, H., & Thiran, J. P. (2001). Text identification in complex background using SVM. *Proceedings - IEEE Computer Society Conference on Computer Vision and Pattern Recognition, 2*, 611–621.

Chief, Z. S., Mustafa, R. A., & Maryoosh, A. A. (2020). Hiding Encrypted Text in Image using Least Significant Bit Image Steganography Technique. *International Journal of Engineering Research and Advanced Technology, 6*(8), 63–75. doi:10.31695/IJERAT.2020.3642

Detlev, M., & Cycon, H. L. (1999). Very Low Bit-Rate Video Coding Using Wavelet-Based Techniques. *IEEE Transactions on Circuits and Systems for Video Technology, 9*(1), 85–94. doi:10.1109/76.744277

Duan, X., Jia, K., Li, B., Guo, D., Zhang, E., & Qin, C. (2019). Reversible image steganography scheme based on a U-Net structure. *IEEE Access, 7*, 9314-9323.

Duchowski, A. T. (1998). Representing Multiple Region of Interest with Wavelets. *Proceeding of International Conference on Visual Communications and Image Processing, 3309.*

Fakhredanesh, M., Rahmati, M., & Safabakhsh, R. (2019). Steganography in discrete wavelet transform based on human visual system and cover model. *Multimedia Tools and Applications, 78*(13), 18475–18502. doi:10.100711042-019-7238-8

Farrag, S., & Alexan, W. (2019). A high-capacity geometrical domain-based 3d image steganography scheme. *IEEE International Conference on Advanced Communication Technologies and Networking CommNet*, 1-7. 10.1109/COMMNET.2019.8742346

Fayez, I., & Ferat, A. (2006). An Efficient Method for Region of Interest Coding in JPEG2000. *Proceedings of the 5th WSEAS International Conference on Signal Processing.*

Feng, B., Weng, J., Lu, W., & Pei, B. (2017). Steganalysis of content-adaptive binary image data hiding. *Journal of Visual Communication and Image Representation, 46*, 119–127. doi:10.1016/j.jvcir.2017.01.008

Gllavata, J., Ewerth, R., & Freisleben, B. (2003, September). A robust algorithm for text detection in images. *ISPA, 2*, 611-616. 10.1109/ISPA.2003.1296349

Gupta, S., & Jain, R. 2015, December. An innovative method of Text Steganography. In *2015 Third International Conference on Image Information Processing (ICIIP)* (pp.60-64). IEEE. 10.1109/ICIIP.2015.7414741

Hussain, M., Wahab, A. W. A., Idris, Y. I. B., Ho, A. T., & Jung, K. H. (2018). Image steganography in spatial domain: A survey. *Signal Processing Image Communication, 65*, 46–66. doi:10.1016/j.image.2018.03.012

Jagtap, K., & Manjare, C. (2015). An Ancient Degraded Images Revamping Using Binarization Technique. *International Journal of Soft Computing and Engineering*, *4*(6), 10–15.

Jalood, N. S., Jasim, A. N., & Shareef, A. H. (2019). New method of image steganography based on particle swarm optimization algorithm in spatial domain for high embedding capacity. *IEEE Access: Practical Innovations, Open Solutions*, *7*, 168994–169010. doi:10.1109/ACCESS.2019.2949622

Jayapandiyan, J. R., Kavitha, C., & Sakthivel, K. (2020). Enhanced Least Significant Bit Replacement Algorithm in Spatial Domain of Steganography Using Character Sequence Optimization. *IEEE Access: Practical Innovations, Open Solutions*, *8*, 136537–136545. doi:10.1109/ACCESS.2020.3009234

Jung, K., Kim, K. I., & Jain, A. K. (2004). Text information extraction in images and video: A survey. *Pattern Recognition*, *37*(5), 977–997. doi:10.1016/j.patcog.2003.10.012

Keun, H. P., & Hyun, W. P. (2002). Region-of-Interest Coding Based on Set Partitioning in Hierarchical Trees. *IEEE Transactions on Circuits and Systems for Video Technology*, *12*(2), 106–113. doi:10.1109/76.988657

Kim, K. I., Jung, K., & Kim, J. H. (2003). Texture-based approach for text detection in images using support vector machines and continuously adaptive mean shift algorithm. *IEEE Transactions on Pattern Analysis and Machine Intelligence*, *25*(12), 1631–1639. doi:10.1109/TPAMI.2003.1251157

Manne, R., Kantheti, S., & Kantheti, S. (2020). Classification of Skin cancer using deep learning, ConvolutionalNeural Networks - Opportunities and vulnerabilities- A systematic Review. *International Journal for Modern Trends in Science and Technology*, *6*(11), 101-108. doi:10.46501/IJMTST061118

Mansour, R. F., & Abdelrahim, E. M. (2019). An evolutionary computing enriched RS attack resilient medical image steganography model for telemedicine applications. *Multidimensional Systems and Signal Processing*, *30*(2), 791–814. doi:10.100711045-018-0575-3

Marc, A., & Michel, B. (1992). Image coding using wavelet transform. *IEEE Transactions on Image Processing*, *1*(2), 205–220. doi:10.1109/83.136597 PMID:18296155

Mishra, A. (2013). Enhancing security of caesar cipher using different methods. *International Journal of Research in Engineering and Technology*, *2*(09), 327–332. doi:10.15623/ijret.2013.0209049

Pandey, D., Pandey, B. K., & Pandey, S. (2011). Survey of Bioinformatics Applications on Parallel Architectures. *International Journal of Computers and Applications*, *23*(4), 21–25. doi:10.5120/2877-3744

Pandey, D., Pandey, B. K., & Wairya, S. (2020). Hybrid deep neural network with adaptive galactic swarm optimization for text extraction from scene images. *Soft Computing*. Advance online publication. doi:10.100700500-020-05245-4

Pandey, D., Pandey, B. K., & Wariya, S. (2019). Study of Various Techniques Used for Video Retrieval. *Journal of Emerging Technologies and Innovative Research*, *6*(6), 850–853.

Pandey, D., Pandey, B. K., & Wariya, S. (2019). Study of Various Types Noise and Text Extraction Algorithms for Degraded Complex Image. *Journal of Emerging Technologies and Innovative Research*, *6*(6), 234–247.

Pandey, D., Pandey, B. K., & Wariya, S. (2020). An Approach To Text Extraction From Complex Degraded Scene. *IJCBS, 1*(2), 4–10.

Park, Sahng, Delp, & Yu. (2004). Adaptive lossless video compression using an integer wavelet transform. *IEEE International Conference on Image Processing*, 2251-2254.

Patani, K., & Rathod, D. (2021). Advanced 3-Bit LSB Based on Data Hiding Using Steganography. In K. Kotecha, V. Piuri, H. Shah, & R. Patel (Eds.), *Data Science and Intelligent Applications. Lecture Notes on Data Engineering and Communications Technologies*. Springer. doi:10.1007/978-981-15-4474-3_42

Pramanik, S., & Bandyopadhyay, S. K. (2013). Application of Steganography in Symmetric Key Cryptography with Genetic Algorithm. *International Journals of Engineering and Technology, 10*, 1791–1799.

Pramanik, S., & Bandyopadhyay, S. K. (2014). Hiding Secret Message in an Image, International Journal of Innovative Science. *Engineering and Technology, 1*, 553–559.

Pramanik, S., & Bandyopadhyay, S. K. (2014). An Innovative Approach in Steganography, Scholars. *Journal of Engineering Technology*, 276–280.

Pramanik, S., Singh, R. P., & Ghosh, R. (2020). Application of Bi-orthogonal Wavelet Transform and Genetic Algorithm in Image Steganography. *Multimedia Tools and Applications, 79*(25-26), 17463–17482. Advance online publication. doi:10.100711042-020-08676-1

Pramanik, S., Singh, R. P., Ghosh, R., & Bandyopadhyay, S. K. (2020). A Unique Way to Generate Password at Random Basis and Sending it Using a New Steganography Technique. *Indonesian Journal of Electrical Engineering and Informatics, 8*(3), 525–531.

Rahmani, M. K. I., Arora, K., & Pal, N. (2014). A crypto-steganography: A survey. *International Journal of Advanced Computer Science and Applications, 5*, 149–154.

Rashmi, N., & Jyothi, K. (2018). An improved method for reversible data hiding steganography combined with cryptography. *IEEE 2nd International Conference on Inventive Systems and Control (ICISC)*, 81-84. 10.1109/ICISC.2018.8398946

Rather, M., & Sengupta, A. (2020). IP Core steganography using switch-based key-driven hash-chaining and encoding for securing DSP kernels used in CE systems. *IEEE Transactions on Consumer Electronics, 66*(3), 251–260. doi:10.1109/TCE.2020.3006050

Restrepo, A., & Bovik, A. (1988). Adaptive trimmed mean filters for image restoration. Acoustics. *IEEE Transactions on Speech and Signal Processing, 36*(8), 1326–1337. doi:10.1109/29.1660

Sauvola, J., & Pietikäinen, M. (2000). Adaptive document image binarization. *Pattern Recognition, 33*(2), 225–236. doi:10.1016/S0031-3203(99)00055-2

Shapiro, J. M. (1993, December). Embedded Image Coding Using Zerotrees of Wavelet Coefficients. *IEEE Transactions on Signal Processing, 41*(12), 3445–3462. doi:10.1109/78.258085

Shen, K., & Edward, J. D. (1999). Wavelet-Based Rate Scalable Video Compression. *IEEE Transactions on Circuits and Systems for Video Technology, 9*(1), 109–122. doi:10.1109/76.744279

Singla, D., & Juneja, M. (2014). An analysis of edge-based image steganography techniques in spatial domain. *IEEE International Conference on Recent Advances in Engineering and Computational Sciences (RAECS)*, 1-5. 10.1109/RAECS.2014.6799604

Sreekutty, M. S., & Baiju, P. S. (2017). Security enhancement in image steganography for medical integrity verification system. *IEEE International Conference on Circuit, Power and Computing Technologies (ICCPCT)*, 1-5. 10.1109/ICCPCT.2017.8074197

Strom, J., & Cosman, P. (1997). Medical Image Compression with Lossless Regions of Interest. *Signal Processing*, *59*(2), 155–171. doi:10.1016/S0165-1684(97)00044-3

Taburet, T., Bas, P., Sawaya, W., & Fridrich, J. (2020). Natural steganography in JPEG domain with a linear development pipeline. *IEEE Transactions on Information Forensics and Security*, *16*, 173–186. doi:10.1109/TIFS.2020.3007354

Tyagi, M. V. (2012). Data Hiding in Image using least significant bit with cryptography. *International Journal of Advanced Research in Computer Science and Software Engineering*, *2*(4), 120–123.

Vellaiappan, E., Kumaravelu, N., Shiva, G., & Vijayabhaskar, P. V. M. (2012). Comparison of Wavelet Filters in Image Coding and Denoising using Embedded Zerotree Wavelet Algorithm. *Research Journal of Applied Sciences, Engineering and Technology*, *4*(24), 5449–5452.

Westin, C. F., Richolt, J., Moharir, V., & Kikinis, R. (2000). Affine adaptive filtering of CT data. *Medical Image Analysis*, *4*(2), 161–177. doi:10.1016/S1361-8415(00)00011-6 PMID:10972328

Yang, Z., Wang, K., Li, J., Huang, Y., & Zhang, Y. J. (2019). TS-RNN: Text steganalysis based on recurrent neural networks. *IEEE Signal Processing Letters*, *26*(12), 1743–1747. doi:10.1109/LSP.2019.2920452

Yongbing, Xu., & Linbo, Xu. (2011). The Performance Analysis of Wavelet in Video coding System. *International Conference on Multimedia Technology (ICMT)*. 10.1109/ICMT.2011.6002109

Zaynalov, N. R., Kh, N. U., Muhamadiev, A. N., Bekmurodov, U. B., & Mavlonov, O. N. (2019). Features of using Invisible Signs in the Word Environment for Hiding Data. *International Journal of Innovative Technology and Exploring Engineering*, *8*(9), 1377–1379.

Zhao, C., Zhao, H., Wang, G., & Chen, H. (2020). Improvement SVM Classification Performance of Hyperspectral Image Using Chaotic Sequences in Artificial Bee Colony. *IEEE Access: Practical Innovations, Open Solutions*, *8*, 73947–73956. doi:10.1109/ACCESS.2020.2987865

Chapter 8
Modern Approaches to Creating Highly Undetectable Stegosystems (HUGO Systems)

Vladimir N. Kustov

Saint Petersburg State University of Railway Transport of Emperor Alexander I, Russia

Alexey G. Krasnov

Nexign, Russia

Ekaterina S. Silanteva

NST LLC, Russia

ABSTRACT

This chapter's primary goal is to provide a comprehensive approach to the development of new highly undetectable stegosystems that greatly complicate their steganalysis. The authors propose several implementations of highly undetectable stegosystems, the so-called HUGO systems, using an integrated approach to their synthesis. This approach most fully considers the features of transmitting hidden messages over highly noisy communication channels. At the stage of embedding hidden messages, the authors suggest actively using their discrete transformations. The authors also propose increasing the secrecy of secret messages by converting them to a form that resembles natural noise. The authors use a discrete chaotic decomposition of the Arnold cat map (ACM) to do this. The authors also suggest using highly efficient noise-tolerant encoding and multi-threshold decoding to combat interference in the communication channel and an embedding algorithm. The authors also describe two original stegosystems ±HUGO and ⊕HUGO and test results confirming their effectiveness.

DOI: 10.4018/978-1-7998-7160-6.ch008

INTRODUCTION

Steganography is a specific field of scientific activity related to creating and researching methods for concealing and detecting information transmission. Similar to cryptography, steganography has also existed since ancient times. But the analogies end there, especially in the field of theory. Over the past half-century, a new discipline called mathematical cryptography or cryptology has been created and successfully developed, in which mathematical models of cryptographic systems are studied. The time has come to develop a new steganography and steganalysis mathematics branch, which should be called steganology. Such attempts in this direction have recently been made more often but still fragmented and insufficient.

The reason for this situation is the increasing complexity of problems arising in steganography. Attempts to construct mathematical models of steganographic systems are associated with considering many cases and sub-cases that do not allow a uniform and straightforward interpretation. In other words, the external environment in which steganographic systems should function has a much larger number of freedom degrees compared to the external environment of cryptographic schemes.

If you want to summarize the new trends in modern steganography briefly, you can list the following distinctive features:

- The Increasing use of still digital photographs as covering objects, with their preliminary conversion using discrete transformations combined with already well-known steganography methods.
- Research in creating new stegosystems with higher data transmission secrecy (Shelukhin & Kanaev, 2018).
- Increased attention to taking into account the presence of interference in communication channels and ways to deal with them (Amirtharajan et al., 2010), (Muttoo & Sushil Kumar, 2011).
- Active use of new self-orthogonal noise-tolerant codes for encoding covering objects with embedded hidden messages when transmitting them over highly noisy communication channels. (Zolotarev et al., 2012).
- Increased attention to new developments of efficient multi-threshold decoders with optimal characteristics of energy consumption, speed and reliability of decoding processes (Zolotarev & Ovechkin, 2016), (Zolotarev & Averin, 2007).
- The transition from a preliminary cryptographic transformation of a hidden message before embedding it in the covering object to using cryptographic transformations directly in the algorithm for embedding a hidden message (Kustov & Krasnov, 2020).
- Active expansion of research in the synthesis of highly detectable stegosystems – Hugo systems (Kustov & Silanteva, 2020).

In this Chapter, the authors have tried to align their research with these areas that characterize steganography's current state.

In their research, the authors tried to fully consider all the features listed above and present their research results in developing mathematical and software models of modern, highly undetectable stegosystems.

Theoretical research in steganography and steganalysis continues to be including the authors of this Chapter.

This Chapter's primary goal is to provide a comprehensive approach to developing new, highly undetectable stegosystems that greatly complicate their steganalysis and present some of these studies' results.

This Chapter's authors consider this content a definite contribution to the newly emerging mathematical sciences branch – steganology.

RESEARCH UNDERGROUND OF HUGO TECHNOLOGY

Let's look in chronological order at the well-known scientific publications that make up the foundation on which the authors conducted their research.

The beginning of research in the field of highly undetectable stegosystem should probably be attributed to the early twentieth century when it was published an article (Westfeld, 2001) which proposed a modification of the algorithm F5 providing high stability from visual attacks at a low degree of detection by statistical attacks and high capacity of embedded messages. The fact is that all existing stegoalgorithms up to this time could not provide a high capacity of hidden messages with a low degree of detection. The proposed F5 algorithm used matrix coding to increase embedding capacity by reducing necessary changes and used permutations with offset. The developed new F5 algorithm withstood visual attacks but simultaneously provided a large embedding capacity. The algorithm F5 used permutation bias to distribute the embedded bits of the hidden message in the DCT (Discrete Cosine Transform)-coefficients of the covering object in JPEG format throughout the steganogram. Thus, an attacker's task to detect a hidden message embedded in the covering object became complicated.

In the following paper (Fridrich et al., 2005), the authors use so-called wet paper codes and introduce the concept of perturbed quantization to describe a new approach to steganography's passive safety. The sender in perturbed quantization embeds the hidden message in the covering object by a quantization operation using loss compression or the so-called down-sampling function. It requires the use of so-called wet paper codes. The authors present a heuristic algorithm, which provides higher steganographic security for covering objects in JPEG format. The results also indicate that the proposed method provides better steganographic security than previously existing stegosystems for JPEG.

In the paper (Fridrich et al., 2007), the authors determine the maximum steganographic capacity of covering objects in JPEG format (that is, the largest payload embedded undetectable) relative to the best methods of steganalysis. When testing stegoalgorithms, the authors evaluate the impact of various parameters, such as JPEG compression, matrix embedding, adaptability of channels, and minimal information on the sender's side. The authors claim that the undetectability of embedding hidden messages for black-and-white covering objects in JPEG format is about 0.05 bits / per one factor for non-zero DCT coefficients.

In further research (Filler & Fridrich, 2010), the authors established a connection between synthesizing a stegosystem that minimizes distortion during embedding and statistical physics. A distinctive feature of this work from previous works is that the authors introduced an arbitrary nature of the distortion function. It allowed the authors to describe changes in the embedding as spatially dependent. As a theoretical basis for constructing stegosystems, the authors used thermodynamic integration to calculate the distortion level and a Gibbs sampler to evaluate the proposed embedding schemes' optimality. The research method reduced the problem of stegosystem synthesis to find the minimum values of the distortion function potentials that determine the statistical undetectability of a hidden message. Having described this method of selecting a specific variant of the distortion function, the authors present experimental justification of the proposed approach and discuss various practical application options in practice.

The authors described another new approach to using additive steganographic embedding in the covering object's spatial domain (Holub & Fridrich, 2012). The authors propose determining the level of change in pixel values in the high-frequency regions of the covering object by its weight and aggregation using the inverse Helder norm to determine individual pixel changes. Unlike other stegosystems, the aggregation rule allows you to embed secret message bits only in highly structured forcibly, natural-noise regions like the covering object, avoiding uniform areas. It allowed to significantly increasing the stability of the proposed scheme for steganalysis. The algorithm's actual implementation is based on the use of syndrome-lattice codes, which would minimize the expected distortion at the payload's specified values.

In previous publications, the authors usually calculated the costs of embedding a hidden message in the covering object's spatial area either one-time or by estimating the total consequences of embedding in the used feature space. In this paper (Fridrich & Kodovsky, 2013), the authors used a different strategy to represent the covering object as some independently distributed quantized Gaussians. The probabilities of making a change in the covering object's pixels are calculated to minimize the total divergence for a given embedding operation and a given payload. The proposed model's apparent simplicity does not prevent the synthesis of stegosystems providing security very close to modern methods for a relatively acceptable range of payloads.

In the paper (Holub et al., 2014), the authors propose a universal approach to describing distortions, called universal wavelet relative distortion (UNIWARD), and apply it to embed a hidden message in both the spatial and frequency domains of the covering object. As a distortion, the sum of changes in the coefficients in various implementations of the covering object's directional filters is taken. The directivity of filtering allows you to explore areas of the covering object, such as textures or natural noise, while avoiding smooth areas for embedding. The authors present experimental results confirming that the stegosystems built based on UNIWARD either match or exceed the existing methods, both for the spatial domain and the JPEG domain.

In most stegosystems for still digital images that use raster formats, the amplitude of the changes made is usually limited to the minimum value when implementing a hidden message. However, in the paper (Sedighi et al., 2015), the authors explore ways to increase the embedding volume in highly textured areas of the covering object by significantly growing the embedding amplitude, which leads to an increase in payload. The authors' approach is based on the fact that the probabilities of changes in the covering object's pixels by a certain amount are calculated on the model of the covering object for an optimal statistical test. Embedding consists of two steps. At the first step, the sender evaluates the covering object's statistical parameters, such as pixel variances and pixel values, as independent random variables subject to the Gaussian distribution. The possibility of changing each pixel's value by 1 or 2 is determined, which is converted into the cost of using the embedding of the syndrome-lattice codes, and a system of two nonlinear algebraic equations is solved. The use of the proposed model is demonstrated by the example of two well-known embedding algorithms: HILL and S-UNIWARD.

The view that adding additional information to a hidden message increases the security of the stegosystem has long been indisputable. Additional confirmation of this is the article (Denemark & Fridrich, 2017). The authors investigate the use of a priori information provided by several JPEG images for the same scene if there is no pre-recording access. Authors can use a priori known images in JPEG format to choose changing the separate DCT coefficients in the embedding algorithm. The authors describe the test data obtained by processing conventional images with the addition of synthesized noise, indicating a significant increase in the safety of the stegosystem compared to using a single image. The simulation was carried out by the Monte Carlo method.

They further developed the authors' results in the previous publication in the article (Denemark et al., 2018). As in the last case, the secret message is hidden in the covering object in the form of adding a noise signal to it, which is a heteroscedastic noise introduced naturally on the recipient's side. This method's main requirement is that the covering image is available in raw form (this operation is called "sensors capture"). This article suggests embedding the hidden message in the DCT coefficients of a JPEG file by adding random values of heteroscedastic noise to the corresponding pixels to make the embedding look like the covering object's same image (switch the original covering objects). The authors suggest using two digital cameras to demonstrate the proposed method, monochrome, and the other is color. The authors investigated several algorithms for embedding different added noise models into DCT coefficients and use cases of demosaicing for converting raw values of the covering object. The experiment results demonstrated that the use of the developed models significantly increases the safety of the stegosystem. A substantial payload can be embedded for monochrome covering objects or low JPEG quality factors while providing a high-security level.

The most recent work results in JPEG steganography are published in (Boroumand & Fridrich, 2020). The article discusses two different strategies for improving the security of stegosystems, which allow modifying each selected pixel of the DCT coefficients of the covering object by +1 or -1 with unequal probabilities. The first strategy involves knowing quantization errors in the covering object's design/processing before implementing the hidden message. The second strategy uses embedding in disjoint sublattices while using heuristics to align the polarity of neighboring changes. In this article, the authors propose a combined method for using both strategies. The new results obtained by the authors experimentally confirm an increase in security for several types of additional information in steganalysis on two data sets using the mathematical apparatus of convolutional neural networks.

THEORETICAL BACKGROUND OF HUGO TECHNOLOGY

Stegosystem Model Description

To describe the mathematical model of the stegosystem, the authors use an information-theoretic approach.

A pair of reversible transformations define the stegosystem: Emb and Ext, which are used respectively to embed a hidden message in the covering object and to extract this message from the stego:

stego = Emb(covering object, hidden message, key),

hidden message = Ext(stego, key).

It is required that, for any given key, it is likely enough to extract from the stego exactly the hidden message that was embedded in it.

The Emb transformation is, generally speaking, not universally defined. For simplicity, we define it further by assuming that for every triple (the covering object, hidden message, key) that is not in the scope of the definition, the Emb transformation value is equal to the empty string λ.

Usually, models of stegosystems assume the presence of an opponent who controls the communication channel. The opponent's main assumption is that he will pass through the communication channel those covering objects that will seem natural to him.

Creating a mathematical model of a natural covering object (container) is a significant research problem in steganography.

Authors have tried in their research to at least partially try to contribute to the solution of this problem. The authors attempt to disguise the hidden message under the channel's natural noise by discrete chaotic mapping to the hidden message.

The following three types of opponents are mentioned in the steganography literature (Simmons, 1984):

- **passive** - acts as described in the classical Simmons model;
- **active** - can make small changes to the passed container. As a rule, he is assumed that his intervention should remain invisible to the recipient;
- **malicious** - there are no restrictions on his actions. He can change containers or even block the communication channel.

The lack of clear criteria that distinguish active opponents from malicious ones is another serious problem when building a mathematical theory of steganographic systems.

The main threats to the security of steganographic systems include:

- **Detection of the steganographic channel.** It is the weakest of the security threats to stegosystems. A passive opponent can carry it out.
- **Retrieving a hidden message.** The opponent must find the hidden message contained in this stego. There is also a weaker version of this threat: the opponent must get partial information about the hidden message. A passive opponent can also carry out this threat.
- **The destruction of the hidden message.** Such a threat exists only from an active enemy. In this case, opponents must make such acceptable changes to the container that the recipient cannot extract the hidden message from him.
- **The substitution of a hidden message.** It is the most powerful of threats; an active opponent can only carry it out. The opponent must replace the hidden message in the container with another message that benefits him so that recipient does not suspect the substitution.

The following main types of attacks on steganographic systems are known (Johnson & Jajodia, 1998):

- **Attack with a known stego.** The weakest of all possible attacks, which a passive opponent can always carry out.
- **Attack with a known container.** The opponent receives a container sent from the sender to the recipient and the corresponding empty container.
- **Attack with a known hidden message.** This attack is only possible in a steganographic channel with repetitions and can be carried out by a passive opponent. It's assumed that the opponent knows stego and maybe the corresponding empty container.
- **Attack with a choice of a hidden message.** Similar to the previous one, but the opponent can choose the hidden message.

Formally, the stegosystem must meet the following requirement. Let C be the set of all containers (empty – covering objects, and stego - containers with hidden messages), and K is a key, M — the set of hidden messages, and $S = \{s = \text{Emb}(c,m,k), s \neq \lambda \mid c \in C, m \in M, k \in K\}$ is the set of stegos. Note that $S \in C$.

One of the essential characteristics of a steganographic channel is the payload (or capacity), which is the maximum possible length of a hidden message in bits embedded in a single covering object to this covering object's size in bytes.

Experts involved in the analysis of stegosystem to detect vulnerabilities in their structures are called steganalytics, and the scope of their activities is called steganalysis.

In their studies of the stability of stegosystem to hacking, the authors believe that the probability distributions on the sets of stego and covering object, in this case, should be almost indistinguishable. The authors define indistinguishability as a statistical characteristic relative to various stegoalgorithms. The authors would then use the following terminology. The sender uses the cover object (container) and the G function to noise the cover object. The covering object is a still digital copy of a photograph of the object. The purpose of the G function is to apply noise distortion to this digital photocopy. Further in their research, the authors propose to create a steganography channel by masking the embedding of a secret message under distortions resembling natural noise generated by the G function.

Discrete Transformations of the Covering Object

Steganography methods that use a still digital image as a covering object consist of two broad classes: the first class of methods embeds a secret message into the covering object's spatial area. The second class of methods does this in the frequency area. The first class of methods changes the covering object's spatial area, such as its pixels. However, these methods are susceptible to certain graphical transformations of the covering object, such as zooming out or zooming in, noise, compression, and other changes that make it impossible to extract the hidden message.

The second group of methods embeds hidden messages in the frequency spectrum of the covering object. This group of methods uses preliminary discrete transformations of the covering object's frequency spectrum into the spectrum's low-frequency and high-frequency parts. The embedding of a secret message is usually carried out in the high-frequency area of the spectrum. The researcher can use this group of methods for various formats of covering objects. The following discrete transformations are applied:

- Discrete Cosine Transform (DCT);
- Discrete Hadamard Transform (DHT);
- Discrete Wavelet Transform (DWT);
- Discrete Fourier Transform (DFT);
- Singular Value Decomposition (SVD).

Note that DWT and DCT are most commonly used. It is because researchers used these methods to develop widely used compression algorithms JPEG2000 and JPEG.

Discrete Chaotic Transformations of a Hidden Message

Chaos theory is a branch of mathematics that deals with systems that exhibit chaotic behavior under certain conditions. Even for the random behavior of some deterministic systems, the concept of chaos is applicable. In this case, this behavior is called deterministic chaos. It also is referred to as a branch of mathematics called deterministic chaos theory.

The description of deterministic chaos usually uses the chaotic transformation (decomposition or map). At the moment, there are more than 150 different chaotic maps. Chaotic maps are classified according to the following classification features:

- Time-domain: continuous, discrete;
- Space domain: real, rational, complex, discrete;
- Number of space dimensions: 1, 2. 3, arbitrary;
- Number of parameters: 0, 1, 2, 3, 4, 6, 9, 10, 18, variable.

Discrete chaotic transformations of hidden messages presented as still images disguise them as natural noise in the steganography communication channel.

To convert a hidden message presented as a still digital image, you need to convert it to a form that closely resembles the communication channel's noise. It is usually gone using discrete chaotic maps.

It should be emphasized that to use a chaotic discrete mapping to mask a hidden message under natural noise, it must, among other things, have the encryption property (to ensure confidentiality) of a two-dimensional object. When performing a chaotic mapping, a secret key must be generated. Using the key ensures that the mapping is reversible. Besides, the mapping must be deterministic, finite, and easily calculated.

From the complete satisfaction with the above properties, the authors in their research chose the chaotic mapping of the Arnold Cat Map (ACM) to mask hidden messages under natural noise.

ACM has the following values for the listed classification features:

- Time-domain: discrete;
- Space domain: discrete;
- Number of space dimensions: 2;
- Number of parameters: 2.

Self-Orthogonal Error-Correcting Codes and Error-Correcting Multi-Threshold Decoding

Error correction in communication channels with noise is usually performed by applying noise-tolerant codes. The theory of noise-tolerant coding offers a wide range of codes and corresponding decoding methods, characterized by error correction efficiency. The most promising class of codes in this regard is self-orthogonal codes (SOC), which are usually decoded using multi-threshold decoders (MTDs). For correctly selected codes, these decoders have optimal decoding and polynomial decoding complexity.

In their research, the authors suggest using SOC for the noise-tolerant encoding of the covering object in 2 stages.

At the first stage, the noise-tolerant encoding of the source coverage object is performed. Then, using the ACM algorithm, a discrete chaotic transformation of the hidden message is performed. After that, the hidden message looks like a natural noise. Next, the Emb operation is performed, which results in the required stego. If the communication channel had ideal characteristics and had zero intrinsic noise, it would be possible to send the received stego to the communication channel. However, there is always noise in the communication channel in practice, introduced into the transmitted stego as interference.

Therefore, the second stage of repeated noise-tolerant coding of the stego using SOC is necessary. After the second stage of encoding, the stego is transmitted to the communication channel, interfered with by noise.

The noisy stego on the receiver side from the communication channel goes to the multi-threshold decoder (MTD). The interference introduced into the stego by the communication channel is eliminated.

Next, the ACM-encoded hidden message is extracted by re-decoding the interference-free stego using the MTD. Note that the hidden message is a collection of interference removed at this stage. Also, note that the repeated extraction of noise from the stego at this stage is the Ext operation to extract hidden messages.

The hidden message is now ready to perform the reverse ACM conversion (RACM), which it undergoes. After that, the hidden message takes its original form and is passed to the recipient.

Given the use of a binary synchronous channel (BSC) for data transmission in the model, this stegosystem can be briefly described in the following notation: SOC&ACM&SOC&**BSC**&MTD&MTD&RACM.

This approach was called the integrated approach by the authors and is described below.

AN INTEGRATED APPROACH TO THE SYNTHESIS OF STEGOSYSTEM

In this section, the authors present an attempt to move to an integrated solution of problems in the field of modern stegosystems synthesis. The authors generalize the concept of a software simulation model that uses transmitting secret messages in digital still images, taking into account all its aspects. From the sender to the recipient, all the hidden stages of message processing are also considered. The simulation model uses DWT and new algorithms of hiding that support ACM decomposition. Also, the effectiveness of noise-resistant cryptography and multi-threshold decoders ensures the reliability and integrity of secret messages transmitted over high-noise communication channels are shown.

In this stegosystem model, the authors use the LSB methodology in conjunction with the DWT (LSB&DWT).

Figure 1 shows a generalized simulation model of the stegosystem. In the proposed model, a digital image presented in bmp format is used as a hidden message.

Figure 1. A generalized model of stegosystem

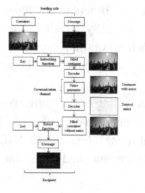

Selecting a graphic object as a secret message ensures that it is more resistant to interference with transformations.

The block shown in Figure 2 implements hidden message embedding functionality and is the main block of the simulation model. Let's take a closer look at its functions.

Figure 2. Embedding function block

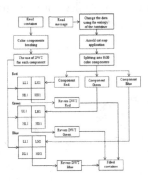

First of all, it is intended for executing a DWT of a covering object and embedding in it a pre-converted hidden message file using the stegoalgorithm.

For each level of decomposition of the covering object, the DVT is first performed vertically and horizontally. The result of the first decomposition is a 4x4 block, illustrated in Figure 3a.

Figure 3. The DWT, after two steps

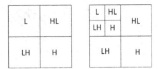

The DWT is then performed exclusively within the part (L) obtained in the previous DWT step (see Figure 3b).

The hidden message, meanwhile, is being decomposed by the ACM. In discrete chaotic maps, the ACM is known as the chaotic transformation on the torus surface. Vladimir Arnold (Saxena, 2011) first proposed ACM.

ACM can also be described as a chaotic two-dimensional transformation by the following formulas:

$p'=q(\mod 1)$,

$q'=p+2q(\mod 1)$.

The matrix representation of these relations has the following form:

$$\begin{Vmatrix}1 & 1 \\ 1 & 2\end{Vmatrix}\begin{Vmatrix}p \\ q\end{Vmatrix} = \begin{Vmatrix}0 & 1 \\ 0 & 1\end{Vmatrix}\begin{Vmatrix}0 & 1 \\ 1 & 1\end{Vmatrix}\begin{Vmatrix}p \\ p\end{Vmatrix}.$$

These relationships show the dynamics of changes in parameter values over a sequential time step.

Because a torus's surface usually represents the ACM space, the variation of each parameter's values is limited to the range from zero to one. It is usually a square with sides equal to one with coordinates q and p. For ACM, it is its graphic illustration. ACM got its name because Vladimir Arnold illustrated it with an image that resembles a cat's head (Fig. 4).

Figure 4. Graphical representation of ACM

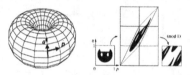

Note that the image subjected to ACM always retains its space and is usually used to describe the chaotic processes dynamics (Figure. 5).

Figure 5. ACM chaotic processes dynamics of the hidden message

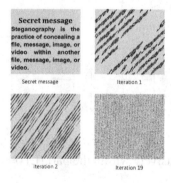

After the hidden message becomes very similar to the noise in iteration 19, it is sent to the input of the embed block, as shown in Figure 1.

After the hidden message is divided into RGB-components, it is introduced using the LSB method in the LH1 area (Figure 2). Then the reverse DWT, designated as (RDWT), is performed, the individual parts of the coverage object are assembled, and as a result of these operations, a new stego is obtained in the form of a filled coverage object/

ACM, during this case, is employed to extend safety. ACM decomposition makes it easy to extract a hidden message, but only if the authorized recipient has a secret key, i.e., iteration number 19. The stego is then sent to the communication channel after applying noise-tolerant coding (Figure 1). The communication channel additionally imposes noise in the stego from the noise generator.

A multi-threshold decoder decodes the noisy stego received from the communication channel to clear the noise introduced in the communication channel by the noise generator and then transmitted to the extraction unit (Figure 1). Then, the extraction unit first performs DWT again. After that, the hidden message components are extracted from the LH1 blocks and used to reverse LSB transformation. Finally, the extracted hidden message using the key is converted to its original form using reverse ACM (RACM) and delivered to the recipient.

One specific feature in the transmission of secret messages over a noisy communication channel is noise-resistant coding.

It is worth noting that for transmitting messages over high-noise communication channels such as radio channels, noise-tolerant coding methods are based on new self-orthogonal codes (SOC) combined with multi-threshold decoders (MTD) are actively used. The well-known simple decoder Messi (Messi, 1963) (Messi, 1969) is considered the MTD prototype. MTD is a new technical design that is based on the efficient use of noise-tolerant codes. The main advantages of MTD are the following:

- Polynomial complexity of calculations;
- High probability of error correction;
- Continuously approaching the optimal of iterative type error correction process;
- Simple design;

Figure 6. MTCBE scheme

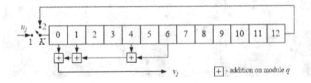

- Ability to use a wide range of code speed, including for high-noise communication channels;
- Lower energy costs with higher productivity.

The device of the multi-threshold encoder considered by the authors was first proposed by Professor Zolotarev (Zolotarev et al., 2012). To synthesize the self-orthogonal code, he developed a multi-threshold

Figure 7. MTCBD with one verification and one information branches

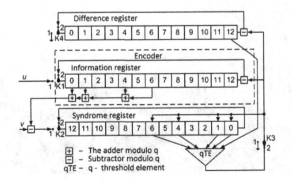

character block encoder (MTCBE) scheme with a single information branch shown in Figure 6. The structure of the encoder is straightforward. The encoder consists of only three adders, modulo q (where q = 256) and one shift register.

Professor Zolotarev also proposed a multi-threshold character block decoder (MTCBD) scheme for this code, shown in Fig. 7. In this scheme, the function of the verification branch is assigned to the syndrome register, and the information register is used as the information branch.

The MTCBD contains the following components: a shift register, a threshold element (TE), and an adder and subtractor modulo q. TE counts the most common characters in the checked current positions of the shift and syndrome registers in this scheme. Let the symbol q_1 occur k_1 times, and the symbol q_2 occur n_1 times. In this case, TE compares the value $|k_1 - n_1|$ with the specified threshold value in TE and corrects the corresponding elements if their values exceed the threshold value.

Figure 8. Covering object

In their research, the authors will use to model the communication channel its representation in the form of a binary synchronous channel (BSC), the so-called channel without memory, with an exponential law of error flow distribution.

Figure 9. Stego with 25% noise

The image file shown in Figure 8 was used as the covering object.

Figure 9 shows a 25% noise level stego at the BSC output, which results from embedding a hidden message in the covering object and then making it noisy in the BSC.

The noisy stego is passed to MTCBD for processing. After the noise is eliminated, the cleared stego is sent to the hidden message extraction block. It is extracted using the reverse LSB transformation and then applied to the RACM. It takes its original form and is transmitted to the recipient.

According to the authors, the conducted research is a successful attempt of an integrated approach to solving highly undetectable systems synthesis. In their study, the authors use a simulation model of the stegosystem, which includes the following main components: ACM, DWT, LSB, and MTD.

Thus, the stegosystem proposed by the authors can be described by the following notation: ACM& DWT&LSB&RDWT&SOC&**BSC**&MTD&DWT&LSB&RDWT&RACM.

STEGOSYSTEM ±1HUGO

As before, the authors in this section consider covering objects represented by digital still images for transmitting hidden messages and suggest using a highly undetectable model of the stegosystem. The main distinguishing feature of this stegosystem is the minimization of distortions introduced when embedding a hidden message into the covering object by applying an effective embedding algorithm. By distortion, the authors mean a ± 1 operation applied to the bytes of the covering object selected specially and providing a devaluation of the value of the penalty function, which is calculated from the nearest neighborhood of the selected byte. The algorithm proposed by the authors ensures that the covering object remains almost unchanged, even if hidden messages of a sufficiently large volume are embedded in it. In this case, the stego obtained from the embedding operation is practically indistinguishable from the covering object, making it very difficult to solve steganalysis. The authors named the proposed stegosystem model as ± 1Highly Undetectable SteGOsystem model or ± 1HUGO model for short. In the model under study, the implementation of secret messages in the covering object is much more efficient and higher than the LSB algorithm while providing significantly higher stability of stego to steganalysis.

Stegosystem Model

Let three finite sets be denoted as C, M, K. The authors assume that in the proposed stegosystem, they are defined by random values C, M, K and representing the container, hidden message, and key.

Let P be a random value of a variable from a set $\acute{P}$. This variable is intended to introduce to the stego some randomness.

In the stegosystem under consideration, the secret key k, senders, and recipients transmit hidden messages using a random value on the set K. The sender to transmit a message m (a random value of M) creates a stego $s = \mathrm{Emb}(c, m, k, p)$ sends it to the recipient, who, in turn, extracts m, using the extract function $\mathrm{Ext}(s, k)$. The authors also believe that there is a function G of $C \times D$ in C, where D is a random value on the set D that performs the role of noise. Then the sender can also pass a random value $G(c, D)$ to the recipient.

In this formal model, the opponent is represented by a set of binary functions $\{A_c | c \in C\}$, and $A_c: C \to \{0, 1\}$. The opponent must learn to know the value of C to distinguish stego ($S = \mathrm{Emb}(C, M, K, R)$) from noise-free ($C' = G(C, D)$). Then if C is the original covering object (it is assumed that it is known to the opponent), then the expression $A_c(x) = 1$ means that the opponent believes that the covering object $x \in C$ is stego, otherwise if $A_c(x) = 0$, the opponent considers $x \in C$ to be the original covering object.

The first time, the resistance of a stegosystem (to the threat of being hacked by a known container attack) was considered (Johnson & Jajodia, 1998).

An opponent can make two mistakes during an attack, commonly referred to in mathematical statistics as the first and second kind errors. The result of a situation where the opponent takes an empty container (covering an object) for a stego is *an error of the first kind. The second kind of error* occurs when the opponent takes the stego for an empty container. For set C, the average probabilities of the first and second kind errors are usually denoted as α and β, respectively.

The works of (Anderson & Petitcolas, 1998) and (Anderson, 1996) are also well-known. In these works, an upper bound on the channel steganography capacity is formulated using the entropy difference. But it should be noted that this approach is not strictly mathematical. Let's focus on a summary of it. The above authors consider X, Y, and Z as random values respectively on the sets $\mathbf{X}$, $\mathbf{Y}$, and $\mathbf{Z}$. Further, the authors denote the Shannon entropy of a variable X as Ent(X) and the entropy of X under the condition Y as Ent($X|Y$). The ratio Ent($X|Y$) $\leq$ Ent(X) is well-known. The expression Ent($X|Y$) = Ent(X) is valid only if X and Y are independent. *The entropy of X* concerning Y, denoted as REnt($X\|Y$), is a measure of the two distributions equivalence of random variables X and Y and is defined by the following relation:

$$\text{REnt}\left(X \parallel Y\right) = \sum_{x \in \mathbf{X}} \Pr\{X = x\} \log_2 \frac{\Pr\{X = x\}}{\Pr\{Y = x\}}.$$

As $\text{REnt}((X \mid Z) \parallel (Y \mid Z))$, we denote the conditional entropy of X relative to Y under the condition, Z. It is formally described by the following expression:

$$\text{REnt}((X \mid Z) \parallel (Y \mid Z)) = \sum_{z \in \mathbf{Z}} \Pr\{Z = z\} \text{REnt}\left((\mathrm{X}|Z = z) \parallel (Y|Z = z)\right).$$

It is well known that the ratio REnt($X\|Y$) $\geq$ 0 is always true, and REnt $(X\|Y)$ = 0 only when X and Y are the same distributions. From this, it follows that REnt($X|Z$)$\|$($Y|Z$)) $\geq$ 0 and REnt(($X|Z$)$\|$($Y|Z$)) = 0 only if ($X|Z = z$) and ($Y|Z = z$) have the same distributions for any $z \in \mathbf{Z}$. Let ε be an arbitrary real value.

In this case, the following wording is correct (Frith, 2007):

The stegosystem (Emb, Ext) will be called (Cachin, 2004)

- ○ *ε-stable (under the condition of a passive enemy attack)* if REnt ($C'\|S$) $\leq \varepsilon$;
- ○ *stable (under a passive enemy attack)* if it is *0-stable*, i.e., if the random variables S and C' are equally distributed.

Note that the established stability limits of the stegosystem given above are based on the exact knowledge of the distribution laws values S and C'. It is often complicated to fulfill this requirement. Therefore, the authors used the following more straightforward estimates for the statistical effectiveness of their proposed stegosystems.

Figure 10. The neighborhood 3x3 of the specially selected byte

A₁	A₂	A₃
A₄	Bᵢ	A₅
A₆	A₇	A₈

The peak signal-to-noise ratio (PSNR) can be calculated according to the formula below and can be used to show the difference between an empty container and a stego:

$$\text{PSNR} = 10 \log_{10}\left(\frac{255^2}{MSE}\right).$$

This expression determines the ratio between the possible maximum value of the useful signal and the noise's power that distorts this value.

To determine the difference between the pixel intensities of the covering object and the stego, *the Mean-Square Error (MSE)* usual used denoted by the symbol 6 in the following relation:

$$6 = \frac{1}{M*N}\sum_{i=1}^{M}\sum_{j=1}^{M}\left(f(i,j) - f'(i,j)\right)^2,$$

where $f(i, j)$ and $f'(i, j)$ represent the pixel brightness of the covering object and the stego, respectively. A high value of 6 corresponds to a low image quality, and Vice versa.

Capacity is the ratio of the hidden message size V_m calculated in bits to of the covering object size V_c calculated in bytes as indicated in the following formula:

$$\text{Capacity} = \frac{V_m}{V_c}.$$

Correlation (r_{cs}) is used to display the degree of tightness of the paired linear relationship between the covering object C_i and the stego S_i:

Table 1. ±1HUGO algorithm illustration

Type	Bits								
c_i	0	1	0	1	1	0	1	0	0
m_i	1	0	x	0	x	1	0	1	1
k_i	0	1	x	1	x	0	1	0	0
s_i	1	1	x	1	x	1	1	1	1
k_i	0	1	x	1	x	0	1	0	0
m_i	1	0	x	0	x	1	0	1	1
c_i	0	1	0	1	1	0	1	0	0
i	1	2	3	4	5	6	7	8	9

$$r_{cs} = \frac{\sum_{j=1}^{:}(c_j - \bar{c})(s_j - \bar{s})}{(n-1)1_c 1_s},$$

where: c_j is j byte of covering object C_i; s_j is j byte of stego S_i; $\bar{c}$, $\bar{s}$ - respectively average values of C_i, S_i; 6_c is MSE for C_i; 6_s is MSE for S_i; n is the number of observations; k is the number of bytes in C_i.

Table 2. KPIs of simulation modeling

No.	C	M	$PSNR_c$	$PSNR_s$	r_{cs}	Capacity
1	1670x1040	634x716	45.0551	15.2342	0.9998	0.261
2	1450x980	634x716	47.8424	20.4325	0.9997	0.206
3	1370x758	610x408	49.3422	12.2343	0.9998	0.239

±1HUGO Algorithm

Operation ±1 is performed when embedding the next bit of the hidden message in the lower bit of the specially selected byte of the secret message. The selected B_i byte is the geometric center of the 3x3 neighborhood (see Figure 10).

A byte Bi is considered suitable for embedding operation performing if the inhomogeneity condition specified by relation (1) is met on its 3x3 neighborhood:

$$\varepsilon \geq \left| \frac{\sum_{j=1}^{8} A_j}{8} - B_i \right|, \tag{1}$$

where ε is called sensitivity and is the minimum allowable value of the 3x3 neighborhood inhomogeneity.

The authors believe that improve the proposed stegosystem for steganalysis and is necessary to abandon secret message bits in the covering object's monotone regions. It is the whole point of fulfilling condition 1. As a result, only those areas of the covering object with an acceptable level of heterogeneity are those that have a sufficient frequency of changing pixel brightness levels to embed the hidden message. And in this way, the effect of practical indistinguishability of the covering object from the stego will be achieved.

Note that more straightforward neighborhoods can also be used, such as three consecutive bytes distributed vertically, horizontally, diagonally, or a cross 3x3.

Next, assume that the key K and secret message M are represented by bits k_i and m_i strings, respectively (Kustov & Protsko, 2017). The analogy with the LSB algorithm bits s_i and c_i of S and C, respectively, are also used.

Then for the ± 1HUGO algorithm, the forward and reverse transformations using the bijective eXclusion OR (XOR) operation can be described in the following sequence of steps:

1. The stego calculating operation $s_i = \text{Emb}(c_i, m_i, k_i)$ is performed in the following two steps:

    a. $s_i = XOR(c_i, m_i)$;
    b. $k_i = \neg m_i$,

    if $c_i = m_i$ (indicated by the symbol "x" in Table 1), then the bit is skipped, and the next bit is selected.

1. The operation of a hidden message extracting from the stego $m_i = \text{Ext}(s_i, k_i)$ is performed as follows:

    a. $m_i = XOR(s_i, k_i)$.

Simulation Model Structure and Results

The simulation modeling results in the form of values of key performance indicators (KPIs) obtained in the process are presented in Table 2. These results demonstrate that the developed method successfully performs the task of hiding data. The correlation coefficients' values are very close to 1 with an accuracy

Figure 11. The general simulation model of the stegosystem

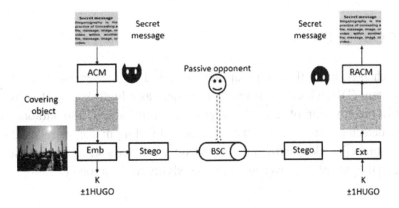

of up to the fourth decimal place. This fact indicates that steganalysis's task becomes complicated since S and C are almost indistinguishable even with a sufficiently high capacity exceeding the value of 0.2.

Figure 11 shows a general simulation stegosystem model.

In this model, the hidden message transformed using the ACM algorithm until it reaches iteration 19 is passed to the embed module, which receives the covering object on another input. By the ±1HUGO method, the embedding module embeds the hidden message in the covering object. It generates stego S and the secret key K. After that; the stego is sent to the BSC from the output passed to the block that extracts the hidden message. The extracted hidden message is then passed to the RACM block to perform reverse ACM using the secret key *K*. As a result, the extracted hidden message is transmitted to the recipient in a non-changeable form.

Figure 12. Forward and reverse stego transformations according to the ⊕HUGO algorithm

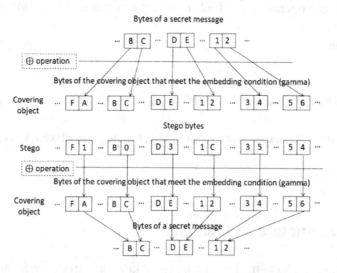

Thus, the stegosystem proposed by the authors can be described by the following notation:

ACM&±1HUGO&**BSC**&±1HUGO&RACM.

⊕HUGO STEGOSYSTEM

In this part of the chapter, the authors present their proposed simulation model of the new highly undetectable stegosystem ⊕HUGO. This simulation model has a high degree of secrecy in embedding a secret message in the covering object. The stegosystem proposed by the authors uses the principle of minimizing the detected changes using the original embedding mechanism based on the use of the mathematical operation ⊕ - addition modulo two used for character strings of the hidden message and specially selected half-bytes of the covering object satisfying the relation (1).

Figure 13. The Class Diagram of the software simulation model

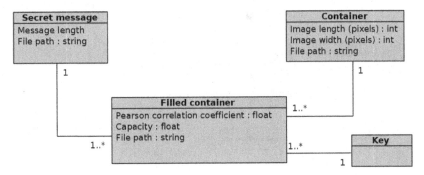

From the point of view of mathematics, the operation $\oplus$ is bijective, which makes it possible for the recipient simply to extract the secret message from the stego using the same operation, of course, if the recipient has the key developed by the sender at the embedding stage. The authors present the results of statistical tests of the simulation model of the developed stegosystem, which confirm its high resistance to steganalysis.

In the next part of the chapter, the authors present a simple example of the $\oplus$HUGO algorithm that demonstrates forward and reverse stego transformations in the stegosystem they developed.

Figure 14. The Use Case Diagram of the software simulation model

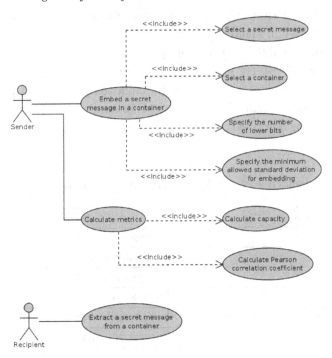

Figure 15. The Activity Diagram of the software simulation model

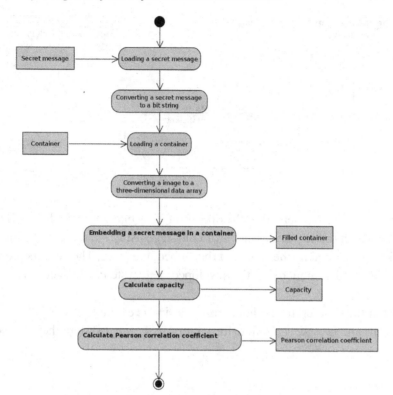

⊕HUGO Algorithm

According to the ⊕HUGO algorithm, the sequence of performing the operations of forward and reverse stego transformations is shown in Figure 12.

Let us describe in more detail the sequence of operations when using the ⊕HUGO algorithm. Let us denote the hidden message - M; the sequence of bytes of the covering object satisfying the formula (1) - C; and the sequence of m bytes of stego used for embedding - S. Let us assume that C, m, and S are strings of bytes of limited length. The sequence of forwarding and reverse stego transformations presented in Figure 12 can be described as follows.

Table 3. The functional dependence of the Pearson correlation coefficient on the capacity

Capacity	Pearson correlation coefficient
0,0020938271604938	0,999999778871843
0,0057975308641975	0,999999395816408
0,0181827160493827	0,999998071126027
0,0613234567901235	0,999993505057878
0,1976049382716049	0,999979058609949
0,5933086419753086	0,999937203360553

Figure 16. The functional dependence of the Pearson correlation coefficient on the capacity

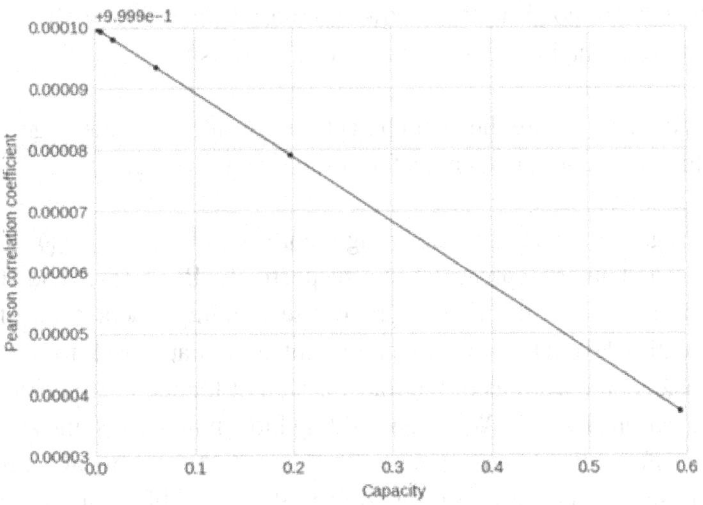

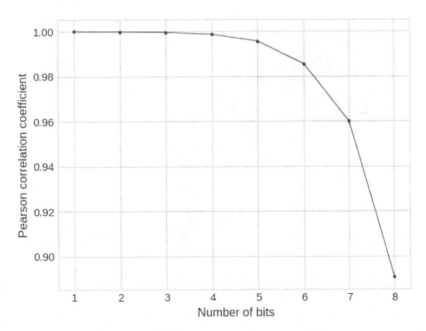

For direct stego transformation (Emb - embedding):

1. The character (half-byte) m_i of the secret message, represented in binary form, is added using the addition operation modulo two $\oplus$ with the right half-byte of the byte ci satisfying the condition (1) of the covering object C. Thus, the right half-byte of the next byte of the stego s_i is formed. This operation corresponds to the mathematical expression: $s_i = m_i \oplus c_i$.
2. Step 1 must be performed for all the mi half-bytes of the secret message.

Figure 17. The functional dependence of the Pearson correlation coefficient from the number of embedded bits

Thus, for $i = 1$, we can write: $s_1 = m_1 \oplus c_1$. In hexadecimal format (for half-bytes) this will look like this: $1 = B \oplus A$, which corresponds to the following binary form: $0001 = 1011 \oplus 1010$.

The reverse stego transformation (Ext - extraction) is done as follows:

1. The operation is done to restore the next character m_i of the secret message: $m_i = s_i \oplus c_i$.
2. Step 1 is done for each subsequent character of the secret message.

For the secret message symbol m_1, the following record is valid: $m_1 = s_1 \oplus c_1$. This entry will look like this in hexadecimal and binary representations, respectively: $B = 1 \oplus A$ and $1011 = 0001 \oplus 1010$.

Thus, in this part of the chapter, the authors propose several implementations of highly undetectable stegosystems, the so-called HUGO systems, using an integrated approach to their synthesis. This approach most fully considers the features of the transmission of hidden messages when transmitted over highly noisy communication channels. When embedding hidden messages, the authors suggest actively using their discrete transformations to mask them. To this end, the authors also propose to increase the secrecy of a secret message by converting it into a form that resembles natural noise. The authors use the discrete chaotic decomposition of the Arnold Cat map (ACM). The authors also suggest using high-performance noise-tolerant coding and multi-threshold decoding to combat interference in the communication channel and an embedding algorithm. The authors also describe the two original stegosystems ± 1HUGO and $\oplus$HUGO and test results confirming their effectiveness.

Figure 18. Plotting 3D graphs based on the Pearson correlation coefficient - sensitivity - the number of implemented bits

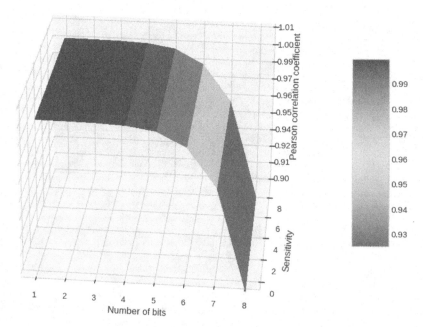

Software Simulation Model

The software simulation model in structural form was implemented in the Universal Modeling Language (UML). The model structure consists of three main components: model Class Diagram, model Use Case Diagrams, and model Action Diagram. Let us take a closer look at these three main components.

The structure of the Class Diagram of the software simulation model is explained in Figure 13.

The structure of the Use Case Diagram of the software simulation model is explained in Figure 14.

The structure of the Activity Diagram of the software simulation model is explained in Figure 15.

The simulation model software package is written in the high-level Python programming language. The choice of this programming language is because it has extensive capabilities in digital still image processing. The Python language's relative laconism allows you to use it to create software simulation models that have a more compact size than their counterparts do. Therefore, Python programs are developed much faster. Also, extensive libraries of programs for scientific research have been created for the Python language.

Simulation Results

The main objectives of the simulation were:

1. Obtaining the Pearson correlation coefficient's functional dependence on the capacity measured as the bit/pixel ratio.
2. Obtaining functional dependence of the Pearson correlation coefficient from the number of embedded bits (1, 2, ..., 8) of a hidden message in every pixel of the covering object, satisfying ratio (1).
3. Plotting 3D graphs based on the Pearson correlation coefficient - sensitivity (given by equation (1)) - the number of implemented bits.

Table 3 and Figure 16 show the results of calculations of the functional dependence of the Pearson correlation coefficient on the capacity.

Figure 17 shows the functional dependence of the Pearson correlation coefficient from the number of embedded bits.

Figure 18 shows plotting 3D graphs based on the Pearson correlation coefficient - sensitivity (given by equation (1)) - the number of implemented bits.

Based on the results of the simulation, the following conclusions can be drawn:

1. The covering object is almost indistinguishable from the stego, even with a sufficiently high degree of capacity. Therefore, even with a very significant load approaching the value of 0.6 bits/pixel, the Pearson correlation coefficient is almost equal to the value of 1.0. The difference is less than 0.00007.
2. These results make it very difficult to solve steganalysis, even with the most modern statistical methods.

Therefore, the following notation can describe the stegosystem proposed by the authors in this part of the Chapter: ACM&$\oplus$HUGO&SOC&**BSC**&MTD&$\oplus$HUGO&RACM.

FUTURE RESEARCH DIRECTIONS

The authors expect to do the following in their further research:

1. Carry out thorough statistical tests of the stability of the developed methods using the following technologies:
   a. "Break Our Stego System" (BOSS);
   b. The assemble method;
   c. The support vector machine (SVM) method.
2. For the synthesis of new stegosystems, significantly expand the list of:
   a. Discrete transformations for covering objects;
   b. Discrete chaotic decompositions for hidden messages.
3. Develop new schemes for SOC encoders and multi-threshold decoders using parallel data processing methods that significantly increase their performance when working in online mode.

CONCLUSION

At the beginning of the Chapter, the authors briefly described the state of research in steganography, based on which the authors conducted their investigation. Then, within the framework of the information-theoretical approach, the authors outlined the main fundamental concepts in steganography, which formed the study's theoretical basis. The authors also outlined the main elements of an integrated approach to synthesizing stegosystems, including discrete transformations of covering objects, chaotic decompositions of hidden messages, noise-tolerant encoding, and multi-threshold decoding of stego transmitted over noisy communication channels. Further, the authors presented an example of the synthesis of the original stegosystem, which can be briefly described in the following form using the notation proposed by the authors: ACM&DWT&LSB&RDWT&SOC&BSC&MTD&DWT&LSB&RDWT&RACM. The authors then describe the two highly undetectable stegosystems they offered, designated by the authors as ±1HUGO and $\oplus$HUGO. Each of the authors' stegosystems is accompanied by a detailed description of their functioning using visual examples. The presentation of the description of the developed stegosystem ends with a discussion of the results of software simulation, confirming their high resistance to steganalysis.

ACKNOWLEDGMENT

The authors sincerely thank the companies they work with to provide an enabling environment for the research presented in this Chapter, despite the Covid-19 pandemic limitations. Among such companies, the authors consider it necessary to mention: Saint Petersburg State University of railway transport of Emperor Alexander I, "GIS CA" LLC, "Gasinformservice" LLC, JSC "Nexign" and NST LLC.

REFERENCES

Amirtharajan, R., Akila, R., & Deepikachowdavarapu, P. (2010). Comparative Analysis of Image Steganography. *International Journal of Computers and Applications*, *2*(8), 41–47.

Anderson, R. (1996). Stretching the limits of steganography. *Proceeding of the 1st International Workshop on Information Hiding*, *1174*, 39–48. 10.1007/3-540-61996-8_30

Anderson, R., & Petitcolas, F. (1998). On the limits of steganography. *IEEE Journal on Selected Areas in Communications*, *16*(4), 474–481. doi:10.1109/49.668971

Boroumand, M., & Fridrich, J. (2020). Synchronizing Embedding Changes in Side-Informed Steganography. *Proc. IS&T, Electronic Imaging, Media Watermarking, Security, and Forensics*, *290*, 1-12.

Cachin, C. (2004). An Information-Theoretic Model for Steganography. *Information and Computation*, *192*(1), 41–56. doi:10.1016/j.ic.2004.02.003

Denemark, T., Bas, P., & Fridrich, J. (2018). Natural Steganography in JPEG Compressed Images. *Proc. IS&T, Electronic Imaging, Media Watermarking, Security, and Forensics*, *316*, 1-10.

Denemark, T., & Fridrich, J. (2017). Steganography with Multiple JPEG Images of the Same Scene. *IEEE TIFS*, *12*(10), 2308–2319. doi:10.1109/TIFS.2017.2705625

Filler, T., & Fridrich, J. (2010). Gibbs Construction in Steganography. *IEEE Transactions on Information Forensics and Security*, *5*(4), 705–720. doi:10.1109/TIFS.2010.2077629

Fridrich, J., Goljan, M., & Soukal, D. (2005). Perturbed quantization steganography. *ACM Multimedia System Journal*, *11*(2), 98–107. doi:10.100700530-005-0194-3

Fridrich, J., & Kodovsky, J. (2013). Multivariate Gaussian model for designing additive distortion for steganography. *Proc. IEEE, ICASSP*, 2949–2953. 10.1109/ICASSP.2013.6638198

Fridrich, J., Pevný, T., & Kodovský, J. (2007). Statistically undetectable JPEG steganography: Dead ends, challenges, and opportunities. *Proceedings of the 9th ACM Multimedia & Security Workshop*, 3–14. 10.1145/1288869.1288872

Frith, D. (2007). Steganography Approaches, Options and Implications. *Network Security*, *2007*(8), 4–7. doi:10.1016/S1353-4858(07)70071-5

Holub, V., & Fridrich, J. (2012). Designing Steganographic Distortion Using Directional Filters. *IEEE Workshop on Information Forensics and Security*, 234-239.

Holub, V., Fridrich, J., & Denemark, T. (2014). Universal Distortion Function for Steganography in an Arbitrary Domain. *EURASIP Journal on Information Security*, *2014*(1).

Johnson, N. F., & Jajodia, S. (1998). Steganalysis of images created using current steganography software. *Proceeding of 2nd International Workshop on Information Hiding*, 1525, 273–289. 10.1007/3-540-49380-8_19

Kustov, V., & Krasnov, A. (2020). *Software model of a highly undetectable stegosystem - ⊕HUGO model. Journal of Physics: Conference Series*.

Kustov, V., & Silanteva, E. (2020). ±1Highly Undetectable Stegosystem Model Using Digital Still Images. *Proceeding of 43rd International Conference on Telecommunications and Signal Processing (TSP)*, 6-9. 10.1109/TSP49548.2020.9163587

Kustov, V. N., & Protsko, D. K. (2017). A Software model of steganography on the basis of a combination of methods LSB and DCT. In *Science and education in the XXI century. Collection of scientific papers on the materials of the XVIII international scientific-practical conference*, (part 3, pp. 49-54). Tambov, LLC "Ucom Consulting Company". https://ukonf.com/doc/cn.2017.02.03.pdf

Kustov, V. N., & Protsko, D. K. (2018). Using a discrete wavelet transform to embed information in images. In *Science and education in the XXI century Collection of scientific papers based on the materials of the XVII international scientific conference* (pp. 15-20). Center for Scientific Conferences "International Research Federation Public science". https://www.elibrary.ru/item.asp?id=35398976

Massey, J. (1969). Shift-register synthesis and BCH decoding. *IEEE Transactions on Information Theory, IT-15*(1), 122–127. doi:10.1109/TIT.1969.1054260

Messey, J. (1963). *Threshold decoding* (Dissertation). Dept. of Electrical Engineering, Massachusetts Institute of Technology, Technical report. http://dspace.mit.edu/handle/1721.1/4415

Muttoo & Kumar. (2011). A multilayered secure, robust and high capacity image steganographic algorithm. *World of Computer Science and Information Technology Journal, 1*(6), 239–246.

Saxena, D. (2011). Digital Watermarking Algorithm based on Singular Value Decomposition and Arnold Transform. *International Journal of Electronics and Computer Science Engineering, 1*(1), 22–27.

Sedighi, V., Fridrich, J., & Cogranne, R. (2015). Content-Adaptive Pentary Steganography Using the Multivariate Generalized Gaussian Cover Model. *Proc. SPIE, Electronic Imaging, Media Watermarking, Security, and Forensics 2015*, 9409, 13.

Sheluhin, O. I., & Kanaev, S. D. (2018). *Steganography. Algorithms and software implementation.* Hotline – Telecom.

Simmons, G. J. (1984). The prisoners' problem and the subliminal channel. *Publishing in Crypto, 83*, 51–67. doi:10.1007/978-1-4684-4730-9_5

Westfeld, A. (2001). High capacity despite better steganalysis (F5 – a steganographic algorithm). In *Information Hiding, 4th International Workshop*, volume 2137 *of Lecture Notes in Computer Science* (pp. 289–302). Springer-Verlag.

Zolotarev, V. V., & Averin, S. V. (2007). Non-Binary MulKustjvtithreshold Decoders with Almost Optimal Performance. Report at 9-th ISCTA'07.

Zolotarev, V. V., & Ovechkin, P. V. (2016). High-Speed Viterbi decoder based on graphic processors. *Proceedings of the all-Russian scientific and technical conference "Intellectual and information systems"*, 7-10.

Zolotarev, V. V., Zubarev, Y. B., & Ovechkin, G. V. (2012). *Multi-Threshold decoders and optimization theory of coding.* Hotline – Telecom.

Chapter 9
IoT Security Using Steganography

Atrayee Majumder Ray
Netaji Subhash Engineering College, India

Anindita Sarkar
Netaji Subhash Engineering College, India

Ahmed J. Obaid
University of Kufa, Iraq

Saravanan Pandiaraj
King Saud University, Saudi Arabia

ABSTRACT

Internet of things (IoT) is one of those emerging technologies, which are going to rule the world in the next few decades. Due to the advancement of low-cost computing systems and mobile technologies, these physical things are now capable of sharing and collecting data with minimal human interference. However, these devices are exposed to various security threats regarding privacy and data confidentiality as they are openly accessible to all in the network. Moreover, many IoT devices have low processing power and weak security level which could be the main targets for hackers. Lightweight cryptographic schemes are used to meet the security needs in IoT environment. Steganography is used as another security tool for IoT devices. This chapter is an attempt to analyze the various steganography techniques used to strengthen the security needs of IoT devices as per their applications. IoT security schemes using different steganography models and algorithms are outlined here with their relative advantages and disadvantages.

DOI: 10.4018/978-1-7998-7160-6.ch009

I INTRODUCTION

In recent times IoT plays an important and crucial part in the domain of information and communication technology. Internet Of Things is a scheme of dissimilar components which are linked over internet and each having unique identifier. These connected devices or 'things' which are also called the smart objects(ex IP cameras) are implanted with different software and sensors having computing ability those are able to collect and exchange data without human interference with other devices or systems over the internet. The number of such connected devices is increasing every day and there is an estimation that the number would exceed 25 million within a year. These devices include medical devices, household appliances, smart TVs, IP cameras, vehicles, electric meters and controls, traffic controls, street lights as well as digital assistants like Amazon Alexa and Google Home. The connectivity of these devices now not only restricted to the traditional end users such as mainframes, desktops and laptops but also expanded to hand hold smart phones and tablets. As a result use of these IoT devices has enormously increased in our daily life and that's why there is an enhanced requirement to scrutiny the security issues of IoT devices. It is really a very challenging task to maintain the data security in IoT. It should not be neglected specially in case of home appliances, smart televisions, IP cameras, remote health monitoring etc where there is a lack of confidentiality and could be easily hacked (Atamli & Martin, 2014). Due to the significant improvement of computing facility several vulnerabilities and threats have occurred for IoT devices which led to implement strong security systems for them.From the security threats of view IOT devices were amongst the top five in 2015 (Bradley, 2015). However, IoT devices have the limitations of having lower battery capacity, less computing power and less memory. Due to this resource constrained environment, traditional strong cryptographic models would not work for it. Lightweight cryptographic models may be a solution. Researchers are still looking for alternative solutions. It is found that Steganography may be a good solution for specific IoT applications. The main focus of this section is to investigate the different ways to achieve security in IoT devices using Steganography.

IoT devices are handled both internally (for Software upkeep) and externally (to communicate with other devices) by a management unit which is called command and control (C&C) centre. These units are accountable for the configuration of the software, upkeep, upgradation of the firmware to cover bugs and vulnerabilities, and finally for the authentication and provisioning of tasks. Communication among devices is facilitated by application program interface (API). Once the manufacturer declares its API, the data exchange and communication process can process with different devices or other applications . Even some APIs are able to govern other devices. For example, a construction manager are able make use of an API to remotely lock any doors inside a definite room/office. C&C centres and APIs use to manage daily IoT operations. An IoT device generates a vast amount of data, a subsequent portion of which is related to exclusive information of its individual users. This information includes credit card details, online browsing/ purchases records, personal health information etc. If the device is not properly secured then these personal information would be left vulnerable for hackers. These vulnerable devices are also exploited by hackers to capture the areas of the system where they are organised to extract more delicate data. The use of IoT in medical field is also very common now. Medical uses of IoT includes remote heart monitoring, remote tuning of pacemakers and defibrillators act. These devices are also exposed to security threats and could be exploited by hackers to hinder a patient's medical health. The centralized nature of IoT devices generates a number of new vulnerabilities and threats. Sometimes the end-users need to physically copy the updates from C&C centre directly due to connectivity issues. This may introduce new vulnerabilities to the devices which are running on outdated software. As APIs are the gateway to a C&C centre, they use to face various threats such as middle man attack, distributed denial of service, code injections etc. Moreover, Manufacturers provide weak or easily decipherable passwords. Devices with such passwords may become a easy target for hackers while left for remote access. Improperly secured Internet Of Things devices are also susceptible to being captured by hackers and can be use in a bonnet – a collection of malware – infected devices connected over internet. As IoT devices are more erudite now, they have become open to all types of cyber attacks, including widespread spam and phishing attacks as well as distributed denial of service attacks. The latter have been growing in the current scenarios mainly due to availability of large number of less protected IoT devices. So, an enormous and progressive research actions are required to accomplish complete security of IoT devices and variety of new security schemes could be experimented to find the most suitable one. This section depicts the ways to achieve security aspects of IoT devices via different Steganographic applications. Definition of IoT is explained in the given below Figure .

Figure 1. Definition of Internet Of Things

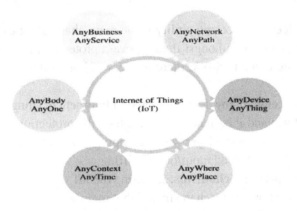

Figure 2. IoT Ecosystem

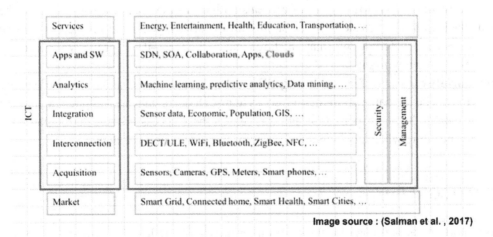

Image source : (Salman et al. , 2017)

Internet of Things Ecosystem

The IoT devices cannot exist in void. It can be defined as an ecosystem of different web devices that can transfer information. IoT is also well-organized with Big Data and also Cloud Computing,, Embedded processing and Connectivity and Sensing are also part of it. The IoT ecosystem can sense the surrounding temperature, gyroscope, pressure, etc. and make the surrounded processing using IoT devices. Figure 2 describes an IoT ecosystem.

Smart Yet Flawed-Vulnerabilities of IoT

The vulnerabilities of IoT are summarized as follows:

Weak and easily recognized passwords: Maximum IoT devices that we get from the market have predetermined authorisations (usernames and passwords) given by the manufacturer. These default identifications are easily available to the outsiders and can be disturbed by the attackers. Thus for more security purpose IoT devices must be customary with new login criteria by the administrators before making it public.

Unsafe network services: Networking ability is the main characteristics of IoT devices which permits the end nodes to interconnect amongst them above a protected internet connection. Whenever a device come across any unsecured network, there is a loss of important data and verification processes may be avoided.

Corruption IoT ecosystems: If any devices related to Internet Of Things are amalgamated with any central organisation platform and inheritance systems, then the protection vulnerabilities are easily introduced by the users at the application layer which comprises of negotiated verification controls, weak encryption procedures and unenhanced input/output sifting.

Absence of proper updating mechanisms: Updating the IoT devices is an essential part of security. But sometimes there is a lack of this mechanism and that mainly involves the lack of firmware authentication and also safe delivery. In order to prevent the IoT related devices from any compromisation the companies must have the eligibility to send real-time updates to every end nodes at the moment they're made available.., IoT devices may run with outdated if this error is not corrected.

Lack of confidentiality: IoT devices often deals with user's personal details, which may be like hot cake to the hackers if they can sidestep the significant security aspects and verification measures. The broader IoT system - including information stores and API edges –if not properly secured can also be leveraged to leak the important data.

Inappropriate data transfer and storage: Even the vast IoT components can be browbeaten if operators fail to encode the data within their IT ecosystems. Delicate data are whipped at collection point, while in the path or during dispensation. For this reason these access accounts are regarded as the top priority for controlling when handling a collection of interconnected IoT devices.

II. STEGANOGRAPHY

The two important methodology for information protection in the IoT scenario are Cryptography and Steganography. While classical cryptography deals with concealing the message content, Steganography deals with covering the statistic that the secret information is actuality sent together with the message

Figure 3. Steganography Process

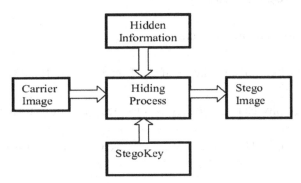

content. Mainly Steganography deals with walloping messages in a manner that the potential monitors are not even aware that the message has been sent. The word Steganography means "covered writing" deriving from Greek' Steganographia ("stegos" meaning "cover" and "grafia" meaning "writing")) (Khosravi et al., 2011).In the past invisible ink or hidden tattoo were used for conveying steganography content but now a days different computer networks are used as communication channel in Steganography. Steganography process is depicted in Figure-3.

There are two aspects in Steganography –message and carrier. Message is the secret information that is to be concealed and carrier is where the message to be hidden(Cachin, 2005).

Figure 4. Classification of Steganography

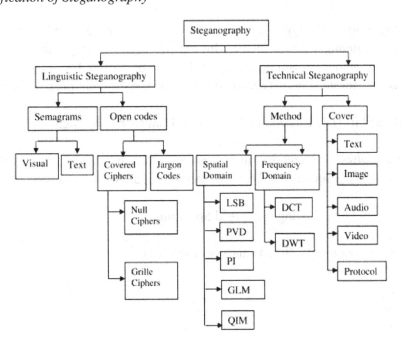

A. Classification of Steganography

Steganography is mainly divided into three classes,

- Pure Steganography–Here no stego key is used. It is considered that the message is unknown to any one else
- Secret key Steganography-Here stego key is swapped preceding to message. This is excessive vulnerable to interruption.
- Public key Steganography-Here both public key as well as private key is used for protected communication.

Few Important Types of Steganography in Digital Mediums

a)Text Steganography- It is obtained either by altering the full text format or by replacing characters in the text. Different types of text Steganography are:

i)Format Based Method; ii) Random and Statistical Method; iii) Linguistics Method

In text Steganography three types of coding are used:

1. **Line-Shift Coding**: In this type the coding is done by moving the areas of content lines vertically, finally we can embed the secret word from the format file
2. **Word-Shift Coding**: this type of coding is one where the word inside the text are moved horizontally
3. **Feature Coding**: This coding technique picks the text topographies after the image have been investigated . the highlights those depends on the password cannot be changed or adjusted,

Image Steganography-In this type the cover or the carrier is an image in which data is hidden. Pixel intensities are used for hiding the data. Image. This type of Steganography is the most popular one because of the enormous amount of automated image data can be accessed with the increase availability of digital cameras and elevated internet speed .distribution. The different image Steganography are

i).Data Hiding Method ii).Data Embedding Method iii).Data Extracting Method

Audio Steganography-The secret data in this case is hidden in an audio file. Mainly these data are hidden in WA,AU and MP3 sound files. Different methods of audio Steganography are:

i) Low Bit Encoding ii) Phase Coding iii) Spread Spectrum

Types of Audio Steganography:(Bhattacharyya et al., 2011)

1. Echo Hiding
2. Phase Coding
3. Parity Coding

4.   Spread Spectrum
5.   Tone insertion
    a.   ***Video Steganography****-Secret data or files in this type are hidden in digital video format and the video combined with the pictures are used as the carrier. H.264, Mp4, MPEG, AVI are different video Steganography formats.
    b.   ***Network and Protocol Steganography****-Here the information hiding is done by using the network protocol such as TCP, UDP, ICMP, IP, etc. as the carrier object.

Classification of Steganography Methods

Steganography can be implemented mainly in six methods which are depicted in figure 5.

Figure 5. Steganography Methods

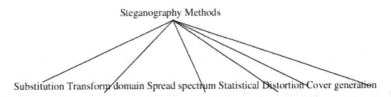

- Substitution process substitute duplicate parts of a cover with a secret message mainly in the spatial domain.
- Transform domain method implant secret information in a transform space of the signal in the frequency domain
- Spread spectrum techniques accept concepts from the spread spectrum communication.
- Statistical methods encrypt data by altering several statistical assets of a cover and use suggestion testing in the extraction process.
- Distortion techniques store data by signal misrepresentation and measure the aberration from the original cover in the decoding step.

III. SCOPE OF STEGANOGRAPY IN DIFFERENT IOT APPLICATIONS

The main aim of IoT is to shape a smart environment and self-conscious independent scenario such as smart living, smart items, smart health, and smart cities among others (Abomhara & Køien, 2014)

Now in this section use of Steganography for providing security to different applications of IoT is discussed.

IOT in Different Fields

Security is mandatory in each IoT application. Steganography is employed in different IoT fields for protecting against the threats. Conventionally, Steganography was mainly based on hiding secret infor-

Figure 6. Different fields of IoT

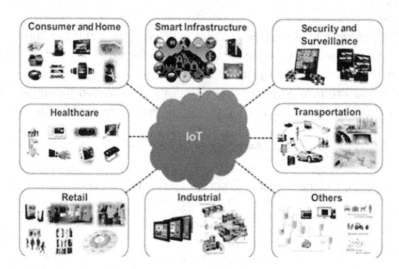

mation in image files but now, awareness in applying stenographic techniques to video files as well as audio files is growing. The advantage of using video files in hiding data is to be added security against hacker attacks due to the relative complication of video compared to image files and audio files

A. IoT in Smart Homes and Industries

Day by day The IoT smart home services are becoming more popular for its comfort and security purposes while away from home. (Yoon et al., 2015), digital components are efficiently communicating with one other using Internet Protocol (IP) addresses. The devices in the smart home are connected through the internet. Due to the increase of smart devices malevolent attacks also increases. But now most of the smart home devices are independent and can be accessed from anywhere anytime, thus decreasing the malicious attacks. A smart home comprises of four sections: service platform, smart devices, home gateway, and home network. There is home gateway that controls the flow of data among the internal devices and the external network.

The IoT also provides a fair chance to build significant industrial systems and applications. Through intelligent IOT one can track the transportation system, can predict the road traffic and future location of the vehicle, allow only the authorized person to access the secured and protected data etc. Global Positioning System (GPS) devices, mobile devices, and actuators and sensors are IoT smart devices used with the transportation and authentication in the industries. The amenities of new IoT technologies are more secured and reliable but still the confidentiality is a more serious issue.

Security Threats in Smart Homes And Industries and few solutions through Steganography:

In the early stages smart homes and industries were more exposed to cyber –attacks as no security parameters were given by the provider and thus these fields are easily prone to cyber-attacks. Snooping is the major security threat in smart home and industries. Few Steganography techniques are discussed below for protecting against the IOT threat.

IP cameras, smart tv and many other home appliances are part of the smart homes. These smart IoT devices lack of proper security. In industries also illegal admittance have significant impact on information privacy and user confidentiality. So in both in homes and industries different access authentication options are used for controlling the unauthorized access. The competence of an authentication system to detect frauds define the confidence level in the IoT Environment.

- Previously tokens and passwords were used for authentication. But these were not so reliable. Those can be lost or stolen. So now a days biometric authentication is becoming more popular like face, fingers, palm prints, iris etc. Least Significant Bit (LSB)Image Steganography and inverted LSB methods are highly used in smart homes for transmission of the secured sensitive data like user face image, between the cameras and home server using within the LAN. The transmission between the home server and the devices those are outside the LAN are encrypted(Yin, Fen, Mughal, & Iranmanesh, 2015).

- Among the different authentication techniques more reliable is through iris because of its unique features (Lai et al., 2017).But still apart from many advantages of these biometric authentication methods the major drawback is that the biometric characters are not replaceable. If once lost it is lost forever and it affects all others applications associated with that feature (Yang, Hu, Wang et al, 2014; Yang, Hu, & Wang, 2014).so for the protection of the biometric features the technique known as cancellable biometrics is practised. Since iris authentication is very reliable so a Steganography based cancellable iris- user authentication system is used... Due to the rotation of the iris a iris feature is set. If this set iris feature is sent directly without any protection to the server and is acquired by the opponent there can be serious problem in security. So a random projection based alteration is employed directed by a user precise key. At the time this confirmation system receives the user's iris image a, a specific security key is generated and a matrix is produced. Then, the non-invertible alteration is functional to each element of the set feature. Finally Steganography technique is use to skin the user-specific security key, which is needed by cancellable biometrics.

The segmented data i.e. only the isolated image of the iris region of the eye after unwrapping into a fixed dimension rectangle is extracted. This extracted data is hidden in the least significant bits (LSBs) of a cover image, in the frequency domain. Sometimes we apply an online Steganography program (Online Steganography Program, 2019) for this purpose.

- ZigBee, a wireless sensor also have adverse application in the field of IOT and is used in GSM based home automation. Its network specification is based on IEEE 802.14.5 wireless protocol and is developed by the ZigBee Alliances .ZigBee is the wireless personal area network standard having low cost, less complexity, and low power consumption .this ZigBee is protected against different IOT threats through public key Steganography which is a protocol of sending hidden message between two unknown parties over a public channel. ZigBee has mainly four layers-Physical layer, Media Access Control layer(MAC),Network layer and Application Sublayer(APS). Each layer has its own tasks. Though different Steganography approaches uses communication protocols for data hiding purposes and the communication layer fields is considered as the cover object but in this Steganography technique the reserved field bits in the layers of IEEE 802.14.5

are used for hiding the secret message. This process triggers the overall security of the ZigBee protocol. Here mainly the reserved field of MAC layer are used for secret message hiding (Backes & Cachin, n.d.).

B. IoT in Health Sector

In healthcare system also the IoT devices are taking its important position for monitoring and assessment of patients (Tarouco et al., 2012) medical condition, Personal Medical Devices (PMDs) are either embedded in patients' body internally or externally. This PMD s are very much common now a days.

Advancement of these Remote digital healthcare based IOT system, medical data transmission is becoming more popular and it's a great challenge for securing the patients' data transmitted and received in the IOT environment (Shehab et al., 2018; Bairagi et al., 2016; Anwar et al., 2015; Abdelaziza et al., 2018; Paschou et al., 2013; Sajjad, Nasir, Khan et al, 2017; Kumar & Lee, 2011).

There are three major aspects in the health care sector for data implanting that employs an IoT distributed structure over various settlements and metropolises.

The aspects are

1. Despatcher position (Patient side): The evidence is managed to ensure its confidentiality and security.
2. Cyberspace (Internet layer) – The grid or storage space which may be disposed to to bouts and information misuse.
3. Headset position (Hospital side) - Interprets the secret data from a stego-image.

Few Steganography Techniques for Its Protection

- A very effective approach in the health sector is by using three colour image Steganography for protecting the medical data in the IOT environment. Here in the first and the third approach all the three colours (red green and blue) and in the second approach two colours (green blue) were used as channels for carrying the secret data. Dynamic positioning technique and by using a shared secret key the information is hidden in the more deeper layer of the image for more security.
- Amalgamation of Steganography with encryption and watermarking is another medical data security technique in the IOT field (Razzaq et al., 2017).this is a very efficient and secured method. The method is divided in three parts-the cover image is first encrypted I using XOR operation then least significant bit (LSB is a steganography process)is used for embedding to produce the stego image and finally the watermarking of the stego image in both spatial and frequency domain is done.
- Another secured stenographic method with minimal dilapidation of the quality is where symmetric RC4 encryption is used for encrypting the confidential patients' information and implanting it within the cover image using portioning approach .the total cover image is partitioned mainly into 8*8 blocks and then manipulated with the help of Integer Lifting Wavelet Transform (ILWT) method. Lastly to locate the exact position of the confidential data, a scanning method called Tree Scan Order (TSO) Is smeared to each operated block (Seyyedi et al., 2016).
- A domain specified mobile cloud based framework is also in use for the outsourcing the medical stego image to the cloud for discriminatory encryption. The visual saliency model type is very

efficient here for detecting the region of interest(ROI) from the transmitted image. A stenographic method known as the directed edge Steganography is used for entrenching the detected ROI in the cover image producing the stego image that is sent to the cloud for specific encryption. This method also helps in the security of the medical data (Sajjad, Muhammad, Baik et al, 2017).

- Inverted Least Significant Bit(LSB) Steganography method has been also used for medical image security purposes.in this process the medical images are employed in terms of the spatial domain and have five subdivisions (Hashim et al., 2020).
  - Affine cipher is utilized for patients secret information to confirm data safety;
  - Huffman Coding is used for encoded lossless information compression preceding for implanting;
  - After selection of the random pixel it is arranged in sub pixels of 8*8 for hiding the LSB of the each pixel. The patients data are also fragmented into blocks of 64 bits, now the LSB bits of the subpixels are replaced within 64 bits of the patients confidential data. The Reverse Bit Function(RBF) is used to verify the resemblance amongst the top-secret bits twosomes preceding to the substitution; if the figure of matching bits is less compared to the mismatched bits, then in this circumstance, there will be a inversion of the patient's confidential data before entrenching, otherwise, there will be a direct implantation of the confidential bits by the RBF system
  - Hiding technique for inserting the patients compressed secret information within the LSB portion of the pixel within a medical image to yield a stego images . This is completed in two stages –random pixel selection and data embedding .Stages are done simultaneously.
  - The abstraction procedure for recovery the implanted patient bits from the stego image.
- DES scheme of Cryptography and LSB scheme of Steganography together boost the medical data security Firstly the secret information encrypted using DES method and then that encoded data and the key are implanted in the concealed image using the LSB scheme at the transmitter side. Reverse Steganography is used in the receiver side to translate the information and the key and finally with the recovered key the data is decrypted.
- There is an interesting scheme where patient data is concealed in the abnormal Electrocardiogram (ECG) signal using Steganography technique. Specifically the medical data is entrenched in a 2D ECG medium of an arrhythmic ECG signal.
- Simple Least Significant Bit Substitution (SLSBS),Variable Least Significant Bit Substitution (VLSBS), Most Significant Bit –Least Significant Bit (MSB-LSB) Substitution Scheme are also different methods of data security in the health sector.
- Hybrid Robust Image Steganography is a secure transmission scheme of biomedical images. The Biomedical images are encoded by means of the logistic chaotic map to interpret it to the cipher image. Cipher image is fragmented into blocks of 8 x 8 pixels. to hide our biomedical images an RGB cover image is taken .the cover image selected is separated into three image planes and each plane is segmented into blocks of 16*16 pixels. Now co occurrence measurement is done for each block in each plane. This co occurrence value of each block, DCT, RIWT is implemented on that block for the embedding process. Embedding map is then calculated in the sender side and sent to the receiver side. Finally QR decomposition method is used on encrypted secret image blocks and RIWT transformed blocks of cover image planes.
- Again in medical field in accompany with Elliptic Curve Cryptography which includes very less number of bits suitable for resources, Least Significant Bit (LSB) Encoding Steganography meth-

od is used to implant the encrypted data into a less complicated image. This method produces a very high level security under IOT cloud devices(Lakshmi Kanth & Siva Narayana, 2020)

- A blend of cryptography (NTRU encryption algorithm) and Steganography (LSB Audio encoding technique) also increase the information security in health care sector. Here healthcare data are entrenched into the cover audio that can easily be retrieved without any doubt of the carrier. Audio file is chosen as replacement features such as LSB are available in different formats in this type of file. The Steganography here uses the Discrete Wavelet Transform (DWT) and NTRU Encrypt to pre-process, compress and transform both the secret message and the cover medium for more security against any attack(Boukari & Bobbo, n.d.).

C. IoT in Defence and Steganography Technology for Its Security

IOT is not only restricted only in physical components used in smart homes health or industry sector. Rapid development of variety of devices and internet communication lead into a new embedded technology for Internet of Things. The things in this embedded global network are considered as isolated objects involved in different operations (Sumi & Ranga, 2016).

IOT is tremendously used on logistics and chain management. Every field like agriculture, health are benefitted by this. In military sector also the connected sensors and the digital analytics that IOT provides are used for tracking and sharing information between the transmitter and receiver but it is highly confidential and the important databases should be securely protected from the enemy countries. The soldiers also utilize the IOT concept in punitive RF environments like in battlefields. These scenario contains hundreds of control, communications, computers, intelligence and investigation systems with numbers of antennas/sensors and RF circuitries Here enormous amount of big data is to be handled and the data is to be stored in the safe surroundings free from interloper.

- A hybrid crypto stegano scheme that combines the crypto and stegano techniques is used in defence sector. Asymmetric based ElGamal cryptography was used to provide high level security during transmission secret data. The embedding technique used here is the quantum Steganography which is very powerful and advanced data hiding method. Eagle strategy particle swarm optimization help the huge amount of data to be transferred securely over the wireless medium. Best pixel position Is selected here for embedding the secret information on the image cover blocks.it also have a secured secret key option for more security purpose (Sharma & Mohan, 2020).
- dual-layered based Reversible Image Hiding (RIH) based Steganography method using modified least significant bit (LSB) is used in Internet of Things(IoT) enabled communications mainly In military applications.it is so effective that there is no loss of single information. Here two layers based data concealing technique is used to achieve high EE with strong anti-steganalysis ability. In the first layer two bits of data are hidden separately in each pixel to crop the intermittent pixel(IPP).then again four bits of data are hidden using IPP. In this way dual layer information embedding technique is used to produce high EE compared to other method(Sahu & Swain, 2020).

D. Steganography Used in Other IoT Scenarios

- The CycleGAN is a very recent technology to study alteration between two image distribution, i.e., the task of taking an image from one class of images and interpreting it in the elegance of another class .actually it is the automatic training of image-to-image translation prototypes without paired examples. . It contains two basic sub-structures a generator and a discriminator.

- A CycleGAN based Steganography algorithm called S-CycleGAN (Meng et al., 2019) is used in industrial control, military investigation, identification technology and pervasive computing for embedding the secret messages.. Here image –to image translation is done by the amalgamation of the steganolysis module and the Steganography module. To thwart the stego image generated and to make it more secured steganolysis module is used. By easing the cycle consistency loss the generated stego image(generated mainly by S-CycleGAN since it can resist SPA detection more efficiently.) becomes very similar to the cover image. Cycle constant in CycleGAN not only produces a good quality stego image but it also makes the stego images more sturdy for detection. This method is very effective for secured communication in IoT environment.

- Associative pixel Steganography is a Steganography technique used with different encryption methods also confirm a better data security in the IOT environment

- IOT and Artificial Intelligence (AI) are blended together.AI makes the devices those are connected with the internet learn from their data and experience.so AI security system is also very important.AI system make use of USB Webcam for getting the image. The electric entryway act as an actuator that gives the application programming interfaces (APIs) to collect game plans which is perfect with IoT basis of enhancement for video Steganography circulation for Raspberry Pi.

Few Terminologies Related to Steganograpgy and IoT

1. **1.Steganography substitution method-** Least Significant Bit is a Steganography practice in which the least significant bit of pixels of the image is replaced with information bits. This approach is very simple to understand, easy to apply and results in stego-images that contain embedded hidden data.

2. **2. Edge Steganography-**A Steganography method where edges in the cover image are used to embed secret messages.

3. **Eagle strategy-**Eagle strategy was developed by Yang and Deb .It is a is a two-stage method for optimization. It uses an amalgamation of basic global search and rigorous local search through a equilibrium combination of different algorithms to fit different purposes.

4. **Discrete Cosine Transform (DCT) –** DCT expresses the finite sequence of data points in terms of cosine functions oscillating at different frequencies. it is widely used in signal processing and data compression.

5. **Generative Adversarial Network (GAN) –** GAN is an algorithm based architecture which utilizes two neural networks contesting one against another to generate new form of synthetic data that can play as real data. They are widely used for image, audio and video generation.

IV USE OF DIFFERENT TYPES OF STEGANOGRAPHY IN IOT

Though IoT technology has become very popular now a day yet its global deployment is still deferred due to the presence of many security challenges. These security issues need to be overcome first before the deployment of these networks. As these networks use to deal with a wide range of heterogeneous devices such as sensors, laptops, RFID etc. so adopted security schemes should be capable to accommodate this heterogeneity without affecting the functionality of devices. The security schemes should be also scalable to include the massive number of IoT devices. The IoT networks suffer from the limitations of having low storage capacity, low processing power, less communication facility as well as small battery size. Hence, simple security schemes with low complexity are suitable for IoT devices. Moreover, these huge number of IoT devices use to generate a large volume of data on regular basis. So, the security system should able to handle high payload of secure data. To address all these issues, lightweight algorithms are found most suitable. It is found that audio signals require less transmission energy and data rate compared to images and videos and this in turn lead to advantages like lower processing time, improved energy consumption rate and much reduced storage requirement. That is why among different types of Steganography techniques audio Steganography have used in maximum IoT applications. Image Steganography is also used in many applications related to home appliances like IP camera. In this section few proficient steganographic schemes are discussed which involve either audio or image Steganography.

A Noise Resilient Lightweight Steganography Scheme:

This steganographic scheme as depicted in (Djebbar & Abu-Ali, 2017) is specially designed for IoT applications which generate a stego-signal by hiding information in another signal known as cover-signal. This stego-signal is modulated using Orthogonal Frequency Division Multiplexing or Quadrature Phase Shift Keying and transmitted through an AWGN channel. At destination, the received signal is detected to extract the implanted information. So, this proposed algorithm could make use of variety of wireless communication technologies viz. cellular, WiFi and vehicular techniques. The main focus of the proposed scheme is to locate secure hiding areas in the frequency spectrum (Djebbar et al., 2010). The signal property which is utilized here to find proper signal spectrum to implant data states that the noise values less than 13 dB from the original signal spectrum are ineffective in all frequencies (Ayad, 2011). This would certainly influence the stego audio quality. The foundation of steganographic systems is formed by the unpredictability criterion and the payload capacity. So, multiple keys are used in this technique to hide the payload inside the frequency component of the signal. Generally, parameters like Frequency band limits, Threshold value, distortion level, least bit layer etc. are used to find specific number of embedding locations and to control the payload capacity. The quantity and the dimension of the locations may vary according to the number of the frequency components, their energy and the chosen distortion level in a selected band. The cover signal is split into X frames of 4 ms and Y samples each and is defined as $sc(x, y)$, where $1 \pounds x \pounds X$ and $1 \pounds y \pounds Y$. *FFT* is applied on each frame such that $Sc(x, y) = F(sc(x, y))$ and the magnitude spectrum $|Sc(x, k)|$ is isolated. The hiding band varies in between *FHDmin* and *FHDmax*, where *FHDmin* and *FHDmax* are the minimum and the maximum value of the hiding band respectively. The lowest energy required for data hiding of a frequency component is selected as the threshold value. The threshold is set to make a trade off among payload capacity and stego quality. Frequency components with energy more than or equal to the threshold value are selected. The distortion amount of the signal is selected as ρdB from the energy of $|Sc(x, k)|$. ρdB is the amount attenuated from the original signal frequency band and the value is about 13 dB so that: $\Delta(x, k) = (|Sc(x, k)|) - \rho dB$. The embedding locations found in the magnitude of the phase spectrum are replicated by the payload to hide in the phase spectrum. The phase components are then modified by introducing implanted bits in a selected phase module following an algorithm to generate stego-phase spectrum $|\phi s(x, k)|$. The amount of implanted bits in the frequency component varies depending on the energy of the frequency component. Ultimately the new phase is multiplied with its magnitude to produce the stego-spectrum. The inverse IFFT transformation is applied on the spectrumt to get the new stego-signal (x, n). The newly generated stego-signal is then modulated using *OFDM/QPSK* with *AWGN* which creates the stego-channel. Considering the capabilities of the IoT devices different modulations and coding schemes may be applied. This proposed scheme has few advantages as follows:

1. The reduction in stego-signal quality is minimized because of modification of small number of bits in a given module of signal spectrum. This would also provide a smooth transition while preserving phase continuity.
2. Due to the utilization of phase coding better signal-to noise ratio (Bender et al., 1996) is achieved by this scheme which in turn reduces the probability of retransmission and makes the scheme reliable for mass deployment of smart devices.
3. Phase coding is strong for few regular techniques such as amplification, attenuation, filtering, re-sampling (Bender et al., 1996) etc. and provides much better quality without any additional complexity and cost.
4. There are scopes to increase hiding capacity which in turn discover new ways to accommodate huge IoT devices and to handle higher traffic.

Use of Discrete Cosine Based Steganography for achieving Privacy and Authenticity in IoT:

To overcome the confidentiality and authenticity issues in IoT it is found that simple encryption techniques based on symmetric and asymmetric keys as well as digital signature and authentication schemes have a crucial limitation that mathematical operations and machine learning techniques cannot be applied directly to the encrypted form as it leads to exposure of the keys to the intermediate hops and cloud providers. This is because cloud providers need to work on the original data to maintain the security measures. The confidentiality concern may be solved by different types of new cryptographic techniques such as homomorphic encryption as well as utilizing approaches involving random perturbation and K-anonymity. However, these techniques could not solve both the issues of confidentiality and authentication simultaneously. So, researchers are now looking for techniques which could solve both the issues together and permit machine learning techniques and mathematical operations to be easily applied without revealing the secret information. A special type of Steganography scheme has been proposed by authors of (Abuadbba et al., n.d.) which is found to meet all these requirements. They have introduced a novel privacy protection scheme based on Steganography which is superior to the existing models in maintaining proper balance in amount of implanted data which is up to 10 bits per coefficients. This scheme has reduced the mathematical and computational complexity by employing a linear steganographic algorithm which utilizes a simple one dimensional Discrete Cosine Transformation (DCT). This light algorithm defined as O(n) randomly hides the original information inside the periodically assembled normal streams so that it could be accessed by authorized users only. DCT is applied to the normal stream to reshape the resulting co-efficient into two dimensional M x N matrix with the help of an integrated random key. This key would conceal the private data employing a fast symmetric key encryption followed by a random sequence of co-efficient. An inverse DCT is used to decrypt the secret data and reconstruct the normal stream. The person having the key can only encrypt or decrypt the secret information.

Hiding Steps Summary:

1. The information is encrypted to secret bits using the key.
2. Hiding order is generated using the key which is a random progression of co-efficients in the form of a 2D matrix of order P × Q.
3. Discrete Cosine Transform is applied on the normal stream.
4. Observations are listed from three different experimental datasets and least important coefficients are selected on that basis.
5. Rescale these coefficients in integer format to exclude the negative- positive differentiation issue. Also this makes sure that the selected coefficients are ready for Steganography. This is done by adding a threshold Θ and multiplied by φ.
6. The key is utilized to redistribute the resultant DCT coefficients from a vector to 2D P × Q matrix.
7. The hiding process is initiated.
8. When the hiding process finishes, the resultant coefficients are recalculated and then rescaled by dividing all stego coefficients by φ and subtracting the threshold Θ.
9. Re-arrange the coefficients and apply inverse DCT.

This is a strong and robust end-to-end privacy protection scheme which provides strong authentication simultaneously. It ensures highest hiding capacity with minimum distortion. One advantage of this scheme is that mathematical operations as well as machine learning techniques could be applied easily on stego streams without revealing the hidden data. Another advantage of this scheme is that one may use the stego IoT stream without eliminating the secret data.

Securing Data Using Image Steganography

In IoT home automation applications IP camera is used to verify user face to open the locked doors (e.g. house front door, office server room door etc.). In this specific scheme (Yin, Fen, Mughal, & Iranmanesh, 2015), the IP camera use to capture user face images and send them to the server for verification and store them in devices which are not connected to the LAN network (cloud storage). Any hacking attack in the LAN breaches the confidentiality and integrity of the transmitted information. The focus of the proposed scheme is the secure transmission of images from IP camera to the local area network using the IoT devices. A server is kept inside the home which is connected to the LAN use to collect the encrypted face image and stores it in the cloud. As smart devices are unable to handle tough and complicated encryption algorithm, lightweight cryptographic techniques are best suited for them. Even though the secret information is encrypted, yet attackers may decode it if acquire an adequate amount of time and high processing power. Moreover, encryption is not enough to hide the information from the hackers (Tiwari & Shandilya, 2010). Steganography may be an alternative approach for secure data transfer. In this scheme, image Steganography is utilized to secure essential images (face) captured by the IP camera and transmits that to the home server. IP camera detects the face of the house owner successfully when he approaches for face detection and stores it as an image. At the same time it randomly captures another image which is not detecting any face. These images are known as cover image. The face image is first hidden into the cover to produce the encrypted image using a Steganography technique and then sends it to the home server. Later, the same stego image is converted to the original captured image by the home server by adopting the reverse Steganography technique. On the other hand, a hacker may attack the home network to interrupt the data conduction between the camera and the home server. He knew about the existence of the IP camera in the front door of the house. Therefore, he tries to capture all images of the camera which also includes the encrypted image, but he can't trace the hidden image as this seems alike other arrested images. This proposed scheme is based on least significant bit (LSB) Steganography. LSB is a popular image steganography technique (Paik, 2010) which is basically a replacement method. In this scheme, the pixel value of the cover image is presented as a sequence of one and zeroes. Similarly, the secret face image may be represented as a separate bit string which uses to replace few bits of the cover image. This replacement use to occur on the LSBs of the cover image pixel values, which is not able to bring any significant modification on the image body(up to 4 LSBs). On the other hand, if any modification is made on most significant bits (MSB) pixel that would significantly degrade the image quality and that could be recognized even through manual acuity (Akhtar et al., 2014). However, statistical analysis could be used to identify the LSB hiding scheme. This is because the process of choosing the LSBs for information hiding could not be fully randomized (Paik, 2010) and that can instigate the attacker to utilize statistical analysis for finding out the modification of the image. To mitigate this possibility, inverted LSB image Steganography is used in spite of the LSB scheme (Akhtar et al., 2014).

V CONCLUSION

This chapter focuses on the use of Steganography to strengthen IoT security. IoT technology is based on an amalgamation of various technologies, protocols and devices like a variety of wireless sensors, recently developed wearable and implanted sensors. IoT also includes various kinds of hardware, communication protocols and services. This diversity of IoT provides comfort to the users but at the same time lead to a significant number of security challenges and attacks. In this chapter vulnerabilities of IoT devices are discussed and probable solutions are discussed to mitigate the security issues using Steganography. Though it is relatively easy to scramble a secret message in a media like an image, audio or video, the retrieval of such embedded message is a bit difficult because of the use of many different methods and the continuous development of latest Steganography algorithms. Application of Steganography for various IoT applications are discussed in detail with relative comparisons. Recently, research on image Steganography has exhibited its prospect in adopting neural network techniques. Image Steganography scheme introducing Generative Adversarial Network (GAN) [e,f] and its application in IoT may grab future research attention. There are several types of audio steganograhy schemes such as eco hiding, phase coding, parity coding, Least Significant Bit (LSB), using DCT etc. Audio Steganography is most suitable for IoT applications as it requires less transmission energy. Audio Steganography is also used to secure IoT in 5G platform. More research could be performed to implement dual Steganography techniques which would provide more security to the IoT data.

REFERENCES

Abdelaziza, A., Elhoseny, M., Salama, A.S., & Riad, A.M. (2018). A Machine Learning Model for Improving Heal*thcare services on Cloud Computing Environment. Academic Press.*

Abomhara, M., & Køien, G. M. (2014). Security and privacy in the internet of things: Current status and open issues. In Privacy and Security in Mobile Systems (*PRISMS), International Conference on. IEEE.*

*Abuadbba, S., Ibaida, A., & K*halil, I. (n.d.). IoT Sign: Protecting Privacy and Authe*nticity of IoT using Discrete Cosine Based Steganography. arXiv:1911.00604[cs.CR].*

Akhtar, N., Khan, S., & Johri, P. (2014). An improved inverted LSB image steganography. Issues and Challenges in Intelligen*t Computing Techniques (ICICT), International Conference on, 749-745. 10.1109/ ICICICT.2014.6781374*

Anwar, A. S., Ghany, K. K. A., & Mahdy, H. E. (2015). Improving the security of images transmission. International Journal (Toronto, *Ont.), 3(4).*

Atamli, A. W., & Martin, A. (2014). Threat-Based Security Analysis for the Internet of Things. Secure Internet of Things (S*IoT), International Workshop, 35-43.*

*Ayad, B. (2011). N*oise Suppressor. U.S. Pa*tent 7,889,874 B1.*

Backes, M., & Cachin, C. (n.d.). Public-Key Steganograp*hy with Active Attacks. IBM Research,* Zurich Research Laboratory.

Bairagi, A. K., Khondoker, R., & Islam, R. (2016). An efficient stegan*ographic approach for protecting communication in the Internet of Things (IoT) critical infrastructures. Academic Press.*

Bender, W., Gruhl, D., Morimoto, N., & Lu, A. (1996). Techniques for Data Hiding. IBM Systems Jour*nal, 35(3-4), 13-33.*

Bhattacharyya, S., Banerjee, I., & Sanyal, G. (2011). Data Hiding Through Multi Level Steganography and SSCE. Journal of Gl*obal Research in Computer Science, 2(2), 38–47.*

Boukari & Bobbo. (n.d.). ceeol.com

Bradley, T. (2015). Experts pick the top 5 security threats for 2015. PC Worl*d.*

*Ca*chin, C. (2005). Digital Steganography. Ency*clopaedia of Cryptography and Security.*

Djebbar, F., Abed-Maraim, K., Guerchi, D., & Hamam, H. (2010). Dynamic energy based text-in-speech spectrum hiding using speech masking properties. *2nd International Conference on Industrial Mecha-tronicsand Automation (ICIMA), 2, 422-426.* 10.1109/ICINDMA.2010.5538279

Djebbar, F., & Abu-Ali, N. (2017). Lightweight Noise Resilient Steganography Scheme for Internet of Things. *IEEE Global Communications Conference (GLOBECOM 2017), 1-6.* 10.1109/GLO-COM.2017.8255039

Hashim, M., Rhaif, S., Abdulrazzaq, A., Hussein Ali, A., & Taha, M. (2020). *Based on IoT Healthcare Application for Medical Data Authentication: Towards A New Secure Framework Using Steganography.* Academic Press.

Khosravi, S., Mashallah, A. D., & Hossein, Y. M. (2011). A new Steganography method based HIOP (Higher Intensity Of Pixel) algorithm and Strassen's matrix multiplication. *Journal of Global Research in Computer Science, 2*(1).

Kumar, P., & Lee, H. J. (2011). Security issues in healthcare applications using wireless medical sensor networks: A survey. *Sensors (Basel), 12*(1), 55–91. doi:10.3390120100055 PMID:22368458

Lai, Y. L., Jin, Z., Teoh, A. B. J., Goi, B.-M., Yap, W.-S., Chai, T.-Y., & Rathgeb, C. (2017). Cancellable iris template generation based on Indexing-First-One hashing. *Pattern Recognition*, *64*, 105–117. doi:10.1016/j.patcog.2016.10.035

Lakshmi Kanth, K., & Siva Narayana, R. (2020). *Integrating Steganography and Cryptography techniques in IoT cloud for secure data transfer*. Academic Press.

Meng, R., Cui, Q., Zhou, Z., Fu, Z., & Sun, X. (2019). A Steganography Algorithm Based on CycleGAN for Covert Communication in the Internet of Things. *IEEE Access: Practical Innovations, Open Solutions*, *7*, 90574–90584. doi:10.1109/ACCESS.2019.2920956

Online Steganography Program. (2019). https://stylesuxx.github.io/Steganography

Paik, M. (2010). Blacknoise: Low-fi Lightweight Steganography in Service of Free Speech. *M4D*, 150.

Paschou, M., Sakkopoulos, E., Sourla, E., & Tsakalidis, A. (2013). Health Internet of Things: Metrics and methods for efficient data transfer. *Simulation Modelling Practice and Theory*, *34*, 186–199. doi:10.1016/j.simpat.2012.08.002

Razzaq, M. A., Sheikh, R. A., Baig, A., & Ahmad, A. (2017). Digital image security: Fusion of encryption, Steganography and watermarking. *International Journal of Advanced Computer Science and Applications*, *8*(5).

Sahu, A. K., & Swain, G. (2020). Reversible Image Steganography Using Dual-Layer LSB Matching. *Sensing and Imaging*, *21*(1), 1. doi:10.100711220-019-0262-y

Sajjad, M., Muhammad, K., Baik, S. W., Rho, S., Jan, Z., Yeo, S. S., & Mehmood, I. (2017). Mobile-cloud assisted framework for selective encryption of medical images with Steganography for resource-constrained devices. *Multimedia Tools and Applications*, *76*(3), 3519–3536. doi:10.100711042-016-3811-6

Sajjad, M., Nasir, M., Khan, M., Khan, S., Jan, Z., Sangaiah, A.K., Elhoseny, M., & WookBaik, S. (2017). Raspberry Pi assisted face recognition framework for enhanced law-enforcement services in smart cities. In Future Generation Computer Systems. Elsevier.

Seyyedi, S. A., Sadau, V., & Ivanov, N. (2016). A Secure Steganography Method Based on Integer Lifting Wavelet Transform. *International Journal of Network Security*, *18*(1), 124–132.

Sharma, A., & Mohan, N. (2020). Article. European Journal of Molecular & *Clinical Medicine*, *7*(4), 376–384.

Shehab, A., Elhoseny, M., Muhammad, K., Sangaiah, A. K., Yang, P., Huang, H., & Hou, G. (2018). Secure and Robust Fragile Watermarking Scheme for Medical Images. *IEEE Access: Practical Innovations, Open Solutions*, *6*, 10269–10278. doi:10.1109/ACCESS.2018.2799240

Sumi, L., & Ranga, V. (2016). Sensor enabled Internet of Things for smart cities. *Fourth International Conference on Parallel, Distributed and Grid Computing (PDGC)*, 295-300. 10.1109/PDGC.2016.7913163

Tarouco, L., Bertholdo, M. R., Granville, L. Z., & Carbone, L. M. R. (2012). Internet of things in healthcare: Interoperability and security issues in Communications (ICC). *IEEE International Conference on. IEEE*, 6121–6125.

Tiwari & Shandilya. (2010). Evaluation of Various LSB based Methods of Image Seganography on GIF File Format. *International Journal of Computer Applications.*

Yang, W., Hu, J., & Wang, S. (2014). *An Alignment-free Fingerprint Bio-cryptosystem based on Modified Voronoi Neighbour Structures.* Academic Press.

Yang, W., Hu, J., Wang, S., & Delaunay, A. (2014). Quadrangle-Based Fingerprint Authentication System with Template Protection Using Topology Code for Local Registration and Security Enhancement. *IEEE Transactions on Information Forensics and Security, 9*(7), 1179–1192. doi:10.1109/TIFS.2014.2328095

Yin, Fen, Mughal, & Iranmanesh. (2015). Internet of Things: Securing Data Using Image Steganography. *3rd International Conference on Artificial Intelligence, Modelling and Simulation (AIMS),* 310-314. .. doi:10.1109/AIMS.2015.56

Yin, J. H. J., Fen, G. M., Mughal, F., & Iranmanesh, V. (2015). Internet of Things: Securing Data Using Image Steganography. *3rd International Conference on Artificial Intelligence, Modelling and Simulation (AIMS),* 310-314. 10.1109/AIMS.2015.56

Yoon, S., Park, H. Y. H., & Yoo, H. S. (2015). Security issues on smarthome in IoT environment. In Computer Science and its Applications. Springer.

Chapter 10
An Integration of Keyless Encryption, Steganography, and Artificial Intelligence for the Secure Transmission of Stego Images

Digvijay Pandey

(iD) https://orcid.org/0000-0003-0353-174X

Department of Technical Education, IET, Dr. A. P. J. Abdul Kalam Technical University, India

Vinay Kumar Nassa

(iD) https://orcid.org/0000-0002-9606-7570

South Point Group of Institutions, Sonepat, India

Ayushi Jhamb

Department of IT, College of Engineering, Roorkee, India

Dashrath Mahto

Central University of Jharkhand, Ranchi, India

Binay Kumar Pandey

College of Technology, Govind Ballabh Pant University of Agriculture and Technology, Pantnagar, India

A. S. Hovan George

Masters IT Solutions, India

A. Shaji George

Crown University International Chartered Inc., Argentina

Samir Kumar Bandyopadhyay

GLA University, India

ABSTRACT

Protected stored data as well as transfer in this virtual environment have been a significant thing since this world wide web has been used for information exchange. The need for data security rises as the level of personal data exchanged on the web is becoming more susceptible. To protect information from malicious use as well as alteration, services like confidential information but also data integrity have been needed. So many traditional cryptographic methods have been proposed by numerous studies throughout

DOI: 10.4018/978-1-7998-7160-6.ch010

recent times to maintain multimedia data communicated over public networks. The chapter proposes a novel keyless picture encryption algorithm focused on a chaotic map. Almost every picture element is encoded by shuffling pixel values, which would be measured by an adapted cat map. In this suggested technique, steganography is used to transfer keyless encrypted information using a cover picture with encrypted information inserted in picture, audio, and video files.

1. INTRODUCTION

At the present time, the entire globe tends to revolve round the World Wide Web. The web revolutionized the concept while becoming widely known for data transmission through one person to the other. The World Wide Web had already drastically changed around the globe. Time, space and average distance had also changed drastically. Information has become quickly available at any time and with almost any place. Individuals are nowadays digitally savvy, as illustrated mostly by internet and mobile phones. A World Wide Web that is overflowing to new technologies has been expanding rapidly.

The two-dimensional input is used to encrypt a digital image. The Digital Image's (DI's) equations to describe would be usually binary, of a two-dimensional image (Kamboj et al., 2013). Each kinds of image resolution defines that whether picture is vector or raster. The word "digital image" generally refers with vector graphics and bitmapped images when used solely. A DI has been generally denoted by f(x,y), in which x and y will be mutually perpendicular as well as the valuation with f at a certain factor (x,y) would be commensurate to a image's gray scale at a certain moment. Digital images were also classified into three categories (Kamboj et al., 2013).

1.1. Binary images

Binary images are images which are characterized only by one bit by each pixel. As each pixel only has two values ('0' or '1'), such images are quite effective besides database processing.

1.2. Grayscale Images

The grayscale (or grey level) picture merely conveys the color schemes as grayscale colors. Logic underneath differentiating these pictures from other kinds with color photos is that less data is provided to every and almost every pixel. Because the red, green, and blue components of grey have equal intensity in R G B space, each pixel only requires a single pixel intensity, as opposed to the three intensities required to define each pixel in a full color image.

1. 3 Colour Images

In a color image, each pixel has a distinct color, which is represented by the three primary colors present in an image: red, green, and blue. A linear combination of the three fundamental colors, red, green, and blue, can be used to describe a color, recognized by the human eye. The R G B based color-space is built around these three basic colors. The 24-bit information in an RGB image represents millions of colors.

1.4 Image Processing

Image Processing (IP) is indeed a method of conducting some few operations on an image with the particular objective of getting a better picture as well as extracting the large range of valuable information from all of this. This is a type with signal processing where an image is being used as the input as well as the outcome is an image or even a characteristic related to such an image. IP is among the quickest technologies in recent years. It also is a focal point with study throughout computer engineering scientific fields. Analogous to pictures, it's a form of signal indulgence. Generally, the whole method presents pictures as two-dimensional signals while still going to employ signal processing techniques. Its own applications are found in several areas of a business, and this is one of today's quickest technologies (El-kouny, A. et. al., 2002). A Digital Image Processing has been involved in the process of building a visual scheme but also, as a result, an established platform conducting maneuverability on even a digital image.

1.5 Image Processing Techniques

In image analysis, there have been two techniques accessible:

1.5.1 Processing of Analog Images

The word "image processing" relates to the procedure with changing an image utilizing electromagnetic methods. The television image is the most well-known explanation. The voltage level of a television signal differs in amplitude to reflect luminosity through picture. On even a television, the intensity as well as contrast regulates and modifies the amplitude and mention of the video signal, likely to result throughout the brightening, obfuscating, and variance of a presented image's light intensity threshold (Chung, K. L., et al., 2001).

1.5.2 Digital Image Processing

The image is processed by utilizing computers that used a scanner-digitizer. The image will be converted to digital form and afterwards analyzed. It's also described as confining mathematical objects to the series of processes, while keeping the accurate goal in mind in order to produce the desired outcome. This begins with a single image and ends with such a slight modification of the same image. In the way, a method changes an image into a distinct sort of image. A main advantage of Digital Image Processing is its ability to adapt, repeatability, but also sustainability with original image accuracy (Chung, K. L., et al., 2001).

1.6 Processing Methods for Text - Based Encrypting Data

Text - based encryption process employs a variety of strategies, including:

1.6.1. Cryptography

Cryptosystem has been historically described as the procedure with converting plain text to coded text. The globe is also now globally connected through internet protocol, and information sharing would be critical. Everybody uses its website to speed up business in a different number of ways. The networks are built to become more resistant with crucial functions and much more vulnerable with malevolent purposes (Fridrich, 1998). The rapid expansion of computer networks enabled big files, such as digital photos, is transferred seamlessly over internet. Encrypted data has been widely used to maintain safety; nevertheless, the huge chunk of an available encryption calculation can be used for textual information. With the ever-increasing growth of multimedia applications, security is becoming an increasingly important issue in image communication as well as storage space, so there is a common approach known as cryptography to maintain image safety. With help of cryptographic algorithms, this will attempt to transform an actual image that would be difficult to understand to another image; to keep the image secret between two parties, or we can say that no one is capable of decrypting the information without the need for a key for decryption. The method of transforming original messages into the encrypted messages is defined as encrypted data, and also the conversion process such as encrypted message being back into their original file is regarded as decryption. Color images are really quite large when distributed over the internet and wireless networks, which take advantage of rapid advances in multimedia as well as network technologies. Until now, it seems to have a wide range of data encryption anticipated for color image. Recent times, various data encryption techniques, for example, AES, RSA, or IDEA, have been planned and commonly used, the vast majority of which are developed as a part of the text or paired data. It's indeed a challenge to be using them directly in multimedia data and inefficient for color encryption algorithm leading to enhanced pixel correlation. Besides multimedia data, high repetition, huge quantities, and real-time interactions were also required (Fridrich, 1998). In today's world, data security has risen to a top of the priority list for any commercial enterprise environment. Cryptography is required to ensure the privacy of data sent in a network. Data encryption could be achieved in two ways:

1.6.1.1 Cipher Block

In block ciphers, a block of plaintext is encrypted together creating a group ofcipher text of the same size. So if the key is comprised of various values, it is used to encrypt the entire plain-text block. A cipher text block depends on the whole plain text block. There is one to one mapping between a plaintext block and a ciphertext block (Chen, W. et. al., 2016). Block ciphers are using the same transitions to encode fixed-length blocks of bits, however block cipher execute slowly and it is more complex.

1.6.1.2 Stream Ciphers

Encryption and decryption are mainly performed along the same emblem in cryptographic algorithms (such as a character). This generates one cipher text character through one unencrypted character. The character to character encrypted image comes next (Chen, W. et. al., 2016).Stream ciphers are still thusly named as they have three streams: plaintext, cipher-text, and key-stream. One after the other, plaintext

Figure 1. Symmetric Key Encryption

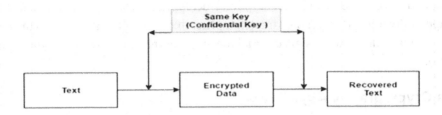

characters are fed into the encryption algorithm. Characters for cipher text are also generated one by one. Stream ciphers utilize different transformations depending mostly on engine's state. Ciphers are less complex than block ciphers and execute faster. Mostly on the basis of key management, there have been primarily two types of cryptographic algorithms.

1.7 Algorithms for Key-Oriented Cryptography

The two broad types of key-oriented cryptographic techniques are (Kocarev,2001):

1.7.1 Cryptographic Algorithms with a Secret-Key

Symmetrical key cryptosystem also is known as cryptographic algorithms because it uses a single key for both encryption and decryption. Information is encrypted by the sender using the key, and deciphered by recipient that uses the same key. In this case, both the sender and the receiver have access to the same secret key. The sender encrypts the information and data with the secret key, and also the recipient decrypts the data with the same secret key (Kocarev 2001). The key plays an important role throughout symmetric cryptography, which would be dependent on the type of a key.

Figure 2. Asymmetric Key Encryption

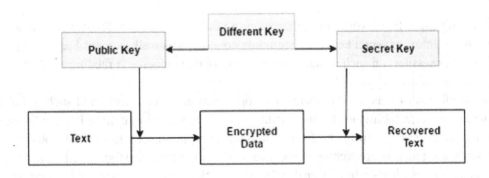

1.7.2 Cryptography Using Public Keys

This cryptography utilizes a key pair for encryption / decryption, relating to public and private keys. The cryptography fully utilized secret data transition, first in one location and then to the next location via networks. Several methods are designed for all the cryptography method to encrypt the information (Bernd, J. 1993).

1.8 Keyless Cryptography Algorithms

The Keyless method further encrypts relevant data; there really is no flexibility associated with key creation and sharing. Simply apply accessible rational operations in a manner by which information could be deciphered by an intruder whilst also sending over public domain in such types of approaches. It is used to encode information from a variety of aspects. Such techniques could also be categorized as symmetric or asymmetric. The very same rational operations are being used to encrypt or decrypt information in such a symmetric keyless method. The sender and recipient of an asymmetric keyless method utilizes distinct logical operations with encrypted and decrypted information (Malik, S.,2012)

1.8.1 Theory of Chaos

The chaos theory is really the evaluation of complex nonlinear methodologies which demonstrate persuasive supportability to starting conditions and also have arbitrary practices, even though established by Edward Lorenz (Lorenz, E.N., 1993), an influence which is exquisitely signalized as butterfly effect which has an elaboration. Does the fold of a butterfly's wings in Brazil cause a tidal wave in Texas? The fluttering two wings communicate to a minor transition and in the structure's start point that also causes the attachment of situations to cause large-scale concepts. If the butterfly hadn't been flitting its wings, the structure's trajectory may have been extremely distinguishable (Kellert, H.S., 1993). In the most part, this indicates that high solubility in starting conditions produces typically isolating outcomes for chaotic systems, making long-term forecasting usually intolerable. The above concept occurs despite the fact that these structures or systems are deterministic, which means which one's future behavior has been completely determined by ones initial conditions, without any arbitrary defined considerations involved. Finally, the conclusive nature of these frameworks or structures helps make someone to be mutable (Kellert,H.S.,1993).

There have been two common approaches to interpolating the chaos map in such a cipher framework, according to (Kocarev, L., 2001):

- Utilizing chaos framework to generate pseudo-random key clauses for stream ciphers.
- Using plaintext or secret key(s) as beginning conditions as well as control parameters recognize a few other sessions on such a chaotic structure to obtain cipher-text relating to block ciphers.

This is referred to it as deterministic chaos or important chaos. Abnormal such as behavior, non-anticipating, and affectability to starting condition are three aspects that make it a good candidate for an encryption connection. The primary distinction is that encryption operations are denoted by constrained components of figures, whereas chaos maps have been denoted by actual figures. Chaotic maps exemplify chaotic behaviors. Such maps have been divided into two types: constant maps and discrete maps. Iterated processes are commonly used as the interpretation for discrete maps. Iterates are similar with rounds in cryptosystems, so discrete chaotic dynamic constructions are being used as a part of cryptography. Each map is made up of dependent variable that is new to cryptography and correlate to an encrypted data key. As per (Kocarev, L. 2001), there are two general approaches to apply a chaos map in a cipher system:

- Utilization chaotic constructions to generate pseudo-arbitrary key stream, similar to stream ciphers.
- Using the plaintext or the mystery key(s) as the starting conditions as well as control variables, some few rounds on chaotic constructions are being used to acquire cipher content related to block ciphers.

1.9 Architecture of Chaotic Image Cryptography

Chaos based two-based cryptographic architectural design seems to be mirror images of each other (Chong, Fu et. al., 2016). When the measurements of all change, but the positions of pixels remain the same, the image becomes chaotic. From here, a starting points as well as the sequence behave as the key. It is far less susceptible to also be permutation-less now as it is susceptible to any attack to enhance the pixilation. The significance of each and every pixel is altered after it has been encrypted. In particular, the implementation method of diffusion is focused on the beginning requirements as well as the management variables. The pixel values throughout the diffusion state series change consecutively from the chaotic system (Chong, Fu et. al., 2016). The whole confusion-diffusion method is carried thoroughly to ensure security. Figure 3 represents the proposed architecture.

Figure 3. Architecture of chaos-based image encryption

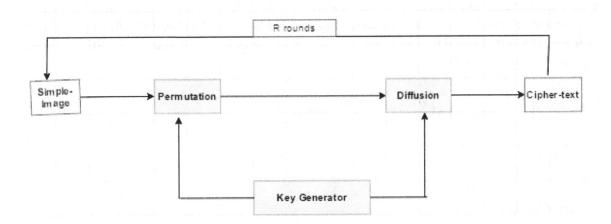

1. 10 Keyless Chaos Based Image Encryption

Sooner or later, keyless techniques will become even more popular. There really is no administrative cost. Just the simple and obvious operations are used in such a way such that the information cannot be perceived throughout transit. Utilizing traditional computer security methods as just a means of authentication is just as unlikely as relying on Quantum Cryptography (Chin-Chang et al., 2001). All the time they could be classified as probabilistic, stochastic. Such behavior can indeed be readily detected using chaotic behaviors and even small perturbations can yield great deviational changes. Even now, the outcomes of such constructions will be predicted since they're focused mostly on initial conditions, so their activity must be referred to as pattern of chaos.

Due to the extreme close relationship among chaos and cryptography, the best methods for encrypted images tend to be based on it. The two important features of the true ciphers seem to be complex and distributive. Take some real functions to minimal computation, and yet constant modification is impossible. The chaotic key-based encryption method blends a lot of speed, security, and complexity, and uses less power.

Pseudo-random number generation must be used to create a series of unpredictable numbers which are then used it as an encryption key. Preliminary conditions (Lu, Jun-an. et al., 2004) differ in to the distinct routes. Encryption and decryption could be applied to such variables. Under such complex initial conditions, the resulting confusion can increase the vulnerability. Due to the extreme unpredictable behavior, the system is likely open to an attacker.

Numerous cryptographic algorithms are developed by scientists for cryptography; however the majority of them will be designed to encode text messages. But since images possess unique characteristics in comparison to text documents, their information capacity seems to be enormous. As just a result, encryption algorithm necessitates a large amount of computing power. One method for delivering effective security to images has been mentioned below.

1.11 Arnold's Cat Map (ACM)

Arnold's cat map is a chaotic mapping transformation. An image is subjected to the transition which changes the pixel position of an image without removing other information. Nevertheless, after much iteration, the original image reappears. Arnold's period is the number of iterations required. Fig4 shows the example of effects of ACM on an image. The duration has been determined by the image size, as such Arnold's period would then vary according to the size of an image (Abbas, N. A., 2015) Arnold's Cat Map equation are as follows:

$$\begin{bmatrix} x_{n+1} \\ y_{n+1} \end{bmatrix} = A \begin{bmatrix} x_n \\ y_n \end{bmatrix} (\text{mod } N) = \begin{bmatrix} 1 & P \\ Q & PQ+1 \end{bmatrix} \begin{bmatrix} x_n \\ y_n \end{bmatrix} (\text{mod } N)$$

Where,

N=Sizeofimage
pandq=Positiveintegersdet(A) =1
(x_n,y_n)=Positionofpixelsinimage
(x_{n+1},y_{n+1})=Transformedposition

The secret data is mainly encrypted using just a novel key-less chaotic encryption method. The heuristic approach's cover image can then be used to embed this into a cover image. After this, the secure

Figure 4. ACM effects on an image

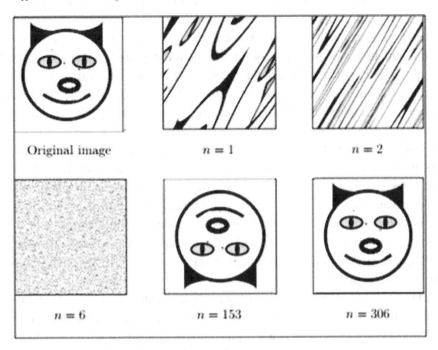

text hidden within the cover image is performed using steganalysis. In addition, the efficiency of the proposed method is illustrated by launching several attacks (Rather, M. and Sengupta, A., 2020).

The proposed embedding process is spatially divided into two stages. Chaos based key less cryptography is being used to generate the cipher data. After that, the cipher-data is placed in the cover image's first few bytes, and the encoded secret message is enciphered elsewhere. The text retrieved from a steganographic image is called steganalysis. Detection, assessment, as well as message extraction could be three different steps of the same procedure. Textual text only gets in the way of the image's texture fetch. To work, noise must be taken out of the image in the beginning and then feature extraction and message extraction is performed. The message is retrieved using the decryption process of keyless chaos based enciphering and a hybrid convolution integrated network

2. LITERATURE REVIEW

The existing literature assists throughout the exploration as well as summarization of investigation on a particular subject. The literature review is defined as a consistent way for the major area of testing, either quantitative or qualitative, in a mixed methods study. For such a review of the literature, reliable sources on chaotic map image encryption, steganography (Pramanik, S., Bandyopadhyay, S. K., 2013), deep learning have been used to collect relevant data. To fulfill the standards with safe image transfer, (Pareek, N. K. et al., 2006) proposed a new approach for image cryptography based on chaotic logistic maps. An external 80-bit secret key and two chaotic logistic maps are used for the proposed image's cryptographic system. Both logistic maps' initial conditions are derived using an exterior secret key that assigns a different weight to each of its bits.

In (Abdul, N., et al., 2015) have proposed the novel process for encrypting images that is both useful and accurate. For encryption, the said suggested methodology used Arnold cat map to adjust the mixing matrix in Independent Component Analysis. The combining matrices first were created from the ACM by inserting the square image of any dimension throughout this proposed method. Second, for encryption algorithm, the mixing process was implemented using the mixing matrix. Third, ICA techniques were used to decode the image. The outcomes of many studies, including PSNR, SDR, and SSIM, when particularly in comparison to a standard mixing matrices, show that the proposed encryption method is an efficacious manner to encrypting images.

In (Garcia-Bosque, et al., 2016) this new method uses a rearrangement of pixels throughout plaintext to encode a picture. The cat map as well as Lorenz system was used to shuffle the positions of pixel values, leading to the creation of the diffusion key. The hash value of the plaintext message is used as a permutation key, which is measured by the control parameters of the cat map. The shuffle image is generated by a hash function property. The observational results reveal that the improved method just requires either one two rounds to achieve good diffusion properties, whereas the traditional method needed two or more sessions. The proposed algorithm passed all security analyses, making it more secure than the traditional method.

In (Pandey, D. et. al., 2020) gives details of the whole research that analyzes various algorithmic methods for removing noise from an image as well as increasing the equality enhancement of a sophisticated corrupted images. The complicated deteriorated image is one in which different kinds of unwanted signal, such as impulse noise, Brownian Noise (Fractal Noise), Rayleigh Noise, Gamma Noise, and Structured Noise, have been introduced. An objective of this research is to reassess a number of text extraction techniques as well as de-noise a complicated degraded image. To remove noise from posh corrupted images, a variety of filters are used.

As per (Song, Y., et al., 2017) proposed a two-stage method for embedding a sequence of binary bits into a gray scale image. This day, information security is extremely important. The primary objective of security is to keep important information hidden. The pattern(Pandey, B. K.,2011) has been split in to the few more equal-length substrings in the first stage of the proposed strategy. The binary bit in the pattern has been shuffled using a set of one-dimensional logistic matrices. A shuffled pattern was divided into smaller regions throughout the second stage, as well as the regions were sequentially embedded into the corresponding pixels in the gray-scale image. The least significant bits of the grey value of the current pixel were replaced with the bits in the region to implement a region throughout the rotated pattern. The suggested algorithm's findings demonstrate it can securely embed information into a gray-scale image without drastically changing the image's material, and therefore it could even possibly be seen in practice for protected image-based hiding data.

In (Mostafa, S. et.al,.2017) have proposed a new chaos encryption approach for medical images. In present time encryption provide the security of our information. The proposed algorithm uses control parameters to generate the secret key. The permutation of the pixel has been done in a way that minimum distance between each pixel is 10. This proposed algorithm enhances the security of the data with the help of control parameters. Through experimental results analysis provides the good performance of the proposed algorithm. This algorithm also provides the good results compared to another typical approach which is based on the similar chaotic map. They have found that proposed approach provides high security, key sensitivity and the randomness of the encrypted image. The proposed algorithm is big enough for any type of attack.

In (Pandey, D. et. al., 2019) presented, the review of different techniques of algorithms that make a picture free from the noise and increase the equality enhancement of the complex degraded image. Complex degraded image is a picture that's suffering from differing types of unwanted signal like impulse noise, Brownian Noise (Fractal Noise) Rayleigh Noise, Gamma Noise, and Structured Noise. The main effort of this paper is that the revise of a variety of text extraction techniques and de-noising the complex degraded image. Different sort of filter is employed to get rid of noise from a posh degraded image. The most motivation of the paper is that the latest application of the automated text extraction process followed by text recognition is receiving huge demand.

According to (Attaby, A. A. et. al., 2018) cryptography is the primary method of data protection, with steganography serves as a replacement in some cases. The science and art of steganography is the art and science of confidential communication between two parties that attempt to maintain the message from being discovered. Most of them provoke statistically meaningful changes in the cover carrier's properties, particularly whenever the text payload is huge. This study proposes a novel transform domain JPEG image steganography technique that effectively improves embedding performance whilst also needing minor modifications to the cover carrier image. The DCT-M3 method incorporates two bits of the compact form of a hidden code utilizing modulus 3 of the difference of two DCT coefficients.

In (Pandey, D. et. al., 2020) gives details about deep learning-based weighted Naive Bayes classifier (WNBC) that is being used to efficaciously identify text as well as recognize characters from image data. Ordinarily, (Manne, R. et. al., 2020) natural scene files represent a few little noises, as well as the guided image filter is used during the preprocessing stage to remove this. The Gabor transform as well as stroke width transform techniques have been used to retrieve useful features throughout the classifier. Eventually, using such extracted features, WNBC and deep neural network-based adaptive galactic swarm optimization successfully achieves text detection and character recognition. The suggested method's adeptness would then be assessed using performance metrics such as accuracy, F1-score, precision, mean absolute error, mean square inaccuracy, but also recall measurements.

4. SUGGESTIVE OBJECTIVES OF PROPOSED METHOD

Following are a few objectives of the proposed method for secure text extraction from complex degraded image by applying steganography and deep learning.

- Tostudyandanalyzevariousimageencryptionalgorithmtotransmitoverunsecuredchannels.
- To create a dataset of images.
- To apply chaotic image encryption algorithm to shuffle the pixel position and permute the pixel value.
- To enhance image encryption algorithm and encrypt the image.
- To create new methods for providing high-quality stego images by using encrypted text data in data security via image steganography.
- To provide highly secure transmission of secret data over an internet.
- At receiver end, by using new techniques, extracting secret data from stego images with high quality.
- Then create an AI based algorithm that extracts text from a cover image with minimal error and high accuracy.

- Using an adaptive optimization algorithm improves the effectiveness of the text extraction technique.
- After modeling and simulation, the proposed approaches must be validated.

Finally, the performance of the proposed approaches will be compared to all currently available methods.

3. METHODLOGY USED

As shown in figure 5, a model is constructed for secure transmission of images. Firstly the pixel value and position are changing. After this conversion encrypted (Pramanik, S., Bandyopadhyay, S. K., 2014) image to stego-image using eLSB based stenography and transmit (Pramanik, S. et. al., 2020) on public internet.

Figure 5. Suggested Methodology used

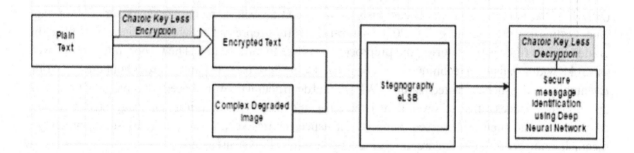

3.1 Model for Execution

Almost every model is run, and this is checked to see whether the modeling is running as anticipated. Whatever impediment in this respect has been erased

3.2 Model Evaluation

Throughout this case, the method has been evaluated in terms of various metrics that have already been described, and then conclusions can be drawn.

3.3 Algorithm for proposed encryption

The proposed encryption algorithms performed following steps to encrypt text data without using any key.

3.3. 1 Steps of Reading HDR Images

There are various methods for reading High-Dynamic-Range (HDR) images. MATLAB has an in-built method to read images. For this research in-built function of MATLAB was used to read HDR images and for flat HDR images. Following method was used:

f1¬open fileinreadmode

[Filetypeno. ofbits]¬getformatoff1fsensor¬get information of f1filluminant ¬get illumination of f1himage¬makeimagereadable

[himage,Gluminance]¬ convert highdynamic tolowusingReinhardglobaltonemapalgo.

3.3.2 Working Process of Image Encryption

Step 1: Deploynodes

Step2: Readanimage

Step3: Convert the RGB imageto grayscale

Step4: [number_of_pixelnY]¬Size (image (i, j)) // nY varible hold size of image

Step 5: loop through rows of image (i, j) // outer row wise for loop

Step 6: loop through columns of image (i, j) // inner column wise loop

Step7:pixel_values¬image(i,j) // pixel_values store value pixel in row and column wise dimension

Step 8: new_pixel_value ¬(pixel_value + i^ columns)/256

// Shuffling of each pixel value is performed in step 8 to keep pixel value more complex

Step9:t_image(i,j)¬newpixelvalue // variable t_image(i, j) hold total new value of each pixel after performing shuffling of each pixel.

Step 10: end columnloop

Step11:endrow loop

Step 12: loop through rows of image (i, j)

Step 13: loop through columns of image(i, j)

Step 14: ImgXx(i,j)¬image(i,j)+245;

Step15: end columnloop

Step16:end row loop

Step17:imgxXor¬unit8(ImgXx(i, j)); // i, j represent dimension of image

Step18:newXx¬xor imgxXor(i, j)// bitwise Xor operation performed on image imgxXor(i, j);

Step19: Secret message is stored in an optimized way in the cover-Image by using enhanced LSB (eLSB) based stegnography

Step 20: Transmit text data embedded cover image on public network

3.3.3 At the receiver end for encryption

Step 1:Convert Stego image into normal image and text by applying reverse e LSB method

Step2:Retrieveencrypted textual data (imgxXor(i,j)) from stego image by applying reverse eLSB process.

Step3: ImgXx(i, j)¬unit8 imgxXor((i, j)); // unit8 bitwise operation performed

Step4:: loop through rows of image (i, j);

Step 5: loop through columns of image (i, j):

Step 6: image(i,j)¬ImgXx(i,j) -245;

Step 7: end columns loop;

Step 8: end row loop;

Step 9: loop through rows of image (i, j);

Step 10: loop through columns of image (i, j);

Step 11: new_pixel_value ¬t_image (i, j);

Step 12: pixel_value¬(new_pixel_value - i^ columns)/256 ;

Step 13: image (i,j)¬pixel_values;

Step 14: end columnloop;

Step 15: end row loop;

Step 16: Convert the grayscale image to RGB

Step17: Apply the guided image filter is initially used to improve the contrast of a textual-image.

Step 18: Over the contrast, a marker-based watershed segmentation is applied to further improved image.

Step 19:A Gabor-transform is used to feature extraction needed for the classification task.

Step 20: A weighted-naïve-bayes model is used to identify the textual data from degraded image.

Step21:Using an adaptive optimization technique like gradient descent, further the performance of the such model is further improve

3.4 Performance Analysis on the Basis of PSNR, NPCR

Peak signal to noise ration and statistics are used to verify the proposed image encryption method's efficiency:

3.4.1 Peak Signal to Noise Ratio

It is also the ratio of the maximum likely power of corrupting noise affecting image representation coherence. Sometimes in cases, even though the PSNR is significantly smaller, one restoration could appear to be closer to the original than the other. Greater PSNR is usually associated with higher reconstruction quality (Dey et al., 2011). The mean square error shown in equation 1, is calculated for two dimension m*n monochrome images I and K, is used to define peak signal to noise ratio.

$$\text{Mean Square Error} = \frac{1}{MN} \sum_{y=1}^{M} \sum_{x=1}^{N} \left[I(x,y) - I'(x,y) \right]^2 \dots\dots\dots\dots \tag{1}$$

Where,

Oneoftheimagesiswellthought-outasnoisyimageoftheotheroriginalimage.

The equation (1)is used to calculate the peak signal to noise ratio:

$$\text{Peak Signal to Noise Ratio: } 10 \log_{10}\left(\frac{MAX}{\sqrt{MSE}} \right) \text{db} \text{-----------------------} \tag{2}$$

MAX seems to be the image's maximum available value of pixel. MAX is 255 once pixels are represented using 8 bits per specimen. This is a very useful indicator of a decoding procedure's efficiency. The ratio of the MSE of the component for the two images to the maximum mean square difference that can exist between two images is the peak signal to noise ratio of an image. The decibel valuation is used to articulate something that (db). The better the image quality retrieved, a much higher the peak-signal-to-noise value.

3.4.2 Analytical Statistics

It is well known that passing the statistical analysis on cipher text is critical for a cryptographic algorithm. In fact, an ideal cipher must be essential against any statistical attack. The previous statistical methods have been performed in order to demonstrate the proposed image encryption scheme for security.

3.4.3 Pearson's Linear Correlation Coefficient

It is most commonly used in statistical analysis, image encryption, and image processing. It seems to have application areas like comparing these two images for object recognition, image registration, and disparity measurement (Yen et al., 1998). The Pearson-correlation coefficient for monochrome digital images has been defined as:

$$\frac{\sum_i (x_i - x_m)(y_i - y_m)}{\sqrt{\sum_i (x_i - x_m)^2}\sqrt{\sum_i (y_i - y_m)^2}} \dots\dots\dots\dots\dots\dots\dots\dots\dots\dots\dots\dots \quad (3)$$

Where x_i is the quantity of the ith pixel of image 1, y_i is the strength of the ith pixel of image 2, x_m is the mean amount of image 1, and y_m seems to be the average strength of image 2, and x_m is the average quantity of image 1 and y_m is the average strength of image 2. Unless the two images have become completely identical, the correlation seems to be r=1 or close to 1, r=0 whether they are completely uncorrelated, and r=-1 if they are completely anti-correlated, such as if one image is the negative of the other. The correlation-coefficient is often used in security systems such as evaluation, agreement verification, temper identification with a security seal, and tagging.The correlation coefficient is typically used when combining similar images of the same object depending on the time. The value of r indicates whether or not entity has also been relocated or altered.

3.4. 4 Number of Pixel Change Rate

It's a common metric for determining an effect of a specific pixel change on the entire image. Let Ior(i,j) and Ienc(i,j) be the pixel values of an original and encoded image, respectively, to calculate the percentage of pixel values between the two images. Ior and Ienc, respectively, is the ith pixel row and j^{th} pixel column. Number of Pixel Change Rate defined through the following formula as (Abdullah, H.A.et al,.2017):

Figure 6. Example of used Image Data Set

$$\text{Number of Pixel Change Rate} = \frac{\sum_{i=1}^{M}\sum_{j=1}^{N} d(i,j)}{T} \times 100 \dots\dots\dots\dots\dots\dots \tag{4}$$

where,

The cipher- image's total number of pixels is denoted by the symbol T. The following is the definition of d (i, j):

$$d(i,j) = \begin{cases} 0 & Ior(i,j)=Ienc(i,j) \\ 1 & Ior(i,j)\neq Ienc(i,j) \end{cases} \dots\dots\dots\dots\dots\dots\dots\dots\dots \tag{5}$$

3.4.1 Unified Average Changing Intensity

A minor alteration in the unencrypted image must lead to a significant alteration to the encrypted image. For both the plaintext image Ior(i,j) and encrypted image Ienc(i, j), unified average changing intensity (UACI) is useful in determining the average intensity of difference in pixels between the two images (i,j). The following mathematical expression is used to define unified average changing intensity (Abdullah,H.A.etal., 2017):

$$UACI = \left[\sum_i \sum_j \frac{Ior(i,j) - Ienc(i,j)}{L.T} \right] \times 100\% \dots\dots\dots\dots\dots\dots\dots \tag{6}$$

Table 1. HDR image PSNR and MSE values

Image	MSE values of proposed Algorithm for HDR	PSNR values of proposed Algorithm for HDR images
1	0.07999	93.91
2	0.08011	93.92
3	0.08201	94.62
4	0.08101	94.71
5	0.08100	94.73
6	0.08222	94.81
7	0.08334	94.91
8	0.08314	94.93
9	0.08324	94.93
10	0.08214	94.83

Where L stands for the maximum pixel value compatible with the cipher text image format, T stands for the maximum pixel value compatible with the original text image formatand i, j stands for the absolute value function.

Figure 7. HDR image PSNR and MSE values

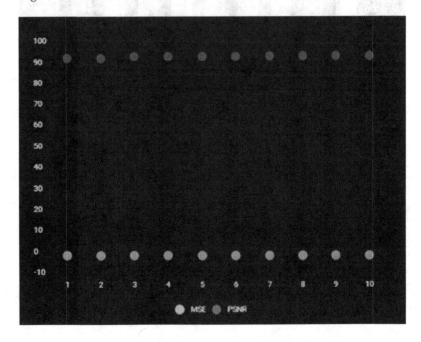

Table 2. HDR images for NPCR and UACI values

Image	NPCR of proposed algorithm for	UACI of proposed algorithm
	HDR image(%)	For HDR image (%)
1	98.90	33.32
2	98.609	33.46
3	99.61	33.51
4	99.65	33.46
5	99.66	33.53
6	99.70	33.54
7	99.69	33.55
8	99.69	33.56
9	99.72	33.57
10	99.76	33.56

4. RESULTS AND ANALYSIS

A general purpose database is used to run several tests on the proposed work in a systematic manner. HDR images (Xiao et al., 2002), JPEG images of the building, building inside, building front, flowers,

Figure 8. shows the values of NPCR and UACI of cipher images for proposed algorithm of HDR images.

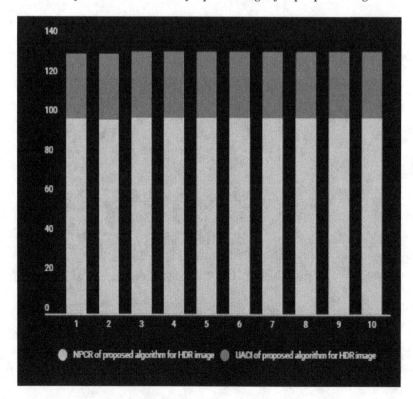

Table 3. PSNR and MSE values for JPEG images

Image	MSE of proposed algorithm for jpeg	PSNR of proposed algorithm for jpeg
1	0.084784	82.961948
2	0.083497	83.028356
3	0.084306	82.986500
4	0.085644	82.918107
5	0.084380	82.982690
6	0.085141	82.943691
7	0.085822	82.898454
8	0.083333	82.865474
9	0.084455	82.329104
10	0.085536	82.999453

gallery, and other images with a size of 256256 are one of the images stored in the database. Figure 6 below shows some examples of images from of the database.

The PSNR and MSE values of the proposed algorithm for HDR images are shown in Table 1. These are all the results of the chaotic map-based image encryption strategy. The MSE between the original and decrypted image was found to have been 0.086, as well as the PSNR was found to be 94.9282, indicating close restoration(Kanafchian, Mohadeseh, 2017).

The results of the proposed algorithm for HDR images are shown in Table 2 and Figure 7. By changing a pixel of a plain image, the real values of NPCR and UACI of cipher imagescan be obtained.

The values of NPCR and UACI for the experimental dataset are shown in figure 8. The closer NPCR can get to 100 percent, and the sensitive the cryptosystem is to plain image changes and the more effective it is at resisting simple text attacks. The larger the value of UACI, the better the cryptosystem's

Table4. NPCR and UACI values for JPEG images

Image	NPCR of Proposed Algorithm For JPEG (%)	UACI of proposed algorithm for JPEG(%)
1	99.609375	33.463541
2	99.609603	33.463541
3	99.609455	33.463541
4	99.609446	33.463541
5	99.587530	33.463541
6	99.609551	33.463541
7	99.609241	33.463541
8	99.609517	33.463541
9	99.607442	33.463541
10	99.605072	33.463541

resistance to various attacks. The findings show that the proposed algorithm is extremely sensitive to even minor changes in the plaintext message.

The PSNR and MSE results of the proposed algorithm for jpeg images are shown in Table 3 and figure 11. These are the results of a chaotic map-based image encryption approach along with enhanced LSB Stenography (Pramanik, S. et. al., 2020). The MSE between the original and decrypted image has been found to be 0.083, and the PSNR was found to be 83.99, indicating near-perfect feature extraction.

Table3 shows the values of PSNR and MSE of proposed algorithm for jpeg images. These evaluated values of image encryption approach based on chaotic map. Analysis of the value MSE between the original and decrypted image observed as 0.085 and PSNR observed as 82.9619 which is near good retrieval of image.

Figure 9. Shows the values of NPCR and UACI of cipher images for proposed algorithm of jpeg images.

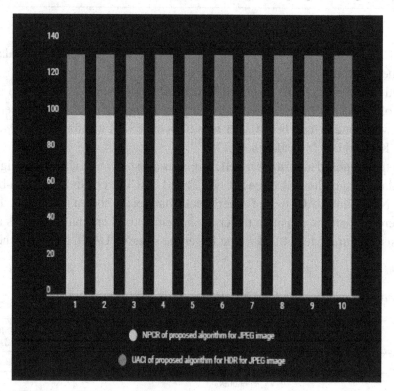

Figure 9 and table 4, shows the values of NPCR and UACI of cipher images for proposed algorithm of JPEG images. The values of NPCR and UACI for the experimental dataset are shown in Figure 9. The closer NPCR can get to 99% approximately, and the sensitive the cryptosystem is to plain image changes and the more effective it is at resisting simple text attacks. The larger the value of UACI the better the cryptosystem's resistance to various attacks. As shown in figure 10, it reveals that the proposed algorithm is extremely sensitive to even minor changes in the plaintext message.

Figure 10. shows that proposed algorithm has also good results for jpeg image. High PSNR value and low MSE value show the proposed algorithm is secure to transmit data

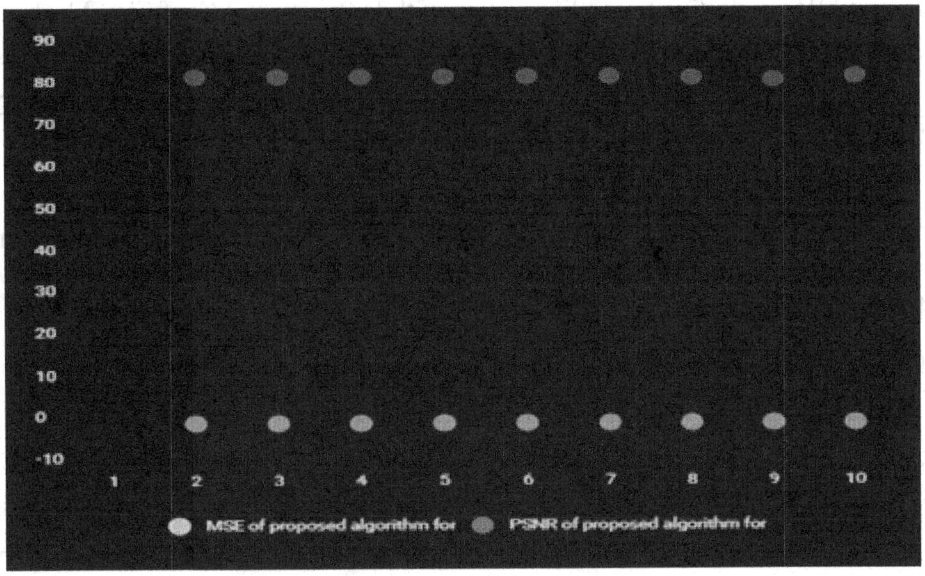

CONCLUSION

At existing eras where the most important communication is through wireless techniques using internet net work to transfer data, domain concerns are on the subject of the security of such personal or countries defense data. In this method, chaotic based encryption, enhanced LSB (e-Least Significant Bit) steganography, a deep learning based weighted naive bayes classifier along with and adaptive optimization technique is utilized for secure transmission, extraction, and identification of textual data on public network of computers.

Chaotic encryption techniques, steganography, and weighted naive bayes classifier based deep learning method are used to secure data transmission in a public network-based data transmission channel in three stages. In the first phase, a chaotic based image encryption scheme applied to encrypt the secured information. The encrypted data is implanted inside the cover-image by utilizing an improved LSB steganography procedure. The logic of chaotic keyless encryption and secret-key obtained by the steganography algorithm is shared with the message retrieval algorithm on the receiver side to retrieve the message, and the embedded text message is finally identified using a weighted naive bayes classifier. Furthermore, the weighted naive bayes classifier performance is enhanced through the use of adaptive optimization techniques. In the proposed method a high value of peak signal to noise ratio of stego image reflected the difficulty of retrieving the original image without the knowledge of proposed approach. NPCR of stego image is close to100% means high and has robust performance against the noisy attack. Performance analysis is used to review and assess the effectiveness of existing approaches and it is found that the proposed algorithms has a better result than the traditional algorithms for performance parameter peak signal to noise ratio and NPCR.

REFERENCES

Abdul & Naser. (2015). Selective Image Encryption with Diffusion and Confusion Mechanism. *International Journal of Advanced Research in Computer Science and Software Engineering, 4*(7), 5-12.

Abdullah, H. A., & Abdullah, H. N. (2017). Image encryption using hybrid chaotic map. *2017 International Conference on Current Research in Computer Science and Information Technology (ICCIT)*, 121-125. 10.1109/CRCSIT.2017.7965545

Attaby, A. A., Ahmed, M. F. M., & Alsammak, A. K. (2018). Data hiding inside JPEG images with high resistance to steganalysis using a novel technique: DCT-M3. *Ain Shams Engineering Journal, 9*(4), 1965–1974. doi:10.1016/j.asej.2017.02.003

Bernd, J. (1993). Digital Image Processing. In Concepts, Algorithms, and Scientific Applications. Springer-Verlag.

Chen, W. (2016). Optical Multiple-Image Encryption Using Three-Dimensional Space. *IEEE Photonics Journal, 8*(2), 1–8.

Chong, F., Bian, O., Jiang, H-y., Ge, L-h., & Ma, H-f. (2016). A New Chaos-Based Image Cipher Using a Hash Function. *IEEE/ACIS 15th International Conference on Computer and Information Science (ICIS)*.

Chung, K. L., Shen, C. H., & Chang, L. C. (2001). A novel SVD based image hiding scheme. *Pattern Recognition Letters, 22*(9), 1051–1058. doi:10.1016/S0167-8655(01)00044-7

Dey, N., Roy, A. B., & Dey, S. (2011). A Novel Approach of Color Image Hiding Using RGB Color Planes and DWT. *IJCA, 36*(5), 19–24.

Elkouny, A., Zakaria, N. S., & Sobhy, M. I. (2002). Communication Security using Chaotic Generator. *IEEE 45th Midwest Symposium on Circuits and Systems (MWSCAS)*. 10.1109/MWSCAS.2002.1187200

Fahim, Islam, & Aowlad. (2017). A new chaos based medical image encryption scheme. *2017 6th International Conference on Informatics, Electronics and Vision & 2017 7th International Symposium in Computational Medical and Health Technology (ICIEV-ISCMHT)*, 1-6.

Fridrich, J. (1998). Symmetric Chaos Based on Two-Dimensional Chaotic Maps and Chaos. *International Journal of Bifurcation, 8*(6), 1259–1284. doi:10.1142/S021812749800098X

Garcia-Bosque, M., Sánchez-Azqueta, C., & Celma, S. (2016). Secure communication system based on a logistic map and a linear feedback shift register. *IEEE International Symposium on Circuits and Systems (ISCAS)*, 2016, 1170-1173, 10.1109/ISCAS.2016.7527454

Kamboj, P., & Rani, V. (2013). Image Enhancement Using Hybrid Filtering Techniques. *International Journal of Scientific Research, 2*(6), 12–18.

Kanafchian, M., & Vajargah, B. F. (2017). A Novel Image Encryption Scheme Based on Clifford Attractor and Noisy Logistic Map for Secure Transferring Images in Navy. *International Journal of e-Navigation and Maritime Economy*, 53-63.

Kellert, H. S. (1993). In the Wake of Chaos: Unpredictable Order in Dynamical Systems. University of Chicago.

Kocarev, L. (2001). Chaos-based cryptography: a brief overview. *IEEE Circuits and Systems Magazine, 1*(3), 6–21. doi:10.1109/7384.963463

Lorenz, E. N. (1993). *The Essence of Chaos*. University of Washington Press.

Lu, J-a., Deng, X., Xie, J., & Chang, L. (2004). Secure Communication Based on Synchronization of a Unified Chaotic System. In *Fifth World Congress on Intelligent Control and Automation*. IEEE.

Malik, S., & Sardana, A., & Jaya. (2012). A Keyless Approach to Image Encryption. *2012 International Conference on Communication Systems and Network Technologies*, 879-883. 10.1109/CSNT.2012.189

Manne, R., Kantheti, S., & Kantheti, S. (2020). Classification of Skin cancer using deep learning, ConvolutionalNeural Networks - Opportunities and vulnerabilities- A systematic Review. *International Journal for Modern Trends in Science and Technology, 6*(11), 101-108. doi:10.46501/IJMTST061118

Pandey, B. K., Pandey, D., & Pandey, S. (2011). Survey of Bioinformatics Applications on Parallel Architectures. *International Journal of Computers and Applications, 23*(4), 21–25. doi:10.5120/2877-3744

Pandey, D., & Pandey, B. K. (2020). Analysis of Text Detection,Extraction and Recognition from Complex Degraded Images and Videos. *Journal of Critical Reviews, 7*(18), 427–433.

Pandey, D., Pandey, B. K., & Wariya, S. (2019). Study of Various Types Noise and Text Extraction Algorithms for Degraded Complex Image. *Journal of Emerging Technologies and Innovative Research, 6*(6), 234–247.

Pandey, D., Pandey, B. K., & Wariya, S. (2020). An Approach To Text Extraction From Complex Degraded Scene. *IJCBS, 1*(2), 4–10.

Pareek, N. K., Patidar, V., & Sud, K. K. (2006). Image Encryption using ChaoticLogisticMap. *Image and Vision Computing, 24*(9), 926–934. doi:10.1016/j.imavis.2006.02.021

Pramanik, S., & Bandyopadhyay, S. K. (2013). Application of Steganography in Symmetric Key Cryptography with Genetic Algorithm. *International Journals of Engineering and Technology, 10*, 1791–1799.

Pramanik, S., & Bandyopadhyay, S. K. (2014). Hiding Secret Message in an Image, International Journal of Innovative Science. *Engineering and Technology, 1*, 553–559.

Pramanik, S., & Bandyopadhyay, S. K. (2014). An Innovative Approach in Steganography, Scholars. *Journal of Engineering Technology*, 276–280.

Pramanik, S., Singh, R. P., & Ghosh, R. (2020). Application of Bi-orthogonal Wavelet Transform and Genetic Algorithm in Image Steganography. *Multimedia Tools and Applications, 79*(25-26), 17463–17482. Advance online publication. doi:10.100711042-020-08676-1

Pramanik, S., Singh, R. P., Ghosh, R., & Bandyopadhyay, S. K. (2020). A Unique Way to Generate Password at Random Basis and Sending it Using a New Steganography Technique. *Indonesian Journal of Electrical Engineering and Informatics, 8*(3), 525–531.

Rather, M., & Sengupta, A. (2020). IP Core steganography using switch-based key-driven hash-chaining and encoding for securing DSP kernels used in CE systems. *IEEE Transactions on Consumer Electronics*, *66*(3), 251–260. doi:10.1109/TCE.2020.3006050

Song, Y., & Song, J. (2017). A secure algorithm for image based information hiding with one-dimensional chaotic systems. *2017 3rd IEEE International Conference on Computer and Communications (ICCC)*, 1824-1829.

Chapter 11
Multimedia Data Protection Using Hybridized Crystal Payload Algorithm With Chicken Swarm Optimization

Sivanantham Kalimuthu
Crapersoft, India

Farid Naït-Abdesselam
University of Missouri, Kansas City, USA

Jaishankar B.
KPR Institute of Engineering and Technology, India

ABSTRACT

This research consists of three phase. The first model includes a crystal payload encryption method watermarking scheme and an attack-free encryption scheme called international data encryption algorithm (IDEA). The second model is a binary grey scale image in chicken swarm optimization (CSO) applied to copyright production parameter optimized swarm intelligence domain-based approach, which is compared to conventional approaches. The work performance has been evaluated for conventional machine learning approach using MATLAB. The simulation results show that proposed hybridized crystal payload algorithm with chicken swarm optimization (HCPECSO) scheme achieves a high copyright production with the lowest mean square error values and highest peak signal noise ration when compared with the existing approaches schemes like machine learning SVM, logistic regression, and neural network. The proposed HCPECSO attained less processing time of 32.33s and processing cost compared to existing schemes.

DOI: 10.4018/978-1-7998-7160-6.ch011

INTRODUCTION

In recent days, most of the image processing applications are implemented for security purposes. In that manner, the face detection process will help in providing an effective solution to security issues. The digital media stands over the analogue media because digital media can be reproduced easily and infinitely without any loss of fidelity. This boon, however, can also lead to a headache for copyright owners who need their work to be protected from unauthorised reproduction. The area of research concentration of this research is on hybrid schemes and dual watermarking. Dual protection scheme which means combination of encryption method with watermarking and dual watermarking schemes are analysed. It gives emphasis on robustness, embedding capacity, and rate of embedding and the visual perceptibility of the digital content. Foremost, the research analyses a model for assigning copyright protection to the image using crystal payload encryption method and Chicken Swarm Optimization watermark scheme. The watermark scheme used is a frequency domain algorithm which ensures high robustness to the input data. This model withstands almost all the watermarking attacks. Even though the CPE encryption scheme is faster, it is exposed to attacks.

This Research Consist of Three Phase. The first model includes an Crystal payload encryption method watermarking scheme and an attack free encryption scheme called International Data Encryption Algorithm. In this model the input is a image file which undergoes frame extraction before it is processed. This results in improved robustness when compared with the former, Least Significant Bit (LSB) based on image and text (multimedia) steganography and Secure image steganography using cryptography and image transposition model, but the overall model consumes more processing time due to the increased encryption time. Second model Binary Grey scale image in Chicken Swarm Optimization applied to copyright production parameter optimized swarm intelligence domain based approach and compared to conventional approaches.

The advancement of the Internet has accepted multimedia content to become accessible in digital form and is a major factor in the increased use of copyright marking. Though digital content can be distributed easily, it is also easy to misuse copyrighted material. Internet copies can be easily shared (Usman and Lemo, 2007). To peer to peer network, the stago values convert and stored on a server, make it though for the accredited users to locate and litigate offenders. Steganography can be fragile steganography or robust steganography. Fragile Steganography destroys the file on modification. It is incompatible for recording the copyright instruction, but helps to demonstrate that the file has been tampered (Panwar, Purwar and Jain, 2019). Fragile steganography methodologies are easier to demonstrate. Robust steganography embeds instructions into a data that is not easily eradicated. Although no mark is truly indestructible, a file can be considered safe, when changes in the file make it unusable.

The simplicity and the easiness of using digital content may result in breach of digital content. In the current era, rights managements for digital content are of huge important and were researched over decades. The multidimensional digital content transmitted over the internet should be protected to assure that it is not corrupted. The multidimensional contents are 2D/3D images, Video files and Image files. Hence there is a need for copyright protection, since the owners of the digital content need their property to be protected from illegal copying and illegal access. Digital watermarking techniques and cryptographic techniques have drawn more attention because of the need for copyright protection (Gong, He, Cheng, Hua, and Zhou, 2016).

Steganography is a method where by the digital secret content is embedded in the host content, So that the secret message is hidden from accessing and it is recoverable. The steganography schemes used should be very robust and should be resistant to all types of attacks on watermarks. The use of the encryption is to protect the digital content with the help of the key such that only the intended for person access to it. The cryptographic method used should not be prone to any kind of attacks and should execute faster.

A few paramilitary elements have been arrogating to themselves unscrupulous methods to harm innocent people the world over and one such modus operandi is hacking. Steganography is one of the digital deterrents to stop unethical people from attacking law-abiding citizens. This is the prime motivation behind settling on steganography. Moreover the contemporary market opportunities created by the state-of-the-art digital distribution coupled with apprehensions that digital works would be easy to copy is another reason for fixing on steganography (Siar, Alirezazadeh, and Jalali, 2018). Many a time people who seek complete confidentiality, look for steganography in place of cryptography. Although powerful encryption tools are available, the downside is that an encrypted message divulges itself that it carries a piece of information and this prompts the hackers to start investigating possible links. Encryption ensures confidentiality but not secrecy, while steganography disguises information and by looking at a picture, it would be difficult even to guess that it has secret information. The scope of steganography combined with encryption is additional security and invokes interest in the subject (Srinath, Usha, Sonia Maria, and Bangalore, 2018).

The spirit that virtuous engineers should also burn the midnight oil with courage and determination to thwart the plans of equally hard-working hackers is yet another reason to pursue the research on this area. The chicken swarm optimization process is ordinarily called the pre-processing stage in image processing applications (Rustom and Farah, (2017). Hence, optimization process is a significant prompt for determining pixels in an input image. Identification of a human optimization is entitled to a lot of issues that have attracted an impressive consideration of researchers in years. Crystal payload encryption method is very robust and it withstands invariant scaling attacks. Binary Grey scale image in modified discrete wavelet domain is highly robust and has high embedding capacity (Ye and Wong 2012). Hybrid crystal payload with chicken swarm optimization algorithm is faster than crystal payload encryption method and modified discrete wavelet domain. To enhance the embedding procedure crystal payload encryption based cryptographic Chicken Swarm Optimization method taken into account to fulfil the requirements of copyright protection. CPE is faster and is less prone to attacks also reversible block cipher which is very strong and it is not exposed to any kind of attacks. Hence the motivation of this work is developing the platform that can analysis various models for copyright protection with the combination of cryptographic (Wang, Lin, and Yang 2011).

The reminder of paper is organized as follows Section 2, Multimedia Data Protection and its related work, Section 3 discussed to Hybridized Crystal Payload Algorithm with Chicken Swarm Optimization algorithm, section 4 presents proposed system and existing systems experimental results comparison. Finally, section fifth provides the concluding remarks and future scope of the Multimedia DATA encryption.

LITERATURE REVIEW

The term cryptography characterizes as the procedure of secret communication between the sender and beneficiary where individual or group messages are contributed in an encrypted way, which will be unscrambled to get the principal message. Similarly, Cryptanalysis is the converse procedure of cryptography. The term cryptology is containing both Cryptography and cryptanalysis terms together.

Abed, H. N (2017) presented the concept of strategy for the identification of twofold JPEG compression and a maximum-likelihood estimator of the essential quality factor. These strategies are fundamental for the development of precisely focused on and daze steg-analysis strategies for JPEG pictures. The proposed strategies use Super Vector Machine classifiers with vectors shaped by histograms of low-recurrence DCT coefficients. The execution of the calculations is contrasted with selected existing methods. Initially, the identification of twofold compression is a legal device that is helpful for the restoration of the handling history.

Tiwari.N & Shandilya.M (2010) proposed Double compressed images are additionally created during image processing control. By distinguishing the intimations of recompression in singular picture portions, they might have the option to recognize the fashioned district because the non-tampered some portion of the picture will show hints of twofold compression Popescu and Farid (2004). Second, some steganographic calculations consistently decompress the cover JPEG format into the spatial space before inserting it. During installation, the image is compacted once more, normally with a default quantization framework.

Deb, K et al, (2012) proposed a stego-analysis strategy based on measurable perceptions on contrast picture histograms for the dependable recognition of LSB steganography. A physical quantity is acquired from the progress coefficients between distinction picture histograms of a picture and its prepared adaptation delivered by setting all bits in the LSB plane to zero. This amount is a decent proportion of the powerless relationship between's progressive piece planes and can be utilized to segregate stego-pictures from spread pictures. Further examinations show that there exists a practical connection between this amount and the implanted message length.

Hassoon.N.H, (2018) presented the strategy depends on the experimental Benford's Law and, all the more explicitly, on its summed up structure. They have been demonstrated and broaden the legitimacy of the logarithmic principle in shading pictures and present a visually impaired steganographic strategy that can hail a document as a suspicious stego-transporter. The proposed technique accomplishes high precision and speed and depends on the appropriations of the primary digits of the quantized Discrete Cosine Transform coefficients present in JPEGs. To approve and assess our calculation, we created steganographic instruments that can examine image records and altogether it is famous for the Uncompressed Color Image Database.

The historical backdrop of cryptography was ordinarily given to a specific occasion or association. For example military, wars, spies, and lords, whom they used its need also, knowing the methods. Then, the term of Steganography isn't to be mistaken for cryptography or on the other hand encryption. Irrespective of whether they consider the primary objective of the two procedures are secret, where steganography discussed how to conceal the presence of the message altogether, while, encryption discuss how to cloud the substance of the message, the two systems attempting to accomplish most extreme security regardless of whether they have various objectives.

Cryptography is not just protecting the information from attacker or modification, yet can likewise be utilized for customer verification. There are three kinds of cryptographic plots regularly used to achieve these objectives as shown below

- Secret key (or symmetric) cryptography
- Public key cryptography, and
- Hashmechanisms.

In all cases, the fundamental decoded information is referred to as plaintext. It is scrambled into ciphertext, which will (ordinarily) be decoded into usable plaintext.

Joshi.S.V et al, (2012) proposed the steganographic method, it utilizes human vision sensitivity to conceal secret bits. To make this, the unknown information is changed over into a progression of images to be implanted in a documentation framework with different bases. Hence, specific bases utilized are controlled by the level of neighbourhood variety of the pixel extents in the host picture.

A.Sharif, (2017) proposed a concept of secure information transmission utilizing video Steganography. They discussed this method at a very basic level to transmit data like less cost and military information in a secure way. Video Steganography is the strategy for covering some uncertainty information inside a component. The extension of this information to the quality isn't apparent by the human eye as the change of pixel concealing is irrelevant. They proposed to give a profitable and secured methodology for highlight Steganography. The proposed framework makes a neglected for the puzzle information and the record is placed in the packaging of the video itself. With the help of this record, the housings contain the puzzle information is to be found. Therefore, in the middle of the extraction procedure, rather than looking at the entire element, the packaging containing the challenge data is explored with the help of the list at the not exactly attractive end.

Wang et al, (2011) proposed a concept of Video Steganalysis against Motion Vector. This will be adding or subtracting one movement vector Value. They concentrated more on providing the system for a group of gathering vector-based element steganography. To start with the change on the least sum imperative piece of the development vector is discussed. I.S.Sam et al (2012) the crash of the introducing procedure on the aggregate of a total of an outright gap is discussed, which licenses us to focus on the contrast between the genuine total of the outright gap and nearby measures perfect total of outright gap after the including or-subtracting-one activity on the development regard. Assessments are finished on highlights corrupted by disparate steganography systems and encoded by various development conclusion frameworks, in various bit rates, and various element codecs.

H.Sa et al (2015) proposed an exceptionally secure video steganography utilizing Hamming code. Because of the fast web and propels in advancement, people are finding the shortest path to hack by an attacker. Since, numerous estimations of steganography and data detection have been proposed. Steganography is a system of introducing the secrecy information inside the host medium. Swain.G (2019) also explained version same time, an enormous segment of the extreme steganographic assessment programming ventures has been given to unapproved customers to get well the huge challenge information that was embedded in the transporter archives. Some steganography computations can be viably common place by step analytical locators taking into account the absence of security and introducing efficiency.

A change to the LSB steganography was presented by Y.Liu et al (2015). This change gives the ideal decision of a paired capacity of two spread pixels as opposed to being arbitrary as in LSBM. To build the degree of security, a joined information encoding and concealing procedure was proposed by Maheswari& Hemanth (2017). This procedure was utilized to beat the issue of picture shading changes after the installing process. The LSB steganography system was created by Malik et al., (2017), it dependent on installing the mystery message into the more extreme edge locales of the picture to guarantee its obstruction against picture steganalysis dependent on measurable examination. A tale picture steganography was proposed by Montalbo & Barfeh,(2019), it is based on Integer Wavelet Transform, and it is utilized to insert different mystery pictures and keys in shading cover image.

The steganography methods are studied in this chapter have their own merits and demerits. Most of the researchers suggested various concepts/suggested new enhancement instead of the traditional steganography module. Since, the merits and demerits of every article were studied. It is observed that single research is not enough to meet all requirements for steganography and watermarking. The major problems that are identified in the review are the security of information.

SYSTEM DESIGN

Taking the preferred position of the input stgo picture and the rest of optimization techniques about similar hues, shading dispersion of distinguished input data districts is figured and utilized for consequently building an input image shading model under the crystal payload encryption system. The proposed model optimized the image parameters and calculation checks whether the input stgo image condition of the following edge has changed or not.

Input region is utilized to test image hues and a dynamic thresholding procedure is utilized to refresh the image shading model just if the brightening condition has changed. At the point when the enlightenment condition has changed yet there is no face distinguished, shading rectification procedure is utilized to change over the shades of the current casing to those as they show up under the equivalent illuminant of the last model refreshed casing. The image shading arrangement is then performed on the shading rectified picture. The stream chart of the proposed strategy is outlined in figure 1.

Initially, the image is sampled and processed with illumination variations and face detections. The Discrete-Time Dynamic System is added additionally that the fundamental structure utilized by (Muhammad, Ahmad, Sajjad, and Zubair, 2015). As per the technique, it is critical to take note that since the calculation employments a determinant in its procedure; the information framework must be square.

Usman and Lemo (Usman and Lemo, 2007) proposed based on the issue which may be to apply the calculation on square squares of a given picture drearily. However, that would produce recognizable impossible to miss occasional square examples given the idea of the procedure, and obviously, this isn't an intriguing certainty as it clashes with the point of producing riotous maps. Most definitely, the combination of the interpretation of pixels into their underlying areas, i.e., picture accurate recreation after certain emphasis, is likewise not an engaging variable. This is a watched wonder in an assortment of disordered based calculations. Given one of the emphasis is utilized, if an aggressor picks up information on the calculation and gets the parameter "l", which is not hard to break utilizing a savage power assault, the aggressor will have the option to include further cycles which will uncover the unique image.

The calculation is very much defined and sufficiently introduced, it yields great outcomes for RGB pictures as announced by the creators. It was seen that they utilized an adjusting administrator which was applied recursively along with the various emphases. The significant concern would be in recouping the specific power estimations of the information picture as the recuperated picture that appeared in their work may be only an estimate due to the previously mentioned administrator. This is significant, particularly in the use of steganography where the goal is to recuperate the specific installed record as opposed to its estimation.

Based on the image encryption review, the encryption suggestions are to be followed. It is necessary to convert image standards by considering the various considerations discussed in (Shet 2017).

- Change the image and video encryption plans that are commonly unreliable against known and selected plaintext assaults.
- Mystery change is certainly not an essential.

- An image content criticism is exceptionally valuable for improving the security.
- Image content criticism can be improved further whenever joined with stage.
- Consolidating a basic stream image and a basic square figure can help improve security.
- The diffusion methods used in most chaos-based encryption methods that are very slow.
- Specific encryption may give enough security given the conditions between the decoded and scrambled information.

Based on the above considerations, the following algorithm is framed hybrid crystal payload encryption with chicken swarm optimization algorithms.

In the case of selecting the entire payload, encryption will result in the simplest code and easy to retrieve the image or text. The chance of detection will be high and help in resolving the data transfer issues. Since the payload may extend for the function of encryption. Even though that is not a function of encryption and it does not ensure the data integrity. Since there are some limitations such as the whole payload becomes incoherent, maybe delaying functionality and it will lead to misleading the data. Similarly, the encrypted data must require various indexes while decrypting the respective images. The size of the encryption will become complex and provide communication overhead. The adoption of the crystal payload concept is because of its granular control over the source. This will help in providing the encryption and decryption of an image. The storage of the management cannot read the original payload data. Hence, this is more efficient and named it as Payload Encryption (PE).

The merits of PE are described as follows:

- The data or information stores in the cloud can be decrypted only on the client-side. Hence, it will be more secure.
- It is easy to handle the data both in the movement phase and the pause phase.
- In case of storing the data in public cloud storage, then it will have the second level of encryption to avoid any attack from hackers.
- It will support data integrity on different storage and maintain compatibility.
- Payload encryption provides a high level of privacy.

Three common color spaces are Red, Green and Blue. Apart from that, the Orthogonal color space indicates that Luminance (Y), Chromatic blue (Cb) and Chromatic red, (Cr). This is a change that has a place with the group of Television (TV) transmission shading spaces. This shading space is utilized broadly in video coding and pressure, for example, Moving Picture Experts Group (MPEG) and is perceptually uniform. Besides, it gives a fantastic space for luminance and chrominance detachability. Y is an added substance mix of R, G and B segments and consequently saves the high recurrence picture substance.

$$YC_bC_r \begin{cases} Y = 0.299R + 0.587G + 0.114B \\ \quad C_b = 0.56(B - Y) \\ \quad C_r = 0.71(R - Y) \end{cases} \tag{1}$$

Equation (1) subtracts the Y component and balances the high recurrence (Y). As per the triplet RGB, the YCbCr change can be determined to utilize the framework. The next parameter is Illumination. It is consistently tarnished along with the RGB frame on a given colourimage. Finally, the effectishardly distributed here. It is possible to segregate the color images, gray level and 3D images. There are different approaches to segregate such illumination.

To express to advance images, most normally utilized shading space is RGB as most image gadgets have an RGB yield. RGB shading space is utilized in each framework just as cameras, recordings and so forth. The benefit of RGB is its straight forwardness and likewise, it is anything but difficult to actualize. The hindrances are the high connection between the channels, critical perceptual non-consistency, blending of chrominance and luminance information. Figure 2 proposed RGB color space.

Initially, the input images are collected from a dataset. Then process with the aforementioned steps on anyone color space transformations. Since, the color transformation will be carried out by I(x). This process will include matrix multiplication and reduces the color representation for 3-Dimensional to Single Dimension space. This process will help in reducing the hue and saturation details. The outcome will be in terms of the grayscale colour. This process is carried out using the Equation (2). Initially, the decoding concept involves a generated keymap and mapping unit. Since the encryption must be equal to null set{$\emptyset$}.

$$Encryption = \left\{ Encryptedmatrix - Decoding\left(A', Map \right) \right\} \tag{2}$$

To achieve the transformation from sensitivity to the spatial domain, the hybrid DCT and FFT methods are applied. Accordingly, pictures can be handily encoded safely with secret word security. Note that this plan productively encodes greyscale and double pictures. Anyhow, for RGB pictures it is seen that utilizing a similar secret key for the three primaries yields a few detectable examples acquired from the first picture, RGB hues are exceptionally associated. This is effectively defeated through the accompanying two decisions: either the client supplies three passwords every one of which scrambles one shading channel or all the more helpfully Steganoflage creates another two exceptional keys from the first provided secret word. For example, a solitary key can be used to create the accompanying distinctive hash functions.

Next, the calculation attempts to acquire another form of the luminance however this time without bringing the R vector into account.Most input image shading will in general redinterchannel. The disposing of red shading is purposeful, as in the last stage it will help to figure the mistake signal.Therefore, the new vector will have the biggest components taken from G or B. The elimination of the Red colors will be achieved through the HSV modification.Figure 3 shows the HSV color space system.Figure 2 shows the YCrCb color space system. In figure 1 expalined the proposed Hybrid Crystal Payload Encryption with Chicken Swarm Optimization algorithm flow chart and data communication. The figure 2 explain proposed skin detection input image dataset rgb colour prediction model, in 3D color representation block color starts value (0,0,0) accordance to the color values varied. The 3 explain the proposed skin detection angular roataion, HSV model used to predict the each colour rotation.

$$e(x) = I(x) - I(x) \tag{3}$$

As shown in the Equation (3.3), the error signal will be derived for each value. The error value e(x) will be either eliminated or rounded off to the nearest value.

Figure 1. Proposed Hybrid Crystal Payload Encryption with Chicken Swarm Optimization Flow chart

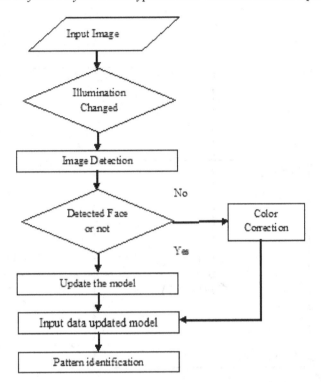

Creating an Encryption Probability Map that utilizes an unequivocal limit based Chicken Swarm Optimization group classifier which characterizes the lower and upper limits of the input image group is vital to the achievement of the proposed strategy. A collection of some pixel samples was gathered from distinctive input image districts displaying a scope of races with an extraordinary variety of lighting effects. After change utilizing the proposed strategy, the projection of information concedes a distribution that could be easily fit into a Gaussian curve utilizing the Expectation-Maximization method which is an approximation of Gaussian Mixture Models as appeared in Figure 5. It is also clear that there are no other Gaussians covered up in the appropriation.

The face or encryption detection will be carried out through some statistics with the help of mean (μ) and standard deviation (σ). By embedding the crystal payload encryption standard from this image detection will result in an excellent performance. The outer layer is identified by detecting the dark red spots to extract. Since, the color space will be changed based on the given input image standard. This will separate the optimization and non-optimization clusters. To verify this proposed hybrid concept, the algorithm was adopted with various color images with different RGB image standards.

The following steps will discuss more the embedding and identification of the reliable regions in the encrypted process.

Step 1: Initially, Illumination is equally spread along with RGB hues in some random shading picture. Consequently, its impact is hardly recognized here. There are various ways to deal with isolate such light.

Figure 2. RGB color space

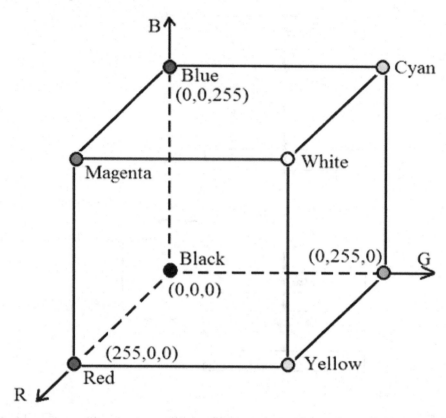

Step 2: Next, the calculation attempts to acquire another form of the luminance however this time without considering the R vector. Most input image shading will in the general group in the red channel.

Step 3: The disposing of the shading red is intentional, as in the last stage it will assist with computing the blunder signal.

Step 4: Making a Chicken Swarm Optimization Map(SPM), which utilizes an unequivocal edge-based Chicken Swarm Optimization group classifier which characterizes the lower and upper limits of the input image regions, is essential to the accomplishment of the proposed procedure.

Step 5: An assortment of some pixel tests was collected from various input encrypted areas showing a scope of races with an outrageous variety of lighting impact.

Step 6: After change utilizing the proposed strategy, the projection of information concedes an appropriation that could without much of a stretch fit a Gaussian curve utilizing an Expectation-Maximization, a technique which is an estimation of crystal payload encryption. It is likewise evident that there are no different Gaussians covered up in the conveyance.

To initialize the normalization process with the given image as per the crystal payload encryption. Identify the outer layer with the given input image with the chicken swarm optimization orientation, border, etc,. Some edges are automatically detected with the feature points and find the midpoint. It will be segregated with the grayscale image standard. The measures will help with Chicken Swarm Optimization optimized feature and identify the matches between each outer.

Figure 3. HSV color space

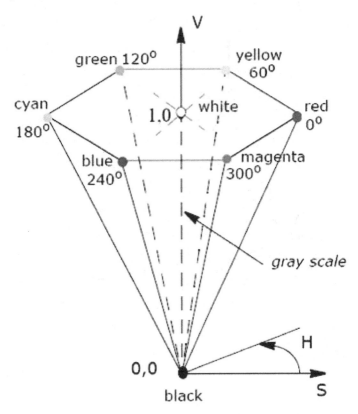

RESULT DISCUSSION

In this chapter, the experimental consequences of the proposed strategy are introduced and examined. In the investigation, images of various resolutions comprising of color pictures are utilized as source pictures. To implement crystal payload encryption module performance is presented with the threshold concept to identify the Chicken Swarm Optimization outer layer. The assessment of the pictures is utilized for direct execution examination of the proposed technique that encourages prompt power against assaults. In the test work, the messages are effectively inserted into the spread pictures like Deblur, Mandrill, Lena, and peppers. It is necessary to detect any type of image with various illuminance. Hence, the image with face, object and irregular 4 types of input images are selected for examination. These images are processed into the following types.

- Image detection
- Embedding
- Extraction

Initially, the image selection process will be taken place. Detect the Input image with the help of a payload encrypted style, followed by cropping and estimate the Histogram details of each image. The embedding concept will be carried out by the following process,

Figure 4. YCrCb color space system

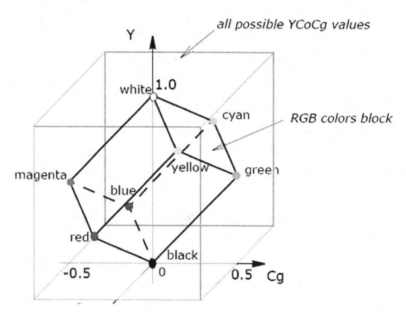

- The key generation process
- Transformation
- Embedding
- Inverse transform
- Reconstruction

The extraction process started with Stego-image and the size is adjusted based on the requirement. Again, the transformation is applied as per the encryption standard. Finally, extract the original image with a high-efficiency factor.

The input image is sampled by both color and grayscale. The two test sets will help in achieving the input image color model. Figure 6 is used as a normal image given as an input, assuming that each image in it is obtained under normal lighting conditions. Similarly, Figure 7 is used as a grayscale input image which is inverted in the original color images.

The bit can be generously focused comparative with the image, focused however balance to below focus, or arranged in another area. In a subsequent model, the bit can be each nth pixel in an area, for example, the rectangular locale depicted in the main model. In a third model, the part can be choosen dependent on the shading, splendor, or another part of the pixels, any strategy can be utilized to select the part.

Figure 8 illustrates the input image which is implemented with the proposed methodology. This will segment the input images regions based on the wide variation in illumination conditions. Because of the embedding concept of crystal payload, the image is encrypted with a high-security feature. The addition of keys will result in a high level of security. With that, the skin tone detection will help predict the surface of the face and non-image area.

Figure 5. Extraction process

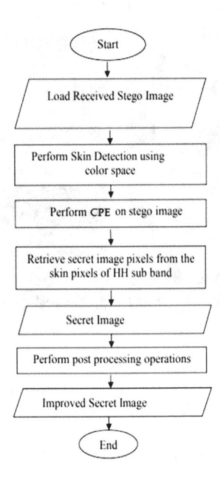

The image identification framework can separate a bit from the given image. The extraction can be preceded as depicted concerning Figure 8 Extracting the part can incorporate choosing a bit, duplicating a segment, or alluding to a segment of the image. The bit can be a particular locale of the image. Then again, the part can incorporate individual pixels disseminated all through the picture or pixels situated inside at least one explicit segment of the image.

Initially, the proposed HCPECSO algorithm was tested on all four images. Occlusion-free images were used for training. The features of the HCPECSO algorithm were also tested for comparative performance evaluation. The computerized image encryption based cryptography is the determination of a goodchaotic map for an encryption plot. In this examination, the three stages of image encryption plans are structured and broke down by standard tests. The plans show great confusion and dispersion properties of encryption. The security levels of the structured plans are examined well. The security level is high and they can withstand any potential attacks.

Information Entropy

The information entropy is computed for the original secret image and its recovered secret image. Its value should be 8 for grayscale image. The security level of proposed system is high if the value of informa-

Figure 6. Original Images used for proposed encryption method

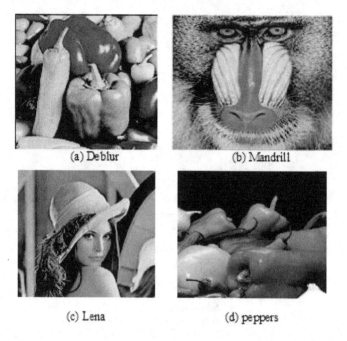

tion entropy is equal or greater than 8 proposed system compared to three different types of algorithm, listed as table1 shows the value of IE for different secret images and cover images.

Figure 7. Grayscale input image-standard

Figure 8. Input dataset Mask images

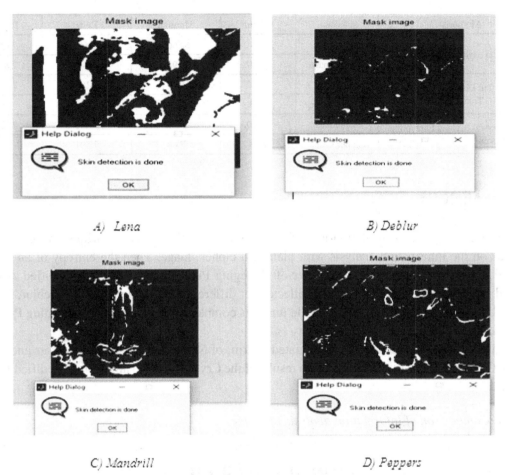

An Efficient Encryption is of dominant importance to almost all forms of cryptography applications. The simple encryption standardis developed to avoid the insecurity. Various methods like efficient encryption standard using crystal payload algorithm, an efficient encryption standard by using Modified Discrete Wavelet Domain and Crystal Payload Encryption with Chicken Swarm Optimization. In this section, a near report is done of the three proposed plans that have just been communicated about independently in the past parts. Consequently, hybrid methods are considered. The Information analyses of these methods are listed as shown in Table 1 and figure 9. The parameter IE is measured after applying steganography algorithm on cover and secret images. The need of cryptography is based on the parameter IE.

The IE values after steganography has values less than the threshold '8' and IE values after cryptography has values greater than the threshold '8'. The security of the proposed system is high when the value of IE is greater than the threshold value 8. It is very clear from Table 1, that the security of the proposed system is optimum by applying the cryptography technique on the stego image

Table 1. Information entropy of Image

Methods	Type	Deblur	Mandril	Lena	Pepper
Crystal payload algorithm	Plain image	6.7210	6.8661	7.0687	7.0545
	Cipher image	7.4318	7.4985	7.4809	7.8869
Modified Discrete Wavelet Transform	Plain image	6.810	6.99	7.108	7.0545
	Cipher image	7.33	7.68	7.591	7.98
Hybrid Crystal Payload Encryption with Chicken Swarm Optimization	Plain image	6.810	6.99	7.108	7.0545
	Cipher image	7.33	7.68	7.591	7.98

Entropy Analysis

In the present study, experimentation is carried out to analyze the effect of various image encryption standards on the information analysis with plain and cipher image. Then the entropy of an image is reviewed with two parameters like Number of Changing Pixel Rate (NPCR) and Unified Averaged Changed Intensity (UACI). The data are collected for different image standards like Deblur, Mandril, Lena and Pepper. The entropy analysis of the image is compared with Number of Changing Pixel Rate (%) and Unified Averaged Changed Intensity (%).

The quality of the decoded image is evaluated interms of Number of Pixels Change Rate and Unified Average Changing Intensity. The simulation results of the Crystal payload algorithm, Modified Discrete

Figure 9. Comparison of Information analysis of Image

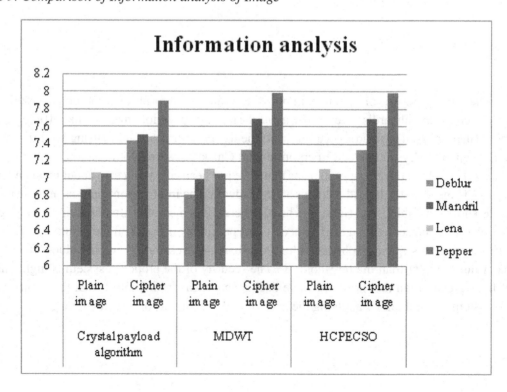

Table 2. Entropy Analysis of Image

Parameters	Methods	Deblur	Mandril	Lena	Pepper
Number of Changing Pixel Rate (%)	Crystal payload algorithm	99.4209	99.4786	99.46608	99.4521
	Modified Discrete Wavelet Transform	99.50	99.55	99.56	99.55
	Hybrid Crystal Payload Encryption with Chicken Swarm Optimization	99.62	99.64	99.69	99.70
Unified Averaged Changed Intensity (%)	Crystal payload algorithm	31.4106	31.5355	31.4943	31.4918
	Modified Discrete Wavelet Transform (MDWT)	31.518	31.52	31.54	31.50
	Hybrid Crystal Payload Encryption with Chicken SwarmOptimization (HCPECSO)	31.623	31.645	31.78	31.73

Wavelet Transform, and HCPECSO approach on a gray-level image displayed in table 2 and figure 10 the high speed, performance on the sensitivity and security. NPCR, UACI are used to evaluate the strength of image encryption algorithms. Even in the Crystal payload algorithmthe change of the number of pixels in the cipher-image rate when only one pixel of the plain-image is modified and the Unified Average Changing Intensity is already very high (NPCR99.4209, UACI 31.4106).

Execution Time

As general prerequisites, any image encryption calculation should oppose all sorts of referred to assaults, for example, the known-plaintext assault, the factual assault, the differential assault, the figure text-just assault and the different types of real-time attacks. The proposed approaches utilize various sizes of hued pictures for the investigation. The security investigation acted in these methodologies is a visual examination, histogram examination, correlation coefficient. All these analyses demonstrate that the proposed techniques satisfy all the outcomes totally and appropriately. The average time of these images is observed with all methodologies and shown in Figure 11.

Peak Signal Noise Ratio

To achieve a secure and robust watermarking using a hybrid crystal payload encryption scheme with a Chicken swarm optimization process is implemented.

Since, from the observations, the enhanced HCPECSO algorithmic concept of encryption shows that they are performing better in the case of NPCR and UACI values. Since the value decides the security feature that will help in blocking the attack. Further, the PSNR metrics are equated in Figure 12.

PSNR with Variable Amount of Embedded Cipher

The PSNR is further estimated with different sizes of embedded data in KBs, as shown in figure 13.The comparative results of the proposed HCPECSO algorithm as compared to the previous Least Significant

Figure 10. Comparison of Entropy Analysis

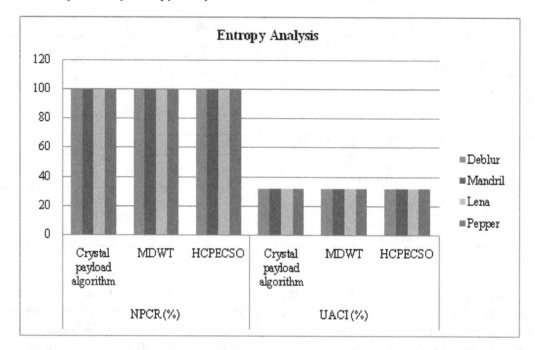

Bit, Modified Discrete Wavelet Transform based on image steganography,and secure image steganography using cryptography and image transposition. The HCPECSO algorithm clearly shows its better results in terms of PSNR which validate the effectiveness of the proposed method.

From the above experiments, which are discussed in chapters 3, 4, and 5 respectively, it is strongly recommended that an HCPECSO provides better accuracy and high-security level when compared to other existing methods. Conventional encryption standards are not adequate for authentication because of its low security. So, the research focuses on implementing the CSO and crystal payload algorithm hybridized to improve the security in plain and cipher images also compared conventional steganography algorithms for data security performance evaluation parameters.

CONCLUSION

With the quick improvement of innovations and technology frameworks give on-going protection to various applications. Data is a benefit which should be made sure about. The subject of securing data or images by changing plaintext into an unintelligible configuration is called cipher text. Just the individuals who have a mystery key can decode the message into plain content. In the ever-increasing development of media applications, security is a crucial job in communication and the capacity of an image. Encryption is one of the approaches to guarantee security. It changes the substance into an incomprehensible and un-visible group.

For the most part, Communication utilizing image guarantees secure communication. Information transmitted through the channel should contain security, integrity, and authenticity through the exposed system. So to keep the mystery of the information is getting increasingly more consideration. An origi-

Figure 11. Comparison of various methods with execution time

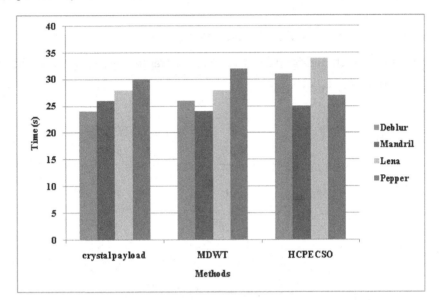

nal image or document needs more space to store. If extra space or transmission time is significant, at that point images should be compacted. Therefore, the images are compressed and removed unwanted portions to adapt to such an objective. Based on this motivation, the proposed research methodology responded with the following objectives.

- Privacy
- Integrity
- Less execution time
- More security

To achieve these objectives, the crystal payload detection algorithm is implemented with various stages. The original images are processed by RGB hues and equate the luminance factor. Later, the Encryption Probability Map (EPM) is framed to achieve edge classification. With the help of Expectation-Maximization and DWT, an efficient crystal payload encryption is formed. The encoded key will help decide the histogram analysis. The Correlation Co-efficient analysis decides the relationship of the encryption process. The DWT process contains Layered image, sub chaos image added with the key to process Multi chaotic encryption. Finally, the encryption image is recovered through a scrambling image. Finally, the crystal payload encryptions with Chicken Swarm Optimization algorithms are proposed with the training phase and detection phase. The factor called illumination change and face detection will decide the outer layer and further classification model is updated.

The experimental results were carried out in MATLAB tool with Crystal Payload Encryption, Modified Discrete Wavelet Transform, and crystal payload encryption with CSO algorithms. The observations are processed with four types of test images are collected namely Deblur, Mandrill, Lena, and peppers. The research conducted is applied by using Crystal Payload Encryption with Chicken Swarm Optimization

Figure 12. Comparative analysis of three methods using PSNR with different images

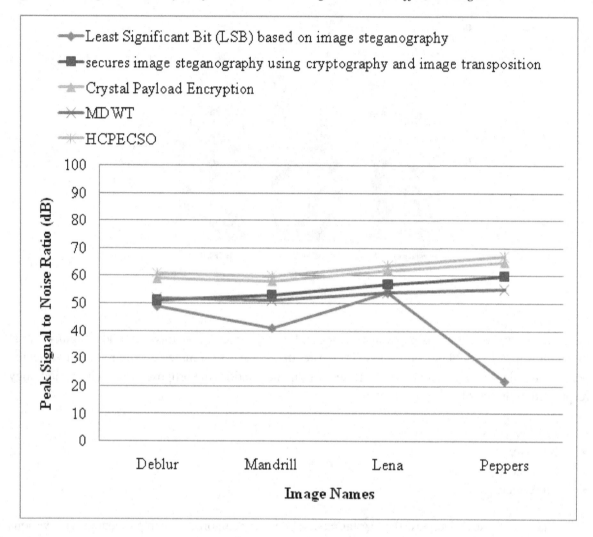

which can be extended to serve the security. It is experimental with the graphical test, that it consumes very less time to execute and holds data security.

FUTURE WORK

Further improvements of the presented framework in this thesis are described as follows. In the future, this hybrid method must be combined with some secure image standards to compress the size and processing time. The proposed model has experimented with 8 KB of image size. In the future, it will be further extending the design and that must check the complex image formats.

Figure 13. Comparative analysis using PSNR with a variable amount of embedded cipher

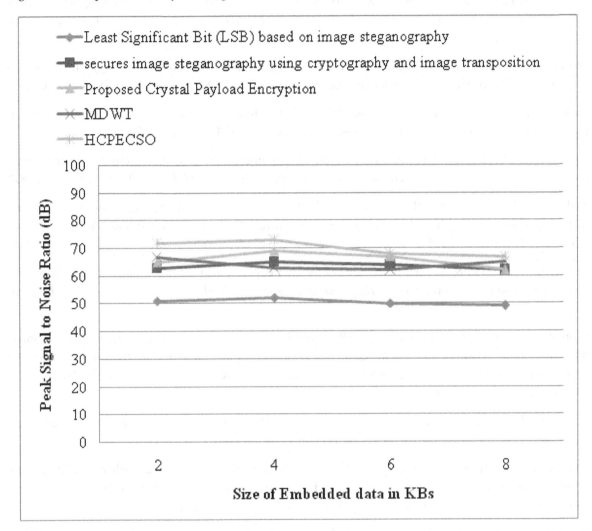

REFERENCES

Abed, H. N. (2017). Robust and secured image steganography using lsb and encryption with qr code. *Journal of Al-Qadisiyah for Computer Science and Mathematics, 9*(2), 1-9.

Deb, K., Al-Seraj, M. S., Hoque, M. M., & Sarkar, M. I. H. (2012, December). Combined DWT-DCT based digital image watermarking technique for copyright protection. In *2012 7th International Conference on Electrical and Computer Engineering* (pp. 458-461). IEEE. 10.1109/ICECE.2012.6471586

Gong, L. H., He, X. T., Cheng, S., Hua, T. X., & Zhou, N. R. (2016). Quantum image encryption algorithm based on quantum image XOR operations. *International Journal of Theoretical Physics, 55*(7), 3234–3250. doi:10.100710773-016-2954-6

Hassoon, N. H., Ali, R. A., Abed, H. N., & Alkhazraji, A. A. J. (2018). Multilevel hiding text security using hybrid technique steganography and cryptography. *IACSIT International Journal of Engineering and Technology*, *7*(4), 3674–3677.

Hemalatha, S., Acharya, U. D., & Renuka, A. (2015). Wavelet transform based steganography technique to hide audio signals in image. *Procedia Computer Science*, *47*, 272–281. doi:10.1016/j.procs.2015.03.207

Joshi, S. V., Bokil, A. A., Jain, N. A., & Koshti, D. (2012). Image steganography combination of spatial and frequency domain. *International Journal of Computers and Applications*, *53*(5).

Liu, Y., Yang, T., & Xin, G. (2015). Text steganography in chat based on emoticons and interjections. *Journal of Computational and Theoretical Nanoscience*, *12*(9), 2091–2094. doi:10.1166/jctn.2015.3992

Maheswari, S. U., & Hemanth, D. J. (2017). Performance enhanced image steganography systems using transforms and optimization techniques. *Multimedia Tools and Applications*, *76*(1), 415–436. doi:10.100711042-015-3035-1

Malik, A., Sikka, G., & Verma, H. K. (2017). A high capacity text steganography scheme based on LZW compression and color coding. *Engineering Science and Technology, an International Journal*, *20*(1), 72-79.

Montalbo, F. J. P., & Barfeh, D. P. Y. (2019, December). Classification of Stenography using Convolutional Neural Networks and Canny Edge Detection Algorithm. In *2019 International Conference on Computational Intelligence and Knowledge Economy (ICCIKE)* (pp. 305-310). IEEE. 10.1109/ICCIKE47802.2019.9004359

Muhammad, K., Ahmad, J., Sajjad, M., & Zubair, M. (2015). *Secure image steganography using cryptography and image transposition.* arXiv preprint arXiv:1510.04413.

Panwar, K., Purwar, R. K., & Jain, A. (2019, September). Design of a SHA-2 Hash Based Image Encryption Scheme using 1D chaotic systems and DNA sequences. In *2019 International Conference on Computing, Power and Communication Technologies (GUCON)* (pp. 769-773). IEEE.

Rustom, N. A. H., & Farah, N. A. A. (2017). A Review in Using Steganography Applications in Hiding Text Inside Digital Image (BMP). *International Journal (Toronto, Ont.)*, *7*(1).

Sam, I. S., Devaraj, P., & Bhuvaneswaran, R. (2012). An intertwining chaotic maps based image encryption scheme. *Nonlinear Dynamics*, *69*(4), 1995–2007. doi:10.100711071-012-0402-6

Sharif, A., Mollaeefar, M., & Nazari, M. (2017). A novel method for digital image steganography based on a new three-dimensional chaotic map. *Multimedia Tools and Applications*, *76*(6), 7849–7867. doi:10.100711042-016-3398-y

Shet, K. S., Aswath, A. R., Hanumantharaju, M. C., & Gao, X. Z. (2017). Design and development of new reconfigurable architectures for LSB/multi-bit image steganography system. *Multimedia Tools and Applications*, *76*(11), 13197–13219. doi:10.100711042-016-3736-0

Siar, F., Alirezazadeh, S., & Jalali, F. (2018). A novel steganography approach based on ant colony optimization. In *2018 6th Iranian Joint Congress on Fuzzy and Intelligent Systems (CFIS)* (pp. 215-219). IEEE.

Srinath, N. K., Usha, B. A., Sonia Maria, D. S., & Bangalore, B. B. (n.d.). *Image Steganography Using Neural Networks*. doi:10.1109/CFIS.2018.8336653

Swain, G. (2019). Very high capacity image steganography technique using quotient value differencing and LSB substitution. *Arabian Journal for Science and Engineering*, *44*(4), 2995–3004. doi:10.100713369-018-3372-2

Tiwari, N., & Shandilya, M. (2010). Secure RGB image steganography from pixel indicator to triple algorithm-an incremental growth. *International Journal of Security and Its Applications*, *4*(4), 53–62.

Usman, S., & Lemo, T. (2007). *Policy Statement by the Government of Nigeria on the Nigerian Economic Reform Program After Completion of the Policy Support Instrument*. Academic Press.

Vani, B. G., & Prasad, E. V. (2013). A Novel Method of 3D Image Steganography Using LZW Technique and Chaotic Neural Network. *International Journal of Computer Science and Network Security*, *13*(6), 1.

Wang, Y. R., Lin, W. H., & Yang, L. (2011). An intelligent watermarking method based on particle swarm optimization. *Expert Systems with Applications*, *38*(7), 8024–8029. doi:10.1016/j.eswa.2010.12.129

Ye, G., & Wong, K. W. (2012). An efficient chaotic image encryption algorithm based on a generalized Arnold map. *Nonlinear Dynamics*, *69*(4), 2079–2087. doi:10.100711071-012-0409-z

Zhang, Q., Guo, L., Xue, X., & Wei, X. (2009, October). An image encryption algorithm based on DNA sequence addition operation. In *2009 Fourth International on Conference on Bio-Inspired Computing* (pp. 1-5). IEEE. 10.1109/BICTA.2009.5338151

Chapter 12
Secure Framework Data Security Using Cryptography and Steganography in Internet of Things

Kannadhasan S.
ⓘ https://orcid.org/0000-0001-6443-9993
Cheran College of Engineering, India

R. Nagarajan
Gnanamani College of Technology, India

ABSTRACT

The exponential development of the internet and the internet of things (IoT) applies to the next step of the information transition, which entails billions of integrated smart devices and sensors to enable the speedy sharing of information and data under soft real-time restrictions. Significant improvements in data sharing also sparked the digital information movement. This transmission of data can include private, reliable, and often private communication. The exponential development of the internet and the internet of things (IoT) applies to the next step of the information transition, which entails billions of integrated smart devices and sensors to enable the speedy sharing of information and data under soft real-time restrictions. Significant improvements in data sharing also sparked the digital information movement. This transmission of data can include private, reliable, and often private communication.

1. INTRODUCTION

The Internet of Things (IoT) provides a mix of multiple sensors and artifacts that without human mediation, will communicate explicitly with each other. Physical devices, such as sensor gadgets, combine the stuff in the IoT, which screen and arrange a broad range of computer and human social life details. The IoT landing has caused the steady-wide distribution of humans, products, sensors, and administrations

DOI: 10.4018/978-1-7998-7160-6.ch012

to be linked. The IoT main objective is to include an interoperable correspondence and programming system platform to enable physical/virtual sensors, (PCs), keen appliances, vehicles, and stuff, such as refrigerators, dishwashers, microwave broilers, food, and solutions, to be combined and consolidated anytime and on any system (Ian F Akyildiz et al., 2002)-(Machanavajjhala et al., 2007). A large number of IoT systems are already experiencing diverse traffic challenges, such as congestion. The IoT network data is dropped where the learning mechanisms are used to categories the congestion, when the congestion is expected. In such instances, IoT systems will eliminate the need to incorporate the distributed learning of end devices in potential work. Knowledge that is detected is collected and analyzed in the network cloud (Huang et al., 2018)-(Marvel, 1999).

The Internet of Medical Stuff (IoMT) has recently to develop successfully for healthcare applications involving the incorporation of product life management (PLM) to control the flow of knowledge from one organization to another. A modern combined IoMT- and PLM-based architecture for medical health care technology has been adopted into the model. Enhancing mobile technologies makes it possible for countless objects to be a part of the IoT by special mobile sensors. Nevertheless the specifications for the large-scale operation of the IoT are increasing exponentially, which then affects in a big security problems. The main issues in IoT environments involve protection concerns, including protection, authentication, encryption, device setup, access control, data management and control. IoT applications, such as smartphone and embedded systems, for instance, promote a digital ecosystem for global communication that simplifies people's lives by simplifying them (Zaidan et al., 2010)-(Li et al., 2015).

2. INTERNET OF THINGS

These IoT attacks and risks need to be taken into consideration in order to provide consumer data with protection and privacy. IoT production is primarily focused on resolving security issues. The sensor node detects the data that has passed through the LAN to cloud storage. Data would be allowed utilizing the authorization server before saving data for cloud storage. By attacking the LAN, the attacker will eavesdrop the details. Due to its heterogeneity and wide collection of interconnected devices, ensuring protection for the IoT ecosystem is a daunting job. You may group the attacks against IoT into four groups. There are physical threats, network attacks, attacks on devices, and attacks on cryptography. While the internet is the most consistent platform for the dissemination of sensitive details, the absence of infrastructure that concerns computer hackers makes for malicious activities. In comparison, numerous existing encryption algorithms are currently found to be fragile. Also with the protection offered by recent encryption technology, by the brute force attack method and dictionary or rainbow table attack, hackers always disrupt the hidden letter. In order to escape these assaults, one would need to move details inconspicuously. Steganography is a known technique for the sensitive transmission of results.

In the Internet of Things (IoT) networks, wireless links link things, often called intelligent, Networks, data generation and utilization in order to execute their tasks. In the IoT, smart objects are typically connected to sensors and computational capabilities that enable them to feel the world around them, engage with each other and probably make a decision without or with limited) human interference. In the case of remote surveillance IoT networks, because of the energy and computing constraints of smart objects (e.g. cameras), rather than relying on their limited resources, data needs to be collected and transmitted wirelessly by smart objects to remote central servers for further processing. However, security risks such as unauthorized access will seriously affect data confidentiality and consumer privacy for such IoT networks. User authentication for access control purposes therefore plays a key role in maintaining trust between smart object users and remote servers. A secure authentication mechanism guarantees that real valid users are the users of smart objects, such that trust can be built and data security can be assured. An authentication system's capacity to identify impostors dictates the degree of faith in the IoT setting.

IoT sensor network protection issue: sensors are not only liable for the processing of data, but also for the acquisition, integrity and cooperation of data. Therefore, malicious code attacks and security threats can occur while transmitting information. In the networking environment, IoT system protection plays a primary function. IoT is a bond between the virtual and the real environment that determines our quality of life. IoT security may be well described here as a technical sector alarmed by the Internet of Things (IoT) defence of related devices and networks. With the support of internet links, automated and mechanical computers, persons etc it offers a framework of interconnected computing devices. Here every entity is provided with a unique identifier and also with the capacity to automatically transfer data over a network. When we enable these machines to link to the open internet, they are open to a broad spectrum of serious liability, and for that, we need security. Our proposed scheme uses an X.509 certificate that uses the regular Public Key Infrastructure (PKI) to authenticate whether the public key belongs to the certificate's device, consumer or other service identification. It is the most adaptive authentication method used by millions of users to provide technology incorporation with a quick, business-driven approach. When it is introduced to the framework, users can have their RSA ID within the time period if the ID changes during the authentication process. Users will provide a safe link from this through the interconnected networks.

IOT is known to be one of the most applicable innovations in the world today. The author indicated that the comprehensive controls, the capacity to track from any location and at any time in an appropriate manner can be managed efficiently with the assistance of IIOT industries. With the assistance of specific radio frequency fingerprint technology, distinctive user identification is created. They exploit the wireless networks that serve as cryptographic keys between the source and the destination. This approach is extended to the physical layer of the network protocol. Their framework is very powerful, offering a protection mechanism for attacks such as denial of service, tampering, resource depletion, etc. Through pointing out the major threats in any device module, they have established a specific protection framework for the IoT system and they are also minimizing them in the same process. There would be several limitations on the hardware of smart toys, but they have implemented a particular encryption technique that has proven to provide the delicate IoT ecosystem with a stable solution. They also suggested a technique of three protection steps. The first step manages light weight data with non-interfered communications. The next step improves data protection at the stage of source and destination. The last stage would have longer-term protection with reciprocated authentication. They have also used cryptographic schemes to support the MQTT protection system. Through contrasting it with different fields such as smart house, fitness, consumer devices etc., they also studied the power and shortcomings of the cryptographic norms. Of all these, they are still deliberating about the potential issues confronting the IoT in the future. At this layer, they concentrate on RFID and the sensor network and identify different attacks by taxonomic grouping and deliberate on the solution needed. In the end, they focus on the problems of the interpretation layer and efficiently identify effective corrections.

3. STEGANOGRAPHY

Steganography is a hidden communication science that hides the secret information inside an entity such as text, audio and video inside another object. One of the robust strategies for shielding sensitive knowledge is known to be steganography. Current steganographic strategies utilize digital technology to keep concealed details as a cover medium. Audio, photograph, video and text are various forms of cover media. The value of the cover medium is not only encrypting information into a media file of a carrier source, but also vague awareness of eavesdroppers as confidential information is exchanged by the recipient. Without revealing it explicitly to the eavesdroppers, it will build the encrypted files. This strategy is attainable because online media is so familiar. In order to improve the robustness of the confidential details, audio steganography makes a major contribution. In order to improve the audio recording, audio steganography attempts to insert hidden codes into an audio file. While it is one of the successful ways to protect steganography technique is the most difficult process.

Such approaches range from basic algorithms that put information in the form of audio signal noise to a more influential approach that utilizes information concealment methods of signal processing. Instead of the messages embedded in the picture cover medium, the hidden message embedded in the audio cover medium is more difficult. Various approaches are used to incorporate audio steganography strategies for embedding hidden messages in order to hide secret messages. Audio steganography is a masking under which the human ear's properties manipulate unnoticed to conceal the hidden message so the human system can only detect between 20 and 20000 HZ in the frequencies. Many steganographic methods use the modulation method of the least significant bit (LSB) to hide the hidden message in the cover medium. To conceal the hidden details in IoT, the streamlined audio embedding technique (OAET) in audio steganography is suggested. In order to shuffle hidden data and wave media, this approach utilizes random bit collection.

Steganography is the analysis of hiding knowledge in such a way that no one but the sender and recipient, can predict about it. Unlike cryptography, where the messages are hidden with encryption and not accessible to the world, it provides an alternative concept for hiding the credential details. Using a mixture of steganography and other approaches, such as cryptography, the protection of knowledge has now greatly improved. Many soft computing-based smart algorithms, such as Fuzzy Logic (FL), Adaptive Neural Networks (ANN), Genetic Algorithms (GA), are used to achieve stable and optimal solutions in steganography. Steganography basically requires three elements, i.e. the carrier, the data and the key. The carrier may be any format, such as audio, video, visual pictures, TCP/IP packets, etc., and the hidden message is included. Any cipher or pattern which is used to code/decode the secret message may be a key. Steganography includes all forms of records, including text, pictures, audio or video. Spatial steganography is available in many variants, all of which explicitly transform a few bits of image pixel values into masking data. One of the easiest methods to conceal a hidden message in LSPs without obvious distortion of pixel values is the Least Important Bit (LSP). To the human eye, shifts in the LSP value are not apparent. It is possible to easily or arbitrarily add message bits. LSP, matrix modulation, methods for certain spatial domains. Masking and filtering is a method of data masking which can be used in grey scale.

The location of watermarks on a written image is equivalent to hiding and filtering. In the most critical areas of the noise level, these strategies provide details. The methods for watermarking are integrated with the image and can be used without risk of compromising the image due to compression failure. In the transformed transactions, the frequency field message is added, granting it the power to mask additional details and have stronger intensity against records. Transform Domain Embedding - Since all of these effective imaging systems today function in the area of conversion, several methods may be referred to as suggested embedding technologies. The pieces that are less exposed in the shot. There is no dependency on picture format on certain metamorphic field technology, which could be more than lossless interface adjustments.

4. CRYPTOGRAPHY TECHNIQUES

Through interacting with both the inner and real world together, IoT produces a synchronized correspondence process of integrated devices and phases. In the approach to IoT systems focused on remote computerized human care, the transfer of clinical knowledge becomes a daily schedule. Subsequently, in order to ensure the protection and uprightness of the patient's demonstrative knowledge conveyed and retrieved from the IoT situation, it is necessary to develop an efficient model. Another word for protection of knowledge is cryptography. The way to encode messages is by encrypting cryptography. The two theory formulas used for knowledge encryption are the Advanced Encryption Standard (AES) measurement. AES is a symmetric on the two sides where a similar key is used. It has a square set message size of 128 content bits (plain), and length keys of 128,192, or 256 bits. They are partitioned into 128-piece squares at the stage where longer messages are sent. Longer keys certainly make the figure more challenging to crack, but they often endorse a more elaborate method of encoding and unscrambling. AES encryption encrypts hidden plain text data that is then inserted using Discrete Wavelet Transform into a cover image. The resulting steno-image is then transmitted using OFDM to the other end. Encrypted data is retrieved from the steno-image on the recipient end and then it is decrypted.

The medical data transfer model of a protected patient utilizing both color and gray-scale photos as a cover carrier for the IoT setting focused on health care has been suggested. Either 2D-DWT-1L or 2D-DWT-2L steganography and hybrid mixing AES cryptographic techniques were involved in the suggested model. Based on statistical parameters (BER and SNR), the output was evaluated. In recent years, tremendous concern has been demonstrated in remotely capturing data to efficiently track numerous events such as climate change, violation of boundaries, battlefield situations, nuclear installations or traffic screening. Using tiny sensors named Internet of Things (IoT), the streams are captured wirelessly and redirected to their ultimate destination (e.g. activity centers). Continuous streams generally include two categories of data: (1) common samples (e.g. operation data) and (2) highly classified details (e.g. geometric location of the nuclear plant or boundary screen, facility IDs, and tiny photographs of positions combined with date and time). Given the obvious gains of these practices, the protection of the hidden details and the authenticity of the ordinary readings raise different issues. The transmitted knowledge cannot be breached with the aid of this algorithm. In addition, little value may be gathered from the knowledge exchanged if it has been revealed to anyone. We also formulated this algorithm as a cell phone framework such that when sharing personal and confidential details such as account numbers and passwords with other devices, any individual will profit from it. The concerns around computer management are not fresh. These problems have continued at all times, and scientists and researchers have been interested in the quest to preserve the privacy and confidentiality of knowledge regardless of its form. These problems will continue to exist and are likely to persist through the years, when everyone has an innate tendency to preserve sensitive knowledge and privacy.

Researchers had to operate in parallel with the advancement of computer science and the sophistication of the underlying fields and the invasion of knowledge in all aspects of existence, as it became important to maintain protection and secrecy, to evolve this science in this period. The incorporation of intelligence has contributed to the exposure to individuals and corporations of secrets that trigger injury and significant losses. This allows, without creating some kind of question, to share the requisite confidential and sensitive details. Users of this kind of science may submit digital data (text, audio or video files...) to other parties without giving them an impression that they involve very confidential, hidden and sensitive details. The science of steganography has thus given a marvelous approach focused on circumventing some of the human being's senses to give in a soft, seamless and isolated way what they might want. Furthermore, even though attackers obtain transmitted contact or knowledge in the form of an image by finding or gaining direct access to this material, the coding techniques and skills are sufficient to deter attacks.

IoT is the technology of the decade and in fact, still has several possible data breach points. This protection issue and suggests an improved IoT computer steganography system. A big influence on knowledge and connectivity is the evolution of the IoT and ubiquitous computing. There appears to be an exponential rise in the growth rate of smart phones. With the advent of new-age gadgets, the provision of quality facilities for the end consumer. Steganography occurs where a file, document, picture, or video is fully hidden within another file, message, image or video. The value of steganography in cryptography overload alone is that expected hidden correspondence should not call attention to itself as a target of investigation. Seeing encrypted texts, no matter how unbreakable they are will obviously be alive, arouse interest and can in itself be incriminating in places where encryption is illegal. This indicates a process that can conceal the hidden data in picture layers and IoT steganography. LSB substitution ciphers for the IoT are the technique.

The AES algorithm is used by the microcontroller to encrypt and decrypt info. However, any physical modifications, such as dry, injured, or dirty skin, can cause an error in the user's fingerprint function information detection. Asymmetric encryption utilizes a key pair, which consists of a public key that is open to anybody that is a possible sender and a private key that is only accessible to the recipient. The sender uses the public key to encrypt a letter, whereas decryption involves a corresponding private key. Asymmetric encryption is exemplified by Cipher text-Policy Attribute-Based Encryption (CP-ABE) and Elliptic Curve Cryptosystem (ECC). The encrypt or in CP-ABE will intelligently determine which individuals have access to the data and which do not.

Because of the existence of the Internet of Things, resource-constrained devices may assign expensive exponentiation computations to trustworthy neighbor devices identified as assistant nodes. TinyPK's RSA has been replaced with ECC, which offers improved protection and performance. Furthermore, since IoT devices can interact wirelessly, Computational Intelligence (CI) is used to build a Wireless Intrusion Detection System (WIDS) that is more scalable, stable, has quicker computation speeds, and adapts well to evolving conditions. It also increases tolerance for imprecision, ambiguity, and approximation while minimizing overhead, improving latency, and enabling users to understand their preferences. The aim of CI is to substitute unstable cryptography. Self-jamming may be used as a protection measure to shield data from leakage while the Wireless Sensor Network (WSN) is inserted into IoT devices in order to capture neighboring devices, which contributes to better efficiency of the IoT devices inside the network. In reality, self jamming is a strategy by which a recipient avoids a passive assault by jamming and corrupting incoming messages that are obtained by an eavesdropper. This can be calculated by applying noise to data transmission. Furthermore, since the receiver is the one that introduces noise, he will know the difference between the initial message and the noise in order to retrieve the message. Furthermore, it is shown that the receiver must sustain a low rise in obtained power of 3dB or it would not work properly. It was also stated that if the sender's signal is 20dB away from the eavesdropper's receiver sensitivity, even if the receiver retains the low rise, the framework would be ineffective.

By linking the inner and real realms, IoT produces a coordinated correspondence state with intertwined devices and levels. With the introduction of IoT systems focused on remote computerized human services, clinical data sharing has become a regular occurrence. As a consequence, it is crucial to create an appropriate model that guarantees the reliability and consistency of the patient's demonstrative knowledge conveyed and derived from the IoT condition.

The Advanced Encryption Norm (AES) approximation is one of the two key formulas used in this work for knowledge encryption. AES is a symmetric figure in which the two sides use the same key. It uses keys with lengths of 128,192, or 256 bits and a defined message square size of 128 bits of content (plain or figure). When receiving longer messages, the messages are split into 128-piece squares. Longer keys, of course, make the figure more difficult to crack, but they also allow for a longer encode and unscramble process. Secret plain text data is encrypted with AES encryption and then inserted in a cover image using Discrete Wavelet Transform. The resulting stego-image is then transmitted using OFDM to the other end. Encrypted data is retrieved from the stego-image and then decrypted at the receiver point.

The scheme is widely used in the healthcare sector for medical data transfer. The protection between the rings was developed utilizing a hybrid ring. Re-encryption is done by these tightly secured rings in order to shield themselves against unwanted entry, time-based data owner demands, and user revocation. The hybrid ring paradigm increases the security and performance of data security applications, according to the findings.

It has an embedding algorithm for covering encrypted messages in nonadjacent and irregular pixel areas in picture edges and smooth regions. An enhanced edge detection filter is used to identify the edges in the cover image. The encrypted message bits are then inserted in the least important byte of arbitrarily chosen edge pixels, as well as some unique LSBs of red, green, and blue components. Traditional steganography detection methods have a rough time estimating the true message duration using this form of steganography technique since there are less chances of doubt regarding message bits embedded in the picture.

The cloud service provider repeats the details in order to increase information accessibility, accuracy, and power. Cloud storage is the most commonly deployed administration that provides a range of processing properties, ranging from servers and power to large enterprise apps such as email, protection, and backup, all distributed over the internet. Cloud software controls the client's IT assets and even implements the IT assets in a convincing fashion. Through the advancement of web cloud storage, it is now possible to efficiently handle and leverage vast volumes of data. Because they would ascend to security threats to big business data by using cloud storage, a vast amount of risks have arisen. As a consequence of the high-quality initiative, cloud infrastructure is commonly used. To ensure data spillage, benefit deliberation, and so on, confirmation and access power administration are vital considerations.

5. MODERN COMMUNICATION, STEGANOGRAPHY AND CRYPTOGRAPHY

Increasing opportunities for modem communications need specific means of protection, especially on the network. The protection of the network is becoming increasingly critical as the volume of data being shared on the Internet grows. Therefore to protect against unauthorized entry, confidentiality and data integrity are needed. Moreover the increasing growth of publishing and broadcasting technologies also demands an alternate hide-information approach. Any invisible material is also incorporated in the digital media to address this question in such a way that it cannot be readily accessed without a specialist technique. Knowledge hiding is an evolving field of study, and involves technologies such as digital media copyright security, watermarking, fingerprinting, and stenography. All these data hiding technologies are very diverse. With exponential change in the field of communications, it is of primary importance to provide improved data protection. Using encryption, steganography or a combination of both, protection is sometimes increased. Although cryptography renders the secret unreadable to the third party, the mere presence of the secret does not mask it. In the other side, steganography masks the very same thing, but the secret is revealed until found. Using the lightweight encryption method, a given plaintext is translated into cipher text that guarantees that none of the data (as a byte) is in its original place in the cipher. There is a need for a position map to insert the text within the graphic. For the same reason, a Super-tour knight's algorithm has been proposed and has also discussed the issues raised by the new Knight's tour algorithm. Consequently, this technique is called Document as Hidden (TAS).

Lately, a variety of algorithms for image encryption have been suggested that are either based on pixel level or bit level encryption. Nevertheless, not only permutation of the pixel level, but even permutation of the bit level has its inherent disadvantages. To counter these pitfalls, this paper introduces a modern cryptosystem. Various forms of permutation algorithms are first studied and compared comprehensively. Since an image may be considered as a natural three-dimensional (3D) bit matrix (width, height, and bit length) from a bit level viewpoint, a new 3D bit matrix permutation is suggested, in which the Chen system is used to create a random visiting mechanism to the plain-image bit level. A new mapping rule is generated to map one random location to another random position (i.e. double random position permutation) in the 3D matrix rather than utilizing conventional sequential visits to the plain image by integrating elements of the Chen method with a 3D Cat chart in the permutation point. Simulations are carried out and the findings affirm our latest cryptosystem's protection and performance. An increasing curiosity in knowledge hidden in multimedia details as the host has been observed in the research community in recent years. This secret knowledge, including source recognition, copyright rights and clandestine data transmission, can be used for several different purposes.

Encryption is the method of translating data into a cipher code, such that it can only be read by permitted parties. In which 2-D pictorial data is protected, picture encryption is fundamentally an important feature of encryption; therefore all the encryption procedure is done on it. Any extension to a previous picture encryption solution focused on SCAN patterns is achieved in this paper in such a clear manner that it provides protection to a large degree. The carrier image is created by using a distinctive code known as four out of eight codes in the SCAN technique and attaching the carrier image to the original image that results in the encrypted image. Instead of encrypting an image in its original pattern, this another solution in which the image is separated into entirely separate components in order to combine into a pattern that is only understood to authorize parties and then complete more methods of encryption and decryption. In this approach outlined provides security to a greater extent. In MATLAB, both encryption and decryption methods are applied and an overview has been developed for different picture characteristics. Visual audio steganography, where encrypted covert data is embedded in the host audio signal wavelet coefficients. The least important bits of lifting wavelet coefficients are inserted in the data bits according to this threshold. The transformation of the inverse lifting wavelet is added to modified coefficients to create the time domain steno signal. The need for data integrity and privacy has been stronger than ever for a few days now. These considerations were prerequisites, from minor bank transfers to large-scale secret military details. With the aid of a faux confidential, this sensitive knowledge may be purposely faked by the sender in order to raise the degree of protection. Cryptography makes this data unreadable and the same is hidden by steganography. Using the AES algorithm, the secret image or text file is encrypted and then camouflaged into the pseudo-secret image using a modified chess-based algorithm inspired by Knight's Tour that improves data diffusion. The pseudo-secret image/text is then encrypted using the AES algorithm again and is masked using a checkerboard-based location map into the cover image/text. For different types of image extension, lossless, highly secure, nested-layer steganography is thus achieved with high complexity and high PSNR.

The recent surge in web technology has resulted in increased social networking and online media sharing. Data such as pictures, audio and video is transferred across the web in huge volumes. Obviously, data and confidentiality must be secured. To remove this obstacle, the way around is to use chaotic image encryption systems to increase safety in the field of steganography. In information hiding and extraction, steganography and steno analysis play an important role. A Steganography deal with information hiding techniques and with little or no knowledge about the steganography algorithm or its parameters, steganalysis detects the hidden information. Steganography is the method in which a secret image is embedded in a cover image without affecting the cover image's perceptual quality. It is classified as image steganography, audio steganography and video steganography, based on the medium used in steganography to embed the message.

Using domain transformations such as Discrete Fourier Transform (DFT), Discrete Cosine Transform (DCT), Discrete Wavelet Transform (DWT), Fourier Mellin Transform (FMT), Fractal Transform, etc the carrier image is first converted into the frequency domain method in frequency domain steganography. Then through implementing embedding techniques, the message is concealed inside the transformed cover image. But in spatial-domain steganography, by adding some modulation over the multiple pixels of the image, the hidden message is concealed within the image. The chaos-based data hiding method is applied in this paper to achieve high-level security. By utilizing disorderly coding as part of authentication, the first degree of authentication is obtained. The explanation behind the usage of chaotic maps is that chaotic map properties involve dynamic actions, ergodicity, initial conditions-sensitive, and nonlinear deterministic existence that provides strong encryption methods for uncertainty and diffusion. The second degree of authentication is accomplished by applying picture steganography by forcing a transformation on the cover image prior to embedding. In order to improve the degree of security, the Discrete Wavelet Transform (DWT) frequency domain steganography approach is used in this article. The addition of the least significant bit (LSB) is used to implant the hidden image within the converted cover image. In the spatial domain in which the payload bits are inserted in the least important bits of the cover image, the LSB algorithm is used to obtain the steno-image.

Standard device verification mechanisms are codes and tokens. It can be missed quickly and tokens can be stolen or misplaced. As an alternative, since biometric traits cannot be lost and do not need to be remembered, biometric authentication is becoming more attractive. Biometric identification systems achieve "who you are"-based authentication since the biometrics of every person, such as iris and fingerprints, are unique. For biometric identification, certain biometric features, such as fingerprints, ears, iris, and palm prints, may be used. Among these options, due to its unique and stable characteristics, the iris is highly reliable. One of the new technologies that will be the best agents for transforming the current environment is the Internet of Things (IoT). It comprises mobile, interactive and instantaneous communications for machine-to-machine contact. The IoT framework comprises of household equipment and several other sensors for capturing data, not just traditional computer devices. With IoT, with only a few taps on their smart gadgets, people will power their home appliances. The simplicity and "smartness" of IoT devices allows the number of such devices to rise. Any persons, though, could still be terrified of having these machines in their houses. While IoT devices can make it a lot simpler for citizens, security analysts have stated their worries regarding future security issues (The Vulnerability of Things), rendering IoT devices one of the top five security threats. As a matter of truth, the key protection challenges in the IoT framework that must not be ignored are knowledge disclosure. In addition, the key targets for hackers would be IoT devices with a poor degree of protection and computing capacity, such as IP cameras, smart TVs and other home appliances, which lack privacy features. Therefore, active and passive assaults in the IoT scheme may be rendered simpler with a heterogeneous framework and its characteristics spread across the Internet in order to hack private information or harm human beings.

Through engaging the simulated and real environments together, IoT provides an interactive networking system with linked technologies and networks. The transfer of medical details is becoming a regular occurrence with the introduction of remote automated healthcare-based IoT systems. Therefore to ensure the confidentiality and privacy of the patient's diagnostic data transmitted and retrieved from the IoT environment, an effective model must be established. Another word for data encryption is cryptography. Encryption cryptography is the encoding method for messages. On both sides, the key is used . It has a led message block size of 128 bits of text (plain or cipher), and keys of length 128,192, or 256 bits. They are broken into 128-bit blocks as longer messages are submitted. Depending about what you are concerned with how you treat things and what your tools are, it can be described in several different forms. It covers several aspects of life-from different components (such as refrigerator, oven, and washing machine) to well-equipped semi-detached homes, from travelling tools to advanced equipment to track the behavior of an individual to his or her degree of thinking and gathering relevant information and applying services. The next step in the virtualization of digital data is IoT, as it can be visualized as the interaction between several data packets from different devices and their exchange between machines and objects. As emerging global Internet-based information architecture, the Internet of Things (IoT) is something that connects 100 million people, facilitating the global exchange of data and information.

In the era of computing, Radio Frequency Identification (RFID) and sensor network technologies can be used to address the new challenge of the next wave, in which information and communication systems are invisibly embedded in the environment around us. This adds to the production of large volumes of data that need to be effectively analyzed and delivered in a smooth and understandable manner. Data, channel, medium, etc. security is an important aspect that, despite the theoretical concept of secured servers and smart devices, the IT organizations are most concerned about, practical implementation of these security features is minimal. IoT terminal security problem: terminal devices are readily accessible and can trigger harm or alterations to records. The prior issue is the authentication and credibility of the records. Because passive RFID tags are unable to share so many messages with authentication servers, the key issue being that the awareness terminal contains the terminal of the authentication server. Sensitive leakage, tampering, copying, terminal virus and other issues of knowledge.). SHA has been used in multiple protocols, such as TLS, SSL, PGP, SSH, MIME and IPSec. There are possibilities for security breaches as several devices are linked in the IoT setting. In a situation where the user provides the controller with the original 'On Device 2' command, the user's original message is hacked and the controller only receives the fake 'ON Device 3' command. The link is completely blocked or violated by the hackers here, and therefore there will be no confidentiality.

Hackers, without their consent, are definitely taking the user's original order. Users would have little awareness of the case, and that's a huge asset for hackers. The integrity of the data is completely abandoned here. The hacker can now create a false order and direct it to the controller. The controller also has zero knowledge of the situation and the fake command received will continue with the processing phase. All the information processed can now be transmitted to the computer present in the IoT setting. This whole security violation sends the consumer a specific order to the controller, but the hacker blocks the link. A false order is generated by the hacker and transmitted to the end of the recipient. The user and the controller will have zero knowledge of it and security is breached in the entire IoT environment. Our suggested scheme uses RSA, SHA and X.509 authentication mechanisms to include a safe link in the IoT environment in order to secure the connection between the consumer and the controller on all devices in the IoT environment. Instead of HTTP, we also use a protected MQTT protocol because it is slow and delivers more overhead compared to MQTT. In the IoT world, we use the AMES encryption scheme for safe communication methods.

A cryptographic technique for encrypting patient knowledge acquired from multiple medical sources. With the assistance of XOR stenography encoding methodology, they insert the encrypted data and transform it into a low-complexity picture. The secret data in the picture is decrypted and retrieved at the last point. The device showed that DOS attacks and replay attacks were immune. The technique is often light and advanced in terms of methods. It is well linked to other growing developments, such as IoHT, IoE, IoC, blockchain, and IoT. In the IoT environment, each sub-sector offers a brief comparison of the blockchain mechanism with protection measures, efficiency, difficulty, etc. The IoT would keep any object that takes place in our lives every day. Smart objects control the whole universe, and as a service provider, the Internet plays a broad role in the sector. Only sensors such as smart objects and the Internet have created the IoT. Increased sensor use contributes to higher amounts of raw data and dispersed data. The data are obtained utilizing Mobile Devices using the Internet. Because of the advances in the area of wireless networking methods, and because of the speed of the internet, it is a dangerous job to encourage progress. The purpose would be to imagine all the sensors as intelligence in the IoT architecture. Like any computer incorporated to be linked to the internet, the IoT is changing absolutely quite rapidly.

In IoT, the most important role is to have some data and protection. The IoT strengthens sensing, nano-technology, RFID technology, and embedded devices. From its simple nature, any danger can take place. RFID (Radio Frequency Identification) is one of the main markers when referring to IoT. It automatically identifies items containing tags using electromagnetic fields. In this layer, big attacks from WSNs can take place. When improving protection, RSN, WSNs, RFID, and RSN security must be obtained. In the transport layer, the protection of the local network, core network, and access network is protected. The protection of 5G, 4G, 3G, 2G, EDGE and Wi-Fi networks is also part of later identification, transportation, and access. The Framework layer would have the total protection inside the IoT. The protection of IoT devices correlated with creating such end-to-end security in an IoT system has been hampered by many challenges. In every business enterprise, hacking security can occur. When injecting a patient's drug, if the beliefs are wrong, the loss of human life will occur. Hacking the device and modifying the principles may be achieved quickly. In the smart refrigerator, for example, if malware exists and the temperature value varies, the medications stored on the refrigerator will be wasted as this dilemma raises the protection thread that is more vulnerable to the industry than most other threats.

The Internet of Things (IOT) is just an immense collection of gadgets connected with the internet. The well-being section connected to the network of things is IOT protection and it aims to secure IOT devices and systems against programmers. Through enabling them to relay knowledge and computerize activities, IOT renders daily articles amazing, without needing any manual intercession. At present, the aim of designers is to maximize the possibility of these applications, with little attention on the protection of the devices. If there is no identity protection, there are ways for data to infiltrate at that level and therefore personal data can be easily stolen from the device. IOT requires identifiable documentation and verification as an essential concept. As cryptographic skills that have to ensure that the data is spoken with the proper gadget, these concepts are interrelated to each other. The presentation of knowledge by intruders may be maintained through encryption. Data can be easily encrypted with the help of cryptography, which is the mechanism that scrambles coherent content so that the accepted entity or unscrambled key can be scanned. This offers information protection with confidential details. Cryptography is used to offer our knowledge mystery and authenticity and both clarification and obscurity to our communications. Most of the most remarkable kinds of cryptography is elliptic bent cryptography (ECC). H.264/adaptable AVC's full-scale demanding square (FMO) illuminate to cover up notification bits. Regarding the content of the message bits to be protected, the macro blocks are allocated to self-assertive cut bunches. The fundamental system used in this paper is to safeguard, however fairly anticipated, the discrepancies between distinct cosine shift (DCT) coefficients in a related situation in neighbouring DCT obstructs.

The Internet of Things (IoT) is a network that connects the physical and digital worlds together to provide services to users via interconnected infrastructures and devices. The IoT allows consumers, computers, and apps that are spread in numerous areas across the globe to connect effortlessly. In the IoT, citizens are surrounded by wide varieties and amounts of electronic devices of varying sizes and communication capabilities. In this modern world, a vast amount of mobile devices such as cell phones, computers, tablets and other smart devices link to the Internet every day to access various resources for people's everyday lives. The Internet of Services (IoS) is the core component of the potential Internet, where for greater competitiveness; any conceivable service can be readily and extensively open to consumers through the Internet.

Cloud infrastructure is supposed to be the next big trend. However, in addition to its benefits, protecting privacy is one of the big problems that has been a roadblock in the development of Cloud Storage. In Cloud Storage, one of the most common security-preserving strategies was used to protect privacy, but none of the techniques sufficiently resolved the problems. In the networking world, IoT system protection is important. IoT functions as a connector between the virtual and real realms, deciding our quality of life. IoT security, in this context, can be described as a technical field concerned with the safety of connected devices and networks in the Internet of Things (IoT). It offers an internet-connected framework of interconnected computer devices, digital and mechanical computers, artifacts, and individuals, among other items. Every entity is granted a unique identifier as well as the capability of automatically transmitting data over a network. When we enable these machines to link to the open internet, they become susceptible to a broad range of dangerous threats, for which we need security.

TLS, SSL, PGP, Tcp, MIME, and IPSec are only a handful of the protocols that use SHA. Where a large number of devices are linked in an IoT environment, there is a chance of a security breach. When a user sends the controller an original instruction, such as "On System 2," the original request is hacked, and the controller then gets the bogus command "ON Device 3." There is no secrecy since the link is absolutely broken or compromised by the hackers. Without the user's awareness, hackers are taking the user's initial order. The customer would be totally ignorant of the case, which is a major advantage for the hackers. The credibility of the data is totally overlooked in this situation. The hacker can now generate a false order and send it to the controller. The controller is still unaware of the situation and will continue to the processing step utilising the obtained false order. The whole processed data can now be transmitted to the IoT computer in the IoT environment.

We looked through a number of analysis materials to find out what the latest and past approaches were for enhancing network protection in the IoT area. IIOT is recognized as one of the most commonly adopted inventions in today's world. The suggestion is that businesses can easily manage extensive monitors, as well as the prospect of surveillance from any venue and at any time, with the aid of IIOT. They also suggested a clear and safe system for providing secure communication and authentication in the IoT world. Special radio frequency fingerprint processing is used to establish distinct user identification. As cryptographic keys, they exploit the wireless networks between the source and the target. The actual layer of the network protocol is exposed to this approach. The technique employs CoAP, which enables clients to control the server's capital in an energy-efficient fashion. To build a stable network session, use AES with a key duration of 128 bits. Their scheme is very effective, with little network link overhead and a protection system against attacks such as denial of service, tampering, resource depletion, and so on. They've built a special protection framework for the IoT device, which includes detecting and mitigating major threats in each system module at the same time. There would be various drawbacks for smart toy hardware, but they have proposed a novel encryption technique that has proven to be a safe approach for the delicate IoT climate. They also suggested a three-phase security approach. The first step deals with non-interfering light-weight data messages. The following process enhances data protection at both the source and destination stages. With reciprocated authentication, the final step would have protection over a longer period of time. They have used the MQTT encryption platform, which is capable of supporting cryptographic schemes. They spoke about existing protocol specifications for cryptographic schemes that are typically found in IoT devices. They compared the cryptographic standards' strengths and shortcomings to a number of fields, like smart homes, fitness, consumer electronics, and so on. We also address the upcoming problems that the Internet of Things will encounter in the future. They concentrate on the most relevant IoT elements as well as the protection specifications at the perception layer. At this layer, they concentrate on RFID and sensor networks, classifying a range of attacks using taxonomic classification and debating the appropriate response. Finally, they focus on the vision layer issues and successfully identify acceptable rectifications.

They encrypt personal data collected from a number of medical outlets using a cryptographic technique. They use the XOR stenography encoding technique to insert the encrypted data and transform it into a low-complexity picture. They often employ the adaptive firefly algorithm to refine complex picture blocks. The image's secret data is decrypted and retrieved in the final step. They propose a novel protected authentication scheme for heterogeneous IoT in which enables them to migrate between PKI and CLC environments. The proposed scheme will provide reliable contact to authorized users, ensuring their protection. Other features such as non-repudiation, consumer privacy, and so on would be enabled by this scheme. The suggested scheme showed DOS and replay assault tolerance. The technique is also a basic and sophisticated strategy. They have a cross-sectional view of the block chain mechanism. It works well with other increasingly emerging innovations such as IoHT, IoE, IoC, blockchain, and IoV. Every subsector in the IoT ecosystem compares the blockchain framework in terms of stability, efficiency, and complexity. The primary purpose of this paper is to offer a detailed description of all block chain protocols that are explicitly developed for use in the IoT context. Encryption and decryption security is enhanced utilising grasshopper optimization and particle swarm optimization.

In HIP – BEX, they also propose an adaptive distribution protection computational load framework. To achieve end-to-end protection in IoT, they merge both E2E and HIP. The recommended approach CD

– HIP is energy effective and consistent with normal HIP, according to the findings of the assessment. They suggest a more stable network design with a main delivery system assisted by automated and local authorization agencies. They fix a number of IoT-related problems while still taking into consideration resource constraints. The overhead rate of the proposed model scales at a much slower rate than TLS after measurement, and it also fits well for resource limited devices. They look at routing protocols and encapsulation in the sense of IoT networking technologies. They offer a layer-based taxonomy as well as an overview of how the network protocols can operate and how they will satisfy current IoT specifications. Interoperability, compatibility, and problems relating to the configuration of current and new protocols are among the many networking concerns. All of this was done with the aid of IPV6. They suggest an efficient framework based on authentication and permission for smart objects during their life cycle. The proposed approach is consistent with the EU EP7 IoT architectural guide model. As a consequence, they have lightweight smart object architecture for authentication. They recommend an ECC-based protocol for verifying the reader's identity prior to issuing the certificate, which will provide user security and enable them to use the cloud interface in an RFID environment.

Sensitive personal details can be collected during web-based data transfer. Furthermore, there are a multitude of applications accessible on the internet, and several websites enable users to upload photos containing confidential personal details such as phone numbers, emails, and credit card numbers. Customers can participate in personal and protected exchanges for a number of reasons, such as protecting sensitive details from programmers while ignoring an accessible channel, necessitating rating and information respectability against unwanted entry and usage. Cryptography and steganography are two popular methods for checking communication. Cryptography is the method of encoding and decoding data using arithmetic to hold posts safe by converting a consistent data structure (plaintext) into an opaque (cipher text) framework. Encryption is the method of modifying plaintext to locate text by utilising keys. Figure content that has been protected using the plaintext encryption key. Decoding is the method of recovering the plaintext from the chart's content.

The Diffie-Hellman Key Trade Convention was the main mechanism for utilising public key or two-key cryptography. As a consequence, it is often referred to as asymmetric encryption. This was the most commonly spread way of creating a mutual mystery relevant along a checked (but not personal) route of interchanges without depending on a previously shared mystery. Steganography and cryptography are two techniques for maintaining confidentiality that have been in use for quite some time. Both are continually being researched and developed, much like anything else in the data engineering industry. While incorporating these methods in a common context is a relatively recent path, we can find a few excellent pieces of literature.

Cryptography and steganography was basically inspired by the ability to deliver hidden messages. Steganography, on the other hand, is not the same as cryptography. The content of a noxious person's mystery text is hidden by encryption, while steganography requires the message's presence. Steganography is not to be associated with encryption, in which the signal is distorted to make it undecipherable to a malicious party who intercepts it. As a consequence, the importance of splitting the system differs. The mechanism is broken in cryptography because the aggressor gains access to the hidden signal. Except when the button to decrypt is accessible, the structure of a text is blended in cryptography to render it great for nothing and deceptive. The concealed signal is not hidden or disguised in any way. Cryptography is simply the ability to transfer knowledge amongst people in such a way that an alien cannot decipher it. Cryptography may also be used to validate a person's or thing's identity. Steganography, on the other hand, does not modify the structure of the enigmatic; rather it encases it in a cover picture such that it is covered. A message sent in ciphertext, for example, can create questions about the receiver, while a message sent using steganographic techniques would not be undetectable. Steganography, in other terms, stops the data from being identified by an unwanted receiver. The data encoding framework's mystery often contributes to the steganography system's security. As the encoding system is found, the steganography method is vanquished. It is necessary to merge the approaches by saving text using cryptography and then covering the removed signal using steganography. The resulting stego picture may be passed without disclosing the mystery material is being exchanged.

This paper proposes a modern secure communication model that blends cryptography and steganography to have two layers of protection, guaranteeing that the steganalyst cannot decipher the ciphertext without understanding the mystery button. The mystery data was first captured using the AES MPK, and then the deleted data in the grim picture was covered up using hybrid methods. Because of this combination, the mystery's data may be distributed through an accessible path, despite the fact that the ciphertext does not seem aimless, but rather conceals its existence by utilising steganography to mask ciphertext in pictures. Our proposed model will shroud substantially more details than other current methods, and the graphic character of the stego picture is also improved, considering its strength in transmitting mystery detail, according to test results. In a potential initiative, we intend to apply the proposed approach to noise and broadcasting. In addition, we anticipate the proposed approach to be changed such that the threshold is lower while the PSNR stays the same or higher.

The Internet of Things (IoT) is a completely controlled internet boundary generated through the connectivity of smart objects and cloud policies (IoT). The aim of this new model is to change the modern world through technology. The Internet of Things (IoT) is the smart interconnection of basically connected artifacts in order to build a Smart Cyberspace, achieve great networking, and conduct powerful computation with fast data evaluation. Reduced energy usage, increased certainty, automation regulation, and undemanding facilities are all benefits of a well-designed IoT.

Different types of data are propagated via the IoT structure; these data forms are usually connected to medical and military knowledge and are in the form of (text records, photograph, video, audio, and recordings) sourced from various sensors and processed via an application. The guarantee of the computation's functionality, security, and productivity is needed to achieve a faster, smarter, and more durable framework that fully encompasses an application in relation to control and intelligence.

Several attacks may often arise as a consequence of knowledge propagation through an unstable channel; such attacks can result from the systems' total computerization. The volume of data propagated through IoT systems necessitates addressing the associated issues, particularly those relating to the system's certainty, discreteness, protection, and authentication. IoT networks may render digitalized data more available, copyable, exploitable, and disseminated, possibly raising the likelihood of multimedia assaults. Today, data protection practices are already immature, although there are several reports of active data compromises on the part of major multinational organizations.

These breaches exist in a number of fields, including healthcare and security, and are not accepted in these industries due to the importance of healthcare and defense-related records, where even small improvements will result in inaccurate decisions. IoT is the technology of the decade, but it still has a number of possible points for data breaches. This study looks at the topic of protection issues and suggests an advanced steganography system for IoT computers. The Internet of Things (IoT) and ubiquitous computing are having a huge effect on knowledge and connectivity. The pace of system development tends to be growing exponentially. With the introduction of modern age gadgets, the ultimate aim tends to be to offer quality facilities to the end consumer. Steganography is the practice of encrypting a file, document, picture, or video and covering it inside another file, message, image, or video. The value of steganography in the overabundance of cryptography is that expected confidential messages do not call attention to themselves as a subject of inspection. In places where cryptography is unlawful, being able to see encrypted texts, no matter how unbreakable they are, arouses curiosity and can be incriminating in and of itself. This thesis suggests a system for covering hidden data in picture layers, as well as steganography for IoT. LSB replacement ciphers are the suggested IoT technique. Experiments of multiple aspect ratio photos reveal that the proposed algorithms tend to do better. The proposed approach works especially well in RGB mode. In terms of MSE and PSNR, the basic LSB approach tends to have a drawback, which is solved by the proposed Vacillating LSB method.

If the Internet becomes more prevalent in our everyday lives, security challenges must be addressed; scalable security for emerging network implementations is needed. This project aims to merge conventional network protection with data hiding, an evolving technique. For data hiding, several methods of knowledge hiding are used, such as cryptography, in which all parties encrypt the information and pass a cipher. In recent years, these strategies have been even more accessible and public. Steganography, in contrast to cryptography, helps to preclude a third party from detecting any covert contact. Steganography is described as the art and science of concealing information by sending hidden messages through harmless cover carriers in such a way that their presence is undetectable. Only those with awareness of the encoded data and access to a "key" would be able to decipher and interpret the data. This key can come in a range of shapes and sizes. It may vary from an appreciation of how to decipher details to a transfer for electronic stegnography.

It is known as the art and science of concealing content, which is a method of concealing a message in a suitable courier, such as a text file. The carrier will then be delivered to a recipient without someone else being informed of the coded letter. Steganography is a generic concept that includes all strategies for embedding additional material into any type of carrier. The carrier may be anything from an ancient piece of parchment to a network protocol header. While modern steganographic approaches are much more advanced than their forerunners, the basic concepts have stayed the same. They normally encrypt hidden data using digital media archives or network protocols as a courier. Steganography is a broad concept that applies to any technique for embedding additional hidden material into any type of carrier with the intention of hiding the inserted changes. The carrier's choices are virtually limitless; it may be an antique piece of parchment or a network protocol header. It was created over time, influenced by biological phenomena and embraced by man in ancient times. While modern steganographic methods are much more advanced than their forerunners, the basic concepts remain the same. They normally encrypt hidden data using digital media archives or network protocols as a courier.

Steganography is a strategy for concealing secret knowledge such as text, passwords, pictures, and audio in a cover disc. The embedded device can assist in the encryption of the message stored inside the picture format. The message is even more protected in an embedded device so even though an unauthorized user is able to hack the picture, the person would not be able to interpret the message. Through designing an application that uses the LSB algorithm on an ARM architecture computer, hidden data such as photographs may be encrypted into cover data. Images with embedded data can be used to communicate secrets using simple, fast, and stand-alone novel algorithms that, when combined, generate a more complex algorithm. This paper uses a significant bit XOR encryption with a recursive diagonal transformation as a pre-processing stage, followed by steganography using the Least Significant Bit (LSB). Using the Raspberry Pi in a creative way in the process. The outcomes were found to be lossless, stable, and yielded high image metric values.

The emerging capacities of modem communications necessitate special protection measures, especially on networks. If the volume of data being shared on the Internet expands, network protection becomes more essential. To protect against unauthorized entry, confidentiality and data integrity are needed. As a consequence, the data-hiding industry has evolved at a breakneck rate. Furthermore, the rapid development in publishing and broadcasting technologies necessitates a new way to conceal knowledge. To fix this problem, certain intangible data is often encoded within digital media in such a way that it cannot be readily retrieved through the use of a sophisticated technique. Material concealment is a recent field of study that involves copyright security for interactive media, watermarking, fingerprinting, and stenography. Many of these information-hiding implementations are very diverse. With the exponential development in technology in the field of communications, the need for improved data protection has never been more critical. Cryptography, steganography, or combinations of the two are widely used to boost protection. Although cryptography renders the secret unreadable to a third party, it does not conceal the secret's nature. On the other side, steganography conceals the same details, but once found, the secret is uncovered. The suggested lightweight encryption method transforms plaintext into cypher text, meaning that none of the data (as a byte) is in its original place in the cypher.

Encryption is the act of translating data into a cypher text that can only be read by registered parties. Picture encryption is a critical feature of encryption in which 2-D pictorial data is secured, and therefore the whole encryption method is carried out on it. Some improvements to an earlier picture encryption solution focused on SCAN patterns are performed in such a clear way that they have a high degree of protection. The carrier picture is created in the SCAN technique by using a special code known as the four out of eight-code and applying it to the original image, which results in the encrypted image. Rather than encrypting an image in its original pattern, this paper suggests a system in which the image is broken into entirely separate elements and then combined into a pattern that is only understood by approved parties, accompanied by the encryption and decryption phase. The method mentioned in this paper improves protection to a greater degree. All of the encryption and decryption methods are applied in MATLAB, and an analysis for different image qualities has been developed.

Encrypted covert data is embedded in the wavelet coefficients of the host audio signal in this process for optical audio steganography. Lifting wavelet transform is used to prevent extraction errors. We measure listening threshold in wavelet domain to utilize the full potential of audio signals. The data bits are then inserted in the least important bits of lifting wavelet coefficients according to this threshold. In order to create a stego signal in the time domain, modified coefficients are subjected to the inverse lifting wavelet transform.

Data integrity and privacy are more important than ever these days. These considerations have been prerequisites for anything from minor bank transfers to large-scale sensitive military details. To improve the degree of confidentiality, the sender may intentionally fake this sensitive information with the aid of a faux secret. This knowledge is made unreadable by cryptography, and it is hidden by steganography. The hidden picture or text file is encrypted with the AES algorithm and then camouflaged into the pseudo-secret image with an updated Knight's Tour-inspired chess-based algorithm that boosts data diffusion. The pseudo-secret image/text is then masked into the cover image/text using a checkerboard-based position chart and encrypted again using the AES algorithm. The Internet of Things (IOT) is a vast array of web-connected computers. IOT protection is the wellbeing section of the internet of things, and it seeks to secure IOT devices and systems from programmers. The task of IoT is to have an IT framework for the secure and legal exchange of gadgets. The web is the IoT's backbone and lifeblood. As a consequence, nearly all of the security threats that occur on the Internet have spread to IoT. The advantages of IOT are infinite, and its implementations are transforming the way we function and live through saving time and energy and creating new avenues for growth, progress, and knowledge sharing between organizations. The fact of such a massive structure of interconnected components would present new challenges to defence, safety, and confidence.

Daily papers became amazing due to the Internet of Things, which helps them to transmit data and automate activities without the need for human interference. Designers are currently concentrating on rising the likelihood of these products, with little concern for their security. When there is no computer protection, there is a risk that information will be compromised, and sensitive details will be easily extracted from the system. There are essential principles in IOT that provide familiar evidence and verification. These principles are linked as cryptographic features that must be utilised to ensure that data is transmitted to the correct computer.

When two gadgets interact with one another, knowledge is transferred between them. The details may also be highly sensitive and personal. So there's the basis for data encryption. Intruders won't be able to see the details as it's secured. Data may be easily encrypted with the aid of cryptography, which is the method of scrambling coherent information such that it can be interpreted by an authenticated person or unscrambled key. It guarantees the privacy of confidential data. Cryptography is used to offer our data mystery and authenticity, as well as clarification and obscurity in our communications. One of the most impressive forms of cryptography is elliptic bend cryptography (ECC). This is used for pre-planned jobs. ECC is a tool for open key encryption that uses the science of elliptic bends to achieve equal protection.

For intended job, a method known as steganography is used. The other approach is steganography, which involves hiding a hidden message within a spread bearer such that it is undetectable. As a spread transporter, steganography is frequently investigated with image, video, or sound. If there is sufficiently redundancy to mask the mystery message, the scatter message is valuable. Knowledge is secured using sophisticated cryptographic techniques. Then, using excellent formulas, you may apply details to unnecessary data that is part of the database format, such as a JPEG image. The existing study necessitates additional protections for network steganography. With the aid of the Adaptive firefly algorithm, the image square is advanced, and the scrambled knowledge is avoided the frame, which is obstructed by an enormous picture square.

The elliptic Galois cryptography (EGC) convention is used to encrypt data during transmission across the Internet of Things. In the proposed work, specific IoT devices transfer data through the proposed protocol as part of the controller. With the aid of the Steganography technique, the encoded measurement within the controller encodes the details using the EGC protocol, and then the scrambled and assured message is covered up in layers of the image. The image could then be easily transferred around the Internet, with the intention of stopping a gatecrasher from deleting the message contained within the image. Initially, the EGC protocol encrypts sensitive details. The Steganography technique embeds the encoded mystery message within the image in this manner. Then, to choose a square in the picture, an enhancement calculation called the Adaptive Firefly calculation is used.

Various angle proportion pictures are included in the experiments, which demonstrate that the proposed equations seem to perform better. The Internet of Things (IoT) seems to be guiding the planet over the next decade. The IoT's different definitions result in significantly more security bugs. This thesis suggests a modern method for maintaining the confidentiality of data using steganography. Since only the ECC mystery key can recover the first details, the information that is concealed by the proposed strategy can't be accessed by someone who isn't approved.

The Elliptic Galois cryptography (EGC) Protocol attained notable amounts of data protection during data transfer in the Internet of Things. The proposed EGC display provides better protection thanks to the novel EGC Galois sector. Improved knowledge concealing capacity can be obtained through enhanced inserting efficiency. Any amount of data could be conveniently propagated via IOT organize protection covered up in profound layers of pictures with the aid of the given convention and scalable firefly streamlining. Boundaries are used to test execution, such as adding proficiency, PSNR bearer limit, MSE, and time multifaceted design. Finally, guided work on Java obscure devices is finished, and inserting proficiency is attained. The proposed convention's results are compared to those of current strategies.

6. CONCLUSION

Cryptography and steganography are two of the most important methods used in communication to encrypt knowledge. Through preventing eavesdroppers from having something valuable from the system and unreliable contact channel, cryptography protects against attacks. Cryptography, though, has a range

Table 1. Number of Papers Published in Data Security

Year	Number of Papers Published					
	IEEE	**IET**	**ELSEVIER**	**SPRINGER**	**WILEY**	**ACM**
2000	2	8	1	3	1	3
2001	4	5	2	2	5	2
2002	8	12	5	6	8	6
2003	2	8	8	7	10	7
2004	8	9	6	2	12	2
2005	2	4	16	5	15	5
2006	4	5	18	7	12	7
2007	8	10	19	8	14	8
2008	5	12	22	3	16	3
2009	8	13	16	10	18	10
2010	6	12	10	12	12	12
2011	7	17	12	16	15	16
2012	8	18	16	6	16	6
2013	9	20	6	18	18	18
2014	8	21	18	25	20	25
2015	5	22	14	29	10	29
2016	7	24	16	30	20	30
2017	9	22	18	35	20	35
2018	8	25	12	34	10	34
2019	6	25	15	38	10	38
2020	7	26	16	40	20	40

Figure 1. Papers Published in Secure Framework Data Security

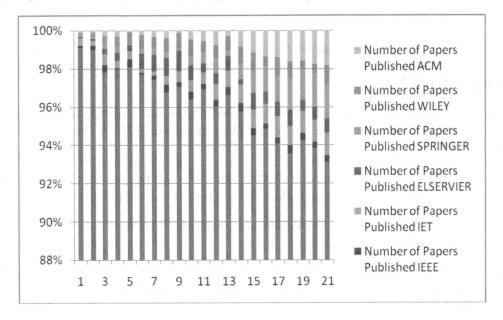

of limitations; the presence of cryptographic knowledge may trigger suspicion itself. Three (R, G, B) channels are used for transporting knowledge in the first and third techniques, and the second strategy uses G and B channels for transmitting. For embedding details, all approaches select a higher-order location in the channel. Steganography, on the other hand, preserves data by hiding it inside a carrier without allowing attackers to suspect it. It provides more identity protection and safety than encryption, since it conceals the very presence of secrets rather than only shielding the material.

REFERENCES

Altaay, A. J. (2012). An Introduction to Image Steganography Techniques. *International Conference on Advanced Computer Science Applications and Technologies*, 122 - 126. 10.1109/ACSAT.2012.25

Daemen, J., & Rijmen, V. (1999). *AES Proposal: Rijndael*. Available in http://csrc.nist.gov/archive/aes/rijndael/Rijndael-ammended.pdf#page=1

Huang, C.-T., Tsai, M.-Y., Lin, L.-C., Wang, W.-J., & Wang, S.-J. (2018). VQ-based data hiding in IoT networks using two-level encodingwith adaptive pixel replacements. *The Journal of Supercomputing*, *74*(9), 4295–4314. doi:10.100711227-016-1874-9

Ian F Akyildiz, W. S., Sankarasubramaniam, Y., & Cayirci, E. (2002). Wireless sensor networks: A survey. *Computer Networks*, *38*(4), 393–422. doi:10.1016/S1389-1286(01)00302-4

Kargupta, H., Datta, S., Wang, Q., & Sivakumar, K. (2003). On the privacy preserving properties of random data perturbation techniques. In *Data Mining, 2003. ICDM 2003. Third IEEE International Conference* (pp. 99–106). IEEE. 10.1109/ICDM.2003.1250908

Li, S., Da Xu, L., & Zhao, S. (2015). The internet of things: a survey. *Information Systems Frontiers, 17*(2), 243-59.

Liao, X., Yin, J., Guo, S., Li, X., & Sangaiah, A. K. (2018). Medical JPEGimage steganography based on preserving inter-block dependencies. *Computers & Electrical Engineering, 67*, 320–329. doi:10.1016/j.compeleceng.2017.08.020

Liu, Kargupta, & Ryan. (2006). Random projection based multiplicative data perturbation for privacy preserving distributed data mining. *Knowledge and Data Engineering, IEEE Transactions on, 18*(1), 92–106.

Machanavajjhala, Kifer, Gehrke, & Venkitasubramaniam. (2007). Privacy beyond k-anonymity. *ACM Transactions on Knowledge Discovery from Data, 1*(1), 3. doi:10.1145/1217299.1217302

Marvel, L. M. (1999). Spread Spectrum Image Steganography. IEEE Transactions on Image Processing, 8(8), 1075 – 1083. doi:10.1109/83.777088

Sfar, A. R., Natalizio, E., Challal, Y., & Chtourou, Z. (2018, April 1). A roadmap for security challenges in the Internet of Things. *Digital Communications and Networks., 4*(2), 118–137. doi:10.1016/j.dcan.2017.04.003

Shanableh, T. (2012). Data hiding in MPEG video files using multivariateregression and flexible macroblock ordering. *IEEE Transactions on Information Forensics and Security, 7*(2), 455–464. doi:10.1109/TIFS.2011.2177087

Shoukat. (2011). A Survey about the Latest Trends and Research Issues of Cryptographic Elements. *International Journal of Computer Science Issues, 8*(3), 140-149.

Yick, J., Mukherjee, B., & Ghosal, D. (2008). Wireless sensor network survey. *Computer Networks, 52*(12), 2292–2330. doi:10.1016/j.comnet.2008.04.002

Zaidan, Zaidan, Al-Frajat, & Jalab. (2010). On the Differences between Hiding Information and Cryptography Techniques: An Overview. *Journal of Applied Sciences, 10*(15), 1650-1655.

Chapter 13
Application of Steganography for Secure Data Transmission Using Lossless Compression

Kylyn Fernandes
Dwarkadas J. Sanghvi College of Engineering, India

Ankit Rishi Gupta
Dwarkadas J. Sanghvi College of Engineering, India

Pratik Panchal
Dwarkadas J. Sanghvi College of Engineering, India

Ramchandra Mangrulkar
iD https://orcid.org/0000-0002-9020-0713
Dwarkadas J. Sanghvi College of Engineering, India

ABSTRACT

Steganography is the art of hiding messages or files in a way that prevents the detection of the existence of these hidden messages. It encompasses several techniques, including physical methods like invisible ink on paper and digital techniques like hiding text on multimedia files like images and music files. In the modern digital era, steganography has become a useful tool to evade detection and perusal of secret messages. With the advent of social media, it is very easy to encode a message or file onto an image and upload it online for the intended recipients to access, decode, and read or use. In this case of digital steganography of messages or files onto images, an important factor to consider is the effect of image compression on the hidden message. Since most social media and other online image posting websites run some sort of compression, cropping, and other image transformations on the uploaded images, understanding these techniques and their effect on the hidden text can help one choose the most suitable steganography technique to use for a particular use case.

DOI: 10.4018/978-1-7998-7160-6.ch013

INTRODUCTION

Before getting into Steganography lets first get into Cryptography. What is Cryptography? It is a technique that converts a plain readable text into something which is either not readable or readable with the real message hidden. This technique can be found as far back as 1900 B.C. Ancient Egyptians used to scribe hieroglyphics in the inscription. Cryptography was being used from 500-600 BC with simple techniques like ATBASH, reversed alphabet, simple substitution. Today the methods of cryptography used are far more complicated than these simple techniques, as they are implemented by computers. As cryptography was evolving over time Steganography thrived independently.

The origin of Steganography was with the 2 Greek words 'Steganos' which means secret or cover and 'grafia' which means drawing or writing (Khosravi et al., 2011). It is basically a technique which is used to hide any sensitive information into other harmless messages, audio files or pictures. It is hard to tell just by looking at some pleasing image that some sensitive information is hidden within it. This is the most important aspect of steganography that differentiates it from cryptography. In cryptography, the presence of the message is known, only contents are unknown, but steganography also hides the existence of the message. Just by looking at some encrypted text, it is apparent that there is a message encoded in it that can be read if decryption is achieved. Given enough time and resources, this may be possible or even easy to do, but in case of steganography, the message is hidden completely, and its presence itself also may not be known (Robert Krenn, 2004).

The first technique for steganography was developed around 440 B.C in ancient Greece. The Greek ruler used to shave the head of slaves, tattoo the secret message on the scalp, wait till the hair grows back and then send the slave to deliver the message. The receiver then again shaves the head of the slave and the original message was visible on their scalp. The next Steganography technique used by Demaratus was that the message is carved in the wood of wax tablet and then covered with another wax layer. It continued to develop in the early 1600s.

Steganography was heavily used during the American Revolutionary wars. Both the forces used various forms of Invisible Ink. This special Ink was visible under light or heat. Another technique from these times is the Null cipher which embeds unencrypted messages within some text (Siper et al., 2005).

For example, consider the carrier text, "Fishing freshwater bends and saltwater coasts rewards anyone feeling stressed. Resourceful anglers usually find masterful leapers fun and admit swordfish rank overwhelming any day." By extracting the third character from every word, the real encoded message is decoded as "Send Lawyers, Guns, and Money" (Johnson, 1995)

Here the carrier text does not make much sense, so it may arouse suspicion in readers that some hidden message may exist in it. Often when the carrier text also conveys some meaning and is not nonsensical gibberish, even the existence of the hidden message is not suspected. In the techniques that shall be discussed further, avoidance of detection of the hidden message or its existence via visual inspection will also be considered as a factor to compare them. Before that, some of the terminologies used for steganography must be discussed. The knowledge of the exact meaning of these can help understand the techniques used for steganography quicker.

The payload, or message, is the information that is to be hidden and covertly communicated. This is facilitated by encoding it onto the carrier or cover, which is a signal, textual data, image or other type of file that can hide the message on it. The resulting signal, textual data or file with the payload encoded in it is called the stego file or covert message. Terms like plaintext, key and ciphertext are also borrowed from cryptography when both techniques are used in conjunction.

The payload is then called the plaintext, which can be encrypted using cryptography techniques before embedding in the cover, requiring a key to encode and decode it. This is done so that even if the hidden message is detected, it will not be easy to read and interpret, adding another layer of security. This is often done in cases where the hexadecimal ciphertext produced can be added to the message, for example, it will be much more difficult to encode the 128 or 256 bit ciphertext that is usually outputted by algorithms that are like the null cipher described above.

In this chapter the types of Steganography are discussed next and the scope and uses of Steganography after that. The techniques used for image steganography are covered next, followed by 3 case studies on the real-world use and detection of Steganography for covert communication via social media. Compression with a focus on Image Compression using Lossy and Lossless Techniques is discussed after this. This information is used to compare image steganography techniques with specific focus on compression and manual inspection. The authors highlight the Experimentation and its results in the penultimate section and reach the Conclusion of the Chapter after that.

Table 1. Comparison of secret communication techniques (Kaur and Behal, 2014)

Secret Communication Technique	Confidentiality	Integrity	Un-removability
Encryption	Yes	No	Yes
Digital Signatures	No	Yes/No	No
Steganography	Yes/No	Yes/No	Yes

Background of Steganography

Masoud Mosrati et al. (2011) have provided a succinct yet informative introduction to steganography, followed by a compilation of numerous steganography techniques, primarily focusing on text, image and audio steganography. Some of those techniques have been enlisted further in this chapter. As additional reference, the work of Navneet Kaur and Sunny Behal (2014) compares Steganography to Encryption and Digital Signatures and provides a more thorough compilation of its types.

R. J. Mstafa et al. (2017) and Bobade and Goudar (2015) have clearly explained the techniques and working of Video and Protocol Steganography, respectively. Neil F. Johnson and Sushil Jajodia (1998) have provided the most complete document on steganography yet discussed, throwing light on not just introductory information and thorough descriptions of various techniques with examples and pictorial representations, but also compared tools available for the same as of February 1998.

Kumar Arvind and Km. Pooja (2010) explain that due to the advancement of technology, the conventional method of sending encrypted messages has become less and less secure. Any third party or eavesdropper can intercept the message and decoding it has also become much easier. Hence steganography provides a more secure foundation for exchange of secret messages.

They explain how the third party or eavesdropper has no idea which image has a hidden message. Even if the eavesdropper somehow manages to find the image with the hidden message, decrypting it is a tedious task as one needs to know the tools, technique, password, etc. required. (Kumar and Km, 2010)

In the case studies performed by Trotter, Lindsey Kathryn (2019) the focus is to identify the best tools and methods for the encryption and decryption of stego images and how social media can be used to send secret messages using stego images.

In the first case study, it is observed that for most social media sites, the stego images go through a compression process, thus disrupting the hidden secret message. Facebook and Twitter were found to be the most effective social media sites for transfer of these stego images. For Facebook it was observed that uploading these images on the timeline results in image compression thus a more effective method would be to upload it as a Cover Photo.

In the second case study, different methods are studied to find which is the most effective in decrypting the stego image. Here, it was found that the Quantization Matrix method proved the most effective to decrypt stego images created by JP Hide & Seek tool and SilentEye tool for stego images posted on Twitter. This method however, proved ineffective for stego images posted on Facebook.

These bring out the need for reliable steganography techniques for use as a covert communication medium, especially via social media. The biggest challenge here was compression of images to make them viable for internet transmission and avoiding platforms that would apply transformations on the image that can cause the message to be lost.

Types of Steganography

Due to the long history of steganography, there are a lot of different types and techniques available. Over the years, steganography has seen use across all types of communication media, be it letters being transmitted via pigeons and messengers, or telegrams used during wartimes. Some common ways to categorize steganography will be discussed in this section.

The biggest categorization of steganography is based on whether it is digital or physical. For physical steganography, printed and handwritten material is usually used. Historically this was the most used method, but with the advent of computers and digital steganography techniques, covert communication now needs to be using computers and the internet, hence the need for digital steganography. A subclass of digital steganography, literal steganography, deals with such physical steganography techniques carried over to the digital domain. It includes open codes like the null cipher and semagrams that modify the look and presentation of information, such as visual semagrams (for example, modifying the layout of items on a webpage) and textual semagrams (for example, modifying the size of spacing between words). (Kaur and Behal, 2014)

Technical Steganography consists of some specialized techniques useful only for computers that encode data as bits, i.e., zeroes and ones. It works by modifying the cover in a way such that some bits of it are modified to be the bits representing the payload. They are classified either according to the method or the cover used.

Some Text steganography techniques include Format Based Method and Random and Statistical Generation. There are also Line-Shift Coding, Word-Shift Coding and Feature Coding techniques for text Steganography.

- Line-Shift Coding is a method of altering a document by vertically shifting the locations of text lines to encode the document uniquely. Encoding the format file or the bitmap of a page image using Line-Shift Coding is possible. The embedded codeword may be extracted from the format file or bitmap.

Figure 1. Classification of Steganography

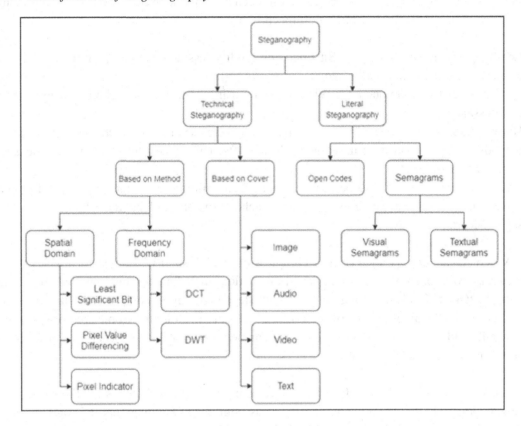

- Word-Shift Coding is a method of altering a document by horizontally shifting the locations of words within text lines to encode the document uniquely. Encoding the format file or the bitmap of a page image using Word-Shift Coding is possible. The embedded codeword may be extracted from the format file or bitmap. Documents must have variable spacing between adjacent words for this technique. (Mosrati et al., 2011)
- Feature Coding is a coding method in which the image is examined for chosen text features, and depending on the codeword, those features are either altered, or not altered. Encoding the format file or the bitmap of a page image using Feature Coding is possible. Decoding requires a specification of the change in pixels at a feature. Any text feature can be modified, for example, alter the tops of letters, b, d, h, etc. by extending or shortening their lengths by one (or more) pixels. (Brassil et al., 1995)

Some Image steganography techniques include Least Significant Bit Insertion, Masking and Filtering, Redundant Pattern Encoding, Encrypt and Scatter and Coding and Cosine Transformation. The basic idea for image steganography is embedding an image or message within a photo through the addition of digital noise. Detailed explanations for the same are available in the Techniques section of this chapter.

For Audio steganography, some Image Steganography techniques like Least Significant Bit Manipulation can be reused. Audio signals are represented as sampled and quantized signals digitally, so the binary data can be modified in a very similar manner to images. Playing an audio track backwards or at higher speeds to reveal a secret message has also been a technique used for audio steganography, but here the track to use as carrier must be carefully chosen.

- Least Significant Bit and Parity Bit Encoding modify less noticeable bits in the audio. Another technique is to add noise to the signal.
- Spread Spectrum technique adds White noise by using higher parts of the bandwidth to encode the message.
- Human Auditory Systems (HAS) can detect such noise, so instead the phase of the audio signal is modified, by encoding the message as phase shifts. This makes the encoding unnoticeable and is called Phase Coding.
- The secret message can also be encoded using Echo Hiding. Here the audio signal amplitude, decay rate and offset are modified to create an echo of the original and the echo contains the message. (Mosrati et al., 2011)

For Video steganography, the effect of compression, which shall be studied for images further in the chapter, is more apparent. There are 2 major distinctions in techniques, ones applied after compression using H.264 or HEVC encoding (called Video steganography in compressed domain), and ones applied before the encoding (called Video steganography in raw domain). Some Audio steganography techniques like hiding a message in the video that can be seen by playing it faster, slower or in reverse are also available for video steganography.

- Since video is essentially a collection of frames in order, the techniques are the same as image steganography in the raw domain, namely, Least Significant Bit encoding, Histogram manipulation and Transformation techniques like DCT and DWT.
- In the compressed domain, transformation techniques can still be used, but instead of bit manipulation on image frames of the video, encoding is done on the compression algorithm encoded frames. (Mstafa et al., 2017)

Protocol Steganography lets us encode messages in various network layer protocols of the OSI or TCP/IP model. There are many redundant, deprecated, or empty parts of the headers of TCP, IPv4 and IPv6. IPv6 also contains many covert data channels, which too can be used to secretly transmit information. Bobade and Goudar (2015) propose encoding data into these locations for military applications of steganography.

Scope and Uses of Steganography

Steganography is used to send secret messages or data without being censored and is not easy to track or intercept or traced back to parties involved. It can be an effective alternative to cryptography, or at least be used in conjunction with it. Some uses as elaborated by Kumar Arvind and Km. Pooja (2010) are as follows:

1. Steganography can also be used to watermark images. There are several techniques used in steganography that can store watermarks in data. While steganography focuses on hiding information, watermarking only extends the original image with extra information. This digital watermarking

helps us detect whether an image has been copied. For example, if someone downloads some digital art that was digitally watermarked, and uploads it as his own creation, the watermark can be used to prove true ownership.

2. Steganography is also used to store information about a particular topic. For example, private banking accounts and details, military secrets, government secrets, can be stored in source image so finding this information becomes more difficult in case device is breached.

3. Hidden exchanges can also be carried out using steganography. For example, Business trade secrets, Government communication, etc. Even via an unsecure communication channel, the existence of the hidden text will not be noticeable to any hackers who may get access to the data via attacks like Man in the Middle.

4. Broadcast of hidden data is also possible with the help of steganography. It overcomes the drawback of cryptography where an eavesdropper knows which messages are encrypted and which are not. Combining cryptography and steganography can prove to be a very useful tool to combat compromise of data.

5. Biometrics including fingerprint scanning, retinas, blood-type, when used alongside personal session IDs allow inserting fingerprint images through steganography, hence increasing the security during E-Commerce transactions.

One real world example of steganography was by jihadists to covertly communicate online using an app called MuslimCrypt. It has been covered in case study 3 of this chapter. (Newman Lily Hay, 2018)

Techniques of Image Steganography

Image steganography involves the cover image, which is an image file that shall be manipulated in such a way that a second file, the message, can be hidden in it retrievably. This output with the message hidden inside is the stego image. A key or a password, commonly called a stego-key can optionally be required to hide the message in the image, requiring the knowledge of the stego-key to decode the message from the image.

Information can be encoded serially in the first few bytes of the image, or selectively in noisy areas of the image to draw less attention. One could also pseudo randomly scatter the message across the image. This helps prevent loss due to actions like cropping.

Prominent Image Steganography techniques include Least Significant Bit manipulation, Masking and Filtering/Redundant Pattern Encoding, Encrypt and Scatter, Discrete Cosine transform and Discrete Wavelet Transform. (Johnson and Jajodia, 1998)

Bit Manipulation or Spatial Techniques involve modifying the intensity of individual pixels to encode the message. The simplest and most common such technique is Least Significant Bit (LSB) Manipulation. For a message as a stream of bits, the least significant bit of each byte in the image is changed to be the bit of the message. This can be applied to both grayscale and color images.

Grayscale images represent each pixel as 1 byte or 8 bits. Hence to store a message of n bytes, 9n pixels are needed in the grayscale image. 9 bits per byte are used, not 8 to indicate whether the message has terminated or not, using the extra bit. If this bit is not used, the decoding algorithm will also read gibberish from the rest of the image.

$$number\_of\_pixels\_needed = 9 \times message\_length \tag{1}$$

Figure 2. Image Steganography Techniques

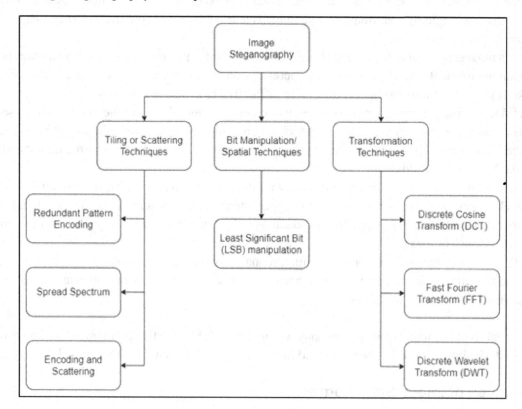

For color images with each pixel as 3 bytes, 1 byte each for Red, Green and Blue respectively, exactly 3 pixels are needed to store 1 byte of the message. Hence the number of pixels required reduces by a factor of 3. See the implementation section of this chapter for a live example of this technique.

$$\text{number\_of\_pixels\_needed} = 9 \times \text{message\_length} \tag{2}$$

The LSB manipulation technique works fine for encoding data onto a lossless compression filetype and is not at all resistant to transformations of the image. Any type or rotation, cropping or editing of the image can cause the message to be lost. Even simple image transformations like contrast enhancement can lead to complete loss of the message. (Mosrati et al., 2011)

Tiling and Scattering techniques are comparatively more robust as compared to LSB manipulation. Tiling techniques repeat the message over the image multiple times. Here the total number of pixels must be much larger than the number of pixels required to store the message. One way to do this is as a mask over the image containing the text. This mask with higher than 15% luminance is visible to the human eye, but with very low luminance, it is practically invisible. The mask can be detected and separated to increase luminance and make the hidden text visible. This is more useful for text that is needed to be human read, such as using steganography for digital watermarking. Masking is more robust than LSB insertion with respect to compression, cropping, and some image processing.

Scattering techniques pseudo randomly scatter the message across the message, so it resembles noise. The Spread Spectrum technique also scatters the message across the image using multiple channels.

Scattering and Encryption make the message more robust against being read even if it is extracted as the stego-key is required to read it. (Johnson and Jajodia, 1998)

Transformation techniques do not work in the spatial domain. The message is instead embedded into the wavelet, cosine or Fourier transform of the image. This is a very robust method of watermarking and steganography. The DCT is used by the JPEG compression algorithm as well, and the same reason that obfuscates the message in LSB manipulation of JPEG images prevents it in the case of DCT transformation. Xiang-Gen Xia et al. demonstrate the JPEG2000 compression using DWT and IDWT and the process for watermarking and extracting the watermark for JPEG2000 images and MPEG4 videos. (Xia, Boncelet and Arce, 1997)

Some attempts have been made to further improve this LSB substitution, like this RGB based technique by M. Tanvir Parvez and A. Abdul-Aziz Gutub (2008). They store variable number of bits in each color (R, G or B) channel of the pixels based on the actual color values of that pixel, where a lower color component stores higher number of bits. This algorithm offers very high capacity for cover media compared to other existing algorithms.

S. Ohmaya et al. (2009) further work on the DCT based technique to achieve image alteration detection for JPEG2000 compressed data. They embedded not just the message and the JBIG2 bit-stream of a part of the LSB plane but also the bit-depth of the quantized coefficients on some code-blocks to reach this result. After the extraction steps, the secret data was extracted and they retrieved a bit-plane structure of quantized wavelet coefficients, which was found to be identical to the original bitstream.

CASE STUDIES

Social media is defined as computer technology that facilitates the sharing of ideas, thoughts, and information through the building of virtual networks and communities. By design, social media gives users quick electronic communication of content via the internet. Users can post updates about themselves, their travels, their hobbies, and share it with everyone using their online accounts through Online Social Networks (OSNs). Some common social media outlets are Facebook, Instagram, Twitter, etc. Social Media can become an effective means of discrete communication when combining its use with steganography.

Suppose a suspect wants to send a message to his crime partner. If he sends a direct message or email to his partner, then it can be easily flagged by investigators post-crime. Even if the message is encrypted, it can be cracked by investigators, if they figure out the decryption key. The address of the recipient is also readily available in the message.

Now, considering the extensive use of social media by billions of users throughout the world, it will be easier to hide the message by encrypting it in an image and sharing it as a normal post. To any other user, it is just a harmless post, but to the partner having the decryption key, it is the perfect method to distribute the messages.

Investigators neither have the time nor the resources to pull off such a task of analyzing billions of images appearing on social media. Even if they did manage to find the encrypted image, they still have no way of identifying the partner, as millions of users can view the image.

Case Study 1: How to share Stego Messages on Social Media (Trotter, 2019)

Recent study proved that when stego images are shared through social media, the data is generally lost or corrupted due to image compression used by most social media sites. The following table by Trotter, Lindsey Kathryn (Trotter, 2019) shows the ranking of most common sites and whether they were explored in their paper.

Table 2. Ranking of Social Media Websites for Steganography (Trotter, 2019)

Rank	Network	Will Research	Reasoning
1	Facebook	Yes	Most popular app
2	YouTube	No	Shares videos, not images
6	Instagram	No	Does not allow to download images, hence can't retrieve stego image
8	QZone	No	Foreign App
9	Douyin/TikTok	No	Foreign App
10	Sina Weibo	No	Foreign App
11	Twitter	Yes	Second most popular app not disqualified

During the analysis of Facebook, recent studies found that sometimes the entire data was unchanged after being posted on Facebook. When they used JP Hide & Seek app on Windows and SilentEye on Mac and uploaded the stego image to Facebook, they were found to retain most stego messages on downloading the uploaded image and decoding the message. They also found maximum success with Facebook when stego images were kept as the user's Cover Photo.

Methodology

Recent studies have been able to determine the credibility of using steganography via social media on basis of whether the payload is retained or lost during the communication. This case study was based on research to find more effective sharing of stego images through social media accounts. To study the success of steganography, 2 methods were used:

1. Upload image using phone to social media.
2. Upload image to PC, then PC to social media.

A test was conducted according to the following diagram by uploading image containing same text file for all trials of Facebook and Twitter. JP Hide & Seek was used for Windows trials while SilentEye was used for Mac trials. Both tools are DCT transformation-based tools.

Each image was encoded with a message, uploaded on a social media site, downloaded from the site and then checked for retention of the encoded message.

Findings

Figure 3. Technique used to test the Social Media platforms (Trotter, 2019)

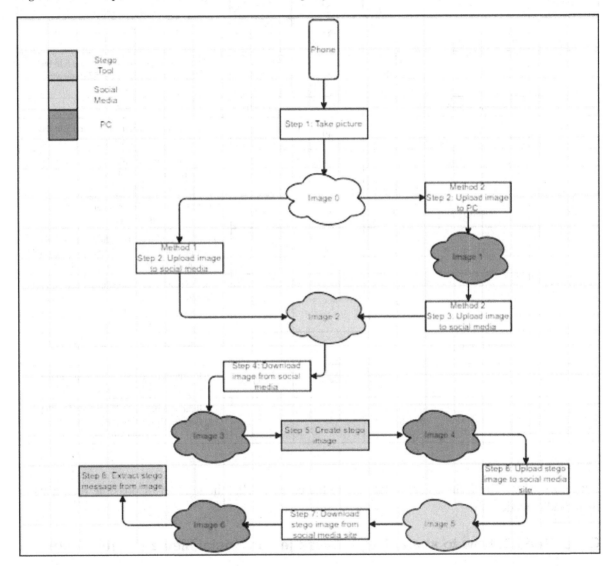

Conclusion of Case Study 1

From case study 1, it is evident that stego images can be created and shared on social media platforms like Facebook and Twitter. But, for such execution, a specific set of instructions need to be followed. Here, it is also observed that steganography works mostly with Facebook cover photos. Hence, for an investigator it is easier from one point of view while increases tasks from another point of view. Since the number of cover photos in much less compared to the timeline images, it is easier to find the encrypted

Table 3. Success rate with various tools and social media platforms (Trotter, 2019)

Social Media	Stego App	Method	Number of Trials	Success Rate	Where Failure Occurred
Facebook	SilentEye	1	20	80.00	All failures occurred during step 5 in the diagram above.
		2	37	91.90	All failures occurred during step 5 in the diagram above.
		Both	57	87.71	All failures occurred during step 5 in the diagram above. 50 of the 57 trials were successful.
	JP Hide & Seek	1	15	100.00	N/A
		2	40	32.50	All failures occurred during step 8 in the diagram above.
		Both	55	50.90	All failures occurred during step 8 in the diagram above. 28 of the 55 trials were successful
Twitter	SilentEye	1	15	86.70	All of the failures occurred during step 5 in the diagram above
		2	40	67.50	4 of the failures occurred during step 5 in the diagram above and 9 of the failures occurred during step 8 in the diagram above.
		Both	55	72.72	6 of the failures occurred during step 5 in the diagram above and 9 of the failures occurred during step 8 in the diagram above. 40 of the 55 trials were successful
	JP Hide & Seek	1	15	20.00	All failures occurred during step 8 in the diagram above.
		2	40	5.00	All failures occurred during step 8 in the diagram above.
		Both	55	9.09	All failures occurred during step 8 in the diagram above. 5 of the 55 trials were successful.

image. But since cover photos are accessible to the entire public, the number of possible recipients is increased considerably.

Case Study 2: How to share Stego Messages on Social Media (Trotter, 2019)

This case study focused on searching for a way to find which images on social media are encrypted. Through Quantization Matrices analysis, some images including the ones generated in case study 1 were put to the test. The feasibility of social media as a platform for covert communication using steganography relies heavily upon the ease and speed of detection of such steganography and the likelihood of the message not being caught.

A Quantization matrix is possessed only by images having JPEG file extension. The JPEG image is first transformed into an 8x8 matrix. This matrix then undergoes 3 steps:

1.   A Discrete Cosine Transfer.

2. Divided by a Quantizer table.
3. Put through an Entropy Encoder.

Methodology

Once creation of images was done, QMs were found by using the following tools:

- For Mac:- https://29a.ch/photo-forensics/#jpeg-data
- For Windows:- https://www.impulseadventure.com/photo/jpeg-snoop.html (JPEG Snoop app)

Findings

All images downloaded before stego image creation was same for Twitter but not all were same for Facebook. Also, every image generated using SilentEye had the same QM. This was true for the images before they were uploaded on Facebook or Twitter. Some of the images had the same QM as the SilentEye photos. This indicates that these images are most probably encrypted with stego message.

When QM method was tested for JP Hide & Seek tool, it was observed that this tool does not have a standard QM of its own. Hence this method was not effective for images generated using JP Hide & Seek tool.

Conclusion of Case Study 2

Quantization Matrices can be used to gather image data and find out if that is an encrypted image. In short, if QM of an image matches that of a standard SilentEye, then the image is generally an encrypted image.

Case Study 3: A Real-World use of Steganography for Covert Communication

This case study focuses on how jihadi terror groups like ISIS took complete advantage of secure communication tools, using common social platforms in a way that no common person would expect. These groups create technology for themselves to use normal software and alter it for encryption purposes depending on their requirements. One of their most prominent software is the communication tool MuslimCrypt. It follows steganography techniques to send secrets to each other. Generally, software developed at home has quite a shortage of resources and reliability. However, while studying MuslimCrypt, it was found that it is actually effective.

According to Simon Wiseman, who is the chief technology officer at Deep Secure, a British network security firm, working to protect against bad use of steganography said, "Steganography's value as a secret communication tool makes it unsurprising that jihadis would eventually adopt the technique." (Newman Lily Hay, 2018)

Methodology

MuslimCrypt was originally introduced in a private, pro-ISIS Telegram channel. It uses the same technology as other steganography techniques. It is encrypting a digital message in a distinguished piece of technology, similar to the concept of invisible ink. MuslimCrypt encrypts these messages in images posing no threat to be shared or posted freely on social media since only the intended person will know which image is the encrypted one. Even if the correct image is intercepted, the decryption key would be required to access the embedded the message.

By using the simple concept of steganography, and using a custom implementation of it, they have managed to elude deciphering of the messages despite its existence having been revealed. Not only does it rely on the idea that the existence of the covert message is hidden, but by keeping the technique of steganography secret, they add an extra layer of difficulty to cracking the system.

MEMRI researcher Marwan Khayat traced the tool's history on Telegram, found it's users, and after verifying that downloading it wouldn't be dangerous, examined it in a software sandbox to determine how to use the tool. He then tested its ability to encode information in image files and extract that data on the receiver's end. Given that ISIS and its sympathizers use active multimedia propaganda campaigns, there are a lot of places for messages to be hidden. (Newman Lily Hay, 2018)

Findings

1. The tool is so effective, that the exact technique of steganography it uses is also unknown.
2. It has made a huge impact as it has provided an effective communication channel for the jihadis.
3. The program's interface is extremely simple, with fields to enter which image should be used, the message to hide, and then to enter a password.
4. It also supports hashes, so any tampering of the file in between can be identified. (Cox Joseph, 2018)

Conclusion of Case Study 3

MEMRI (Middle East Media Research Institute) researcher Marwan Khayat will continue to dig inside MuslimCrypt, but the conclusions only point out the fact that this technology is a huge breakthrough in jihadist communication channels. (Newman Lily Hay, 2018)

"There's no good reliable technique to find this stuff if the data is encrypted and the techniques are smart. It just looks like noise, and photos have a lot of noise," Matthew Green, a cryptographer and Assistant Professor at the Johns Hopkins Information Security Institute told Motherboard in a Twitter message. (Cox Joseph, 2018)

COMPRESSION

In general Compression is a technique where the size of the data is somehow reduced so that the space required to store the data is minimum. This reduced data is possible to recover completely in case of lossless technique or if lossy compression is applied it cannot be recovered. Also, when the size is reduced it becomes even easier to transfer the file. (Christensson, 2011)

There are mainly two types of data where compression is done:

1. File Compression: Any general computer file including text and binary files
2. Media File Compression: This include files such as images, videos, and audio.

Figure 4. Block diagram of lossy compression

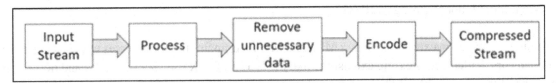

File Compression

The most common types of file compressions utilities are Zip, RAR, 7z etc. By using these lossless compression utilities, the size reduces to 10% to 50% of the original size. This can be done on a single or a group of files. Although the compression algorithm is different for different utilities the main goal is to eliminate the redundant data. For example, a particular word like 'The' is repeated many times in a file which required 3 bytes per word. So, by replacing 'The' with '1' which requires only 1 byte of space, with this simple replacement technique the overall size of the file is decreased. It can also be used on binary files with repeated binary patterns. Since the compression applied is lossless any compressed file can be fully recovered back to its original state. (Christensson, 2011)

Media Compression

In media compression the algorithm used is rather different than what was used in File compression. It works on specific type of media file such as image compression, video compression, etc. At times it is even possible to use lossy compression on media file thus it cannot be recovered to its original state. Some common type of compressed image extensions is:

1. JPEG which is more of a lossy compression which uses DCT (Discrete Cosine Transform), this lessens the variations in pixel intensities making it more redundant. (Raid A. et al., 2014) This obviously causes issues to any text hidden using spatial steganography techniques like LSB manipulation. A detailed explanation of steps involved in JPEG compression has been discussed below. (X Zhou, 2011)
2. PNG which uses lossless compression technique which predicts the pixel color based on its surrounding pixels. It is a file format based on raster graphics that also supports transparent backgrounds. It

Figure 5. Block diagram of loss less compression and decompression

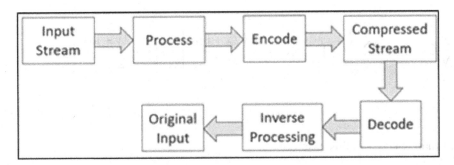

supports RGBA and was created for transferring files across the network, so it has strong compression, though not as strong as JPEG.

Audio Compression extension such as MP3 and M4A eliminates the frequencies which is not audible to human ears. Video compressing extensions like MPEG and DivX use specific coder and decoder that removes redundant data like if the background is same for multiple frames then instead of redrawing it at every frame it simply draws it only once. (Amandeep Singh Sidhu et al., 2014)

JPEG Compression

1. The whole JPEG image is been divided into 8x8 blocks which are processed individually using DCT. Let O be the following 8x8 matrix.

$$O = \begin{pmatrix} 65 & 55 & 55 & 54 & 49 & 48 & 47 & 49 \\ 62 & 56 & 54 & 52 & 48 & 47 & 48 & 53 \\ 41 & 60 & 52 & 48 & 48 & 47 & 49 & 54 \\ 63 & 61 & 60 & 60 & 63 & 64 & 70 & 65 \\ 67 & 67 & 70 & 74 & 79 & 85 & 91 & 92 \\ 82 & 95 & 101 & 106 & 114 & 115 & 112 & 117 \\ 96 & 110 & 115 & 130 & 128 & 128 & 130 & 128 \\ 109 & 121 & 127 & 133 & 139 & 141 & 140 & 140 \end{pmatrix}$$

2. Here all values are ranging from 0 to 256, we subtract 128 from it. So that the values will range from -128 to +127. Let the matrix be O'.

$$O' = O - 128 = \begin{pmatrix} -63 & -73 & -73 & -74 & -79 & -80 & -81 & -79 \\ -66 & -72 & -74 & -76 & -80 & -81 & -80 & -75 \\ -87 & -68 & -76 & -80 & -80 & -81 & -79 & -74 \\ -65 & -67 & -68 & -68 & -65 & -64 & -58 & -63 \\ -61 & -61 & -58 & -54 & -49 & -43 & -37 & -36 \\ -46 & -33 & -27 & -22 & -14 & -13 & -16 & -11 \\ -32 & -18 & -13 & 2 & 0 & 0 & 2 & 0 \\ -19 & -7 & -1 & 5 & 11 & 13 & 12 & 12 \end{pmatrix}$$

3. 3. Now the DCT is computed using the following formula,

$$F(u,v) = \frac{2}{N} C(u) C(v) \sum_{x=0}^{N-1} \sum_{y=0}^{N-1} f(x,y) \cos\left[\frac{\pi(2x+1)u}{2N}\right] \cos\left[\frac{\pi(2y+1)v}{2N}\right] \tag{3}$$

Here,

N: the size of matrix i.e., 8 in this case

u, v, x, y: ranges from 0 to N-1

f(x,y): O'(x,y)

$$C(k): \begin{cases} \dfrac{1}{\sqrt{2}} \; for \; k = 0 \\ 1 \; for \; k = 1 \, to \, N - 1 \end{cases}$$

Hence the matrix becomes.

$$F = \begin{pmatrix} -370 & -32.9 & -6.8 & -6.1 & -1.8 & -3.2 & -3.6 & -1.7 \\ -236 & 45.9 & 21.6 & 2.3 & 3.5 & 2.9 & 2.8 & 1.6 \\ 65.5 & 11 & -6.3 & -1.3 & 3.5 & 1.5 & 2 & -1.9 \\ 14.9 & -6.2 & -1.7 & 3 & 5.1 & 3.6 & 3.9 & 0.2 \\ -2.8 & -0.1 & 6.6 & 7.7 & 1.4 & 6 & 2.5 & 3.2 \\ 0 & 4.5 & -5.6 & -0.6 & -0.8 & 1.7 & -3.6 & -1.1 \\ -0.4 & -2 & -3.3 & -3.6 & -4.3 & -8 & 0.3 & 0 \\ -12.7 & -4.7 & 0.3 & -3.9 & -1.8 & -0.9 & -2.5 & -2.5 \end{pmatrix}$$

4. There is a standard Quantization table defined known as Luminance matrix. (Cogranne Rémi, 2018) Let Q be the luminance matrix.

$$Q = \begin{pmatrix} 16 & 11 & 10 & 16 & 24 & 40 & 51 & 61 \\ 12 & 12 & 14 & 19 & 26 & 58 & 60 & 55 \\ 14 & 13 & 16 & 24 & 40 & 57 & 69 & 56 \\ 14 & 17 & 22 & 29 & 51 & 87 & 80 & 62 \\ 18 & 22 & 37 & 56 & 68 & 109 & 103 & 77 \\ 24 & 35 & 55 & 64 & 81 & 104 & 113 & 92 \\ 49 & 64 & 78 & 87 & 103 & 121 & 120 & 101 \\ 72 & 92 & 95 & 98 & 112 & 100 & 103 & 99 \end{pmatrix}$$

5. Here matrix B is computed as F/Q.

$$
B = \begin{pmatrix}
-23 & -3 & -1 & 0 & 0 & 0 & 0 & 0 \\
-20 & 4 & 2 & 0 & 0 & 0 & 0 & 0 \\
5 & 1 & 0 & 0 & 0 & 0 & 0 & 0 \\
1 & 0 & 0 & 0 & 0 & 0 & 0 & 0 \\
0 & 0 & 0 & 0 & 0 & 0 & 0 & 0 \\
0 & 0 & 0 & 0 & 0 & 0 & 0 & 0 \\
0 & 0 & 0 & 0 & 0 & 0 & 0 & 0 \\
0 & 0 & 0 & 0 & 0 & 0 & 0 & 0
\end{pmatrix}
$$

6. After this the matrix is flatten by traversing it in zig zag way as shown in below image

After this it is encoded using Huffman Encoding as discussed in the next section.

Figure 6. Zigzag Pattern to flatten the matrix

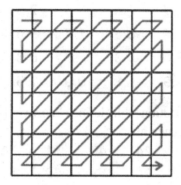

7. The image is recovered back by performing all this steps in reverse order and by computing Inverse DCT. Following is the recovered 8x8 image matrix.

$$
Recovered = \begin{pmatrix}
69 & 67 & 62 & 60 & 66 & 79 & 96 & 113 \\
65 & 64 & 61 & 62 & 69 & 82 & 98 & 114 \\
61 & 62 & 66 & 73 & 82 & 94 & 106 & 117 \\
71 & 75 & 85 & 97 & 107 & 114 & 118 & 123 \\
97 & 103 & 116 & 129 & 136 & 136 & 132 & 129 \\
126 & 132 & 144 & 156 & 158 & 152 & 142 & 134 \\
143 & 147 & 156 & 164 & 163 & 154 & 143 & 134 \\
141 & 143 & 148 & 152 & 150 & 145 & 137 & 132
\end{pmatrix}
$$

Hence, after comparing Recovered matrix with Original matrix O, the values are though similar but not exactly same. Therefore, any information embedded in the image via steganography techniques will get corrupted and the message will be irretrievably lost.

LOSSY AND LOSSLESS TECHNIQUES OF IMAGE COMPRESSION

Figure 7. Types of compression techniques

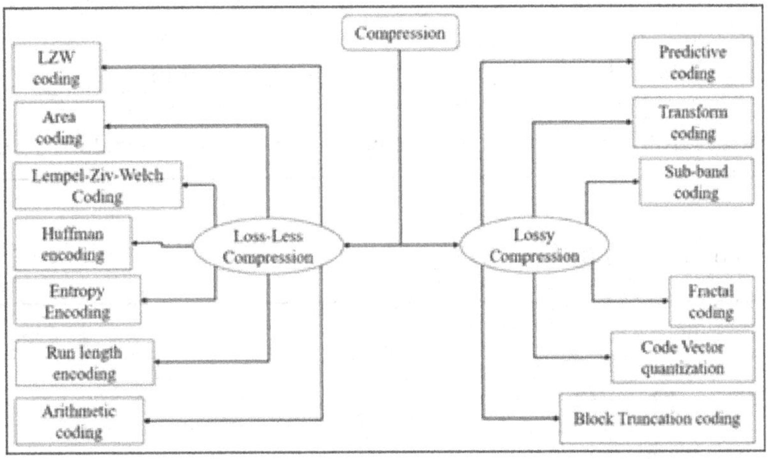

Lossy Compression

Block Truncating Coding

Here the image is divided into a block of N x N and each block is processed individually. First the mean is of all the pixels in that block is taken out, this is certainly the threshold value. After the mean calculation, the bitmap of that block is generated by putting '1' where the pixel is greater than mean and '0' otherwise. Then two values are decided 'a' and 'b' which will be replaced in place of '1' and '0' (Zhe-Ming Lu and Shi-Ze Guo, 2017). For example

Loss Less Compression

Huffman Encoding

This works on the principle on variable length bit code. First the frequencies of all the pixels are taken out and it is sorted in ascending order of their frequencies. Then a tree is constructed by combining minimum pairs and marking left side as 1 and right branch as 0. For example, let us consider a 4x4 image as given below (Dinesh V. Rojatkar et al., 2015)

After the tree is constructed, the encoding of each pixels is as follows

Figure 8. Block Truncating coding example

125	60	48	125
230	60	125	230
100	120	60	100
120	60	60	120

mean = 109

1	0	0	1
1	0	1	1
0	1	0	0
1	0	0	1

bitmap

230	60	60	230
230	60	230	230
60	230	60	60
230	60	60	230

a = 230, b = 60

Figure 9. Sample Image and it's Huffman Tree

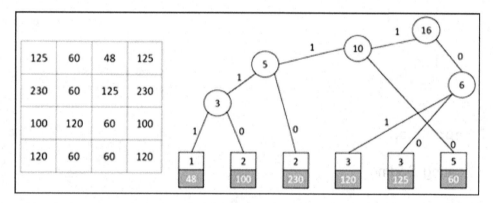

Comparison of Image Steganography Techniques

Due to its lossy compression, most steganography software does not support JPEG format images. PNG, BMP and GIF files are preferred over JPEG for steganography purposes. The ideal files for steganography are grayscale 8-bit images. Each pixel is represented as one byte, with 256 different gray levels available to it. This is because the shade of colors shifting by a little may be noticeable, but for grayscale images, the distortion is less noticeable and can be perceived to be noise if detected.

Figure 10. Huffman encoding for above example

Pixels	48	60	100	120	125	230
Frequencies	1	5	2	3	3	2
Codes	1111	10	1110	01	00	110

Bit manipulation techniques like LSB manipulation usually only have the message in the cover image only once. They also only manipulate the least significant bit, which may change due to compression. For example, JPEG uses DCT and DWT to compress huge images into small sizes, making them ideal for sharing on the internet. This means that depending on the precision of the float cosine, the exact value of the pixel on uncompressing might change. These changes are expected to bring as little distortion as possible, but the LSB can change without bringing significant noticeable difference in color. Hence the JPEG compression can change the LSB of pixels, which can lead to corruption of the hidden message within the stego image.

An advantage of these techniques is that for lossless compression or compression-less file formats like PNG and BMP, the message is not at all noticeable via manual inspection. It is also not viable to run automated analysis of images to detect these messages such as the Quantization Matrix used in Case Study 2 of this chapter. Added encryption such as AES 256 requiring a key to decode the message make this method extremely difficult to detect if the image is not being cropped, edited, transformed, or compressed. A python3 implementation of this technique is available further in this chapter.

Watermarking and Masking techniques do not just hide the data in noise, but rather significant parts of the image as well, making it more suitable than LSB for lossy JPEG images. This still is not perfect, but considerably more reliable than LSB manipulation for cropping and compression resistance.

Transformation techniques like DCT and DWT are most robust to tackle JPEG's lossy compression by integrating with the compression technique itself. These become very noticeable by humans, as patches of varied luminosity on the image.

The basis of comparison for image steganography techniques from an application perspective includes:

1. Lossless Compression Resistance
2. Lossy Compression Resistance
3. Detection by Human Eye
4. Automated Detection
5. Capacity (size of message a certain size of image can store)
6. Perceptual transparency (affects quality of image after embedding the message)
7. Robustness (immunity to general image manipulations like cropping, rotation etc)
8. Tamper resistance (difficulty in manipulating the message after hiding)
9. Computational complexity (the time complexity of the steganography algorithm to hide the message)

(Hussain Mehdi and Hussain Mureed, 2013)

Experimental Setup and Results

With a focus on simplicity and effectiveness, the LSB manipulation technique was implemented using python3 to hide a text message onto image files. AES256 encryption was provided as an option using the open source simple-crypt package to encrypt the message before encoding and provide more security in case the message was detected.

```
From PIL import Image
import simplecrypt
```

Table 4. Comparison of Image Steganography techniques

Basis of Comparison of Techniques	LSB Manipulation	Masking and Scattering	DCT/DWT Transformation
Lossless Compression Resistance	Yes	Yes	Yes
Lossy JPEG Compression Resistance	Low	Medium	High
Visibility to Human Eyes	Low	Medium (depends on luminosity)	High
Automated Detection	Difficult	Difficult	Easily by Quantization Matrix method
Capacity	High	Low	Low
Perceptual Transparency	No	Depends on Luminosity	Yes
Robustness	No	Yes	No
Tamper Resistance	No	No	Yes
Computational Complexity	Low	Low	High

```python
def increment(x, y, w):
    if x == w-1:
        x=0
        y+=1
    else:
        x+=1
    return x, y




def hide_text(image, text, output_image_path, encryption_key=None, show_
working=True):
    if encryption_key != None:
        enc_data = simplecrypt.encrypt(encryption_key, text)
        data = [format(I, '08b') for I in bytearray(enc_data)]
        if show_working:
            print(bytearray(enc_data), list(enc_data))
    else:
        data = []
        for I in text:
            data.append(format(ord(i), '08b'))

    if image.size[0] * image.size[1] / 3 < len(data):
        raise Exception("data too long for image")

    encoded_image = image.copy()
```

```python
    width = image.size[0]
    x, y = 0, 0

    for bytecount, byte in enumerate(data):
        p = None
        if show_working:
            print(byte)
        for bitcount, bit in enumerate(byte):
            if bitcount % 3 == 0:
                p = list(image.getpixel((x,y)))
                if show_working:
                    print(p, end=", ")

            if bit == "0" and p[bitcount % 3] % 2 != 0:
                p[bitcount % 3] -= 1
            elif bit == "1" and p[bitcount % 3] % 2 != 1:
                p[bitcount % 3] += 1

            if bitcount % 3 == 2:
                encoded_image.putpixel((x, y), tuple(p))
                if show_working:
                    print(p, (x, y))
                x, y = increment(x, y, width)

        if bytecount != len(data) - 1:
            if p[2] % 2 != 0:
                p[2] -= 1
        else:
            if p[2] % 2 != 1:
                p[2] += 1
        encoded_image.putpixel((x, y), tuple(p))
        if show_working:
            print(p, (x, y))
        x, y = increment(x, y, width)

    encoded_image.save(output_image_path, str(output_image_path.split(".")[1].
upper()))

def retrieve_text(image, encryption_key=None, show_working=True):
    data = []
    imgdata = iter(image.getdata())

    while (True):
        pixels = [value for value in imgdata.__next__()[:3] + imgdata.__next__
```

```
() [:3] + imgdata.__next__() [:3]]

        binstr = ''

        for I in pixels[:8]:
            if (I % 2 == 0):
                binstr += '0'
            else:
                binstr += '1'

        data.append(int(binstr, 2))
        if (pixels[-1] % 2 != 0):
            break

    print(data)
    if encryption_key != None:
        try:
            return (True, simplecrypt.decrypt(encryption_key,
bytes(bytearray(data))).decode("utf-8"))
        except simplecrypt.DecryptionException:
            return (False, "Wrong Encryption Key")
    else:
        return (True, ''.join([chr(i) for I in data]))
```

As evident, in the SilentEye Masking technique that uses some form of Transformation technique to add the data as noise, human eye can clearly notice that some form of manipulation has occurred in

Figure 11. Hiding "My msg" in 5x5 cover image

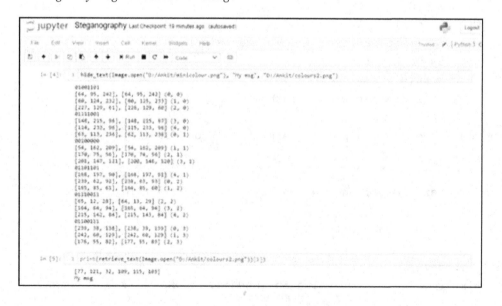

Figure 12. Juxtaposition of cover image and stego image using LSB manipulation

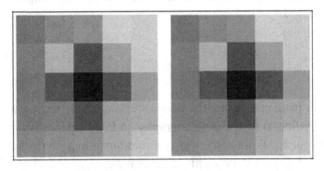

Figure 13. Hiding an AES encrypted message in a 25x25 image

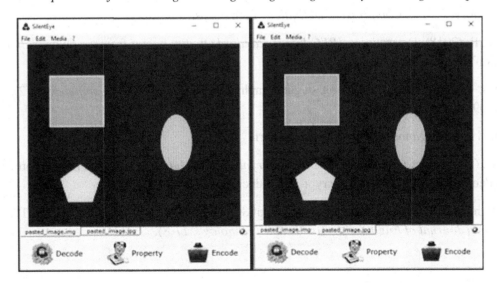

Figure 14. Juxtaposition of cover image and stego image using SilentEye Masking technique

the form on spots on the image. On the other hand, in the LSB python3 implementation, the images are virtually indistinguishable.

CONCLUSION

Based on the observations from comparing the image steganography techniques and conduction of experimentation, LSB manipulation image steganography on PNG images is the most reliable technique for steganography. Since our focus was on covertly communicating via the internet, and more specifically, social media, we will restrict the conclusion to that use case. Small size PNGs encoded using a stegokey for encryption are found to be ideal for this purpose. These are supported by major social media websites like Facebook and Twitter and are most resistant to detection as seen by the comparison done in this chapter. While JPEG images find a larger use on social media and on the internet in general due to their 60-75% compression, PNGs are also widely accepted, and the only drawback is that the size of the image is large for higher resolution images. When the purpose of steganography is sharing a message embedded in an image that does not need to have a large file size, PNGs can be used most reliably.

REFERENCES

Arvind & Pooja. (2010). Steganography– A Data Hiding Technique. *International Journal of Computer Applications, 9*(7).

Bobade, S., & Goudar, R. (2015). Secure Data Communication Using Protocol Steganography in IPv6. *International Conference on Computing Communication Control and Automation*, 275-279. 10.1109/ICCUBEA.2015.59

Brassil, J. T., Low, S., Maxemchuk, N. F., & O'Gorman, L. (1995, October). Electronic Marking and Identification Techniques to Discourage Document Copying. *IEEE Journal on Selected Areas in Communications, 13*(8), 1495–1504. doi:10.1109/49.464718

Christensson, P. (2011). *Compression Definition*. TechTerms.

Cogranne, R. (2018). *Determining JPEG Image Standard Quality Factor from the Quantization Tables*. Academic Press.

Johnson & Jajodia. (1998). Exploring steganography: Seeing the unseen. *Computer, 31*(2), 26-34. . doi:10.1109/MC.1998.4655281

Johnson. (1995). *Steganography*. Technical Report.

Joseph, C. (2018). *This Custom-Made Jihadi Encryption App Hides Messages in Images*. https://www.vice.com/en/article/ne4x7w/muslim-crypt-jihadi-encryption-app

Kaur & Behal. (2014). A Survey on various types of Steganography and Analysis of Hiding Techniques. *International Journal of Engineering Trends and Technology, 11*(8).

Khosravi, S., Dezfoli, M. A., & Yektaie, M. H. (2011). A new steganography method based HIOP (Higher Intensity of Pixel) algorithm and Strassen's matrix multiplication. *Journal of Global Research in Computer Science, 2*(1).

Krenn. (2004). *Steganography and steganalysis.* Internet Publication.

Lu, Z.-M., & Guo, S.-Z. (2017). *Lossless Information Hiding in Block Truncation Coding–Compressed Images.* Lossless Information Hiding in Images.

Mehdi & Mureed. (2013). A Survey of Image Steganography Techniques. *International Journal of Advanced Science and Technology, 54.*

Mosrati, Karimi, & Hariri. (2011). An introduction to steganography methods. *World Applied Programming, 1*(3), 191–195.

Mstafa, R. J., Elleithy, K. M., & Abdelfattah, E. (2017). Video steganography techniques: Taxonomy, challenges, and future directions. *2017 IEEE Long Island Systems, Applications and Technology Conference (LISAT)*, 1-6. 10.1109/LISAT.2017.8001965

Newman. (2018). *Mysterious 'MuslimCrypt' App Helps Jihadists Send Covert Messages.* https://www.wired.com/story/muslimcrypt-steganography/

Ohyama, Niimi, Yamawaki, & Noda. (2009). Lossless data hiding using bit depth embedding for JPEG2000 compressed bit-stream. *Journal of Communication and Computer, 6*(2).

Raid, A., Khedr, W., El-Dosuky, M., & Ahmed, W. (2014). Jpeg Image Compression Using Discrete Cosine Transform - A Survey. *International Journal of Computer Science & Engineering Survey, 5.* Advance online publication. doi:10.5121/ijcses.2014.5204

Rojatkar. (2015). Image Compression Techniques: Lossy and Lossless. *International Journal of Engineering Research and General Science, 3*(2).

Siper, Farley, & Lombardo. (2005). The Rise of Steganography. In *Proceedings of Student/Faculty Research Day, CSIS.* Pace University.

Su, & Kuo. (2003, November). Steganography in JPEG2000 compressed images. *IEEE Transactions on Consumer Electronics, 49*(4), 824–832. doi:10.1109/TCE.2003.1261161

Tanvir Parvez, M., & Abdul-Aziz Gutub, A. (2008). RGB Intensity Based Variable-Bits Image Steganography. *IEEE Asia-Pacific Services Computing Conference*, 1322-1327.

Trotter, L. K. (2019). A case study involving creating and detecting steganographic images shared on social media sites. *Graduate Theses and Dissertations. 17798.*

Xia, X.-G., Boncelet, C. G., & Arce, G. R. (1997). A Multiresolution Watermark for Digital Images. In *IEEE Int'l Conf. Image Processing.* IEEE Press.

Zhou, X. (2011). Research on DCT-based image compression quality. *Proceedings of 2011 Cross Strait Quad-Regional Radio Science and Wireless Technology Conference*, 1490-1494. doi: 10.1109/CSQRWC.2011.6037249

Chapter 14
Applications of Machine Learning in Steganography for Data Protection and Privacy

Mahip M. Bartere

ⓘ https://orcid.org/0000-0002-2703-1638

G. H. Raisoni University, Amravati, India

Sneha Bohra

ⓘ https://orcid.org/0000-0001-5090-8920

G. H. Raisoni University, Amravati, India

Prashant Adakane

G. H. Raisoni University, Amravati, India

B. Santhosh Kumar

GMR Institute of Technology, India

ABSTRACT

Data security is one of the most important aspects in today's scenario. Whenever we send our data from source to destination, data protection is one of the prime components. With the help of data hiding and data extraction techniques, we are able to provide the solution of different types of problems whenever we transfer our data. Steganography is a process where we can hide our data and maintain the quality of the image. At the same time, we think about data alteration. With the help of stegtanalysis method, we reverse engineer and extract the original data. In this chapter, data hiding and data extraction techniques are explained in the combination of machine learning architecture. The combination of steganography and steganalysis along with machine learning is used to identify protected data using different techniques.

DOI: 10.4018/978-1-7998-7160-6.ch014

INTRODUCTION ABOUT STEGANOGRAPHY AND STEGANALYSIS

Advanced information installation in computerised media is an area of data advancement for the accelerated growth of enterprises and, moreover, national protection of intrigue. The dissemination of mechanised media objects through online techniques is increasingly becoming unmistakable. They also promote the creation of cutting-edge theft, as the electronic media can be supportively distributed and replicated lossless. Various data hiding techniques are used to tackle this problem. Converted messages or steganography resembles a Greek phrase which actually means 'secured voice' .It is the process to conceal data beneath a wrap form (also referred to as host, such as, photograph, film, or noise, to build up secret communication among confident conclave and to mask the existence of inserted data. i.e. The fundamental purpose of preserving instruction is to supply the observer conveniently in such a manner that the actual data introduced in each of the propelled channel is not apparent to the viewer. That is unwelcome social occasions unable to perceive involving cover (picture without any riddle note) and stego picture (balanced cover picture containing puzzle message) in any way. The stego image should then not vary a lot from the main cover image. There are 4 basic feature of Data Hiding (A. E. Mustafa, 2011), various information concealing systems can be evaluated: i) payload – Data Hiding capacity; (ii) vigour - blurred facts imperviousness to commotion; (iii) straightforwardness - low host castration for disguise objective; and (iv) security- To provide security to our Hidden Data.

OVERVIEW OF STEGANOGRAPHY

As of late, it is suspected that creating data concealing technologies, particularly as steganography, poses a danger to individual defence, enterprise, what's more, national security interests. As Data extraction process can be represented in two ways: passive and dynamic, the countermeasure advancement to steganography protection is constantly suggested. The basic operation that an idle steganalysis should perform is to select the closeness or non-appearance of covering data in some media items (double theory testing issue). Dynamic steganalysis (otherwise referred to as criminology steganalysis) refers to the attempt of unintentional receivers to remove/evacuate/change legitimate secret information. The process of Dynamic Data Extraction Process is not at all similar to watermarking defence assaults in this particular case.

Steganography is one of the security in which information is covertly implanted in a cover picture, where the real message need to be sent is totally changed to another shape, shrouded information under a cover picture and sent to the goal. Just the individual who knows the method can without much of a stretch unscramble the message. The execution of Steganography strategies can be evaluated by three Parameters: limit, security and indistinctness. So "Steganography implies concealing one bit of information inside another."

The equations of steganography help conduct mystery correspondence. The most used mainstream data classes are .bmp, .jpeg, .mp3, .txt, .pdf, .gif. The way to hide a mystery message inside the cover medium, for example, image, film, content, sound, is to store knowledge away. Concealed image has various uses, particularly in the new creative world of today. For a great many users on the site, privacy and mystery are a problem. Two meetings to convey furtively and secretly take care of the hidden photograph. During transition, the secret data must be protected and know how to be acquired by 2 means: cipher and data hiding. In order to expand information security, a hybrid of the two methods should be used.

Techniques of Steganography.

Dependent upon the kind of the cover question there are various fitting steganographic systems which are taken after with a specific end goal to get security.

- **Steganography in Image:** Identify the Image for the process of Data hiding is one of the big concern as picture in steganography is known as picture steganography. For the most part, in this procedure pixel forces are utilized to shroud the data.
- **Network Steganography:** When seeking shelter question as system convention, for example, Transmission Control Protocol, User Datagram Protocol, and so on, where convention is utilized as bearer, is known as system convention steganography. In OSI model, the idle header bits of Transmission Control Protocol/Internet Protocol fields are the field where steganography can be proficiently implemented.
- **Video Steganography:** It is a process of hiding any sort of information into electronic video. It is used as bearer for shrouded data. For the most part discrete cosine transform (DCT) modify a value which is utilized to shroud the data in every frames of the video, which is not detectable by the third party. This steganography is used, for H.264, AVC (Advance Video Coding), and Audio Video Interleaved or other video groups.
- **Audio Steganography:** The process of considering the sound as a transporter for data concealing it is called sound steganography. It has turned out to be extremely huge medium because of voice over IP (VOIP) fame. Sound steganography utilizes advanced sound arrangements.
- **Text Steganography:** General procedure in content steganography, for example, number of tabs, void areas, and capital letters, much the same as Morse code is utilized to accomplish data covering up. Figure 1.1 demonstrates diverse sorts of Image Steganography.

Figure 1. Types of Image Steganography.

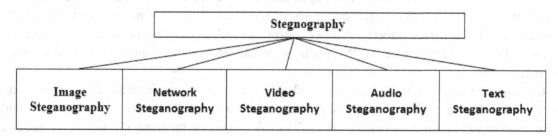

Model of Image Steganography

This type of technique is used for the process of Data hiding using an image and generates a stego-picture as output. This stego-picture at that point sent to the next gathering by known medium, where the intruder doesn't understand covered message hidden in this stego image. In order to retrieve the message in stego-image simply removes with or without stego-key (contingent upon implanting calculation) by the less than desirable end (N. Johnson and S. Jajodia, 1998).

The basic structure of data hiding is shown in Figure 1.2. For data hiding process the most important step is to identify the input image by virtue of which we can go for data hiding. This image is considered as input image. The data is stored behind this image using embedding process, to provide the security to our data we provide additional security using key, this key is nothing but stego key. If anyone wants to extract the information from the input image at that time stego key is must.

Figure 2. Basic Diagram of Image Steganography

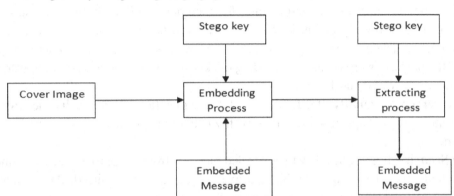

Cryptography vs. Steganography

Cryptography and Steganography vary to each other in light of the fact that cryptography is utilized to keep the substance of the message mystery while steganography is utilized to shroud the presence of mystery message. The two methods are utilized to shield data from the unapproved utilize however at some point it is utilized as a part of illicit means and neither cryptography is distant from everyone else idealize nor steganography. Both methodologies can be utilized with each other, to give better security since cryptography makes the message mystery and steganography make presence of message imperceptible. On the off chance that somebody attempt to discover the presence of mystery message and finds yet that message would not be comprehended on the grounds that it would be encoded because of the utilization of cryptography. Thus, by consolidating these two methodologies, data can be influenced more to secure.

Image Steganography Classifications.

By and large picture steganography is ordered in following perspectives (E Lin and E Delp, 1999)

- **High Capacity**: the capacity to put away Maximum size of Data into picture.
- **Perceptual Transparency:** To check the quality of image, perceptual quality will be undermined into stego-picture as diverge from cover-picture.
- **Strength:** After installing, information should remain in place if stego-picture goes into some change, for example, editing, scaling, separating and expansion of clamor.
- **Inviolable:** It ought to be hard to change the message once it has been introduced into stego-picture.

- **Processing cost:** What amount costly it is computationally to insert and isolating a covered message?

Performance Measure

- **Payload Capacity**: It implies the measure of data that can be installed into cover media without disintegrating its uprightness. The payload is the information secretly imparted. The transporter is the flag, stream, or information record that shrouds the payload—which varies from the channel (which commonly implies the kind of info, for example, a JPEG picture). The subsequent flag, stream, or information document with the encoded payload is in some cases called the bundle, stego record, or incognito message. The rate of bytes, tests, or other flag components adjusted to encode the payload is known as the encoding thickness, and is regularly communicated as a number in the vicinity of 0 and 1.
- **Picture Perceptual quality**: It is fundamental that to maintain a strategic distance from doubt the implanting ought to happen without noteworthy debasement or loss of perceptual quality of the cover media.
- **Image Security**: It gives Security to concealed message from unapproved. Since boundless number of duplicates of a unique can be effectively circulated or produced, the assurance and requirement of licensed innovation rights is another imperative issue. An advanced watermark is proposed to supplement cryptographic procedures, and is a vague flag added to mechanized substance that can be later recognized or expelled with a specific end goal to make some statement about the substance. On the off chance that computerized watermarks are to be utilized as a part of steganography applications, identification of their essence by an unapproved specialist overcomes their exceptionally reason. Indeed, even in applications that don't require shrouded correspondence, yet just strength, it is alluring to first distinguish the conceivable nearness of a watermark before attempting to expel or control it. For instance, supplanting a copyright check with the one asserting legitimate proprietorship.

Steganalysis

One process in image steganography is to hide the data consider as image steganography and the process is data extraction. The process of data extraction using any algorithm or method is called as steganalysis.

In the growing era Data hiding process is used by most people to provide the security to secret data. As we have different methods for the same it is having various use and applications in various fields. Lots of work has been done in last decade which shows various algorithms and methods to perform Data hiding & extraction process.

The main aim of this process is to detect the secret data behind image. At the same time we have to think about how much amount of data is hide behind image to identify the payload capacity of the image. In steganalysis different tools are available online and offline to extract secret data.

MACHINE LEARNING ARCHITECTURE

It is a process in which calculations are done to detect valuable outlines & connections from information. When attempting to tackle an issue, there are some rules which we have to define. For example, on the off chance that we need to distinguish if the thing in an image is an apple or guava, we can accomplish something like:

if(no._red_pixels>89%)
return"apple"
else
return"guava"

There are some straightforward guideline be supposed to function admirably and take care of work. We have to design a framework and analyses the same regarding perceive green apples too. Our past principle will presently don't work, and we should incorporate extra guidelines and thresholds. Then again, a Machine Learning calculation will naturally learn such standards dependent on the refreshed information. We have to update our data to check the instances with respect to apples which is in green color at that time we have to reset and retrain the model.

Sometimes it may be happen this architecture can generate new challenges as we get the new images of fruits from the data sets. For this scenario we have to improve our structure to identify new images of fruits, Figure 3 shows this overall thought

Figure 3. General Model of Machine Learning

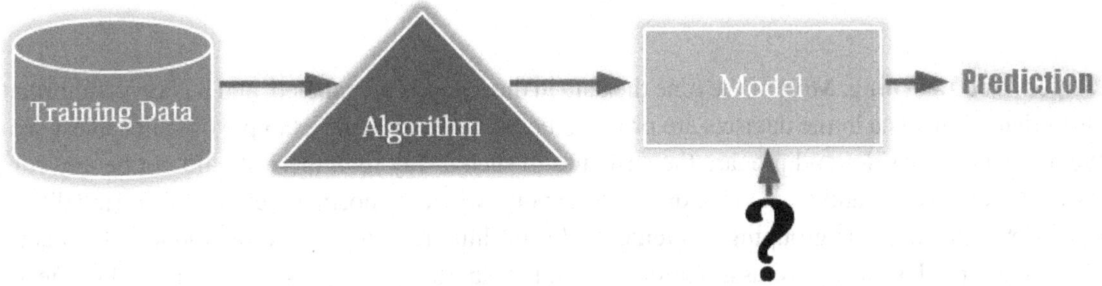

Machine Learning techniques depend on three building blocks of primary structure:

- Information available in Data Sets
- Methods to process the data
- Models to define the structure of the system.

For different machine learning process we have to analyse all the images in the data sets to gain some information from the images. In some cases it may be possible that you have to identify images which are not applicable for your algorithm, at that time we have to retrain the model in such a way that it can accept and gives appropriate output as per the input received by your system. Once the system is developed and identify the images then we can go for further calculations with respect to different images we are having in Data sets.

Commonly, a calculation will utilize the information to gain proficiency with a template. This stage is known as the preparing stage. This educated model is used to utilize & to create forecasts when given new information. The information nearly new and now to prepare new model in the architecture and this model is nothing but your training set. Until we require an approach to check the performance of model, whenever it is sent in a genuine setting (underway), we additionally need what is known as the test set. The test set is utilized to gauge the model's exhibition on information it has never observed.

Machine Learning and its Types

There are three different types of machine learning.

Figure 4. Types of Machine Learning

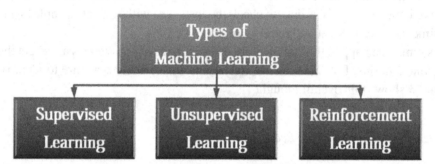

Supervised Learning. Most of the time the data in the datasets are labeled, and it is very important to identify that all the data in the datasets are proper labeled. if we took the example of fruits, every image in the datasets is consider and prepare the structure in such a way that, there should not be any confusions when we generate and labeled the data. At the point when the normal yield is a class (the different kind of flowers), called as grouping of elements. In machine learning create the model which is used to classify the model called as classification model, for classification there are different classifiers are available like NN, RF (Random Forest), Clustering algorithms, decision trees and so on. Sometimes we have to build the model so that it can perform predict the weather report which is available in the form of Numbers (Weather Prediction) it is called regression. It can be formalized as follows:

f(z) = x

In the above expression f(z) is used for mapping the function of different variable as z so that we can get the output an x to identify different types of flowers. This function is used for sorting. Basically this model is used to identify best suitable model so that we can extract some valuable information which consist of n sets (z,x) of models. At the time of learning phase, the calculation approaches the normal yield for each information z. At inference time, that is, the point at which we need to make expectations for new models, we can utilize the learned model f and feed it with another information z to acquire the relating anticipated value x.

- **Unsupervised Learning**. In these types of machine learning most of the data in the datasets where labels are not mentioned. If the data inside the datasets is not labelled then it is very difficult to extract some knowledge form the data sets in machine learning. In this case valuable information is not get extracted which is main aim of machine learmning.can we extract some information from such type of datasets? Yes we can. Imagine you have flowers pictures without any label. What is the approach so that the information gets automatically aggregate? The classifications could be simply the sorts of fruits, i.e., attempting to frame bunches in which pictures inside a similar class have a place with a similar kind. In the flowers example, we could derive the genuine kinds by outwardly assessing the pictures, yet by and large, visual review is troublesome and the framed gatherings might not have a simple translation, yet at the same time, it is valuable and can be utilized as a training step (like in vector quantization). These sorts of calculations that discover gatherings (hierarchical category sometimes). This is called as clustering techniques.

- **Reinforcement Learning**: Another type of machine learning is called Reinforcement Learning (RL) which has considerable contrasts from the past. Such type of learning doesn't depend on model information as the past ones however on boosts from the agent's current circumstances. At some random tip as expected, a negotiator can play out an activity which will lead it to another state where a reward is collected. The point is to become familiar with the arrangement of activities that increase the reward. Reinforcement learning brings up to the issue of inducing ideal successive choices dependent on rewards or punishments got because of past activities. Reinforcement Learning (RL) is utilized, as a rule, to address applications, for example, robotics, finance, inventory management, where the objective is to get familiar with an arrangement, i.e., a planning between conditions of the environment into activities to be performed, while straightforwardly associating with the environment.

ARCHITECTING THE MACHINE LEARNING PROCESS

Figure 5. Machine Learning Process

Data Acquisition

It depends on accessible information in favor of the framework toward settle on a choice henceforth the initial step characterized shown in the framework act as data acquisition. This includes information assortment, getting ready and isolating the case situations dependent on specific features associated with the dynamic succession and sends information to the handling phase for the process of classification.

Such process is considered as data preprocessing stage. In the next phase of ML the information phase is required which anticipate authentic, quick & versatile information. Whatever the versatile information we received from previous phase it is then transfer for the preparation of stream framework (persistent information) that put away in data warehouses in the form of groups (for discrete information) prior to be given to information model or handling stages.

Data Processing

This stage took the input from the previous stage that is Data Acquisition. The said information is delivering to the neat layer (data processing layer). The role of this layer is too exposed to cutting edge coordination and handling. It includes standardization of the information, cleaning the information, change the information, and encoding. This process is likewise subject to sort of getting the hang of being utilized. For e.g., whenever supervised learning is used for utilizing the information, it will be isolated into numerous means of test information needed for preparing of the framework and the information hence made. This process is called as training sample data. Additionally, this phase is needy upon the sort of handling required and may include decisions going as of activity in the lead of consistent information which includes utilization of explicit task based on architecture, for instance, lambda design, it may also include activity based on distinct information. This information is used for preparing the memory bound. This phase is used to preprocess the information if it is available in proper available format. If it is not then the information on the way or in rest.

Data Modeling

In the Data Modeling phase, it is having different choices are available in terms of different algorithms that require to create the model based on the information. These algorithms are advanced or acquired from various libraries. These algorithms are used to show the information in different manner; this prepares the framework for the next stage.

Execution

This stage in machine learning is the place where the experimentation is done, testing is included and tunings are performed. The overall objective behind being to upgrade the algorithm to separate the necessary machine result and amplify the framework execution, the yield of the progression is a refined arrangement equipped for giving the necessary information to the machine to decide.

Deployment

Like some other programming yield, ML yields should be operationalized or be sent for additional exploratory preparing. The yield can be considered as a non-deterministic inquiry which should be additionally conveyed into the decision-making framework.

WHEN TO USE MACHINE LEARNING?

As we know that in digital world everything is based on data, so it is very important to predict something for business point of view with this data. For the said reason there is a need of Machine Learning. There are some classical techniques are available but they are not providing good results.

Figure 6. Flow chart of when to use Machine Learning

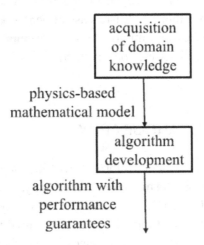

As represented in above figure, the first step in the traditional method is to acquire domain specific knowledge: The matter of concern is determined in respect, creating numerical copy that catches the material science of the arrangement beneath investigation. With respect to this representation, an improved algorithm is delivered. This algorithm is used for the execution & ensures the suspicion that the specified model based on Physical model is a precise portrayal of the real world (Osvaldo Simeone, 2018)

The accompanying models, offer helpful rules on the kind of designing undertakings that can profit by the utilization of machine learning devices. (Osvaldo Simeone, 2018)

1. The classical working flow isn't appropriate because of a model deficiency or to design insufficiency.
    a. If the said model is insufficient, then there is no other model is available to check such models. There is no mathematical models be present for the issue because of inadequate space information. Therefore, a regular model based plan is unimportant.
    b. if the algorithm in the said model is insufficient, a grounded numerical model is accessible, yet existing algorithms advanced based on such model are too multifaceted to be in any way executed. For such situation, the utilization of assumption module with productive equipment, for example, neural network of restricted dimension or with custom fitted equipment executions can yield lower-multifaceted nature arrangements. (Osvaldo Simeone, 2018)
2. Sometimes we need to train the datasets using training huge amount of data. Sometimes the index of the data is available sometimes we have to made.
3. The task doesn't need the use of rationale, good judgment, or unequivocal thinking dependent on foundation information.

4. The assignment doesn't need point by point clarifications with respect to choice made. The training model consists of various algorithms and methods so that no one knows what is going on. Thus, it doesn't give straight intends to learn why the given set of model has been generated, because of an information, albeit ongoing exploration has gained some progress on this front. These differentiations with designed ideal arrangements, which can be regularly deciphered based on actual execution standards. For example, a greatest probability decoder picks a given yield since it limits the likelihood of mistake under the expected model.

5. The function or phenomenon being found out is fixed for an adequately extensive stretch of instance. The said function is used to authorize statistics assortment & knowledge.

6. The task has either loose necessity limitations, or, on account of an algorithm insufficiency, the necessary execution certifications can be given by means of mathematical models. (Osvaldo Simeone,2018)

WORKING MODEL OF STEGANOGRAPHY

Data Hiding is the ability of concealing hidden information inside a separate, ordinary point. Pictures, text, video, audio, etc. may be the messages. In modern steganography, the goal is to convey a digital message covertly. The primary function of steganography is to prevent a secret message from being intercepted. To maximise the protection of the secret message, it is also paired with cryptography. Steganalysis is the study of steganography (breaking) to detect messages hidden. Steganography is used in applications such as sensitive correspondence, secret storage of data, digital watermarking, etc.

Figure no 7 represent the basic plan of steganography process. The sender gives the carrier file and secret message to be send to the encoding module .This encoding module embeds the secret message and carrier file using the embedding techniques. This stego file is then transmitted through communication carrier and given as an input to decoding module. The decoding module uses the key given by the encoding module and decoding algorithm to regenerate the secret message from the stego file.

As discussed earlier the carrier file can be of any format like text, image, audio, video etc. There are various embedding algorithms that can be used for various format of carrier file.

Embedding Algorithms for Images

The most commonly used embedding algorithm is LSB steganography. LSB steganography is the approach which substitutes the LSB of the carrier medium. LSB is the traditional method to hide the data. In this process the secret data is hiding in the carrier image using number of bits. In LSB method the embedding power is limited to only 2 or 3 bits. While, for example, there are some LSB techniques for embedding, a pseudo-random number is selected for the sample value to be embedded to defy visual shells or sequential steganography. (W. Bender et.al, 1996) (H. Farid, 2002) (Rainer Böhme and Andreas Westfeld, 2004) (J. Fridrich et al, 2004) .

Another strategy suggested by (J. Zhang et.al, 2007) is LSBMR, in this methods two or more pixel elements are considered for embedding purpose. Each pixel in image is one bit. The hidden data and the combination in the form of even & odd of the 2 pixel element values are consider by remaining part of secret data. It deals with for the given pixel element in the image the different pixels are kept into ac-

Figure 7. Block Diagram of Steganography Process

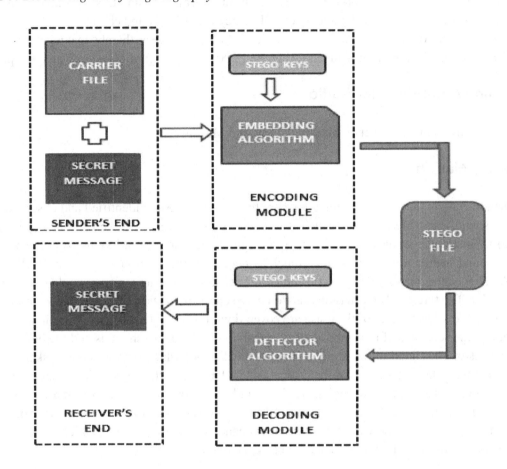

count and the difference between the two neighbouring values are calculated and considered. There are various features to be considered for evaluation of the quality of image and to identify the secret content.

It initialises some of the parameters used for initial processing and section variety of subsequent data and then checks the ability of the particular sections. The selected region is broad as per the image size then the secret message is cover. Then in the particular region the information concealment is carried out. At the receiver side if you need the secret file, it require some post production. If not, the system must amend the specifications & then repeat the area range and power measurement in anticipation of it can be totally integrated.

The initial stage in this process is to identify the features of image that is how much number of blocks can be created, size of the blocks and to identify the threshold value of the image. This is very important as far as data hiding process is concerned. The stego is separated into blocks and then arbitrary degrees are centred on the blocks rotated by the hidden key. The resultant picture is regrouped as a vector of rows. At last, the resultant module is used in merging by splitting into non-overlapping blocks of two successive pixels (J. Zhang et.al, 2007)

Author in (T. Pevný,2010) implements another modified type of data embedding technique. Generally regular Data hiding technique used in this paper is the LSB substitutions, where the Least Significant Bits of each cover components are supersede with message bits. LSB Matching (of-10 referred to as ±1 embedding) (T. Pevný, 2010) updates the LSB Substitution form. By using this algorithm thee values of the pixels by ±1 in such a way that the pixel LSBs obeys the transmitted code.

Furthermore, the components of image can be used to hide the message thereby making it difficult for steganalysis. When selecting healthy pixels (A. D. Ker, 2005) in the high-dimensional imaging process.

Embedding Algorithms for Audio

These algorithms include Frequency Masking, Temporal Masking.

Frequency Masking

It is a phenomenon in the frequency domain where the signal values are identified and observed as the low audio signal, e.g. a clean sound (which is to be used for masking), can be exhibited as inaudible (masked) by a stronger signal (masker) that occurs simultaneously, e.g. a low noise pure sound and inaudible sound having noise are close as much as necessary they appear in frequency (UKEssays, 2018). A value called threshold can be considered for masking. The audio signal would not be detectable beyond it. The thresholds for masking rely on pure sound and inaudible sound characteristics. The components of low-level signal of the noise are covered within and outer surface. Noise inputs may be noise coding, the sequence of the embedded watermark, etc. The audio signal is audible only with the help of a masker. The signal-to-mask ratio (SMR) is the distance which separates the masker level and the masking threshold. The value near the critical band's left side is the highest. Inside a critical band, noise generated by watermark embedding would be audible as long as the signal-to-noise ratio (SNR) for the critical band is greater than its SMR. The NMR (m) noise-to-mask ratio represents the difference between the noise of the watermark in a given critical band and the frequency at which a distortion can only be heard; NMR value is and in dB should be negative (Noll P, 1993).

Temporal Masking

Along with Frequency masking, the phenomena of the Human Auditory System in the time domain also play an important role in human auditory perception. Those are in time, pre-masking and post masking. Before and after a masking signal has been turned on and off, the temporal masking effects occur, respectively. The time taken before masking is slightly less than one-tenth of the post-masking duration. It is generally within the range of 50 to 200 milliseconds (Chandramouli R & Memon N, 2001)

Embedding Algorithms for Video

In 2015, (S. A. Abbas et.al, 2015) introduced an approach for video steganography based on the algorithm called Cuckoo search. The hidden message was divided into bytes by bytes in this process, and then five different forms were used for presenting each byte's bits. Subsequently, by measuring the resemblance between the pixels and different byte forms, the Euclidian distance was used to select a better pixel. Subsequently, the Levy Random walk flight used to spontaneously move from pixels to another in the hidden message and used the LSB technique for embedding within the video clip.

(U. Sahu and S. Mitra, 2015) introduced a visual steganography system in 2015 which combined the features of the least significant bit algorithm and the encryption standard of AES .The encryption of the hidden data was achieved using the AES method . In the next step, the frames for embedding the data were randomly selected and the algorithm for swapping the pixel was selected. It has been used to strengthen defence. After that the process of LSB was used to implant the hidden data inside the preferred video clip.

A system for video steganography was suggested by (K. Sudeepa et.al, 2016). The hidden message in this process Using a key and a feedback change register (FSR) used to randomly pick the window, it is encoded to prevent Dismissal. Redundancy. The hidden message was subsequently embedded inside a video using the LSB process.

In 2016, authors (P. Sethi and V. Kapoor, 2016) proposed a method for video steganography which used AES cryptographic algorithm and the genetic algorithm. The hidden message was compressed in this process to decrease the size. The AES algorithm was used to convert the compressed image into cypher text. After this the genetic algorithm and LSB was used to integrate the encoded message into image which selects the pixel used to add data using the LSB process.

In 2016, authors (A. Saleema and T. Amarunnishad, 2016) introduced a picture steganography technique through the use of an arbitrary collection of image pixels to be used to embed the hidden message and to use the LSB Method to integrate the data inside the image and to improve the use of hybrid Fuzzy Neural Networks Image consistency.

Researchers (] Z. S. Y. Alsaffawi, 2016) suggested a process in 2016 with the use of LZW to minimise the scale of the secret message and embed the secret message using the EMD and knight tour algorithm within the image's hidden message.

In (A. Solichin and Painem,2016), authors developed a methodology for video steganography in 2016. This approach is notified as less important frame (LSF). In this form, the choice of the frame that was selected and the hidden message was based on the movement of the frame using the optical stream functionality.

For 2016, (K. Rezagholipour and M. Eshghi, 2016) proposed a system based on the motion of the frame in video steganography where the hidden message has been incorporated into the moving picture motion vectors.

In 2017, (A. Putu et.al, 2017) implemented a video steganography process, using an AES-128 bit system to encrypt an image. The LSB procedure was then used to embed the encoded image within the video.

Authors in (S. Mumthas and A. Lijiya, 2017) developed a new video steganography process in 2017 by using RSA and random DNA to encrypt the hidden message, and after that, using the Huffman encoding, the encoded message is compressed. The 2D DCT is then used to embed the hidden data to improve the system's protection.

PROPOSED METHODOLOGY

The following figure shows the block diagram of proposed system. The proposed system is divided into two parts: Steganography Block and Steganalysis Block. The Steganography block is responsible to embed the text into the selected image file whereas the Steganalysis Block will reverse the process and extract the hidden text from the stego-image.

Image Acquisition and Pre-processing Block: This block reads the jpeg image in which the hidden text will be embedded. Pre-processing is the important step since it yields to better performance in future steps. The input image is resized to the desired size of 512 x 512 pixels. Cover image was prepared

Figure 8. Block diagram of proposed system

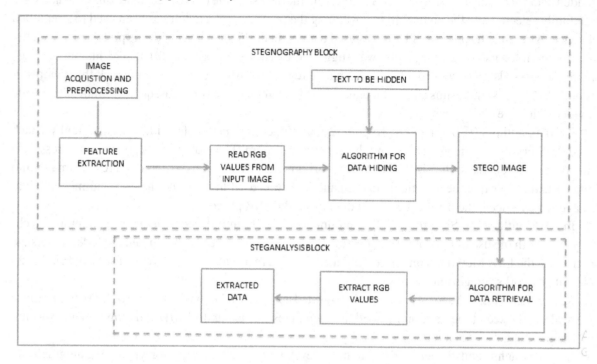

by flipping nearly 50% of the LSB pixels of the input image. This method adds in the unwanted data embedding and thereby ensuring that the intruder does not get the correct size of the hidden data.

Feature Extraction: The convolutional neural network (CNN) is a machine learning approach that has been used to successfully classify images. CNN is nothing but a form of artificial neural networks which can be applied to images and has a special structure which is shown in figure 9.

Figure 9. CNN structure for feature extraction

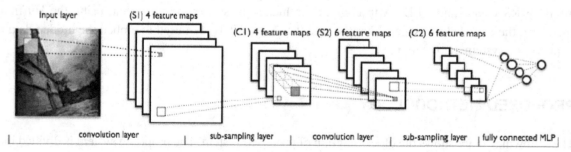

One or more convolutional layers are preceded by a pooling layer, followed by one or more fully connected layers in the hidden layers of a CNN. The function extraction layers are convolutional layers, and the classifier is the last fully connected layer. The filter bank layer and the non-linearity layer are the two layers that make up the convolutional layers. Since, the input image is a RGB image, the dimensions of the matrix is 512x512x3 where 3 is the number of feature maps. The pixel values of the input

Figure 10. Comparison of Input vs. Stego Image

 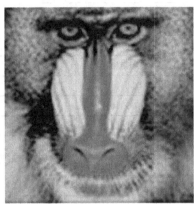

Input image   Stego Image

image acts as the input for each color channel in the first layer. Each of the kernels detects a particular feature at every location on the input.

Data Hiding: The text to be hidden will be first converted to binary. XOR keys will be generated using pseudo random key generator. This key will perform basic XOR operation on the binary data and image. This will generate the stego image.

Steganalysis Block performs the reverse process on the stego image and retrieves the original image and hidden text.

EXPERIMENTAL RESULTS

Following is the comparison of the actual image and stego image.

Following table give image analysis of the input and stego image.

Table 1. Image Analysis

Image Type	Red Mean	Green Mean	Blue Mean	Mean	Entropy
Input	151	110	78	28026	534.19
Stego	150	110	79	27983	534.19

Table 2. Image Comparative Analysis

Red Average	Green Average	Blue Average	Mean Square Error (MSE)	PSNR
1.57	0.84	1.48	18.19	35.53

Table 3. Image Quantization Error

Image No	RGB-Original	RGB-Original-Binary	RGB-Stego	RGB-Stego-Binary	RGB-Quantization-Error	RGB-Quantization-Error Binary
1	51	00110011	18	00010010	33	100001
2	75	01001011	108	01101100	33	100001
3	125	01111101	124	01111100	1	1
4	139	10001011	166	10100110	27	11011
5	62	00111110	25	00011001	37	100101
6	46	00101110	36	00100100	10	1010
7	97	01100001	68	01000100	29	11101
8	162	10100010	134	10000110	28	11100
9	117	01110101	72	01001000	45	101101
10	145	10010001	178	10110111	8	1000

From the table and the figures, the bit locations in the error do not fit the normal significance ordering. In other words, the hidden image's information is scattered through the color streams, which is why it was not identified earlier. The fully convolutional networks were able to achieve combined classification rates of 90-92%. As a reference, the same networks were retrained to find Least-Significant-Bit substitution (where the L least significant bits of each color channel in the cover image are replaced with the L most significant bits from the secret image). The networks were eligible and checked with L = 1, 2, 3, 4, and all achieved combined ratings of over 92%.

Figure 11. Graph of Quantization Error of RGB values.

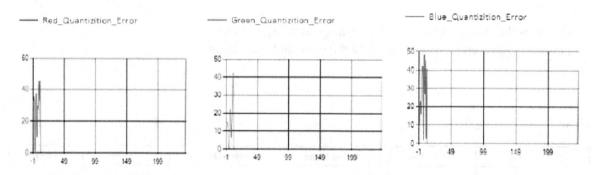

Figure 12. Graph for comparison of RGB values of Input image vs. Stego Image

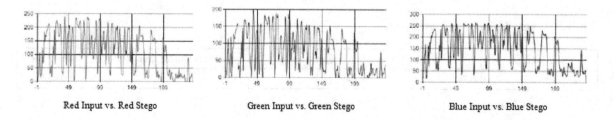

APPLICATIONS

Steganography can be used to mask data whenever you like. There are several explanations for withholding content, but they all come down to the need to discourage unwanted entities from being aware of a message's presence. A secret message is indistinguishable from white noise using these new strategies. Steganography can be used in the industrial world to conceal a hidden chemical solution or proposals for a new technology (The WEPIN Store, 1995).

To keep their messages confidential and plan attacks, terrorists may even use steganography. Much of this seems pretty nefarious, and the obvious applications of steganography are really for stuff like surveillance. But there are a range of implementations that are peaceful. In map making, the easiest and oldest are used, where cartographers often apply a tiny imaginary street to their maps, causing copycats to be punished.

The addition of fictitious names to mailing lists is a similar trick, such as a search against resellers who are illegal. Many of the newer apps use steganography, such as a watermark, to shield information from copyright. Photograph sold on CD, collections also have secret messages in the images that enable illegal use to be identified. The same technology on DVD is much more effective, as the industry develops DVD recorders to track and avoid copying of DVDs that are covered.

To implement watermarking, steganography can also be used. While steganography is not inherently the idea of watermarking, there are many steganography methods that are used to store watermarks in data. The key difference is deliberate, while the object of steganography is to mask information, watermarking merely extends additional information to the cover source. Since individuals will not accept visible modifications attributable to a watermark in images, audio or video files, steganography techniques may be used to mask this (UKEssays, 2018).

CONCLUSION

Steganography is an interesting and powerful tool that has been used throughout history to cover records. Methods to expose such devious strategies may be used, but the first move is knowledge that there are indeed such methods. There are also several good reasons for using this kind of data hiding, including watermarking or a more reliable central storage system for stuff like codes, or for main operations.

Various strategies for embedding data in text, photograph, and audio/video signals as cover media are explored in this article. A quick summary of a very exciting and fast-paced field of computer security has been given. In the defense sector, this technology has many concerned about the potential damage that can be done to both government and private sectors. This technology will expand significantly as PC's get stronger and become even more popular.

Hundreds of steganography applications are now available and can be used on text, audio and graphic media. The nation and plenty of people, private organizations are exploring ways to best detect the use of file steganography. As steganalysis becomes more advanced, the way firewalls, virus detection applications and intrusion detection systems are at present will be introduced as a standard security technique.

REFERENCES

Abbas, S. A., El Arif, T. I., Ghaleb, F. F., & Khamis, S. M. (2015). Optimized video steganography using Cuckoo search algorithm. *IEEE Seventh International Conference on Intelligent Computing and Information Systems (ICICIS'15)*. doi: 10.1109/IntelCIS.2015.7397279

Alsaffawi, Z. S. Y. (2016). Image steganography by using exploiting modification direction and knight tour algorithm. *J. Al-Qadisiyah Comput. Sci. Math.*, *8*, 1–11.

Bender, W., Gruhl, D., Morimoto, N., & Lu, A. (1996). Techniques for data hiding. *IBM Systems Journal*, *35*(3-4), 313–336.

Böhme, R., & Westfeld, A. (2004). Statistical Characterisation of MP3 Encoders for Steganalysis. *Proceedings of the Multimedia and Security Workshop*, 25-34.

Chandramouli, R., & Memon, N. (2001). Analysis of lsb based image steganography techniques. *Proc. IEEE International Conference on Image Processing*, 1019–1022.

Che-Wei, L. W.-H. T. (2012, January). A Secret-Sharing-Based Method for Authentication of Grayscale Document Images via the Use of the PNG Image With a Data Repair Capability. *IEEE Transactions on Image Processing*, *21*(1), 207–218. doi:10.1109/TIP.2011.2159984 PMID:21693424

Farid, H. (2002). Detecting hidden messages using higher-order statistical models. *International Conference on Image Processing*.

Fridrich, J. (2003). Quantitative steganalysis of digital images: estimating the secret message length. ACM Multimedia Systems Journal, 9(3), 288-302.

Hong Caoand Alex, C. K. (2013, September). On Establishing Edge Adaptive Grid for Bilevel Image Data Hiding. *IEEE Transactions on Information Forensics and Security*, *8*(9).

Johnson, N., & Jajodia, S. (1998, February). Exploring steganography: Seeing the unseen. *IEEE Computer*, *31*(2), 26–34. doi:10.1109/MC.1998.4655281

Ker, A. D. (2005, June). Steganalysis of LSB matching in grayscale images. *IEEE Signal Processing Letters*, *12*(6), 441–444.

Li, M., Kulhandjian, M. K., Pados, D. A., Batalama, S. N., & Medley, M. J. (2013, July). Extracting Spread-Spectrum Hidden Data From Digital Media. *IEEE Transactions on Information Forensics and Security*, *8*(7).

Lin, E., & Delp, E. (1999). A Review of Data Hiding in Digital Images. *Proceedings of the Image Processing, Image Quality, Image Capture Systems Conference (PICS'99)*.

Mumthas, S., & Lijiya, A. (2017). Transform domain video steganography using RSA, random DNA encryption and Huffmanencoding. *7th International Conference on Advances in Computing and Communications ICACC-2017*, 115, 660–666.

Mustafa, ElGamal, ElAlmi, & Ahmed. (2011). *A Proposed Algorithm For Steganography in Digital Image Based on Least Significant Bit*. Academic Press.

Noll, P. (1993). Wideband speech and audio coding. *IEEE Communications Magazine, 31*(11), 34–44.

Pevný, T., Filler, T., & Bas, P. (2010). Using high-dimensional image models to perform highly undetectable Steganography. In Information Hiding. New York: Springer.

Putu, A., Gusti, M., & Ni, M. (2017). A MP4 video steganography using least significant bit (LSB) substitution and advanced encryption standard (AES). *J. Theor. Appl. Inform. Technol., 95*, 5805–5814.

Rezagholipour, K., & Eshghi, M. (2016). Video steganography algorithm based on motion vector of moving object. *IEEE Eighth International Conference on Information and Knowledge Technology (IKT)*. doi: 10.1109/IKT.2016.7777764

Sahu & Mitra. (2015). A secure data hiding technique using video steganography. *Int. J. Comput. Sci. Commun. Netw.*, 348–357.

Saleema, A., & Amarunnishad, T. (2016). A new steganography algorithm using hybrid fuzzy neural networks. International Conference on Emerging Trends in Engineering, Science and Technology (ICE-TEST-2015), 24, 1566–1574.

Sethi, P., & Kapoor, V. (2016). A proposed novel architecture for information hiding in image steganography by using geneticalgorithm and cryptography. *Int. Conf. Comput. Sci.*, 87, 61–66.

Simeone. (2018). A Very Brief Introduction to Machine Learning With Applications to Communication Systems. *IEEE Transactions on Cognitive Communications and Networking, 4*(4).

Solichin & Painem. (2016). Motion-based less significant frame for improving lsb-based video steganography. *IEEE International Seminar on Application for Technology of Information and Communication (ISemantic)*. doi:10.1109/ISEMANTIC

Sudeepa, K., Raju, K., Ranjan, K., & Ghanesh, A. (2016). A new approach for video steganography based on randomization and parallelization. *International Conference on Information Security and Privacy*, 78, 483–490.

Yang, C., & Liu, F. (2013, January). Pixel Group Trace Model-Based Quantitative Steganalysis for Multiple Least-Significant Bits Steganography. *IEEE Transactions on Information Forensics and Security, 8*(1).

Zhang, J., Cox, I., & Doerr, G. (2007). Steganalysis for LSB matching in images with high-frequency noise. *Proc. IEEE Workshop MultimediaSignal Process.*, 385–388.

Chapter 15

Design and Development of Hybrid Algorithms to Improve Cyber Security and Provide Securing Data Using Image Steganography With Internet of Things

Abhishek Rajeshkumar Mehta

Parul Institute of Computer Application, Parul University, India & DCIS, Sabarmati University, India

Trupti Pravinsinh Rathod

Vidyabharti Trust College of Master in Computer Application, India

ABSTRACT

Internet of things (IoT) is a typical thing (object) in this day and age, which fills in as a component of our standard life exercises. In spite of the fact that it benefits the private region in a few different ways, different difficulties, for example information classification and protection, are made. Web of things (IoT) is all over the place and utilized in a lot more advantageous functionality. It is utilized in our homes, clinics, fire counteraction, and announcing and controlling of ecological changes. Information security is an urgent prerequisite for IoT since the number of late advances in various spaces is expanding step by step. Different endeavors have been set to sate the client's expectations for greater security and protection.

OUTLINE

Internet-of-Things (IoT) is amongst the rising advancements be the best operators to alteration the cutting-edge ecosphere. It includes system-to-system interchanges versatile, computer-generated and momentary associations. It's simply normal processing gadgets, IoT framework comprises of family gadgets and

DOI: 10.4018/978-1-7998-7160-6.ch015

numerous other information meeting devices. With IOT, individuals switch their family apparatus with only couple of trace on shrewd gadgets. Moreover, Cisco's Internet BSG had anticipated measure of IOT gadgets to be twofold (50 billion gadgets) by 2020 (). The comfort and "insightfulness" of IoT gadgets helps in the development of number of these gadgets. Notwithstanding, a few people may in any case be hesitant to have these gadgets in their homes. In spite of the fact that IoT gadgets may make individuals' life a ton simpler, security specialists had referenced their interests on the potential security issues (The Uncertainty of Belongings), which brand the IOT gadgets amongst top five sanctuary dangers in 2016 ().

In actuality, data divulgence principle safety issues in IoT framework that necessity not be disregarded (). Additionally, IOT gadgets with feeble safety level then handling control, for example, IP photographic camera, brilliant Television and other home apparatuses, which consume the absence classification highlights can be fundamental focuses programmers. Consequently, with varied construction and it's quality of appropriated over the Net, dynamic aloof assaults could be complete simpler in the IOT framework so as take secluded data compromise humanoid resources contrasted with different organizations that contain just ground-breaking processing gadgets. For instance, the aggressors have a more prominent opportunity to block and mediate on information broadcast between IOT gadgets as it needs a wide circulation of organizations to associate them composed, which as a rule includes the Internet. The data that the programmers may be intrigued are identified with verification, installment or even authoritative privileged insights. By getting validation data through snooping or capturing with an association, the aggressor can get to or have regulator of convinced IOT gadgets utilizing the recovered data for additional misuses () To tackle the issue of classification in the IoT organization, we propose a security conspire that includes associations with the Net. Meanwhile the IP photographic camera is painstaking as the IoT gadget in this examination, communicating the delicate data between IP cameras and home worker is depended on utilizing picture steganography inside the LAN, while information transmission between a home worker and different gadgets out of the LAN (Internet) will be scrambled. This can give greater security on the sent delicate information, for example, picture of client face in the LAN network since the presence of touchy data can be concealed utilizing picture steganography. Consequently, the assailants have a smaller amount dubious of the communicated information so as to snoop them (inhaling).

The rest of the newspaper is organized as shadows. Segment 2, a few related deals with how the data revelation in IOT gadgets settled. Segment 3 delineates the future conspire. At long last, a conversation and end are attracted segment IV.

Electronic information transmission may incorporate touchy individual information that might be caught. Moreover, there are innumerable applications on the web, and numerous locales power clients to do pictures that incorporate touchy individual data, for example, portable figures, places, and card data charging. For certain reasons, clients may include individual and safe exchanges, for example, protecting their classified information from developers amidst disregarding an open channel, hence requiring positioning and data decency against unapproved section and use. The intermittent methodologies for checking correspondence are cryptography and steganography. (). Cryptography is the act of utilizing math to encode and unscramble information to keep up posts checked by changing predictable information structure (plaintext) into muddled (ciphertext) system. The term cryptography originated from the Greek word 'cryptos' signifying' wrapped up' and' diagramming ' hugeness' composing.' thusly, cryptography's most noteworthy plausible noteworthiness is "covered stating" (). Any cryptosystem incorporates plaintext, figuring of encryption, computation of unscrambling, material of code, and key. Plaintext is a sign or information that is clear (not compacted) in its ordinary structure. Encryption is the course using catches to change over plaintext to discover text.

Figure material outcomes from encryption by executing the plaintext encryption key. Disentangling is the course to get the plaintext back from the material of the outline the key is utilized to manage the cryptosystem (setting) information, and just () is perceived by the sender and beneficiary. While cryptography is exceptionally unbelievable to check information; cryptanalysts may have the option to break the numbers by looking at the amount component material to return the plaintext (). The paper has a clear structure and is figured out as the going with. In fragment II, we talk about the substance modules of steganography to related work. In section III, show the III. Similar investigation. Section VI show the proposed approach and results investigation. We close the whole paper, and present the end in Section V.

LITERATURE REVIEW

So as to determine the data revelation among the IoT gadgets, a few strategies recommended. The steganography procedure comprises a couple calculations, changes over simple text (mystery messages) into ciphertext (encryption) at the despatcher side and changes over it back to simple text (unscrambling) beneficiary side (). Nevertheless, because of the imperative regular steganography in IOT gadgets, which requests all the more preparing and memory, lightweight cryptography is utilized (). Lightweight cryptography is a technique had some expertise compelled conditions, for example, RFID labels, sensors, contactless brilliant vehicles and medical services gadgets. In programming usage, inconsequential submissions are favored with littler cypher and RAM scope, which doesn't generally misuse the security-effectiveness compromises. Also, lightweight cryptography needs to embrace in IOT on the grounds that it has a tall effectiveness of start to finish correspondence and applications to low asset gadgets. The difficulties that looked by insubstantial steganography is a level of security, because of diminishing the encryption adjusts just as key distance ().

By and large, the frivolous steganography calculations separated into symmetrical and unbalanced classifications. In symmetrical encoding, the two players essential to grip a mutual important and the key e utilized for encryption and decoding. A few instances of symmetrical encryption are, PRESENT, HIGHT and SM1/SM3 in security framework. A lightweight cryptography convention dependent on XOR activity is proposed to forestall information show snooping in labels and perusers. The method can shield information transmission from any inactive assault. Other than that, the analysts proposed a plan for encryption hub in IoT gadgets dependent on unique mark highlights and CC2530 () which is a genuine framework on chip (SoC) microcontrolle, created by

Texas Gadgets. Miniature regulator permits information encryption and unscrambling utilizing AES calculation. In any case, client's unique mark highlight data recognition whitethorn have mistake with any corporeal transformed, for example, harmed, essy skin. Likewise, it is suggested utilizing network estimations, all the more especially, uses, to achieve key abstraction, and consequently, any main circulation component isn't fundamental. The creators likewise proposed to utilize the keys from encryption/decoding in packed detecting hypothesis to permit encryption and pressure to be done at the same time with CS-based encryption. With it documents trivial and pressure to be achieved at the same time with tall -proficiency. However, downside technique is that if there is any obstruction or vindictive changes in the properties of the remote channel, the remaking mistake high as the answers won't be comparative. Other than the snoop situated an exceptionally (inside a large portion of recurrence frequency) the transporter, he would have the option shrewdly choose the substances that permitted admittance information and the 1s not. Another procedure additionally improve CPABE is Obliging Cipher Rule Characteristic

Founded Encoding. The idea of IOT permits asset compelled gadgets to designate expensive exponentiation calculation to other confided in neighbor gadgets which is known as "partner hubs. Scientists effectively executed of into validation and security conspire confirmation and important trade dependent which gives healthier safety execution with proficiency. Furthermore, the correspondence between IOT gadgets remote, Computational insight (CI) is acquainted with make that is more adaptable, heartiness, higher calculation speed and great adaptively in changing conditions.

This button, which was held entirely mysterious by the two meetings, could then be used to trade hidden texts. In this manner, various enormous problems to the ground arise to cope with dispersing buttons. Open key cryptography tends to these disadvantages so clients can impart safely over an open channel without concurring upon a mutual key in advance. Whitfield Diffie and Martin Hellman published a lopsided main cryptosystem in 1976, which, influenced by Ralph Merkle's job on accessible main distribution, revealed an accessible main comprehension method. This main trade approach, which utilizes exponentiation in a restricted area, has become regarded as the main trade of Diffie–Hellman. The primary structure for using public key or two-key cryptography was the Diffie Hellman Key Trade Convention. Consequently, it is at some point called as Asymmetric encryption. This was the main dispersed down to ground method to build a mutual mystery important over a verified (although not personal) route of interchanges without using an previous shared mystery. Steganography and cryptography speak to two strategies for guaranteeing security that have been utilized for quite a while now. Like everything else in the data innovation region, the two are in ceaseless research and improvement. Joining these strategies inside a similar framework is a moderately new heading however we can locate a few extraordinary works in writing. One such work is exhibited in paper (). The creators propose a framework that will improve the least critical piece (LSB) technique, which is likely the most well known steganographical strategy. The portrayed framework has a private key transmitted between the sender and the recipient and used to remove the shrouded message. () will detail four conceivable starting evaluation viewpoints of outer, DMZ, interior and basic purposes of essence. Next, every point of view will be differentiated by its capacity to evaluate and abuse vulnerabilities in an association. At that point, the four viewpoints will be thought about by their proficiency and way of assault surface investigation. Finally, inconveniences and preferences of every point of view will be illustrated. Note that aggressive safety assessment is a human-directed process involving both trade and skills, as well as impotence identification and tools of misuse. In that ability, the method is more workmanship than science, but then it is one of the most important apparatuses that can be accessed to proactively check a scheme owing to the use of subsequent findings that could provide proactive protection of defenselessness (). In the present investigation, an endeavor is made to address this hole by exhibiting an increasingly thorough examination of past security occurrences on basic foundation and modern control frameworks, both as far as the scope of alternatives considered in arranging assaults and the quantity of episodes tested. An aggregate of 242 revealed security occurrences on basic foundation and modern control frameworks are studied and broke down dependent on a proposed arrangement plan introduced in the accompanying approach segment (). Alongside the advancement of data security, steganography has gotten progressively consideration. It has turned into a pattern that an ever-increasing number of foundations offer steganography strategies in cybersecurity training.

In this paper, we propose coordinating steganography into cybersecurity educational programs. Stenography modules and hands-on labs are planned. It covers the standards of steganography, steganographic strategies, and the premise of steganalysis. Three lab activities incorporate steganography execution in HTML, TCP/IP, and computerized picture. () demonstrates an audit on various calculations utilized for steganography. As it is appeared, every strategy utilizes changed strategies, for example, LSB encoding, pseudo irregular encoding systems, other piece addition procedures to install and various calculations, for example, AES, RSA, RC4, Blowfish calculation, and so forth to change over the plaintext into ciphertext. Every technique has its very own points of interest and burdens. So it is hard to decide the best and the most exceedingly awful one.

This paper likewise looks at some of them from various perspectives and furthermore can be useful to decide an appropriate technique for explicit utilization. It helps in understanding which calculation is superior to another in a particular circumstance (). These days, legal picture examination apparatuses and systems goal is to uncover the hardening techniques and reestablish the firm faith in the unwavering quality of advanced media. This paper examines the difficulties of identifying steganography in PC crime scene investigation. Open source devices were utilized to examine these difficulties. The trial examination centers around utilizing steganography applications that utilization same calculations to shroud data only inside a picture. The exploration finding signifies that, if a specific steganography device An is utilized to conceal some data inside an image, and after that apparatus B which uses a similar strategy would not have the option to recuperate the inserted picture (). A somewhat new methodology as far as framework's security and furthermore the one utilized in this paper is to join cryptography with steganography. When utilizing cryptography alone, the message is encoded, its structure is changed and a key is expected to decode it. When that key is found by a pernicious outsider, the data is undermined. With steganography, the message's presence is covered up yet the structure isn't changed. When somebody understands there is a concealed message in whatever record was utilized to shroud it, the data is again traded off. Be that as it may, if the two techniques are consolidated, the security level is a lot higher as both steganalysis and cryptanalysis should be performed so as to locate the first information. A solid security level as portrayed above is the thing that frameworks, for example, CPS need because of their basic application regions ().

Comparison Study

Essentially, giving secret letters is the motive behind cryptography and steganography. Steganography, however, is not equal to cryptography. Cryptography overshadows the content of a noxious person's mystery text, while steganography even includes the message's existence. Steganography should not be confused for cryptography, where we alter the signal to render it obscure to a vindictive person who catches it. The significance of violating the structure is therefore diverse In cryptography, when the aggressor can peruse the secret signal, the structure is breached. Breaking a steganographic structure requires the assailant to define the use of steganography and the implanted text to be perused. (). The composition of a text is blended in cryptography to create it great for nothing and misleading except when the button to decode is available. It does not attempt to hide or disguise the hidden signal. Cryptography essentially provides the ability to transmit information between individuals in a way that prevents an alien from knowing it. Cryptography can also verify that a individual or thing's character is confirmed. Steganography, on the other hand, does not change the structure of the message of mystery, yet it envelops it within a cover image so that it can not be seen. For example, a message in ciphertext may raise doubts about the beneficiary while a message made with steganographic strategies will not be "undetectable." Steganography, in other words, prevents an unintended recipient from suspecting the data occurs. The safety of the steganography system developed also relies on the data encoding framework's mystery (). The steganography system is defeated when the encoding system is recognized.

Consolidating the approaches is conceivable by storing text using cryptography and hiding the deleted signal using steganography afterwards. Without discovering that mystery information is being traded, the subsequent stego image can be transferred. Moreover, irrespective of whether an aggressor would overcome the steganographic approach and recognize the signal from the stego object, it would involve the cryptographic unraveling button to translate the written message in any event. () demonstrates that the two advancements have counter favorable circumstances and disservices. Shockingly most employments of steganography and research around the point of steganography revolve around the ill-conceived purposes. The three greatest zones of ill-conceived steganography advance around based oppression, erotic entertainment and information robbery. Amid the exploration for this site the ill conceived employments of steganography were likewise observed to be on a worldwide scale, included national security or were done on a scholarly premise so as to all the more likely comprehend the potential risk of steganography whenever made by people with sick aims.

Proposed Methodology

Genuine situation, the IP photographic camera gives this ability to verify client expression to open entryways (for example worker room entryway, house front entryway). For this situation, the IP photographic camera can acquire face pictures of the clients and direct them to employee for validation reason different gadgets outside LAN organization (for example distributed storage) for capacity as appeared in figure 1. Any listening in assault, particularly in the network abuses privacy data communicated. instance, achieved picture is as touchy data in fig one and any programmer that can effectively get it done listening in assault have the option confirm with the verification.

Figure 1. Actual arrangement

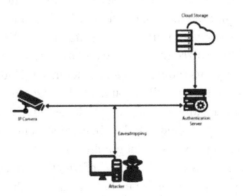

Fig 2 shows the projected conspire so as make sure about communicated pictures touchy information utilizing IoT gadget. For this situation, picture steganography is utilized so as to make sure about delicate data, for example, client face picture, organization. Furthermore, a home-based worker utilized as an incorporated gadget inside the LAN organization to get the face picture, which are now concealed utilizing picture steganography to scramble all together them to the gadgets are situated on the Net (distributed).

Referenced previously, the IOT gadgets can't handle solid and multifaceted encoding plans, subsequently, frivolous encoding coding techniques utilized. In spite of the fact that the touchy data is in

Figure 2. Future arrangement

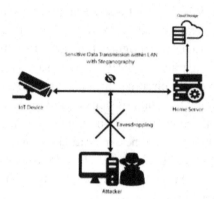

incoherent organization, aggressors may in any case have the option to reveal or decode it with adequate time or handling power. What's more, the encryption doesn't conceal the presence of data or messages from seeing the assailants. Therefore, cryptography method utilized elective safety instrument for moving the information safe way. As needs be, since the IP camera for the most part manages the picture in our plan, henceforth, we acquaint picture steganography with secure any touchy picture (expression), which needs communicated worker. So as to type the plan basic, think about Bod, who has the proprietor house, moves toward the IP photographic camera for face identification. After IP photographic camera recognized Bod's face effectively, it supplies it is a picture haphazardly catches picture with no distinguished, it is called spread picture. Rather than transfer the look picture legitimately to the homebased worker, the look picture covered up (inserted) trendy the chose arbitrary picture (spread picture) with cryptography method create additional picture (stage picture), It covers first look picture. Advanced on, the stage picture shipped off the homebased worker so as recover first expression picture from the stage picture utilizing a similar steganography procedure, yet in an opposite way. Then again, a busybody, Eve, has effectively assaulted in Bod's organization capture information broadcast amid IP photographic camera and home worker for any delicate data. She realized that the IP camera capacities as a face discovery authenticator for Bob's home in front entry way. Accordingly, catches pictures, including steno picture, yet he doesn't speculate with that picture as it seems, by all accounts, to be like other caught pictures. Cryptography is technique to brand private data and mails imperceptible keep programmers after recognizing. With steganography, assailants won't know about the data being communicated through a channel. Furthermore, a few analysts have utilized picture steganography on low handling power gadgets, for example, inserted gadgets and cell headphones for concealing information. In accompanying, least noteworthy piece (LBS) procedure is depicted as one of the picture steganography strategies for the proposed conspire. It is because of its fewer intricacy contrast with convoluted cryptography techniques just as high limit so as to move more information. to characterize the utilization of steganography and the embedded content to be examined. (). The synthesis of a book is mixed in cryptography to make it extraordinary in vain and deluding aside from when the catch to translate is accessible. It doesn't endeavor to stow away or mask the concealed sign. Cryptography basically gives the capacity to communicate data between people in a manner that keeps an outsider from knowing it. Cryptography can likewise check that an individual or thing's character is affirmed. Steganography, then again, doesn't change the structure of the message of secret, yet it encompasses it inside a cover picture with the goal that it can not be seen.

For instance, a message in ciphertext may raise questions about the recipient while a message made with steganographic methodologies won't be "imperceptible." Steganography, all in all, keeps a unintended beneficiary from suspecting the information happens. The security of the steganography framework grew likewise depends on the information encoding system's mystery (). Least noteworthy piece (LBS) is kind of substitution strategy that one the most well-known picture steganography strategies. Actually, the spread picture pixel esteem (for example 100) can be spoken to as a line of zeroes and ones (bits). Correspondingly, the touchy data (picture face) can be appeared as the other series of pieces (1, 0) so as to be supplanted with a portion of the pieces of the spread picture. Indeed, this substitution can be happened on the least huge pieces of spread picture pixels, which can't create a critical change on the presence of the picture (up to 4 LSBs). Conversely, any alteration on most noteworthy piece (MSB) of pixel can prompt make a significant corruption on the nature of picture, which can be distinguished through human discernment Nonetheless, utilizing the LSBs of pixel to shroud the delicate data can be perceived utilizing measurable examination, for example, $x2$ investigation as opposed to human vision. This is because of the way that choosing the LSBs for concealing the data isn't viewed as randomized, which can produce a marker for the assailant to utilize factual investigation on the picture to discover the modification. To take care of the above issue, rearranged LSB picture steganography is proposed to use in this plan. With this strategy, the delicate data has less opportunity to be identified by aggressors due the utilizing of spot reversal that prompts improve the nature of stego picture. The creators have proposed 2 plans for LBS reversal strategy, which conspire 2 required the spread picture to be gotten by the beneficiary in earlier. Since the IP camera is utilized to send the face (delicate data) of the client just a single time, thus, the main plan is adjusted as the picture steganography procedure in this plan. The clarification of the referenced procedure with a model is given as follows. worker is utilized. In this way, a solitary home worker is adequate in proposed plan and it would be more cost proficient. Moreover, utilizing a brought together worker is recommended in where the remote hubs are utilized to encode the information while the concentrated worker is utilized to decode the information as it were.

Data Hiding is firmly identified with software engineering, correspondence hypothesis, PC illustrations and picture handling, coding, signal preparing, scientific measurements, various media recognition properties and different fields of information and innovation. As it traverses different subjects, the substance shrouded in this class are of a wide range. The necessities on the course essentials and the premise of information are higher. Not the same as advanced watermarking and encryption innovation, the most noticeable component of stenography is that the private data is implanted into bearers yet not pull in the consideration of the others. Went with the steady battle of steganalysis, new steganographic advancements are rising. In the meantime, new strategies have a solid handy necessity. Notwithstanding educating sgeganography hypothesis, it is likewise important to structure certain exploratory and work on preparing for understudies so as to ace the framework hypothesis and innovation Steganography should not be confused for cryptography that involves altering the signal to cloud its meaning to vindictive people that prevent it. The significance of violating the structure is distinctive in this particular scenario. In cryptography, when the assailant can peruse the signal of mystery, the structure is breached. Breaking a steganographic structure requires the assailant to acknowledge the use of steganography and the implanted text to be perused. Steganography, as indicated, provides methods for mystery correspondence that cannot be evacuation without substantially altering the data it is entered into. Similarly, the safety of the defined structure for steganography relies on the data encoding framework's mystery. The steganography system is defeated when the encryption system is recognized. Nonetheless, using cryptography and steganography together to include multiple levels of safety is reliably a good method. By entering, a company should be able to encrypt the data and then mount the point signal with the help of the stego button in a noise or some other medium. The combination of these two methods will enhance the safety of the embedded data. For instance, restriction, safety and authority for safe data communication over an accessible circuit will be met by this united study. The amount below delineates the cryptography and steganography mix. The methods to steganography can be split into three kinds: 1) Pure Steganography; It is a scheme that only utilizes the strategy of steganography without consolidating various approaches. It takes a snap to dissimulate information within the distributed holder. 2) Secret Key Steganography; The mixture of mystery important cryptography and steganography strategy is used. This kind of option is to scramble the mystery signal through the mystery key system and hide the hidden data within the distributed carrier afterwards. 3) Community Key Steganography; It is a mixture of the strategy to public important cryptography and steganography. This kind of option is to encode the mystery data using the accessible important methodology and then cover up the stored data within the distributed holder. The Difference between Cryptography and Steganography (): Cryptography prevents unapproved parties from discovering the contents of mail, but Steganography anticipates revelation of the existence of letters (i.e., Cryptography babbles data and realizes that the text passes while Steganography generally hides the proximity of hidden data and obscures the signal moving through) Cryptography shifts the mystery text framework while the mystery text system is not adjusted by Steganography. Cryptography is a more characteristic development than technology in steganography. Cryptography's most calculations are excellent, yet Steganography's calculations are still being generated through particular settings. The solid calculation in cryptography depends on the key size, the greater the key size ; mixed by the AES-MPK computation, and thereafter the substance is camouflaged by the count PVD-MSLDIP-MPK. The covered sign is procured from the transmitter and subsequently unscrambled. Assessment Parameters: A measure of subtlety (Stego-picture worth) and payload (masking constraint) is used to review the demonstration of the solidified calculation. the more expensive processing force is required to decode ciphertext. In Steganography, the signal turns out to be recognized when the hidden text is recognized. Cryptography can provide all safety objectives by updating individuals with hash capabilities or verification codes or sophisticated labels in particular and personal key(s). Steganography can not provide a big part of safety objectives (integrity, validity, nonrevocation) autonomous of anyone else without using cryptographic systems. Anyway, it provides autonomous ranking from anyone else on the basis that most of the person concerned understands that the text is wrapped up in what kind of form. The mystery key steganography method is used in this document to enhance safety by using modified AES and method in[1] that includes PVD MPK and MSLDIP-MPK approaches to encode and hide the signal in the distributed image. In this way, if an aggressor asks about the stego picture and attempts to identify the message from the stego picture, the encoded message would in any case require the way to unravel. Proposed Hybrid Algorithm Input: input the Secret information in the format of message (SI), to define the Cipher Key (CK). Output: to represent the message in the format of Cipher Communication CC. Phase 1: Step 1. Create for (CK) for expand this is created by combination of two list. Step 2. Partition SI to slabs (S1, S2, S3 .... Sn) each and every slabs have the information about 16 byte . Step 3. To perform the operation for each Si block do Step 4. Change every byte to MP(CK) digits (two digits for every byte). Step 5. to segment Si to two state arrays (4*4). Step 6 Applying the filter the each and every state. Stage 7. Make pre round AddRoundKey which is a humble bitwiseXOR of the current two states through two sub keys Step 8. rehash Step 9. Apply the four changes (SubBytes, ShiftRows, MixColumns, and AddRoundKey) in two states. Stage 10. To play out the nine round . Stage 11. At last round actualizes SubBytes, ShiftRows, andAddRoundKey yet MixColumns is erased. Stage 12.

Return the digits 9 and 8 in their place in each state. Stage 13. Blend two states to be one square. Stage 14. Convert square to characters by utilizing MPK deciphering (i.e.two digits speak to character). The outcome speaks to cipherblock Step 15. end Step 16. Link the right now figure block with the past code squares to gather CC. Second Phase: 2 Input: Secret Message M, Cipher Key K, Cover Image C. Yield: Stego Image S. Stage: Phase 1. M has been encoded by utilizing the AES_MPK that takes M and K at that point produces figure text. Stage 2. The code text has been covered up in C by utilizing the strategy in () that is consolidating PVD-MPK technique with MSLDIP-MPK strategy and afterward delivers S Experimental Environment: The pre-owned PC with windows 10 and furnished with a Genuine Intel(R) Core(TM) i5-4210U CPU 1.70 GHz 240 GHz with 8 GB RAM memory. MATLAB R2015b and Matlab code are utilized to execute the calculation Benchmarks: Several investigations with size 512 * 512 and 256 * 256 standard dark scale pictures (Cameraman, Lena, Peppers, Lake, Airplane, and Baboon) were utilized to install a book encoded message. The message is initially scrambled by AESMPK calculation, and afterward it is covered up by PVD-MSLDIPMPK calculation to be sent. At the recipient, the concealed message is extricated and afterward unscrambled. Benchmarks: Several tests with sizes 512* 512 and 256* 256 typical dark scale pictures (Cameraman, Lena, Peppers, Lake, Airplane and Baboon) were utilized to encode a sms signal. To begin with, the content is scrambled by the AES-MPK calculation, and afterward the content is disguised by the calculation PVD-MSLDIP-MPK. The covered sign is acquired from the transmitter and afterward unscrambled. Evaluation Parameters: A gauge of nuance (Stego-picture worth) and payload (disguising limitation) is utilized to survey the show of the consolidated computation. Nuance (Stego-picture quality) gauges how regularly contrast (bending) was achieved by data that was put away in the primary spread, where the higher the nature of stegoimage, the more subtle the message is. The stego-picture exactness could be chosen by utilizing the circumstance (2) characterized by Peak Signal to Noise Ratio (PSNR).On the remote possibility that dim scale picture PSNR is bigger than 36 dB, the human visual structure (HVS) can not recognize the dispersed picture and the stego picture at that stage. Payload (Hiding Capacity) shows how much information can be topped off inside a disseminated picture without unmistakably reshaping the estimation of the scatter picture. Realize that it doesn't infer that a figuring hides colossal measures of information and produces huge bending in the presentation of the picture. Along these rows, it can be said that a steganographic operation is an extension in the case that it illustrates the development of the payload while maintaining a satisfying verbal character of the stegopicture or improving the performance of the stegopicture at the appropriate, concealing threshold or off possibility that both can be improved(). We actualized the open key steganography dependent on coordinating technique in various chose areas of a picture to demonstrate the presentation of the proposed strategy. In our execution, we utilized 600×400 bitmap picture record to conceal 5 KB content information. As talked about before, both of the two correspondence gatherings should locate the mystery key (stegokey) first by applying Diffie-Hellman open key trade convention to perform abnormal state of security. As in, the 8 bits information will be covered up inside 1 pixel, subsequently the 600x400, 24 bit picture record can acknowledge roughly 240000 bytes of information. This is contrasted and surely understood stego strategy, for example, LSBs which needs 3 pixels to conceal 1 byte of information. We can likewise alter the bit-rate at which we can shroud the information in the chose district. All things considered, the proposed steganographic convention is more effective than LSBs, since the calculation utilized the coordinating strategy to get indistinguishable pixel's bytes. Be that as it may, the proposed strategy resorts to the LSBs technique to appropriate the mystery information on the off chance that if the 8 bit of information isn't coordinated with any of the past three bytes (red, green, and blue).

Information Hiding is solidly related to programming designing, correspondence speculation, PC representations and picture taking care of, coding, signal planning, logical estimations, different media acknowledgment properties and various fields of data and development. As it navigates various subjects, the substance covered in this class are of a wide reach. The necessities on the course basics and the reason of data are higher. Not equivalent to cutting edge watermarking and encryption advancement, the most observable segment of transcription is that the private information is embedded into carriers yet not draw in the thought of the others. Went with the consistent clash of steganalysis, new steganographic progressions are rising. Meanwhile, new systems have a strong helpful need. Despite teaching sgeganography theory, it is in like manner critical to structure certain exploratory and work on getting ready for understudies in order to pro the system speculation and development Steganography ought not be mistaken for cryptography that includes changing the sign to cloud its importance to noxious individuals that forestall it. The criticalness of abusing the structure is unmistakable in this specific situation. In cryptography, when the aggressor can scrutinize the sign of secret, the structure is penetrated. Breaking a steganographic structure requires the aggressor to recognize the utilization of steganography and the embedded content to be perused. Steganography, as shown, gives strategies to secret correspondence that can not be clearing without generously changing the information it is gone into. Also, the security of the characterized structure for steganography depends on the information encoding structure's mystery. The steganography framework is crushed when the encryption framework is perceived. In any case, utilizing cryptography and steganography together to incorporate different degrees of wellbeing is dependably a decent technique. By entering, an organization should have the option to scramble the information and afterward mount the point signal with the assistance of the stego button in a commotion or some other medium. The mix of these two strategies will improve the wellbeing of the installed data. For occasion, limitation, security and authority for safe information correspondence over an available circuit will be met by this assembled study. The sum beneath depicts the cryptography and steganography blend. The techniques to steganography can be part into three sorts: 1) Pure Steganography; It is a plan that just uses the procedure of steganography without uniting different methodologies. It takes a snap to dissimulate data inside the circulated holder. 2) Secret Key Steganography; The combination of secret significant cryptography and steganography system is utilized. This sort of alternative is to scramble the secret sign through the secret key framework and conceal the shrouded information inside the disseminated transporter thereafter. 3) Community Key Steganography; It is a combination of the procedure to public significant cryptography and steganography.

CONCLUSION

Internet-of-Things (IoT) is a standard in the 21st period. It is receiving more significant and utilized it as a component of every day life. 1 of the significant worries that essential to investigate it data classification or security. Requirements for a safe, reliable savvy climate crucial. What's more, programmers can assault the organization because of the presence of weakness inside IOT and little preparing control gadgets, can compromise security of the clients. In this paper, a plan proposed dependent picture cryptography meanwhile the IP photographic camera with low handling memory capacities utilized as IOT gadget settle security issues during the transmission between brilliant gadget and home worker. Because of constraints brilliant gadgets, particularly memory computational force, least critical cycle strategy being adjusted. With strategy, least critical piece not bring about significant debasement value human discernment just measurable investigation. Also, the likelihood of having a doubt on sent information by the aggressor is utilizing cryptography contrast with the frivolous encoding meanwhile the arrangement information is in coding. Also, tall measure information because use of picture just as upset LSB picture steganography strategy, which requires fewer pieces for implanting. Since the LBSs choice is in this strategy, the safety of the cryptography calculation can expanded. Notwithstanding, choosing correct bay picture to the picture is one of the downsides of the conspire. As it were, the size of spread picture and its substance (pixels) must be large enough so as to install the face picture inside itself. Additionally, since the safe correspondence utilizing picture steganography is a single direction component, for a situation that the worker is needed to send any data (for example checking the validation) to IOT gadget (IP photographic camera), data determination be sent simple text, it be caught abused assailant. examination ought to completed execute the frivolous coding related to steganography strategies (double steganography) to give greater security on the communicated information utilizing IOT devices over the group. What's more, the expression picture (creation its scope littler the spread picture) be valuable choose picture by IP photographic camera as the spread picture. Another safe correspondence model was introduced in this paper that consolidates methods of cryptography and steganography to give two layers of security, so that the steganalyst can not achieve plaintext without knowing the mystery button to decode the ciphertext. Initially, the mystery data was recorded using the AES MPK, then using hybrid methods to cover up the deleted data in the bleak image. Because of this mixture, the data of the mystery can be transmitted over the open channel in view of the reality that the ciphertext does not appear aimless but rather disguises its nature by using steganography to conceal ciphertext in the images.Test findings showed that our suggested model can be used to shroud considerably more data than other existing methods and that the graphic character of the stego image is also enhanced, although it is strong for communication of mystery information. We anticipate adding the suggested method to noise and television in subsequent job. In addition, we expect the suggested method to be upgraded to render the threshold lower than it, while maintaining the PSNR equal or greater.

REFERENCES

Han, D., Yang, J., & Summers, W. (2017). Inject Stenography into Cybersecurity Education. *2017 31st International Conference on Advanced Information Networking and Applications Workshops (WAINA)*. 10.1109/WAINA.2017.30

Kekre, West, Khanna, & Hussaini. (2012). *Comparison between the basic LSB Replacement Technique and Increased Capacity of Information Hiding in LSB's Method for Images*. Academic Press.

Kumar, A., & Sharma, R. (2013). International Journal of Advanced Research in A Secure Image Steganography Based on RSA Algorithm and Hash-LSB Technique. *International Journal of Advanced Research in Computer Science and Software Engineering*, *3*(7), 363–372.

Menon, N., & Vaithiyanathan. (2017). A survey on image steganography. *2017 International Conference on Technological Advancements in Power and Energy (TAP Energy)*. doi:10.1109/TAPENERGY.2017.8397274

Oakley, J. (2018). Improving hostile digital protection appraisals utilizing shifted and novel instatement viewpoints. *Proceedings of the ACMSE 2018 Conference on - ACMSE '18*. 10.1145/3190645.3190673

Ogie, R. I. (2017). Cyber Security Incidents on Critical Infrastructure and Industrial Networks. *Proceedings of the 9th International Conference on Computer and Automation Engineering - ICCAE '17.* 10.1145/3057039.3057076

Sharma, Mithlesharya, & Goyal. (2013). Security Image Hiding Algorithm using Cryptography and Steganography. *Journal of Computer Engineering, 13*(5), 1–6.

Vegh, L., & Miclea, L. (2014). Securing communication in cyber-physical systems using steganography and cryptography. *2014 10th International Conference on Communications (COMM).* 10.1109/ICComm.2014.6866697

Yadav, V., Ingale, V., Sapkal, A., & Patil, G. (2014). Cryptographic Steganography. *Computer Science and Information Technology*, 17–23.

Yari, I. A., & Zargari, S. (2017). An Overview and Computer Forensic Challenges in Image Steganography. *2017 IEEE International Conference on Internet of Things (iThings) and IEEE Green Computing and Communications (GreenCom) and IEEE Cyber, Physical and Social Computing (CPSCom) and IEEE Smart Data (SmartData).* doi:10.1109/ithingsgreencom-cpscom-smartdata.2017.60

Compilation of References

Yang, W., Hu, J., Wang, S., & Delaunay, A. (2014). Quadrangle-Based Fingerprint Authentication System with Template Protection Using Topology Code for Local Registration and Security Enhancement. *IEEE Transactions on Information Forensics and Security*, *9*(7), 1179–1192. doi:10.1109/TIFS.2014.2328095

Yang, W., Hu, J., & Wang, S. (2014). *An Alignment-free Fingerprint Bio-cryptosystem based on Modified Voronoi Neighbour Structures*. Academic Press.

Online Steganography Program. (2019). https://stylesuxx.github.io/Steganography

Backes, M., & Cachin, C. (n.d.). *Public-Key Steganography with Active Attacks*. IBM Research, Zurich Research Laboratory.

Tarouco, L., Bertholdo, M. R., Granville, L. Z., & Carbone, L. M. R. (2012). Internet of things in healthcare: Interoperability and security issues in Communications (ICC). *IEEE International Conference on. IEEE*, 6121–6125.

Shehab, A., Elhoseny, M., Muhammad, K., Sangaiah, A. K., Yang, P., Huang, H., & Hou, G. (2018). Secure and Robust Fragile Watermarking Scheme for Medical Images. *IEEE Access: Practical Innovations, Open Solutions*, *6*, 10269–10278. doi:10.1109/ACCESS.2018.2799240

Bairagi, A. K., Khondoker, R., & Islam, R. (2016). *An efficient steganographic approach for protecting communication in the Internet of Things (IoT) critical infrastructures*. Academic Press.

Anwar, A. S., Ghany, K. K. A., & Mahdy, H. E. (2015). Improving the security of images transmission. *International Journal (Toronto, Ont.)*, *3*(4).

Abdelaziza, A., Elhoseny, M., Salama, A.S., & Riad, A.M. (2018). *A Machine Learning Model for Improving Healthcare services on Cloud Computing Environment*. Academic Press.

Paschou, M., Sakkopoulos, E., Sourla, E., & Tsakalidis, A. (2013). Health Internet of Things: Metrics and methods for efficient data transfer. *Simulation Modelling Practice and Theory*, *34*, 186–199. doi:10.1016/j.simpat.2012.08.002

Atamli, A. W., & Martin, A. (2014). Threat-Based Security Analysis for the Internet of Things. *Secure Internet of Things (SIoT), International Workshop*, 35-43.

Sajjad, M., Nasir, M., Khan, M., Khan, S., Jan, Z., Sangaiah, A.K., Elhoseny, M., & WookBaik, S. (2017). Raspberry Pi assisted face recognition framework for enhanced law-enforcement services in smart cities. In Future Generation Computer Systems. Elsevier.

Kumar, P., & Lee, H. J. (2011). Security issues in healthcare applications using wireless medical sensor networks: A survey. *Sensors (Basel)*, *12*(1), 55–91. doi:10.3390120100055 PMID:22368458

Razzaq, M. A., Sheikh, R. A., Baig, A., & Ahmad, A. (2017). Digital image security: Fusion of encryption, Steganography and watermarking. *International Journal of Advanced Computer Science and Applications*, *8*(5).

Seyyedi, S. A., Sadau, V., & Ivanov, N. (2016). A Secure Steganography Method Based on Integer Lifting Wavelet Transform. *International Journal of Network Security, 18*(1), 124–132.

Sajjad, M., Muhammad, K., Baik, S. W., Rho, S., Jan, Z., Yeo, S. S., & Mehmood, I. (2017). Mobile-cloud assisted framework for selective encryption of medical images with Steganography for resource-constrained devices. *Multimedia Tools and Applications, 76*(3), 3519–3536. doi:10.100711042-016-3811-6

Hashim, M., Rhaif, S., Abdulrazzaq, A., Hussein Ali, A., & Taha, M. (2020). *Based on IoT Healthcare Application for Medical Data Authentication: Towards A New Secure Framework Using Steganography.* Academic Press.

Lakshmi Kanth, K., & Siva Narayana, R. (2020). *Integrating Steganography and Cryptography techniques in IoT cloud for secure data transfer.* Academic Press.

Boukari & Bobbo. (n.d.). ceeol.com

Sumi, L., & Ranga, V. (2016). Sensor enabled Internet of Things for smart cities. *Fourth International Conference on Parallel, Distributed and Grid Computing (PDGC)*, 295-300. 10.1109/PDGC.2016.7913163

Sharma, A., & Mohan, N. (2020). Article. European Journal of Molecular & *Clinical Medicine, 7*(4), 376–384.

Bradley, T. (2015). Experts pick the top 5 security threats for 2015. *PC World.*

Meng, R., Cui, Q., Zhou, Z., Fu, Z., & Sun, X. (2019). A Steganography Algorithm Based on CycleGAN for Covert Communication in the Internet of Things. *IEEE Access: Practical Innovations, Open Solutions, 7*, 90574–90584. doi:10.1109/ACCESS.2019.2920956

Djebbar, F., & Abu-Ali, N. (2017). Lightweight Noise Resilient Steganography Scheme for Internet of Things. *IEEE Global Communications Conference (GLOBECOM 2017)*, 1-6. 10.1109/GLOCOM.2017.8255039

Djebbar, F., Abed-Maraim, K., Guerchi, D., & Hamam, H. (2010). Dynamic energy based text-in-speech spectrum hiding using speech masking properties. *2nd International Conference on Industrial Mechatronicsand Automation (ICIMA), 2*, 422-426. 10.1109/ICINDMA.2010.5538279

Ayad, B. (2011). *Noise Suppressor.* U.S. Patent 7,889,874 B1.

Bender, W., Gruhl, D., Morimoto, N., & Lu, A. (1996). Techniques for Data Hiding. *IBM Systems Journal, 35*(3-4), 13-33.

Abuadbba, S., Ibaida, A., & Khalil, I. (n.d.). *IoT Sign: Protecting Privacy and Authenticity of IoT using Discrete Cosine Based Steganography.* arXiv:1911.00604[cs.CR].

Yin, Fen, Mughal, & Iranmanesh. (2015). Internet of Things: Securing Data Using Image Steganography. *3rd International Conference on Artificial Intelligence, Modelling and Simulation (AIMS)*, 310-314. .. doi:10.1109/AIMS.2015.56

Tiwari & Shandilya. (2010). Evaluation of Various LSB based Methods of Image Seganography on GIF File Format. *International Journal of Computer Applications.*

Khosravi, S., Mashallah, A. D., & Hossein, Y. M. (2011). A new Steganography method based HIOP (Higher Intensity Of Pixel) algorithm and Strassen's matrix multiplication. *Journal of Global Research in Computer Science, 2*(1).

Paik, M. (2010). Blacknoise: Low-fi Lightweight Steganography in Service of Free Speech. *M4D*, 150.

Akhtar, N., Khan, S., & Johri, P. (2014). An improved inverted LSB image steganography. *Issues and Challenges in Intelligent Computing Techniques (ICICT), International Conference on*, 749-745. 10.1109/ICICICT.2014.6781374

Cachin, C. (2005). Digital Steganography. *Encyclopaedia of Cryptography and Security.*

Bhattacharyya, S., Banerjee, I., & Sanyal, G. (2011). Data Hiding Through Multi Level Steganography and SSCE. *Journal of Global Research in Computer Science, 2*(2), 38–47.

Abomhara, M., & Køien, G. M. (2014). Security and privacy in the internet of things: Current status and open issues. In *Privacy and Security in Mobile Systems (PRISMS), International Conference on.* IEEE.

Yoon, S., Park, H. Y. H., & Yoo, H. S. (2015). Security issues on smarthome in IoT environment. In Computer Science and its Applications. Springer.

Lai, Y. L., Jin, Z., Teoh, A. B. J., Goi, B.-M., Yap, W.-S., Chai, T.-Y., & Rathgeb, C. (2017). Cancellable iris template generation based on Indexing-First-One hashing. *Pattern Recognition, 64*, 105–117. doi:10.1016/j.patcog.2016.10.035

Abbas, S. A., El Arif, T. I., Ghaleb, F. F., & Khamis, S. M. (2015). Optimized video steganography using Cuckoo search algorithm. *IEEE Seventh International Conference on Intelligent Computing and Information Systems (ICICIS'15).* doi: 10.1109/IntelCIS.2015.7397279

Abd El-Latif, A. A., Abd-El-Atty, B., Hossain, M. S., Rahman, M. A., Alamri, A., & Gupta, B. B. (2018). Efficient quantum information hiding for remote medical image sharing. *IEEE Access: Practical Innovations, Open Solutions, 6,* 21075–21083. doi:10.1109/ACCESS.2018.2820603

Abdel Wahab, O.F., Hussein, A.I., Hamed., H.F., Kelash., H.M., Khalaf., A.A., & Ali, H.M. (2019). Hiding data in images using steganography techniques with compression algorithms. *Telkomnika, 17*(3), 1168-1175. . doi:10.12928/telkomnika.v17i3.12230

Abdul & Naser. (2015). Selective Image Encryption with Diffusion and Confusion Mechanism. *International Journal of Advanced Research in Computer Science and Software Engineering, 4*(7), 5-12.

Abdulla, A. A. (2015). *Exploiting similarities between secret and cover images for improved embedding efficiency and security in digital steganography.* Buckingham E-Archive of Research.

Abdullah, H. A., & Abdullah, H. N. (2017). Image encryption using hybrid chaotic map. *2017 International Conference on Current Research in Computer Science and Information Technology (ICCIT),* 121-125. 10.1109/CRCSIT.2017.7965545

Abed, H. N. (2017). Robust and secured image steganography using lsb and encryption with qr code. *Journal of Al-Qadisiyah for Computer Science and Mathematics, 9*(2), 1-9.

Abikoye, O. C., Adewole, K. S., & Oladipupo, A. J. (2012). Efficient data hiding system using cryptography and steganography. *International Journal of Applied Information Systems (IJAIS), 4*(11), 6–11.

Achkoun, K., Hanin, C., & Omary, F. (2019) SPF-CA: A new cellular automata based block cipher using key-dependent S-boxes. *Journal of Discrete Mathematical Sciences and Cryptography.* Doi:10.1080/09720529.2019.1649031

Ahmad, B., Kamili, A., Gull, S., & Parah, S. A. (2021). Data Embedding in Color Images: A Secure Data Communication Framework Based on Modular Arithmetic. In *Multimedia Security* (pp. 157–176). Springer. doi:10.1007/978-981-15-8711-5_8

Ahvanooey, M. T. (2018). AITSteg: An innovative text steganography technique for hidden transmission of text message via social media. *IEEE Access: Practical Innovations, Open Solutions, 6,* 65981–65995. doi:10.1109/ACCESS.2018.2866063

AithalP. S. (2016). A Review on Various E-Business and M-Business Models & Research Opportunities. *International Journal of Management, IT and Engineering, 6*(1), 275-298. Available at SSRN: https://ssrn.com/abstract=2779175

Alajmi, M. E.-S., Elashry, I., El-Sayed, H. S., & Farag Allah, O. S. (2020). Steganography of Encrypted Messages Inside Valid QR Codes. *IEEE Access: Practical Innovations, Open Solutions, 8,* 8. doi:10.1109/ACCESS.2020.2971984

Alam, S. S. (2014). Entropy Based Visual Cryptographic Encryption Technique for Medical Images Security. ERCICA, 75-78.

Al-Huwais, N. H. (2020). An Improved Least Significant Bit Image Steganography Method. In *International Conference on Multimedia Computing, Networking and Applications* (pp. 90-96). IEEE.

Ali, Y. M. B. (2021). A Steganographic Embedding Scheme Using Improved-PSO Approach. In *Heuristics for Optimization and Learning* (pp. 199–210). Springer. doi:10.1007/978-3-030-58930-1_13

Al-Nofaie, S. M., & Gutub, A. A.-A. (2020). Utilizing pseudo-spaces to improve Arabic text steganography for multimedia data communications. *Multimedia Tools and Applications*, 79(1-2), 19–67. doi:10.100711042-019-08025-x

Alsaffawi, Z. S. Y. (2016). Image steganography by using exploiting modification direction and knight tour algorithm. *J. Al-Qadisiyah Comput. Sci. Math.*, 8, 1–11.

Al-Sanjary, O. I., Ibrahim, O. A., & Sathasivem, K. (2020, June). A New Approach to Optimum Steganographic Algorithm for Secure Image. In *2020 IEEE International Conference on Automatic Control and Intelligent Systems (I2CACIS)* (pp. 97-102). IEEE. 10.1109/I2CACIS49202.2020.9140186

Altaay, A. J. (2012). An Introduction to Image Steganography Techniques. *International Conference on Advanced Computer Science Applications and Technologies*, 122 - 126. 10.1109/ACSAT.2012.25

Alwan, A. A. (2019). *A Survey On Combined Various Data Hiding Techniques*. Open International Journal of Informatics.

Aman, M. K. (2017). *A hybrid text steganography approach utilizing Unicode space characters and zero-width character*. International Journal on Information Technologies and Security.

Amirtharajan, R., Akila, R., & Deepikachowdavarapu, P. (2010). Comparative Analysis of Image Steganography. *International Journal of Computers and Applications*, 2(8), 41–47.

Anand, A. (2020). Watermarking techniques for medical data authentication: A survey. *Multimedia Tools and Applications*, 1–33.

Anderson, R. (1996). Stretching the limits of steganography. *Proceeding of the 1st International Workshop on Information Hiding*, 1174, 39–48. 10.1007/3-540-61996-8_30

Anderson, R., & Petitcolas, F. (1998). On the limits of steganography. *IEEE Journal on Selected Areas in Communications*, 16(4), 474–481. doi:10.1109/49.668971

Angelopoulos, G., & Pitas, I. (1991). Multichannel Wiener filters in color image restoration based on AR color image modelling. *IEEE International Conference on Acoustics, Speech, and Signal Processing, ICASSP-91*. 10.1109/ICASSP.1991.150913

Antonio, H., Prasad, P. W. C., & Alsadoon, A. (2019). Implementation of Cryptography in Steganography for Enhanced Security. *Multimedia Tools and Applications*, 78, 32721–32734. doi:10.100711042-019-7559-7

Anusha, M., Bhanu, K. N., & Divyashree, D. (2020, July). Secured Communication of Text and Audio using Image Steganography. In *2020 International Conference on Electronics and Sustainable Communication Systems (ICESC)* (pp. 284-288). IEEE. 10.1109/ICESC48915.2020.9155715

Arvind & Pooja. (2010). Steganography–A Data Hiding Technique. *International Journal of Computer Applications, 9*(7).

Attaby, A.A., Ahmed, M.F.M., & Alsammak, A.K. (2018). Data hiding inside JPEG images with high resistance to steganalysis using a novel technique: DCT-M3. *Ain Shams Engineering Journal, 9*(4), 1965-1974.

Attaby, A. A., Ahmed, M. F. M., & Alsammak, A. K. (2018). Data hiding inside JPEG images with high resistance to steganalysis using a novel technique: DCT-M3. *Ain Shams Engineering Journal, 9*(4), 1965–1974. doi:10.1016/j.asej.2017.02.003

Atta, R., & Ghanbari, M. (2021). A high payload data hiding scheme based on dual tree complex wavelet transform. *Optik (Stuttgart), 226*, 165786. doi:10.1016/j.ijleo.2020.165786

Ayub, N., & Selwal, A. (2020). An improved image steganography technique using edge-based data hiding in DCT domain. *Journal of Interdisciplinary Mathematics, 23*(2), 357–366. doi:10.1080/09720502.2020.1731949

Azza, A. A., & Lian, S. (2020). *Multi-secret image sharing based on elementary cellular automata with steganography. Multimed Tools Appl.* doi:10.100711042-020-08823-8

Babu, D. V., & Alamelu, N. R. (2009). Wavelet-Based Medical Image Compression Using ROI EZW. *Int. J. of Recent Trends in Engineering and Technology, 1*(3), 97–100.

Baluja, S. (2017). Hiding images in plain sight: Deep steganography. *Proceedings Neural Information Processing Symposium*, 2069–2079.

Bandekar, P. P., & Suguna, G. C. (2018). LSB Based Text and Image Steganography Using AES Algorithm. *3rd International Conference on Communication and Electronics Systems (ICCES)*, 782-788. doi: 10.1109/CESYS.2018.8724069

Banik, B. G., & Banik, A. (2020). Robust, Imperceptible and Blind Video Steganography using RGB Secret, Maximum Likelihood Estimation and Fibonacci Encryption. *International Journal of Electronic Security and Digital Forensics, 12*(2), 174–199.

Bas, P., Filler, T., & Pevny, T. (2011). Break our steganographic system: The ins and outs of organizing BOSS. *LNCS, 6958*, 59–70.

Bender, W., Gruhl, D., Morimoto, N., & Lu, A. (1996). Techniques for data hiding. *IBM Systems Journal, 35*(3-4), 313–336.

Bennett, C. H. (1984): Quantum cryptography: public key distribution and coin tossing. *IEEE International Conference on Computers, Systems and Signal Processing*, 175(1), 175-179.

Bernd, J. (1993). Digital Image Processing. In Concepts, Algorithms, and Scientific Applications. Springer-Verlag.

Bhargava, S., & Mukkhija, M. (2019). Hide Image and Text using LSB, DWT and RSA based on Image Steganography. *ICTACT Journal on Image and Video Processing, 9*(3), 1940–1946.

Bhoi, N., & Meher, S. (2008). Circular spatial filtering under high-noise-variance conditions. *Computers & Graphics, 32*(5), 568–580. doi:10.1016/j.cag.2008.07.006

Biswas, R., Mukherjee, I., & Bandyopadhyay, S. K. (2019). Image feature-based high capacity steganographic algorithm. *Multimedia Tools and Applications, 78*(14), 20019–20036. doi:10.100711042-019-7369-y

Bobade, S., & Goudar, R. (2015). Secure Data Communication Using Protocol Steganography in IPv6. *International Conference on Computing Communication Control and Automation*, 275-279. 10.1109/ICCUBEA.2015.59

Böhme, R., & Westfeld, A. (2004). Statistical Characterisation of MP3 Encoders for Steganalysis. *Proceedings of the Multimedia and Security Workshop*, 25-34.

Bonavoglia, P. (2020). A Partenio's Stegano-Crypto Cipher. In *International Conference on Historical Cryptology HistoCrypt* (pp. 36-45). Linköping University Electronic Press. 10.3384/ecp2020171006

Boroumand, M., Chen, M., & Fridrich, J. (2018). Deep residual network for steganalysis of digital images. *IEEE Transactions on Information Forensics and Security*, *14*(5), 1181–1193. doi:10.1109/TIFS.2018.2871749

Boroumand, M., & Fridrich, J. (2020). Synchronizing Embedding Changes in Side-Informed Steganography. *Proc. IS&T, Electronic Imaging, Media Watermarking, Security, and Forensics*, *290*, 1-12.

Boughaci, D., & Douah, H. (2020). A Variable Neighborhood Search Based Method with Learning for Image Steganography. In *Sustainable Development and Social Responsibility—Volume 2* (pp. 7–18). Springer. doi:10.1007/978-3-030-32902-0_2

Brar, R. K., & Sharma, A. (2020). Improved Steganography Using Odd Even Substitution. In *Cognitive Computing in Human Cognition* (pp. 1–8). Springer. doi:10.1007/978-3-030-48118-6_1

Brassil, J. T., Low, S., Maxemchuk, N. F., & O'Gorman, L. (1995, October). Electronic Marking and Identification Techniques to Discourage Document Copying. *IEEE Journal on Selected Areas in Communications*, *13*(8), 1495–1504. doi:10.1109/49.464718

Cachin, C. (2004). An Information-Theoretic Model for Steganography. *Information and Computation*, *192*(1), 41–56. doi:10.1016/j.ic.2004.02.003

Cai. (2004). Improving the capacity of the Boström-Felbinger protocol. *Phys. Rev. A, 69.*. doi:10.1103/PhysRevA.69.054301

Cao, Y., Zhao, X., Feng, D., & Sheng, R. (2011). Video steganography with perturbed motion estimation. *Proceedings Information Hiding*, *6958*, 193–207.

Cao, Y., Zhou, Z., Sun, X., & Gao, C. (2018). Coverless information hiding based on the molecular structure images of material. *Computers. Materials & Continua*, *54*(2), 197–207.

Chaharlang, J., Mosleh, M., & Rasouli-Heikalabad, S. (2020). A novel quantum steganography-Steganalysis system for audio signals. *Multimedia Tools and Applications*, *79*, 17551–17577. doi:10.100711042-020-08694-z

Chahar, V. (2020). Steganography Techniques Using Convolutional Neural Networks. *Review of Computer Engineering Studies*. doi:10.18280/rces.070304

Chakrabarti, S. D. S. (2015). A Novel Approach to Digital Image Steganography of Key-Based Encrypted Text. Communication and Optimization (EESCO), 24 - 25.

Chakraborty, S., & Jalal, A. S. (2020). A novel local binary pattern based blind feature image steganography. *Multimedia Tools and Applications*, *79*(27-28), 1–14. doi:10.100711042-020-08828-3

Chandramouli, R., & Memon, N. (2001). Analysis of lsb based image steganography techniques. *Proc. IEEE International Conference on Image Processing*, 1019–1022.

Chandra, N. S. R., Sneha, V., & Paul, P. V. (2020). A Novel Image Steganography Model Using LSB with Extended ASCII Codes. In *Smart Intelligent Computing and Applications* (pp. 107–116). Springer. doi:10.1007/978-981-13-9282-5_11

Changqing, L. (2004). ROI and FOI algorithms for Wavelet-Based Video Compression. *Proceedings Of The 5th Pacific Rim Conference On Advances In Multimedia Information Processing*, *3*, 241-248.

Charalampos, D., & Ilias, M. (2007). Region of Interest Coding Techniques for Medical Image Compression. *IEEE Engineering in Medicine and Biology Magazine*. PMID:17941320

Chaudhary, S. D. (2016). Text steganography based on feature coding method. In *The International Conference on Advances in Information Communication Technology & Computing* (pp. 1-4). ACM.

Chaumont, M. (2019). *DL in steganography and steganalysis from 2015 to 2018*. Academic Press.

Chavada, P., Patel, N., & Patel, K. (2014). Region of Interest Based Image Compression. *IJIRCCE, 2*(1), 10-20.

Chen, D., Bourlard, H., & Thiran, J. P. (2001). Text identification in complex background using SVM. *Proceedings - IEEE Computer Society Conference on Computer Vision and Pattern Recognition, 2*, 611–621.

Chen, W. (2016). Optical Multiple-Image Encryption Using Three-Dimensional Space. *IEEE Photonics Journal, 8*(2), 1–8.

Che-Wei, L. W.-H. T. (2012, January). A Secret-Sharing-Based Method for Authentication of Grayscale Document Images via the Use of the PNG Image With a Data Repair Capability. *IEEE Transactions on Image Processing, 21*(1), 207–218. doi:10.1109/TIP.2011.2159984 PMID:21693424

Chief, Z. S., Mustafa, R. A., & Maryoosh, A. A. (2020). Hiding Encrypted Text in Image using Least Significant Bit Image Steganography Technique. *International Journal of Engineering Research and Advanced Technology, 6*(8), 63–75. doi:10.31695/IJERAT.2020.3642

Chong, F., Bian, O., Jiang, H-y., Ge, L-h., & Ma, H-f. (2016). A New Chaos-Based Image Cipher Using a Hash Function. *IEEE/ACIS 15th International Conference on Computer and Information Science (ICIS).*

Chowdhuri, P., Pal, P., Jana, B., & Giri, D. (2020). A New Repeated Pixel Value Difference-Based Steganographic Scheme with Overlapped Pixel. In *Intelligent Computing: Image Processing Based Applications* (pp. 103–118). Springer. doi:10.1007/978-981-15-4288-6_7

Christensson, P. (2011). *Compression Definition*. TechTerms.

Chung, K. L., Shen, C. H., & Chang, L. C. (2001). A novel SVD based image hiding scheme. *Pattern Recognition Letters, 22*(9), 1051–1058. doi:10.1016/S0167-8655(01)00044-7

Cogranne, R. (2018). *Determining JPEG Image Standard Quality Factor from the Quantization Tables*. Academic Press.

Cogranne, R., Giboulot, Q., & Bas, P. (2019). The ALASKA steganalysis challenge: A first step towards steganalysis. In *Proceedings Information Hiding and Multimedia Security* (pp. 125–137). ACM., doi:10.1007/978-3-642-24178-9_14.

Couchot & Couturier. (2016). *Steganalysis via a Convolutional Neural Network using Large Convolution Filters*. Academic Press.

Daemen, J., & Rijmen, V. (1999). *AES Proposal: Rijndael*. Available in http://csrc.nist.gov/archive/aes/rijndael/Rijndael-ammended.pdf#page=1

Dalal, M. (2020). Steganography and Steganalysis (in digital forensics): A Cybersecurity guide. *Multimedia Tools and Applications*, 1–49.

Damrudi, M., & Aval, K. J. (2019). Image Steganography using LSB and Encrypted Message with AES, RSA, DES, 3DES and Blowfish. *International Journal of Engineering and Advanced Technology, 8*(63), 204–208.

Dang-Nguyen, D., Pasquini, C., Conotter, C., & Boato, G. (2015). RAISE: a raw images dataset for digital image forensics. In *Proceedings ACM SIGMM Conference on Multimedia Systems* (pp. 219–224), ACM. 10.1145/2713168.2713194

Das, D., & Basak, R. K. (2020). Rank Based Pixel-Value-Differencing: A Secure Steganographic Approach. In *Proceedings of the Global AI Congress 2019* (pp. 501-514). Springer. 10.1007/978-981-15-2188-1_39

Davey, M. C., & MacKay, D. J. C. (2001). Reliable Communication over Channels with Insertions, Deletions, and Substitutions. *IEEE Transactions on Information Theory, 47*(5), 687–698. doi:10.1109/18.910582

Deb, K., Al-Seraj, M. S., Hoque, M. M., & Sarkar, M. I. H. (2012, December). Combined DWT-DCT based digital image watermarking technique for copyright protection. In *2012 7th International Conference on Electrical and Computer Engineering* (pp. 458-461). IEEE. 10.1109/ICECE.2012.6471586

Debnath, B., Das, J. C., & De, D. (2018). Design of Image Steganographic Architecture using Quantum-Dot Cellular Automata for Secure Nanocommunication Networks. *Nano Communication Networks*, *15*, 41–58.

Debnath, D., Ghosh, E., & Banik, B. G. (2020). Multi-Image Hiding Blind Robust RGB Steganography in Transform Domain. *International Journal of Web-Based Learning and Teaching Technologies*, *15*(1), 24–52. doi:10.4018/IJWLTT.2020010102

Denemark, T., Bas, P., & Fridrich, J. (2018). Natural Steganography in JPEG Compressed Images. *Proc. IS&T, Electronic Imaging, Media Watermarking, Security, and Forensics*, *316*, 1-10.

Denemark, T., & Fridrich, J. (2017). Steganography with Multiple JPEG Images of the Same Scene. *IEEE TIFS*, *12*(10), 2308–2319. doi:10.1109/TIFS.2017.2705625

Denemark, T., & Fridrich, J. (2017). Steganography with two JPEGs of the same scene. *2017 IEEE International Conference on Acoustics, Speech and Signal Processing (ICASSP)*, 2117-2121. 10.1109/ICASSP.2017.7952530

Detlev, M., & Cycon, H. L. (1999). Very Low Bit-Rate Video Coding Using Wavelet-Based Techniques. *IEEE Transactions on Circuits and Systems for Video Technology*, *9*(1), 85–94. doi:10.1109/76.744277

Devlin, J. C. (2018). *Bert: Pre-training of deep bidirectional transformers for language understanding.* arXiv preprint.

Dey, N., Roy, A. B., & Dey, S. (2011). A Novel Approach of Color Image Hiding Using RGB Color Planes and DWT. *IJCA*, *36*(5), 19–24.

Dhawan, S. (2020). Analysis of various data security techniques of steganography. A survey. Information Security Journal: A Global Perspective, 1-25.

Dhawan, S., & Gupta, R. (2021). Analysis of various data security techniques of steganography: A survey. *Information Security Journal: A Global Perspective, 30*(2), 63-87.

Dolhansky, B., Howes, R., Pflaum, B., Baram, N., & Canton-Ferrer, C. (2019). *The deepfake detection challenge (DFDC) preview dataset.* abs/1910.08854.

Douglas, M., Bailey, K., & Leeney, M. (2018). An overview of steganography techniques applied to the protection of biometric data. *Multimedia Tools and Applications*, *77*, 17333–17373. doi:10.100711042-017-5308-3

Duan, X., Jia, K., Li, B., Guo, D., Zhang, E., & Qin, C. (2019). Reversible image steganography scheme based on a U-Net structure. *IEEE Access, 7*, 9314-9323.

Duan, X. (2020). A New High Capacity Image Steganography Method Combined with Image Elliptic Curve Cryptography and Deep Neural Network. *IEEE Access: Practical Innovations, Open Solutions, 8*, 25777–25788.

Duan, X., Guo, D., Liu, N., Li, B., Gou, M., & Qin, C. (2020). A New High Capacity Image Steganography Method Combined with Image Elliptic Curve Cryptography and Deep Neural Network. *IEEE Access: Practical Innovations, Open Solutions, 8*, 25777–25788. doi:10.1109/ACCESS.2020.2971528

Duchowski, A. T. (1998). Representing Multiple Region of Interest with Wavelets. *Proceeding of International Conference on Visual Communications and Image Processing*, *3309*.

Easttom, W. (2021). Steganography. In *Modern Cryptography*. Springer. doi:10.1007/978-3-030-63115-4_16

Elharrouss, O., Almaadeed, N., & Al-Maadeed, S. (2020, February). An image steganography approach based on k-least significant bits (k-LSB). In *2020 IEEE International Conference on Informatics, IoT, and Enabling Technologies (ICIoT)* (pp. 131-135). IEEE. 10.1109/ICIoT48696.2020.9089566

Elkouny, A., Zakaria, N. S., & Sobhy, M. I. (2002). Communication Security using Chaotic Generator. *IEEE 45th Midwest Symposium on Circuits and Systems (MWSCAS).* 10.1109/MWSCAS.2002.1187200

El-Latif, A. A. A., Abd-El-Atty, B., Hossain, M. S., Elmougy, S., & Ghoneim, A. (2018). Secure Quantum Steganography Protocol for Fog Cloud Internet of Things. *IEEE Access: Practical Innovations, Open Solutions, 6,* 10332–10340. doi:10.1109/ACCESS.2018.2799879

Embaby, A. A., Mohamed, A., Shalaby, W., & Elsayed, K. M. (2020). Digital Watermarking Properties, Classification and Techniques. *International Journal of Engineering and Advanced Technology, 9*(3), 2742–2750.

Evsutin, O., & Kultaev, P. (n.d.). An algorithm for embedding information in digital images based on discrete wavelet transform and learning automata. *Multimedia Tools and Applications,* 1-23.

Eyssa, A. A., Abdelsamie, F. E., & Abdelnaiem, A. E. (2020). An Efficient Image Steganography Approach over Wireless Communication System. *Wireless Personal Communications, 110,* 321–337. doi:10.100711277-019-06730-2

Fahim, Islam, & Aowlad. (2017). A new chaos based medical image encryption scheme. *2017 6th International Conference on Informatics, Electronics and Vision & 2017 7th International Symposium in Computational Medical and Health Technology (ICIEV-ISCMHT),* 1-6.

Fakhredanesh, M., Rahmati, M., & Safabakhsh, R. (2019). Steganography in discrete wavelet transform based on human visual system and cover model. *Multimedia Tools and Applications, 78*(13), 18475–18502. doi:10.100711042-019-7238-8

Farid, H. (2002). Detecting hidden messages using higher-order statistical models. *International Conference on Image Processing.*

Farrag, S., & Alexan, W. (2019). A high-capacity geometrical domain-based 3d image steganography scheme. *IEEE International Conference on Advanced Communication Technologies and Networking CommNet,* 1-7. 10.1109/COMMNET.2019.8742346

Fayez, I., & Ferat, A. (2006). An Efficient Method for Region of Interest Coding in JPEG2000. *Proceedings of the 5th WSEAS International Conference on Signal Processing.*

Feng, B., Weng, J., Lu, W., & Pei, B. (2017). Steganalysis of content-adaptive binary image data hiding. *Journal of Visual Communication and Image Representation, 46,* 119–127. doi:10.1016/j.jvcir.2017.01.008

Filler, T., & Fridrich, J. J. (2010). Gibbs construction in steganography. *IEEE Transactions on Information Forensics and Security, 5*(4), 705–720. doi:10.1109/TIFS.2010.2077629

Fortes, R., & Rigolin, G. (2015). Fighting noise with noise in realistic quantum teleportation. *Physical Review A, 92*(1), 1. doi:10.1103/PhysRevA.92.012338

Fridrich, J. (2003). Quantitative steganalysis of digital images: estimating the secret message length. ACM Multimedia Systems Journal, 9(3), 288-302.

Fridrich, J. (1998). Symmetric Chaos Based on Two-Dimensional Chaotic Maps and Chaos. *International Journal of Bifurcation, 8*(6), 1259–1284. doi:10.1142/S021812749800098X

Fridrich, J., Goljan, M., & Soukal, D. (2005). Perturbed quantization steganography. *ACM Multimedia System Journal, 11*(2), 98–107. doi:10.100700530-005-0194-3

Fridrich, J., & Kodovsky, J. (2013). Multivariate Gaussian model for designing additive distortion for steganography. *Proc. IEEE, ICASSP*, 2949–2953. 10.1109/ICASSP.2013.6638198

Fridrich, J., Pevný, T., & Kodovský, J. (2007). Statistically undetectable JPEG steganography: Dead ends, challenges, and opportunities. *Proceedings of the 9th ACM Multimedia & Security Workshop*, 3–14. 10.1145/1288869.1288872

Frith, D. (2007). Steganography Approaches, Options and Implications. *Network Security, 2007*(8), 4–7. doi:10.1016/S1353-4858(07)70071-5

Gaba, J., & Kumar, M. (2013). Design and analysis of Compress-Encrypt-Stego technique for steganography. *IEEE International Conference in MOOC, Innovation and Technology in Education (MITE)*, 32-36. 10.1109/MITE.2013.6756300

Ganiev, A. A. (2020). The analysis of text steganography methods. *International Scientific Journal of Theoretical & Applied Science*, 85-88.

Garcia-Bosque, M., Sánchez-Azqueta, C., & Celma, S. (2016). Secure communication system based on a logistic map and a linear feedback shift register. *IEEE International Symposium on Circuits and Systems (ISCAS)*, 2016, 1170-1173, 10.1109/ISCAS.2016.7527454

Geabanacloche, J. (2002). Hiding messages in quantum data. *Journal of Mathematical Physics, 43*(9), 4531–4536. doi:10.1063/1.1495073

Gllavata, J., Ewerth, R., & Freisleben, B. (2003, September). A robust algorithm for text detection in images. *ISPA, 2*, 611-616. 10.1109/ISPA.2003.1296349

Gong, L. H., He, X. T., Cheng, S., Hua, T. X., & Zhou, N. R. (2016). Quantum image encryption algorithm based on quantum image XOR operations. *International Journal of Theoretical Physics, 55*(7), 3234–3250. doi:10.100710773-016-2954-6

Gowda, S. N. (2016). An advanced Diffie-Hellman approach to image steganography. *2016 IEEE International Conference on Advanced Networks and Telecommunications Systems (ANTS)*, 1-4. doi: 10.1109/ANTS.2016.7947849

Guan, X. W., Chen, X. B., Wang, L. C., & Yang, Y. X. (2014). Joint remote preparation of an arbitrary two-qubit state in noisy environments. *International Journal of Theoretical Physics, 53*(7), 2236–2245. doi:10.100710773-014-2024-x

Guo, G. C., & Guo, G. P. (2012). Quantum data hiding with spontaneous parameter down-conversion. *Physical Review A, 68*(4), 4343–4349.

Gupta Banik, B. (2020). Novel text steganography using natural language processing and part-of-speech tagging. *Journal of the Institution of Electronics and Telecommunication Engineers*, 12.

Gupta, M.K., & Chandra, P. (2020). A comprehensive survey of data mining. *Int. J. Inf. Tecnol.* doi:10.100741870-020-00427-7

Gupta, S., & Jain, R. 2015, December. An innovative method of Text Steganography. In *2015 Third International Conference on Image Information Processing (ICIIP)* (pp.60-64). IEEE. 10.1109/ICIIP.2015.7414741

Hadipour, A. &. (2020). Advantages and disadvantages of using cryptography in steganography. In *International ISC Conference on Information Security and Cryptology* (pp. 88-94). IEEE.

Hambouz, A., Shaheen, Y., Manna, A., Al-Fayoumi, M., & Tedmori, S. S. (2019). Achieving Data Integrity and Confidentiality Using Image Steganography and Hashing Techniques. *2nd International Conference on new Trends in Computing Sciences (ICTCS)*, 1-6. doi: 109/ICTCS.2019.892306010.1

Han, D., Yang, J., & Summers, W. (2017). Inject Stenography into Cybersecurity Education. *2017 31st International Conference on Advanced Information Networking and Applications Workshops (WAINA).* 10.1109/WAINA.2017.30

Handoko, W. T. (2020). IOP Conf. Ser. *Mater. Sci. Eng., 879.*

Han, J., Ji, X., Hu, X., Zhu, D., Li, K., Jiang, X., Cui, G., Guo, L., & Liu, T. (2013). Representing and retrieving video shots in humancentric brain imaging space. *IEEE Transactions on Image Processing, 22*(7), 2723–2736. doi:10.1109/TIP.2013.2256919 PMID:23568507

Hassoon, N. H., Ali, R. A., Abed, H. N., & Alkhazraji, A. A. J. (2018). Multilevel hiding text security using hybrid technique steganography and cryptography. *IACSIT International Journal of Engineering and Technology, 7*(4), 3674–3677.

Hemalatha, S., Acharya, U. D., & Renuka, A. (2015). Wavelet transform based steganography technique to hide audio signals in image. *Procedia Computer Science, 47*, 272–281. doi:10.1016/j.procs.2015.03.207

Holub, V., Fridrich, J., & Denemark, T. (2014). Universal Distortion Function for Steganography in an Arbitrary Domain. *EURASIP Journal on Information Security, 2014*(1).

Holub, V., & Fridrich, J. (2012). Designing Steganographic Distortion Using Directional Filters. *IEEE Workshop on Information Forensics and Security*, 234-239.

Holub, V., & Fridrich, J. J. (2012). Designing steganographic distortion using directional filters. *Proceedings International Workshop on Information Forensics and Security*, 234–239.

Holub, V., Fridrich, J. J., & Denemark, T. (2014). Universal distortion function for steganography in an arbitrary domain. *EURASIP Journal on Information Security, 2014*(1), 1. doi:10.1186/1687-417X-2014-1

Hong Caoand Alex, C. K. (2013, September). On Establishing Edge Adaptive Grid for Bilevel Image Data Hiding. *IEEE Transactions on Information Forensics and Security, 8*(9).

Hossen, M. S., Islam, M. A., Khatun, T., Hossain, S., & Rahman, M. M. (2020, September). A New Approach to Hiding Data in the Images Using Steganography Techniques Based on AES and RC5 Algorithm Cryptosystem. In *2020 International Conference on Smart Electronics and Communication (ICOSEC)* (pp. 676-681). IEEE. 10.1109/ICOSEC49089.2020.9215442

Huang, C.-T., Tsai, M.-Y., Lin, L.-C., Wang, W.-J., & Wang, S.-J. (2018). VQ-based data hiding in IoT networks using two-level encoding with adaptive pixel replacements. *The Journal of Supercomputing, 74*(9), 4295–4314. doi:10.100711227-016-1874-9

Huang, Y. F., Tang, S., & Yuan, J. (2011, June). Steganography in Inactive Frames of VoIP Streams Encoded by Source Codec. *IEEE Transactions on Information Forensics and Security, 6*(2), 296–306. doi:10.1109/TIFS.2011.2108649

Hussain & Hussain. (2013). *A survey of image steganography techniques.* Academic Press.

Hussain, I. (2020). A Survey on Deep Convolutional Neural Networks for Image Steganography and Steganalysis. *Transactions on Internet and Information Systems (Seoul), 14*(3), 1228–1248. doi:10.3837/tiis.2020.03.017

Hussain, M., Wahab, A. W. A., Idris, Y. I. B., Ho, A. T. S., & Jung, K. (2018). Image steganography in spatial domain: A survey. *Signal Processing Image Communication, 65*, 46–66. doi:10.1016/j.image.2018.03.012

Ian F Akyildiz, W. S., Sankarasubramaniam, Y., & Cayirci, E. (2002). Wireless sensor networks: A survey. *Computer Networks, 38*(4), 393–422. doi:10.1016/S1389-1286(01)00302-4

Jagtap, K., & Manjare, C. (2015). An Ancient Degraded Images Revamping Using Binarization Technique. *International Journal of Soft Computing and Engineering, 4*(6), 10–15.

Jalood, N. S., Jasim, A. N., & Shareef, A. H. (2019). New method of image steganography based on particle swarm optimization algorithm in spatial domain for high embedding capacity. *IEEE Access: Practical Innovations, Open Solutions, 7*, 168994–169010. doi:10.1109/ACCESS.2019.2949622

Jan, A., Parah, S. A., & Malik, B. A. (2020, June). A Novel Laplacian of Gaussian (LoG) and Chaotic Encryption Based Image Steganography Technique. In *2020 International Conference for Emerging Technology (INCET)* (pp. 1-4). IEEE.

Jan, A., Parah, S. A., & Malik, B. A. (2021). Logistic Map-Based Image Steganography Using Edge Detection. In *Innovations in Computational Intelligence and Computer Vision* (pp. 447–454). Springer. doi:10.1007/978-981-15-6067-5_50

Jayapandiyan, J. R., Kavitha, C., & Sakthivel, K. (2020). Enhanced Least Significant Bit Replacement Algorithm in Spatial Domain of Steganography Using Character Sequence Optimization. *IEEE Access: Practical Innovations, Open Solutions, 8*, 136537–136545. doi:10.1109/ACCESS.2020.3009234

Jeevitha, S., & Prabha, N. A. (2020). Effective payload and improved security using HMT Contourlet transform in medical image steganography. *Health and Technology, 10*(1), 217–229. doi:10.100712553-018-00285-1

Johnson & Jajodia. (1998). Exploring steganography: Seeing the unseen. *Computer, 31*(2), 26-34. . doi:10.1109/MC.1998.4655281

Johnson. (1995). *Steganography*. Technical Report.

Johnson, N. F., & Jajodia, S. (1998). Steganalysis of images created using current steganography software. *Proceeding of 2nd International Workshop on Information Hiding, 1525*, 273–289. 10.1007/3-540-49380-8_19

Joseph, C. (2018). *This Custom-Made Jihadi Encryption App Hides Messages in Images.* https://www.vice.com/en/article/ne4x7w/muslim-crypt-jihadi-encryption-app

Joshi, K. (2018). A new approach of text steganography using ASCII values. *International Journal of Engineering Research & Technology, 7*(5).

Joshi, K., & Yadav, R. (2016). New approach toward data hiding using XOR for image steganography. *2016 Ninth International Conference on Contemporary Computing (IC3)*, 1-6. 10.1109/IC3.2016.7880204

Joshi, S. V., Bokil, A. A., Jain, N. A., & Koshti, D. (2012). Image steganography combination of spatial and frequency domain. *International Journal of Computers and Applications, 53*(5).

Jung. (2019). *A Study on ML for Steganalysis.* . doi:10.1145/3310986.3311000

Jung, K., Kim, K. I., & Jain, A. K. (2004). Text information extraction in images and video: A survey. *Pattern Recognition, 37*(5), 977–997. doi:10.1016/j.patcog.2003.10.012

Kadhim, I. J., Premaratne, P., & Vial, P. J. (2020). High-capacity adaptive image steganography with cover region selection using dual-tree complex wavelet transform. *Cognitive Systems Research, 60*, 20–32. doi:10.1016/j.cogsys.2019.11.002

Kadhim, I. J., Premaratne, P., Vial, P. J., & Halloran, B. (2019). Comprehensive survey of image steganography: Techniques, Evaluations, and trends in future research. *Neurocomputing, 335*, 28. doi:10.1016/j.neucom.2018.06.075

Kalaichelvi, T., & Apuroop, P. (2020). Image Steganography Method to Achieve Confidentiality Using CAPTCHA for Authentication. In *2020 5th International Conference on Communication and Electronics Systems (ICCES)* (pp. 495-499). IEEE. 10.1109/ICCES48766.2020.9138073

Kalaichelvi, V., Meenakshi, P., Devi, P. V., Manikandan, H., Venkateswari, P., & Swaminathan, S. (2020). A stable image steganography: A novel approach based on modified RSA algorithm and 2–4 least significant bit (LSB) technique. *Journal of Ambient Intelligence and Humanized Computing*, ●●●, 1–9.

Kalsi, S. K., Kaur, H., & Chang, V. (2018). DNA cryptography and deep learning using genetic algorithm with NW algorithm for key generation. *Journal of Medical Systems*, *42*(1), 17. doi:10.100710916-017-0851-z PMID:29204890

Kalubandi, V. K. P., Vaddi, H., Ramineni, V., & Agilandeeswari Loganathan, A. (2016). A Novel Image Encryption Algorithm using AES and Visual Cryptography. *Proceedings of NGCT 2016*. DOI: 10.1109/NGCT.2016.7877521

Kamaruddin, N. S., Kamsin, A., Por, L. Y., & Rahman, H. (2018). A review of text watermarking: Theory, methods, and applications. *IEEE Access: Practical Innovations, Open Solutions*, *6*, 6. doi:10.1109/ACCESS.2018.2796585

Kamboj, P., & Rani, V. (2013). Image Enhancement Using Hybrid Filtering Techniques. *International Journal of Scientific Research*, *2*(6), 12–18.

Kanafchian, M., & Vajargah, B. F. (2017). A Novel Image Encryption Scheme Based on Clifford Attractor and Noisy Logistic Map for Secure Transferring Images in Navy. *International Journal of e-Navigation and Maritime Economy*, 53-63.

Kargupta, H., Datta, S., Wang, Q., & Sivakumar, K. (2003). On the privacy preserving properties of random data perturbation techniques. In *Data Mining, 2003. ICDM 2003. Third IEEE International Conference* (pp. 99–106). IEEE. 10.1109/ICDM.2003.1250908

Kaur & Behal. (2014). A Survey on various types of Steganography and Analysis of Hiding Techniques. *International Journal of Engineering Trends and Technology*, *11*(8).

Kaur, B., Kaur, B., & Singh, J. J. (2011). Steganographic approach for hiding image in DCT domain. *International Journal of Advances in Engineering and Technology*, *1*, 72–78.

Kaur, M., Kumar, V., & Singh, D. (2020). An efficient image steganography method using multi-objective differential evolution. In *Digital Media Steganography* (pp. 65–79). Academic Press. doi:10.1016/B978-0-12-819438-6.00012-8

Kazi, J. A. R., Kiratkar, G. N., Ghogale, S. S., & Kazi, A. R. (2020). A novel approach to Steganography using pixel-based algorithm in image hiding. *International Conference on Computer Communication and Informatics (ICCCI)*, 1-6. 10.1109/ICCCI48352.2020.9104072

Kekre, West, Khanna, & Hussaini. (2012). *Comparison between the basic LSB Replacement Technique and Increased Capacity of Information Hiding in LSB's Method for Images*. Academic Press.

Kelash, H. M., Abdel Wahab, O. F., Elshakankiry, O. A., & El-sayed, H. S. (2013). Hiding data in video sequences using steganography algorithms. *2013 International Conference on ICT Convergence (ICTC)*, 353-358. 10.1109/ICTC.2013.6675372

Kellert, H. S. (1993). In the Wake of Chaos: Unpredictable Order in Dynamical Systems. University of Chicago.

Ker, A. D. (2005, June). Steganalysis of LSB matching in grayscale images. *IEEE Signal Processing Letters*, *12*(6), 441–444.

Keun, H. P., & Hyun, W. P. (2002). Region-of-Interest Coding Based on Set Partitioning in Hierarchical Trees. *IEEE Transactions on Circuits and Systems for Video Technology*, *12*(2), 106–113. doi:10.1109/76.988657

Khairullah, M. (2019). A novel steganography method using transliteration of Bengali text. *Journal of King Saud University-Computer and Information Sciences*, 348-366.

Khosravi, B. K. (2019). A new method for pdf steganography in justified texts. Journal of Information Security and Applications, 61-70.

Khosravi, S., Dezfoli, M. A., & Yektaie, M. H. (2011). A new steganography method based HIOP (Higher Intensity of Pixel) algorithm and Strassen's matrix multiplication. *Journal of Global Research in Computer Science*, *2*(1).

Kim, K. I., Jung, K., & Kim, J. H. (2003). Texture-based approach for text detection in images using support vector machines and continuously adaptive mean shift algorithm. *IEEE Transactions on Pattern Analysis and Machine Intelligence, 25*(12), 1631–1639. doi:10.1109/TPAMI.2003.1251157

Kocarev, L. (2001). Chaos-based cryptography: a brief overview. *IEEE Circuits and Systems Magazine, 1*(3), 6–21. doi:10.1109/7384.963463

Koren, I., & Mani Krishna, C. (2010). *Fault-tolerant systems*. Morgan Kaufmann.

Kothari, L., Thakkar, R., & Khara, S. (2017). Data hiding on web using combination of Steganography and Cryptography. *International Conference on Computer, Communications and Electronics (Comptelix)*, 448-452. 10.1109/COMPTELIX.2017.8004011

Krenn. (2004). *Steganography and steganalysis*. Internet Publication.

Krishnan, R. B. (2017). An overview of text steganography. In *International Conference on Signal Processing, Communication and Networking* (pp. 1-6). IEEE.

Kui, X. S., & Wu, J. (2018). A Modification Free Steganography Method Based on Image Information Entropy. *Security and Communication Networks*, 1–8. doi:10.1155/2018/6256872

Kukharska, N., Lagun, A., & Polotai, O. (2020, August). The Steganographic Approach to Data Protection Using Arnold Algorithm and the Pixel-Value Differencing Method. In *2020 IEEE Third International Conference on Data Stream Mining & Processing (DSMP)* (pp. 174-177). IEEE. 10.1109/DSMP47368.2020.9204108

Kumar, A., & Sharma, R. (2013). International Journal of Advanced Research in A Secure Image Steganography Based on RSA Algorithm and Hash-LSB Technique. *International Journal of Advanced Research in Computer Science and Software Engineering, 3*(7), 363–372.

Kumar, R. (2020). *Recent Trends in Text Steganography with Experimental Study*. Springer. doi:10.1007/978-3-030-22277-2_34

Kumar, S., Singh, A., & Kumar, M. (2019). *Information Hiding with Adaptive Steganography based on Novel Fuzzy Edge Identification*. Defence Technology.

Kustov, V. N., & Protsko, D. K. (2017). A Software model of steganography on the basis of a combination of methods LSB and DCT. In *Science and education in the XXI century. Collection of scientific papers on the materials of the XVIII international scientific-practical conference*, (part 3, pp. 49-54). Tambov, LLC "Ucom Consulting Company". https://ukonf.com/doc/cn.2017.02.03.pdf

Kustov, V. N., & Protsko, D. K. (2018). Using a discrete wavelet transform to embed information in images. In *Science and education in the XXI century Collection of scientific papers based on the materials of the XVII international scientific conference* (pp. 15-20). Center for Scientific Conferences "International Research Federation Public science". https://www.elibrary.ru/item.asp?id=35398976

Kustov, V., & Krasnov, A. (2020). *Software model of a highly undetectable stegosystem - ⊕HUGO model. Journal of Physics: Conference Series*.

Kustov, V., & Silanteva, E. (2020).'±1Highly Undetectable Stegosystem Model Using Digital Still Images. *Proceeding of 43rd International Conference on Telecommunications and Signal Processing (TSP)*, 6-9. 10.1109/TSP49548.2020.9163587

Laishram, D., & Tuithung, T. (2020). A novel minimal distortion-based edge adaptive image steganography scheme using local complexity. *Multimedia Tools and Applications*, 1–24. doi:10.100711042-020-09519-9

Lanza-Cruz, I., Berlanga, R., & Aramburu, M. J. (2018). Modelling Analytical Streams for Social Business Intelligence. *Informatica (Vilnius)*, *5*, 33.

Lerch-Hostalot, D., & Megías, D. (2016, April). Unsupervised Steganalysis Based on Artificial Training Sets. *Engineering Applications of Artificial Intelligence*, *50*(C), 45–59. doi:10.1016/j.engappai.2015.12.013

Li, S., Da Xu, L., & Zhao, S. (2015). The internet of things: a survey. *Information Systems Frontiers*, *17*(2), 243-59.

Li, W., Zhang, W., Chen, K., Zhou, W., & Yu, N. (2018). Defining Joint Distortion for JPEG Steganography. *Proceedings of the 6th ACM Workshop on Information Hiding and Multimedia Security, IH&MMSec'2018*, 5–16. 10.1145/3206004.3206008

Li, Wang, Li, Tan, & Huang. (2015). A Strategy of Clustering Modification Directions in Spatial Image Steganography. *IEEE Transaction on Information Forensics and Security*, *10*(9), 1905–1917. doi:10.1109/ICIP.2014.7025854

Liao, X., Yin, J., Guo, S., Li, X., & Sangaiah, A. K. (2018). Medical JPEGimage steganography based on preserving inter-block dependencies. *Computers & Electrical Engineering*, *67*, 320–329. doi:10.1016/j.compeleceng.2017.08.020

Li, B., Wang, M., Huang, J., & Li, X. 2014. A New Cost Function for Spatial Image Steganography. *Proceedings of IEEE International Conference on Image Processing, ICIP'2014*, 4206–421.

Li, B., Wei, W., Ferreira, A., & Tan, S. (2018, May). ReST-Net: Diverse Activation Modules and Parallel Subnets-Based CNN for Spatial Image Steganalysis. *IEEE Signal Processing Letters*, *25*(5), 650–654. doi:10.1109/LSP.2018.2816569

Li, L., Hossain, M. S., Abd El-Latif, A. A., & Alhamid, M. F. (2019). Distortion less secret image sharing scheme for Internet of Things system. *Cluster Computing*, *22*(1), 2293–2307. doi:10.100710586-017-1345-y

Li, M., Kulhandjian, M. K., Pados, D. A., Batalama, S. N., & Medley, M. J. (2013, July). Extracting Spread-Spectrum Hidden Data From Digital Media. *IEEE Transactions on Information Forensics and Security*, *8*(7).

Lin, E., & Delp, E. (1999). A Review of Data Hiding in Digital Images. *Proceedings of the Image Processing, Image Quality, Image Capture Systems Conference (PICS'99)*.

Lingyun Xiang, S. Y. (2020). Novel linguistic steganography based on character-level text generation. *Mathematics*, 18.

Liu, Kargupta, & Ryan. (2006). Random projection based multiplicative data perturbation for privacy preserving distributed data mining. *Knowledge and Data Engineering, IEEE Transactions on*, *18*(1), 92–106.

Liu, Zoph, Neumann, Shlens, Hua, Li, Li, Yuille, Huang, & Murphy. (2018). Progressive Neural Architecture Search. In *Proceedings of the European Conference on Computer Vision, ECCV'2018: Vol. 11205. Lecture Notes in Computer Science*. Springer. 10.1007/978-3-030-01246-5_2

Liu, J. C., Chen, W., & Wen, Y. (2018). A Robust and Flexible Covert Channel in LTE-A System. *Journal of Physics: Conference Series*, *1087*, 6. doi:10.1088/1742-6596/1087/6/062027

Liu, Y., Yang, T., & Xin, G. (2015). Text steganography in chat based on emoticons and interjections. *Journal of Computational and Theoretical Nanoscience*, *12*(9), 2091–2094. doi:10.1166/jctn.2015.3992

Li, X., Kong, X., Wang, B., Guo, Y., & You, X. (2013). Generalized Transfer Component Analysis for Mismatched JPEG Steganalysis. *Proceedings of IEEE International Conference on Image Processing, ICIP'2013*, 4432–4436. 10.1109/ICIP.2013.6738913

Lockwood, R. (2017). Text based steganography. *International Journal of Information Privacy. Security and Integrity*, *3*(2), 134–153.

Lorenz, E. N. (1993). *The Essence of Chaos*. University of Washington Press.

Lu, J.-a., Deng, X., Xie, J., & Chang, L. (2004). Secure Communication Based on Synchronization of a Unified Chaotic System. In *Fifth World Congress on Intelligent Control and Automation*. IEEE.

Lubenko & Ker. (2012). Steganalysis with Mismatched Covers: Do Simple Classifiers Help? *Proceedings of the 14th ACM Multimedia and Security Workshop, MM&Sec'2008, MM&Sec'2012*, 11–18.

Lubenko, I., & Ker, A. D. (2012). Going From Small to Large Data in Steganalysis. *Proceedings of Media Watermarking, Security, and Forensics III, Part of IS&T/SPIE 22th Annual Symposium on Electronic Imaging, SPIE'2012, 8303.* 10.1117/12.910214

Lu, W., Zhang, J., Zhao, X., Zhang, W., & Huang, J. (2020). Secure Robust JPEG Steganography based on AutoEncoder with Adaptive BCH Encoding. *IEEE Transactions on Circuits and Systems for Video Technology*, 1. doi:10.1109/TCSVT.2020.3027843

Lu, Z.-M., & Guo, S.-Z. (2017). *Lossless Information Hiding in Block Truncation Coding–Compressed Images*. Lossless Information Hiding in Images.

Machanavajjhala, Kifer, Gehrke, & Venkitasubramaniam. (2007). Privacy beyond k-anonymity. *ACM Transactions on Knowledge Discovery from Data, 1*(1), 3. doi:10.1145/1217299.1217302

Madhavi, K. K. (2018). A Robust and Efficient Steganography Using Skin Tone as Biometric for Real Time Images. *International Research Journal of Engineering and Technology*, 4.

Mahato, S. K., Khan, D. A., & Yadav, D. K. (2020). A modified approach to data hiding in Microsoft Word documents by change-tracking technique. *Journal of King Saud University-Computer and Information Sciences, 32*(2), 216–224. doi:10.1016/j.jksuci.2017.08.004

Mahato, S., Khan, D. A., & Yadav, D. K. (2020). A Modified Approach to Data Hiding in Microsoft Word Documents by Change-Tracking Technique. *Journal of King Saud University-Computer and Information Sciences, 32*(2), 216–224.

Maheswari, S. U., & Hemanth, D. J. (2017). Performance enhanced image steganography systems using transforms and optimization techniques. *Multimedia Tools and Applications, 76*(1), 415–436. doi:10.100711042-015-3035-1

Majumder, A. C. (2020). A New Text Steganography Method Based on Sudoku Puzzle Generation. In *Proceedings of ICETIT* (pp. 961-972). Cham: Springer. 10.1007/978-3-030-30577-2_85

Malik, A., Sikka, G., & Verma, H. K. (2017). A high capacity text steganography scheme based on LZW compression and color coding. *Engineering Science and Technology, an International Journal, 20*(1), 72-79.

Malik, S., & Sardana, A., & Jaya. (2012). A Keyless Approach to Image Encryption. *2012 International Conference on Communication Systems and Network Technologies*, 879-883. 10.1109/CSNT.2012.189

Mallat. (2016). Understanding Deep Convolutional Networks. *Philosophical Transactions of the Royal Society. Series A, Mathematical, Physical, and Engineering Sciences, 374.*

Mandal, K. K. (2020). Applying Encryption Algorithm on Text Steganography Based on Number System. In Computational Advancement in Communication Circuits and Systems (pp. 255-266). Springer.

Mandal, K. K. (2014, March). A new approach of text Steganography based on mathematical model of number system. *International Conference on Circuits, Power and Computing Technologies [ICCPCT-2014]*, 1737-1741. 10.1109/ICCPCT.2014.7054849

Manne, R., Kantheti, S., & Kantheti, S. (2020). Classification of Skin cancer using deep learning, ConvolutionalNeural Networks - Opportunities and vulnerabilities- A systematic Review. *International Journal for Modern Trends in Science and Technology, 6*(11), 101-108. doi:10.46501/IJMTST061118

Mansor, F. Z. (2018). An Antonym Substitution-based Model on Linguistic Steganography Method. *Indonesian Journal of Electrical Engineering and Computer Science, 12*.

Mansour, R. F., & Abdelrahim, E. M. (2019). An evolutionary computing enriched RS attack resilient medical image steganography model for telemedicine applications. *Multidimensional Systems and Signal Processing, 30*(2), 791–814. doi:10.100711045-018-0575-3

Marc, A., & Michel, B. (1992). Image coding using wavelet transform. *IEEE Transactions on Image Processing, 1*(2), 205–220. doi:10.1109/83.136597 PMID:18296155

Martin, K. (2007). Steganographic communication with quantum information. *International Conference on Information Hiding, 4567*(1), 32-49. 10.1007/978-3-540-77370-2_3

Marvel, L. M. (1999). Spread Spectrum Image Steganography. IEEE Transactions on Image Processing, 8(8), 1075 – 1083. doi:10.1109/83.777088

Ma, S. Y., Gao, C., Zhang, P., & Qu, Z. G. (2017). Deterministic remote preparation via the brown state. *Quantum Information Processing, 16*(4), 93. doi:10.100711128-017-1542-x

Massey, J. (1969). Shift-register synthesis and BCH decoding. *IEEE Transactions on Information Theory, IT-15*(1), 122–127. doi:10.1109/TIT.1969.1054260

Mathivanan, P. (2021). QR code based color image stego-crypto technique using dynamic bit replacement and logistic map. *Optik (Stuttgart), 225*, 165838. doi:10.1016/j.ijleo.2020.165838

Mazumder, J. A., & Hemachandra, K. (2019). Image Steganography Using the Fusion of Quantum Computation and Wavelet Transformation. *2019 3rd International Conference on Computing Methodologies and Communication (IC-CMC)*, 226-232. 10.1109/ICCMC.2019.8819681

Mehdi & Mureed. (2013). A Survey of Image Steganography Techniques. *International Journal of Advanced Science and Technology, 54*.

Meng, R., Rice, S. G., Wang, J., & Sun, X. (2018). A fusion steganographic algorithm based on faster R-CNN. *Computers, Materials & Continua, 55*(1), 1–16.

Meng, Ruohan & Cui, et al. (2018). A Survey of Image Information Hiding Algorithms Based on DL. *Computer Replicaing in Engineering & Sciences., 117*, 425–454.

Menon, N., & Vaithiyanathan. (2017). A survey on image steganography. *2017 International Conference on Technological Advancements in Power and Energy (TAP Energy)*. doi:10.1109/TAPENERGY.2017.8397274

Messey, J. (1963). *Threshold decoding* (Dissertation). Dept. of Electrical Engineering, Massachusetts Institute of Technology, Technical report. http://dspace.mit.edu/handle/1721.1/4415

Mihara, T. (2012). Quantum steganography embedded any secret text without changing the content of cover data. *Journal of Quantum Information Science, 2*(1), 10–14. doi:10.4236/jqis.2012.21003

Mihara, T. (2015). Quantum steganography using prior entanglement. *Physics Letters. [Part A], 379*(12-13), 952–955. doi:10.1016/j.physleta.2015.01.038

Mishra, Mishra, & Adhikary. (2014). *Digital Image Data Hiding Techniques: A Comparative Study*. Academic Press.

Mishra, A. (2013). Enhancing security of caesar cipher using different methods. *International Journal of Research in Engineering and Technology, 2*(09), 327–332. doi:10.15623/ijret.2013.0209049

Montalbo, F. J. P., & Barfeh, D. P. Y. (2019, December). Classification of Stenography using Convolutional Neural Networks and Canny Edge Detection Algorithm. In *2019 International Conference on Computational Intelligence and Knowledge Economy (ICCIKE)* (pp. 305-310). IEEE. 10.1109/ICCIKE47802.2019.9004359

Morkel, T., Eloff, J. H. P., & Olivier, M. S. (2005). *An overview of image steganography.* Proceedings Information Security for South Africa.

Mosrati, Karimi, & Hariri. (2011). An introduction to steganography methods. *World Applied Programming, 1*(3), 191–195.

Mstafa, R. J., Elleithy, K. M., & Abdelfattah, E. (2017). Video steganography techniques: Taxonomy, challenges, and future directions. *2017 IEEE Long Island Systems, Applications and Technology Conference (LISAT)*, 1-6. 10.1109/LISAT.2017.8001965

Muhammad, K., Ahmad, J., Sajjad, M., & Zubair, M. (2015). *Secure image steganography using cryptography and image transposition.* arXiv preprint arXiv:1510.04413.

Mukherjee, M. (2014). Fibonacci Based Text Hiding Using Image Cryptography. Lecture Notes on Information Theory, 2(2).

Mukherjee, N., Paul, G., Saha, S. K., & Burman, D. (2020). A PVD based high capacity steganography algorithm with embedding in non-sequential position. *Multimedia Tools and Applications, 79*(19), 13449–13479.

Mukherjee, S., Roy, S., & Sanyal, G. (2018). Image Steganography using Mid Position Value Technique. *Procedia Computer Science, 132*, 461–468. doi:10.1016/j.procs.2018.05.160

Mumthas, S., & Lijiya, A. (2017). Transform domain video steganography using RSA, random DNA encryption and Huffman encoding. *7th International Conference on Advances in Computing and Communications ICACC-2017*, 115, 660–666.

Mustafa, ElGamal, ElAlmi, & Ahmed. (2011). *A Proposed Algorithm For Steganography in Digital Image Based on Least Significant Bit.* Academic Press.

Muttoo & Kumar. (2011). A multilayered secure, robust and high capacity image steganographic algorithm. *World of Computer Science and Information Technology Journal, 1*(6), 239–246.

Nag, A. (2019). Low-tech steganography for covert operations. *IJCNIS, 2*(1), 21–27.

Naqvi, N. A. (2018). *Multilayer partially homomorphic encryption text steganography (MLPHE-TS): a zero steganography approach.* Springer.

Nasereddin, H. H. (2016). Enhancing Open Space Method in Data Hiding. *International Journal of Computers and Applications*, 5–17.

Nechta, I. (2017). Steganography in social networks. *Siberian Symposium on Data Science and Engineering*, 33-35. 10.1109/SSDSE.2017.8071959

Nedal, Kafri, & Suleiman. (2009). Bit-4 of Frequency Domain DCT Steganography Technique. *IEEE Proc. 1st Int. conf. on Networked Digital Technologies*, 286-291.

Neogi, P. P. G., Goswami, S., & Mustafi, J. (2020). Intelligent Water Drops Based Image Steganography. In *Proceedings of the Global AI Congress 2019* (pp. 363-375). Springer. 10.1007/978-981-15-2188-1_29

Newman. (2018). *Mysterious 'MuslimCrypt' App Helps Jihadists Send Covert Messages.* https://www.wired.com/story/muslimcrypt-steganography/

Nie, Q., Xu, X., Feng, B., & Zhang, L. Y. (2018). Defining embedding distortion for intra prediction mode-based video steganography. *Computers, Materials & Continua, 55*(1), 59–70.

Nisha, C. D., & Monoth, T. (2020). Analysis of Spatial Domain Image Steganography Based on Pixel-Value Differencing Method. In *Soft Computing for Problem Solving* (pp. 385–397). Springer. doi:10.1007/978-981-15-0184-5_34

Nolkha, A., Kumar, S., & Dhaka, V. S. (2020). Image Steganography Using LSB Substitution: A Comparative Analysis on Different Color Models. In *Smart Systems and IoT: Innovations in Computing* (pp. 711–718). Springer. doi:10.1007/978-981-13-8406-6_67

Noll, P. (1993). Wideband speech and audio coding. *IEEE Communications Magazine, 31*(11), 34–44.

Oakley, J. (2018). Improving hostile digital protection appraisals utilizing shifted and novel instatement viewpoints. *Proceedings of the ACMSE 2018 Conference on - ACMSE '18.* 10.1145/3190645.3190673

Ogie, R. I. (2017). Cyber Security Incidents on Critical Infrastructure and Industrial Networks. *Proceedings of the 9th International Conference on Computer and Automation Engineering - ICCAE '17.* 10.1145/3057039.3057076

Ohyama, Niimi, Yamawaki, & Noda. (2009). Lossless data hiding using bit depth embedding for JPEG2000 compressed bit-stream. *Journal of Communication and Computer, 6*(2).

Ozcan, S., & Mustacoglu, A. (2018). Transfer Knowledge Effects on Image Steganalysis with Pre-Trained Deep Residual Neural Network Replica. doi:10.1109/BigData.2018.8622437

Ozighor, E. R., & Izegbu, I. (2020). Information Protection against Security Threats in an Insecure Environment using Cryptography and Steganography. *Computing in Science & Engineering, 8*(5), 1671–1692.

Padmavathi, B., & Kumari, R. (2013). A Survey on Performance Analysis of DES, AES and RSA Algorithm alongwith LSB Substitution Technique. *International Journal of Scientific Research, 2*(4), 170–174.

Pandey, D., & Pandey, B. K. (2020). Analysis of Text Detection,Extraction and Recognition from Complex Degraded Images and Videos. *Journal of Critical Reviews, 7*(18), 427–433.

Pandey, D., Pandey, B. K., & Pandey, S. (2011). Survey of Bioinformatics Applications on Parallel Architectures. *International Journal of Computers and Applications, 23*(4), 21–25. doi:10.5120/2877-3744

Pandey, D., Pandey, B. K., & Wairya, S. (2020). Hybrid deep neural network with adaptive galactic swarm optimization for text extraction from scene images. *Soft Computing.* Advance online publication. doi:10.100700500-020-05245-4

Pandey, D., Pandey, B. K., & Wariya, S. (2019). Study of Various Techniques Used for Video Retrieval. *Journal of Emerging Technologies and Innovative Research, 6*(6), 850–853.

Pandey, D., Pandey, B. K., & Wariya, S. (2019). Study of Various Types Noise and Text Extraction Algorithms for Degraded Complex Image. *Journal of Emerging Technologies and Innovative Research, 6*(6), 234–247.

Pandey, D., Pandey, B. K., & Wariya, S. (2020). An Approach To Text Extraction From Complex Degraded Scene. *IJCBS, 1*(2), 4–10.

Pandey, J., Joshi, K., Sain, M., Singh, G., & Jangra, M. (2021). Steganographic Method Based on Interpolation and Cyclic LSB Substitution of Digital Images. In *Advances in Communication and Computational Technology* (pp. 731–744). Springer. doi:10.1007/978-981-15-5341-7_55

Panwar, K., Purwar, R. K., & Jain, A. (2019, September). Design of a SHA-2 Hash Based Image Encryption Scheme using 1D chaotic systems and DNA sequences. In *2019 International Conference on Computing, Power and Communication Technologies (GUCON)* (pp. 769-773). IEEE.

Panwar, S., Damani, S., & Kumar, M. (2018). Digital Image Steganography using Modified LSB and AES Cryptography. *International Journal of Recent Engineering Research and Development, 3*(6), 18–27.

Pareek, N. K., Patidar, V., & Sud, K. K. (2006). Image Encryption using ChaoticLogisticMap. *Image and Vision Computing, 24*(9), 926–934. doi:10.1016/j.imavis.2006.02.021

Park, Sahng, Delp, & Yu. (2004). Adaptive lossless video compression using an integer wavelet transform. *IEEE International Conference on Image Processing,* 2251-2254.

Patani, K., & Rathod, D. (2020). Advanced 3-Bit LSB Based on Data Hiding Using Steganography. In *Data Science and Intelligent Applications* (pp. 383–390). Springer.

Patani, K., & Rathod, D. (2021). Advanced 3-Bit LSB Based on Data Hiding Using Steganography. In K. Kotecha, V. Piuri, H. Shah, & R. Patel (Eds.), *Data Science and Intelligent Applications. Lecture Notes on Data Engineering and Communications Technologies.* Springer. doi:10.1007/978-981-15-4474-3_42

Patil, A. S., Patil, R. M., & Shinde, M. M. (2020). DWT Based Mosaic Image Steganography. In *Techno-Societal 2018* (pp. 95–107). Springer. doi:10.1007/978-3-030-16848-3_10

Pevný, T., Filler, T., & Bas, P. (2010). Using high-dimensional image models to perform highly undetectable Steganography. In Information Hiding. New York: Springer.

Pevny, T., Filler, T., & Bas, P. (2010). Using high-dimensional image models to perform highly undetectable steganography. *LNCS, 6387,* 161–177.

Pibre, L., Pasquet, J., Ienco, D., & Chaumont, M. (2016). *Deep learning is a good steganalysis tool when embedding key is reused for different images, even if there is a cover source mismatch. In Proceedings Media Watermarking, Security, and Forensics.* Ingenta.

Pradeep, A., Mridula, S., & Mohanan, P. (2016). High security identity tags using spiral resonators. *Computers, Materials & Continua, 52*(3), 185–195.

Pradhan, A., Sekhar, K. R., & Swain, G. (2018). Digital Image Steganography Using LSB Substitution, PVD and EMD. *Mathematical Problems in Engineering.* Advance online publication. doi:10.1155/2018/1804953

Pradhan, A., Sekhar, K. R., & Swain, G. (2020). Image steganography using add-sub based QVD and side match. In *Digital Media Steganography* (pp. 81–97). Academic Press. doi:10.1016/B978-0-12-819438-6.00013-X

Pramanik, S., Bandyopadhyay, S. K., & Ghosh, R. (2020). Signature Image Hiding in Color Image using Steganography and Cryptography based on Digital Signature Concepts. *2020 2nd International Conference on Innovative Mechanisms for Industry Applications (ICIMIA),* 665-669.

Pramanik, S., Bandyopadhyay, S. K., & Ghosh, R. (2020, March). Signature Image Hiding in Color Image using Steganography and Cryptography based on Digital Signature Concepts. In *2020 2nd International Conference on Innovative Mechanisms for Industry Applications (ICIMIA)* (pp. 665-669). IEEE.

Pramanik, S., Singh, R.P., & Ghosh, R. (2019). A New Encrypted Method in Image Steganography. *Indonesian Journal of Electrical Engineering and Computer Science, 14*(3), 1412–1419. .v13.i3.pp1412-1419 doi:10.11591/ijeecs

Pramanik, S., Bandyopadhayay, S. K., & Ghosh, R. (2020). Signature Image Hiding in Color Image using Steganography and Cryptography based on Digital Signature Concepts. *IEEE International Conference on Innovative Mechanisms for Industry Applications (ICIMIA)*, 665-669.

Pramanik, S., & Bandyopadhyay, S. (2013). Application of Steganography in Symmetric Key Cryptography with Genetic Algorithm. *International Journal of Computers and Technology, 10*(7).

Pramanik, S., & Bandyopadhyay, S. K. (2013). Application of Steganography in Symmetric Key Cryptography with Genetic Algorithm. *International Journals of Engineering and Technology, 10*, 1791–1799.

Pramanik, S., & Bandyopadhyay, S. K. (2014). An Innovative Approach in Steganography, Scholars. *Journal of Engineering Technology, 2*(2B), 276–280.

Pramanik, S., & Bandyopadhyay, S. K. (2014). Hiding Secret Message in an Image, International Journal of Innovative Science. *Engineering & Technology, 1*(3), 553–559.

Pramanik, S., & Bandyopadhyay, S. K. (2014). Hiding Secret Message in an Image, International Journal of Innovative Science. *Engineering and Technology, 1*(3), 553–559.

Pramanik, S., & Bandyopadhyay, S. K. (2014). Hiding Secret Message in an Image. *International Journal of Innovative Science, Engineering & Technology, 1*(3), 553–559.

Pramanik, S., & Singh, R. P. (2017). Role of Steganography in Security Issues. *International Journal of Advance Research in Science and Engineering, 6*(1), 1119–1124.

Pramanik, S., & Singh, R. P. (2017). *Role of Steganography in Security Issues. International Journal on Advance Studies in Engineering and Science.*

Pramanik, S., Singh, R. P., & Ghosh, R. (2020). *Application of bi-orthogonal wavelet transform and genetic algorithm in image steganography. Multimed Tools Appl.* doi:10.100711042-020-08676-1

Pramanik, S., Singh, R. P., Ghosh, R., & Bandyopadhyay, S. K. (2020). A Unique Way to Generate Password at Random Basis and Sending it Using a New Steganography Technique. *Indonesian Journal of Electrical Engineering and Informatics, 8*(3), 525–531.

Putu, A., Gusti, M., & Ni, M. (2017). A MP4 video steganography using least significant bit (LSB) substitution and advanced encryption standard (AES). *J. Theor. Appl. Inform. Technol., 95*, 5805–5814.

Qian, Y., Dong, J., Wang, W., & Tan, T. (2015). Deep learning for steganalysis via convolutional neural networks. *SPIE Proceedings, 9409.*

Qin, J., Wang, J., Tan, Y., Huang, H., Xiang, X., & He, Z. (2020). Coverless Image Steganography Based on Generative Adversarial Network. *Mathematics, 8*(9), 1394. doi:10.3390/math8091394

Qu, Z., Cheng, Z., Luo, M., & Liu, W. (2017). A robust quantum watermark algorithm based on quantum log-polar images. *International Journal of Theoretical Physics, 56*(11), 3460–3476. doi:10.100710773-017-3512-6

Qu, Z., Cheng, Z., & Wang, X. (2019). Matrix Coding-Based Quantum Image Steganography Algorithm. *IEEE Access: Practical Innovations, Open Solutions, 7*, 35684–35698. doi:10.1109/ACCESS.2019.2894295

Qu, Z., Chen, S., & Ji, S. (2017). A novel quantum video steganography protocol with large payload based on MCQI quantum video. *International Journal of Theoretical Physics, 56*(2), 1–19. doi:10.100710773-017-3519-z

Qu, Z., Chen, S., Ji, S., Ma, S., & Wang, X. (2018). Anti-noise bidirectional quantum steganography protocol with large payload. *International Journal of Theoretical Physics, 1*(2), 1–25. doi:10.100710773-018-3716-4

Qu, Z., Li, Z., Xu, G., Wu, S., & Wang, X. (2019). Quantum Image Steganography Protocol Based on Quantum Image Expansion and Grover Search Algorithm. *IEEE Access: Practical Innovations, Open Solutions, 7*, 50849–50857. doi:10.1109/ACCESS.2019.2909906

Raghavendra, C. S., Sivasubramanian, S., & Kumaravel, A. (2019). Improved image compression using effective lossless compression technique. *Cluster Computing, 22*(S2), 6. doi:10.100710586-018-2508-1

Rahmani, M. K. I., Arora, K., & Pal, N. (2014). A crypto-steganography: A survey. *International Journal of Advanced Computer Science and Applications, 5*, 149–154.

Raid, A., Khedr, W., El-Dosuky, M., & Ahmed, W. (2014). Jpeg Image Compression Using Discrete Cosine Transform - A Survey. *International Journal of Computer Science & Engineering Survey, 5*. Advance online publication. doi:10.5121/ijcses.2014.5204

Ramalingam, M., Isa, N. A. M., & Puviarasi, R. (2020). A Secured Data Hiding using Affline Transformation in Video Steganography. *Procedia Computer Science, 171*, 1147–1156. doi:10.1016/j.procs.2020.04.123

Rashid, A., & Rahim, M. K. (2016). Critical Analysis of Steganography "An Art of Hidden Writing". *International Journal of Security and Applications, 10*(1), 259–282. doi:10.14257//ijsia.2016.10.3.24

Rashid, M. R.-H. (2014). Combining SPF and source routing for an efficient probing solution in IPv6 topology discovery. In *Global Information Infrastructure and Networking Symposium*. IEEE.

Rashmi, N., & Jyothi, K. (2018). An improved method for reversible data hiding steganography combined with cryptography. *IEEE 2nd International Conference on Inventive Systems and Control (ICISC)*, 81-84. 10.1109/ICISC.2018.8398946

Rather, M., & Sengupta, A. (2020). IP Core steganography using switch-based key-driven hash-chaining and encoding for securing DSP kernels used in CE systems. *IEEE Transactions on Consumer Electronics, 66*(3), 251–260. doi:10.1109/TCE.2020.3006050

Reshma, V. K., Kumar, R. V., Shahi, D., & Shyjith, M. B. (2020). Optimized support vector neural network and contourlet transform for image steganography. *Evolutionary Intelligence*, 1–17. doi:10.100712065-020-00387-8

Restrepo, A., & Bovik, A. (1988). Adaptive trimmed mean filters for image restoration. Acoustics. *IEEE Transactions on Speech and Signal Processing, 36*(8), 1326–1337. doi:10.1109/29.1660

Rezagholipour, K., & Eshghi, M. (2016). Video steganography algorithm based on motion vector of moving object. *IEEE Eighth International Conference on Information and Knowledge Technology (IKT)*. doi: 10.1109/IKT.2016.7777764

Ritala, P., Schneider, S., & Michailova, S. (2020). Innovation management research methods: embracing rigor and diversity. *R&D Management*. doi:10.1111/radm.12414

Rojatkar. (2015). Image Compression Techniques: Lossy and Lossless. *International Journal of Engineering Research and General Science, 3*(2).

Rustom, N. A. H., & Farah, N. A. A. (2017). A Review in Using Steganography Applications in Hiding Text Inside Digital Image (BMP). *International Journal (Toronto, Ont.), 7*(1).

Sah, H. R., & Gunasekaran, G. (2015). Privacy preserving data mining using visual steganography and encryption. *10th International Conference on Computer Science & Education (ICCSE)*, 154-158. doi: 10.1109/ICCSE.2015.7250234

Sahu & Mitra. (2015). A secure data hiding technique using video steganography. *Int. J. Comput. Sci. Commun. Netw.*, 348–357.

Sahu, A. K., & Swain, G. (2020). Reversible image steganography using dual layer LSB matching. *Sensing and Imaging*, *21*(1), 1. doi:10.100711220-019-0262-y

Saleema, A., & Amarunnishad, T. (2016). A new steganography algorithm using hybrid fuzzy neural networks. International Conference on Emerging Trends in Engineering, Science and Technology (ICETEST-2015), 24, 1566–1574.

Salomon, M., Couturier, R., Guyeux, C., Couchot, J.-F., & Bahi, J. (2017). Steganalysis via a convolutional neural network using large convolution filters for embedding process with same stego key: A deep learning approach for telemedicine. *European Research in Telemedicine*, *6*(2), 79–92. doi:10.1016/j.eurtel.2017.06.001

Samanta, M. M. (2014). Fibonacci Based Text Hiding Using Image Cryptography. *Lecture Notes on Information Theory*, *2*(2), 172–176. doi:10.12720/lnit.2.2.172-176

Samanta, S. (2020). A Significant Survey on Text Steganalysis Techniques. *International Journal on Computer Science and Engineering*, 187–193.

Sam, I. S., Devaraj, P., & Bhuvaneswaran, R. (2012). An intertwining chaotic maps based image encryption scheme. *Nonlinear Dynamics*, *69*(4), 1995–2007. doi:10.100711071-012-0402-6

Sauvola, J., & Pietikäinen, M. (2000). Adaptive document image binarization. *Pattern Recognition*, *33*(2), 225–236. doi:10.1016/S0031-3203(99)00055-2

Saxena, D. (2011). Digital Watermarking Algorithm based on Singular Value Decomposition and Arnold Transform. *International Journal of Electronics and Computer Science Engineering*, *1*(1), 22–27.

Sedeeq, I. C. (2017). A prediction model based approach to open space steganography detection in HTML webpages. *International Workshop on Digital Watermarking*, 235-247. 10.1007/978-3-319-64185-0_18

Sedighi, V., Fridrich, J., & Cogranne, R. (2015). Content-Adaptive Pentary Steganography Using the Multivariate Generalized Gaussian Cover Model. *Proc. SPIE, Electronic Imaging, Media Watermarking, Security, and Forensics 2015*, 9409, 13.

Segal, Y., Hadar, O., Birman, R., & Hadas, E. (2017). Defence from Covert Channel Cyber-attack over video stream payload. *Proceedings RESCUE 2017 – Workshop on Reliability, Security and Quality*. https://www.academia.edu/download/53973023/Cyber_abstract_v-3.7.pdf

Sethi, P., & Kapoor, V. (2016). A proposed novel architecture for information hiding in image steganography by using geneticalgorithm and cryptography. *Int. Conf. Comput. Sci.*, 87, 61–66.

Setyono, A., & Setiadi, D. R. I. M. (2019). Article. *Journal of Physics: Conference Series*, *1196*, 012039.

Sfar, A. R., Natalizio, E., Challal, Y., & Chtourou, Z. (2018, April 1). A roadmap for security challenges in the Internet of Things. *Digital Communications and Networks.*, *4*(2), 118–137. doi:10.1016/j.dcan.2017.04.003

Shah, V., & Kumbharana, C. K. Design, Development, and Implementation of an Image Steganography Algorithm for Encrypted (Using AES) and Non encrypted Text into an Image. In *Rising Threats in Expert Applications and Solutions* (pp. 313–320). Springer. doi:10.1007/978-981-15-6014-9_36

Shanableh, T. (2012). Data hiding in MPEG video files using multivariateregression and flexible macroblock ordering. *IEEE Transactions on Information Forensics and Security*, *7*(2), 455–464. doi:10.1109/TIFS.2011.2177087

Shankar Prasad, S., Hadar, O., & Polian, I. (2020). Detection of malicious spatial-domain steganography over noisy channels using convolutional neural networks. In *Proceedings International Symposium on Electronic Imaging 2020: Media Watermarking, Security, and Forensics.* Society for Imaging Science and Technology.

Shankar, S. S., & Rengarajan, A. (2017). Puzzle based highly secure steganography. *2017 International Conference on Algorithms, Methodology, Models and Applications in Emerging Technologies (ICAMMAET)*, 1-5. 10.1109/ICAMMAET.2017.8186742

Shapiro, J. M. (1993, December). Embedded Image Coding Using Zerotrees of Wavelet Coefficients. *IEEE Transactions on Signal Processing, 41*(12), 3445–3462. doi:10.1109/78.258085

Sharif, A., Mollaeefar, M., & Nazari, M. (2017). A novel method for digital image steganography based on a new three-dimensional chaotic map. *Multimedia Tools and Applications, 76*(6), 7849–7867. doi:10.100711042-016-3398-y

Sharma, Mithlesharya, & Goyal. (2013). Security Image Hiding Algorithm using Cryptography and Steganography. *Journal of Computer Engineering, 13*(5), 1–6.

Sharma, V., Shukla, M., Srivastava, S., & Mandal, R. (2020, May). Generative Network Based Image Encryption. In *2020 4th International Conference on Intelligent Computing and Control Systems (ICICCS)* (pp. 1-5). IEEE. 10.1109/ICICCS48265.2020.9121060

Sharma, S. G. (2016). Analysis of different text steganography techniques: a survey. In *International Conference on Computational Intelligence & Communication Technology* (pp. 130-133). IEEE. 10.1109/CICT.2016.34

Sheluhin, O. I., & Kanaev, S. D. (2018). *Steganography. Algorithms and software implementation*. Hotline – Telecom.

Shen, K., & Edward, J. D. (1999). Wavelet-Based Rate Scalable Video Compression. *IEEE Transactions on Circuits and Systems for Video Technology, 9*(1), 109–122. doi:10.1109/76.744279

Shet, K. S., Aswath, A. R., Hanumantharaju, M. C., & Gao, X. Z. (2017). Design and development of new reconfigurable architectures for LSB/multi-bit image steganography system. *Multimedia Tools and Applications, 76*(11), 13197–13219. doi:10.100711042-016-3736-0

Shoukat. (2011). A Survey about the Latest Trends and Research Issues of Cryptographic Elements. *International Journal of Computer Science Issues, 8*(3), 140-149.

Siar, F., Alirezazadeh, S., & Jalali, F. (2018). A novel steganography approach based on ant colony optimization. In *2018 6th Iranian Joint Congress on Fuzzy and Intelligent Systems (CFIS)* (pp. 215-219). IEEE.

Siddiqui, G. F., Iqbal, M. Z., Saleem, K., Saeed, Z., Ahmed, A., Hameed, I. A., & Khan, M. F. (2020). A Dynamic Three Bit Image Steganography Algorithm for Medical and e-Healthcare Systems. *IEEE Access: Practical Innovations, Open Solutions, 8*, 181893–181903. doi:10.1109/ACCESS.2020.3028315

Simeone. (2018). A Very Brief Introduction to Machine Learning With Applications to Communication Systems. *IEEE Transactions on Cognitive Communications and Networking, 4*(4).

Simmons, G. J. (1983). The prisoners problem and the subliminal channel. In D. Chaum (Ed.), Advances in Cryptology – CRYPTO 83 (pp. 51–67). Academic Press.

Simmons, G. J. (1984). The prisoners' problem and the subliminal channel. *Publishing in Crypto, 83*, 51–67. doi:10.1007/978-1-4684-4730-9_5

Singh, P. K., Jana, B., & Datta, K. (2021). Robust Watermarking Scheme for Compressed Image Through DCT Exploiting Super pixel and Arnold Transform. In *Proceedings of the Sixth International Conference on Mathematics and Computing* (pp. 43-54). Springer. 10.1007/978-981-15-8061-1_4

Singh, R. K., T. B. (2017). Text Encryption: Character Jumbling. *Proc. of IEEE International Conference on Inventive Systems and Control,* 19-20.

Singla, D., & Juneja, M. (2014). An analysis of edge-based image steganography techniques in spatial domain. *IEEE International Conference on Recent Advances in Engineering and Computational Sciences (RAECS)*, 1-5. 10.1109/RAECS.2014.6799604

Siper, Farley, & Lombardo. (2005). The Rise of Steganography. In *Proceedings of Student/Faculty Research Day, CSIS*. Pace University.

Solichin & Painem. (2016). Motion-based less significant frame for improving lsb-based video steganography. *IEEE International Seminar on Application for Technology of Information and Communication (ISemantic)*. doi:10.1109/ISEMANTIC

Song, Y., & Song, J. (2017). A secure algorithm for image based information hiding with one-dimensional chaotic systems. *2017 3rd IEEE International Conference on Computer and Communications (ICCC)*, 1824-1829.

Soni, T., Baird, R., Lobo, A., & Heydari, V. (2020, June). Using Least Significant Bit and Random Pixel Encoding with Encryption for Image Steganography. In *National Cyber Summit* (pp. 139–153). Springer.

Soto, Reinel & Pollán. (2019). DL Applied to Steganalysis of Digital Images: A Systematic Review. IEEE Access. doi:10.1109/ACCESS.2019.2918086

Sreekutty, M. S., & Baiju, P. S. (2017). Security enhancement in image steganography for medical integrity verification system. *IEEE International Conference on Circuit, Power and Computing Technologies (ICCPCT)*, 1-5. 10.1109/ICCPCT.2017.8074197

Srinath, N. K., Usha, B. A., Sonia Maria, D. S., & Bangalore, B. B. (n.d.). *Image Steganography Using Neural Networks*. doi:10.1109/CFIS.2018.8336653

Stanescu, D., Stangaciu, V., & Stratulat, M. (2010). Steganography on new generation of mobile phones with image and video processing abilities. *International Joint Conference on Computational Cybernetics and Technical Informatics*, 343-347. 10.1109/ICCCYB.2010.5491253

Stoyanov, B., & Stoyanov, B. (2020). BOOST: Medical Image Steganography Using Nuclear Spin Generator. *Entropy (Basel, Switzerland)*, 22(5), 501. doi:10.3390/e22050501 PMID:33286274

Strom, J., & Cosman, P. (1997). Medical Image Compression with Lossless Regions of Interest. *Signal Processing*, 59(2), 155–171. doi:10.1016/S0165-1684(97)00044-3

Sudeepa, K., Raju, K., Ranjan, K., & Ghanesh, A. (2016). A new approach for video steganography based on randomization and parallelization. *International Conference on Information Security and Privacy*, 78, 483–490.

Su, & Kuo. (2003, November). Steganography in JPEG2000 compressed images. *IEEE Transactions on Consumer Electronics*, 49(4), 824–832. doi:10.1109/TCE.2003.1261161

Swain, G. (2018). *High Capacity Image Steganography Using Modified LSB Substitution and PVD against Pixel Difference Histogram Analysis*. Security and Computer Networks. doi:10.1155/2018/1505896

Swain, G. (2019). Very high capacity image steganography technique using quotient value differencing and LSB substitution. *Arabian Journal for Science and Engineering*, 44(4), 2995–3004. doi:10.100713369-018-3372-2

Syed, K. A., & Khadri, D. (2014). Message Encryption Using Text Inversion plus N Count: In Cryptology. International Journal of Information Science and Intelligent System, 3(2), 71-74.

Szczypiorski, K. (2016). *StegHash: new method for information hiding in open social networks*. arXiv preprint.

Taburet, T., Bas, P., Sawaya, W., & Fridrich, J. (2020). Natural steganography in JPEG domain with a linear development pipeline. *IEEE Transactions on Information Forensics and Security, 16*, 173–186. doi:10.1109/TIFS.2020.3007354

Taha, M. S., Rahim, M. S. M., Lafta, S. A., Hashim, M. A., & Alzuabidi, H. M. (2019). Combination of Steganography and Cryptography: A Short Survey. *ICSET, 2019*. Advance online publication. doi:10.1088/1757-899X/518/5/052003

Tanvir Parvez, M., & Abdul-Aziz Gutub, A. (2008). RGB Intensity Based Variable-Bits Image Steganography. *IEEE Asia-Pacific Services Computing Conference*, 1322-1327.

Thakur, A., Gill, G. S., & Saxena, S. (2020, February). Analysis of Image Steganography Performance Check Using Bit Selection. In *2020 7th International Conference on Signal Processing and Integrated Networks (SPIN)* (pp. 1-5). IEEE. 10.1109/SPIN48934.2020.9071251

Thangadurai, K. &. (2014, January). An analysis of LSB based image steganography techniques. In *International Conference on Computer Communication and Informatics* (pp. 1-4). IEEE. 10.1109/ICCCI.2014.6921751

Tiwari, N., & Shandilya, M. (2010). Secure RGB image steganography from pixel indicator to triple algorithm-an incremental growth. *International Journal of Security and Its Applications, 4*(4), 53–62.

Tran, N. (2019). *Deep Neural Networks Based Invisible Steganography for Audio-into-Image Algorithm.* doi:10.1109/GCCE46687.2019.9015498

Trithemius, J. (1606). Steganographia. Academic Press.

Trotter, L. K. (2019). A case study involving creating and detecting steganographic images shared on social media sites. *Graduate Theses and Dissertations. 17798*.

Tyagi, M. V. (2012). Data Hiding in Image using least significant bit with cryptography. *International Journal of Advanced Research in Computer Science and Software Engineering, 2*(4), 120–123.

Usman, S., & Lemo, T. (2007). *Policy Statement by the Government of Nigeria on the Nigerian Economic Reform Program After Completion of the Policy Support Instrument.* Academic Press.

Vani, B. G., & Prasad, E. V. (2013). A Novel Method of 3D Image Steganography Using LZW Technique and Chaotic Neural Network. *International Journal of Computer Science and Network Security, 13*(6), 1.

Vegh, L., & Miclea, L. (2014). Securing communication in cyber-physical systems using steganography and cryptography. *2014 10th International Conference on Communications (COMM).* 10.1109/ICComm.2014.6866697

Vellaiappan, E., Kumaravelu, N., Shiva, G., & Vijayabhaskar, P. V. M. (2012). Comparison of Wavelet Filters in Image Coding and Denoising using Embedded Zerotree Wavelet Algorithm. *Research Journal of Applied Sciences, Engineering and Technology, 4*(24), 5449–5452.

Vishnu, B., Namboothiri, L. V., & Sajeesh, S. R. (2020, March). Enhanced Image Steganography with PVD and Edge Detection. In *2020 Fourth International Conference on Computing Methodologies and Communication (ICCMC)* (pp. 827-832). IEEE. 10.1109/ICCMC48092.2020.ICCMC-000153

Von Leipzig, T. (2017). Initialising customer-orientated digital transformation in enterprises. *Procedia Manufacturing, 8*, 517–524.

Vyas, A. O., & Dudul, S. V. (2020). A Novel Approach of Object Oriented Image Steganography Using LSB. In *ICDSMLA 2019* (pp. 144–151). Springer. doi:10.1007/978-981-15-1420-3_16

Wang, J., Geng, Y.-C., Han, L., & Liu, J.-Q. (2017). Quantum Image Encryption Algorithm Based on QuantumKey Image. *International Journal of Theoretical Physics.* Advance online publication. doi:10.100710773-018-3932-y

Wang, K., & Gao, Q. (2019). A coverless plain text steganography based on character features. *IEEE Access: Practical Innovations, Open Solutions, 7*, 95665–95676. doi:10.1109/ACCESS.2019.2929123

Wang, M., Gu, W., & Ma, C. (2020). A Multimode Network Steganography for Covert Wireless Communication based on BitTorrent. *Security and Communication Networks*. Advance online publication. doi:10.1155/2020/8848315

Wang, Y. R., Lin, W. H., & Yang, L. (2011). An intelligent watermarking method based on particle swarm optimization. *Expert Systems with Applications, 38*(7), 8024–8029. doi:10.1016/j.eswa.2010.12.129

Wei, Z. H., Chen, X. B., Niu, X. X., & Yang, Y. X. (2013). A novel quantum steganography protocol based on probability measurements. *International Journal of Quantum Information, 11*(7), 1350068. doi:10.1142/S0219749913500688

Wei, Z. H., Chen, X. B., Niu, X. X., & Yang, Y. X. (2015). Erratum to: The quantum steganography protocol via quantum noisy channels. *International Journal of Theoretical Physics, 54*(8), 2516–2516. doi:10.100710773-015-2686-z

Westfeld, A. (2001). High capacity despite better steganalysis (F5 – a steganographic algorithm). In *Information Hiding, 4th International Workshop*, volume 2137 *of Lecture Notes in Computer Science* (pp. 289–302). Springer-Verlag.

Westin, C. F., Richolt, J., Moharir, V., & Kikinis, R. (2000). Affine adaptive filtering of CT data. *Medical Image Analysis, 4*(2), 161–177. doi:10.1016/S1361-8415(00)00011-6 PMID:10972328

Wu, P., Yang, Y., & Li, X. (2018). StegNet: Mega Image Steganography Capacity with Deep Convolutional Network. *Future Internet., 10*(6), 54. Advance online publication. doi:10.3390/fi10060054

Xiang, L. W. (2017). A novel linguistic steganog-raphy based on synonym run-length encoding. *IEICE Transactions on Information and System, 100*(2), 313-322.

Xia, X.-G., Boncelet, C. G., & Arce, G. R. (1997). A Multiresolution Watermark for Digital Images. In *IEEE Int'l Conf. Image Processing*. IEEE Press.

Yadahalli, S. S., Rege, S., & Sonkusare, R. (2020, June). Implementation and analysis of image steganography using Least Significant Bit and Discrete Wavelet Transform techniques. In *2020 5th International Conference on Communication and Electronics Systems (ICCES)* (pp. 1325-1330). IEEE.

Yadav, V., Ingale, V., Sapkal, A., & Patil, G. (2014). Cryptographic Steganography. *Computer Science and Information Technology*, 17–23.

Yang, C., & Liu, F. (2013, January). Pixel Group Trace Model-Based Quantitative Steganalysis for Multiple Least-Significant Bits Steganography. *IEEE Transactions on Information Forensics and Security, 8*(1).

Yang, Z. L. (2018). RNN-stega: Linguistic steganography based on recurrent neural networks. *IEEE Transactions on Information Forensics and Security*, 6.

Yang, Z., Wang, K., Li, J., Huang, Y., & Zhang, Y. J. (2019). TS-RNN: Text steganalysis based on recurrent neural networks. *IEEE Signal Processing Letters, 26*(12), 1743–1747. doi:10.1109/LSP.2019.2920452

Yari, I. A., & Zargari, S. (2017). An Overview and Computer Forensic Challenges in Image Steganography. *2017 IEEE International Conference on Internet of Things (iThings) and IEEE Green Computing and Communications (GreenCom) and IEEE Cyber, Physical and Social Computing (CPSCom) and IEEE Smart Data (SmartData)*. doi:10.1109/ithingsgreencom-cpscom-smartdata.2017.60

Ye, D., Jiang, S., Li, S., & Liu, C. (2019). Faster and transferable deep learning steganalysis on GPU. *Journal of Real-Time Image Processing, 16*(3), 623–633. doi:10.100711554-019-00870-1

Ye, G., & Wong, K. W. (2012). An efficient chaotic image encryption algorithm based on a generalized Arnold map. *Nonlinear Dynamics, 69*(4), 2079–2087. doi:10.100711071-012-0409-z

Yick, J., Mukherjee, B., & Ghosal, D. (2008). Wireless sensor network survey. *Computer Networks, 52*(12), 2292–2330. doi:10.1016/j.comnet.2008.04.002

Yongbing, Xu., & Linbo, Xu. (2011). The Performance Analysis of Wavelet in Video coding System. *International Conference on Multimedia Technology (ICMT).* 10.1109/ICMT.2011.6002109

Younes, M. A. B., & Jantan, A. (2008). A New Steganography Approach for Image Encryption Exchange by using the LSB insertion. *Int. J. of Comput. Sci. and Network Security, 8*(6), 247–254.

You, W., Zhang, H., & Zhao, X. (2020). A Siamese CNN for Image Steganalysis. *IEEE Transactions on Information Forensics and Security, 16*, 291–306. doi:10.1109/TIFS.2020.3013204

Yu, C., Hu, D., Zheng, S., Jiang, W., Li, M., & Zhao, Z. Q. (n.d.). An improved steganography without embedding based on attention GAN. *Peer-to-Peer Networking and Applications,* 1-12.

Zaidan, Zaidan, Al-Frajat, & Jalab. (2010). On the Differences between Hiding Information and Cryptography Techniques: An Overview. *Journal of Applied Sciences, 10*(15), 1650-1655.

Zakaria, A. (2018). Quantitative and Binary Steganalysis in JPEG: A Comparative Study. *Proceedings of the European Signal Processing Conference,* 1422–1426. 10.23919/EUSIPCO.2018.8553580

Zaynalov, N. R., Kh, N. U., Muhamadiev, A. N., Bekmurodov, U. B., & Mavlonov, O. N. (2019). Features of using Invisible Signs in the Word Environment for Hiding Data. *International Journal of Innovative Technology and Exploring Engineering, 8*(9), 1377–1379.

Zenati, A., Ouarda, W., & Alimi, A. M. (2019). SSDIS-BEM: A New Signature Steganography Document Image System based on Beta Elliptic Modeling. *Engineering Science and Technology, an International Journal, 23*(3), 470-482.

Zeng, J., Tan, S., Li, B., & Huang, J. (2018). Large-Scale JPEG Image Steganalysis Using Hybrid Deep-Knowledge Structure. *IEEE Transactions on Information Forensics and Security, 13*(5), 1200–1214. doi:10.1109/TIFS.2017.2779446

Zhang, Q., Guo, L., Xue, X., & Wei, X. (2009, October). An image encryption algorithm based on DNA sequence addition operation. In *2009 Fourth International on Conference on Bio-Inspired Computing* (pp. 1-5). IEEE. 10.1109/BICTA.2009.5338151

Zhang, R., Zhu, F., Liu, J., & Liu, G. (2018). *Efficient feature learning and multi-size image steganalysis based on CNN.* arXiv preprint arXiv:1807.11428.

Zhang, Yiwei & Zhang. (2018). *Adversarial Examples Against Deep Neural Network based Steganalysis.* . doi:10.1145/3206004.3206012

Zhang, D., Han, J., Li, C., Wang, J., & Li, X. (2016). Detection of co-salient objects by looking deep and wide. *International Journal of Computer Vision, 120*(2), 215–232. doi:10.100711263-016-0907-4

Zhang, J., Cox, I., & Doerr, G. (2007). Steganalysis for LSB matching in images with high-frequency noise. *Proc. IEEE Workshop MultimediaSignal Process.,* 385–388.

Zhang, L., Gao, Y., Xia, Y., Dai, Q., & Li, X. (2015). A fine-grained image categorization system by cellet-encoded spatial pyramid replicaing. *IEEE Transactions on Industrial Electronics, 62*(1), 564–571. doi:10.1109/TIE.2014.2327558

Zhang, R., Zhu, F., Liu, J., & Liu, G. (2019). Depth-wise separable convolutions and multi-level pooling for an efficient spatial CNN-based steganalysis. *IEEE Transactions on Information Forensics and Security*, *15*, 1138–1150. doi:10.1109/TIFS.2019.2936913

Zhang, S. Y. (2020). *Linguistic Steganography: From Symbolic Space to Semantic Space*. Signal Processing Letters.

Zhao, C., Zhao, H., Wang, G., & Chen, H. (2020). Improvement SVM Classification Performance of Hyperspectral Image Using Chaotic Sequences in Artificial Bee Colony. *IEEE Access: Practical Innovations, Open Solutions*, *8*, 73947–73956. doi:10.1109/ACCESS.2020.2987865

Zhou, L. (2019). Study of Chinese Text Steganography using Typos. In *Asia-Pacific Signal and Information Processing Association Annual Summit and Conference* (pp. 1351-1357). IEEE.

Zhou, Q., Qiu, Y., Li, L., Lu, J., & Yuan, W. (2018). Steganography using reversible texture synthesis based on seeded region growing and LSB. *Computers, Materials & Continua*, *55*(1), 151–163.

Zhou, X. (2011). Research on DCT-based image compression quality. *Proceedings of 2011 Cross Strait Quad-Regional Radio Science and Wireless Technology Conference*, 1490-1494. doi: 10.1109/CSQRWC.2011.6037249

Zolotarev, V. V., & Averin, S. V. (2007). Non-Binary MulKustjvtithreshold Decoders with Almost Optimal Performance. Report at 9-th ISCTA'07.

Zolotarev, V. V., & Ovechkin, P. V. (2016). High-Speed Viterbi decoder based on graphic processors. *Proceedings of the all-Russian scientific and technical conference "Intellectual and information systems"*, 7-10.

Zolotarev, V. V., Zubarev, Y. B., & Ovechkin, G. V. (2012). *Multi-Threshold decoders and optimization theory of coding*. Hotline – Telecom.

Zou, Y. (2018). *Research on image steganography analysis based on DL*. doi:10.1016/j.jvcir.2019.02.034

About the Contributors

Sabyasachi Pramanik is a Professional IEEE member. He obtained a Ph.D. in Computer Science and Engineering from the Sri Satya Sai University of Technology and Medical Sciences, Bhopal, India. Presently, he is an Assistant Professor, Department of Computer Science and Engineering, Haldia Institute of Technology, India. He has many publications in various reputed international conferences, journals, and online book chapter contributions (Indexed by SCIE, Scopus, ESCI, etc). He is doing research in the field of Artificial Intelligence, Data Privacy, Cybersecurity, Network Security, and Machine Learning. He is also serving as the editorial board member of many international journals. He is a reviewer of journal articles from IEEE, Springer, Elsevier, Inderscience, IET, and IGI Global. He has reviewed many conference papers, has been a keynote speaker, session chair and has been a technical program committee member in many international conferences. He has authored a book on Wireless Sensor Network. Currently, he is editing 6 books from IGI Global, CRC Press EAI/Springer and Scrivener-Wiley Publications.

Mangesh Manikrao Ghonge is currently working as Assistant Professor at Sandip Institute of Technology and Research Center, Nashik, India. He received his Ph.D. in Computer Science & Engineering from Sant Gadge Baba Amravati University, Amravati, India in 2019, and an MTech degree in Computer Science & Engineering from Rashtrasant Tukadoji Maharaj Nagpur University, Nagpur, India in 2012. He has been invited as a resource person for many workshops. He has organized and chaired many national/international conferences and conducted various workshops. He received a grant from the Ministry of Electronics and Information Technology (MeitY) for organizing a faculty development program. His more than 40 research papers were published in various international journals including Scopus indexed journals. He has presented a research paper at IEEE conferences in Singapore, Malaysia, also presented more than 10 papers in IEEE conferences. He worked as a reviewer for Scopus/SCIE Indexed journals. Also, a reviewer in various international journals and for international conferences held by different organizations in India and well as abroad. His 02 patent is published by the Indian Patent office. He has also contributed to the Board of Studies, Computer Science & Engineering of Sandip University, Nashik as a Board Member. His research interest includes security in wireless networks, Ad-Hoc networks, Machine learning, Blockchain technology. He is a member of CSI, IACSIT, IAENG, IETE, and CSTA.

Renjith V. Ravi is presently employed as Associate Professor in the department of electronics and communication engineering of MEA Engineering College, Malappuram, Kerala, India. He has published 10 articles in various international journals and conferences and having an experience of around 10 years of in Teaching and Research. He has completed his Ph.D in Electronics and Communication Engineering in 2019, M.E. in Embedded System Technology in 2011 and B.Tech in Electronics and

Communication Engineering in 2007. He is the reviewer of various reputed international journals from Elsevier, Springer, Inderscience, IGI Global, etc.

Korhan Cengiz is an Assistant Professor at the Department of Electrical and Electronics Engineering of Trakya University.

* * *

Gaurav Agarwal has been working as an assistant professor at Invertis University for 14 years. Currently working as the head of the department in CSE. The research area is cryptography and network security.

Jaishankar B. completed his B.E. (ECE) from University of Madras. He obtained M.E and Ph.D from Anna University, Chennai. He is having 2 years of industrial experience and 11 years of teaching as well as research experience. His areas of interest include signal processing, Image processing and Networks. He has published 10 Papers in International Journals and 4 papers in National and International Conferences. He is a Reviewer for International Journal of Advances in Engineering and Technology and an Editorial Board Member for 3 International Journals. He is a member of IEEE, ISTE and BES.

Samir Bandyopadhyay is a distinguished professor of GLA University.

Shawni Dutta is a lecturer in the Computer Science department of Bhawanipur Education Society College, Kolkata. Her research areas are Machine Learning, Deep Learning, Medical Data Analysis and Recommended systems. Currently she is engaged as a reviewer in many reputed journals. She has already received national awards for her research works.

Kylyn Fernandes is a student at Dwarkadas J. Sanghvi college of engineering and is currently in the final year of his undergraduate degree. He is pursuing a Bachelor of Engineering in Computer Engineering. He has a keen interest in advanced algorithms and operational research and is also currently dabbling in Cybersecurity and Cryptography related topics.

Ajay B. Gadicha is currently working as Head of Department and Assistant Professor, Department of Computer Science and Engineering in P.R.Pote College of Engineering and Management Amravati. He becomes First Merit & University Topper in Master of Engineering in Information Technology in 2011. He has completed PhD in Computer Science and Engineering from Sant Gadge Baba Amravati University. He has 10 years of experience in the field of Computer Forensics and Information Technology. He has published 76 research papers in National and International conferences & journals. He has published 2 books (online) and 30 patents filled in the field of Electrical /Electronics and Machine Learning. He has field of interest in Video Forensics, Network Security, Image Processing, Video Summarization. Dr. Gadicha working in 190 editorial and reviewer board of various national and international bodies & communities including ISTE, CSI, IAENG, IEEE, ACM, IFERP, etc. Dr. Gadicha received International Association for Science and Technology Education Awarded "Best Young Research Award-2017" at Tamil Nadu. Dr. Gadicha Received "Best Researcher Award-2019" by Vivekanandha College of Arts and Science for Women (Autonomous), Tiruchengode, Tamil Nadu, India. Dr. Gadicha Received "Young

Researcher in Computer Science and Engineering on 31 July 2019" by Global Outreach Research & Education Association Bangalore.

A. Shaji George is a Professor of Information and Communication Technology, Member Board of Trustees and Representative of Vice-Chancellor, Crown University International in the Middle East, and Asia. Trainer and Counsellor of the National Human Rights and Humanitarian Federation -NHRF / University of the Blue Cross & Blue Crescent Faculty of Entrepreneurship Facilitators (FEF) for FBC Kerala Blue Cross Society and Delegate to the Global Committee Society and District Dean/ Director, and a recognized technical expert in IT Infrastructure Systems, Network & Telecommunication, having worked in almost every aspect of the IT Industry. His research interests include Wireless, Networking, Cloud Computing, Big Data, Data Mining, Automation systems, Microeconomics, Gig Economy, and Labour Economics. In 2020 Dr. A.Shaji George was the recipient of the Race-Bangkok's Award 2020 for Best Research Paper and in addition, was awarded IARDO Academic Excellence Awards-2021 for Best Thesis. He has published more than 50 Journals and is an author of 3 books.

Ankit Rishi Gupta is a student at Dwarkadas J. Sanghvi college of engineering, currently pursuing a Bachelor of Engineering in Computer Engineering. He has worked in fields related to his undergraduate degree, such as Internet of Things (IoT) and Cybersecurity.

Ankur Gupta has received the B.Tech and M.Tech in Computer Science and Engineering from Ganga Institute of Technology and Management, Kablana affiliated with Maharshi Dayanand University, Rohtak in 2015 and 2017. He is an Assistant Professor in the Department of Computer Science and Engineering at Vaish College of Engineering, Rohtak, and has been working there since January 2019. He has many publications in various reputed national/international conferences, journals, and online book chapter contributions (Indexed by Scopus, ESCI, ACM, DBLP, etc.). He is doing research in the field of cloud computing, data security & machine learning. His research work in M.Tech was based on biometric security in cloud computing.

Vrinda Gupta is currently working as System Engineer in Tata Consultancy Services. She has completed her bachelor's in Computer Science and Engineering from Government College of Engineering, Amravati. She has always been excellent in her academics. Besides, she is actively pursuing research in various fields related to computer science.

Ofer Hadar (SM'11) received the B.Sc., M.Sc. (cum laude), and the Ph.D. degrees from the Ben-Gurion University, Negev, Israel, in 1990, 1992, and 1997, respectively, all in electrical and computer engineering. From August 1996 to February 1997, he was in the Center for Research and Education in Optics and Lasers, Central Florida University, Orlando, FL, USA, as a Visiting Research Scientist. From October 1997 to March 1999, he was a Postdoctoral Fellow in the Department of Computer Science, Technion- Israel Institute of Technology, Haifa, Israel. In 1999, he joined the Communication Systems Engineering Department, Ben-Gurion University. He is currently an Associate Professor and the Head of the department. In August 2015, he went for a Sabbatical leave for six months in the Department of Electrical Engineering, University of California, Los Angeles, working with Prof. Rubin on optimizing video streaming over wireless networks. He is also a Consultant for various Hi-Tech companies in Israel. Recently, he established a startup company, Coucou, that focuses on developing algorithms against cyber-attack in video streaming. His research interests include image compression, advanced video coding, H.264, SVC, HECV, packet video, transmission of video over wireless networks, and image processing, data hiding, and cyber in compressed video streaming. Since 2011, he has been an Associate Editor of the Optical Engineering journal. He was the Guest Editor (with his former Ph.D student Dr. D. Grois) of a special section on video compression technology in Optical Engineering, vol. 52, no. 7, July, 2013. He is a Senior Member of SPIE.

Bui Thanh Hung received his M.S. degree and Ph.D. degree from Japan Advanced Institute of Science and Technology (JAIST) in 2010 and in 2013. He is currently the Director of Data Analytics & Artificial Intelligence Laboratory, Director of Master/ Undergraduate Information System Programme, Engineering - Technology School, Thu Dau Mot University. His main research interests are Natural Language Processing, Machine Learning, Machine Translation, Text Processing, Data Analytics, Computer Vision and Artificial Intelligence.

Nicholas Ibenu Jr. is an IT Engineer, Internet Entrepreneur, Investor, and a Security Researcher. He is also a lecturer of Information & Communication Technology, Faculty of Information Technology, ILHR/ESCAE University of Science Technology. He has over 4+ years of experience in IT and most of his area of research interest focuses on military and civil based application on the role of information Technology to combat Cyber Crime, Terrorism & Cyber Espionage protection from foreign spies. He holds different training IT Certifications from different training Institute. He is also Certified from the Institute of Leadership and Human Resource Center, (ILHR), an Institute of Professional bodies governed by top military officer's center of intelligence. He is a graduate student of Technology and Management, Yaba College of Technology with outstanding degrees in view in related area of studies with few publications on International Journal.

Sivanantham Kalimuthu received His Bachlor Engineering In electrical and electronics engineering from Anna University of Coimbatore (2013) and his Master of Business Administration in Project Management System From Bharathiyar University, Coimbatore (2016). From 2016 to 2019 he worked at software developer in Crapersoft, Advanced Products lab Coimbatore. He promoted the senior software developer for Crapersoft R&D Center in 2019. His current research interest include Bigdata /datamining/ encryption and decryption, Database analytics, Embedded IoT developer database.

Alexey Krasnov is a senior analyst, JSC "Naxign", Saint-Petersburg, Russia Education: military space Academy named after A. F. Mozhaisky in 2006 with a degree in computer security. 14 years of professional experience. 2 years of teaching experience. Research interests: information security, cryptography and steganography, noise-proof coding.

Krishan Kumar is shouldering the responsibility as Head of the department in Computer Science & Engineering, National Institute of Technology, Uttarakhand, India. He received Ph. D. for his thesis "Performance Enhancement of Events Detection and Summarization Models in Videos over Cloud," in Computer Science & Engineering, Visvesvaraya National Institute of Technology, Nagpur, India in 2019. He has 6+ years of teaching, research and administrative experience, taught UG and PG courses, guided students in projects & technical paper/reports, competitive contests. He supervised 06 M. Tech. students and 03 Ph. D scholars. He has organized six Workshops /STTP/FDP including one International

Conference. He shouldered many other responsibilities in the Institute like CWN, IT Services, CUG Services, Institute Telephone Services, and CCTV Surveillance etc. He published more than 50 articles in reputed International Conferences and reputed Journals including IEEE Transactions, for more details please refer https://scholar.google.com/citations?user=er5TwRAAAAAJ&hl=en. He is working on a research sponsored project Secret Sharing Scheme Based Technology for Multimedia Security over Cloud from DST, Govt. of India. His research interests include Cloud Computing, Image and Video Processing, Computer Vision, & Artificial Intelligence. He received best paper award in PReMI 2017 ISI Kolkata. He scored 99.05 percentile in the Computer Science & Engineering in GATE 2012. Dr. Kumar received Wall of Fame Award from ULektz as one of the Top 50 Distinguished HoDs CSE/IT in Higher Education across India for the year of 2019. He is chair/member of many committees in the Institute and outside the institute. He is Senior Member IEEE and ACM.

Vladimir Kustov is a doctor of technical sciences in 1994. Specialty: 20.02.12 – System analysis, modeling of military operations and systems, computer technologies in military Affairs (technical Sciences). Professor since 1995. Professor of the Department of Informatics and information security, St. Petersburg state University of Railways of Emperor Alexander I (PGUPS), St. Petersburg, Russia. Education: Perm higher command and engineering militery school in 1972 with a degree in "aircraft control systems and ground-based test and launch electrical equipment for them". More than 40 years of teaching and research experience. 16 candidates of technical Sciences and 4 doctors of technical Sciences were trained. Research interests: information security, electronic signature validation protocols, trusted third-party technology, cryptography and steganography, noise-proof coding, distributed registry technology (blockchain). More than 230 publications with a total volume of more than 80 printed pages, 12 copyright certificates for inventions, 5 copyright certificates for programs. Member of the dissertation Council, member of the IEEE.

Deepak Mane is working as Senior Data Scientist in Global Consulting practice - Performance Engineering Lab at Tata Research Development and Design Center (A Research wing of TCS). In his previous role he was Scientific Officer at Tata Research Fundamental Research (TIFR). He has published 12 papers in Conference Seminars, and has been conducting Seminar/workshop at various colleges in Maharashtra and MP under AIP/FDP activities - TCS . He's also a mentor for KreSIT, Indian Institute of Technology - Mumbai. He is currently pursuing research in Cloud computing, Performance Management, Disaster Recovery and Capacity management.

Ramchandra Mangrulkar, being a post graduate from National Institute of Technology, Rourkela Odisha, received his PhD in Computer Science and Engineering from SGB Amravati University, Amravati in 2016 and presently he is working as an Associate Professor in the department of Computer Engineering at SVKM's Dwarkadas J. Sanghvi College of Engineering, Mumbai (Autonomous College affiliated to University of Mumbai), Maharashtra, India. Prior to this, he worked as an Associate Professor and Head, department of Computer Engineering, Bapurao Deshmukh College of Engineering Sevagram. Maharashtra, India. Dr. Ramchandra Mangrulkar has published 48 papers and 12 book chapters with Taylor and Francis, Springer and IGI Global in the field of interest. Also presented significant papers in related conferences. He has also chaired many conferences as a session chair and conducted various workshops on Artificial Intelligence BoT in Education, Network Simulator 2 and LaTeX and Overleaf. He has also received certification of appreciation from DIG Special Crime Branch Pune and Supretendant of Police. He is also ICSI-CNSS Certified Network Security Specialist. He has also received grant in aid of Rs. 3.5 laks under Research Promotion Scheme of AICTE, New Delhi for the project "Secured Energy Efficient Routing Protocol for Delay Tolerant Hybrid Network". He is active member of Board of Studies in various universities and autonomous institute in India.

Abhishek Mehta is working as an Assistant Professor in Parul Institute of Engineering and Technology. He has 5 years and 7 months of teaching experience. His basic qualification is BCA (Computer Science) from Veer Narmad South Gujarat University & MCA from Shrimad Rajchandra Institute of Management and Computer Application, Uka Tarsadia University. Presently undertaken doctoral (Ph.D) work in Sabaramati University, Ahemdabad on Emerging Technology of Image Processing and Natural Language Processing. Apart from Digital Image Processing, Natural Language Processing, Artificial Intelligence, Source Code Management, Information Systems is the area of interest of his research where could prepare a system that use in educational area. He received Best Research Paper Award in International Conference on Recent Advancement in Engineering and Technology (ICRAET-19) Organized by Institute for Engineering Research and association with Nirma University in June 2019. He also received Research Excellence Award from NASA and ISRO, received Teacher Innovation Award from Zero Investment Innovations for Education Initiatives - ZIIEI, Initiative of Sri Auro bindo Society, Puducherry. He has published 5+ Research Papers in reputed and peer-reviewed National/International Journals, presented 4+ research papers in State/National/International conferences, delivered 5+ expert talks in various refresher course/orientation course/workshop conducted by Parul University, Gujarat Technological University, and many more, attended 50+ workshops/conferences/refresher course/orientation programme/Training Program. He has received fund of Rs. 1,00,000/- for Startup– "Regaclown" from SSIP under GISC Scheme, Government of Gujarat. In periods of lockdown, he received COVID-19 Warrior Award from Bhartiya Vikas Sansthan.

R. Nagarajan received his B.E. in Electrical and Electronics Engineering from Madurai Kamarajar University, Madurai, India, in 1997. He received his M.E. in Power Electronics and Drives from Anna University, Chennai, India, in 2008. He received his Ph.D in Electrical Engineering from Anna University, Chennai, India, in 2014. He has worked in the industry as an Electrical Engineer. He is currently working as Professor of Electrical and Electronics Engineering at Gnanamani College of Technology, Namakkal, and Tamilnadu, India. His current research interest includes Power Electronics, Power System, Soft Computing Techniques and Renewable Energy Sources.

Farid Nait-Abdesselam received his B.Sc. degree from Bab Ezzouar University, Algeria, in 1993, his M.Sc. degree from Paris Descartes University, France, in 1994, and his Ph.D. degree from Versailles University, France, in 2000. He is a Professor at University of Missouri Kansas City. His research interests lie in the field of computer and communication networks with emphasis on algorithms, architectures and protocols for security and optimization in wireless and wired networks.

Vinay Kumar Nassa has dual PhD (CSE) & PhD (ECE). His area of interest are wireless Communication & Data Science, Machine Learning & Deep Learning applications to image Processing, Communication Healthcare, etc. He has published papers in International Journals including scopus and ugc Care.

Ahmed J. Obaid, Asst Professor at the Department of Computer Science, Faculty of Computer Scinece and Mathematics, University of Kufa, PhD in Web Mining and Data Mining from University of Babylon in 2017., Editor in KEM (Key Engineering Material, Scopus) Journal, Editor of MAICT-19, ICMAICT-2020, IICPS 2020, IICESAT, and ICPAS with IOP journal Of Physics, Scopus, ISSUE. An Associate Editor in IJAST Scopus Journal and Reviwers in many Scopus Journals.

Pratik Panchal has completed his four years industry-integrated computer engineering diploma course from Larsen & Toubro Institute of Technology. He is currently pursuing a Bachelor of Engineering degree from Dwarkadas J. Sanghvi College of Engineering in Computer Engineering. He has more than one year of Industry work experience in three different companies. He has also published a research chapter on springer in a book title "Internet of Things, Smart Computing and Technology: A Roadmap Ahead". He has extensive experience on IoT and Cybersecurity projects.

Binay Kumar Pandey is currently working as an Assistant Professor in Department of Information Technology of Govind Ballabh Pant University of Agriculture and Technology Pantnagar Uttrakhand, India. He obtained his M. Tech with Specialization in Bioinformatics from Maulana Azad National Institute of Technology Bhopal M. P. India, in 2008 . He obtained his First Degree B. Tech at the IET Lucknow (Uttar Pradesh Technical University, Uttar Pradesh and Lucknow) India, in 2005. In 2010, he joined Department of Information Technology of College of Technology in Govind Ballabh Pant University of Agriculture and Technology Pantnagar as an Assistant Professor and worked for various UG and PG projects till date. He has more than ten years of experience in the field of teaching and research. He has more than 40 publications in reputed peer journal reputed journal Springer, Inderscience (SCI and Scopus indexed journal and others) and 3 patents. He has many awards such PM Scholarship etc . He session chair in IEEE International Conference on Advent Trends in Multidisciplinary Research and Innovation (ICATMRI-2020) on December 30, 2020 organized by Pankaj Laddhad Institute of Technology and Management Studies; Buldhana, Maharashtra, India.

Digvijay Pandey is currently working in the Department of Technical Education, Kanpur, India and acting HOD in the IT Department. He obtained his M Tech with honours in Digital System and Design at the KNIT Sultanpur (Dr. A.P.J. Abdul Kalam Technical University, Uttar Pradesh and Lucknow) India, in 2016. He obtained his First Degree in BTech in honours at the IERT Allahabad (Dr. A.P.J. Abdul Kalam Technical University, Uttar Pradesh and Lucknow) India, in 2011. In 2012, he joined TCS (IT analyst) and worked for various US/UK/Canada projects till 2016 and also works in IERT Allahabad as a faculty. He has more than ten years of experience in the field industry and teaching. He has been on the reviewing member of many reputed journal like Springer, SCI, IEEE and Scopus indexed journal He has more than 50 publications in reputed peer journal reputed journal Springer, Inderscience, Science Direct (Elsevier) (SCI and Scopus indexed journal), more than 5 book chapters and 4 patents. He has many awards such PM Scholarship, Rajya Prushakar, National Player, NCC C Certificate, NSS and many more. He session chair in IEEE International Conference on Advent Trends in Multidisciplinary Research and Innovation (ICATMRI-2020) on December 30, 2020 organized by Pankaj Laddhad Institute of Technology and Management Studies; Buldhana, Maharashtra, India and International Conference on "Sustainable Business Management Practices and Social Innovation" conducted by SRDC – Vidhyanidhi, CMS, Jain (Deemed-to-be University).

Saravanan Pandiaraj is a Faculty in Department of Self-Development Skills, CFY Deanship King Saud University, Riyadh, Saudi Arabia. His area of Expertise in Artificial Intelligence, Evolutionary Algorithms and IoT based Real Time Applications.

Sana Parveen is currently pursuing her final year undergraduate degree in 'Electronics and Communication Engineering' at M.E.A Engineering College, India, affiliated to the A.P.J. Abdul Kalam Technological University, and will be graduated in 2021 with a B.Tech. degree in Electronics and Communication Engineering. She was awarded the 'Merit Cum Means scholarship' for the meritorious students from India Government for the years 2018, 2019, and 2020. She also received the 'Academic Excellence Award' from M.E.A Engineering College in both years of 2018 and 2019. She is currently the Chairperson of 'IEEE Power and Energy Society' student chapter of IEEE MEA student branch and also member of 'IEEE Industrial Application Society' and 'IEEE Women Engineering Affinity Group'. As an active student member of these IEEE societies, she had volunteered, organized, and participated in many technical events. She had participated in many technical completions since 2014 and was rewarded. She recently certified the course 'Applied Optimization for Wireless, Machine learning, Big Data' from the Indian Institute of Technology, Kanpur, through the National Programme on Technology Enhanced Learning. Moreover, she has a strong interest in the field of information security and assurance.

Ilia Polian is a Full Professor and the Director of the Institute for Computer Architecture and Computer Engineering at the University of Stuttgart, Germany. He received his Diplom (MSc) and PhD degrees from the University of Freiburg, Germany, in 1999 and 2003, respectively. Prof. Polian co-authored over 200 scientific publications and received two Best Paper Awards. He is a Senior Member of IEEE. Prof. Polian is the Speaker of DFG's Priority Program 2253 "Nano Security" and a Director of Gradute School "Intelligent Methods for Test and Reliability" in Stuttgart (funded by Advantest). His scientific interest include hardware-oriented security, emerging architectures, test methods, and quantum computing.

Gurunath R. is a Research Scholar, Department of Computer Science, CHRIST (Deemed to be University) and faculty of Department of Computer Applications, Dayananda Sagar College, India.

Rahul Rastogi has been working as an Assistant Professor at Invertis University since 2006. Area of interest is networking and security issues.

Trupti Pravinsinh Rathod is working as an Assistant Professor in Vidyabharti Trust College of Master in Computer Application. She has 09 years of teaching experience in the field of computer science. Her basic qualification is BCA and MCA (Computer Science and Application) from Veer Narmad South Gujarat University. Operating System, Computer Networks, Software Engineering, Web Design, Cyber Security are the interest area of her. She delivered 2+ expert talks in various colleges of BCA; she has attended 30+ webinars/workshops/Faculty development program/Short term Training Program. She also participated in national and international level quiz got the top rank in the entire quiz. In Lockdown she prepared the video of the subject Operating system for online learning a part from the same, that video approved by the Gujarat Technological University. In periods of lockdown, she received COVID-19 Warrior Award from Bhartiya Vikas Sansthan.

Kannadhasan S. is working as an Assistant Professor in the department of Electronics and Communication Engineering in Cheran College of Engineering, Karur, Tamilnadu, India. He is currently doing research in the field of Smart Antenna for Anna University. He is ten years of teaching and research experience. He obtained his B.E in ECE from Sethu Institute of Technology, Kariapatti in 2009 and M.E in Communication Systems from Velammal College of Engineering and Technology, Madurai in 2013. He obtained his M.B.A in Human Resources Management from Tamilnadu Open University, Chennai. He obtained his PGVLSI in Post Graduate diploma in VLSI design from Annamalai University, Chidambaram in 2011 and PGDCA in Post Graduate diploma in Computer Applications from Tamil University in 2014. He obtained his PGDRD in Post Graduate diploma in Rural Development from Indira Gandhi National Open University in 2016. He has published around 10 papers in the reputed indexed international journals and more than 85 papers presented/published in national, international journal and conferences. Besides he has contributed a book chapter also. He also serves as a board member, reviewer, speaker, advisory and technical committee of various colleges and conferences. He is also to attend the various workshop, seminar, conferences, faculty development programme, STTP and Online courses. His areas of interest are Smart Antennas, Digital Signal Processing, Wireless Communication, Wireless Networks, Embedded System, Network Security, Optical Communication, Microwave Antennas, Electromagnetic Compatibility and Interference, Antenna Wave Propagation and Soft Computing techniques. He is Member of IEEE, ISTE, IEI, IETE, CSI and EAI Community.

Debabrata Samanta is presently working as Assistant Professor, Department of Computer Science, CHRIST (Deemed to be University), Bangalore, India. He obtained his Bachelors in Physics (Honors), from Calcutta University; Kolkata, India. He obtained his MCA, from the Academy of Technology, under WBUT, West Bengal. He obtained his PhD in Computer Science and Engg. from National Institute of Technology, Durgapur, India, in the area of SAR Image Processing. He is keenly interested in Interdisciplinary Research & Development and has experience spanning fields of SAR Image Analysis, Video surveillance, Heuristic algorithm for Image Classification, Deep Learning Framework for Detection and Classification, Blockchain, Statistical Modelling, Wireless Adhoc Network, Natural Language Processing, V2I Communication. He has successfully completed five Consultancy Projects. He has received funding under International Travel Support Scheme in 2019 for attending conference in Thailand. He has received Travel Grant for speaker in Conference, Seminar etc for two years from July, 2019. He is the owner of 18 Indian Patents. He has authored and coauthored over 137 research papers in international journal (SCI/SCIE/ESCI/Scopus) and conferences including IEEE, Springer and Elsevier Conference proceeding. He has received "Scholastic Award" at 2nd International conference on Computer Science and IT application, CSIT-2011, Delhi, India. He is a co-author of 9 books and the co-editor of 3 books, available for sale on Amazon and Flipkart. He has author and co-authored of 16 Book Chapters. He also serves as acquisition editor for Springer, Wiley, CRC, Scrivener Publishing LLC, Beverly, USA. and Elsevier. He is a Professional IEEE Member, an Associate Life Member of Computer Society Of India (CSI) and a Life Member of Indian Society for Technical Education (ISTE). He is a Convener, Keynote speaker, Session chair, Co-chair, Publicity chair, Publication chair, Advisory Board, Technical Program Committee members in many prestigious International and National conferences. He was invited speaker at several Institutions.

Swaroop Shankar Prasad received his B.Eng degree in Instrumentation Technology from Sri Jayachamarajendra College of Engineering, India in 2015 and his master's degree in Information Technology from University of Stuttgart, Germany in 2019. He is currently working as a research assistant at the Institute of Computer Architecture and Computer Engineering, University of Stuttgart, Germany. His main areas of interest include Steganography, Steganalysis, Deepfake video detection and Deep Learning.

Husnain Sherazi is an experienced researcher and academician, with several years of teaching & cutting-edge research experience in communication networks and self-sustained IoT systems, currently working at Tyndall National Institute, University College Cork, Cork, Ireland. During his professional career in Italy, UK, Pakistan, and Ireland, he has been a part of renowned research projects and taught a range of courses at both undergraduate and postgraduate levels. Over 30 articles in top-tier journals and conferences are on his credit. He is serving as Associate Editor (Internet Technology Letter), Topic Editor (Electronics), Editor (Ad Hoc Networks), and Guest Editor for a number of prestigious journals. Moreover, he is a Senior Member IEEE, Member ACM, IEEE Young Professionals, IEEE ComSoc, and the IET.

Ekaterina Silanteva is General Director, New Space of Trade LLC, Moscow, Russia. Education: Lomonosov Moscow State University, Faculty of Public Administration, 2013, Manager in Public and Municipal Administration, Lomonosov Moscow State University, Faculty of public administration, 2017, PhD Candidate. 08.00.05: Economy and Management of the National Economy. More than 10 years of teaching and research experience. A number of studies have been conducted at the intersection of Economics and IT for international organizations such as ECE, UNESCAP and Crown Agents. She is an UNNExT expert and is engaged in research work in the field of cross-border paperless trade. Research interests: information security, electronic signature validation protocols, trusted third-party technology, mutual recognition mechanisms, cryptography and steganography, distributed registry technology (blockchain), IT performance assessment, development of competitive strategies for IT companies. She has more than 10 scientific publications with a total volume of more than 10 printed pages.

Randy Joy Magno Ventayen is the current Director for Public Relations, Publiction and Information of Pangasinan State University. He is also a faculty of PSU Open University Systems, PSU Lingayen Campus, and a mobile faculty of PSU Binmaley Campus. He Graduated his Doctoral Degree in Business Administration in 2010 and Doctor in Information Technology at the University of the Cordilleras in consortium with Ateneo de Manila University in 2019. He served as the University Web Administrator of Pangasinan State University in 2016 to 2018, and the former Dean of the College of Business and Public Administration of PSU Lingayen Campus.

Index

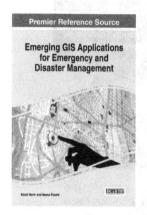

Publisher of Peer-Reviewed, Timely, and
Innovative Academic Research Since 1988

www.igi-global.com

IGI Global's Transformative Open Access (OA) Model:
How to Turn Your University Library's Database Acquisitions Into a Source of OA Funding

Well in advance of Plan S, IGI Global unveiled their OA Fee Waiver (Read & Publish) Initiative. Under this initiative, librarians who invest in IGI Global's InfoSci-Books and/or InfoSci-Journals databases will be able to subsidize their patrons' OA article processing charges (APCs) when their work is submitted and accepted (after the peer review process) into an IGI Global journal.

How Does it Work?

Step 1: **Library Invests in the InfoSci-Databases:** A library perpetually purchases or subscribes to the InfoSci-Books, InfoSci-Journals, or discipline/subject databases.

Step 2: **IGI Global Matches the Library Investment with OA Subsidies Fund:** IGI Global provides a fund to go towards subsidizing the OA APCs for the library's patrons.

Step 3: **Patron of the Library is Accepted into IGI Global Journal (After Peer Review):** When a patron's paper is accepted into an IGI Global journal, they option to have their paper published under a traditional publishing model or as OA.

Step 4: **IGI Global Will Deduct APC Cost from OA Subsidies Fund:** If the author decides to publish under OA, the OA APC fee will be deducted from the OA subsidies fund.

Step 5: **Author's Work Becomes Freely Available:** The patron's work will be freely available under CC BY copyright license, enabling them to share it freely with the academic community.

Note: This fund will be offered on an annual basis and will renew as the subscription is renewed for each year thereafter. IGI Global will manage the fund and award the APC waivers unless the librarian has a preference as to how the funds should be managed.

Hear From the Experts on This Initiative:

"I'm very happy to have been able to make one of my recent research contributions *freely available* along with having access to the *valuable resources* found within IGI Global's InfoSci-Journals database."

— **Prof. Stuart Palmer,**
Deakin University, Australia

"Receiving the support from IGI Global's OA Fee Waiver Initiative *encourages me to continue my research work without any hesitation.*"

— **Prof. Wenlong Liu,** College of Economics and Management at Nanjing University of Aeronautics & Astronautics, China

For More Information, Scan the QR Code or Contact:
IGI Global's Digital Resources Team at eresources@igi-global.com.

Printed in the United States
by Baker & Taylor Publisher Services